Economics
Student Workbook

Economics
Student Workbook

EIGHTH EDITION

John Sloman
University of West of England and the Economics Network

Peter Smith
University of Southampton

Harlow, England • London • New York • Boston • San Francisco • Toronto • Sydney • Auckland • Singapore • Hong Kong
Tokyo • Seoul • Taipei • New Delhi • Cape Town • São Paulo • Mexico City • Madrid • Amsterdam • Munich • Paris • Milan

Pearson Education Limited
Edinburgh Gate
Harlow
Essex CM20 2JE
England

and Associated Companies throughout the world

Visit us on the World Wide Web at:
www.pearson.com/uk

First published in 1991
Second edition published 1994
Third edition published 1997
Fourth edition published 2000
Fifth edition published 2003
Sixth edition published 2006
Seventh edition published 2010
Eighth edition published 2012

© John Sloman and Mark Sutcliffe 1991, 2001
© John Sloman, Mark Sutcliffe and Peter Smith 2006
© John Sloman and Peter Smith 2010, 2012

ISBN: 978-0-273-76510-3

British Library Cataloguing-in-Publication Data
A catalogue record for this book is available from the British Library

ARP Impression 98
Printed in Great Britain by Ashford Colour Press Ltd

Typeset in 8/12pt Stone Serif by 35

Contents

Preface

Welcome to this *Economics Student Workbook*. We hope that the book will help to make your study of the fascinating subject of economics both enjoyable and thought provoking and that it will improve your ability to analyse the economic problems faced by individuals and nations: problems that we hear about daily in the news or come across in our own lives.

Studying economics can be much more rewarding if it is not just seen as a body of knowledge to absorb. Applying the theories, working through problems, analysing data, gathering information, scouring newspapers, reports and official publications and debating with other students can all help to bring the subject alive. This workbook will give you the opportunity to do all these things.

The book may be used with any introductory text, although it is specifically designed to be used with John Sloman, *Economics* (8th edition). Each chapter in the workbook corresponds to a chapter in the main text.

Each chapter is divided into four sections: (A) Review, (B) Problems, exercises and projects, (C) Discussion topics and essays, and (D) Answers. Between them, these sections will help you prepare for all types of examination and assessment currently used at first-year degree level and A level, and on BTEC and professional courses.

Review

This section takes you step-by-step through the material covered in the respective chapter of Sloman, *Economics* (*this edition*), using a mixture of narrative and short questions.

The questions are of seven different types, six of which are signified by symbols.

📃 Multiple choice
These are set out in the standard multiple-choice format. In virtually all cases there are five alternative answers and you are required to circle the correct one. The questions are typical of those used at first-year degree level and at A level.

❓ Written answer
These require you to give one or two words or sentences. Sometimes there will be a list of points for you to give.

◐ Delete wrong word
These are sometimes *true/false* questions, sometimes *yes/no* questions, or sometimes deleting one of two or more alternative answers.

⊖ Diagram/table manipulation
These involve you completing a diagram or table, or reading things off a diagram or table.

⊗ Calculation
These involve short mathematical calculations, usually just simple arithmetic, but in some of the optional, starred questions (see below) they involve simple differentiation.

⬛ Matching/ordering
These are of two types. The first involves matching a set of definitions to a set of descriptions, or a set of answers to a

set of questions. The second involves putting a set of points or events into the correct order.

The final type of question is embedded in the narrative, and involves you deleting the wrong word, phrase or sentence from two or more alternatives given.

Some sub-sections or questions are starred (*). These are on additional topics and may be omitted if desired.

Problems, exercises and projects

This section consists of longer, multi-part questions, often involving simple calculations or the manipulation of graphs. There are also questions involving the gathering and analysis of data. These 'mini-project' questions can be set by your tutor as an assigned piece of work, to be done either individually or in groups. The information gathered can then be used for in-class discussions.

Discussion topics and essays

These questions, as the name suggests, can be used for practice in writing essays or making essay plans (which will help you prepare for exams), or for discussion with fellow students. Most of the questions in this section are designed to raise issues of policy or controversy, and thus should be

more stimulating than the more purely descriptive, theoretical or analytical questions sometimes used for essays. The last question in this section is usually a motion for a debate.

Additional resources

Another way in which you can practise applying economic ideas to practical situations is to think about how economics helps us to interpret events that occur in the world around us. To help you in this, the Sloman website at www.pearsoned.co.uk/sloman contains hot links to a wide range of articles that will be useful to extend your ability to apply economics. All you need to do is go to the website and follow the link to 'Economics News Articles'. In addition, you should make use of the case studies that are on MyEconLab: these are referenced at the end of each chapter in the main text.

Answers

Full answers *plus*, where appropriate, full explanations are given to all section A questions. These will help you check on your understanding as you work your way through the relevant chapter of the main text. They allow section A to be used as a comprehensive revision tool.

TEACHING AND LEARNING: A NOTE TO TUTORS

In devising this Workbook, we intended that it should be both an independent study tool for the student and also a useful teaching aid for tutors. Sections A to C can all be used in a classroom context, adding variety and spice to the delivery of economic principles and policy. Outlined below are some suggestions for ways in which you might use the various sections.

Review

The main purpose of this section is to help reinforce students' learning and understanding of key principles by putting them to use in answering simple questions. The questions are built up in a sequence that mirrors that in the main text.

In addition to being used as a learning tool by students and as a useful revision and practice aid for exams, these questions could also be used in class. Students might be asked, either prior to the class meeting, or in the first part of the class, to complete a set number of questions from this section. Then, preferably in small groups, they would attempt to identify the definitive answer. Groups would be expected to explain the reasoning behind the answers they had chosen.

Alternatively, at the end of a lesson (lecture, seminar or class), a short test based on questions in this section could

be set. This would be quick to administer and mark, and give you feedback on the success of your lesson in meeting its objective(s). With the answers provided to all section A questions at the end of each chapter, students could mark each other's work.

Problems, exercises and projects

As the title of this section suggests, there are three types of question to be found here.

- Multi-part problems. These longer questions provide ideal material for use in very large workshops (of up to 200 students). We have been running workshops similar to these for a number of years and find them very popular with students and a good medium for learning and applying basic economic concepts. Students can work through these multi-part questions (or a portion of them), discussing them with their neighbours as they do so, and then the lecturer can go through the answers from the front. If you leave one row free in every three in the lecture theatre, tutors can go round giving help to students if they are stuck. This is a good way of using postgraduate teaching assistants. Answers to these questions are given on the CD.

- Exercises. Many of these questions require students to look up data or other information from books or electronic media. They are best set in advance of the lesson, unless information collection is one of its main purposes. Once the information has been collected, however, students could work in small groups to devise answers to the questions. This is a very effective way of stimulating debate and discussion.

- Mini projects. These involve students gathering information, sometimes by field work, and then writing a small report or considering a question relating to the information obtained. Again, this work could be done in small groups.

These last two types of question also lend themselves well to group presentations, which help to develop useful communication skills. As part of their presentation, students could be required to consider the method(s) by which they solve problems and construct answers. Telling others how they approached such issues also helps to develop useful skills for themselves and their audience.

The questions in this section also lend themselves very well to being used as assigned pieces of work. They generally require of the student a greater depth of understanding than section A questions.

Discussion topics and essays

These questions can be set as essays, or they can be used as the basis of class discussion. Why not, mid-way through a lecture or class, following a particular point of theory, pose one of the questions for students to discuss and to ascertain its relevance to what they have just been taught? For example, you have introduced your students to the idea of profit maximisation. You now want them to consider its relevance to real-world business decision making. Ask them the following discussion question:

Imagine you were the managing director of a fashion house producing expensive designer clothing. Which of your achievements (or those of your company) would give you special satisfaction?

After a short period of time ask the supplementary question:

Are the achievements consistent with profit maximisation?

You can then proceed to discuss alternative theories of the firm and students can debate whether managerial utility maximisation might be more relevant as a goal of business rather than the maximisation of profit.

The last question in section C is usually a debate. We suggest that the debate is conducted as formally as possible, with two students proposing the motion and two opposing it. After the formal speeches we suggest that the debate is opened to questions and/or contributions from the floor. Finally the proposer and opposer could give a concluding speech. By conducting the proceedings formally, you can develop an atmosphere of theatre, with students acting parts. This can make the learning environment fun.

 ## ACKNOWLEDGEMENTS

The whole team at Pearson Education has been very helpful and we have really appreciated everyone's hard work. A particular thanks to Sally Boyles for her encouragement and careful editorial work and to Liz Johnson for guiding the book through production. Most of all, we owe the book to the unfailing support of Alison and Maureen and the rest of our families.

John Sloman and Peter Smith

Chapter 1

Introducing Economics

 A **REVIEW**

In this first chapter we start by looking at the subject matter of economics. What is it that economists study? How is the subject divided up? What makes a problem an *economic* one?

Although all countries face economic problems, they nevertheless tackle them in different ways. In some countries the government plays a major role in economic decision making. In others decisions are left much more to individuals. Section 1.2 examines how these different types of economy operate.

We then turn to examine types of reasoning employed by economists. Do economists proceed like natural scientists, or does being a *social* science make economics different from subjects like physics and chemistry? We also examine the extent to which economists can contribute to policy making. Can economists tell governments what they *ought* to do?

1.1 What do economists study?

(Page 4) Economists study many issues, but all of them stem from the central economic problem of *scarcity*. Scarcity occurs because there are not enough resources (labour, land and capital) to produce everything that people would like.

Q1. The problem of scarcity is *directly* relevant:
A. only to those times when rationing has been enforced.
B. only to developing countries low in resources.
C. only to those on low incomes.
D. only to those periods of history before mass production.
E. to all countries and all individuals.

Q2. The problem of scarcity will eventually disappear with the development of new technology and resulting higher levels of production. *True/False*

(Page 4) In order to tackle the problem of scarcity, societies produce goods and services for people to consume. This production involves using various resources or *factors of production*.

Q3. It is normal to group factors of production into three broad categories. These are:

1. ....

2. ....

3. ....

Q4. Which one of the following would *not* be classified as a factor of production?

A. Jim Bodget, a bricklayer for a local construction firm.
B. The cement mixer Jim uses.
C. The cement Jim puts in the mixer.
D. The building site Jim works on.
E. The wage Jim gets paid at the end of the week.

(Page 5) One way of understanding the problem of scarcity is in terms of *potential demand and supply*. Potential *demand* relates to the **Q5.** *wants/needs* of individuals, whereas potential *supply* is determined by **Q6.** *the level of resources available/the amount that consumers demand*.

(Pages 5–6) Because of scarcity, people are concerned that society should produce *more* goods and that the resources should be used as *fully* as possible. This is the subject of **Q7.** *microeconomics/macroeconomics*. But given that enough can never be produced to satisfy *potential demands, choices* have to be made: *what* items to produce and in what quantities, *how* to produce them and *for whom*. These choices between alternatives are the subject of **Q8.** *microeconomics/ macroeconomics*.

Q9. Which of the following are macroeconomic issues and which are microeconomic ones?
(a) The level of government spending.
micro/macro
(b) A grant given by the government to the UK film industry. *micro/macro*
(c) The level of investment in the UK by overseas firms.
micro/macro
(d) The price of bricks. *micro/macro*
(e) The rate of inflation. *micro/macro*
(f) The average wage rate paid to builders. *micro/macro*
(g) The total amount spent by UK consumers on house extensions. *micro/macro*
(h) The amount saved last year by households.
micro/macro

Q10. Macroeconomic problems are closely related to the balance between aggregate demand and aggregate supply. Which of the following are likely to result if aggregate demand is too *high* relative to aggregate supply?
(i) Inflation.
(ii) Recession.
(iii) A balance of trade deficit.

A. (i), (ii) and (iii).
B. (i) only.
C. (ii) only.
D. (iii) only.
E. (i) and (iii), but not (ii).

(Pages 7–9) Choices involve sacrifices or *costs*. If as a society we consume more of one good or service then, unless there are idle resources, we will be able to consume less of other goods and services.

Q11. The cost of one good measured in terms of what we must sacrifice is called the:
A. real cost.
B. opportunity cost.
C. average cost.
D. potential cost.
E. social cost.

(Page 8) The notion of opportunity cost is the first of fifteen Threshold Concepts. Once you have come to grips with these, and appreciate their significance, you will begin to think like an economist.

Q12. Your opportunity cost of tackling this question is

....

Q13. Economists assume that economic decisions are made *rationally*. In the case of consumers, rational decision making means:
(a) That consumers will not buy goods which increase their satisfaction by just a small amount.
True/False
(b) That consumers will attempt to maximise their individual satisfaction for the income they earn.
True/False
(c) That consumers buy the sorts of goods that the average person buys. *True/False*
(d) That consumers seek to get the best value for money from the goods they buy. *True/False*
(e) That consumers compare (maybe very casually) the cost of an item they are purchasing with the benefit they expect to gain from it. *True/False*

(Pages 9–10) When we make rational choices, what we are in fact doing is weighing up the marginal benefit of each activity against its marginal (opportunity) cost. If the marginal benefit (i.e. the *extra* benefit of doing a *bit more* of the activity) exceeds its marginal cost (i.e. the extra cost of doing a bit more), it is rational to choose to do that bit more.

Even though we may not be conscious of doing so, we apply this marginal analysis on a regular basis in our day-to-day decision making. This is such an important and widely applicable concept that it is one of our Threshold Concepts, which are designed to help you to think like an economist. It will be examined in Chapter 4.

An important microeconomic objective is to achieve economic efficiency.

Q14. Match each of the following types of efficiency (i)–(iv) with the appropriate definition (a)–(d).
(i) Efficiency in production (productive efficiency)
(ii) Efficiency in consumption
(iii) Efficiency in specialisation and exchange
(iv) Allocative efficiency

(a) Where consumers allocate their expenditures so as to get maximum satisfaction from their income ....

(b) Where firms specialise in producing goods for sale to consumers, and where individuals specialise in doing jobs in order to buy goods, so that everyone maximises the benefits they achieve relative to the costs of achieving them ....

(c) Where production of each item is at minimum costs ....

(d) Where efficiency in consumption and efficiency in specialisation and exchange are both achieved ....

(Pages 10–14) One way in which scarcity, choice and opportunity cost can all be illustrated is via a *production possibility curve.* This depicts a simplified world in which a country produces just two goods. The curve shows all the possible combinations of the two goods that the country can produce in a given period of time.

Figure 1.1 shows the production possibility curve for a country that can produce various combinations of two goods X and Y.

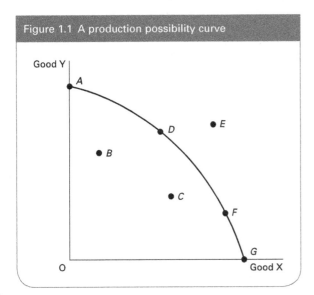

Figure 1.1 A production possibility curve

⊖ Q15. Which point or points illustrate a situation:

(a) Which is efficient? ....

(b) Which is inefficient? ....

(c) Of complete specialisation? ....

(d) Which is unobtainable? ....

Moving from one point to another round a production possibility curve illustrates the concept of opportunity cost.

▤ Q16. Figure 1.2 shows a production possibility curve. Production is currently at point *A*. The opportunity cost of producing one more unit of good X is:

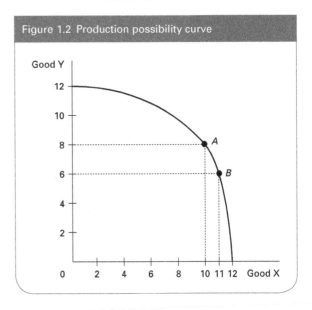

Figure 1.2 Production possibility curve

A. 10 units of X.

B. 1 unit of X.

C. 8 units of Y.

D. 6 units of Y.

E. 2 units of Y.

⑦ Q17. A production possibility curve is typically drawn bowed outward from the origin. This illustrates

....

▤ Q18. Figure 1.3 shows a country's production possibility curves for two years, 2012 and 2015. The production point shifts outward from point *A* in 2012 to point *B* in 2015. The following possibilities might have happened:

(i) Potential output has increased.

(ii) Actual output has increased.

(iii) A fuller use has been made of resources.

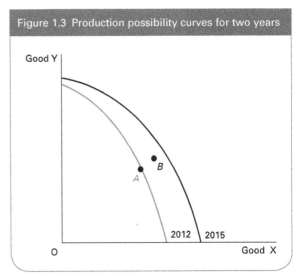

Figure 1.3 Production possibility curves for two years

Which is correct?

A.   (i), (ii) and (iii).
B.   (i) and (ii), but not (iii).
C.   (ii) and (iii), but not (i).
D.   (ii), but not (i) or (iii).
E.   It is impossible to say from the information given.

Q19. Which one of the following would directly lead to an outward shift of a country's production possibility curve?

A.   An increase in the population of working age.
B.   A reduction in the level of unemployment in the economy.
C.   A reduction in value added tax and duties on petrol and alcohol.
D.   An increase in the general level of prices.
E.   A reduction in government expenditure on education.

A production possibility diagram can illustrate the distinction between microeconomics and macroeconomics.

Q20. Which of the following are microeconomic and which are macroeconomic issues?

(a) Whether the production possibility curve shifts outwards over time.   *micro/macro*
(b) Whether the economy is operating on the production possibility curve or inside it.   *micro/macro*
(c) The choice whether to produce more X and less Y, or more Y and less X (i.e. where to produce on the production possibility curve).   *micro/macro*

(Pages 14–15) Another diagram that can be used to illustrate the distinction between micro- and macroeconomics and the process of satisfying consumer wants is the *circular flow of income diagram*. It shows the inter-relationships between firms and households in a money economy. A simplified circular flow diagram is illustrated in Figure 1.4.

Figure 1.4 The circular flow of incomes and of goods and services

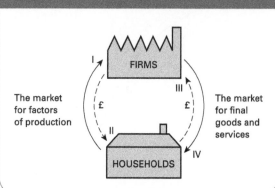

Q21. Which flow (I, II, III or IV) illustrates each of the following?

(a) Goods and services.   *I/II/III/IV*
(b) Wages, rent, profit and interest.   *I/II/III/IV*
(c) Factor services.   *I/II/III/IV*
(d) Consumer expenditure.   *I/II/III/IV*

1.2 Different economic systems

(Pages 16–17) Different countries tackle the problem of scarcity in different ways. One major way in which the economic systems of countries differ is in the extent to which they rely on the market or the government to allocate resources.

Q22. At the one extreme is the *full command economy*. Here all decisions concerning *what* should be produced, *how* it should be produced, and *for whom* are made by

....

Q23. At the other extreme is the completely free-market economy. Here all economic decisions are made by

....

Q24. Which of the following can be seen as economic activities when carried out in the home?

A.   Andrew cooks the evening meal for his family.
B.   Brenda plants runner beans in the back garden so she can enjoy really fresh vegetables in the summer.
C.   Colin, who has retired, volunteers two mornings a week to help at a local charity shop.
D.   None of the above.
E.   All of the above.

(Pages 17–19) There are a number of potential advantages of a command economy.

Q25. Which one of the following is *not* a potential advantage of a command economy?

A.   The planning authority can obtain an overall view of the whole economy and ensure a *balanced* expansion of its various parts.
B.   Resources can be distributed according to need.
C.   The system of planning can ensure that producers respond automatically to consumer wishes.
D.   Resources can be diverted from consumption to investment if it is desired to increase the rate of economic growth.
E.   Unemployment can be avoided.

Q26. Name two potential *disadvantages* of a pure command economy.

1.   ....

2.   ....

(Pages 19–22) In a totally free-market economy the questions of *what*, *how* and *for whom* to produce are determined by the decisions of individual households and firms through the interaction of demand and supply. In goods markets households are **Q27.** *suppliers/demanders/price setters*, whereas in factor markets households are **Q28.** *suppliers/demanders/ neither suppliers nor demanders* of factor services. The way in which people respond to incentives is important in economics. Price is one key incentive in a free market: if the price of a good rises, firms have an incentive to produce **Q29.** *more/less*, and households have an incentive to consume **Q30.** *more/less*.

Demand and supply are brought into balance by the effects of changes in price. If supply exceeds demand in any market (a surplus), the price will **Q31.** *rise/fall/stay the same*. This will lead to **Q32.** *a rise in the quantity both demanded and supplied/a fall in the quantity demanded and supplied/a rise in the quantity demanded but a fall in the quantity supplied/a rise in the quantity supplied but a fall in the quantity demanded*. If, however, demand exceeds supply in any market (a shortage), the price will **Q33.** *fall/rise/stay the same*. This will lead to a **Q34.** *fall/rise* in the quantity demanded and a **Q35.** *fall/rise* in the quantity supplied. In either case the adjustment of price will ensure that demand and supply are brought into equilibrium, with any shortage or surplus being eliminated. This idea of how markets reach equilibrium is the fourth Threshold Concept and will be discussed in Chapter 2.

Goods and factor markets are linked. A change in demand or supply in one market will stimulate changes in other markets.

(?) Q36. What incentives could be set to encourage

(a) firms to produce more?

....

(b) consumers to buy more?

....

(c) motorists to avoid causing congestion?

....

(d) people to smoke fewer cigarettes?

....

(e) you to work harder on your economics course?

....

(?) Q37. If the demand for houses rises, how will this affect the wages of bricklayers?

....

Provided there are many firms competing in each market, the free-market economy can be claimed to lead to a number of advantages.

Q38. These include:
(a) A lack of bureaucracy in economic decision making.
True/False
(b) Producers respond to changes in demand and consumers respond to changes in supply. *True/False*
(c) The competition provides an incentive for producers to be efficient. *True/False*
(d) The interaction of demand and supply ensures that resources are equally distributed. *True/False*
(e) Firms will produce goods that are desirable for society, since only such goods can be sold profitably.
True/False

(Pages 22–4) In reality no economy is a completely planned or completely free market. All economies are *mixed*. The mixture of government and the market varies, however, from one economy to another. It is thus the degree and form of government intervention that distinguishes one type of economy from another.

Threshold Concept 2 highlights the way in which people gain from voluntary economic interaction, but Threshold Concept 3 sounds a warning note that market failure may sometimes prevent society from reaching the best possible market outcomes. Fortunately, we learn from Threshold Concept 6 in Chapter 2 that government may be able to intervene to improve market outcomes.

Q39. Which of the following might be a source of market failure?
A. A giant firm dominates the market for a good, and charges a high price in order to make large profits.
B. A firm becomes complacent from lack of competition and ceases to look for maximum efficiency.
C. A factory producing leather goods causes pollution.
D. Private enterprise is unable to provide street lighting.
E. All of the above.

(?) Q40. List three different ways in which the government can intervene.

1. ....

2. ....

3. ....

1.3 The nature of economic reasoning
(Pages 24–5) The methodology used by economists has much in common with that used by natural scientists. Like natural scientists, economists construct *models*.

Q41. Which one of the following is *not* generally true of economic models?

A. They simplify reality.

B. They provide an explanation of the cause of certain economic phenomena.

C. They enable predictions of the 'if . . . then . . .' variety to be made.

D. They are constructed by conducting experiments under controlled conditions.

E. They can be tested by appealing to the facts.

Building models involves a process known as **Q42.** *deduction/induction*, whereas using a model to make a prediction involves a process known as **Q43.** *deduction/induction*.

Let us assume that an economist was attempting to establish the relationship between the rate of growth in the supply of money in the economy and the rate of inflation (i.e. the annual percentage increase in retail prices) the following year. In the process a number of steps are followed.

Q44. Rearrange the following steps in the correct order:

(a) Predict the rate of inflation next year.

(b) Collect data on the current rate of growth in the money supply.

(c) Collect data on the rate of growth in the money supply and the rate of inflation over a number of past years.

(d) If the prediction is wrong, amend the theory or abandon it.

(e) Establish a hypothesis about the relationship between the two variables.

(f) Continue collecting more evidence.

(g) Conduct observations to establish whether the prediction is correct.

Correct order: ....

(Pages 25–6) Economics concerns human behaviour, which is inherently unpredictable at the individual level. However, *on average*, people are likely to behave predictably. Economists have an important role in helping governments to formulate and assess economic policy. In doing this it is important to separate *positive* questions about what the effects of the policies are, from *normative* ones as to what the goals of policy should be. Economists in their role as economists have no superior right to make normative judgements on the ideological/moral/political basis of the policy. They can and do, however, play a major role in assessing whether a policy meets the political objectives of government (or opposition).

Q45. Which one of the following is a normative statement?

A. The privatisation of the railways has reduced the level of traffic congestion.

B. The privatisation of the railways has led to an increase in fares.

C. Many on the political left believe that the privatisation of the railways is wrong.

D. It is fairer that rail commuters should pay the full costs of the journeys rather than having them subsidised by the government.

E. Rail privatisation has attracted private investment into the industry.

Q46. Which of the following statements are positive and which are normative?

(a) The best policy is one that will maximise the rate of economic growth for the country.   *Positive/Normative*

(b) Government policies give a higher priority to curing inflation than to curing unemployment.
Positive/Normative

(c) The government ought to give higher priority to curing unemployment than to curing inflation.
Positive/Normative

(d) If the government gave a higher priority to curing unemployment, that would be popular with the electorate.   *Positive/Normative*

B   PROBLEMS, EXERCISES AND PROJECTS

Q47. Make a list of five things you did yesterday and any items you purchased. What was the opportunity cost of each? If your fellow students are doing this question, have a look at some of their lists and see if you agree with their estimates of their opportunity costs.

Q48. Imagine that country X could produce just two goods: food and clothing. Assume that over a given time period it could produce any of the following combinations:

Units of clothing	0	1	2	3	4	5	6
Units of food	24	23	21	18	14	8	0

(a) Draw the production possibility curve for country X on Figure 1.5.

(b) What is the opportunity cost of producing one more unit of clothing if the current level of production is (i) 2 units, (ii) 3 units, (iii) 4 units?

(c) Assume that technical innovation in agriculture allows a greater food output per unit of resources devoted to agriculture. What effect will this have on the opportunity cost of producing clothes?

(d) Now assume that there is a drought that halves the amount of food that can be produced per unit of resources. Draw the new production possibility curve.

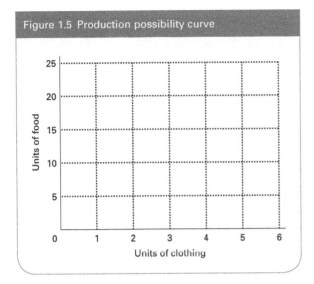

Figure 1.5 Production possibility curve

Q49. Conduct a survey to establish what your fellow non-economics students believe economics to be about. To what extent is their perception of the contents of economics the same as yours (a) was before you started your current course, (b) is now?

Q50. Choose two current economics news items reported in the newspapers. Choose two newspapers of opposing political views which report this item. Give examples from these reports of *positive* statements and *normative* statements. Are there any statements that are not clearly one or the other?

Q51. East European economies have undergone considerable changes since 1989. Using data from the Internet or from your institution's library:
(a) Plot annual economic growth, unemployment and inflation figures since 1989 for three 'transitional' economies.
(b) Describe the patterns.
(c) How might greater reliance on market forces have (i) improved and (ii) worsened the performance of your chosen three economies?
(d) Using the data and other relevant articles, discuss the adverse consequences caused by shifting from a command economy to a market economy.

DISCUSSION TOPICS AND ESSAYS

Q52. Make a list of some current problems that are the concern of economists. Are they microeconomic or macroeconomic problems, or a bit of both? How do they relate to the problem of scarcity?

Q53. Virtually every good is scarce in the sense we have defined it. There are, however, a few exceptions. Under *certain circumstances* water and air are not scarce. When and where might this be true for (a) water and (b) air? Why is it important to define water and air very carefully before deciding whether they are scarce or abundant? Under circumstances where they are *not* scarce, would it be possible to charge for them?

Q54. How can scarcity be a problem when the shops are well stocked, there are well over one million people unemployed (a *surplus* of labour), and there are butter and grain 'mountains' in many countries?

Q55. Using relevant examples, explain what is meant by 'technological progress'. What would cause the rate of technological progress to increase? Will technological progress eventually overcome the economic problem?

Q56. In the past 15 years, many countries have experienced an increase in the proportion of goods and services provided by the private sector.

(a) Why has this occurred?
(b) What are the economic implications of an increase in the proportions of health care and education that are provided by the private sector?

Q57. 'Economists can advise on economic policy and still avoid value judgements.' Explain how this could be so. Is it desirable that economists should avoid value judgements?

Q58. Debate
Each side should prepare a case in support of one of the following two statements (you may wish to use current economics news items).

1. The distinction between positive and normative economics is a very important distinction, since it clearly delineates the boundary between the legitimate areas of enquiry, analysis and pronouncements by economists and those areas where the economist has no superior right of pronouncement to the layperson.
2. The distinction between positive and normative economics is a dangerous and often bogus one. It tends to confer a legitimacy on economists' pronouncements which, while seeming to be 'positive', are in reality highly normative in their implications.

ANSWERS

Q1. E. We define scarcity as the excess of human wants over the means of fulfilling those wants. Virtually everyone would like more than they have. Even very rich people would normally like a higher income, and even if money was no object at all for them, they would still have a shortage of *time* to do everything they would like to do.

Q2. *False.* Human desires are virtually boundless. For example, in 100 years people will want things that have not been invented yet.

Q3. Labour, land (and raw materials), and capital.

Q4. E. All the others contribute towards production. The wages are the *reward* for Jim's labour: they do not add to production.

Q5. *wants.* Potential demand refers to what people would *like* to have and not merely to those items that are thought of as being necessities.

Q6. *the level of resources available.* What society can produce depends on what labour, land and capital are available.

Q7. *macroeconomics.*

Q8. *microeconomics.*

Q9. (a) *macro.*
(b) *micro.*
(c) *macro.* (It would be micro if we were looking at overseas investment in a *specific* industry.)
(d) *micro.*
(e) *macro.*
(f) *micro.* (We are only referring to wages in a *specific* industry.)
(g) *micro.*
(h) *macro.* (We are referring to total household saving in the economy, not to the saving of specific households or to saving in specific financial institutions.)

Q10. E. A recession may result when aggregate demand is too *low* relative to aggregate supply.

Q11. B. The opportunity cost is the cost measured in terms of the next best alternative forgone.

Q12. Your answer to this will depend on what you would most like to be doing instead of tackling this question, perhaps watching TV, or going out with your friends.

Q13. (b), (d), (e) *true*; (a) and (c) *false.* Rational behaviour involves weighing up the costs and benefits of any activity. For consumers this involves comparing the price of a good with the benefit the consumer expects to receive. The consumer will think (however briefly), 'Is this item worth purchasing?' The answer will vary from person to person according to their tastes (i.e. not (c)).

Q14. (a) (ii).
(b) (iii).
(c) (i).
(d) (iv).

Q15. (a) A, D, F and G. All these points lie *on* the production possibility curve and thus show that the country is fully utilising its potential.
(b) B and C. These points lie *inside* the curve and thus illustrate that not as many goods are being produced as could be.
(c) A and G. Point A shows complete specialisation in good Y and point G shows complete specialisation in good X.
(d) E. Point E lies outside the production possibility curve and is thus unobtainable.

Q16. E. When production is initially at point A, producing one more unit of good X (i.e. the 11th unit) will involve reducing production of good Y by 2 units (from 8 to 6 units).

Q17. The phenomenon of *increasing opportunity costs*. As more and more of one good is produced, increasingly larger and larger amounts of the other have to be sacrificed.

Q18. B. The outward shift of the curve illustrates an increase in potential output (i). The movement outward of the production point from A to B illustrates an increase in actual output (ii). But the fact that point A is *on* the earlier curve whereas point B is *inside* the later curve means that resources are being used less fully (or efficiently) than previously.

Q19. A. An increase in the population of working age represents an increase in (human) resources and hence an increase in production potential. Note: B represents a movement outward of the production point towards the production possibility curve; C may encourage increased *consumption* and may as a result stimulate a greater level of production (a movement outward of the production *point*) but does not directly increase *production* potential; D means that the *money* value of output potential has risen, but there is no change in *physical* output potential; E is likely to lead to an *inward* shift of the curve as the quality of the labour force declines.

Q20. (a) and (b) *macro*, (c) *micro*. In the case of (a) and (b) the whole economy is being considered: whether it is growing (a), or whether there is a full use of resources (b). In the case of (c), however, the question is one of the *composition* of production: how much of *each* good is being produced.

Q21. (a) IV.
(b) II.

(c) I.

(d) III.

Q22. The state or some central or local planning agency.

Q23. Individuals: households and firms.

Q24. E: These are examples of activities that carry an opportunity cost but in which no money changes hands. These are taking place in the informal sector.

Q25. C. In a pure command economy, firms do not have the discretion to respond to changes in consumer demand.

Q26. Costly in terms of administration; difficulty in devising incentives to ensure that the plan is carried out as the planners would like; loss of individual liberty; planners may not act in the interests of the people.

Q27. *demanders.*

Q28. *suppliers.*

Q29. *more.*

Q30. *less.*

Q31. *fall.*

Q32. *a rise in the quantity demanded but a fall in the quantity supplied.*

Q33. *rise.*

Q34. *fall.*

Q35. *rise.*

Q36. *(a)* Firms may be encouraged to produce more if the price of the good rises – or perhaps if the firm's costs fall.

(b) Consumers may buy more in response to a decrease in price – or in response to changes in preferences, perhaps as a result of advertising by firms.

(c) One way of discouraging motorists from using congested roads is through road pricing – for instance, as in the London Congestion Charge.

(d) Past experience has suggested that taxing cigarettes has limited effect on smoking behaviour, but that campaigns spreading information about the harmful effects of smoking tobacco can have some effect.

(e) We guess you have some ideas about this! Perhaps your lecturers could make the course even more interesting than it is already – or perhaps they could set you more tests!

Q37. The rise in demand for houses will cause a shortage of houses. This will cause the price of houses to rise. This will increase the profitability of house construction. This in turn will increase the demand for bricklayers. The resulting shortage of bricklayers will lead to a rise in their wages (the 'price' of bricklayers).

Q38. *(a)* True.

(b) True.

(c) True. Competition will help to keep prices down and thus encourage firms to reduce their costs in order to make a satisfactory level of profit.

(d) False. While competition between firms may prevent very high profits in any industry and the competition between workers may prevent very high wages in any type of job, the *ownership* of resources is not equal. Some people own a lot of property; others own none; some workers are skilled and can command high wages; others are unskilled.

(e) False. Goods that are profitable for a firm may not necessarily be socially desirable. For example, the production of certain industrial goods may damage the environment. On the other hand, some things that *are* socially desirable (such as pavements) may not be profitable for private enterprise to supply.

Q39. E. All of the statements describe a possible source of market failure. These – and other – forms of market failure will be discussed later in the book.

Q40. Examples include: state ownership of various industries (nationalisation); legislation to affect production or consumption (e.g. to control pollution); taxation (e.g. high rates on tobacco and spirits); subsidies and benefits (e.g. pensions and other benefits to help the poor); direct provision (e.g. of education and policing); price controls and controls over interest rates and exchange rates.

Q41. D. Although experimental economics has made great progress in recent years, in many circumstances it is usually not possible to conduct controlled experiments in economics since, unlike certain of the natural sciences, it is not a *laboratory* science. It is not possible to hold other things constant. Instead, we simply have to *assume* that other things are constant (*ceteris paribus*). Note: although economic models can usually be tested by appealing to the facts (answer E), there will be a delay if a prediction of the future is being tested.

Q42. *induction.*

Q43. *deduction.*

Q44. (c), (e), (b), (a), (g), (d), (f).

Q45. D. This statement is a question of *value*. Some people may regard it as fair, some may not: it depends on what they believe to be right or wrong. The other statements in principle can all be tested by an appeal to facts. They may be correct or incorrect, but they are statements about what is or is not the case. Note that statement C is positive because it is not a statement about whether privatisation is desirable or not, but about what those on the left believe.

Q46. (b) and (d) are *positive*. The person making the statements is not saying whether government policies are good or bad, or what the government ought to do. In both cases the statements can be assessed by an appeal to the facts (albeit in the case of (d) you would have to wait to see how the electorate responded). (a) and (c), on the other hand, are *normative*. The person making the statements is saying what the government *ought* to do or what the *goals* of government policy *should* be. Note: in the case of (d), there *is* the implication that if the government wants to be popular with the electorate, it would be wise to give a higher priority to curing unemploy-ment, but that does not make it a normative state-ment. The statement as it stands is only about means to ends, not whether those ends are desirable. Only if the person making the statement is *implying* that the government *ought* to do what is popular with the electorate does the statement have norma-tive overtones.

Supply and Demand

A REVIEW

In this chapter we examine the workings of the *free market*. The *market* simply refers to the coming together of buyers (demanders) and sellers (suppliers). We look first at *demand*, then at *supply* and then put the two together to show how price is determined.

In the real world, the government often intervenes in the market. This intervention can take various forms. Examples include: price fixing, taxes or subsidies on various goods and services, directly taking over production, and rules and regulations governing the supply of certain goods.

2.1 Demand

(Page 32) There are several determinants of consumer demand for a product. The relationship between demand and one of these determinants is expressed in the *law of demand*.

Q1. The law of demand states that:
A. quantity demanded increases as price decreases.
B. demand rises as income rises.
C. producers respond to an increase in demand by producing more.
D. an increase in demand causes an increase in price.
E. the amount purchased depends on the amount demanded.

(Page 32) The effect of a change in price on the quantity demanded can be divided into an *income* effect and a *substitution* effect.

Q2. The income effect refers to the effect on price and quantity demanded of a change in consumer income.
True/False

Q3. The substitution effect refers to the effect on the quantity demanded of a change in the price of a substitute good.
True/False

(Pages 33–4) The relationship between price and the quantity demanded can be shown graphically on a *demand* curve. A demand curve can be an individual's demand curve, or that of a group of individuals (a *section* of the market) or that of the whole market.

Q4. Consider the (imaginary) data in Table 2.1. This shows the annual demand for tennis shoes in three sections of the market.
(a) Fill in the column for annual market demand.
(b) Draw the annual demand curve for each of the three groups and the annual market demand on Figure 2.1.

(Pages 34–5) But price is not the only factor that determines how much of a good people will demand. Let us take the case of a particular product:

 Multiple choice   *Written answer*   *Delete wrong word*   *Diagram/table manipulation*   *Calculation*  *Matching/ordering*

Table 2.1 The demand for tennis shoes

Price	Tennis club members (annual) (000s)	Players but not club members (annual) (000s)	Non-tennis players (annual) (000s)	Total market (annual) (000s)
£100	6	1	0	...
£80	7	3	0	...
£60	8	6	2	...
£40	9	10	8	...
£20	10	18	20	...

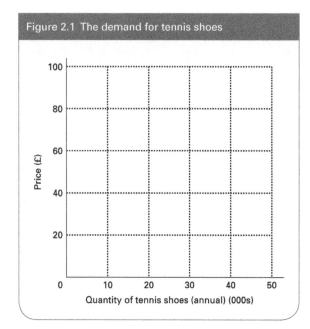

Figure 2.1 The demand for tennis shoes

🏁 **Q5.** It is normal to group the various determinants of demand into categories. The categories include:
  (i) The price of the good.
 (ii) The price of substitute goods.
(iii) The price of complementary goods.
 (iv) Tastes.
  (v) Income.
 (vi) Expectations of future price changes.

Into which of the above categories would you put the following determinants of the demand for tennis shoes?
(a) The price of tennis rackets.

....

(b) The amount shops charge for tennis shoes.

....

(c) The earnings of people who might possibly buy tennis shoes.

....

(d) The price of running shoes.

....

(e) The likelihood that the government will impose a tax on imported sportswear in order to protect the domestic sportswear industry.

....

(f) The amount of coverage to tennis given on the television.

....

(Pages 35–8) When the price of a good changes, we say that this causes the **Q6.** *demand/quantity demanded* to change. This is shown by **Q7.** *a shift in the demand curve/a movement along the demand curve*. When one of the other determinants changes, however, we say that this causes the **Q8.** *demand/quantity demanded* to change. This is shown by **Q9.** *a shift in the demand curve/a movement along the demand curve*.

◗ **Q10.** Consider the demand curve for petrol. What effect will the following have?
(a) An increase in the price of cars. *Rightward shift/leftward shift/movement up along/movement down along/need more information to say.*
(b) An increase in the proportion of the population owning cars. *Rightward shift/leftward shift/movement up along/movement down along/need more information to say.*
(c) A rise in transport costs of shipping oil. *Rightward shift/leftward shift/movement up along/movement down along/need more information to say.*
(d) A growing concern for environmental issues by the general public. *Rightward shift/leftward shift/movement up along/movement down along/need more information to say.*
(e) An increase in duty on diesel. *Rightward shift/leftward shift/movement up along/movement down along/need more information to say.*
(f) A reduction in duty on petrol. *Rightward shift/leftward shift/movement up along/movement down along/need more information to say.*

One of the most important determinants of demand is the level of consumer income. When considering the effect of a change in income on demand, we distinguish between *normal* goods and *inferior* goods.

⑦ **Q11.** We define a normal good as one

....

⑦ **Q12.** On the other hand, we define an inferior good as one

....

2.2 Supply

(Page 39) The relationship between supply and *price* is **Q13.** *a direct/an inverse* relationship.

Q14. Which of the following are explanations of this relationship between price and market supply (there are more than one)?

(a) Costs tend to rise over time. *Yes/No*

(b) As price rises, producers find that it is worth incurring the higher costs per unit associated with producing more. *Yes/No*

(c) At higher prices it is worth using additional, less productive factors of production. *Yes/No*

(d) The lower the price, the more firms will switch to producing other products which are thus now relatively more profitable. *Yes/No*

(e) Technological improvements mean that more can be produced and this in turn will affect prices. *Yes/No*

(Pages 39–40) Given that the quantity supplied is likely to rise as price rises, the supply curve is likely to be upward sloping.

(Pages 40–1) As with demand, price is not the only thing that affects supply.

Q15. Other determinants of supply include:

1. ....

2. ....

3. ....

4. ....

5. ....

(Pages 41–2) If price changes, the effect is shown by **Q16.** *a shift in/a movement along* the supply curve. We call this effect a change in **Q17.** *supply/the quantity supplied*. If any other determinant of supply changes, the effect is shown by **Q18.** *a shift in/a movement along* the supply curve. We call this effect *a change in* **Q19.** *supply/the quantity supplied*.

Q20. Consider the case of the supply curve of organically grown wheat. What effect would the following have?

(a) A reduction in the cost of organic fertilisers. *Rightward shift/leftward shift/movement up along/movement down along.*

(b) An increase in the demand for organic bread. *Rightward shift/leftward shift/movement up along/movement down along.*

(c) An increase in the price of organic oats and barley. *Rightward shift/leftward shift/movement up along/movement down along.*

(d) The belief that the price of organic wheat will rise substantially in the future. *Rightward shift/leftward shift/movement up along/movement down along.*

(e) A drought. *Rightward shift/leftward shift/movement up along/movement down along.*

(f) A government subsidy granted to farmers using organic methods. *Rightward shift/leftward shift/ movement up along/movement down along.*

2.3 Price and output determination

(Pages 42–4) If the demand for a good exceeds the supply, there will be a **Q21.** *shortage/surplus*. This will lead to a **Q22.** *fall/rise* in the price of the good. If the supply of a good exceeds the demand, there will be a **Q23.** *shortage/surplus*. This will lead to a **Q24.** *fall/rise* in the price.

Price will settle at the equilibrium. The equilibrium price is the one that clears the market. The way that markets equate demand and supply is the fourth Threshold Concept.

Q25. This is the price where

....

(Pages 44–51) If the demand or the supply curve *shifts*, this will lead either to a shortage or to a surplus. Price will therefore either rise or fall, **Q26.** causing a *shift in/movement along* the other curve, until a new equilibrium is reached at the position where the supply and demand curves *now* intersect. This is an example of Threshold Concept 5, which is that people respond to incentives – in this case, both consumers and firms respond to prices.

Q27. The demand and supply schedules for organically grown wheat in a free market are shown in Table 2.2.

(a) Draw the demand and supply curves on Figure 2.2.

(b) What would be the size of the shortage or surplus at a price of €180 per tonne?

Shortage/surplus of ....

(c) What would be the size of the shortage or surplus at a price of €340 per tonne?

Shortage/surplus of ....

(d) What is the equilibrium price and quantity?

P = ... ; *Q* = ...

Table 2.2 The market for organically grown wheat (imaginary figures)

Price per tonne (€)	100	140	180	220	260	300	340	380
Tonnes supplied per week	220	260	320	400	500	640	880	1400
Tonnes demanded per week	770	680	610	550	500	460	400	320

Figure 2.2 The market for organically grown wheat

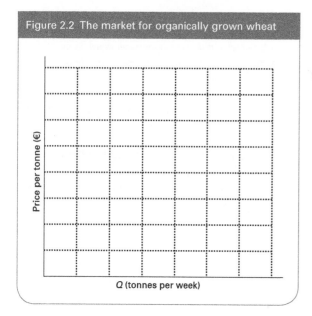

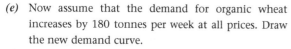

Figure 2.3 The market for new flats

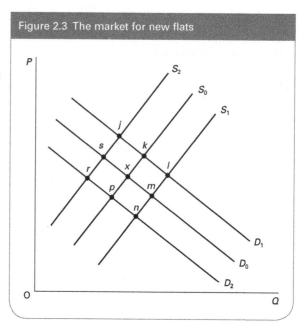

(e) Now assume that the demand for organic wheat increases by 180 tonnes per week at all prices. Draw the new demand curve.

(f) What is the size of the shortage or surplus at the original equilibrium price?

Shortage/surplus of ....

(g) What is the new equilibrium price?

(h) Has the equilibrium quantity increased by more or less than the 180 tonnes per week increase in demand?

More/Less

Assume that supply now changes by an equal amount at all prices.

(i) What would this change have to be to restore the original equilibrium price?

Increase/Decrease of ....

(j) What would this change have to be to restore the original equilibrium quantity?

Increase/Decrease of ....

(k) Is there any shift in the supply curve that could restore both the original equilibrium price and the original quantity? *Yes/No*

Explain ....

....

Q28. If income increases, then for an inferior good, the quantity sold will decrease and the price will increase.

True/False

Q29. Figure 2.3 shows the demand for and supply of new purpose-built flats.

The supply and demand curves are initially given by S_0 and D_0. The market is in equilibrium at point x. Various factors then change which have the effect of shifting the demand curve to D_1 or D_2 and/or the supply curve to S_1 or S_2. What is the new equilibrium point in each of the following cases? (Remember that in each case the market is initially in equilibrium at point x.)

(a) A rise in the price of building materials.

Point ....

(b) Flat living becomes more fashionable.

Point ....

(c) A fall in the price of new houses.

Point ....

(d) A rise in the price of old houses and flats.

Point ....

(e) The imposition of a new construction tax on houses (but not flats).

Point ....

(f) The belief that the price of flats will soon rise substantially.

Point ....

(g) An increase in mortgage interest rates.

Point ....

Q30. Suppose that it is observed that the price of butter falls but that the quantity sold rises. From this we can deduce:

A. That the demand curve has shifted to the right, but we cannot deduce whether or not the supply curve has shifted.

B. That the demand curve has shifted to the left, but we cannot deduce whether or not the supply curve has shifted.

C. That the supply curve has shifted to the right, but we cannot deduce whether or not the demand curve has shifted.

D. That the supply curve has shifted to the left, but we cannot deduce whether or not the demand curve has shifted.

E. Nothing. Either curve could have shifted either way depending on which way the other shifted.

(Pages 38, 42) Demand and supply curves can be represented by equations.

(?) *Q31.* Suppose you are told that the demand curve for bus journeys takes the general form:

$$Q_d = a - bP - cY + dP_r$$

where:

Q_d is quantity demanded of bus journeys, P is the price of bus journeys, Y is consumer incomes and P_r is the price of rail journeys. (Note: the parameters a, b, c and d are all positive.) How would quantity demanded be affected by the following?

(a) A fall in bus fares.

....

(b) A recession that leads to a fall in consumer incomes.

....

(c) An increase in rail fares.

....

(d) An advertising campaign emphasising the convenience of bus travel.

....

(⊖) *Q32.* The supply and demand curves for commodity X are given by the following equations:

$$Q_s = 2 + 3P$$
$$Q_d = 50 - 5P$$

(a) Without drawing a diagram or completing a table, find the equilibrium price and quantity.
(You will need to use simultaneous equations.)

....

(b) Using the two equations, fill in the figures in Table 2.3.
(c) Draw a graph of the two curves on Figure 2.4.
(d) Assume that the demand equation now becomes: $Q_d = 66 - 5P$. Draw the new demand curve on Figure 2.4 and find the equilibrium. How is the shape of the demand curve affected?
(e) Assume that the demand equation now becomes: $Q_d = 50 - 9P$. Draw the new demand curve and find the equilibrium. How is the shape of the demand curve affected this time?

Table 2.3 $Q_s = 2 + 3P$; $Q_d = 50 - 5P$

P	0	1	2	3	4	5	6	7	8	9	10
Q_s	.	.	.	11	.	.	.	.	.	.	.
Q_d	.	.	40	.	.	.	.	.	.	.	.

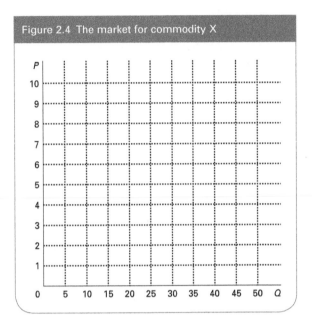

Figure 2.4 The market for commodity X

2.4 The control of prices

(Pages 52–4) The commonest form of price control is the setting of minimum or maximum prices.

If a minimum price (a price floor) is set above the equilibrium price, a *Q33.* shortage/surplus will result. If a maximum price (a price ceiling) is set below the equilibrium price, a *Q34.* shortage/surplus will result.

(⊖) *Q35.* Figure 2.5 shows the demand and supply for petrol. The market is initially in equilibrium with a price of £1.30 per litre and sales of 40 million litres per day.

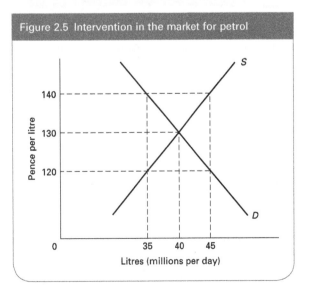

Figure 2.5 Intervention in the market for petrol

(a) Assume that the government is worried about inflation and decides to set a maximum price for petrol. What will be the effect if it sets this price at:

(i) £1.40? ....

(ii) £1.20? ....

(iii) Is a black market in petrol likely to emerge in either case?

£1.40:   *Yes/No*

£1.20:   *Yes/No*

(iv) Explain your answer to (iii).

....

....

(b) Assume now that, worried about the effect of excessive fossil fuel consumption on global warming, the government passes a law forcing companies to sell petrol at £1.40 per litre, but agrees to buy (at £1.40) any surplus and put it into store.

(i) What will be the effect on consumer expenditure?

....

(ii) How much will the government have to buy from the petrol companies?

....

(iii) How much revenue will the petrol companies earn?

....

Q36. Which one of the following controls would involve setting a minimum price rather than a maximum price (where 'price' can include the price of the services of a factor of production)?

A. Controls on rents to protect tenants on low incomes.

B. Controls on wages to protect workers on low incomes.

C. Controls on basic food prices to protect consumers on low incomes.

D. Controls on transport fares to protect passengers on low incomes.

E. None of the above.

Q37. Give three problems that can occur when the government imposes maximum prices.

1. ....

2. ....

3. ....

Q38. Give three problems that can occur when the government imposes minimum prices.

1. ....

2. ....

3. ....

B   PROBLEMS, EXERCISES AND PROJECTS

Q39. Clearly defining the market may be crucial in explaining the effect of a price change on the quantity of a good demanded.

The market for petrol is a good example. The demand for all petrol is relatively inelastic to changes in price: there are few substitutes and it takes time for consumers to change their consumption patterns. Yet if you consider the demand for a single brand of petrol, it becomes far more elastic, as there are several substitute brands available.

Consider the two diagrams in Figure 2.6.

If the price of *all* petrol rises from £1.20 per litre to £1.40 as in diagram (a), total revenue increases from area *abc*0 to area *def*0: from (£1.20 × 50m) = £60m to (£1.40 × 45m) = £63m.

Alternatively, if a *particular company* raises its price *independently* of its competitors, the demand for its particular brand will fall dramatically. In diagram (b), when the

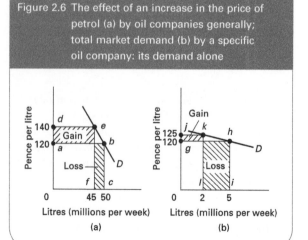

Figure 2.6 The effect of an increase in the price of petrol (a) by oil companies generally; total market demand (b) by a specific oil company: its demand alone

company raises its price to £1.25 its total revenue falls from area *ghi*0 to area *jkl*0: from (£1.20 × 5m) = £6m to (£1.25 × 2m) = £2.5m.

Generally, the more narrowly we define a market, the more substitutes there will be outside that market and therefore the more elastic the demand will be.

(*a*) Using the arc method of calculating elasticity, what is the price elasticity of demand between the two points on each of the two curves in Figure 2.6?

(*b*) Which would you expect to have the higher price elasticity: the demand for a particular brand of petrol or the demand for petrol from a particular filling station? Explain your assumptions.

Q40. Collect data for the annual percentage changes in house prices and GDP (gross domestic product: the value of national output) and for the average annual level of interest rates for the UK from 2000. You should use data from the ONS website and in the Treasury Pocket Databank on the Treasury site (see the hotlinks section on the book's website).

(*a*) Plot a time-series graph for the three indicators. Plot the years on the horizontal axis, the percentage changes in house prices and GDP on one vertical axis and the percentage interest rate on the other vertical axis.

(*b*) Describe the pattern of house price changes over the period.

(*c*) What is the likely relationship between the rate of house price inflation and (i) the rate of interest; (ii) the rate of growth in GDP? Use diagrams to support your answer.

(*d*) Discuss two other factors that might have caused the change in house prices. Draw diagrams to illustrate your analysis.

(*e*) Forecast what will happen to house prices over the next two years, identifying the factors that are likely to influence demand and/or supply.

Table 2.4 Demand and supply of solar panels

Price (per sq. metre) (£)	Quantity demanded (sq. metres per year) (000s)	Quantity supplied (sq. metres per year) (000s)
100	5	40
90	10	30
80	15	25
70	20	20
60	25	15
50	32	9
40	40	2
30	58	0

Q41. Table 2.4 gives (imaginary) information about the market for solar panels.

(*a*) What is the equilibrium price?

(*b*) Over what price range(s) is the demand curve a straight line?

(*c*) Assume that the government wants to promote the purchase of solar panels by householders in order to save energy. As a result it decides to impose a maximum price. What will be the effect if the maximum price is: (i) £90, (ii) £60?

(*d*) Will a maximum price of £50 lead to a higher or lower level of panels being sold than if the price was left free to be determined by the market?

(*e*) Assume that the government abandons the use of maximum prices and instead decides to grant a subsidy to producers. What size subsidy must be granted in order to reduce the price to £60?

(*f*) How much will this subsidy cost the taxpayer?

(*g*) What will be the incidence of this subsidy between consumers and producers?

C DISCUSSION TOPICS AND ESSAYS

Q42. Using supply and demand diagrams, illustrate the effects of a substantial fall in the world output of oil and gas on the prices of (a) oil, (b) coal, (c) cars, and on (d) bus fares.

Q43. Is the following statement true? 'An increase in demand will cause an increase in price. This increase in price will then cause a reduction in demand, until demand is reduced back to its original level.' Explain your answer.

Q44. Under what circumstances are black markets likely to develop? What will determine the level of the black market price?

Q45. Compare the relative merits of alternative means of reducing waiting lists for operations in National Health Service hospitals.

Q46. Give three examples of price controls. In each case identify the reasons for these controls and whether any other form of intervention could have achieved the same objectives.

Q47. Identify some measures the government could take to encourage energy conservation. Would any of these measures prevent a market equilibrium being achieved? What effects would there be in other markets from the various measures?

Q48. Debate
The price of manufactured goods will always be more stable than that of agricultural goods in the short term, but will be less stable in the long term.

ANSWERS

Q1. A. There is an inverse relationship between price and quantity demanded. The higher the price, the less the quantity demanded; the lower the price, the greater the quantity demanded.

Q2. *False.* It refers to the effect of a change in the *price* of the good on quantity demanded as a result of the consumer becoming better or worse off as a result of the price change: in other words, because of the effect of the price change on the purchasing power of the consumer's income.

Q3. *False.* It refers to the effect of a change in the price of the *good itself*, not to a change in the price of a substitute. The point is that if a good comes down in price, it will now be cheaper relative to the substitute than it was before, and thus people are likely to switch to it from the substitute.

Q4. *(a)* See table below.

Price (£)	Annual market demand (000s)
100	7
80	10
60	16
40	27
20	48

(b) See Figure A2.1.

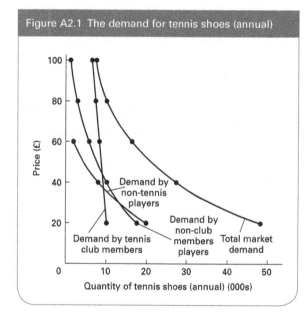

Figure A2.1 The demand for tennis shoes (annual)

Q5. (a) (iii), (b) (i), (c) (v), (d) (ii), (e) (vi), (f) (iv)

Q6. *quantity demanded.*

Q7. *a movement along the demand curve.*

Q8. *demand.*

Q9. *a shift in the demand curve.*

Q10. *(a)* *Leftward shift.* There will be a reduction in the demand for cars and hence for petrol. (Petrol and cars are complements.)

(b) *Rightward shift.* With more car owners the demand for petrol will be higher.

(c) *Movement up along.* This pushes up price (a shift in the supply curve). A change in price causes a movement along the demand curve.

(d) *Need more information to say.* An increased concern for the health hazards from diesel (e.g. asthma from diesel fumes) would cause people to switch from diesel to petrol (a *rightward* shift in the demand for petrol). On the other hand, an increased concern for the problems of traffic congestion, global warming, etc. will cause people to use cars less and thus use less petrol (a *leftward* shift in the demand curve).

(e) *Rightward shift.* People will switch to petrol (a substitute for diesel).

(f) *Movement down along.* This will reduce the price of petrol.

Q11. *whose demand increases as income increases.*

Q12. *whose demand decreases as income increases.*

Q13. *direct.*

Q14. What we are looking for is explanations of why a higher price will lead to a greater quantity being supplied (or why a lower price will lead to a smaller quantity). (b), (c), (d) are correct because they all explain this direct relationship. (a) does not provide an explanation because these cost increases are not associated with extra output. (e) is not an explanation because changes in technology are independent of price changes. They may cause price to change, but they are not a reason why a price change affects output.

Q15. The *costs* of production; the profitability of *alternative products*; the profitability of goods in *joint supply*; *random shocks*; and *expectations* of future price changes.

Q16. *a movement along* the supply curve.

Q17. a change in *the quantity supplied.*

Q18. *a shift in* the supply curve.

Q19. a change in *supply.*

Q20. *(a)* *Rightward shift.* A reduction in the cost of producing organic wheat.

(b) *Movement up along.* The demand for organic wheat has increased and hence also its price.

(c) *Leftward shift.* These goods are in *alternative supply*.

(d) Immediate effect: *leftward shift*. Anticipating higher prices, farmers put more organic wheat into store, hoping to sell later when the price has gone up. This reduces current supplies on the market. Subsequent effect: *rightward shift*. Farmers switch to organic methods in

anticipation that they will be more profitable. Supply increases.

(e) *Leftward shift.* The supply of wheat (of all types) decreases.

(f) *Rightward shift.* (As (a) above.)

Q21. *shortage.*

Q22. *rise.*

Q23. *surplus.*

Q24. *fall.*

Q25. *Demand equals supply.*

Q26. *movement along.*

Q27. (a) See Figure A2.2.

(b) *Shortage of 290 tonnes per week.*

(c) *Surplus of 480 tonnes per week.*

(d) *P = €260; Q = 500 tonnes per week.*

(e) See Figure A2.2.

(f) *Shortage of 180 tonnes per week.*

(g) *P = €300.*

(h) Less. It has only increased by 140 tonnes per week.

(i) *Increase (rightward shift) of 180 tonnes per week.* This would mean that at the old price of €260, 680 tonnes per week would now be both demanded and supplied.

(j) *Decrease (leftward shift) of 900 tonnes per week.* This would mean that at a new equilibrium price of €380, 500 tonnes per week would once again be both demanded and supplied.

(k) *No.* Given that the demand curve slopes downwards, a rightward shift in supply is essential to restore the old equilibrium price, and a leftward shift is essential to restore the old equilibrium quantity. (Only a leftward shift in *demand* could restore both simultaneously.)

Q28. *False.* The demand curve will shift to the left. This will cause a decrease in the quantity sold *and also* a decrease in the price.

Q29. (a) *Point s.* Increased costs shift the supply curve to the left. No shift in the demand curve.

(b) *Point k.* A shift in tastes towards flats shifts the demand curve to the right. No shift in the supply curve.

(c) *Point n.* The fall in house prices reduces the demand for flats (a substitute). The demand curve shifts to the left. The fall in house prices makes their construction less profitable relative to flats (which are in alternative supply). The supply curve of new flats therefore shifts to the right.

(d) *Point k.* This will increase the demand for *new* houses and flats. The demand curve for new flats shifts to the right. No shift in the supply curve. (Builders cannot switch to building *old* houses and flats!)

(e) *Point l.* The construction tax on houses will make building flats more profitable. The supply curve will shift to the right. The higher price of houses resulting from the tax will increase the demand for flats. The demand curve shifts to the right.

(f) *Point j.* People will rush to buy flats now before prices rise. Demand shifts to the right. Builders will wait to sell their new flats until the price has risen. Supply will shift to the left.

(g) There are two possible answers here:

(i) *Point p.* If higher mortgage interest rates reduce the demand for *all* types of property, the demand curve for flats will shift to the left.

(ii) *Point k.* If flats are seen as an inferior good (to houses), the demand may *rise* as purchasers switch from houses to flats.

Q30. C. A shift in the demand curve alone must cause price and quantity to change in the *same* direction. Thus if price and quantity change in opposite directions, the *supply* curve must have shifted, causing a movement along the demand curve. In this case there must be a rightward shift in the supply curve causing a movement down along the demand curve. There may have been a less significant shift in the demand curve too, but we cannot tell.

*Q31. (a) A fall in bus fares induces an increase in demand for bus journeys, as there is a negative relationship between quantity demanded and the price of bus journeys.

(b) The equation also shows a negative relationship between the demand for bus journeys and consumer incomes – i.e. bus travel is an *inferior good*. Thus a recession that leads to a fall in consumer incomes leads to an increase in the quantity demanded of bus journeys.

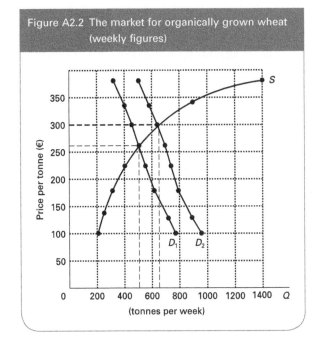

Figure A2.2 The market for organically grown wheat (weekly figures)

Price per tonne (€) / (tonnes per week)

(c) As bus and rail travel are substitutes, an increase in rail fares leads to an increase in the demand for bus journeys.

(d) If successful, the advertising campaign will increase the popularity of bus travel, shifting the demand curve by affecting the size of the parameter *a*.

*Q32. (a) Set the two equations equal (given that in equilibrium supply equals demand).

$2 + 3P = 50 - 5P$

$\therefore 8P = 48$

$\therefore P = 6$

Substituting $P = 6$ in either of the two equations (since demand *equals* supply) gives:

$Q = 20$

(b) See table below.

P	0	1	2	3	4	5	6	7	8	9	10
Q_s	2	5	8	11	14	17	20	23	26	29	32
Q_d	50	45	40	35	30	25	20	15	10	5	0

(c) See Figure A2.3.

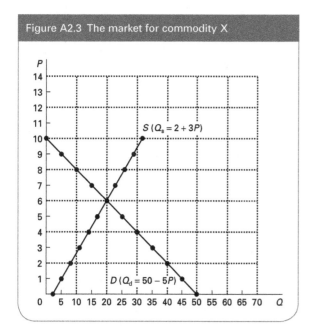

Figure A2.3 The market for commodity X

(d) *Parallel shift to the right by 16 units*. The interception point with the horizontal axis (given by the constant term) increases from $Q = 50$ to $Q = 66$. The equilibrium point now becomes $P = 8$, $Q = 26$.

(e) *The curve flattens*. The interception point with the horizontal axis remains at $Q = 50$, but the slope (given by the inverse of the P term) flattens from $-1/5$ to $-1/9$. The equilibrium point is now $P = 4$, $Q = 14$.

Q33. *surplus*. If the minimum price is set at any point above the equilibrium, supply will exceed demand.

Q34. *shortage*. If the maximum price is set at any point below the equilibrium, demand will exceed supply.

Q35. (a) (i) *No effect*. Maximum price is above existing price.

(ii) *Shortage of 10 million litres per day* (i.e. 45 − 35).

(iii)/(iv) £1.40: *No*. Price remains at the equilibrium of £1.30. £1.20: *Possibly*. There will remain unsatisfied demand of 10 million litres, with, no doubt, some people being prepared to pay considerably more than £1.20. Whether black marketeers can operate depends on whether there are any sources of supply that can avoid detection. This would clearly be difficult in the case of petrol.

(b) (i) *Decrease from £52 million per day (40m × £1.30) to £49 million (35m × £1.40)*.

(ii) *10 million litres per day*.

(iii) *£63 million per day (45m × £1.40)*.

Q36. B. Wage control to help those on low incomes will involve setting a minimum wage *above* the equilibrium wage in low-paid occupations. In the other three cases, the purpose of price controls would be to keep prices *below* the equilibrium if the aim was to help those on low incomes afford the particular type of good or service. In such cases, therefore, a *maximum* price (or rent) would be appropriate.

Q37. If the maximum price is set below the equilibrium, the following problems could occur: producers' income will be cut and thus supplies of an already scarce product (e.g. food supplies in a drought) are likely to be reduced further (a movement down the supply curve); firms will also be discouraged from investing and thus *future* supplies are likely to be less; unless a system of rationing is in place, some consumers may be unable to obtain the product (given that there will be a shortage at the maximum price), and this clearly could be unfair; a black market may develop; queues may develop and this is time consuming.

Q38. If the minimum price is set above the equilibrium, the following problems could occur: surpluses will be produced, which is wasteful (in the case of minimum wages, levels of unemployment in such occupations could rise); the government may have to spend taxpayers' money on purchasing the surpluses; high prices may cushion inefficiency, with firms feeling less need to find more efficient methods of production and to cut costs; firms may be discouraged from producing alternative goods which they could produce more efficiently or which are in higher demand, but which nevertheless have a lower (free-market) price; firms may find ways of evading the price controls and dumping the surpluses onto the market.

Chapter 3

Markets in Action

 REVIEW

Chapter 2 examined the working of the free market. We now turn to examine just how responsive demand and supply are to their various determinants and particularly to changes in price; in doing this we will examine the important concept of *elasticity*.

The response of demand, supply and price to changing market conditions is unlikely to be instantaneous. In the second section, therefore, we examine the *time dimension* of markets. We look at the process of adjustment after the elapse of different periods of time.

In the third section we examine the 'incidence' of taxes and subsidies on goods and services: who ends up paying the tax or receiving the subsidy – the producer or the consumer? To do this we must see what happens to price and this will depend on the price elasticities of demand and supply. In the fourth section we look at the extreme case of where the government rejects allocation by the market and either prohibits the production of certain goods or takes over production directly. Finally, we look at agriculture as a case study of different types of government intervention.

3.1 Elasticity

Elasticity (ϵ) is a measure of the responsiveness of demand (or supply) to a change in one of the determinants, and is one of the most important concepts we shall come across in the whole of economics. It is defined as the proportionate (or percentage) change in quantity demanded (or supplied) (Q) divided by the proportionate (or percentage) change in the determinant (X).

$\epsilon = \Delta Q/Q \div X/X$

(Pages 58–9) The *price elasticity of demand* measures the responsiveness of **Q1.** *the quantity demanded/price* to a change in **Q2.** *the quantity demanded/the quantity supplied/price*.

Q3. The formula for the price elasticity of demand ($P\epsilon_d$) is

....

If the quantity demanded changes proportionately more than the price, we say that demand is **Q4.** *elastic/inelastic*. If the quantity demanded changes proportionately less than the price, we say that demand is **Q5.** *elastic/inelastic*. Assuming that a demand curve is downward sloping, the price elasticity of demand will have **Q6.** *a positive value ($\epsilon > 0$)/a negative value ($\epsilon < 0$)*.

Let us now ignore the sign (positive or negative) and consider just the value for elasticity: for example $\epsilon = 1.8$ or $\epsilon = 0.43$.

| Multiple choice | Written answer | Delete wrong word | Diagram/table manipulation | Calculation | Matching/ordering |

Q7. Match each of the following figures for elasticity to definitions (a)–(e) below.
  (i) $\epsilon = 1$
 (ii) $1 > \epsilon > 0$ (This means that the figure for elasticity is greater than 0 but less than 1.)
(iii) $\epsilon = 0$
(iv) $\epsilon = \infty$
 (v) $\infty > \epsilon > 1$

(a) Elastic.
(b) Unit elastic.
(c) Totally inelastic.
(d) Inelastic.
(e) Totally elastic.

(Pages 59–60) Demand will be more elastic **Q8.** *the greater/the less* the number and closeness of substitute goods, **Q9.** *the higher/the lower* the proportion of income spent on the good and **Q10.** *the longer/the shorter* the time period that elapses after the change in price.

Q11. Rank the following in ascending order of price elasticity of demand (i.e. least elastic first):

(a) Margarine...

(b) 'Scrummy' low-fat margarine..

(c) Spreads for bread..

(d) Low-fat margarine...

(e) 'Scrummy' low-fat margarine with a token for the current competition..

Q12. The price elasticity of demand for holidays abroad (in general) is likely to be high because
A. people tend to book up a long time in advance.
B. there are plenty of different foreign holidays to choose from.
C. foreign holidays are an expensive luxury.
D. holidays at home provide no real alternative.
E. people need a holiday if they are to cope with the year ahead.

We must be careful when drawing inferences about price elasticity from demand curves.

Q13. Referring to the two demand curves in Figure 3.1, which of the following statements are correct?
(a) Curve D_2 is elastic.   *True/False*
(b) Curve D_1 has a price elasticity of –1.   *True/False*
(c) At point x, curve D_1 has an elasticity of zero.
                                          True/False
(d) At point y, curve D_2 has an elasticity of infinity.
                                          True/False

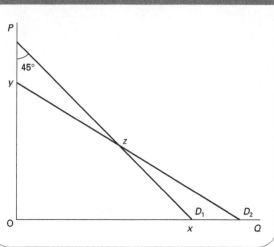

Figure 3.1 Two different demand curves

(e) Curve D_2 is more elastic than curve D_1.   *True/False*
(f) At point z, the two curves have the same price elasticity.
                                          True/False
(g) Curve D_2 is more elastic than curve D_1 over the range yz.   *True/False*

(Pages 62–5) Given that demand curves normally have different elasticities along their length, we can normally only refer to the specific value for elasticity between two points on the curve or at a single point.

Q14. Elasticity measured between two points is known as

....

When applied to price elasticity of demand its formula is:

$$\frac{\Delta Q_d}{\text{average } Q_d} \times \frac{\Delta P}{\text{average } P}$$

where average Q_d is the average value of Q_d at the two points between which we are measuring elasticity. Thus if at one point $Q_d = 6$ and at the other $Q_d = 4$, then average $Q_d = 5$: i.e. average $Q_d = (Q_{d_1} + Q_{d_2})/2$.

Q15. Similarly average $P =$ ....

Q16. Given the equation $Q_d = 20 - 2P$:
(a) Fill in the figures for quantity demanded in Table 3.1.
(b) Estimate the price elasticity of demand between:
   (i) $P = 2$ and $P = 0$
  (ii) $P = 6$ and $P = 4$
 (iii) $P = 9$ and $P = 7$
   In each case state whether demand is elastic or inelastic.
(c) Using this arc method, how would you estimate price elasticity at a single point?

....

(d) Using this method, estimate the price elasticity of demand at:
- (i) $P = 2$
- (ii) $P = 6$
- (iii) $P = 5$
- (iv) $P = 0$
- (v) $P = 10$

(Pages 60–61) One of the most important applications of price elasticity of demand concerns the relationship between the *price* of a good and the total amount of *expenditure* by consumers (and hence the *revenue* earned by firms). We define *total expenditure* as price times quantity sold: $TE = P \times Q$.

⊖ **Q17.** Fill in a new row in Table 3.1 showing the level of total expenditure at each price.

◑ **Q18.** Referring again to Table 3.1:
- (a) What will be the effect on total expenditure of reducing price (and hence increasing the quantity demanded) when demand is price *elastic*?   *rise/fall*
- (b) What will be the effect when demand is price inelastic?   *rise/fall*
- (c) What will be the elasticity at the price where total expenditure is the maximum?

....

Table 3.1 Demand schedule: $Q_d = 20 - 2P$

P(£)	10	9	8	7	6	5	4	3	2	1	0
Q_d	.	.	.	.	8	.	.	.	.	.	.

◑ **Q19.** When the price elasticity of demand for a good is –1.4, then a rise in the price will result in fewer goods being sold but greater consumer expenditure.   *True/False*

◑ **Q20.** When demand is price inelastic, total expenditure will vary directly with price but inversely with quantity demanded.   *True/False*

◑ **Q21.** The elasticity of a straight-line demand curve will fall as you move down the curve, from infinity at the point where it intersects the vertical axis to zero at the point where it intersects the horizontal axis.   *True/False*

*(Pages 64–5) Another way of measuring elasticity is to use the point method. Remember that the arc formula for price elasticity is:

$$\frac{\Delta Q_d}{\text{average } Q_d} \div \frac{\Delta P}{\text{average } P}$$

If we want to measure elasticity at a point, then average P and Q_d simply become P and Q_d, and the 'change' (Δ) in price

and quantity becomes infinitesimally small. An infinitesimally small change is written d. The formula thus becomes:

$$dQ_d/Q_d \div dP/P$$

⑦ *Q22.** Rearranged this formula becomes:

$dQ_d/dP \times$ ....

where dQ_d/dP is the ***Q23.** slope/inverse of the slope* of the tangent to the demand curve at the point in question.

⊖ *Q24.** Given the following equation for a demand curve:

$$Q_d = 50 - 20P + 2P^2$$

- (a) fill in the figures in Table 3.2.
- (b) Draw the demand curve on Figure 3.2.
- (c) Draw the tangent to the curve where $P = 3$, $Q = 8$. What is its slope?

....

- (d) What is the price elasticity of demand where $P = 3$?

....

(Pages 66–8) We turn now to other types of elasticity and start with *price elasticity of supply*.

Table 3.2 Demand schedule: $Q_d = 50 - 20P + 2P^2$

P	5	4	3	2	1	0
Q_d	.	.	.	.	.	.

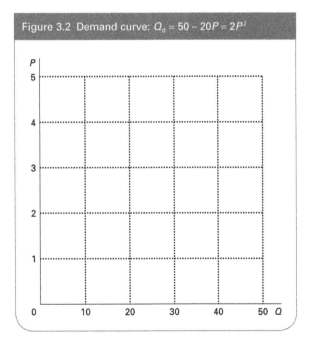

Figure 3.2 Demand curve: $Q_d = 50 - 20P = 2P^2$

◗ Q25. There are two goods A and B. Which is likely to have the more price-elastic supply in each of the following cases?

(a) It is less costly to shift from producing A to another product than it is to shift from B to another product.
A/B/cannot say

(b) The supply of A is considered over a longer period of time than B. *A/B/cannot say*

(c) The cost of producing extra units increases more rapidly in the case of A than in the case of B.
A/B/cannot say

(d) Consumers find it easier to find alternatives to A than to B. *A/B/cannot say*

(e) A is a minor by-product of B. *A/B/cannot say*

(f) A higher proportion of national income is spent on A than on B. *A/B/cannot say*

◗ Q26. Consider the three supply curves in Figure 3.3. Which of the following statements are correct?

(a) Curve S_1 has an elasticity equal to 1 throughout its length. *True/False*

(b) The elasticity of all three curves is the same at point *x*. *True/False*

(c) Curve S_2 has an elasticity greater than 1 throughout its length. *True/False*

(d) Curve S_3 has an elasticity equal to zero at point *z*. *True/False*

(e) Curve S_2 has an elasticity equal to infinity at point *y*. *True/False*

(f) Curve S_3 has a constant elasticity less than 1 throughout its length. *True/False*

(Pages 68–70) Income elasticity of demand measures the responsiveness of demand to a change in income. For normal goods it has a **Q27.** *positive/negative* value.

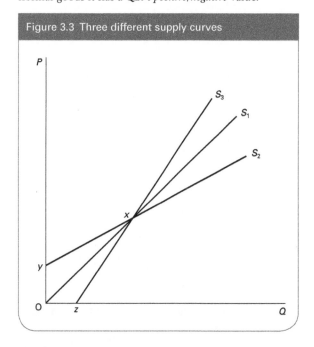

Figure 3.3 Three different supply curves

⊗ Q28. Table 3.3 shows the quantity of three goods (A, B and C) purchased in two years (year 1 and year 2). The only factor affecting demand that changes between these two years is consumer incomes.

Table 3.3 Demand for goods A, B and C in years 1 and 2

	Quantity demanded Good A (000s)	Quantity demanded Good B (000s)	Quantity demanded Good C (000s)	Consumer income (Y) (£bn)
Year 1	30	52	190	45
Year 2	50	48	210	55

(a) What is the income elasticity of demand for the three goods between $Y = £45$ billion and £55 billion? (Use the arc method.)

Good A ....

Good B ....

Good C ....

(b) Which of the three goods has an income-*elastic* demand over the given income range? *A/B/C*

(c) Which of the goods is an inferior good over the given income range? *A/B/C*

◗ Q29. The share of income devoted to a good will increase with income if the good has an income elasticity of demand greater than 1. *True/False*

(Page 70) Cross-price elasticity of demand measures the responsiveness of the demand for one good to a change in the price of another and thus is a means of judging the degree of substitutability or complementarity of two goods.

✪ Q30. Match each of the following five values for cross-price elasticity (i)–(v), to the pairs of products (a)–(e).

(i) Considerably greater than zero
(ii) Slightly greater than zero
(iii) Zero
(iv) Slightly less than zero
(v) Considerably less than zero

(a) Petrol and cars..

(b) Salt and petrol..

(c) Cars and bicycles.....................................

(d) Corsas and Ford Kas.................................

(e) Petrol and cross-Channel ferry crossings...................

3.2 The time dimension

(Page 72) To get a fuller picture of how markets work we must take into account the time dimension. Given that producers and consumers take a time to respond fully to

price changes, we can identify different equilibria after the elapse of different lengths of time. Generally, short-run supply and demand tend to be **Q31.** *more/less* price-elastic than long-run supply and demand. As a result, any shifts in demand or supply curves tend to have a relatively bigger effect on **Q32.** *price/quantity* in the short run and a relatively bigger effect on **Q33.** *price/quantity* in the long run.

Q34. The short-run (retail) supply of freshly cut flowers is much less elastic than that of pot plants because
A. households generally keep pot plants much longer before throwing them away (and often never throw them away).
B. fresh flowers are more likely to be purchased for special occasions.
C. the price of freshly cut flowers fluctuates much more than that of pot plants.
D. supplies of fresh flowers fluctuate much more with the weather and the season.
E. florists cannot keep freshly cut flowers as long as pot plants.

(Pages 72–7) Realising that prices can fluctuate, buyers and sellers are likely to try to anticipate what will happen to prices if they are in a position to wait before buying or selling. In such cases, if people believe that prices are likely to rise, current supply will shift to the **Q35.** *left/right* and current demand will shift to the **Q36.** *left/right.* This will have the effect of causing the price to **Q37.** *rise/fall.*

This activity where buyers or sellers predict price changes and then act on these predictions is called *speculation*. It can be of two types, *stabilising* and *destabilising*.

Q38. Figure 3.4 shows a market where demand has just increased from D_0 to D_1 with a resulting price rise from P_0

to P_1. People then make a judgement from this about future price changes. Which one of the four diagrams represents stabilising speculation and which destabilising?
Stabilising   *(a)/(b)/(c)/(d)*
Destabilising   *(a)/(b)/(c)/(d)*

Q39. Suppose there is a sudden unexpected increase in the price of oil. Which one of the following statements is true in the short run?
A. Motorists will switch to more fuel-efficient cars.
B. Firms will undertake research and development into alternative sources of energy.
C. Motor vehicle producers will develop more fuel-efficient cars.
D. Car drivers will undertake fewer unnecessary journeys.
E. Manufacturing enterprises will convert their factories to use alternative energy sources.

3.3 Indirect taxes
(Pages 78–81) Another form of government intervention in markets is the imposition of taxes on goods (indirect taxes). Such taxes include VAT and excise duties (on items such as cigarettes, alcohol and petrol). The taxes will have the effect of raising prices and thus could be used as a means not only of raising revenue for the government, but also of reducing the consumption of potentially harmful products.

A tax imposed on a good will have the effect of shifting the supply curve **Q40.** *upward/downward.* A specific tax will **Q41.** *make the supply curve steeper/make the supply curve shallower/leave the slope of the supply curve unaffected.* An *ad valorem* tax will **Q42.** *make the supply curve steeper/make the supply curve shallower/leave the slope of the supply curve unaffected.*

Q43. Figure 3.5 shows the effects of imposing taxes or giving subsidies on a good.

Figure 3.4 Speculation

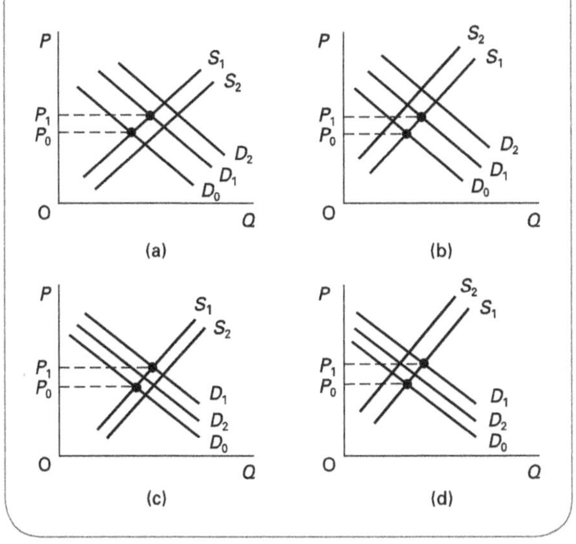

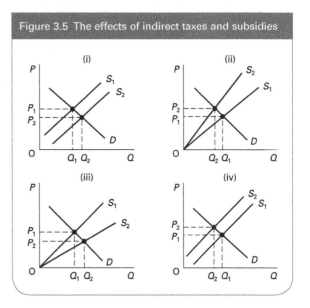

Figure 3.5 The effects of indirect taxes and subsidies

Match each of the following to one of the four diagrams.

(a) An *ad valorem* subsidy   *(i)/(ii)/(iii)/(iv)*
(b) A specific tax   *(i)/(ii)/(iii)/(iv)*
(c) An *ad valorem* tax   *(i)/(ii)/(iii)/(iv)*
(d) A specific (per-unit) subsidy   *(i)/(ii)/(iii)/(iv)*

Q44. If the imposition of a tax (t) on a good has the effect of increasing the price from P_1 to P_2 and reducing the quantity sold from Q_1 to Q_2 then the consumers' share of the total tax paid is:

A. $P_2 \times Q_2$
B. $t \times (Q_1 - Q_2)$
C. $(P_2 - P_1) \times Q_2$
D. $(t - (P_2 - P_1)) \times Q_2$
E. $(P_2 - t) \times (Q_1 - Q_2)$

(Try sketching a diagram and attaching the appropriate labels.)

Q45. Referring to the information in Q44, the producers' share of the tax is:

A. B. C. D. E.

Q46. In which of the following situations would the imposition of a tax on a good involve the highest producers' share of the tax?

A.   An elastic demand and an elastic supply.
B.   An inelastic demand and an inelastic supply.
C.   A unit-elastic demand and a unit-elastic supply.
D.   An elastic demand and an inelastic supply.
E.   An inelastic demand and an elastic supply.

(In each case 'elasticity' is referring to 'price elasticity'.)

3.4 Government rejection of market allocation

(Pages 81–3) With some goods and services, the government may feel that it is best to reject allocation through the market altogether. At one extreme, it may feel that certain products are so important to people that they ought to be provided free at the point of use. This is the equivalent of setting **Q47.** *a maximum price/a minimum price* of zero. The result is that there is likely to be a shortage of provision. This shortage is likely to be greater, the **Q48.** *greater/lower* is the price elasticity of demand for the product.

Q49. In the case of the provision of health care, shortages result in:

(a) Some people taking out private health insurance
          True/False
(b) Waiting lists   *True/False*
(c) Fewer people being treated than if the price were allowed to rise to the equilibrium   *True/False*
(d) Rationing   *True/False*
(e) Non-urgent cases not being treated   *True/False*

(f) Some non-serious cases not being treated   *True/False*
(g) Resources being diverted from education and social security   *True/False*

(Page 82) At the other extreme, the government may feel that some products are so harmful, they ought to be banned.

Q50. Assume that a product (such as a drug) is made illegal. This will have the effect of:

(a) shifting the demand curve to the   *left/right*
(b) shifting the supply curve to the   *left/right*
(c) making the price in the illegal market (compared with the previous legal market)
          higher/lower/either higher or lower (depending on the relative shifts in the demand and supply curves)

Q51. Assuming that making a product illegal has the effect of making the illegal market price higher than the previous legal market price, under which one of the following circumstances would the price rise be the greatest?

A.   A small shift in the supply curve and a large shift in the demand curve.
B.   A small shift in the supply curve and a price-elastic demand.
C.   A small shift in the supply curve and a price-inelastic demand.
D.   A large shift in the supply curve and a price-elastic demand.
E.   A large shift in the supply curve and a price-inelastic demand.

Q52. Assume that the government wishes to reduce consumption of a certain product. To achieve the same level of reduction by using a tax as by banning the product:

(a) A bigger shift in the supply curve will be required.
          True/False
(b) A smaller rise in price will be required.   *True/False*

3.5 Agriculture and agricultural policy

(Pages 83–93) Governments have intervened massively in agricultural markets throughout the world.

Short-term fluctuations in agricultural prices are due to problems on both the demand and supply sides.

Q53. Price fluctuations are likely to be greater,
(a) the more price elastic the supply.   *True/False*
(b) the greater the fluctuations in the harvest.   *True/False*
(c) the more price elastic the demand.   *True/False*

Q54. The following are possible features of the market for wheat.
 (i) There is substantial technical progress leading to increased production over the years.
 (ii) There is an income-inelastic demand for wheat.
 (iii) There is a price-inelastic demand for wheat.
 (iv) Wheat harvests fluctuate substantially with the weather.

Which of the above help to explain why incomes (i.e. revenues) of wheat farmers are likely to grow more slowly than incomes of producers of non-foodstuffs?

A. (ii) and (iii).
B. (i) and (iv).
C. (i), (iii) and (iv).
D. (i), (ii) and (iii).
E. (ii), (iii) and (iv).

(Pages 86–89) There are several different ways a government can intervene to stabilise prices and/or to support farmers' incomes.

Q55. With each of the following schemes decide whether they will stabilise prices, support incomes or both.

(a) Buffer stocks (whose size fluctuates but is not allowed to grow bigger and bigger over the years).
              Stabilise Prices/Support incomes/Both
(b) Output subsidies (of a fixed amount per unit of output).
              Stabilise Prices/Support incomes/Both
(c) Minimum prices with the government buying any resulting surpluses.
              Stabilise Prices/Support incomes/Both
(d) 'Set-aside' schemes (whereby farmers are paid to let land lie fallow).   *Stabilise Prices/Support incomes/Both*
(e) Variable import levies (to bring imported foodstuffs up to an agreed price level).
              Stabilise Prices/Support incomes/Both
(f) Investment grants to farmers.
              Stabilise Prices/Support incomes/Both
(g) A tariff of 10 per cent on imported food.
              Stabilise Prices/Support incomes/Both
(h) Quotas on the numbers of cattle that farmers are allowed to keep.   *Stabilise Prices/Support incomes/Both*
(i) 'Lump-sum' subsidies unrelated to output.
              Stabilise Prices/Support incomes/Both

Q56. Which of the schemes in Q55 will:

1. increase output of domestic producers?......................

2. decrease output of domestic producers? ....

3. either increase or decrease output of domestic producers depending on the circumstances?
    ....

4. have no effect on the output of domestic producers?
    ....

5. increase consumption?..

6. decrease consumption?...

7. either increase or decrease consumption depending on the circumstances?
    ....

8. have no effect on consumption?...................................

If the government wants to support farmers' incomes, rather than merely stabilise prices, then two of the most widely used policies worldwide have been output subsidies and high minimum prices.

Q57. Figure 3.6 shows the market for a foodstuff in which a country is self-sufficient. The market price of P_1 is regarded as too low and the government wants farmers to receive a price of P_2.

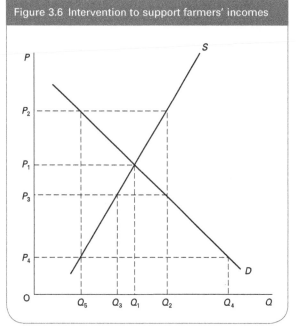

Figure 3.6 Intervention to support farmers' incomes

Assume first that farmers are paid a guaranteed minimum price of P_2.

(a) How much will the government have to buy from producers?
    ....

(b) How much will it cost the taxpayer? ....

Assume now that the government, instead of paying a minimum price, gives an output subsidy.

(c) What must be the size of the subsidy per unit of output to have the same effect on farmers' incomes as the minimum price of P_2?
    ....

(d) How much will it cost the taxpayer? ....

In some cases the country may be a net importer of food, in which case the diagram for such a foodstuff will look like Figure 3.7.

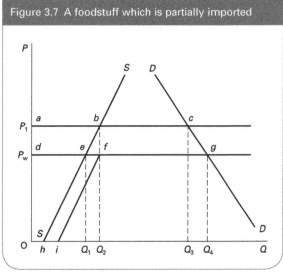

Figure 3.7 A foodstuff which is partially imported

⊖ **Q58.** Assume in Figure 3.7 that the world price is P_w and that initially there is no government intervention. The domestic supply and demand curves are given by SS and DD respectively.

(a) What is the total supply curve (domestic plus world)?

....

(b) What is the level of domestic production? ....

(c) What is the level of domestic consumption?

....

(d) What is the level of imports? ....

....

Now assume that the government imposes an import duty in order to raise the domestic price to P_1.

(e) What will the total supply curve be now?

....

(f) What will be the level of domestic production?

....

(g) What will be the level of domestic consumption?

....

(h) What will be the level of imports?

....

⊖ **Q59.** Continuing from the last question, now assume that instead of import duties, the government gives farmers a *subsidy* to bring their revenue per unit to a level of P_1.

(a) What will the supply curve be now? ....

(b) What will be the market price? ....

(c) What will be the level of domestic production?

....

(d) What will be the level of domestic consumption?

....

(e) What will be the level of imports? ....

▤ **Q60.** Comparing the EU system of high minimum prices (and import levies) with a system of subsidies and free-market prices, the EU system

A. benefits consumers.
B. leads to less waste.
C. leads to less imports.
D. is less damaging to agriculture in developing countries.
E. leads to lower food prices.

◖ **Q61.** Which of the following benefits could be argued to have resulted from the EU system of high minimum prices for agricultural produce?

(a) It has helped to lead to greater European self-sufficiency in food.   *Yes/No*
(b) It has led to lower food prices in the short run. *Yes/No*
(c) It has led to lower food prices in the long run.   *Yes/No*
(d) It has led to increased agricultural investment. *Yes/No*
(e) It has redistributed income more equally than would a system of subsidies.   *Yes/No*
(f) It has benefited developing countries' agriculture.
                                                         Yes/No
(g) It has led to more stable prices.   *Yes/No*
(h) It has given a roughly equal level of agricultural support (per head of the agricultural population) to all the member countries.   *Yes/No*

❓ **Q62.** Give two ways in which the Common Agricultural Policy has harmed the agricultural sector in developing countries.

1. ....

2. ....

Compared with the free-market position, direct income support for farmers has the advantage of leading (in the short run) to **Q63.** *lower/higher/the same* prices and **Q64.** *lower/higher/the same* output.

Q65. The European Commission published a set of policy options for the CAP in 2010. Which of the following was **not** identified as objectives for CAP?

A. Raising the rate of economic growth.
B. Ensuring food supply.
C. Building sustainable economies across Europe.
D. Reducing government debt in European countries.
E. Contributing to employment.

 Q66. The population of the world is currently 7 billion, and expected to increase to 8 billion by 2050. The *Global* *Food and Farming Futures* project report in 2011 identified five key challenges for the future. Which of the following was **not** one of them?

A. Balancing future demand and supply sustainably.
B. Ensuring adequate stability in food prices.
C. Increasing food production to ensure there is enough for all people.
D. Managing the contribution of the food system to the mitigation of climate change.
E. Maintaining biodiversity and ecosystem services.

B PROBLEMS, EXERCISES AND PROJECTS

Q67. Imagine that you were given a rise in grant/pay/allowance of £10 per week.

(a) Make a list of the things on which you would spend this extra income and work out your income elasticity of demand for each.

(b) Are there any items of which you would now buy less? Explain.

Now imagine you had an increase in income of £100 per week.

(c) Answer questions (a) and (b).

(d) Are your answers different this time? Explain.

Q68. Select an item that is purchased by all or most of your class or seminar group. Conduct interviews with everyone to establish the amounts they would buy at six different prices. Now divide the class into two groups (by sex or age or any other feature that you may feel relevant in determining demand).

(a) From the replies given at your interviews, construct a demand curve for each group and a demand curve for the class as a whole.

(b) What is the total expenditure of each group at each price? Explain any differences between the two groups. (You will need to consider both the elasticity and the magnitude of demand.)

Q69. Refer back to the last two Budget speeches by the Chancellor of the Exchequer. (The Budget is usually given in March each year.) The speech is reported in full in *The Times* and in *Hansard*. See also the Treasury website at http://www.hm-treasury.gov.uk.

Examine the Chancellor's justification for any changes in the rate of duty on alcohol, petrol, tobacco or betting. What assumptions are being made about the price and income elasticities of demand for these items? Are the arguments consistent and are there any conflicts of objectives in government policy towards taxing these items?

Q70. Undertake a library or web search to find articles discussing problems and reform of the CAP. Your search could include web addresses in the web appendix in Sloman, *Economics*, this edition (see also the hotlinks section on the Sloman website at http://www.pearsoned.co.uk/sloman), especially sites E14 and G9.

Summarise the alternative agreements or proposals and consider their relative merits and any problems they are likely to cause.

C DISCUSSION TOPICS AND ESSAYS

Q71. It is observed that over time the price and the quantity demanded of a product both rise. Does this mean that the demand curve is upward sloping? What does this tell us about the difficulty of determining the shape of demand and supply curves?

Q72. The demand for pears is more price elastic than the demand for bread and yet the price of pears fluctuates more than that of bread. Why should this be so? If pears could be stored as long and as cheaply as flour, would this affect the relative price fluctuations?

Q73. A fish and chip shop finds that on Friday early evening, Saturday lunch time and between 10.30 and 11.00 every evening it has queues out of the door, whereas at other times it is empty. Would it be a good idea to charge different prices at different times?

Q74. When share prices move upwards on the stock market, people tend to start buying, whereas when they move downward people often sell. Does this mean that the demand curves for shares slope upwards and the supply curves slope downwards?

Q75. How do the price elasticities of demand and supply affect the incidence of an indirect tax?

Q76. Assume that the government wishes to reduce smoking. Compare the relative advantages and disadvantages of (a) increased taxes on cigarettes, (b) making smoking illegal and (c) increased advertising of the health effects of smoking as a means of achieving the government's objective.

Q77. Why are free-market agricultural prices and incomes subject to large fluctuations? What measures could a government adopt (a) to stabilise prices, (b) to stabilise incomes, (c) to stabilise both prices and incomes?

Q78. What would be the likely economic implications for consumers, farmers and the government, in both the short and long run, of totally removing the system of agricultural price support in the EU and replacing it with a system of subsidies unrelated to output: for example, subsidies linked to rural development and the conservation of the environment?

Q79. Consider the relative advantages and disadvantages of alternative means of reforming the CAP.

Q80. Debate
The UK government was correct to abolish rent control in the 1980s.

ANSWERS

Q1. *the quantity demanded.*
Q2. *price.*
Q3. $\Delta Q_d/Q_d + \Delta P/P$.
Q4. *elastic.*
Q5. *inelastic.*
Q6. *a negative value ($\epsilon < 0$).*
Q7. (a) (v), (b) (i), (c) (iii), (d) (ii), (e) (iv).
Q8. *the greater.* The more substitutes there are and the closer they are, the more willing consumers will be to switch from one product to the other as the price of one of them changes.
Q9. *the higher.* The higher the proportion of people's income spent on a good, the more they will be forced to cut back on its consumption as its price rises.
Q10. *the longer.* People will have more time to find alternative products and to change their consumption patterns.
Q11. (c), (a), (d), (b), (e). As we move from (c) to (e) in this order, so the number of substitutes becomes greater. Thus 'Scrummy' low-fat margarine with the current competition token has many substitutes, including: 'Scrummy' low-fat margarine without a token, other brands of low-fat margarine, other brands of margarine, dairy low-fat spreads and butter.
Q12. C. There are two reasons contained in this answer. The first is that foreign holidays are a luxury. This means that people do not regard them as vital, and will thus be prepared to substitute other items (e.g. holidays in their own country or day trips out) if the price of foreign holidays rises. What we are talking about here is a big substitution effect. The second is that, being a large item of people's expenditure, many people may not feel able to afford them if their price rises. What we are talking about here is a big income effect. Note that B would only be an answer if we were talking about a *specific* foreign holiday rather than foreign holidays in general.

Q13. (a) *False.* Except in the case of vertical and horizontal demand curves, the elasticity of straight-line demand curves will vary along their length.
 (b) *False.* Again, downward-sloping straight-line demand curves have varying elasticities along their length. A curve with elasticity = –1 is a rectangular hyperbola (i.e. a curve bowed in toward the origin that approaches but never reaches the two axes).
 (c) *True.* In *proportionate* terms any change in price from zero is an *infinite* change, and thus dividing a proportionate change in quantity by infinity will give a zero elasticity.
 (d) *True.* In proportionate terms any change in quantity from zero is an *infinite* change, and thus elasticity must also be infinity.
 (e) *False.* The elasticities of the two curves differ along their length (getting greater as you move down each curve). There are points high up on curve D_2 which are less elastic than points low down on curve D_1. Only if we specify that we are referring to the *same price range* in each case does the statement necessarily become true (see (g) below).
 (f) *False.* At point *z*, curve D_2 is more elastic than curve D_1.
 (g) *True.* See answer to (e) above.
Q14. *Arc elasticity.*
Q15. $(P_1 + P_2)/2$.
Q16. (a) See table below.

$P(£)$	10	9	8	7	6	5	4	3	2	1	0
Q_d	0	2	4	6	8	10	12	14	16	18	20

 (b) $\Delta Q_d/(Q_{d_1} + Q_{d_2})/2 + \Delta P/(P_1 + P_2)/2$
   (i) $4/18 \div -2/1 = -1/9$ *inelastic*
   (ii) $4/10 \div -2/5 = -1$ *unit elastic*
   (iii) $4/4 \div -2/8 = -4$ *elastic*

(c) Take two points an equal distance either side of the point in question, and calculate arc elasticity between these two points.

(d) (i) $4/16 \div -2/2 = -\frac{1}{4}$
     (ii) $4/8 \div -2/6 = -1\frac{1}{2}$
     (iii) $4/10 \div -2/5 = -1$
     (iv) $4(?)/20 \div -2(?)/0 = 0$
     (v) $4(?)/0 \div -2(?)/20 = \infty$

Q17. See table below.

P(£)	10	9	8	7	6	5	4	3	2	1	0
Q_d	0	2	4	6	8	10	12	14	16	18	20
TR(£)	0	18	32	42	48	50	48	42	32	18	0

Q18. (a) Total expenditure will *rise* (as it does from £10 down to £5).

(b) Total expenditure will *fall* (as it does from £5 downwards).

(c) –1.

Q19. False.

Q20. True.

Q21. True (assuming that both axes start from zero).

*Q22. P/Q.

*Q23. inverse of the slope.

*Q24. (a) See table below.

P	5	4	3	2	1	0
Q_d	0	2	8	18	32	50

(b) See Figure A3.1.

(c) See Figure A3.1. The slope of the tangent is $-4/32 = -1/8$.

(d) $-8 \times 3/8 = -3$.

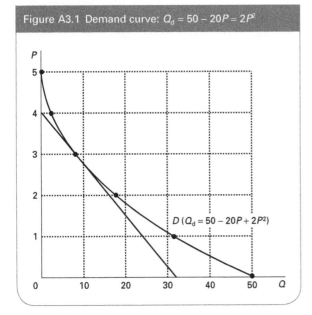

Figure A3.1 Demand curve: $Q_d = 50 - 20P = 2P^2$

$D (Q_d = 50 - 20P + 2P^2)$

Q25. (a) A. This means that for any given percentage fall in price, there will be a greater shift away from producing A than B.

(b) A. There is more time for supply to adjust to changing prices and hence profitability.

(c) B. For any given percentage increase in price, there will be a bigger percentage increase in resources attracted into B than into A before cost increases make it unprofitable to expand further.

(d) *Cannot say.* (A will have a more elastic *demand* than B.)

(e) B. The supply of A is unlikely to be affected much by its price if it is going to be produced anyway as a by-product.

(f) *Cannot say.* This affects elasticity of demand not elasticity of supply.

Q26. (a) *True.* All straight-line supply curves passing through the origin have an elasticity equal to 1 *irrespective of their slope.* (Try drawing some on graph paper and working out their elasticity over various sections.)

(b) *False.* See (c) and (d) below.

(c) *True.* The elasticity equals infinity at point *y* (see (e) below) and then diminishes as you move up the curve, but nevertheless stays above 1. (Again, try drawing it on graph paper and working out its elasticity over various sections.)

(d) *True.* At the point where it crosses the horizontal axis the proportionate change in price is infinite, and thus the elasticity is zero (a number divided by infinity is zero).

(e) *True.* At the point where it crosses the vertical axis, the proportionate change in quantity is infinite.

(f) *False.* It has an elasticity less than 1 throughout its length, but this nevertheless rises towards 1 as you move up the curve.

Q27. *Positive.* A *rise* in income causes a *rise* in demand.

Q28. (a) Good A: $Y\epsilon_d = 20/40 \div 10/50 = 2.5$.
Good B: $Y\epsilon_d = -4/50 \div 10/50 = -0.4$.
Good C: $Y\epsilon_d = 20/200 \div 10/50 = 0.5$.

(b) Good A. ($Y\epsilon_d > 1$.)

(c) Good B. ($Y\epsilon_d$ negative: a rise in income leads to *less* being purchased as people switch to superior goods.)

Q29. *True.* Expenditure on the good increases by a larger proportion than does income.

Q30. (a) (v) (strong complements).

(b) (iii) (unrelated).

(c) (ii) (moderate substitutes).

(d) (i) (close substitutes).

(e) (iv) (mildly complementary).

Q31. *less* price elastic.

Q32. *price.*

Q33. *quantity.*

Q34. E. Once they are cut, the supply is virtually fixed. The florist cannot choose to sell a given bunch of flowers next week or next month instead of today if today's demand is low. Note: A and B refer to *demand.* C is an *effect* of supply inelasticity, not a *cause.* D refers to *shifts* in the supply curve.

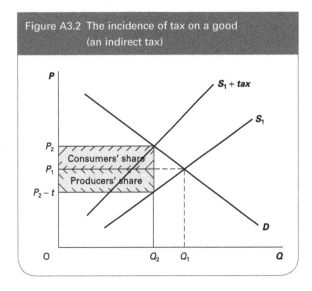

Figure A3.2 The incidence of tax on a good (an indirect tax)

Q35. *left.*

Q36. *right.*

Q37. *rise.* The speculation is thus self-fulfilling.

Q38. Stabilising: (c).

Destabilising: (b).

Q39. D.

Q40. *upward.*

Q41. *leave the slope of the supply curve unaffected.*

Q42. *make the supply curve steeper.*

Q43. (a) (iii), (b) (iv), (c) (ii), (d) (i).

Q44. C. $(P_2 - P_1) \times Q_2$. See Figure A3.2.

Q45. D. $(t - (P_2 - P_1)) \times Q_2$. See Figure A3.2.

Q46. D. Price will rise less, and hence the producers' share will be larger, the more elastic is demand and the less elastic is supply (see cases (2) and (3) in Figure 3.18 on page 79 of Sloman 7th edition).

Q47. *maximum price.*

Q48. *greater.*

Q49. (a) *True.*

(b) *True.*

(c) The answer here depends on the assumptions made. The statement would be *true* if the supply curve were upward sloping (which would occur if money earned from selling health care were ploughed back into a greater level of provision). The statement would be *false* if (i) supply were totally inelastic or (ii) the government responded to the shortage by increasing the level of provision.

(d) *True.* Some sort of rationing will normally occur. For example, specialists may decide which patients will be given expensive treatment and which will have to go without and have a cheaper (but less effective) treatment.

(e) *False.* People would probably have to wait for non-urgent treatment, but most (if not all) serious non-urgent cases would still be treated.

(f) *True.* Some people might be refused treatment. Others may not bother with treatment (or pay for private treatment) rather than wait.

(g) *True* or *false* depending on the government's response to shortages.

Q50. (a) *left.*

(b) *left.*

(c) *either higher or lower (depending on the relative shifts in the demand and supply curves).* Normally, it would be expected that the price would rise. The reason is that the penalties for supplying illegal products are usually higher than those for buying/possessing them. Thus the supply curve would shift to the left more than the demand curve.

Q51. E.

Q52. (a) *True.* The reason is that a tax (unlike making a product illegal) will not shift the demand curve.

(b) *False.*

Q53. (a) *False.* The more elastic the supply, the less will price fluctuate for any given (horizontal) shift in either the demand or the supply curve.

(b) *True.* The greater the fluctuations in the harvest, the bigger the shifts in the actual supply curve, and hence the bigger the fluctuations in price.

(c) *False.* The more elastic the demand, the less will price fluctuate for any given (horizontal) shift in either the demand or the supply curve.

Q54. D. A larger increase over time in supply (i) than demand (ii), combined with a price-inelastic demand (iii) will push prices down and hence lead to a relatively small growth in revenue. Fluctuations in the harvest (iv), on the other hand, will have little effect on *long-term* supply, and may even cause revenues to grow *more* rapidly over time if the fluctuations cause uncertainty and hence a fall in investment and a resultant smaller growth in supply.

Q55. (a) *Stabilise prices.* Prices will be kept up by buying into the stocks in years of good harvest, and selling from stocks in years of poor harvest. If the stocks are not allowed to grow over the years, the average price to the farmer will be no higher, just more stable.

(b) *Support incomes.* Output and hence prices will still fluctuate with the harvest, however.

(c) *Both.* If the minimum price is above the market price, this will both support farmers' incomes and stabilise the price (at the minimum level).

(d) *Support incomes.* Output will be reduced and, with a price-inelastic demand for food, farmers' revenue will thereby increase. Output will still fluctuate with the harvest, however.

(e) *Both.* If the agreed price is above the market level, this will both support farmers' incomes and stabilise the price (at the agreed level).

(f) *Support incomes.* Incomes will be supported in the short run, but in the long run, to the extent that the investment increases output, farmers' incomes will *fall*.

(g) *Support incomes*. This raises price to the farmer, but prices will still fluctuate with supply.

(h) *Support incomes (slight stabilising effect on prices)*. To the extent that supply is reduced, price will rise. Prices will still fluctuate with demand and also with milk yields, even though the number of cattle will be more stable.

(i) *Support incomes*. Output will be largely unaffected, except for those farmers who would not have survived without the subsidy, and thus prices will continue to fluctuate.

Q56. 1. (b), (c), (e), (f) and (g).

2. (d) and (h).

3. (a). In years of good harvest, the government will buy into the buffer stock to keep prices up. This will increase domestic supply above the free-market level (unless supply is totally inelastic). In years of poor harvest, the government will release stocks on to the market to keep prices down. This will reduce domestic supply below the free-market level (unless, again, supply is totally inelastic).

4. (i). A lump-sum subsidy, by definition, does not depend on output. The profitability of producing extra output, therefore, is not affected by the subsidy. Thus the subsidy will have no effect on supply. (The one exception is those farmers who would not have survived without the subsidy.)

5. (b) and (f).

6. (c), (d), (e), (g) and (h).

7. (a). Consumption will be kept below the free-market level in years of good harvests because the government keeps the price up by buying into the buffer stocks. Consumption will be kept above the free-market level in years of bad harvest because the government releases supplies from the stocks to keep prices down.

8. (i).

Q57. *(a)* $Q_2 - Q_5$.

(b) $(Q_2 - Q_5) \times OP_2$.

(c) $P_2 - P_3$. This would shift the supply curve downwards by an amount $P_2 - P_3$ and thus reduce the price to P_3. Sales would increase to Q_2. Farmers would thus earn $(P_3 + \text{subsidy}) \times OQ_2$: the same as with the high minimum price of P_2.

(d) $(P_2 - P_3) \times OQ_2$.

Q58. (a) *heg*, (b) Q_1, (c) Q_4, (d) $Q_4 - Q_1$, (e) *hebc*, (f) Q_2, (g) Q_3, (h) $Q_3 - Q_2$.

Q59. (a) *ifg*, (b) P_w, (c) Q_2, (d) Q_4, (e) $Q_4 - Q_2$.

Q60. C. For any given price to the producer, and hence given domestic supply, the EU system of high minimum prices will lead to a higher price to the consumer and thus a lower level of consumption, and hence a lower level of imports. Note that in the case of A, consumers pay a *higher* price under the EU system; in the case of B, there are surpluses under the EU system and no surpluses under a system of subsidies; in the case of D, the EU system leads to dumped foodstuffs on world markets and involves tariffs on imports of food (including from developing countries); in the case of E, the EU system is specifically designed to lead to higher prices.

Q61. *Yes:* (a), (d), (g).

No: (b), (e), (f), (h).

In the case of (c) the answer could be either *yes* or *no*. It depends on whether the additional agricultural investment resulting from the CAP (and hence a lower *free*-market price) has been sufficient to offset maintaining the price above the equilibrium.

Q62. It has been more difficult for these countries to export to the EU; cheap EU food exports into these countries have made their domestic food production less profitable.

Q63. *the same*.

Q64. *the same*. Since direct income support (as opposed to output subsidies) is unrelated to output, it should have no effect on output, and hence no effect on prices – except that, by enabling farmers to invest more and marginal farmers to survive, it could increase output (and hence reduce prices) in the *long* run.

Q65. D.

Q66. C. It is not sufficient to ensure that there is enough food for all, what is important is that everyone should have global access to food.

Chapter 4

Background to Demand

In Chapter 2 we were concerned with the *total market* demand and supply. In this chapter and the next we go behind the demand and supply curves to examine the behaviour of individuals: individual consumers and individual producers.

In this chapter we consider the behaviour of consumers. We see what determines the quantity of various goods that people will demand at various prices and incomes. By building up a picture of individuals' demand we will then be in a better position to understand total market demand.

There are two major approaches to analysing consumer demand: the marginal utility approach and the indifference approach. We examine both of them in this chapter. We also look at the problem of making rational choices when we only have limited information.

Finally, we consider behavioural economics, an area of economics that has been attracting increasing attention in recent years, especially since the financial crisis of 2007/08. This differs from other approaches by not assuming that consumers will always act rationally.

4.1 Marginal utility theory

(Pages 100–2) People generally buy goods and services because they expect to gain satisfaction from them. We call this satisfaction *utility*. An important distinction we make is between *total* and *marginal* utility.

(?) Q1. Total utility (*TU*) can be defined as

....

(?) Q2. Marginal utility (*MU*) can be defined as

....

Q3. If I gain 20 units of satisfaction from consuming 4 toffees and 23 units of satisfaction from consuming 5 toffees, then my marginal utility from the 5th toffee is

A. 43 units.
B. 23 units.
C. 20 units.
D. 3 units.
E. –3 units.

Q4. Total utility will *fall* whenever
A. marginal utility is falling.
B. marginal utility is rising.
C. marginal utility has reached a maximum.
D. marginal utility is zero.
E. marginal utility is negative.

A problem with the utility approach to analysing consumer demand is that utility cannot be measured.

Table 4.1 Katie's total and marginal utility from cinema visits

Visits	1	2	3	4	5	6	7	8
TU (utils)	12	20	25	28	30	31	31	29
MU (utils)	.	.	.	.	.	.	.	.

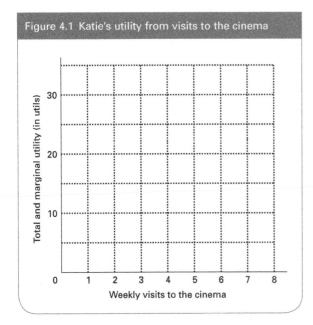

Figure 4.1 Katie's utility from visits to the cinema

Nevertheless in order to understand how utility relates to consumer choice it is convenient to assume that it can be measured. We thus use an imaginary unit of satisfaction called 'utils'.

Q5. Table 4.1 shows the total utility that Katie derives from visits to the cinema per week.
(a) Fill in the figures for marginal utility. (Note that the MU figures are entered midway between the TU figures. This is because marginal utility is the extra utility of going from one level of consumption to the next.)
(b) Draw a graph of the figures for total and marginal utility on Figure 4.1.
(c) Assume that Katie now falls for a guy who also likes going to the cinema. As a result her marginal utility for each visit doubles. What is her total utility now for:
    (i) 3 visits?
    (ii) 6 visits?
    (iii) 7 visits?

You will notice from Figure 4.1 that the marginal utility curve slopes downwards. This is in accordance with the *principle of diminishing marginal utility*.

Q6. Which of the following are directly related to the principle of diminishing marginal utility? Assume that marginal utility remains positive.

(a) Rather than eating one large savoury course at dinner, I prefer to have less first course so as to leave room for a pudding. *Yes/No*
(b) I prefer to spend my time playing sport rather than watching television. *Yes/No*
(c) I like to watch a little television in the evenings. *Yes/No*
(d) I like watching comedy programmes more than documentaries. *Yes/No*
(e) I get bored easily. *Yes/No*

Q7. Diminishing marginal utility implies that total utility:
A. decreases at a decreasing rate.
B. decreases at a constant rate.
C. increases at a constant rate.
D. increases at an increasing rate.
E. increases at a decreasing rate.

(Page 102) When we draw up a utility schedule (like that in Table 4.1) we have to assume *ceteris paribus*. In other words, we assume that other factors which affect the utility gained from the product remain constant.

Q8. Make a list of four things that affect your marginal utility from a glass of orange juice (other than the number of glasses of orange juice you have already had). Will they increase or decrease your marginal utility?

1. .... *Increase/Decrease*

2. .... *Increase/Decrease*

3. .... *Increase/Decrease*

4. .... *Increase/Decrease*

(Pages 102–5) How much of a good will people buy? If they wish to maximise their self-interest (what is known as 'rational' behaviour), they will compare the marginal utility they expect to get from consuming the good with the price they have to pay. This will involve perceiving marginal utility in *money* terms (i.e. how much an extra unit of the good is worth to them). If the marginal utility exceeds the price, rational consumers will **Q9.** *buy more/buy less/not change their level of consumption*. If, however, price exceeds marginal utility, rational consumers will **Q10.** *buy more/buy less/not change their level of consumption*.

What we are saying is that the rational consumer will seek to maximise his or her *total consumer surplus* (*TCS*) from the good.

Q11. Table 4.2 shows the marginal utility a person gets from consuming different quantities of a good. Assume that the good sells for £10.

Table 4.2 Marginal utility for person Y from good X

Quantity consumed	0	1	2	3	4	5	6
Marginal utility (£s)		25	20	16	12	8	4

(a) What is the person's total utility from consuming 4 units?

....

(b) What is the person's total expenditure from consuming 6 units?

....

(c) What is the person's marginal consumer surplus from consuming a second unit?

....

(d) What is the person's marginal consumer surplus from consuming a fifth unit?

....

(e) What is the person's total consumer surplus from consuming 2 units?

....

(f) At what level of consumption is the person's total consumer surplus maximised?

....

(g) What is the marginal consumer surplus at this level?

....

(h) What is the relationship between price and marginal utility at this level?

....

🗐 **Q12.** In Figure 4.2 which area(s) represent total utility at a level of consumption of Q?

A.   1
B.   2
C.   1 + 2
D.   2 + 3
E.   1 + 2 + 3

🗐 **Q13.** In Figure 4.2 which area(s) represent total consumer surplus at a level of consumption of Q?

A.   1
B.   2
C.   3
D.   1 + 2
E.   2 + 3

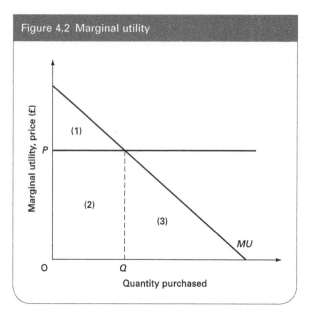

Figure 4.2 Marginal utility

If we assume that an individual's income remains constant, his or her demand curve for a good will be directly related to **Q14.** *total utility/marginal utility*.

(Pages 105–7) Rather than focusing on how much of a *single* good people will buy, it is more satisfactory to examine how people will allocate their incomes *between* alternative goods. *Rational choice* involves comparing the marginal utility of each good relative to its price.

Take the simple case where a consumer buys just two goods, X and Y. If at the current level of consumption $MU_X/P_X > MU_Y/P_Y$, to maximise total utility the consumer should **Q15.** *buy more X relative to Y/buy more Y relative to X/buy whichever item is the cheaper*.

❓ **Q16.** The consumer will continue switching until

....

🗐 **Q17.** Alison loves cheese. She particularly likes Dolcelatte, but also quite likes Cheddar. Her marginal utility from her last gram of Dolcelatte is double that from her last gram of Cheddar. Assuming that she consumes cheese 'rationally', and that Cheddar costs £8.00 per kilo, what is the price per kilo of Dolcelatte?

A.   £2.00
B.   £4.00
C.   £8.00
D.   £16.00
E.   £24.00

🗐 **Q18.** Andrea spends all her income on just three goods X, Y and Z. If at her present level of consumption $MU_X/P_X > MU_Y/P_Y > MU_Z/P_Z$, which one of the following can we conclude?

A.   She will buy more X and Y, and less Z.
B.   She will buy more X, and less Y and Z.
C.   She will buy more X, less Z, and the same amount of Y.

D. She will buy more X and less Z, but we cannot say whether she will buy more, less or the same amount of Y.

E. She will buy more X, but we cannot say whether she will buy more, less or the same amount of Y and Z.

Q19. Which one of the following statements is *not* an example of marginal analysis?

A. If I eat another chocolate bar, I might be sick.

B. If mortgage rates rise by another 1 per cent, some people will no longer be able to afford the repayments.

C. If a firm earns more from selling its products than they cost to produce, it will make a profit.

D. If J. Bloggs (Warehousing) Ltd buys a new forklift truck of the latest design, it should be able to stack another 500 pallets per day.

E. Fitting flue gas desulphurisation equipment to a coal-fired power station in Britain producing *x* kilowatts will reduce the costs of acid rain pollution in Scandinavia by £*y*.

*4.2 Indifference analysis

(Page 108) A problem with marginal utility analysis is that utility cannot be measured. An alternative approach is to use *indifference analysis*. This merely examines a consumer's preferences between different bundles of goods. It does not involve measuring utility.

Q20. Sally, a first-year degree student, lives in a hall of residence and pays a fixed amount for food and accommodation. She spends the money she has left over on books and compact discs. Her preferences between various combinations of books and CDs are shown in Table 4.3. She is indifferent between the combinations in each of the five sets shown, but has preferences between sets.

(a) Plot indifference curves on Figure 4.3 corresponding to each of the sets in Table 4.3.

(b) Which set would Sally like best?

set 1/set 2/set 3/set 4/set 5

(c) Between which two sets is Sally indifferent?

set 1/set 2/set 3/set 4/set 5

(d) Which set does Sally like the least?

set 1/set 2/set 3/set 4/set 5

Table 4.3 Sally's preferences between books and CDs (per year)

Set 1	Books	40	30	23	16	12	10	6	4	2
	CDs	3	5	8	14	19	22	30	37	46
Set 2	Books	33	22	16	13	7	4			
	CDs	7	14	20	25	37	45			
Set 3	Books	40	30	22	20	17	14	11	6	2	1
	CDs	1	2	4	5	7	10	13	20	30	37
Set 4	Books	27	20	11	5					
	CDs	6	10	20	33					
Set 5	Books	30	20	16	12	6	3	1		
	CDs	1	3	4	6	S10	14	20		

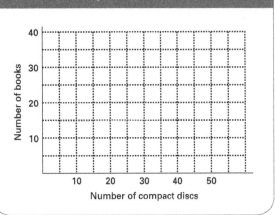

Figure 4.3 Sally's indifference curves between books and compact discs

(e) Given the information in Table 4.3, why would Sally *not* be indifferent between the combinations in the following set: 36 books and 5 CDs, 23 books and 8 CDs, 12 books and 13 CDs, 3 books and 20 CDs?

....

(Page 108) The slope of the indifference curve is given by ΔY/ΔX, where Y is the good measured on the vertical axis and X is the good measured on the horizontal axis. The slope gives the *marginal rate of substitution (MRS)*.

Q21. This can be defined as the amount of one good (Y) that a consumer is prepared to give up for

....

Q22. Referring again to Table 4.3, what is Sally's marginal rate of substitution of books for CDs in set 5 for

(a) the fourth CD?..

(b) the sixth CD? ....

(c) the tenth CD? ....

Q23. Why are indifference curves drawn convex (bowed in) to the origin? Explain this in terms of the marginal rate of substitution.

....

....

Q24. The slope of an indifference curve (the *MRS*) also gives:

A. MU_X/MU_Y

B. MU_Y/MU_X

C. MU_X/P_X

D. MU_Y/P_Y

E. P_Y/P_X

(Pages 109–11)

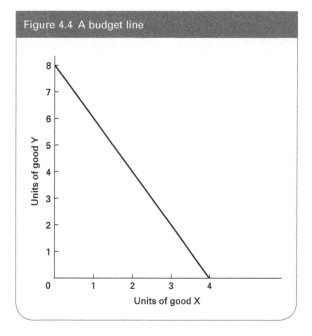

Figure 4.4 A budget line

⊖ **Q25.** Figure 4.4 shows a person's budget to spend on two goods X and Y.

(a) If the size of the budget was £20, what would be the price of X and Y?

P_X=................................. , P_Y= ....

(b) Assume that the price of Y rises to £4 (but that the price of X and the level of money income stay the same). Draw the new budget line.

(c) If the budget line does not shift again, but the price of X is now £10, what must be the size of the total budget now?

....

(d) What will be the price of Y now? P_Y = ...

(e) If the prices of X and Y both double, but the consumer's money income also doubles, what will happen to the budget line?

....

▤ **Q26.** Which of the following gives the slope of the budget line?

A. MU_X/MU_Y
B. MU_Y/MU_X
C. P_X/P_Y
D. P_Y/P_X
E. MRS

(Pages 111–13)

⊖ **Q27.** Referring back to **Q20**, assume that Sally has £300 per year to spend on a combination of books and CDs, and assume that all the books and CDs she wants cost £10 each.

(a) Draw in her budget line on Figure 4.3.

(b) What is the optimum amount of books and CDs for her to buy with this £300?

....................................books, ... CDs

(c) Assume now that the price of CDs rises to £20. Draw in her new budget line.

(d) What is the optimum amount of books and CDs per year for her to buy now?

....................................books, ... CDs

♟ **Q28.** Match each of the following changes in an indifference diagram to the causes (a)–(h) of those changes. (In each case assume *ceteris paribus* and that units of Y are measured on the vertical axis and units of X on the horizontal axis.)

(i) A parallel shift outwards of the budget line.
(ii) The budget line becomes steeper.
(iii) The indifference curves become flatter.
(iv) A parallel shift inwards of the budget line.
(v) A movement along the budget line to a higher indifference curve.
(vi) A pivoting inwards of the budget line round the point where the budget line crosses the X axis.
(vii) The indifference curves become steeper.
(viii) A movement along the budget line from an old tangency point to a new one.

(a) An increase in the price of Y ....

(b) A shift in tastes towards Y and away from X.

....

(c) A rise in income...

(d) A change in the optimum level of consumption resulting from a change in tastes

....

(e) A shift in tastes towards X and away from Y.

....

(f) An increase in utility resulting from a change in consumption.

....

(g) A decrease in the relative price of Y.............................

(h) A fall in income ....

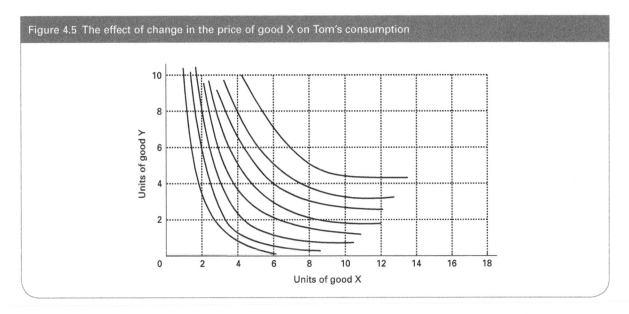

Figure 4.5 The effect of change in the price of good X on Tom's consumption

(Pages 113–14) We can use indifference analysis to show the effects of changes in price of one of the two goods on the quantity demanded of the good. This then enables us to derive an individual's demand curve for that good.

⊖ **Q29.** Tom has an income of £160 to spend on two goods X and Y. Assume that the price of Y is constant at £16.

(a) On Figure 4.5 plot the budget lines corresponding to $P_X = £10$, $P_X = £16$, $P_X = £20$, $P_X = £32$ and $P_X = £40$.

(b) Now show how much X will be consumed at each price. From this construct a *price-consumption curve*.

(c) Use this information to construct Tom's demand curve for good X.

The demand curve you have just derived is for the simple case where the consumer is only buying two goods (X and Y). In the real world people buy many goods.

(?) **Q30.** How can we derive the demand for good X under these circumstances? The answer is to measure good X on the horizontal axis and

....on the vertical axis.

(Pages 114–17) As we saw in Chapter 2, the effect of a change in price can be divided into an income effect and a substitution effect. In examining these effects we can distinguish three types of good: a *normal good*, an *inferior (non-Giffen) good* and a *Giffen good*.

⊖ **Q31.** Figure 4.6 illustrates each of these three types of good measured on the X axis, and the effect in each case of a reduction in the price of good X and a consequent shift in the budget line from B_1 to B_2.

(a) Mark the income and substitution effects in each diagram.

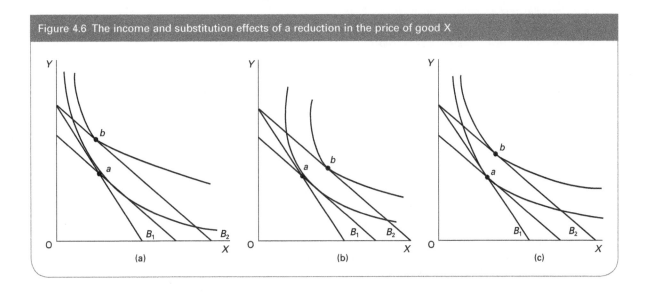

Figure 4.6 The income and substitution effects of a reduction in the price of good X

Table 4.4 Income and substitution effects of a price change

Type of good	Substitution effect	Income effect	Which is the bigger effect?
Normal	*positive/ negative*	*positive/ negative*	*income/substitution/ either*
Inferior (non-Giffen)	*positive/ negative*	*positive/ negative*	*income/substitution/ either*
Giffen	*positive/ negative*	*positive/ negative*	*income/substitution/ either*

(b) In which diagram is X

    (i) a normal good? ....

    (ii) an inferior, but non-Giffen good? ....

    (iii) a Giffen good? ....

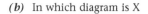 **Q32.** Table 4.4 is used to summarise the direction and relative size of the income and substitution effects. Cross out the incorrect information.

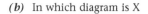 **Q33.** When the price of an inferior (but non-Giffen) good rises, people will consume more of it. *True/False*

4.3 Demand under conditions of risk and uncertainty

(Pages 119–24) When people buy consumer durables they may be uncertain of their benefits and any additional repair and maintenance costs. When they buy financial assets they may be uncertain of what will happen to their price in the future. Buying under these conditions of imperfect knowledge is therefore a form of gamble. Threshold Concept 9 is concerned with the way that people take decisions based on their expectations about the future. A key issue is that those expectations cannot be better than the information on which they are based.

When we take such gambles, if we know the odds, then we are said to be operating under conditions of **Q34.** *probability/possibility/risk/uncertainty/certainty*. If we do not know the odds we are said to be operating under conditions of **Q35.** *probability/possibility/risk/uncertainty/ignorance*.

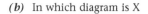 **Q36.** Suppose you are planning to buy a new car in a few weeks' time, as you do not expect your current car to pass its MOT. On which of the following will you *not* need to form expectations?
A. The price of a new car.
B. The interest rate on a loan.
C. The exchange rate.
D. Your income over the last year.
E. The part-exchange value of your present car.

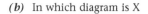 **Q37.** If you are prepared to accept odds of 10/1 on drawing an ace from a pack of cards (i.e. you win £10 for a £1 bet if you draw an ace), then how would your risk attitude be described? *Risk neutral/risk loving/risk averse*

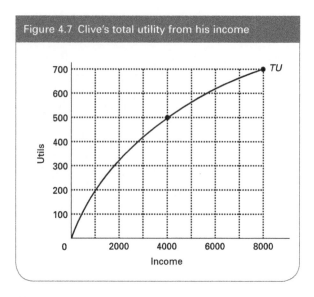

Figure 4.7 Clive's total utility from his income

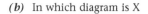 **Q38.** Figure 4.7 shows the total utility that Clive, a first-year degree student, would get from different levels of annual income. Assume at the moment that his annual income (from an allowance from his parents and some part-time work in a burger bar) is £4000. Spending this rationally gives him a total utility of 500 'utils'.

Assume that he is offered the chance to gamble the whole £4000 on the toss of a coin at odds of 2:1 (i.e. if he wins, he doubles his money; if he loses, he loses the lot).

(a) If he takes the gamble, what will be his utility this year if he wins?

....utils.

(b) If he takes the gamble, what will be his utility this year if he loses?

....utils.

(c) What would be his average expected utility from the gamble?

....utils.

(d) Why is it likely that he will not take the gamble, and thus be risk averse?

....utils.

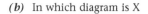 **Q39.** People will be prepared to pay insurance premiums only if the insurance gives them 'fair odds'. *True/False*

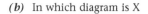 **Q40.** Of the following:
(i) the law of large numbers
(ii) the ability to spread risks
(iii) the independence of risks
(iv) the fact that insurance companies are technically 'risk lovers'

which help to explain why insurance companies are prepared to take on risks that individuals are not?

A. (i).

B. (i) and (ii).

C. (i), (ii) and (iii).

D. (ii), (iii) and (iv).

E. (i), (ii), (iii) and (iv).

Q41. In which of the following cases are the risks independent?

(a) Accident insurance for members of a football team travelling abroad. *Independent/Not independent*

(b) Insurance against loss of income from redundancy (for people working for different companies all over the country). *Independent/Not independent*

(c) Insurance against loss of income from accidents at work (for people working for different companies all over the country). *Independent/Not independent*

(d) House contents insurance for houses in a particular neighbourhood. *Independent/Not independent*

(e) Life assurance for people over 65.
Independent/Not independent

(f) Life assurance for soldiers.
Independent/Not independent

Q42. Identify each of the following as either adverse selection or moral hazard.

(a) Amy does not always bother to lock her bicycle, knowing that it is well insured.
Adverse selection/Moral hazard

(b) Knowing that he has taken out life insurance in favour of his family, Bill continues to smoke heavily.
Adverse selection/Moral hazard

(c) Caroline takes out life insurance, knowing that her smoking habit has given her terminal lung cancer.
Adverse selection/Moral hazard

(d) Dave increases his health insurance just before embarking on a skiing holiday.
Adverse selection/Moral hazard

(e) Having been granted debt forgiveness from the World Bank, the government of a developing country incurs new debt, expecting to be baled out again if necessary.
Adverse selection/Moral hazard

4.4 Behavioural economics

(Pages 124–7) Traditional economic analysis assumes that agents take decisions rationally and that markets operate in such a way as to balance demand and supply. But is this always the case? There is growing recognition that people sometimes respond to emotions and impulses that may seem to go against what economic analysis would suggest to be rational behaviour. *Behavioural economics* explores how people actually behave in reality. Behavioural economists seek not only to identify situations in which people may not behave in a rational manner, but also to explain why they do so.

(Page 125) The way in which choice is presented to people can influence the decisions that they make. For example, consumers tend to buy **Q43.** *less/more* of a good if it is presented as subject to a special offer, even if the price is the same as the identical good that is not 'on offer'. In a famous experiment shoppers were found to be **Q44.** *less/more* attracted to a stall offering a wide choice of samples than a stall offering fewer choices.

Decision makers sometimes make choices under conditions of *bounded rationality*.

Q45. Which of the following statements describe a situation of bounded rationality?

(i) The information needed to make a fully rational decision is not available.

(ii) A decision maker could obtain full information, but judges that it would take too much time to do so.

(iii) A consumer maximises utility from two goods by consuming at the point where the ratio of marginal utilities of the two goods is equal to the ratio of their prices.

(iv) A decision maker is unable to understand the complexity of the situation being faced.

A. (i).

B. (i) and (ii).

C. (i), (ii) and (iii).

D. (i), (ii) and (iv).

E. (i), (ii), (iii) and (iv).

(Page 126) Traditional economic analysis assumes that a consumer's demand for a product depends upon its price, the price of other goods, and on the consumer's preferences and income. Behavioural economics points out that individuals may also be influenced by the behaviour of others. This can lead to *herding* behaviour.

Q46. Which of the following are examples of herding behaviour?

(i) Consumers buy an item in a sale because they see others rushing to buy it.

(ii) People sell a particular share on the stock market because they see others selling it.

(iii) Trying to keep up with the Joneses.

(iv) A fashion for a product catches on.

A. (i).

B. (i) and (ii).

C. (i), (ii) and (iii).

D. (i), (ii) and (iv).

E. (i), (ii), (iii) and (iv).

Q47. Herding behaviour can help to explain destabilising speculative activity. *True/False*

◗ **Q48.** Sunk costs are irrelevant when taking decisions using the marginal principle.   *True/False*

◗ **Q49.** You come home from college on a Friday evening exhausted from a heavy day's study, and feel like having a relaxing time in front of the TV. However, some weeks ago you were persuaded to buy a ticket for a concert. You have to decide whether to collapse in front of the TV or get changed to go to the concert. Is the price you paid for the ticket pertinent to your decision?   *Yes/No*

B   **PROBLEMS, EXERCISES AND PROJECTS**

Q50. Select three items of foodstuff that you purchase regularly (e.g. bread, eggs, potatoes).

(a) In each case estimate how much per week you would purchase at different prices.

(b) In each case work out the amount of consumer surplus you receive per week.

(c) Now ask yourself how much money you would need to be given in each case in order to persuade you not to buy any of the good at all.

(d) Are the answers to (b) and (c) similar? Should they be?

(e) Now choose one of the three goods and select a substitute good for it. How will (i) a 10 per cent rise, (ii) a 20 per cent fall and (iii) a 50 per cent rise in the price of the substitute affect the consumer surplus you gain from the original good?

(f) How will your consumer surplus for each of the three goods be affected by a change in your income?

Q51. Imagine that you have £30 to spend on three goods, A, B and C. The marginal utility you gain from each good is independent of the amount you consume of the other two goods. Your marginal utility from successive units of each of the three goods is shown in Table 4.5.

Table 4.5 Marginal utilities (in utils) from the consumption of three goods A, B and C

Units of good A	1	2	3	4	5	6	7	8	9	10
Marginal utility	45	40	25	20	16	12	9	6	4	2
Units of good B	1	2	3	4	5	6	7	8	9	10
Marginal utility	80	70	60	50	40	30	20	10	0	0
Units of good C	1	2	3	4	5	6	7	8	9	10
Marginal utility	22	20	18	16	14	12	10	8	6	4

(a) Imagine that good A costs £4, good B costs £3 and good C costs £2. How much will you consume of each?

(b) Assume now that the price of A rises to £10, that the price of B falls to £2 and the price of C remains unchanged at £2. How much of each will be consumed now, assuming the budget remains unchanged at £30?

(c) In which situation (a) or (b) is total utility higher?

*Q52. Harry gains equal satisfaction from the following combinations of annual visits to the theatre and visits to football matches:

   14 theatre and 3 football
   11 theatre and 4 football
   8 theatre and 6 football
   6 theatre and 9 football
   4 theatre and 16 football

(a) Using graph paper, plot Harry's indifference curve corresponding to these figures. Plot theatre visits on the vertical axis.

(b) If Harry actually visited the theatre 5 times, how many football matches would he have to attend in order to obtain the same satisfaction as in the other 5 combinations?

(c) What is the marginal rate of substitution of theatre visits for football matches between 4 and 6 football matches?

(d) What is the marginal rate of substitution of theatre visits for football matches at the 8 theatre, 6 football point on the indifference curve?

(e) Assume that Harry decides to allocate a total of £280 per year to these two activities. Assume also that both football matches and theatre visits cost £20. How many visits to the theatre could he make if he attended 9 football matches?

(f) Draw Harry's budget line on your diagram.

(g) How many theatre performances and football matches will he attend?
Why will he not attend an equal number of each?

(h) Assume now that the price of theatre tickets increases to £40, but that Harry unfortunately cannot afford to budget for any more than the £280. Draw Harry's new budget line.

(i) Poor Harry is now going to have to economise on the number of visits to either or both types of event. So he sits down and thinks about alternative combinations that would give him equal satisfaction to each other (but less than before). He comes up with the following combinations:

   12 theatre and 2 football
   9 theatre and 3 football
   6 theatre and 5 football
   3 theatre and 8 football

2 theatre and 11 football

1 theatre and 15 football

Draw this indifference curve on the diagram.

(j) How many theatre performances and football matches will he now attend?

(k) Assume that Harry now wonders whether to try to maintain his previous level of satisfaction by allocating a bigger budget to compensate for the higher price of theatre tickets. If he did do this, what would his new budget line look like? (Draw it.)

(l) How many theatre performances and football matches would he attend under these circumstances?

(m) How much would this cost him?

(n) Had he maintained his original combination of visits, how much would this now have cost him?

(o) On second thoughts he reluctantly decides he will have to restrict himself to the original £280 and thus

the answer to (j) above holds. What will be the size of the income and substitution effects of the rise in the price of theatre tickets from £20 to £40?

(p) Are theatre visits a normal or an inferior 'good' for Harry? Explain.

(q) If Harry meets Sally and she likes going to the cinema with Harry rather than to the theatre, how will this affect Harry's indifference curves between visits to the theatre and visits to football matches?

Q53. Conduct a survey amongst your fellow non-economics students to see whether they ever make spending decisions based on observing other people's spending behaviour, and whether they would take sunk costs into consideration when deciding how to spend their time.

 DISCUSSION TOPICS AND ESSAYS

Q54. If people buy things out of habit, does this conflict with the assumption of rational behaviour?

Q55. In the UK most domestic consumers pay for water through a system of water rates which are based on the value of the person's property. This is a flat sum and does not vary with the amount of water consumed. What would you expect a person's marginal utility for water to be? Make out a case for and against having water meters and charging for water on a per litre basis.

Q56. What are the drawbacks in attempting to measure utility in money terms?

Q57. Explain how goods with little total utility to the consumer can sell for a high price.

*Q58. Could indifference curves ever intersect (i) over the same time period, (ii) over different time periods?

*Q59. Imagine that the price–consumption curve for good X was downward sloping. Are goods X and Y substitutes or complements? Explain.

*Q60. What are the limitations of indifference analysis for (a) explaining and (b) predicting consumption patterns for a given consumer?

Q61. A firm is considering a large investment project. Identify the ways in which expectations about the future will influence the decision, and discuss how

information could be acquired to improve the decision-making process.

Q62. Discuss ways in which the growth of the Internet has influenced consumers and firms in forming expectations.

Q63. Explain the difference between the terms 'risk loving', 'risk neutral' and 'risk averse'. Would a risk-loving person ever be prepared to take out insurance?

Q64. How can insurance companies protect themselves against the problems of adverse selection and moral hazard?

Q65. Discuss the conditions under which an individual may choose to take decisions under bounded rationality rather than trying to maximise utility in a fully rational manner.

Q66. Explain why herding behaviour may arise, and why this may lead people into taking decisions that do not maximise their utility.

Q67. Discuss why individuals may choose to engage in volunteering activities. What incentives might be put in place to encourage more volunteering behaviour?

Q68. Debate

It is wrong for the state to provide services such as health and libraries free at the point of use. With a zero price, people consume a wasteful amount. They consume to the point where marginal utility is zero.

ANSWERS

Q1. The total amount of satisfaction a consumer gains by consuming a given quantity of a good or service over a given time period.

Q2. The additional satisfaction a consumer gains by consuming one more unit of a good or service within the same time period.

Q3. D. By consuming the fifth toffee, my total utility has gone up from 20 units to 23 units: a rise of 3 units.

Q4. E. If total utility is falling then the last unit must *reduce* total utility: its marginal utility must be negative.

Q5. *(a)* See table below.

Visits	1	2	3	4	5	6	7	8
TU (utils)	12	20	25	28	30	31	31	29
MU (utils)	12	8	5	3	2	1	0	-2

(b) See Figure A4.1.

(c) (i) 50; (ii) 62; (iii) 62. A doubling of marginal utility leads to a doubling of total utility.

Q6. (a), (c), (e). In each of these cases I only consume/do a certain amount and then do something else. The implication is that as the marginal utility declines, so it becomes preferable to switch to an alternative. (Note that (b) and (d) simply state a preference without saying how the preference *changes* according to the level of consumption.)

Q7. E. Marginal utility is the extra utility gained from one more unit consumed. If it falls then total utility will still rise (provided that *MU* does not become negative), but will rise *less* than for the previous unit.

Q8. The list could include increased consumption of other drinks (*MU* decreases), the weather (on a hot day the *MU* will increase), increased consumption of dry food (*MU* increases), fashion, etc.

Q9. *buy more.* They are gaining more from extra consumption than it is costing them.

Q10. *buy less.* The last unit being consumed is costing them more than it is benefiting them.

Q11. *(a)* £73 (= £25 + £20 + £16 + £12).

(b) £60 (6 units @ £10 each).

(c) £10 (= £20 (*MU*) – £10 (*P*)).

(d) –£2 (= £8 (*MU*) – £10 (*P*)).

(e) £25 (= £45 (*TU*) – £20 (*TE*)).

(f) 4 units (*TCS* = £33).

(g) (i.e. between +2 (between 3 and 4 units), and –2 (between 4 and 5 units)).

(h) $P = MU = £10$.

Q12. C. It is given by the area under the *MU* curve at the output (*Q*) in question.

Q13. A. It is given by the area between the *MU* curve and the price.

Q14. *marginal utility.* With a constant income and when the consumption of this good is too insignificant to affect the demand for other goods, the demand curve will be the marginal utility curve (where *MU* is measured in money terms).

Q15. *buy more of X relative to Y.* If $MU_X/P_X > MU_Y/P_Y$, then people would be getting a better value (*MU*) for money (*P*) from X than from Y. They would thus consume relatively more of X and relatively less of Y. This would cause MU_X to fall (and MU_Y to rise) until $MU_X/P_X = MU_Y/P_Y$.

Q16. $MU_X/P_X = MU_Y/P_Y$.

Q17. D. If Dolcelatte gives her twice as much marginal utility as Cheddar, it must be costing her twice as much, in order for the equi-marginal principle to be satisfied.

Q18. D. We can say for certain that if she is 'rational' she will switch away from Z and towards X, but whether she alters her consumption of Y and in which direction will depend on how rapidly the marginal utilities of X and Z change.

Q19. C. All the other statements consider the effects of a bit *more* of something (eating another chocolate bar, mortgage rates rising by another 1 per cent, purchasing another forklift truck, installing anti-pollution equipment on one more power station). In the case of C, however, we are considering the effect of *total* revenues for the firm exceeding its *total* production costs.

Q20. *(a)* See Figure A4.2.

(b) *Set 2.* It gives an indifference curve furthest out from the origin.

(c) *Sets 1 and 4.* They lie along the same indifference curve.

(d) *Set 5.* It gives an indifference curve furthest in towards the origin.

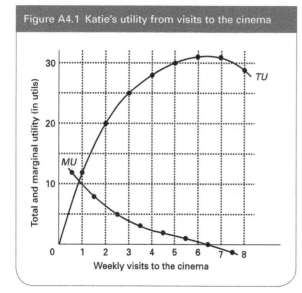

Figure A4.1 Katie's utility from visits to the cinema

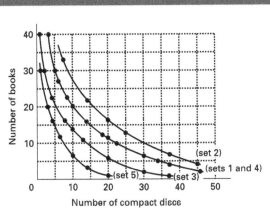

Figure A4.2 Sally's indifference curves between books and compact discs

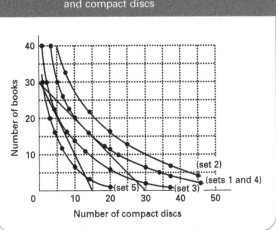

Figure A4.3 Sally's indifference curves between books and compact discs

(e) *Because a curve drawn through these combinations would cross other indifference curves, and indifference curves cannot cross.* 36 books and 5 CDs are preferable to 30 books and 5 CDs (set 1) and yet 3 books and 20 CDs are inferior to 6 books and 20 CDs (set 3) and yet set 1 is preferable to set 3! Thus, given the other sets, 36 books and 5 CDs cannot lie along the same indifference curve as 3 books and 20 CDs.

Q21. The marginal rate of substitution of Y for X is the amount of Y that a consumer is prepared to give up *for a one unit increase in the consumption of X.*

Q22. *(a)* $\Delta B/\Delta CD = 4/1 = 4$.

(b) $\Delta B/\Delta CD = 4/2 = 2$.

(c) $\Delta B/\Delta CD = 6/4 = 1.5$.

Q23. The *MRS* diminishes (e.g. see answer to Q29). The reason is that as more of one good is consumed relative to the other, so its marginal utility will decrease relative to that of the other. Thus the consumer would be prepared to give up less and less of the other good for each additional unit of the first good.

Q24. A. If the slope $(\Delta Y/\Delta X)$ were 2/1, this would mean that the person would be prepared to give up 2 units of Y for 1 unit of X. This would mean that X has twice the marginal utility of Y, i.e. $MU_X/MU_Y = 2$.

Q25. *(a)* $P_X = £5$ (i.e. 4 could be purchased if the whole budget were spent on X).

$P_Y = £2.50$ (i.e. 8 could be purchased if the whole budget were spent on Y).

(b) The new budget line will join 5 on the Y axis with 4 on the X axis. The reason is that, with a new price for Y of £4, if all £20 were spent on Y, 5 units could now be purchased.

(c) £40 (i.e. 4X could be purchased at a price of £10 each).

(d) £8 (i.e. if 5Y can be purchased for £40, the price must be £8).

(e) *Nothing.* The consumer will be able to buy exactly the same quantities as before. Although money income has doubled, *real* income has not changed.

Q26. C. If the slope were 2/1, this would mean that 2 units of Y could be purchased for each 1 unit of X sacrificed. Thus X must be twice the price of Y: $P_X/P_Y = 2$ = slope of budget line.

Q27. *(a)* See Figure A4.3.

(b) 16 books and 14 CDs.

(c) See Figure A4.3.

(d) 20 books and 5 CDs.

Q28. *(a)* (vi).

(b) (iii). (As tastes shift towards Y and away from X so MU_X/MU_Y will fall, and thus the curve will become flatter.)

(c) (i).

(d) (viii).

(e) (vii). (MU_X/MU_Y will rise.)

(f) (v).

(g) (ii).

(h) (iv).

Q29. *(a)* See Figure A4.4.

(b)

P	Q_d
10	8.0
16	5.6
20	5.0
32	3.6
40	3.0

See Figure A4.4 for the price–consumption curve.

(c) The five sets of figures (plus any others you choose to read off from the price–consumption curve) can then be plotted with *P* on the vertical axis and Q_d on the horizontal axis. The points can then be connected to give a demand curve.

Figure A4.4 The effect of a change in the price of good X on Tom's consumption

Price–consumption curve

I_7
I_6
I_5
I_4
I_3
I_2
I_1

$P_x = £40$
$P_x = £32$ $P_x = £20$ $P_x = £16$
$P_x = £10$

Units of good Y

Units of good X

Q30. *expenditure on all other goods.*

Q31. (a) See Figure A4.5. In each diagram the substitution effect is represented by the movement from Q_{X_1} to Q_{X_2} and the income effect by the movement from Q_{X_2} to Q_{X_3}.

(b) (i) diagram (b) (negative income (and substitution) effect), (ii) diagram (c) (positive income effect, but smaller than the negative substitution effect), (iii) diagram (a) (positive income effect which outweighs the negative substitution effect).

Q32. See table below.

Type of good	Substitution effect	Income effect	Which is the bigger effect?
Normal	*negative*	*negative*	*either*
Inferior (non-Giffen)	*negative*	*positive*	*substitution*
Giffen	*negative*	*positive*	*income*

Q33. *False.* People would only consume more if the positive income effect (because the good was inferior) outweighed the (usual) negative substitution effect. This is the case only with a Giffen good.

Q34. *risk.*

Q35. *uncertainty.*

Q36. *D.* All of the other items will not be known until you reach the decision point.

Q37. *Risk loving.* The chances of drawing an ace are 1:13. If for a £1 bet you only won £10 each time you drew an ace, then on average you would lose money. If therefore you were prepared to accept odds of 10/1, you would be risk loving.

Q38. (a) *700 utils* (with a total income of £8000).

(b) *0 utils* (with a total income of £0).

(c) *(700 + 0) ÷ 2 = 350 utils.*

(d) *because, with a diminishing marginal utility of income, by taking the gamble his average expected utility (350 utils) is less than by not taking the gamble (500 utils).*

Q39. *False.* The total amount paid to insurance companies in premiums will exceed the amount received back in claims: that is how the companies make a profit. Thus the odds are inevitably unfair for the client. It is still worthwhile, however, to take out insurance because people are risk averters (given the diminishing marginal utility of income).

Q40. *C.* A company can spread its risks over a large number of policies (ii). The more people the insurance company insures, the more predictable the total outcome (i), provided that the risks are independent (iii). Insurance companies are not risk lovers, because on average they will make a profit.

Q41. (a) *Not independent.* They may all meet with an accident in the coach or on the plane.

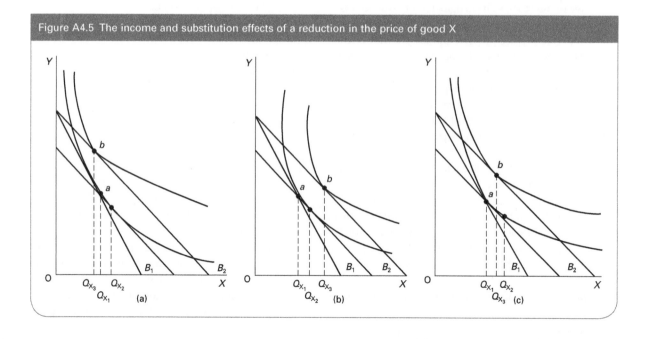

Figure A4.5 The income and substitution effects of a reduction in the price of good X

(b) *Not independent.* In a recession, people in many otherwise unconnected parts of the economy will be under greater threat of redundancy.

(c) *Independent.* One person having an accident will not affect the risks of others having an accident.

(d) *Not independent.* A particular neighbourhood may be more subject to burglaries. (Insurance companies charge house contents premiums based on your postcode. People living in high-risk areas pay higher premiums.)

(e) *Independent.* If a person over 65 dies, this will not affect the chances of other people over 65 dying. Under certain circumstances, however, the risks would *not* be independent. These circumstances would include an epidemic or an exceptionally severe winter.

(f) *Not independent.* In a war, soldiers' lives will generally be at greater risk.

Q42. *(a)* *Moral hazard: knowing that her bicycle is well insured affects Amy's behaviour.*

(b) *Moral hazard.*

(c) *Adverse selection: in this case, Caroline takes out life insurance because she knows that she has terminal cancer. Of course, in practice, the insurance companies are wise to this, and counter it by exclusion clauses for pre-existing medical conditions etc.*

(d) *Adverse selection; again, insurance companies can screen for people who have hazardous hobbies.*

(e) *Moral hazard: several developing countries became burdened with high levels of international debt, which came to a head in the 1990s. The World Bank was reluctant to grant debt forgiveness because of the potential moral hazard issues. Attempts were made to overcome this by imposing conditions on countries that were granted debt relief.*

Q43. *more.*

Q44. *less.*

Q45. D.

Q46. E.

Q47. *True.* For example, people may be induced into buying a risky financial asset because they see others are buying it. This can push the price well above a level that reflects the utility that people will gain.

Q48. *True.*

Q49. *No.* If you are looking to take a rational decision, you should be balancing the marginal benefits and costs of staying at home as opposed to going to the concert. The ticket price is a sunk cost that does not affect this marginal decision.

 A **REVIEW**

We now turn to the theory of supply. We will examine what determines the quantity that firms will produce at various prices and various costs.

In this chapter (and the next two) we will be making the traditional assumption that firms are profit maximisers: that they wish to produce the level of output that will maximise the total level of their profit ($T\Pi$). We define total profit as total revenue (*TR*) minus total costs (*TC*).

In order then to discover how a firm can maximise its profit, we must first consider what determines costs and revenue. We start by examining costs in both the short run and the long run. We then examine revenue. Finally we put the two together to examine profit.

5.1 The short-run theory of production

(Pages 132–5) The cost of producing any level of output will depend on the amount of inputs used. The relationship between output and inputs is shown in a *production function*.

⊗ **Q1.** In the following production function for good A, a good is produced by using two factors, labour (*L*) and capital (*K*). How much will be produced if 6 units of labour and 3 units of capital are used?

$TPP = 10L + 4K$...
(where *TPP* is total physical product: i.e. total output).

Extra output involves using extra input. But increasing the amount of certain inputs may take time: it takes time, for example, to build a new factory or to install new machines. We thus make a distinction between *short-run* production and *long-run* production.

▤ **Q2.** The short run is defined as

A. a period of time less than one year.

B. the shortest time period in which a firm will consider producing.

C. the period of time in which at least one factor of production is fixed in supply.

D. the period of time it takes for raw materials to be converted into finished goods.

E. the length of time taken for a minimum-sized production run.

In the short run, production will be subject to the *law of diminishing (marginal) returns*.

⁇ **Q3.** The law of diminishing marginal returns states that

....

⊖ **Q4.** Imagine that a firm produces good X with just two factors: capital which is fixed in supply, and labour

---

Table 5.1 The relationship between the output (total physical product) of good X and the number of workers employed

(1) Number of workers	(2) TPP	(3)	(4)
0	0		
1	10	.	.
2	26	.	.
3	41	.	.
4	52	.	.
5	60	.	.
6	65	.	.
7	67	.	.
8	67	.	.
9	63	.	.

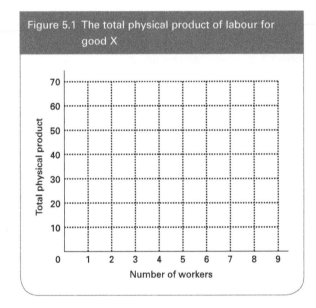

Figure 5.1 The total physical product of labour for good X

which is variable. The effect on total output (*TPP*) of increasing the number of workers is shown in column (2) of Table 5.1. (We will fill in columns (3) and (4) later.)

(*a*) Draw the total physical product curve on Figure 5.1.

(*b*) Beyond what number of workers do diminishing returns set in?

(*Pages 134–8*) We can use total physical product data to derive average and marginal physical product data. We define marginal physical product (*MPP*) as *Q5. the number of units of the variable factor required to produce one more unit of output/the amount of extra output gained from the use of one more unit of the variable factor.*

Q6. If *L* is the quantity of labour, then of the following:

(i) *TPP/L*

(ii) *ΔL/ΔTPP*

(iii) *ΔTPP/ΔL*

(iv) *ΔL/TPP*

(*a*) Which is the formula for the marginal physical product (*MPP*) of labour? (*i*)/(*ii*)/(*iii*)/(*iv*)

(*b*) Which is the formula for the average physical product (*APP*) of labour? (*i*)/(*ii*)/(*iii*)/(*iv*)

Q7. Referring back to Table 5.1, fill in the figures for *APP* and *MPP* in columns (3) and (4) respectively. (Note that the figures for *MPP* are entered between the lines. The reason is that the marginal physical product is the extra output gained from *moving* from one level of input to one more unit of input.)

Q8. Draw the *APP* and *MPP* curves on Figure 5.2.

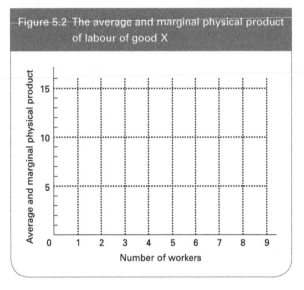

Figure 5.2 The average and marginal physical product of labour of good X

Q9. Why does the marginal product curve pass through the top of the average physical product curve?

....

....

Q10. The total physical product for any given amount of the variable factor is the sum of all the marginal physical products up to that point. *True/False*

Q11. Assume that the following two pieces of information are obtained from a production function for good X. (1) 1000 units of good X can be produced with a combination of 20 units of input A, 30 units of input B and 40 units of input C. (2) 1005 units of good X can be produced with 20 units of input A, 30 units of input B and 41 units of input C. From these two pieces of information it can be deduced that at this point on the production function:

A. the *MPP* of good X is 5 units.

B. the *MPP* of input C is 5 units.

C. the *MPP* of good X is 1005/1000 units.

D. the *MPP* of input C is 1005/40 units.

E. the *MPP* of input C is 1005/41 units.

5.2 Costs in the short run

(Pages 138–9) We now examine how a firm's costs are related to its output. When measuring cost we should be careful to use the concept of *opportunity* cost. In the case of factors not already owned by the firm, the opportunity cost is simply **Q12.** *the implicit/explicit* cost of purchasing or hiring them. In the case of factors that *are* already owned by the firm, we have to impute an opportunity cost when they are used.

Q13. Assume that a firm already owns a machine that has a total life of 10 years. The cost of using the machine for one year to produce good X is:
A. a tenth of what the firm paid for the machine in the first place.
B. a tenth of what it would cost to replace the machine.
C. the value of one year's output of X.
D. the scrap value of the machine at the end of its life.
E. the maximum the machine could have earned for the firm in some alternative use during the year in question.

Q14. The opportunity cost of using a factor owned by the firm that has no other use and whose second-hand or scrap value is not affected by its use is zero.   *True/False*

(Page 140) In the short run, by definition, at least one factor is fixed in supply. The total cost to the firm of these factors is thus fixed with respect to **Q15.** *time/the firm's output*.

Q16. Which of the following are likely to be fixed costs and which variable costs for a chocolate factory over the course of a month?
(a) The cost of cocoa.   *Fixed/Variable*
(b) Business rates (local taxes).   *Fixed/Variable*
(c) An advertising campaign for a new chocolate bar.   *Fixed/Variable*
(d) The cost of electricity (paid quarterly) for running the mixing machines.   *Fixed/Variable*
(e) Overtime pay.   *Fixed/Variable*
(f) The basic minimum wage agreed with the union (workers must be given at least one month's notice if they are to be laid off).   *Fixed/Variable*
(g) Wear and tear on wrapping machines.   *Fixed/Variable*
(h) Depreciation of machines due simply to their age.   *Fixed/Variable*
(i) Interest on a mortgage for the factory: the rate of interest rises over the course of the month.   *Fixed/Variable*

(Pages 139–44) We use a number of different measures of cost: fixed and variable; and average and marginal.

Q17. Which of the measures of cost – total fixed cost (*TFC*), total variable cost (*TVC*), total cost (*TC*), average fixed cost (*AFC*), average variable cost (*AVC*), average (total) cost (*AC*), marginal cost (*MC*) – are described by each of the following?

(a) TC/Q ....

(b) $AC - AFC$ ....

(c) $\Delta TC/\Delta Q$ ....

(d) $\Delta TVC/\Delta Q$ ....

(e) $(TC - TVC) + Q$ ....

(f) $(AFC + AVC) \times Q$ ....

(g) ΣMC ....

(h) $\Sigma MC + TFC$ ....

(Note: Σ means 'the sum of'.)

Q18. Table 5.2 gives the short-run costs for an imaginary firm.

Table 5.2 Short-run costs for firm X

Output	TFC	TVC	TC	AFC	AVC	AC	MC
0	.	.	.				
1	.	8	.	10.0	.	.	.
2	.	12	.	.	.	.	4
3	10	.	25	.	.	.	.
4	.	.	27	.	.	.	.
5	.	.	.	.	4.0	.	.
6	.	.	.	.	4.0	.	5
7	.	.	.	.	.	.	.
8	.	.	.	.	.	5.75	.
9	.	48	.	.	.	6.44	.
10	.	70	.	.	.	.	.

(a) Fill in the figures for each of the columns.
(b) At what output do diminishing marginal returns set in (assuming constant factor prices)?

....

(c) Draw *TFC*, *TVC* and *TC* on Figure 5.3. Mark the point on the *TVC* curve where (i) *MC* is at a minimum, (ii) *AVC* is at a minimum.
(d) Draw *AFC*, *AVC*, *AC* and *MC* on Figure 5.4. Be careful to plot the *MC* figures midway between the figures for quantity (i.e. at 0.5, 1.5, 2.5, etc.).

Q19. If the marginal cost is below the average cost, then:
A. the marginal cost must be falling.
B. the marginal cost must be rising.
C. the average cost must be falling.
D. the average cost must be rising.
E. the average cost could be either rising or falling depending on whether the marginal cost is rising or falling.

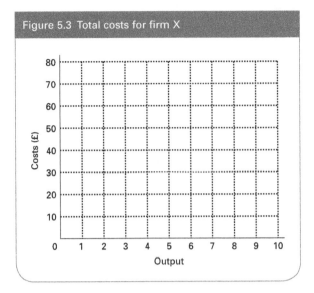

Figure 5.3 Total costs for firm X

Table 5.3 The effects of increasing the amounts of both inputs

Situation (i)			Situation (ii)		
Input 1	Input 2	Output	Input 1	Input 2	Output
1	1	12	1	2	14
2	2	24	2	2	24
3	3	36	3	2	32
4	4	48	4	2	38
5	5	60	5	2	42

(c) Are the figures consistent with the law of diminishing marginal returns? *Yes/No*

Explain ....

If a firm experiences increasing returns to scale, it is also likely to experience *economies of scale.*

Q22. Economies of scale can be defined as:
A. large-scale production leading to bigger profits.
B. large-scale production leading to lower costs per unit of production.
C. large-scale production leading to greater marginal productivity of factors.
D. large-scale production leading to greater output per unit of input.
E. large-scale production leading to a better organisation of the factors of production.

Q23. The following is a list of various types of economy of scale:
   (i) The firm can benefit from the specialisation and division of labour.
  (ii) It can overcome the problem of indivisibilities.
 (iii) It can obtain inputs at a lower price.
 (iv) Large containers/machines have a greater capacity relative to their surface area.
  (v) The firm may be able to obtain finance at lower cost.
 (vi) It becomes economical to sell by-products.
(vii) Production can take place in integrated plants.
(viii) Risks can be spread with a larger number of products or plants.

Match each of the following examples for a particular firm to one of these types of economy of scale.
(a) Delivery vans can carry full loads to single destinations.

....

(b) It can more easily make a public issue of shares.

....

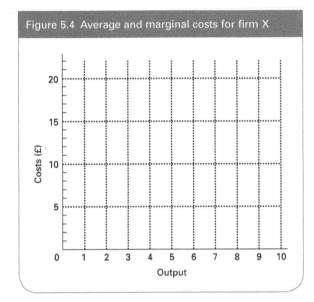

Figure 5.4 Average and marginal costs for firm X

5.3 The long-run theory of production

(Pages 144–7) In the long run, all factors become variable. Given time, more capital equipment can be installed, new techniques of production can be used, additional land can be acquired and another factory can be built.

If a doubling of inputs leads to a more than doubling of output, the firm is said to experience *Q20. decreasing returns to scale/increasing returns to the variable factor/increasing returns to scale.*

Q21. Assume that a firm uses just two factors of production. Table 5.3 shows what happens to output as the firm increases one or both of these inputs.
(a) Which situation represents the long run? *(i)/(ii)*
(b) Does the firm experience increasing returns to scale? *Yes/No*

Explain ....

(c) It can diversify into other markets.

....

(d) Workers spend less time having to train for a wide variety of different tasks, and less time moving from task to task.

....

(e) It negotiates bulk discount with a supplier of raw materials.

....

(f) It uses large warehouses to store its raw materials and finished goods.

....

(g) A clothing manufacturer does a deal to supply a soft toy manufacturer with offcuts for stuffing toys.

....

(h) Conveyor belts transfer the product through several stages of the manufacturing process.

....

Q24. Referring to the list (i)–(viii) of economies of scale in Q23, which arise from increasing (physical) returns to scale?

Q25. Which of the following are *internal* and which are *external* economies of scale for firm A?
(a) Firm A benefits from a pool of trained labour in the area.
Internal/External
(b) Firm A benefits from lower administration costs per unit as a result of opening a second factory.
Internal/External
(c) Firm A is able to sell by-products to other firms.
Internal/External
(d) Firm A benefits from research and development conducted by other firms in the industry.
Internal/External
(e) Other firms benefit from firm A's discovery of a new technique of mass production. *Internal/External*

(Pages 147–8) Given that all factors of production are variable in the long run, a firm will want to choose the least-cost combination of inputs for any given level of output.

Q26. Assuming that a firm uses three factors A, B and C, whose prices are respectively P_A, P_B and P_C, which of the following represents the least-cost combination of these factors?
A. $P_A = P_B = P_C$
B. $MPP_A = MPP_B = MPP_C$
C. $MPP_A \times P_A = MPP_B \times P_B = MPP_C \times P_C$
D. $MPP_A/MPP_B = MPP_B/MPP_C = MPP_C/MPP_A$
E. $MPP_A/P_A = MPP_B/P_B = MPP_C/P_C$

(?) Q27. Table 5.4 gives details of the output of good X obtained from different combinations of the three factors A, B and C.

Table 5.4 Output of good X from various factor combinations

Quantity of input A	Quantity of input B	Quantity of input C	Output of X
100	50	30	1000
100	50	31	1005
100	51	30	1010
101	50	30	1003

Assume that the price of factor A is £6. What must the prices of factors B and C be if the least-cost factor combination to produce 1000 units of X is the one shown in the top row of Table 5.4?

Price of B ....

Price of C ....

⊗ *Q28.* A firm faces a Cobb–Douglas production function represented by the equation:

$$TPP = AK^{1/2}L^{1/3}E^{1/6}$$

where K is capital input, L is labour input and E is energy input.

If $A = 9$, $K = 36$, $L = 27$ and $E = 64$,
(a) Calculate *TPP*.

....

(b) Calculate the *MPP* of labour.

....

(c) Supposing the quantities of all inputs are doubled, calculate *TPP*. (Note that you will need a scientific calculator to work out the cube root of the *L* value. To get the sixth root of the *E* value, you should first take the square root and then the cube root of that.)

....

(d) Comment on the nature of returns to scale.

....

(e) Suppose that labour input is doubled (to 54), but that the other inputs remain at their original level (i.e. $K = 36$ and $E = 64$). Calculate the *MPP* of labour, and compare your results with Part *(b)* of the question

....

(Pages 148–52) The least-cost combination of factors to produce various levels of output can be shown graphically by drawing isoquants and isocosts. This analysis assumes that there are just two factors.

⊖ ***Q29.*** Table 5.5 shows the output of good X obtained from different inputs of factors A and B.

(a) Draw the 100, 200, 300 and 400 unit isoquants on Figure 5.5.

Table 5.5 Various factor combinations to produce different levels of output of good X

100 units of X	
	70*A*, 1*B*; 52*A*, 3*B*; 40*A*, 8*B*; 31*A*, 15*B*; 22*A*, 25*B*; 17*A*, 33*B*; 14*A*, 40*B*; 10*A*, 50*B*; 4*A*, 70*B*
200 units of X	
	70*A*, 3*B*; 58*A*, 5*B*; 45*A*, 10*B*; 33*A*, 20*B*; 26*A*, 30*B*; 18*A*, 45*B*; 10*A*, 63*B*; 5*A*, 80*B*
300 units of X	
	70*A*, 7*B*; 55*A*, 11*B*; 46*A*, 16*B*; 40*A*, 20*B*; 32*A*, 30*B*; 26*A*, 40*B*; 21*A*, 50*B*; 13*A*, 70*B*; 8*A*, 86*B*
400 units of X	
	70*A*, 11*B*; 58*A*, 15*B*; 50*A*, 19*B*; 39*A*, 28*B*; 32*A*, 38*B*; 26*A*, 50*B*; 20*A*, 63*B*; 12*A*, 83*B*

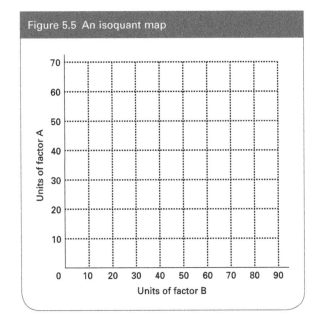

Figure 5.5 An isoquant map

(b) If factor A and factor B both cost £200 each, what is the least-cost combination of A and B to produce 300 units of good X? (You will need to draw the appropriate isocost.)

....

(c) How much will this cost the firm?.............................

(d) Suppose now that the price of factor B rises to £300 but that the firm's total cost remains the same as in (b). What is the maximum output the firm can now produce for this cost?

....

(e) How many units of A and B will it now use?

....

At the point where an isocost is tangential to an isoquant, the firm is producing the highest possible output for a given cost and at the lowest possible cost for a given output.

▤ ***Q30.*** With the quantity of factor A measured on the vertical axis and the quantity of factor B measured on the horizontal axis, the slope of an isoquant gives (for that output):

A. P_A/P_B
B. P_B/P_A
C. MPP_A/MPP_B
D. MPP_B/MPP_A
E. $MPP_A/P_A = MPP_B/P_B$

▤ ***Q31.*** With the quantity of factor A measured on the vertical axis and the quantity of factor B measured on the horizontal axis, the slope of an isocost gives:

A. P_A/P_B
B. P_B/P_A
C. MPP_A/MPP_B
D. MPP_B/MPP_A
E. $MPP_A/P_A = MPP_B/P_B$

5.4 Costs in the long run
(Pages 154–7)

◖ **Q32.** Which of the following assumptions do we make when constructing long-run cost curves? (There may be more than one.)

(a) Factor prices are given.	*Yes/No*
(b) The state of technology is given.	*Yes/No*
(c) All factors are variable.	*Yes/No*
(d) Firms will choose the least-cost factor combination.	*Yes/No*
(e) The firm experiences economies of scale.	*Yes/No*
(f) There are no fixed factors of production.	*Yes/No*
(g) The *MPP/P* ratios for all factors are equal.	*Yes/No*

⊖ **Q33.** Assume that a firm experiences economies of scale up to a certain level of output, then constant (average) costs, and then diseconomies of scale. Sketch its long-run average and marginal cost curves on Figure 5.6.

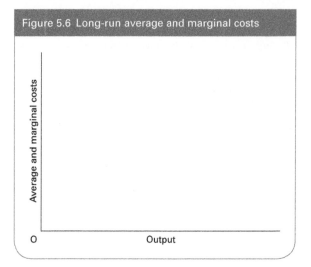

Figure 5.6 Long-run average and marginal costs

◗ **Q34.** The long-run average cost curve will be tangential with the bottom points of the short-run average cost curves. *True/False*

◗ **Q35.** If a firm is achieving maximum economies of scale then its $LRAC = SRAC = LRMC = SRMC$. *True/False*

⊖ ***Q36.** Figure 5.7 shows a (weekly) isoquant map for a firm which uses two factors of production, labour (L) and capital (K), to produce good X. The optimum factor combinations to produce four levels of output are shown by points a, b, c and d. These represent the following factor combinations: $a = 10K, 15L$; $b = 16K, 21L$; $c = 18K, 33L$; $d = 22K, 42L$. The cost of capital is £240 per unit per week. The cost of labour (the wage rate) is £160 per week.

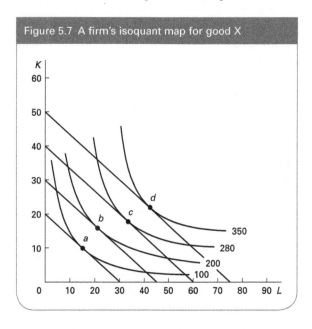

Figure 5.7 A firm's isoquant map for good X

(a) What is the (minimum) total cost of producing:

    (i) 100 units? ....

    (ii) 200 units? ....

    (iii) 280 units? ....

    (iv) 350 units? ....

(b) What is the (minimum) average cost of producing these four levels of output?

    (i) .... ,

    (ii) .... ,

    (iii) .... ,

    (iv) ....

(c) Over what output range does the firm experience economies of scale?

....

5.5 Revenue

(Pages 159–62) Remember we said that profit equals revenue minus cost. We have looked at costs. We now turn to revenue.

Let us assume that firm S is a price taker. In other words it faces a **Q37.** *downward-sloping/horizontal* **Q38.** *demand curve/supply curve.*

⊗ **Q39.** Let us assume that it faces a market price of £2 per unit for its product.

(a) What is its total revenue from selling:

    (i) 5 units? ....

    (ii) 8 units? ....

(b) What shape is its total revenue curve?

....

(c) What will be its marginal revenue from selling:

    (i) the fifth unit? ....

    (ii) the eighth unit? ....

(d) What shape is its marginal revenue curve?

....

Now assume that firm T faces a downward-sloping (straight-line) demand curve. This is shown in Table 5.6.

Table 5.6 The demand curve for the product of firm T

Price (Average revenue) (£)	Quantity (units)	Total revenue (£)	Marginal revenue (£)
20	0	.	
18	1	.	.
16	2	.	.
14	3	.	.
12	4	.	.
10	5	.	.
8	6	.	.
6	7	.	.

(e) Fill in the columns for *TR* and *MR*. (Note that the figures for *MR* are entered between 0 and 1, 1 and 2, 2 and 3, etc.)

(f) What is the price elasticity of demand at *P* = £10?

....

(g) Over what price range is demand price elastic?

....

(h) Over what price range is demand price inelastic?

....

⊗ **Q40.** If a reduction in the price of good X from £20 to £15 leads to a rise in the amount sold from 100 to 130 units, what would be the *MR*?

▤ **Q41.** A wine merchant will supply bottles of Champagne to a wedding at £10 per bottle, but is willing to offer a 10 per cent discount on the total bill if 50 bottles or more are purchased. What would be the firm's marginal revenue for the 50th bottle?

A. £450
B. £9
C. £1
D. –£40
E. –£45

5.6 Profit maximisation

(Page 163) There are two methods of showing the profit-maximising position for a firm. The first uses total revenue and total cost curves.

⊖ **Q42.** Figure 5.8 shows the total cost and revenue curves for a firm on the same diagram.

(a) At what output is the firm's profit maximised?

....

(b) How much profit is made at this output? ....

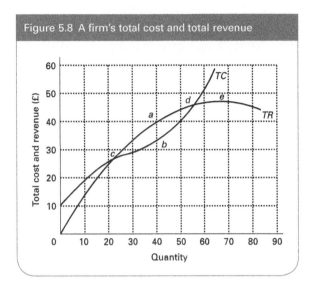

Figure 5.8 A firm's total cost and total revenue

(c) Draw the *TΠ* curve over the range of output where positive profit is made.

(d) How much is total fixed cost? ....

(e) At what output is the price elasticity of demand equal to –1?

....

(f) At what outputs does the firm break even?

(Pages 163–8) The second method of showing the profit-maximising position is to use *AR*, *MR*, *AC* and *MC* curves.

⊖ **Q43.** Table 5.7 gives a firm's average and marginal cost and revenue schedules for the production of good X.

(a) Draw the *AC*, *MC*, *AR* and *MR* curves on Figure 5.9.

(b) Explain the shape of the *AR* curve ....

(c) At what output is profit maximised? ....

(d) How much is average cost at this output?

....

Table 5.7 Costs and revenues for the production of good X

Quantity (units)	Average costs (£)	Marginal costs (£)	Average revenue (£)	Marginal revenue (£)
100	4.80	1.40	3.20	3.20
200	3.60	0.80	3.20	3.20
300	2.90	0.85	3.20	3.20
400	2.45	1.30	3.20	3.20
500	2.30	2.30	3.20	3.20
600	2.55	4.00	3.20	3.20
700	3.05	6.30	3.20	3.20
800	3.80	(above 7.00)	3.20	3.20
900	5.10	(above 7.00)	3.20	3.20

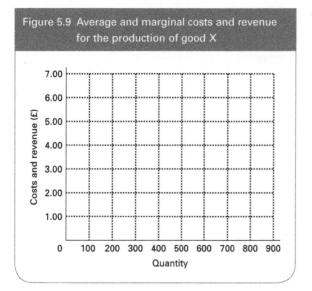

Figure 5.9 Average and marginal costs and revenue for the production of good X

A. AR is less than AC.
B. TR is less than TC.
C. MR is less than MC.
D. TR is less than TFC.
E. AR is less than AVC.

Q48. Figure 5.10 shows a firm's cost and revenue curves. It is currently producing at an output of OX. In order to maximise profits it should:
A. continue to produce at OX in the short run and expand production in the long run.
B. continue to produce at OX in the short run and close down in the long run.
C. reduce output in the short run and expand output in the long run.
D. reduce output in the short run and close down in the long run.
E. close down straight away.

(e) How much is average profit at this output?

....

(f) Shade in the area representing maximum total profit in Figure 5.9.

(g) How much is the maximum total profit?

....

(h) What is the lowest price the firm could receive if it were not to make a loss?

....

Q44. If at the current level of output a firm's price exceeds its marginal revenue and its marginal revenue exceeds its marginal cost, then to maximise profits it should:
A. reduce price and output.
B. raise price and output.
C. reduce price and raise output.
D. keep price the same and reduce output.
E. keep price the same and increase output.

Q45. The optimum point for a profit-maximising firm to produce will be at the bottom of the AC curve.
True/False

Q46. A firm will always maximise profits by charging a price equal to both marginal cost and marginal revenue.
True/False

Q47. A firm will choose to shut down rather than continue to produce in the *short run* when, at any positive output level:

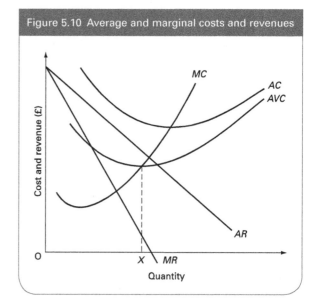

Figure 5.10 Average and marginal costs and revenues

*Q49. A firm faces the following total cost and total revenue schedules:

$$TC = 100 - 20Q + 3Q^2$$
$$TR = 60Q - 2Q^2$$

(a) What is the equation for average cost?.......................

(b) What is the equation for marginal cost?.....................

(c) What is the equation for average revenue?..................

(d) What is the equation for marginal revenue?

....

(e) At what output is profit maximised?...........................

(f) What is average profit at this output?..........................

(g) How much is total profit at this output? ....

(h) What is the equation for total profit? ....

(i) Using this equation, find the output at which profit is maximised (thereby confirming the answer given in (e) above).

....

 PROBLEMS, EXERCISES AND PROJECTS

Q50. Table 5.8 shows the short-run total cost curves of three alternative plants producing luxury cars. The three plants are of different sizes: one small, one medium and one large.

(a) Calculate the (short-run) average cost for each level of output given in the table for each of the three plants.

(b) Plot the (short-run) *AC* curve for each of the three plants (on the same diagram).

(c) From these three short-run *AC* curves sketch the long-run *AC* curve.

(d) Are there increasing, decreasing or constant returns to scale?

(e) Assuming that a firm could choose with what size plants to operate in the long run, which of the three size plants would it choose to produce an output of 10 cars per day?

(f) Assume that a firm is producing 10 cars per day with the optimum-sized plant, and now wishes to increase output to 30 cars per day in response to a temporary increase in demand. What will its average cost of production now be?

(g) Now assume that the rise in demand to 30 cars per day is perceived by the firm to be a permanent increase. After its long-run adjustment, what will its average cost be now?

(h) Now assume that demand increases to 45 cars per day in the long run. Would the firm alter its plant size? Would it alter its plant size if output increased to 50 cars per day? Explain.

Table 5.8 Costs of car production

Output (daily)	TC small plant (£000)	TC medium plant (£000)	TC large plant (£000)
0	35	70	90
5	90	120	200
10	140	170	300
15	180	195	345
20	220	210	360
25	300	225	375
30	420	255	405
35	595	315	455
40	880	400	540
45	1260	585	675
50	1900	950	900
55	2750	1430	1265
60	3900	2400	1800

Q51. Table 5.9 gives details of a firm's total costs and total revenue.

Table 5.9 Costs and revenue for firm X

Q	AR	(AR₁)	TR	(TR₁)	MR	(MR₁)	TC	AC	MC
0	30	–	0	–	...	–	300	–	...
10	...	–	280	–	...	...	350	...	...
20	...	...	520	...	...	...	380	...	...
30	...	...	720	...	...	...	420	...	...
40	...	...	880	...	...	...	480	...	...
50	...	...	1000	...	...	...	600	...	...
60	...	...	1080	...	...	...	780	...	...
70	...	...	1120	...	...	...	980	...	...
80	...	...	1120	...	...	...	1280	...	...
90	...	...	1080	...	...	...	1710	...	...
100	...	...	1000	...	...	...	2300	...	

(a) Fill in the columns for *AR*, *MR*, *AC* and *MC* – but ignore columns for AR_1, TR_1 and MR_1 until you get to (f) below. Remember that *MC* and *MR* are the extra cost and revenue of producing *one* more unit (not ten).

(b) At what output and price is profit maximised?

(c) How much is total profit at this output?

(d) Assume that total fixed cost rises by £200. What effect will this have on the profit-maximising price and output?

(e) What effect will it have on profit?

(f) Now assume that *TFC* returns to its original level and that demand increases by 20 units at each price. Fill in the columns for AR_1, TR_1, and MR_1. (Do not fill in the spaces with a dash.)

(g) What will be the new profit-maximising price and output? (Note: It may help if you draw the *AR*, *MR*, *AC* and *MC* curves on graph paper and then show the effects of shifting the *AR* and *MR* curves.)

The remaining parts of the question continue with the assumption that demand has increased by 20 units at each price.

(h) Now let us assume that the government imposes a *lump-sum* tax of £100 on producers (i.e. a total tax that does not vary with output). What will be the profit-maximising price and output now?

(i) Now assume instead that the government imposes a *specific* tax of £12 per unit. What will be the profit-maximising price and output now? (See if you can spot the answer from the table without entering new cost columns.)

Q52. Should your educational establishment take on more students? The answer given to this question by the administrators of many universities, colleges and schools since the early 1990s has been a resounding 'Yes', as they have avidly competed for students. At the same time the amount of resources they have available per student has declined: and yet many of the administrators have claimed that the quality of education that students have received has not declined and some claim that it has even increased. The arguments they use have partly to do with the marginal cost per student being lower than the average cost and the possibility of achieving economies of scale.

Many of the academic and administrative staff, on the other hand, claim that it is only their harder work that prevents a decline in standards and that a further reduction in moneys earned per student would lead to an inevitable erosion of the service they could provide for students.

Assess these arguments in the context of your own establishment, and in particular consider the following:

(a) What are the fixed and what are the variable costs associated with your particular course? Would the marginal cost be significantly different from the average cost? How will the answer differ in the short run and the long run?

(b) Are there any significant economies of scale associated with (i) courses with large numbers of students; (ii) large educational establishments?

(c) Should your establishment take on extra students at present?

(d) Should there be an expansion of some courses relative to others?

(e) If there were a further decline in the 'unit of resource' (i.e. the money earned per student), should your establishment take on more or fewer students?

(f) Should inefficient educational establishments close down?

Try interviewing teaching staff and administrative staff to help you answer these questions. Explain any differences in the replies they give.

DISCUSSION TOPICS AND ESSAYS

Q53. Imagine that you are a small business person employing five people, and are pleased to find that business is expanding. As a result you take on extra labour: a sixth worker this month, a seventh next month and an eighth the month after. The seventh worker discovers that when she is taken on, output increases more than when either the sixth or eighth worker was taken on. Not surprisingly, she claims that she is a more efficient worker than her colleagues. Do the facts necessarily support her case?

***Q54.** Use isoquant analysis to illustrate the effect on the factor proportions used by a firm of the granting of an employment subsidy (per worker) to the firm.

Q55. What are the likely effects on firms' costs of more people participating in higher education?

Q56. A firm observes that both its short-run and its long-run average cost curves are U-shaped. Explain why the reasons for this are quite different in the two cases.

Q57. Using relevant examples, explain why an increase in the minimum wage is likely to have a greater impact on the price of services than that of manufactured goods.

Q58. Would there ever be any point in a firm attempting to continue in production if it could not cover its long-run average (total) costs?

Q59. The price of personal computers has fallen significantly in recent years, while demand has been increasing. Use cost and revenue diagrams to illustrate these events.

Q60. Debate

It is better to have manufacturing concentrated in just a few large plants in each industry and in just a few parts of the country. That way production will take place at minimum costs.

ANSWERS

Q1. $(6 \times 10) + (3 \times 4) = 72$ units of output.

Q2. C. The actual length of time of the short run will vary from industry to industry depending on how long it takes to vary the amount used of all factors.

Q3. *when one or more factors are held constant, then, as the variable factor is increased, there will come a point when additional units of the variable factor will produce less extra output than previous units.*

Q4. **(a)** See Figure A5.1.

(b) Diminishing returns set in beyond point *a* (beyond 2 workers): i.e. the *TPP* curve rises less rapidly after point *a*.

Figure A5.1 The total physical product of labour for good X

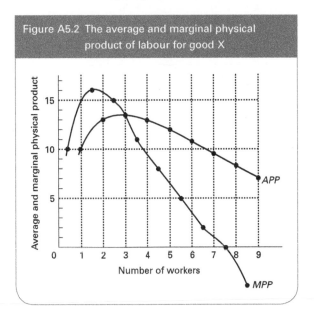

Figure A5.2 The average and marginal physical product of labour for good X

Q5. *the amount of extra output gained from the use of one more unit of the variable factor.*

Q6. **(a)** (iii) Thus if an extra two workers were taken on ($\Delta L = 2$) and between them they produced an extra 100 units of output per period of time ($\Delta TPP = 100$), then the extra output from *one* more unit of the variable factor (i.e. labour) would be 100/2 = 50.

(b) (i) Thus if 200 workers are employed ($L = 200$) and between them they produce a total output of 30 000 units per period of time ($TPP = 30\,000$), the average output per worker would be 30 000/200 = 150.

Q7. See table below.

(1) Number of workers	(2) TPP	(3) APP	(4) MPP
0	0	–	
			10
1	10	10	
			16
2	26	13	
			15
3	41	13.67	
			11
4	52	13	
			8
5	60	12	
			5
6	65	10.83	
			2
7	67	9.57	
			0
8	67	8.38	
			–4
9	63	7	

Q8. See Figure A5.2.

Q9. To the left of this point the *MPP* is above the *APP*. Thus extra workers are producing more than the average. They have the effect of pulling the average up. The *APP* curve must therefore be rising. To the right of this point the *MPP* is below the *APP*. Extra workers produce less than the average and thus pull the average down. The *APP* must be falling.

Q10. *True.* (Try adding the figures in the *MPP* column in Q7.)

Q11. B. *MPP* = $\Delta TPP/\Delta$input C = (1005 – 1000)/(41 – 40) = 5.

Q12. *explicit.*

Q13. E. This is what the firm is having to forgo by using the machine. The alternative forgone may be the production of some other good, or it may be the additional second-hand value from selling it at the beginning of the year rather than after producing X for a year.

Q14. *True.*

Q15. *the firm's output.*

Q16. (a) *variable*, (b) *fixed* (c) *fixed* (unless the firm deliberately chooses to spend more on advertising the more it produces), (d) *variable* (even though the bill may not be paid this month, the total cost of the electricity will nevertheless vary with the amount of chocolate produced), (e) *variable*, (f) *variable* (even though the basic wage is fixed per worker, the amount spent on basic wages will increase if extra workers are taken on to produce extra output, and will fall if workers quitting are not replaced because of falling output), (g) *variable*, (h) *fixed*, (i) *fixed* (the rise in interest rates is not the result of increased output: i.e. the cost is still fixed with respect to output).

Q17. **(a)** *AC.*

(b) *AVC.*

(c) *MC.*

(d) *MC.* (Given that fixed costs, by definition, do not vary with output, marginal costs will consist of variable costs.)

(e) *AFC.*

(f) *TC.*

(g) *TVC.*

(h) *TC.*

Q18. **(a)** See table below.

Output	TFC	TVC	TC	AFC	AVC	AC	MC
0	10	0	10	–	–	–	
							8
1	10	8	18	10.0	8.0	18.0	
							4
2	10	12	22	5.0	6.0	11.0	
							3
3	10	15	25	3.33	5.0	8.33	
							2
4	10	17	27	2.5	4.25	6.75	
							3
5	10	20	30	2.0	4.0	6.0	
							4
6	10	24	34	1.67	4.0	5.67	
							5
7	10	29	39	1.43	4.14	5.57	
							7
8	10	36	46	1.25	4.5	5.75	
							12
9	10	48	58	1.11	5.33	6.44	
							22
10	10	70	80	1.0	7.0	8.0	

(b) 4. After this level of output MC begins to rise.

(c) See Figure A5.3.

(d) See Figure A5.4.

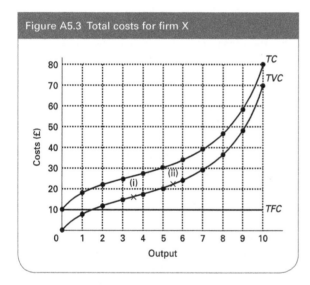

Figure A5.3 Total costs for firm X

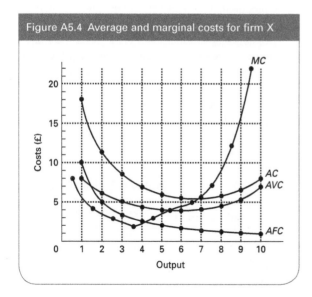

Figure A5.4 Average and marginal costs for firm X

Q19. C. If the marginal cost is below the average cost, then additional units will cost less to produce than the average and will thus pull the average down. You can see that this is the case by looking at Figure A5.4.

Q20. *Increasing returns to scale.* Notice the terminology here. The 'to scale' refers to the fact that *all* the factors have increased in the same proportion: that the whole scale of the operation has increased.

Q21. **(a)** *Situation (i)*: both factors are being varied.

(b) *No.* Output increases proportionately. A doubling of inputs leads to a doubling of output. The firm is experiencing *constant returns to scale*.

(c) *Yes.* The marginal physical product of input 1 diminishes. In other words, when input 2 is held constant, each additional unit of input 1 produces less and less additional output (10, 8, 6, 4).

Q22. B. Economies of scale are defined as lower *costs* per unit of output as the scale of production increases. These lower costs will probably be in part due to increasing returns to scale (answer D), but they may also be the result of lower input prices that large firms can negotiate.

Q23. (a) (ii); (b) (v); (c) (viii); (d) (i); (e) (iii); (f) (iv); (g) (vi); (h) (vii).

Q24. (i), (ii), (iv), (vii).

Q25. External economies of scale occur when a firm experiences lower costs as a result of the *industry* being large. Thus (a) and (d) are external economies of scale for firm A, whereas (b), (c) and (e) are internal economies of scale. Note that (e) is an external economy of scale for *other* firms, but not for firm A.

Q26. E. If the *MPP/P* ratio for any factor were greater than that for another, costs would be reduced by using more of the first factor relative to the second. But as this happened, diminishing marginal returns to the first factor would cause its *MPP* to fall (and the *MPP* of the second to rise) until their *MPP/P* ratios became equal. At that point there would be no further savings possible by substituting one factor for another.

Q27. The *MPP* of A is 3 (i.e. output rises from 1000 to 1003 when one more unit of A is used); the *MPP* of B is 10; the *MPP* of C is 5. If the price of A is £6, then $MPP_A/P_A = 3/6 = 1/2$. If the least-cost combination of factors to produce 1000 units is shown in the top row of Table 5.4 then $MPP_A/P_A = MPP_B/P_B = MPP_C/P_C = 1/2$. Thus:

$P_B = MPP_B/1/2 = 10 \div 1/2 = £20$

$P_C = MPP_C/1/2 = 5 \div 1/2 = £10$

*Q28. **(a)** TPP is $9 \times 36^{1/2} \times 27^{1/3} \times 64^{1/6} = 9 \times 6 \times 3 \times 2 = 324$

(b) $MPP_L = \frac{\partial(TPP)}{\partial L} = \beta AK^\alpha L^{\beta-1} E^\gamma$

i.e. $(9 \div 3) \times 36^{1/2} \times 27^{-2/3} \times 64^{1/6} = 3 \times 6 \times \frac{1}{9} \times 2 = 4$

(c) TPP also doubles to 648.

i.e. $9 \times 72^{1/2} \times 54^{1/3} \times 128^{1/6}$

$= 9 \times 8.485 \times 3.78 \times 2.245 = 648$

(Note that you will need a scientific calculator to work out the cube root of 54. To get the sixth root of 128, you should first take the square root and then the cube root of that.)

(d) If doubling the inputs leads to a doubling of *TPP*, then we have constant returns to scale. We know this anyway, as the sum of the powers on the three inputs is equal to 1.

(e) The MPP_L is now equal to: $3 \times 36^{1/2} \times 54^{-2/3} \times 64^{1/6} = 3 \times 6 \times {}^1/_{14.287} \times 2 = 2.52$.

This is lower than before, as we expect from the law of diminishing returns – as we add more labour input keeping capital and energy constant, we expect lower marginal returns.

Q29. (a) See the four curves in Figure A5.5.

(b) 40*A* and 20*B*. Production will be at point *s*, where the isocost of the slope $(-)P_B/P_A = (-)1$ is tangential to the 300 unit isoquant. This will involve using 40 units of factor A and 20 units of factor B.

(c) £12 000 (i.e. 40*A* @ £200 + 20*B* @ £200).

(d) 200 units of X. If the price of A rises to £300, the £12 000 isocost will pivot inwards on point *u*, so that its slope becomes 300/200. The maximum output that can now be produced is where the isocost touches the highest isoquant: namely at point *t* on the 200 unit isoquant.

(e) 45*A* and 10*B* (point *t*).

*Q30. D. For example, if we move from point *v* to point *w* in Figure A5.5, an extra 4 units of B can replace 8 units of A and output will stay at 400 units. Thus the *MPP* of B must be twice that of A (8/4). Thus the (average) slope of the curve (8/4) must equal MPP_B/MPP_A.

*Q31. B. For example, isocost 2 in Figure A5.5 has a slope of 60/40 = 3/2. But the price of B is £300 and the price of A is £200 and thus $P_B/P_A = 3/2$.

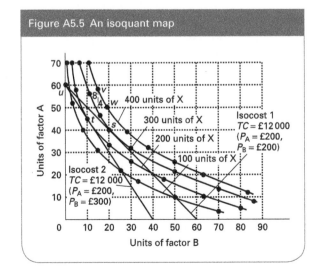

Figure A5.5 An isoquant map

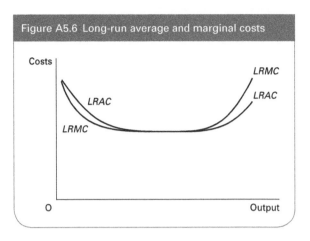

Figure A5.6 Long-run average and marginal costs

Q32. All except (e) are assumed. (In the case of (a) and (b), if factor prices or the state of technology changes, the long-run costs curves will shift. In the case of (e), firms may or may not experience economies of scale. Note that (d) and (g) are the same.)

Q33. See Figure A5.6.

Q34. *False.* This is the so-called 'envelope curve'. It *will* be tangential with the short-run average cost curves, but only with the bottom points where the *LRAC* is horizontal. (Try drawing it.)

Q35. *True.* Maximum economies of scale will be achieved at the bottom of the *LRAC* curve. The *LRMC* must equal *LRAC* at this point – when *LRAC* is neither rising nor falling. At this point the *LRAC* curve is also tangential with the *bottom* of the respective *SRAC* curve, through which point the *SRMC* curve passes.

Q36. (a) (i) 10*K* + 15*L* = £4800.
  (ii) 16*K* = 21*L* = £7200.
  (iii) 18*K* + 33*L* = £9600.
  (iv) 22*K* + 42*L* = £12 000.

(b) (i) £4800 ÷ 100 = £48.00.
  (ii) £7200 ÷ 200 = £36.00.
  (iii) £9600 ÷ 280 = £34.29.
  (iv) £12 000 ÷ 350 = £34.29.

(c) Economies of scale are experienced up until 280 units of output. Thereafter the firm experiences constant costs.

Q37. *horizontal.*

Q38. *demand curve.*

Q39. (a) (i) 5 × £2 = £10; (ii) 8 × £2 = £16.

(b) A straight line out from the origin.

(c) (i) When sales rise from 4 units to 5 units, total revenue rises from £8 to £10. Thus *MR* = 2. (ii) When sales rise from 7 units to 8 units, total revenue rises from £14 to £16. Thus *MR* = 2. *MR* is thus constant and equal to price. The reason is that price is constant. The marginal revenue from selling one more unit, therefore, is simply its price.

(d) A horizontal straight line and equal to the firm's demand 'curve'.

(e) See table below.

P(AR) (£)	Q (units)	TR (£)	MR (£)
20	0	0	
			18
18	1	18	
			14
16	2	32	
			10
14	3	42	
			6
12	4	48	
			2
10	5	50	
			–2
8	6	48	
			–6
6	7	42	

(f) –1. (Where $MR = 0$ and TR is at a maximum, demand is unit elastic.)

(g) Over £10. (A fall in price leads to a proportionately larger rise in quantity demanded and thus a rise in total revenue.)

(h) Under £10. (A fall in price leads to a proportionately smaller rise in quantity demanded and thus a fall in total revenue.)

Q40. $MR = \Delta TR/\Delta Q = ((15 \times 130) - (20 \times 100)) \div (130 - 100)$
$= -50/30 = -£1.67$.

Q41. D. The total revenue for 49 bottles would be $49 \times £10 = £490$. The total revenue for 50 bottles would be $50 \times £9 = £450$. Total revenue thus falls by £40 for the 50th bottle sold.

Q42. (a) 40 (where the two curves are furthest apart).

(b) £7 (the size of the gap, i.e. the distance ab).

(c) The curve should plot the size of the gap, crossing the horizontal axis at outputs of 21 and 56 and reaching a peak of £7 at an output of 40.

(d) £10 (the point where the TC curve crosses the vertical axis).

(e) 65 (the peak of the TR curve: where $MR = 0$ at point e).

(f) 21 and 56 (where $TP = 0$ at points c and d).

Q43. (a) See Figure A5.7.

(b) The firm is a price taker. It has to accept the price as given by the market, a price that is not affected by the amount the firm supplies. The AR curve is thus a horizontal straight line, and the AR also equals the MR, given that each *additional* unit sold will simply earn the market price (AR) as additional revenue (MR) for the firm.

(c) 560 units, where $MC = MR$ (point a).

(d) £2.40 (point b).

(e) £3.20 – £2.40 = £0.80 ($a - b$).

(f) See Figure A5.7.

(g) $560 \times £0.80 = £448.00$.

(h) £2.30 at an output of 500 (the minimum point on the AC curve).

Q44. C. With $MR > MC$, the firm should increase output. With price $> MR$ the firm must face a downward-sloping demand (AR) curve. In order to increase output, therefore, the firm must reduce price.

Q45. *False.* The optimum (profit-maximising) output for the firm will be where $MC = MR$. The profit-maximising firm will thus choose to produce at the bottom of the AC curve *only* if MR and MC happen to intersect at this point. (As we shall see in the next chapter, this *will* be the case in the long run under perfect competition.)

Q46. *False.* It should produce at an *output* where $MR = MC$, but unless it is a price taker whose MR thus equals price, it will sell at a price *above* MR and MC.

Q47. E. If AR is greater than AVC, it will be able to cover the costs arising directly from remaining in production, and will be able to make some contribution to paying its fixed costs which, in the short run, it will have to pay anyway whether it remains in production or not. If it cannot even cover its variable costs, it will lose less by closing down.

Q48. D. In the short run it is covering its average variable cost and therefore it should continue in operation; but it will minimise its losses (i.e. maximise the contribution towards paying off its fixed costs) by producing where $MR = MC$. It should therefore reduce output. In the long run, since it is not covering its average (total) cost (AC) it should close down.

*Q49. (a) $AC = TC/Q = 100/Q - 20 + 3Q$.

(b) $MC = dTC/dQ = -20 + 6Q$.

(c) $AR = TR/Q = 60 - 2Q$.

(d) $MR = dTR/dQ = 60 - 4Q$.

(e) Profit is maximised where $MR = MC$
i.e. where $60 - 4Q = -20 + 6Q$
where $10Q = 80$
where $Q = 8$.

(f) $A\Pi = AR - AC = (60 - (2 \times 8)) - ((100/8) - 20 + (3 \times 8)) = 60 - 16 - 12.5 + 20 - 24 = 27.5$.

(g) $T\Pi = A\Pi \times Q = 27.5 \times 8 = 220$.

(h) $T\Pi = TR - TC = (60Q - 2Q^2) - (100 - 20Q + 3Q^2) = -100 + 80Q - 5Q^2$.

(i) Profit is maximised where $dT\Pi/dQ = 0$
where $80 - 10Q = 0$
where $Q = 8$.

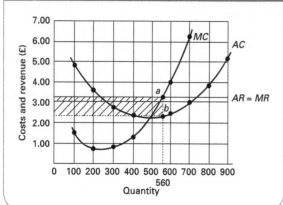

Figure A5.7 Average and marginal costs and revenue for the production of good X

Chapter 6

Profit Maximising under Perfect Competition and Monopoly

A REVIEW

The amount firms will supply and at what price will depend on the amount of competition they face – on the market structure. In this chapter we look at the two extreme types of market structure.

At one extreme is perfect competition. This is where there are so many firms competing that no one firm has any market power whatsoever. Firms are too small to influence market price or have any significant effect on market output. At the other extreme is monopoly, where there is only one firm in the industry, which thus faces no competition at all from inside the industry (although it may well face competition from firms in related industries).

6.1 Alternative market structures

(Pages 172–3) It is usual to divide markets into four categories.

(?) Q1. In ascending order of competitiveness, these are (fill in the missing two):

1. monopoly

2. ....

3. ....

4. perfect competition.

Q2. To which of the four categories do the following apply? (There can be more than one market category in each case.)

(a) Firms face a downward-sloping demand curve.

....

(b) New firms can freely enter the industry.

....

(c) Firms produce a homogeneous product.

....

(d) Firms are price takers.

....

(e) There is perfect knowledge of price and product quality on the part of consumers.

....

Q3. In which of the four categories would you place each of the following? (It is possible in some cases that part of the industry could be in one category and part in another: if so, name both.)

(a) A village post office ....

(b) Restaurants in a large town ....

(c) Banks ....

(d) Hi-fi manufacturers ....

(e) Growers of potatoes ....

(f) Water supply ....

(g) Local buses ....

(h) Local builders ....

(i) The market for foreign currency ....

We can get an indication of the degree of competition within an industry by observing *concentration ratios*.

📖 **Q4.** A five-firm concentration ratio shows:
A. the proportion of industries in the economy that have just five firms.
B. the share of industry profits earned by the five largest firms.
C. the sales of the five largest firms as a proportion of the total industry's sales.
D. the size of the largest firm relative to the total size of the five largest firms.
E. the output of good X produced by the five largest firms as a proportion of their total output of all types of good.

6.2 Perfect competition

(Pages 173–5) The theory of perfect competition is based on very strict assumptions.

◑ **Q5.** These include the following (delete the incorrect one in each case):
(a) Firms are *price makers/price takers* and thus face a horizontal/downward-sloping demand curve.
(b) Firms in the industry produce a *homogeneous/differentiated* product.
(c) Producers and consumers have *complete/limited* knowledge of the market.
(d) Entry of new firms is *free/restricted*.

(?) **Q6.** Before examining what price, output and profits will be, we must distinguish between the short run and the long run as they apply to perfect competition.
(a) The short run is defined as that period which

....

(b) The long run is defined as that period which

....

📖 **Q7.** Which one of the following is true for the marginal firm under perfect competition?
A. It can earn only normal profits in both the short run and long run.
B. It can earn supernormal profits in both the short and long run.
C. It can earn supernormal profits in the long run but only normal profits in the short run.
D. It can earn supernormal profits in the short run but only normal profits in the long run.
E. Whether it earns normal or supernormal profits in the short and long run will depend on the conditions in that particular industry.

(Pages 175–6) Short-run price and output under perfect competition can be found by applying the general rules for profit maximisation that we examined in the last chapter.

📖 **Q8.** Under perfect competition a firm will increase output if:
A. marginal cost is less than price.
B. price exceeds marginal revenue.
C. marginal revenue equals average revenue.
D. marginal cost exceeds marginal revenue.
E. marginal cost equals marginal revenue.

⊖ **Q9.** Figure 6.1 shows the cost and revenue curves faced by a perfectly competitive firm.
(a) What is the maximum profit the firm can earn?

....

(b) What is the maximum output the firm can produce and still earn normal profits?

....

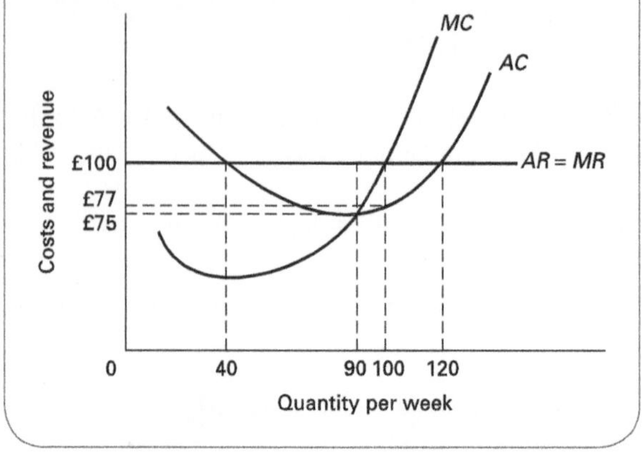

Figure 6.1 Costs and revenue for a perfectly competitive firm

(c) Assuming that there are no internal or external economies or diseconomies of scale, what will be the long-run price and output?

....

⊖ **Q10.** A perfectly competitive firm is currently earning £130 total profit per week from selling 100 units per week. Its total cost schedule is given in Table 6.1.
(a) Fill in its marginal cost schedule in Table 6.1. (Remember that marginal cost is the cost of producing *one* more unit.)
(b) What is the market price? (Clue: find its total revenue from selling 100 units.)
(c) Should the firm alter its level of production if it wishes to maximise its profit? If so, to what? If not, why not?

Table 6.1 Total and marginal costs

Output (Q)	0	20	40	60	80	100	120	140	160	180
TC (£)	100	190	270	340	420	520	640	780	940	1140
MC (£)		...	...	...	...	...	...	...	...	...

(Pages 176–7) The profit-maximising rule tells us how much a firm will produce at any given price. From this we can derive the firm's short-run supply curve.

🖳 **Q11.** A firm's supply curve under perfect competition in the short run will be equal to:
A. the upward-sloping portion of its *AC* curve.
B. the upward-sloping portion of its *MC* curve above its *AC* curve.
C. the upward-sloping portion of its *AVC* curve.
D. the upward-sloping portion of its *MC* curve.
E. the upward-sloping portion of its *MC* curve above its *AVC* curve.

The short-run *industry* supply curve under perfect competition can be derived from the supply curves of the member firms. All we do is simply add up the amounts supplied by each firm at each price to give the total industry supply at each price.

⊖ **Q12.** A perfectly competitive industry consists of 1000 firms. Because of their location, 400 of the firms (type A firms) have higher costs. The cost schedules of the two types of firm are given in Table 6.2.

Table 6.2 Costs for two types of firm in a perfectly competitive industry

Output: weekly (Q)	1	2	3	4	5	6	7	8	9
MC: Type A firm (£)	4	3	4	5	7	10	15	23	40
MC: Type B firm (£)	3	2	3	4	5	7	10	15	23

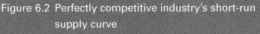

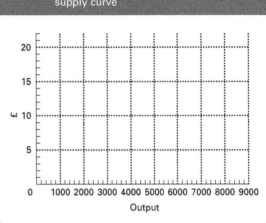

Figure 6.2 Perfectly competitive industry's short-run supply curve

Assume that minimum *AVC* = £4.50 for type A firms and £3.50 for type B firms.
(a) What will short-run industry supply be at each of the following prices?

(i) £15 .... per week

(ii) £7 .... per week

(iii) £4 .... per week

(iv) £3 .... per week

(b) Draw the industry's short-run supply curve on Figure 6.2.

(Pages 177–80) We now turn to the long-run equilibrium under perfect competition.

◖ **Q13.** If the firm is in long-run equilibrium, the market price is equal to its:
(a) long-run average costs. *True/False*
(b) long-run marginal costs. *True/False*
(c) short-run average costs. *True/False*
(d) short-run average variable costs. *True/False*
(e) short-run marginal costs. *True/False*
(f) average revenue. *True/False*
(g) marginal revenue. *True/False*

🖳 **Q14.** A perfectly competitive firm is producing 1000 tins of toffees per week, which it sells for £1.50 per tin. This output on 1000 tins per week incurs the following costs:

Total fixed cost	£1000
Total variable cost	£1200
Marginal cost	£1.00

What should the firm do in the short run?
A. Raise its price.
B. Decrease output.
C. Increase output.

D. Maintain output at its present level.

E. Cease production altogether.

Q15. Referring to the firm in the previous question, assuming that its long-run total cost is £1600, its long-run marginal cost is £1.50 and the price has remained unchanged, what should it do in the long run?

A. Raise its price.

B. Decrease output.

C. Increase output.

D. Maintain output at its present level.

E. Cease production altogether.

The long-run industry supply curve will reflect the changing number of firms as higher prices attract new firms into the industry and lower prices encourage firms to leave the industry.

Q16. If all firms (existing and potential entrants) face the same *LRAC* curves, then the long-run industry supply curve will:

A. necessarily be horizontal.

B. slope upwards if there are external economies of scale.

C. only be horizontal if there are constant external costs with respect to industry size.

D. slope downwards if there are external diseconomies of scale.

E. slope upwards if there are internal diseconomies of scale.

(?) Q17. Why would it be impossible for industries which experience substantial internal economies of scale to be perfectly competitive?

....

....

....

....

(Page 180) Perfect competition is argued to be more in the public interest than other types of market structure.

⊖ *Q18. Figure 6.3 shows a perfectly competitive industry in long-run equilibrium. Industry demand and supply (shown in part (a)) are given by D_0 and S_0, and the typical firm (shown in part (b)) produces q_L and just makes normal profit. Market price is at P_L. Suppose this product suddenly becomes more popular, so that demand increases for any given price. Sketch on the diagram the way in which the market adjusts to this change in the short run and in the long run, under the assumption that entry or exit of firms into or out of the market will not affect the long-run cost curves faced by individual firms.

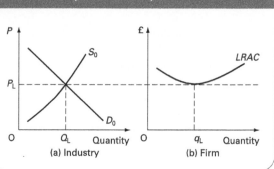

Figure 6.3 An increase in demand in a perfectly competitive industry

(a) Industry

(b) Firm

◗ Q19. Which of the following are claimed to be advantages of perfect competition?

(a) It leads to allocative efficiency. *Yes/No*

(b) It leads to production at minimum short-run *AC*. *Yes/No*

(c) It leads to production at minimum long-run *AC*. *Yes/No*

(d) It leads to the lowest very long-run *AC* curve. *Yes/No*

(e) It leads to high levels of investment. *Yes/No*

(f) It leads to intense non-price competition. *Yes/No*

(g) The competition acts as a spur to X efficiency. *Yes/No*

(h) It leads to firms combining their factors in the least-cost way. *Yes/No*

(i) It leads to consumer sovereignty. *Yes/No*

6.3 Monopoly

(Page 180) A monopoly may be defined as an industry that consists of one firm only. In practice it is difficult to determine whether firms are monopolies or not, because it depends on how narrowly 'the industry' is defined.

(?) Q20. Each of the following firms could be claimed to be *either* a monopoly *or* imperfectly competitive (monopolistic competition or oligopoly) depending on how we define the market (industry) in which it is operating. In each case identify two markets in which the firm operates: (1) where it is a monopoly; (2) where it competes in imperfect competition with other suppliers. Here is an example:

British Telecom (1) Supply of telephone lines to those customers not having access to a competitor (monopoly).

(2) Sale of telephones (imperfectly competitive).

The Post Office (1) ....

(2) ....

Your refectory (1) ....

(2) ....

Car spares manufacturer (1) ....

(2) ....

Local water company (1) ....

(2) ....

Local ice skating rink (1) ....

(2) ....

An ice cream van (1) ....

(2) ....

Q21. A firm would have a 'natural' monopoly if:
A. its average revenue curve were vertical.
B. it controlled the supply of a natural resource essential to the production of the good in question.
C. there were *total* barriers to the entry of new firms.
D. it had gained significant experience of producing the good in question.
E. its long-run average cost curve were downward sloping at the profit-maximising level of output.

(Pages 180–3) In order for a firm to maintain its monopoly position there must be barriers to the entry of new firms.

Q22. Which one of the following would not be a barrier to firms entering an industry?
A. An upward-sloping long-run average cost curve.
B. Patents on key processes.
C. Substantial economies of scale.
D. Large initial capital costs.
E. The threat of takeover by the existing firm(s).

(Pages 183–4) Given its market power, a monopolist will face a downward-sloping demand curve that **Q23.** *is elastic throughout its length/is inelastic throughout its length/must be elastic for some of its length but may be inelastic for part of it.* This downward-sloping demand curve will mean that the monopolist will charge a price **Q24.** *above/below/equal to* its marginal cost of production.

Q25. Because of its market power, a monopolist can choose how much to sell and what price to sell it at.
True/False

Q26. In Figure 6.4 which letter gives the profit-maximising price: A, B, C, D or E?

Q27. Table 6.3 shows the costs and revenues of a monopolist producer of specialist luxury rough terrain cars.

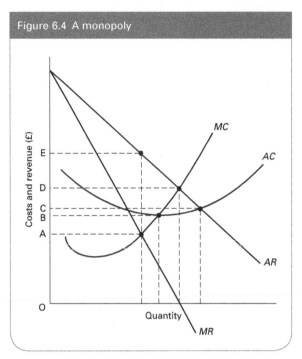
Figure 6.4 A monopoly

Table 6.3 A monopoly car producer

Quantity (cars per day)	AR (£000s)	TR (£000s)	MR (£000s)	AC (£000s)	TC (£000s)	MC (£000s)
1	100	...		110	...	
2	95	...	...	90	...	...
3	90	...	...	80	...	...
4	85	...	...	75	...	...
5	80	...	...	74	...	...
6	75	...	...	76	...	...
7	70	...	...	81	...	...

(a) Fill in the figures for *TR, MR, TC* and *MC.*
(b) At what daily output of cars will the monopolist maximise profits?

....

(c) How much profit will be made? ....

Q28. The profit-maximising monopolist will never produce where *MR* is negative. *True/False*

Q29. At the profit-maximising output, the monopolist's demand will be price inelastic. *True/False*

Q30. Referring to Table 6.3, what is the price elasticity of demand at the profit-maximising point? (Use the mid-point arc method over the price range either side of the profit-maximising price.)

....

(?) Q31. In the long run, a perfectly competitive firm will produce at the bottom of its *AC* curve. Why will a monopolist probably not do so?

....

....

(Pages 184–7) There are several reasons why monopoly may be against the public interest, but several reasons also why the consumer may gain.

Q32. Figure 6.5 shows a perfectly competitive industry for eggs. The egg producers then get together and set up a marketing agency which becomes the monopoly seller of eggs. The agency sets the profit-maximising price and gives each producer an output quota to ensure that total output is kept to the profit-maximising level. Assuming that industry costs are not affected, the consumer will:

A. gain because price falls from P_2 to P_1.
B. gain because price falls from P_3 to P_2.
C. gain because price falls from P_3 to P_1.
D. lose because price rises from P_1 to P_2.
E. lose because price rises from P_2 to P_3.

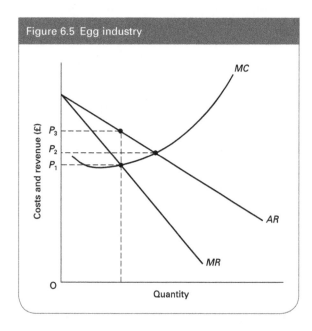

Figure 6.5 Egg industry

Q33. A monopoly will always produce a lower output and at a higher price than if the industry were under perfect competition. *True/False*

Referring again to Figure 6.5, assume now that the egg producers' marketing agency sets up a research laboratory into new efficient methods of egg production and as a result is able to shift the industry *MC* curve downwards. This could result in the profit-maximising industry price being lower than before the agency was set up.

Q34. On Figure 6.5 draw two new *MC* curves below the original curve. Draw them so that one of them results in a lower price than before the agency was set up and the other still results in a higher price.

*Q35. Figure 6.6 shows an industry that can either operate under perfect competition or as a multi-plant monopolist. For this industry, there is no cost advantage in being a monopoly, so costs are the same however the market operates. Long-run average and marginal costs are constant.

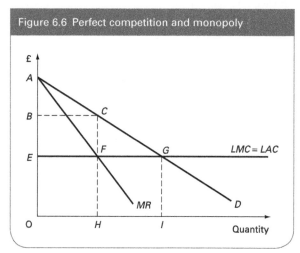

Figure 6.6 Perfect competition and monopoly

(a) Identify the market equilibrium price and quantity under perfect competition. (Hint: remember the nature of long-run industry supply under perfect competition.)

....

(b) Which area in Figure 6.6 represents consumer surplus under perfect competition?

....

(c) Identify the profit-maximising price and output under monopoly.

....

(d) Which area now represents consumer surplus?

....

(e) Comment on the difference in the consumer surplus in the two market situations.

....

⊗ ***Q36.** A monopolist's average revenue and average cost functions are given by:

$$AR = 1200 - 4Q$$
$$AC = 400/Q + 300 - 4Q + 3Q^2$$

where *AR* and *AC* are in £s.

(a) What is the equation for the monopolist's demand curve?

....

(b) What is the equation for total revenue?

....

(c) What is the equation for marginal revenue?

....

(d) What is the equation for total costs?

....

(e) How much are total fixed costs?

....

(f) What is the equation for marginal cost?

....

(g) At what output is profit maximised?

....

(h) What is the price at this output?

....

(i) What is average cost at this output?

....

(j) How much is average profit at this output?

....

(k) How much is total profit at this output?

....

6.4 *The theory of contestable markets*

(Pages 188–91) Even if a firm is currently a monopoly, it may be forced to behave as if it were in a competitive market if there is potential competition: i.e. if the market is contestable. The threat of this competition will be greater **Q37.** *the higher/the lower* the entry costs to the industry and **Q38.** *the higher/the lower* the exit costs from the industry.

(?) **Q39.** A perfectly contestable market is defined as one where

....

....

▤ **Q40.** Which of the following statements is *false*?

A. For a market to be contestable, the product must be produced with a labour-intensive technology.

B. Participants in a contestable market are continuously faced with competition or the threat of competition because entry is cheap.

C. In a contestable market with very few competititors, market forces will guarantee that the firms produce efficiently or be driven out of business.

D. In a contestable market, economic profits cannot persist in the long run.

◗ **Q41.** Classify each of the following markets as highly contestable, moderately contestable, slightly contestable or non-contestable. If it depends on the circumstances, explain in what way.

(a) satellite broadcasting   *highly/moderately/slightly/non*

(b) hospital cleaning services

                        highly/moderately/slightly/non

(c) banking on a university/college campus

                        highly/moderately/slightly/non

(d) piped gas supply   *highly/moderately/slightly/non*

(e) parcels delivery   *highly/moderately/slightly/non*

(f) siting for the Olympic games

                        highly/moderately/slightly/non

(g) bus service to the area where you live

                        highly/moderately/slightly/non

B   PROBLEMS, EXERCISES AND PROJECTS

Q42. A perfectly competitive industry consists of 100 equal-sized firms. The firms fall into three categories according to their cost structures. Their short-run marginal costs are shown in Table 6.4.

Table 6.4 Marginal costs for firms in a perfectly competitive industry

Output per day	40 firms (type A) MC per firm (£)	30 firms (type B) MC per firm (£)	30 firms (type C) MC per firm (£)
1	20	40	20
2	25	45	30
3	30	50	40
4	35	55	50
5	40	60	60
6	45	65	70
7	50	70	80
8	60	75	90
9	70	80	100
10	80	85	110
11	90	90	120

(a)   How much will a type A firm supply at a price of £40?
(b)   How much will total supply of type B firms be at a price of £80?
(c)   What will total industry supply be at a price of £50?
(d)   Assuming that marginal cost is above average variable cost for all firms at all levels of output, construct the total industry supply schedule at £10 intervals between £20 and £90 on the following table.

P	20	30	40	50	60	70	80	90
Q_S	...	...	...	...	...	...	...	...

(e)   What is the industry price elasticity of supply between £50 and £60?
(f)   Assume that the demand schedule facing the industry is given by

$$Q_D = 1100 - 5P$$

Construct the industry demand schedule at £10 intervals between £20 and £90 on the following table.

P	20	30	40	50	60	70	80	90
Q_D	...	...	...	...	...	...	...	...

(g)   What is the equilibrium industry price and output?
(h)   If a tax of £10 per unit is levied on type A firms and a subsidy of £10 is paid to type B firms, how much will each type A and each type B firm supply at a price of £50?

Q43. Look up double glazing, builders, solicitors and taxis in the *Yellow Pages* telephone directory. Approximately how many firms are there in each category? Do any of these industries come fairly close to being perfectly competitive? Look at the advertisements appearing with the telephone numbers.

In what ways are the firms attempting to make their position less like that of firms under perfect competition?

Q44. Figure 6.7 shows cost and revenue curves for a monopolist.
(a)   At what output will the firm maximise profits?
(b)   What price will it charge to maximise profits?
(c)   How much profit will it make?
(d)   Assume that a potential rival had a minimum average cost of £3.70. How much can the monopolist sell if it does not want to attract that firm into the industry?
(e)   How much profit will the monopolist now make?
(f)   What would have to be the position of the monopolist's revenue curves if its maximum profit output were to be at minimum average cost?
(g)   Is there any position of the revenue curves which would give a profit-maximising output at minimum average cost *and* a price equal to minimum average cost?
(h)   At what price and output would this industry produce if it were a perfectly competitive industry (but with the same cost curves and demand curve)?
(i)   Does this represent a long-run equilibrium position for the (perfectly competitive) industry?
(j)   In the long run would *individual* perfectly competitive firms produce more or less than they did in (h)?

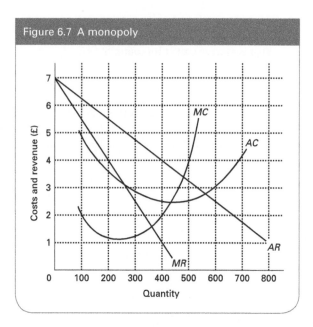

Figure 6.7 A monopoly

Q45. Look through the business sections of the 'quality' newspapers of two or three days and identify those companies that have substantial monopoly power.

What are the barriers to entry in their respective industries? Is there anything in the reports that suggests that these firms act either in or against the public interest? Can this behaviour be explained by their market power?

 C ## DISCUSSION TOPICS AND ESSAYS

Q46. What is the point of studying perfect competition if it does not exist, or only very rarely exists, in the real world?

Q47. Give some examples of markets where the suppliers are price takers. In each case consider whether they are operating under perfect competition.

Q48. Under perfect competition a firm's supply is entirely dependent on its cost of production. In what sense, then, is total industry output the result of the interaction of supply *and* demand?

Q49. Is it possible for a perfectly competitive industry to have falling long-run average costs? Explain.

Q50. Is perfect competition always in the consumer's best interest?

Q51. Using examples, discuss the proposition that whether a firm is regarded as a monopoly or not depends on how narrowly the industry is defined.

Q52. With reference to examples, explain why it is more difficult for firms to enter some markets than others.

Q53. Explain how network economies may make it difficult for other firms to compete with Microsoft's *Windows*.

Q54. 'A monopolist's demand will always be elastic at the profit-maximising output.' 'The greater a monopolist's power, the less elastic its demand curve.' 'The monopolist will try wherever possible to increase its monopoly power.' Reconcile these three statements.

Q55. Assume that an art gallery displaying a unique collection of paintings by old masters finds that all its costs (staffing, heating, lighting, rent, security, etc.) are fixed costs. What price should it charge if it wants to maximise profits?

Q56. How does the level of exit costs from an industry in which there is currently only one firm affect the level of prices the firm will charge?

Q57. You are operating an airline and currently have a monopoly on a route between two destinations that are growing in popularity. You are aware that a competing airline has under-used aircraft available, and is looking for potentially profitable new routes. What pricing strategy do you adopt?

Q58. Debate
Using relevant examples, argue the case for and against the following proposition. *A monopoly that makes supernormal profits is acting against the public interest.*

 D ## ANSWERS

Q1. Monopoly; oligopoly; monopolistic competition; perfect competition.

Q2. *(a)* All except perfect competition.
(b) Perfect competition and monopolistic competition.
(c) Perfect competition and certain oligopolies (e.g. sugar, regular unleaded petrol, cement).
(d) Perfect competition only.
(e) Perfect competition only.

Q3. *(a)* Monopoly for certain items and for certain people. Oligopoly or monopolistic competition for other items where alternative suppliers exist locally, and for people who are mobile.
(b) Monopolistic competition.
(c) Oligopoly.

(d) Oligopoly.
(e) Perfect competition (approximately), assuming no marketing agency.
(f) Monopoly. Although there are several water companies in the UK and in some other countries, there is usually only one company able to supply each customer.
(g) Monopoly if there is only one; oligopoly if there are more than one.
(h) Monopolistic competition.
(i) Perfect competition. (There are many foreign currency dealers; the product is homogeneous; dealers are virtually price takers according to demand and supply from their various customers.)

Q4. C. This measures the market share of the five largest firms in the industry. It is also common to measure the 3-firm or 4-firm concentration ratios.

Q5. *(a)* *price takers; horizontal.*

    (b) *homogeneous.*

    (c) *complete.*

    (d) *free.*

Q6. *(a)* *there is too little time for new firms to enter the industry.*

    (b) *is long enough for new firms to enter the industry.*

Q7. D. Given that in the short run there is not enough time for firms to enter the industry, supernormal profits could be earned by the firm. In the long run, however, supernormal profits would attract new firms to enter, thus driving down the market price until the marginal firm was just earning normal profits.

Q8. A. If marginal cost is less than price (= *MR*), the firm will make additional profits if it produces extra output. Note: price (*AR*) equals marginal revenue and thus B will never occur under perfect competition. C, on the other hand, will always occur, but thus gives no guidance as to whether a firm should expand or contract production. In the case of D, the firm should reduce output. In the case of E, this is the profit-maximising position and hence the firm should not change its output.

Q9. *(a)* £2300 per week. (Profits are maximised where *P* = *MC*, at an output of 100 units per week. Profit per unit equals £100 – £77 = £23. Total profit thus equals 100 × £23 = £2300.)

    (b) 120 units. (Above that *AC* > *P*.)

    (c) *P* = £75; *Q* = 90 (i.e. at the bottom of the *AC* curve: where just normal profits remain).

Q10. *(a)* *MC* = Δ*TC*/Δ*Q* (in this case Δ*Q* = 20).

Q	0	20	40	60	80	100	120	140	160	180
TC(£)	100	190	270	340	420	520	640	780	940	1140
MC(£)		4.50	4.00	3.50	4.00	5.00	6.00	7.00	8.00	10.00

    (b) *P* = £6.50. (100 units are costing £520 to produce and earning £130 profit. The total revenue from these 100 units must therefore be £520 + £130 = £650. Therefore price = *TR*/*Q* = £650/100 = £6.50.)

    (c) *Yes.* At the current output (100), *MR* = £6.50 and *MC* is between £5.00 and £6.00, i.e. *MR* > *MC*. Thus the firm should produce *more*. Profit will be maximised where *MC* = *MR* = £6.50. This will be at an output of approximately 120. At this output, total profit = *TR* – *TC* = (120 × £6.50) – 640 = £140.

Q11. E. The firm, by equating marginal cost and price, will always produce that output for each price that is given by its *MC* curve, but only so long as price, and hence *MC*, is above *AVC*. If price, and hence *MC*, were below *AVC*, the firm would shut down.

Q12. *(a)* (i) 7600 (i.e. 400 firms producing 7 units each plus 600 firms producing 8 units each).

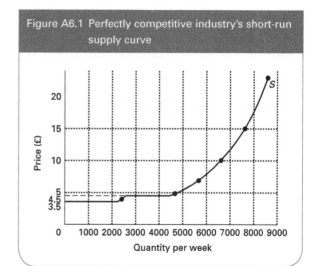

Figure A6.1 Perfectly competitive industry's short-run supply curve

    (ii) 5600 (i.e. 400 firms producing 5 units each plus 600 firms producing 6 units each).

    (iii) 2400 (i.e. 600 firms producing 4 units each; type A firms will not produce as price is below *AVC*).

    (iv) 0 (i.e. price is below *AVC* for all firms).

    (b) See Figure A6.1.

    Note the horizontal sections of the supply curve. These correspond to the prices where the two types of firm leave the industry in the short run because they cannot cover average variable costs.

Q13. All *true* except (d).

Q14. C. The firm is currently making a loss because its *AC* (= £2200/1000 = £2.20) is greater than the price (£1.50). It is nevertheless covering its *AVC* (= £1.20) and should therefore continue in production. It should increase output because *MR* (£1.50) is greater than *MC* (£1.00). This will help to reduce its loss.

Q15. E. The firm's *LRMC* is £1.50, which is also equal to the price. The firm is thus producing at the long-run profit-maximising/loss-minimising point. But with a long-run total cost of £1600, its *LRAC* is £1.60. It is thus making a loss and should therefore cease production.

Q16. C. If there are constant external costs, firms' *LRAC* curves will not shift as the size of the industry changes. If all firms have the same *LRAC* curves, then any increase in demand, and hence any rise in price above the bottom of firms' *LRAC*, will attract new firms. This will simply push price back down to the bottom of the *LRAC* curve. This means that in the long run supply will increase without any increase (or decrease) in price. (Note that E is wrong because higher prices attract *new* firms which can come in at the minimum point of the *LRAC* curve.)

Q17. Because the first firms to take advantage of large-scale production would drive the other firms out of the industry until there were too few firms left for

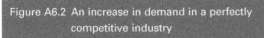

Figure A6.2 An increase in demand in a perfectly competitive industry

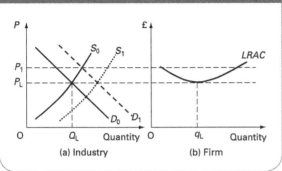

(a) Industry

(b) Firm

them to remain price takers. Markets are not big enough for a large number of large firms.

Q18. When demand increases, the market demand curve in Figure A6.2 shifts from D_0 to D_1, and the equilibrium price rises to P_1. In the short run, the higher price induces existing firms to supply more output, but as time goes by new firms will enter the market in quest of the supernormal profits being made. Thus the industry supply curve moves to the right from S_0 to S_1. Firms continue to enter until price has settled back at its original level of P_L. This occurs because of the assumption in the question that entry of new firms would not affect the long-run cost curves facing individual firms in the market.

Q19. (a), (c), (g), (h) and (i), *yes*.

(b), (d), (e) and (f), *no*. In the case of (b), firms can make supernormal profits or a loss in the short run. In the case of (d) and (e), firms may not be able to afford extensive research and development and investment. As a result their very long-run average costs may not be as low as if they were able to obtain long-run supernormal profits that could be ploughed back into the firm. In the case of (f), there is no non-price competition because, by definition, the firms produce homogeneous products.

Q20. The Post Office: (1) letter mail; (2) stationery.

Your refectory: (1) meals served on site; (2) food retailing.

Car spares manufacturer: (1) for particular makes of car where only one manufacturer produces them; (2) spare parts generally (i.e. general motor accessories) and spare parts for specific cars which are made by more than one manufacturer.

Water company: (1) water supply to a particular area; (2) water supply where the consumer has a choice of location (e.g. a firm setting up in business).

Ice skating rink: (1) ice skating in that area; (2) ice skating nationally; sports facilities.

Ice cream van: (1) ice cream supply at certain events or public places; (2) ice cream supply in the general area or when there is a shop or another van nearby.

Q21. E. If the long-run average cost curve is downward sloping, one firm supplying the whole market would be able to produce at a lower average cost than two firms sharing the market. The established firm would thus be able to undercut the price charged by any new entrant. (Although a downward-sloping *LRAC* curve would be a *sufficient* condition for a firm to have a natural monopoly, it is not a *necessary* condition. A firm could still have a natural monopoly if it was operating at the bottom, or even just beyond the bottom, of its *LRAC* curve, provided that two firms sharing the market would entail moving back up along the *LRAC* curve to a significantly higher level of long-run average cost.)

Q22. A. With an upward-sloping *LRAC* curve, two firms could produce at a lower *AC* than one. A new firm could thus 'steal' some of the monopoly's market by producing at a lower cost.

Q23. *must be elastic for some of its length but may be inelastic for part of it.* Although a monopolist is likely to face a less elastic demand at any given price than an imperfectly competitive firm, its demand curve *must* be elastic along part of its length. The reason is that profits are maximised where *MR* is to equal *MC*. Now *MC* will be positive and thus *MR* must also be positive. But where *MR* is positive, demand is elastic.

Q24. *above.* With a downward-sloping demand curve, price is above *MR*. Thus if *MR* = *MC*, price must also be above *MC*.

Q25. *False.* The monopolist can choose *either* price *or* quantity but not both. Given its demand curve, there is only one price corresponding to each level of sales and only one level of sales corresponding to each price.

Q26. E. The price given by the demand curve at the output where *MR* = *MC*.

Q27. *(a)* See table below.

Quantity (cars per day)	AR (£000s)	TR (£000s)	MR (£000s)	AC (£000s)	TC (£000s)	MC (£000s)
1	100	100		110	110	
2	95	190	90	90	180	70
3	90	270	80	80	240	60
4	85	340	70	75	300	60
5	80	400	60	74	370	70
6	75	450	50	76	456	86
7	70	490	40	81	567	111

(b) 4 cars per day (where *MC* = *MR*).

(c) £40 000 (i.e. *TR* − *TC*).

Q28. *True.* *MC* cannot be negative: it cannot cost less (in total) to produce more. Therefore if *MC* = *MR*, *MR* cannot be negative.

Q29. *False.* Demand is elastic over the output range where *MR* is positive: a rise in output causes a rise in total revenue (quantity rises proportionately more than price falls). Demand is inelastic over the output range where *MR* is negative: a rise in output causes a fall in total revenue (quantity rises proportionately less than price falls). But since *MC* cannot be negative and thus *MR* cannot be negative where it equals *MC*, demand must be elastic at the output where the monopolist maximises profit.

Q30. $P\epsilon_d = \Delta Q/\text{mid}Q + \Delta P/\text{mid}P = 2/4 \div -10/85 = -4.25$ (which is elastic).

Q31. Given the barriers to the entry of new firms, super-normal profits will not be eliminated by competition. Price will remain above *AC*. It will only be chance if *MR* and *MC* happen to intersect at the bottom of the *AC* curve. For example, Figure 6.4 (on page 67) could represent a long-run situation as well as a short-run one. Here *MR* and *MC* intersect to the left of the minimum point of the *AC* curve.

Q32. E. Before the agency was formed, the price was determined by the simple interaction of demand (given by the *AR* curve) and supply (given by the *MC* curve). Price was therefore P_2. Once the agency has been formed, it will sell that quantity where *MC* = *MR*, at a price of P_3.

Q33. *False*. If a monopolist operates with a significantly lower *MC* curve (e.g. because its size allows it to operate more efficiently), this could be sufficient to offset the fact that the monopolist's price will be above the *MC* whereas the perfectly competitive price will equal *MC*.

Q34. See Figure A6.3. Before the agency was set up, the price was P_0, where MC_0 crosses the demand curve. If the agency reduces costs to MC_1, price will fall to P_1. If it only reduces costs to MC_2, however, price will be P_2, which is still higher than the original level.

*Q35. (a) Under perfect competition, long-run equilibrium occurs where market demand equals market supply. This is at a price *E* and level of output *I*.

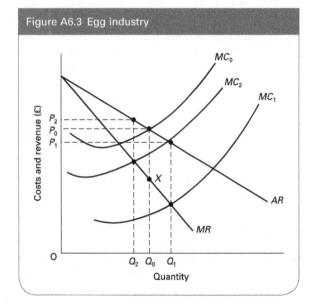

Figure A6.3 Egg industry

(b) Consumer surplus is the area *AEG*.
(c) A profit-maximising monopolist will choose output where *MC* = *MR*, at output level *H* and price *B*.
(d) Consumer surplus is now *ABC*.
(e) Consumer surplus is smaller under monopoly. This is for two reasons: first, the monopoly has appropriated the area *BCFE* as profits; second, the area *CFG* is lost – this represents the social cost of monopoly.

*Q36. (a) $300 - P/4$.
(b) $TR = 1200Q - 4Q^2$.
(c) $MR = 1200 - 8Q$.
(d) $TC = 400 + 300Q - 4Q^2 + 3Q^3$.
(e) $TFC = 400$.
(f) $MC = 300 - 8Q + 9Q^2$.
(g) $MR = MC$
  $\therefore 1200 - 8Q = 300 - 8Q + 9Q^2$
  $\therefore 9Q^2 = 900$
  $\therefore Q = 10$.
(h) $P = AR = 1200 - (4 \times 10) = \pounds1160$.
(i) $AC = 400/10 + 300 - (4 \times 10) + (3 \times 10^2) = \pounds600$.
(j) $A\Pi = \pounds1160 - \pounds600 = \pounds560$.
(k) $T\Pi = \pounds560 \times 10 = \pounds5600$.

Q37. *lower*.

Q38. *lower*. The lower the exit costs, the less risky it will be for new firms to enter the industry: the more easily they can move to some other industry if they fail in their challenge.

Q39. *entry and exit costs are zero*.

Q40. A.

Q41. (a) *slightly*.
(b) *highly* if the cleaning is put out to periodic tender.
  non if the hospital employs its own cleaners or if an outside firm has a permanent contract.
(c) *moderately* if the banks are invited to tender periodically for a site licence.
  non if a single bank is given a permanent site licence.
(d) *non* if the gas pipe grid is owned by a single company and if other companies are not permitted to use it or to establish a rival grid.
  slightly (in densely populated areas) if companies are permitted to construct a rival grid.
  moderately if rival companies are permitted to use the existing grid.
(e) *highly* unless prohibited by law or unless an existing service is heavily subsidised.
(f) *moderately* (at the bidding stage). The failure costs may be high if a city invests a lot on facilities – as several unsuccessful cities can testify (but, of course, the facilities can still be enjoyed by the inhabitants).
(g) as (e).

Chapter 7

Profit Maximising under Imperfect Competition

Imperfect competition is the general term we use to refer to all market structures lying between the two extremes of monopoly and perfect competition. We examine the two broad categories of imperfect competition: *monopolistic competition* and *oligopoly*. We also look at a common practice of firms under imperfect competition (and monopoly too): *price discrimination*.

In this chapter we continue with the assumption that firms want to maximise profits. In the next chapter we will drop this assumption and consider the effects of firms pursuing other goals.

7.1 Monopolistic competition

(Pages 194–6) Monopolistic competition is nearer the perfectly competitive end of the spectrum.

 Q1. From the list of points below, select those which distinguish a monopolistically competitive industry from a perfectly competitive industry.

(a) There are no barriers to the entry of new firms into the market. Yes/No

(b) Firms in the industry produce differentiated products. Yes/No

(c) The industry is characterised by a mass of sellers, each with a small market share. Yes/No

(d) A downward-sloping demand curve means the firm has some control over the product's price. Yes/No

(e) In the long run only normal profits will be earned. Yes/No

(f) Advertising plays a key role in bringing the product to the attention of the consumer. Yes/No

Q2. At which of the following outputs would a monopolistically competitive seller maximise profits?

A. Where marginal revenue equals average cost.
B. Where price equals marginal revenue.
C. Where marginal revenue equals marginal cost.
D. Where average cost is at a minimum.
E. Where price equals average cost.

Q3. Following a rapid growth in the demand for home-delivered fast foods, Pukka Pizza is now earning substantial supernormal profits on its dial-a-pizza business. As a result of this success, a number of other local restaurants and fast-food diners are diversifying into the home-delivery market.

(a) What will be the likely effect on the position and elasticity of Pukka Pizza's demand curve from this increased competition?

....

(b) How will this depend on the type of food that the new competitors are supplying?

....

(c) At what point will firms stop entering the market?

....

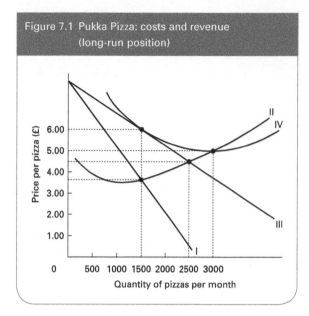

Figure 7.1 Pukka Pizza: costs and revenue (long-run position)

Q4. Figure 7.1 represents Pukka Pizza's long-run equilibrium position.

(a) Label the curves.

Curve I: ....

Curve II: ....

Curve III: ....

Curve IV: ....

(b) What is the long-run equilibrium price? (Tick)
£3.50 ... £4.50 ... £5.00 ... £6.00 ...

(c) What is the long-run equilibrium quantity? (Tick)
1500 ... 2500 ... 3000 ...

(Pages 196–7) Firms under imperfect competition are likely to engage in advertising and other forms of non-price competition. The aim of this is to **Q5.** *shift the demand curve to the right and make it less elastic/shift the demand curve to the right and make it more elastic.*

Q6. For a profit-maximising firm, the amount it should spend on advertising should be:
A. as little as possible because advertising costs money.
B. as much as possible because advertising increases demand.
C. that where the average cost of the advertising equals the average revenue earned from it.
D. that where the average revenue from the advertising minus the average cost of it is at a maximum.
E. that where the marginal revenue from the advertising equals the marginal cost of it.

Q7. Which of the following are reasons why a firm operating under monopolistic competition is inefficient in the long run?

(a) It is only making normal profits. *Yes/No*
(b) It is producing at a price above the minimum average cost. *Yes/No*
(c) It is producing an output below that at minimum average cost. *Yes/No*
(d) It faces a downward-sloping *AR* curve. *Yes/No*
(e) It is producing where marginal cost is below average cost. *Yes/No*
(f) It faces an upward-sloping *MC* curve. *Yes/No*
(g) It sets a price above marginal cost. *Yes/No*

Q8. The monopolistically competitive firm in the long run will produce less than a firm in perfect competition (given the same *LRAC* curve) but will charge a lower price due to the threat of rival firms. *True/False*

Q9. A monopolistically competitive industry in the long run will experience excess capacity. To which one of the following is this due?
A. Firms will only make normal profit.
B. Firms will enter the industry if supernormal profits can be made.
C. Firms will produce along the upward-sloping portion of their marginal cost curve.
D. The tangency point of the firm's *AR* and *LRAC* curves is to the left of the minimum *LRAC*.
E. The point where *AR* equals *LRAC* is vertically above the point where *MR* equals *LRMC*.

Q10. The monopolistically competitive firm in the long run will always produce at a lower price than a monopoly because it only makes normal profits. *True/False*

7.2 Oligopoly

(Pages 197–8) Oligopoly is the most frequently occurring of the four market structures. Oligopolies, however, differ significantly one from another. Nevertheless they do have various features in common.

Q11. Which of the following are characteristics of oligopoly?
(a) There are just a few firms that dominate the industry. *Yes/No*
(b) There are few if any barriers to the entry of new firms into the industry. *Yes/No*
(c) The firms face downward-sloping demand curves. *Yes/No*
(d) There is little point in advertising because there are so few firms. *Yes/No*
(e) Oligopolists tend to take into account the actions and reactions of other firms. *Yes/No*

Q12. Under oligopoly the price charged by one firm is likely to affect the price charged by other firms in the industry. *True/False*

Q13. Because oligopolists are interdependent this makes it easier to predict an oligopolist's price and output.
True/False

(Pages 198–200) Sometimes oligopolists openly compete with each other; sometimes they collude. When they collude they will attempt to act as if they were a monopoly and make monopoly profits which they then must decide how to divide between them.

When oligopolists formally collude this is known as a *cartel*. One way of dividing up the market is to assign each cartel member a quota.

Q14. Assume that a member of a cartel faces the situation shown in Figure 7.2. Assuming that P_c is the price set by the cartel and Q_1 is the firm's allotted quota, why would the firm have an incentive to cheat?

....

....

Figure 7.2 A cartel member

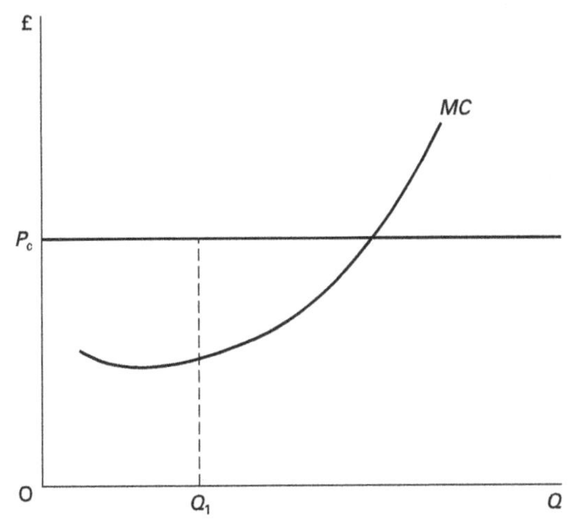

Q15. There will be little point in non-price competition by cartel members if a strict quota system is enforced.
True/False

In most countries there are laws that restrict either the formation of cartels or their activities. When formal or open collusion is against the law, firms may collude tacitly.

Q16. Which of the following are examples of tacit collusion?
(a) Price leadership by a *dominant* firm. *Yes/No*
(b) Agreements 'behind closed doors'. *Yes/No*
(c) Discounts to retailers. *Yes/No*
(d) Setting prices at a well-known benchmark. *Yes/No*
(e) Increased product differentiation within the industry.
Yes/No

(Pages 200–1) One form of tacit collusion is for firms to follow the prices set by the *price leader* in the industry.

Q17. Consider the model of price leadership shown in Figure 7.3.
(a) Which curve represents the market demand curve?
ABC/DBC/DE
(b) Which curve represents the leader's demand curve?
ABC/DBC/DE
(c) Which curve represents the leader's *MR* curve?
ABC/DBC/DE
(d) What price will be set by the price leader if it wishes to maximise profits? *$P_1/P_2/P_3/P_4$*
(e) Q_1 is the output produced by
the leader/all other firms together
(f) Mark total industry output on Figure 7.3.

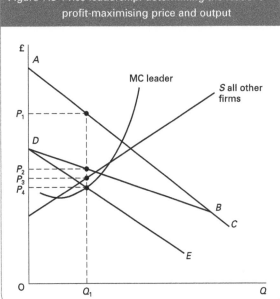

Figure 7.3 Price leadership: determining the leader's profit-maximising price and output

Q18. In the *barometric price leader* model, the price leader is always the largest firm in the industry.
True/False

(Pages 201–4) An alternative form of tacit collusion is for firms to follow simple 'rules of thumb'. An example is that of *average cost pricing*.

Q19. Average cost pricing involves setting price equal to average cost. *True/False*

(Page 204) Sometimes, however, there will be no collusion of any sort between oligopolists, or, if there has been, it may break down.

Q20. Under which of the following circumstances is collusion likely to break down?

(a) There is a reduction in barriers to international trade.

Yes/No

(b) The market becomes more stable. Yes/No

(c) One of the firms develops a new cost-saving technique.

Yes/No

(d) One of the firms becomes dominant in the industry.

Yes/No

(e) The number of firms in the industry decreases.

Yes/No

(Pages 204–9) Under non-collusive oligopoly, firms seeking to maximise profits must make assumptions about the behaviour of their rivals. In the Cournot model, firms make assumptions about their rivals' choice of **Q21.** *price/output,* whereas under the Bertrand model, firms make assumptions about their rivals' choice of **Q22.** *price/output.* Another famous theory of non-collusive oligopoly is that of the *kinked demand curve.* According to this theory, an oligopolistic firm perceives that its demand curve is steeper below the current price than above it: that is, it is kinked at the current price.

⊖ **Q23.** Figure 7.4 shows the market demand curve (D_M) for a product. MC_A is the marginal cost curve facing Firm A, which operates in the market.

(a) Identify the profit-maximising output and price level that would be set by Firm A if it saw itself as a monopolist. *(Hint: you will have to add the marginal revenue curve to the figure.)*

....

Suppose now that Firm A is aware of a competing firm (Firm B) in the market, and assume that Firm A expects Firm B to supply the quantity *OB* regardless of price.

(b) Add to the diagram Firm A's demand curve if Firm B does indeed supply the quantity *OB*.

(c) Identify Firm A's profit-maximising level of output and price.

....

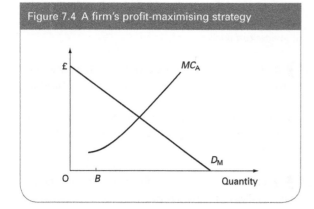

Figure 7.4 A firm's profit-maximising strategy

(d) How does this price level compare with the monopoly price?

....

(e) How does this price level compare with marginal cost?

....

(f) Is this an example of a Cournot or a Bertrand strategy? Explain your answer.

....

⊖ **Q24.** Figure 7.5 shows the reaction curves of two firms in a Cournot duopoly. If in a period, Firm A produces Q_{A1} and Firm B produces Q_{B1}, show on the diagram how the market converges on an equilibrium in the subsequent periods.

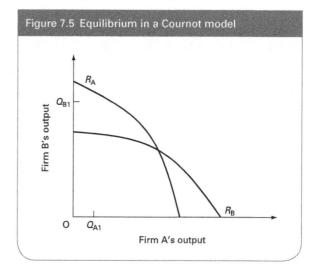

Figure 7.5 Equilibrium in a Cournot model

▤ **Q25.** Which *one* of the following statements is not applicable to the Bertrand model?

A. Firms choose price in response to prices set by rivals.

B. Firms make only a small amount of supernormal profit when the market is in equilibrium.

C. In practice, firms have an incentive to collude.

D. Firms are likely to engage in price-cutting behaviour.

E. Nash equilibrium (in the absence of collusion) is where price is equal to average cost.

▤ **Q26.** In the kinked demand curve model, the kink is due to the firm's belief that its competitors:

A. will set a price at the kink of the demand curve.

B. will match any price increase it makes, but will not match a price reduction.

C. will not match a price increase but will match any price reduction.

D. will match all price increases and reductions.

E. will match neither price increases nor reductions.

The kinked demand curve theory suggests that a firm is likely to keep its price unchanged unless there are substantial shifts in revenue or cost curves.

Q27. Figure 7.6 shows a kinked demand curve. Which of the following represents the *MR* curve?

A. fghi
B. jgkl
C. jghi
D. fgkl
E. jgk,hi

(Pages 207–8) It is not possible to draw firm conclusions as to whether oligopolists act in the public interest given that there are many factors that influence their behaviour and given that circumstances differ from one oligopoly to another.

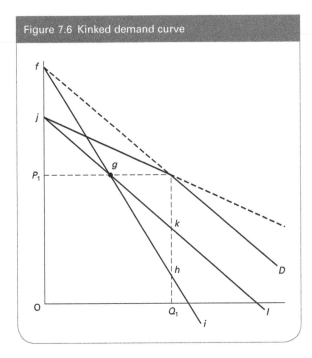

Figure 7.6 Kinked demand curve

Q28. Which of the following aspects of oligopoly can be seen to be in the public interest?

(a) Prices are set collusively.	*Yes/No/Possibly*
(b) Suppliers have countervailing power.	*Yes/No/Possibly*
(c) Customers have countervailing power.	*Yes/No/Possibly*
(d) There is non-price competition in the industry.	*Yes/No/Possibly*
(e) There is substantial advertising.	*Yes/No/Possibly*
(f) The market is contestable.	*Yes/No/Possibly*
(g) The firms' products are highly differentiated from each other.	*Yes/No/Possibly*
(h) There are substantial barriers to entry.	*Yes/No/Possibly*

(Page 208) An oligopsony is a market in which there are **Q29.** *a few/many* **Q30.** *buyers/sellers.*

7.3 Game theory

(Pages 209–10) Rival firms in an oligopoly can be likened to players in a game. One firm's choice of strategy will depend on how it thinks rivals will react and on how willing it is to take risks. Economists have developed game theory to look at this strategic approach in more depth.

The simplest form of game is a single-move game, sometimes known as a **Q31.** *normal-form/extensive-form* game. Such games involve just one move by each firm involved.

Q32. A dominant strategy game is one in which
A. firms collude in order to choose the best strategy.
B. the dominant firm in the market sets the price, and all other firms follow.
C. different assumptions about rival firms' behaviour lead to the adoption of the same strategy.
D. one firm is in a position of market dominance, and dictates market conditions.
E. different assumptions about rival firms' behaviour lead to the adoption of different strategies.

(Pages 210–12) The behaviour of firms under non-collusive oligopoly depends not only on how they think their rivals will react, but also on their attitudes towards taking a risk. Two possible strategies are *maximax* and *maximin*.

Q33. Which *one* of the following is the *maximax* strategy?
A. Choosing the policy whose best outcome is better than the worst outcomes of all alternative policies.
B. Choosing the policy whose best outcome is better than the best outcome of any alternative policy.
C. Choosing the policy whose worst outcome is better than the best outcome of any alternative policy.
D. Choosing the policy whose worst outcome is better than the worst outcomes of all alternative policies.
E. Choosing the policy whose worst outcome is worse than the best outcome of any alternative policy.

Q34. Which *one* of the strategies in Q28 is the *maximin* strategy?

A. B. C. D. E.

Table 7.1 shows the annual profits of two paint manufacturers. At present they both charge £5.00 per litre for gloss paint. Their annual profits are shown in box A. The other boxes show the effects on their profits of one or the other firm or both firms reducing their price per litre to £4.50.

Q35. Which of the two prices should Durashine charge if it is pursuing
(a) a maximax strategy?   £5.00/£4.50
(b) a maximin strategy?   £5.00/£4.50

Table 7.1

		Durashine's price	
		£5.00	£4.50
Supasheen's price	£5.00	A £6m each	B £2m for Supasheen £8m for Durashine
	£4.50	C £9m for Supasheen £3m for Durashine	D £4m each

Q36. Which of the two prices should Supasheen charge if it is pursuing

(a) a maximax strategy? £5.00/£4.50

(b) a maximin strategy? £5.00/£4.50

Q37. Table 7.2 shows the profits that firm A anticipates from three alternative strategies that it could adopt, depending on six possible responses from rival firms.

(a) Identify the maximin strategy for firm A.

(b) Identify the maximax strategy for firm A.

(c) Identify the best compromise strategy for firm A.

Table 7.2 Profit possibilities for firm A (£m)

		Other firms' responses					
		a	b	c	d	e	f
Strategies for firm A	1	120	20	220	60	–40	160
	2	100	60	80	50	40	120
	3	30	50	200	40	60	100

(Pages 212–14) In many situations, firms will find that when they react to what their rivals do, their rivals will react in turn, so the game moves back and forth from one player to the other. Firms still have to think strategically, considering the likely responses of rivals to their own actions. Multiple-move games are known as repeated games or **Q38.** *normal-form/extensive-form* games, such as **Q39.** *fool the rival/tit-for-tat*, in which a firm will only make an aggressive move if the rival does so first.

Q40. Firm X, a department store, announces that it will 'never be undersold' – in other words, it will match the price charged by any competitor in the neighbouring area. If other firms nearby find the promise to be credible, then they will

A. charge a price that is just below that of firm X.

B. charge the same price as firm X.

C. charge a price that is just a little higher than firm X.

D. ignore the promise made by firm X.

E. charge a price that is substantially below firm X.

Q41. Two airlines, Econjet and Whoosh, are choosing whether to buy Boeing or Airbus aircraft for their respective fleets. The profits that each airline will make depend upon the decisions of both – if they both buy the same type of aircraft, then they will fare less well. This is shown in the form of a decision tree in Figure 7.7, which assumes that Econjet chooses first (at point A).

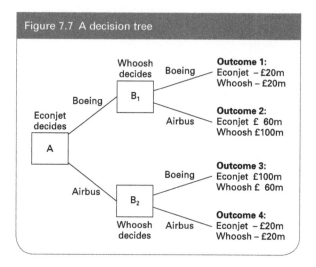

Figure 7.7 A decision tree

(a) What would be the best possible outcome for Econjet?

(b) What would be the best possible outcome for Whoosh?

(c) If Econjet has a first-mover advantage, what will it choose?

(d) So what will Whoosh decide?

7.4 Price discrimination

(Pages 214–19) A firm may practise price discrimination. This is where it sells the same product (costing the same to produce) at different prices in different markets or to different customers.

In order for a firm to practise price discrimination it must be **Q42.** *a price setter/a price taker*. It must be able to distinguish between markets such that the good cannot be resold from the **Q43.** *low-/high*-priced market to the **Q44.** *low-/high*-priced market. In each market, price elasticity of demand will differ. In the low-priced market, demand will be **Q45.** *more elastic/less elastic* than in the high-priced market.

Q46. There are three types of price discrimination:

(i) First-degree price discrimination.

(ii) Second-degree price discrimination.

(iii) Third-degree price discrimination.

Match each of the three types to the following definitions:

(a) When a firm charges a consumer so much for the first so many units purchased, a different price for the next so many units purchased and so on.

(b) When a firm divides consumers into different groups and charges a different price to consumers in different groups, but the same price to all the consumers within a group.

....

(c) When a firm charges each consumer for each unit the maximum price which that consumer is willing to pay for that unit.

....

 Q47. In Figure 7.8 if the firm is able to earn the revenue shown by the shaded area, which of the following must it be practising?

A. First-degree price discrimination.

B. Second-degree price discrimination.

C. Third-degree price discrimination.

D. No price discrimination at all.

E. It is impossible to say without knowing details about its costs of production.

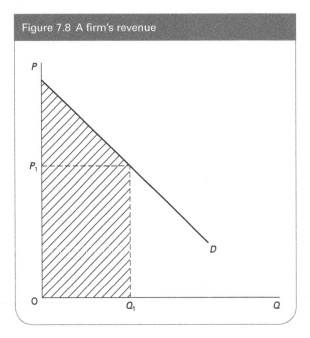

Figure 7.8 A firm's revenue

 Q48. Which of the following are advantages to the firm from practising price discrimination?

(a) Higher total revenue.   *Yes/No/Possibly*

(b) Lower costs.   *Yes/No/Possibly*

(c) Less advertising.   *Yes/No/Possibly*

(d) Helps to drive competitors out of business.

                                         Yes/No/Possibly

(e) Increases sales.   *Yes/No/Possibly*

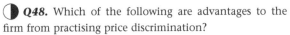

B PROBLEMS, EXERCISES AND PROJECTS

Q49. In recent years it has become fashionable for governments around the world to break up monopolies (sometimes nationalised and sometimes private but protected by licences or other regulations). The argument has been that the introduction of competition will stimulate firms to find ways of reducing costs and of providing a better service or product.

Take the case of buses and coaches. Many routes that were previously guaranteed to a single operator have now been opened up to competition. The immediate advantage is that on the routes used by a lot of passengers, the competition has often driven down the prices.

(a) Demonstrate this diagrammatically for an individual coach operator now finding itself under monopolistic competition.

On the other hand, on many routes facing cut-throat competition, coaches are running with empty seats.

(b) Does the theory of monopolistic competition predict this?

Also there is the danger that companies may cut corners (e.g. in terms of safety) in order to keep their costs as low as possible.

Then there is the problem that the less-used routes may no longer be operated at all. A bus or coach company with a monopoly may be prepared to operate such routes even though it makes a loss on them. It 'cross-subsidises' them with the monopoly profits it gains on the popular routes. When the monopoly is broken up, however, the competitive firms may not be willing or able to carry on operating these routes. Thus country bus services may close down, as may also services early in the morning or late at night on the otherwise well-used routes.

(c) Is it desirable that a monopoly bus company *should* cross-subsidise loss-making routes?

(d) Would a profit-maximising monopoly bus company *choose* to cross-subsidise such routes? How may a local authority ensure that the company does so?

(e) How could a local authority ensure that loss-making routes continued to operate after the industry had become monopolistically competitive?

(f) Use the arguments contained in this case study to compare the relative benefits and costs to the consumer of monopoly and monopolistic competition.

Q50. Find out the prices of a range of foodstuffs and household items sold in two or three different supermarkets and two or three different small foodstores. Which items are sold at similar prices in all the different shops and which are sold at significantly different prices? Account for these similarities or differences.

Q51. Durashine paint company is considering what strategy it should adopt in order to maximise its profits. It is currently considering four options. The first is to introduce a 10 per cent price cut. The second is to introduce a new brand of high-gloss durable emulsion paint. The third is to launch a new marketing campaign. The fourth is to introduce no change other than increasing its prices in line with inflation.

It estimates how much profit each strategy (1–4) will bring depending on how its rivals react. It considers the effects of six possible reactions (a–f).

Other firms' responses		a	b	c	d	e	f
Strategies	1	−25	50	−20	30	40	60
for	2	−20	20	−15	0	15	80
Durashine	3	0	15	30	0	20	30
	4	20	35	−10	40	30	70

(£000s)

(a) Which of the four policies should it adopt if it is pursuing:
   (i) A maximax strategy?
   (ii) A maximin strategy?
(b) Which of the four policies might be the best compromise?

Q52. A firm operating under conditions of oligopoly is currently selling 4 units per day at a price of £30. By conducting extensive market research its chief economist estimates that, if it raises its price, its rivals will not follow suit and that as a result it will face an average revenue curve given by

$P = 40 - 5Q/2$ (where $P = AR$)

On the other hand, if it reduces its price, its rivals will be forced to reduce theirs too. Under these circumstances its average revenue curve will be given by

$P = 50 - 5Q$ (where $P = AR$)

(a) What will be the equation for the firm's *demand* curve if the firm raises its price?

(b) What will be the equation for the firm's demand curve if the firm reduces its price?
(c) How much will be demanded at the following prices?

£40 ....

£35 ....

£30 ....

£20 ....

£10 ....

(d) Plot the two demand curves on Figure 7.9, marking in bold pen the portion of each that is relevant to the firm.
(e) Plot two marginal revenue curves corresponding to each of the demand curves. (Remember that the *MR* curve lies mid-way between the *AR* curve and the vertical axis). Mark in bold pen the portion of each *MR* curve that is relevant to the firm.
(f) Over what range of values can marginal cost vary without affecting the profit-maximising price of £30?

....

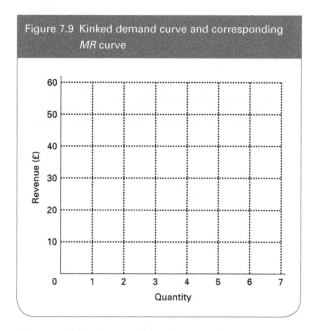

Figure 7.9 Kinked demand curve and corresponding *MR* curve

Q53. Think of some items that are available at different prices depending on *who* is buying them. Analyse the characteristics of these products, and the extent to which these characteristics enable price discrimination to take place.

DISCUSSION TOPICS AND ESSAYS

Q54. Why does monopolistic competition lead to a less than optimal allocation of resources? Does this inevitably mean that the consumer benefits more from perfect competition than monopolistic competition?

Q55. In what ways might the relative ease of firms to enter or exit a market affect the pricing, marketing strategy and productivity of the existing firm(s) in the market?

Q56. How would a firm set about determining the optimum type and amount of advertising? Why is the optimum amount of advertising difficult for a firm to determine?

Q57. Imagine that a group of wall tile manufacturers decide to form a cartel. What factors will determine whether the cartel is likely to be successful in raising prices?

Q58. Assume that an international airline cartel has been operating for a number of years. Imagine various circumstances that could lead to the breakdown of this cartel. What could the members of the cartel do to prevent its breakdown? Under what circumstances is the cartel likely to re-form in the future?

Q59. What are the main strengths and weaknesses of game theory as (a) a theory of oligopoly behaviour and

(b) an aid to a real-world oligopolist in deciding its price and output?

Q60. Using relevant examples, show how the kinked demand curve can be used to demonstrate price stability under oligopoly. According to the kinked demand curve model, what would cause the price to change? Use a diagram to illustrate this.

Q61. Describe what is meant by the *prisoners' dilemma* game. How will the outcome be affected by (a) the number of participants in the game and (b) the degree of similarity between the participants?

Q62. In what ways may the consumer (a) gain and (b) lose from the behaviour of oligopolists?

Q63. Discuss the extent to which there is scope for pharmaceutical companies to use price discrimination in the market for anti-retroviral drugs (used in the treatment of HIV/AIDS), charging lower prices in low-income countries than in high-income countries.

Q64. Debate
Advertising confers no benefits on society. It merely increases costs, eliminates competition and as a consequence pushes up prices.

ANSWERS

Q1. Yes: (b), (d) and (f). The rest ((a), (c) and (e)) apply to both perfect competition *and* monopolistic competition.

Q2. C. This is the universal law for profit maximisation no matter what the type of market structure.

Q3. *(a)* The demand curve will shift to the left as the market will now be divided between a larger number of firms. The curve will probably also become more elastic as there will be a larger number of suppliers to choose from, and hence the demand for Pukka Pizzas will be more price sensitive.

   (b) The more similar the product and the service provided by the competitors, the more elastic will be the demand.

   (c) Firms will stop entering the market when all supernormal profits have been eroded.

Q4. *(a)* Curve I: *marginal revenue (MR)*. Curve II: *marginal cost (MC)*. Curve III: *average revenue (AR)*. Curve IV: *average cost (AC)*.

   (b) £6.00. The price where $MC = MR$ and where $AC = AR$.

   (c) 1500. The quantity where $MC = MR$ and where $AC = AR$.

Q5. *Shift the demand curve to the right and make it less elastic.*

Q6. E.

Q7. Yes: (b), (c), (d), (e) and (g). The long-run equilibrium is where $AR = AC$: i.e. where the AR curve is tangential to the AC curve. But since the AR curve is downward sloping (d), this point of tangency must be to the left of the minimum point of the AC curve (c), at a point where AC is falling and where therefore MC is below AC (e). Thus costs are not as low as they could be and therefore the price is higher (b) and output is lower than it would be (c) if production was at minimum AC. With price set above marginal cost (g), the conditions for allocative efficiency are not met.

Q8. *False.* The monopolistically competitive firm will produce less than the perfectly competitive firm if they both face the same *LRAC* curve, *but* it will charge a *higher* price because it is not producing at the bottom of the *LRAC* curve.

Q9. D. Normal profits will be made where the *AR* curve is tangential to the *LRAC* curve. But because the *AR* curve is downward sloping (unlike under perfect competition), its tangency point with the *LRAC* curve must be to the left of the minimum *LRAC* curve. In other words the firm is producing at less than minimum average cost. It is in this sense that we say the firm and industry experience excess capacity: if industry output were to be expanded, production would take place at lower cost.

Q10. *False.* The monopoly may achieve economies of scale, giving it a lower *LRAC* curve. Also the monopoly may produce further down its *LRAC* curve, depending on where *LRMC = LRMR*.

Q11. Yes: (a), (c) and (e). No: (b) and (d). One of the features that allows oligopolists to maintain their position of power in the market is their ability to restrict the entry of new firms. Advertising is one of the major ways in which oligopolists compete with their rivals in their attempt to gain a bigger market share and bigger profits.

Q12. *True.* As one firm changes its price this will affect the demand for its rivals' products and hence their prices.

Q13. *False.* It is very difficult to predict price and output without knowing what degree of competition or collusion there is between the rival firms.

Q14. By producing more than Q_1, it will earn more profit provided price remains at P_c. At P_c it will maximise its profits where $MR (= P_c)$ equals *MC*.

Q15. *True.* The firm *could* sell more at existing prices if it produced above its quota. There is thus little point in advertising or other types of non-price competition.

Q16. Yes: (a), (b) and (d).

Q17. *(a)* *ABC*;
(b) *DBC*;
(c) *DE*.
(d) P_2: i.e. the price given by the leader's demand curve at the output (Q_1) where the leader's *MC = MR*.
(e) Q_1 is the output produced by the leader.
(f) Total industry output is found by reading across from P_2 to the market demand curve.

Q18. *False.* The barometric firm is simply the one whose prices the other firms are prepared to follow: the one whose price setting is taken as a barometer of market conditions.

Q19. *False.* Price is equal to average cost *plus* a mark-up for profit.

Q20. Yes: (a) and (c). (a) is likely to increase competition from imports. (c) is likely to encourage the firm with

reduced costs to undercut its rivals' prices in order to gain a bigger market share.

Q21. *Output.*

Q22. *Price.*

Q23. *(a)* In Figure A7.1, MR_M is the marginal revenue associated with the market demand curve (D_M). As a monopolist, the firm would maximise profits by choosing output at the point where $MR = MC$, which is at output level Q_0, with the price then set at P_0.
(b) If Firm B supplies *OB*, then Firm A will perceive its demand curve to have shifted left by the distance *OB* – i.e. at D_A.
(c) Given this demand curve and the associated marginal revenue curve (MR_A), the firm will now produce Q_1 output, and set a price at P_1.
(d) The price is now set lower than it had been under monopoly.
(e) However, the price is set above marginal cost, so is higher than would prevail under perfect competition.
(f) This is an example of a Cournot strategy, as Firm A is making assumptions about Firm B's output behaviour.

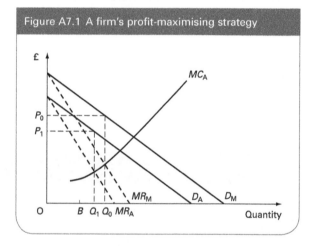

Figure A7.1 A firm's profit-maximising strategy

Q24. The path to equilibrium is shown in Figure A7.2. Starting from point 0, in each period, each firm moves to its reaction curve, so the points 1, 2, 3 . . . show the output path that will be followed. Equilibrium is eventually reached with Firm A producing Q_A^* and Firm B producing Q_B^*. Having reached this point, each firm finds itself on its reaction curve, and each thus sees that it has taken the best strategy given the other firm's decision – it is a *Nash equilibrium.*

Q25. B. In the Bertrand model, each firm sees that it can gain market share by setting price just below that of its rival(s). Price is thus driven down to average cost, and no firm makes supernormal profits.

Q26. C. Competitors will be quite happy to see the firm raise its price and lose market share. They will feel

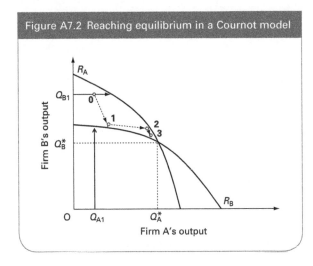

Figure A7.2 Reaching equilibrium in a Cournot model

obliged to match price reductions, however, for fear of losing market share themselves.

Q27. E. The *MR* curve corresponds to the shallower *AR* curve at levels of output lower than that at the kink and to the steeper *AR* curve at levels of output higher than that at the kink.

Q28. (a) *No*; (b) *Yes*; (c) *Yes*; (d) *Possibly*; (e) *No*; (f) *Yes*; (g) *Possibly*; (h) *No*.

Q29. *few.*

Q30. *sellers.*

Q31. *normal-form.*

Q32. C.

Q33. B.

Q34. D.

Q35. *(a)* Cut price to £4.50.
  (b) Cut price to £4.50.

Q36. *(a)* Cut price to £4.50.
  (b) Cut price to £4.50.

Q37. *(a)* The least bad outcome arises for strategy 2, where firm A would make £40m profit. For strategy 1, the worst thing that could possibly happen is a loss of £40m; for strategy 3, the worst possible outcome is a £30m profit.

  (b) The maximax strategy looks for the best possible outcome, which is strategy 1, where the firm could make a £220m profit if the rivals respond with c.

  (c) The best compromise strategy is 3 – the best outcome (c: £200m profit) is only marginally worse than the best possible, but the worst outcome (a: £30m) is only marginally worse than the £40m of strategy 2.

Q38. Extensive form.

Q39. Tit-for-tat.

Q40. B. Charging the same price maximises profits subject to firm X keeping its promise. In other words, the credibility of the promise is crucial.

Q41. *(a)* The best for Econjet is Outcome 3, which maximises profit at £100m.

  (b) For Whoosh, Outcome 2 is best, again because this maximises profit from all possible outcomes.

  (c) If Econjet has a first-mover advantage, it will choose Airbus in order to try to achieve the best outcome (3).

  (d) Once Econjet has chosen Airbus, then Whoosh has to choose Boeing, enabling Econjet to maximise its profits.

Q42. *a price setter.*

Q43. *low.*

Q44. *high.*

Q45. *more elastic.*

Q46. (a) (ii); (b) (iii); (c) (i).

Q47. A. It can charge each consumer the maximum price (above P_1) that he or she is prepared to pay.

Q48. (a) *Yes*; (b) *Possibly*; (c) *No*; (d) *Yes*; (e) *Possibly*.

Chapter 8

Alternative Theories of the Firm

 A **REVIEW**

In this chapter we drop the assumption that firms are always profit maximisers, focusing on the behaviour of decision-makers in firms. Firms may not have the information to maximise profits. But even if they did, they may choose to pursue some alternative aim.

Recognising that firms are complex organisations, with different individuals and departments pursuing their own agenda, we examine what happens when these various goals come into conflict. We look at the effects of pursuing such alternative aims: either a single aim, such as growth or sales, or several aims simultaneously. We also ask how prices are determined in practice.

8.1 Problems with traditional theory

(Page 222) Firms may *want* to maximise profits, but lack the information to do so.

Q1. If firms do not use *marginal* cost and marginal *revenue* concepts, they will not be able to arrive at their profit-maximising output. *True/False*

Q2. If a firm uses accountants' cost concepts that are not based on opportunity cost, then it will only be by chance if it ends up maximising profits. *True/False*

Given the problems in estimating the profit-maximising price and output, the firm may resort to simple rules of thumb. One such rule is the *cost-plus* method of pricing. Under this system a firm merely adds a *mark-up* for profit to its average cost of production. Thus if its average cost were 50p and it wanted to make a 20p profit, it would set a price of

Q3. ....

By a process of trial and error, adjusting the mark-up and adjusting output, the firm can move towards the profit-maximising position.

(Pages 222–3) An even more fundamental criticism of the traditional theory of the firm is that the decision makers in the firm may not even aim to maximise profits in the first place.

Q4. On which of the following is this criticism based?
A. Many shareholders do not want to maximise profits.
B. Owners of firms are not 'rational'.
C. Shareholders are not the decision makers and have different interests from them.
D. Managers prefer to maximise profits because this is usually in their own interest.
E. Shareholders are really utility maximisers.

The divorce between the ownership and control of a firm is likely to be greater if **Q5.** *there are a few large shareholders/*

 Multiple choice   **(?)** Written answer   Delete wrong word   Diagram/table manipulation   Calculation   Matching/ordering

there are many small shareholders. It is also likely to be greater in **Q6.** *partnerships/private limited companies/public limited companies*.

(?) **Q7.** Firms must still make enough profits to survive. But this does not make them profit maximisers.

Instead they are 'profit ....'.

(●) **Q8.** If a firm under *perfect competition* had an aim other than profit maximisation, would this make any difference to the output it would choose to produce?

(*a*) In the short run? *Yes/No*

(*b*) In the long run? *Yes/No*

8.2 Behavioural theories

(Pages 224–7) In section 4.4 we saw that consumers may not always act 'rationally'. Similarly, firms may sometimes deviate from rationality, in particular in relation to behaviour towards competitors and because of asymmetric information and attitudes towards risk.

Firms in a **Q9.** *collusive oligopoly/perfectly competitive market* may take action to **Q10.** *punish/reward* other firms in response to past actions, although this may not result in maximisation of profits.

The problem of managers not pursing the same goals as shareholders is an example of the *principal–agent problem*. Because of asymmetric information and different goals, agents may not always carry out the wishes of their principals. Asymmetric information, in this case, refers to the fact that **Q11.** *principals/agents* have superior knowledge and can, therefore, act against the interests of the other party.

(?) **Q12.** In the following cases, which are the principals and which are the agents?

(*a*) Estate agents and house buyers:

estate agents .... ; house buyers ....

(*b*) Shareholders and managers:

shareholders .... ; managers ....

(*c*) House builders and architects:

house builders .... ; architects ....

(*d*) Employers and workers:

employers .... ; workers ....

(*e*) Shops and their customers:

shops .... ; customers ....

(?) **Q13.** There are two key elements that principals need to consider in order to tackle the principal–agent problem. Name them.

1. ....

2. ....

A moneylender is approached by two potential borrowers. Both expect a return on their respective projects of 10%. Firm A's management team is optimistic about prospects, and sees the possibility of a higher return, albeit risky. Firm B is more cautious, and sees 10% as the best possible outcome.

(●) **Q14.** If the moneylender cannot identify the level of risk attached to the two projects and offers to lend to the two firms at an interest rate of 12%, which of the firms will be prepared to borrow? *Firm A/Firm B/both firms*

(▤) **Q15.** If this scenario were to be repeated throughout the financial system, which of the following would happen?

(i) All firms would be prepared to borrow.

(ii) Only cautious firms would be prepared to borrow.

(iii) Only optimistic firms will be prepared to borrow.

(iv) No firms will be prepared to borrow.

(v) Cautious firms may not survive, and only risky projects will be undertaken.

A. (i).

B. (ii).

C. (iii).

D. (iv).

E. (iii) and (v).

8.3 Alternative maximising theories

(Page 228) Long-run profit maximisation

The traditional theory of the firm assumes that firms are *short-run* profit maximisers. An alternative assumption is that firms seek to maximise *long-run* profits.

(?) **Q16.** In what way might each of the following lead to smaller short-run profits but larger long-run profits?

(*a*) A large-scale advertising campaign ....

....

(*b*) Opening up a new production line ....

....

(*c*) Investing in research and development ....

....

(d) Launching a takeover bid for a rival company ....

....

(e) Installing expensive filter equipment to reduce atmospheric pollution from the factory's chimneys

....

A major problem with the theory of long-run profit maximisation is that it is virtually impossible to test.

Q17. Explain why.

....

Q18. It is also virtually impossible in advance to identify a long-run profit-maximising price and output. Which of the following are reasons for this?
(a) Cost and revenue curves are likely to shift unpredictably as a result of the policy pursued. *Yes/No*
(b) Cost and revenue curves likely to shift as a result of unpredictable external factors. *Yes/No*
(c) The firm is likely to experience economies of scale. *Yes/No*
(d) Some policies may affect both demand *and* costs. *Yes/No*
(e) Different managers are likely to make different judgements about the best way of achieving long-run maximum profits. *Yes/No*

(Pages 228–9) Managerial utility maximisation
Williamson argued that managers would often have the discretion to pursue their own interests and thus seek to maximise their own utility.

Q19. Which *one* of the following was *not* said to be a feature of this situation?
A. Managers would receive higher salaries and spend on company cars or plush offices.
B. Staffing levels would be higher than under profit maximisation.
C. Managers would exercise some discretion over investment expenditure.
D. Expenditure on staff and managerial perks tends to vary with the business cycle.
E. The firm's choice of output and price would be no different from a profit-maximising firm.

(Pages 229–30) Sales revenue maximisation (short run)
The success of many managers may be judged according to the level of the firm's sales. For this reason, sales or sales revenue maximisation may be the dominant aim in a firm. Nevertheless, firms will still have to make sufficient profits to survive. Thus sales or sales revenue maximising firms will also be profit-'satisficing' firms.

Q20. Figure 8.1 shows a firm's short-run cost and revenue curves. (It operates under monopoly or imperfect competition.) The level of output it produces will depend on its aims. For each of the following four aims, identify the firm's output.

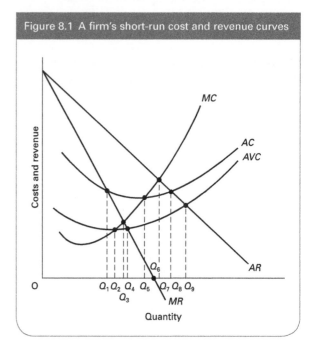

Figure 8.1 A firm's short-run cost and revenue curves

(a) Profit maximisation

....

(b) Sales maximisation (must earn at least normal profits)

....

(c) Sales maximisation (must cover all variable costs)

....

(d) Sales revenue maximisation (must earn at least normal profits)

....

(e) Assume now that the diagram represents a perfectly competitive industry (also in the short run). What will the equilibrium level of output be?

....

(f) Returning to the assumption that the diagram represents a firm under monopoly or imperfect competition, redraw the *AC* (and *AVC*) curves so that (b) and (d) produce the same output.

Q21. The profit-maximising output will never be greater than the (profit-satisficing) sales revenue maximising output. *True/False*

◗ Q22. The (profit-satisficing) sales revenue maximising output will always be greater than the profit-maximising output. *True/False*

(?) Q23. If in the short run the firm could maximise sales revenue and make more than the satisfactory level of profit, this situation would be unlikely to persist in the long run even if other firms were prevented from entering the industry. Why?

....

....

(Pages 230–5) Growth maximisation
Rather than aiming to maximise *short-run* sales revenue, managers may take a longer-term perspective and aim to maximise the rate of growth of their firm. Growth can be by internal expansion, vertical integration, diversification or merger.

If growth is to be by internal expansion, the firm will need to increase both its productive capacity (by investment) and the demand for its product (by advertising). Both will require finance.

(?) Q24. Name three ways in which a firm can finance such expansion.

1. ....

2. ....

3. ....

Firms may be prevented from growing too rapidly by the 'takeover constraint'.

(?) Q25. Why does a takeover become more likely when a firm expands rapidly?

....

....

▤ Q26. Which *one* of the following is a disadvantage of vertical integration?
A. Exploitation of economies of scale.
B. Reduced uncertainty.
C. Enhanced ability to respond to changing market demand, with secure supply sources.
D. Increased barriers to entry.
E. Reduced transport costs.

It is claimed that growth through diversification is beneficial for a firm because it allows the spreading of risks.

(?) Q27. Explain why. ....

....

....

A firm can grow by merging with or taking over another firm. (We will use the term 'mergers' for both mergers and takeovers.) Mergers can be of three types: horizontal, vertical and conglomerate.

♟ Q28. Match each of the three types of merger to the following examples.
(a) A soft drinks manufacturer merges with a pharmaceutical company.

....

(b) A car manufacturer merges with a car distribution company.

....

(c) A large supermarket chain takes over a number of independent grocers.

....

(?) Q29. Various motives have been suggested for mergers other than the simple desire to grow. Name four of them.

1. ....

2. ....

3. ....

4. ....

♟ Q30. Look at the answers to Q29. Which of the motives are consistent with the prime motive of:

(a) long-run profit maximisation? ....

....

(b) growth maximisation? ....

....

▤ Q31. When comparing a growth-maximising firm with a short-run profit-maximising firm, which one of the following (in the short run) is likely for the growth-maximising firm?
A. A lower level of advertising.
B. A lower equilibrium output.

C. A lower price relative to average cost.
D. A lower level of investment.
E. A higher price elasticity of demand at the price charged by the firm.

Q32. Which *one* of the following is *not* an example of a strategic alliance?
A. A joint venture.
B. A network.
C. A franchising agreement.
D. A merger.
E. A subcontracting agreement.

Q33. Which of the following may be seen as an advantage of a strategic alliance?
(a) Facilitates entry to a new market. Yes/No/Possibly
(b) Allows firms to share risk. Yes/No/Possibly
(c) Enables firms to pool capital. Yes/No/Possibly
(d) Less aggressive than an acquisition. Yes/No/Possibly
(e) Help the firms involved to raise finance.
  Yes/No/Possibly
(f) Involves less commitment. Yes/No/Possibly
(g) Enables cost-cutting Yes/No/Possibly

8.4 Multiple aims

(Pages 238–40) Given the complexity of modern firms and the multitude of stakeholders with different – and sometimes conflicting – objectives, firms may seek to achieve multiple aims.

Q34. Is it possible for a firm to *maximise* two objectives simultaneously? Yes/No

Explain ....

....

Sometimes firms may attempt not to maximise any one objective but merely to achieve a target level of several.

Q35. The setting of multiple targets (with no one objective to be maximised) is most likely:
A. when the firm has a complex multi-department organisation.
B. when there is a limited number of large institutional shareholders.
C. when one of the managers in the company is dominant.
D. when firms operate in highly competitive markets.
E. when firms produce a single product.

If targets cannot all be achieved, then a *Q36.* .... procedure will be adopted to find ways of rectifying the problem. This may involve revising the targets to make them less ambitious.

To avoid constant revision of targets, managers may allow *organisational slack* to develop.

Q37. Define organisational slack ....

....

Q38. Which of the following will tend to lead to a higher level of organisational slack?
(a) A greater degree of uncertainty about future demand.
  Yes/No
(b) A more complex organisational structure in the firm.
  Yes/No
(c) The firm does better than planned (in terms of its various targets). Yes/No
(d) Managers become more cautious. Yes/No
(e) The number of rival firms decreases. Yes/No
(f) Industrial relations deteriorate. Yes/No

Q39. A frequent complaint of junior managers is that they are often faced with new targets from above and that this makes their life difficult. If their complaint is true, does this conflict with the hypothesis that managers will try to build in slack? Yes/No

Explain ....

....

Q40. When firms adopt a satisficing approach with multiple targets, their production is likely to be less responsive to changing market conditions. True/False

8.5 Pricing in practice

(Pages 240–5) Whether firms are profit maximisers or are pursuing some alternative objective(s), many set prices, not by referring to marginal cost and marginal revenue, but by adding a profit mark-up to average cost.

Q41. If a firm would like to maximise profits, it will be pure chance if it succeeds in doing so if it uses a mark-up system of pricing. True/False

Q42. A firm that is a profit maximiser is likely to adjust its mark-up more frequently than a firm that is a profit satisficer. True/False

Q43. For a firm which uses mark-up pricing and aims to achieve a particular level of total profit, its supply curve will be:
A. parallel to its average (total) cost curve.
B. parallel to its average variable cost curve.
C. parallel to its demand curve.
D. above its average (total) cost curve, but getting closer to it as output increases.
E. impossible to determine as long as the firm has market power.

PROBLEMS, EXERCISES AND PROJECTS

Q44. A firm has the following total revenue and total cost functions:

$$TR = 32Q - 2Q^2$$
$$TC = 20 + 4Q + Q^2$$

(a) Fill in the figures in Table 8.1.
(b) At what output is profit maximised? ....
(c) At what output is sales revenue maximised?
(d) Assume that the firm regarded £15 as the minimum satisfactory level of profit. How much would it produce now if it were concerned to maximise sales revenue?

....

Assume now that fixed costs increase by £30.

(e) What will be the profit-maximising output now? How much profit would be made at this output?

....

Table 8.1 Total costs, revenue and profit

Quantity (units)	Total revenue (£)	Total cost (£)	Total profit (£)
0	0	20	−20
1	...	...	...
2	...	...	...
3	78	...	...
4	...	52	...
5	...	...	45
6	120	...	...
7	...	...	...
8	128	116	...
9	...	137	...
10	...	...	−40

(f) What would be the sales revenue maximising output assuming that the minimum profit constraint of £15 still applied?

....

*Q45. Given the *TR* and *TC* functions of Q44:
(a) What is the function for *TΠ*?
(b) At what output, to the nearest whole number, is this function maximised? (You will need to use differentiation.)
(c) At what output is the *TR* function maximised?

Check that your answers for (b) and (c) are the same as for Q35 (b) and (c).

Q46. Strategic alliances have become common in the airline business, especially (but not only) on long-haul routes. Find out about the membership of the One World Alliance (www.oneworldalliance.com) and the Star Alliance (www.staralliance.com), and analyse the economic advantages and disadvantages of these alliances for the airlines and their consumers.

Q47. Look through the business pages of two or three quality newspapers for a few days to find reports of companies that are merging, attempting to take over other firms, diversifying or simply expanding fast.
(a) Try to identify the objectives of the companies and whether there are any apparent conflicts in these objectives.
(b) Assess whether the stated aims are 'final' aims or merely the means to achieving other aims (stated or not stated).
(c) In each case try to assess what type of information you would need to have in order to judge (i) whether the companies really were pursuing the objectives stated and (ii) how successful they were in achieving them.
(d) In each case assess the extent to which the company's performance and objectives are in the public interest.

DISCUSSION TOPICS AND ESSAYS

Q48. Under what circumstances is it likely that there will be a divorce between the ownership and control of a company?

Q49. The shareholders of a company realise that their managers have aims that diverge from the best interest of the shareholders. Discuss the steps that they could take to tackle the situation.

Q50. Explain why information asymmetry may have harmful effects.

Q51. Imagine you were the managing director of a fashion house producing expensive designer clothing. What achievements of you or your company would give you special satisfaction? Are these achievements consistent with profit maximisation?

Q52. Are sales revenue maximising firms likely to achieve more than normal profits in the long run (assuming that they have the market power to do so)?

Q53. Make up three seemingly outrageous business decisions and then attempt to justify each as being consistent with a policy of long-run profit maximisation.

Q54. Using a diagram, explain whether a consumer would be better off if a monopoly were a profit maximiser or a sales revenue maximiser.

Q55. To what extent will consumers gain or lose from the three different types of merger?

Q56. Discuss the relative merits of vertical integration and diversification as ways in which a firm may attempt to maximise growth.

Q57. A diversification strategy may allow a firm to grow whilst spreading risks, but may create difficulties for managers having to cope with more complex decisions. Discuss.

Q58. Consider the proposition that satisficing is irrational since it implies that people prefer less of an objective to more.

Q59. Examine the advantages and disadvantages of a strategic alliance as compared with a merger or acquisition.

Q60. 'Ultimately it is not the goals that a firm pursues that determine its price and output but the nature of the competition it faces.' Discuss.

Q61. 'If a firm uses a cost-plus system of pricing, then it is unlikely to be aiming to maximise profits, either in the short run or in the long run.' Discuss this proposition and consider what evidence you would need to have in order to establish what the aims are of a particular firm which uses cost-plus pricing.

Q62. Discuss ways in which firms may be able to increase their profits through understanding that consumers may not always act rationally.

Q63. Debate
Mergers are inevitably against the public interest as they increase monopoly power and reduce the incentive to innovate.

 # ANSWERS

Q1. *False.* Provided a firm measures cost in terms of opportunity cost, it could arrive at the profit-maximising position by a system of trial and error. It does this by sticking with policies that turn out to have increased profits and abandoning policies that turn out to have reduced profits.

Q2. *True.* If the firm does not use opportunity cost concepts, it cannot establish how much profit it is making, and whether profit is therefore at a maximum.

Q3. 70p.

Q4. C. Shareholders may well wish to maximise profits, but if they are separated from managers whose own personal interests may be better served by aiming for some other goal, such as power or prestige, profits will not be maximised. The managers may simply aim to make *enough* profits to keep shareholders quiet.

Q5. *there are many small shareholders.* If there are many of them, individual shareholders will have virtually no say in the firm's decisions.

Q6. *public limited companies.* These are companies where shares are traded publicly. Shareholders (unless they own a large percentage) are unlikely to have any influence on day-to-day decisions. They merely have a vote when broad issues of policy are put at shareholders' meetings.

Q7. *satisficers.*

Q8. *(a) Yes.* Provided it *could* earn supernormal profits, it may choose to sacrifice some or all of these in order to achieve some other aim (e.g. increasing output).

(b) No. It could only make normal profits anyway, which it must make to survive, whether it is a profit maximiser or merely a profit satisficer.

Q9. *collusive oligopoly.*

Q10. *punish.* For example, this may happen where a firm in the oligopoly had reneged on a previous agreement.

Q11. *Agents.*

Q12. *(a)* estate agents, *agents*; house buyers, *principals*.

(b) shareholders, *principals*; managers, *agents*.

(c) house builders, *principals*; architects, *agents*.

(d) employers, *principals*; workers, *agents*.

(e) shops, *agents*; customers, *principals*.

Q13. 1. Have a way of monitoring the performance of their agents.

2. Create appropriate incentives to influence the agents' behaviour.

Q14. *Firm A.*

Q15. E. In this case, asymmetric information exists because the lenders cannot distinguish between potential borrowers, so set a higher rate of interest to guard against risk of default. Cautious firms are forced out of the market, leaving only those prepared to take risks.

Q16. *(a)* Marginal advertising costs exceeding marginal revenue from advertising in the short run; but marginal revenue increasing in the long run as demand steadily grows with the product becoming more established.

(b) Initial high set-up costs and initial 'teething' costs, costs that would fall in the long run. Also if demand is growing and it takes time to open a new production line, the opening of the line may lead to excess capacity in the short run, but not in the long run.

(c) Revenue from new or improved products only occurs in the future *after* the research and development has taken place. Costs occur from the outset.

(d) There may be high administrative and public relations costs associated with the bid. If successful, the acquisition of the new company is likely to lead to bigger profits (sheer size of output; economies of scale; increased monopoly power).

(e) Costs of the filter equipment with little immediate return. In the long run consumers may prefer the firm's 'greener' image and the firm may avoid government-imposed restrictions that might turn out to be more expensive in the long run.

Q17. Because a firm could always, in hindsight, use it to justify virtually *any* decisions, no matter how unprofitable they eventually turn out to be.

Q18. Yes: (a), (b) and (e). Note that (c) and (d) will not in principle make price and output impossible to predict; they are merely factors that would need to be taken into account.

Q19. E.

Q20. *(a)* Q_3; where $MC = MR$.

(b) Q_8; the maximum level of sales consistent with AR being not less than AC.

(c) Q_9; the maximum level of sales consistent with AR being not less than AVC.

(d) Q_6; the point where $MR = 0$ and where, therefore, TR is at a maximum. (Note that in this diagram, the sales revenue maximising point more than satisfies the requirement that at least normal profits should be made. In this case supernormal profits will be made because the AR curve is above the AC curve at Q_6.)

(e) Q_7; the point where MC (the industry supply curve) equals demand (AR).

(f) The AC curve should now intersect the AR curve at, or to the left of, Q_6.

Q21. *True.* At the profit-maximising point, $MC = MR$. Since MC will be positive, MR must also be positive, and thus revenue could be increased by producing *more*.

The revenue-maximising firm will thus produce more than the profit-maximising firm (provided profits are above the satisfactory level and thus allow the firm to increase production).

Q22. *False.* Although the (profit-satisficing) sales revenue maximising output cannot be less than the profit-maximising output, it could be the same. This will occur when the maximum profits are no greater than the satisfactory level (e.g. under perfect competition in the long run).

Q23. Because the firm would be likely to spend the excess profits on advertising or product improvements in order to increase sales. It would continue doing this, even when the MC from advertising exceeded MR, as long as MR was positive and as long as profits were still above the minimum level.

Q24. 1. from borrowing.
2. from a new issue of shares.
3. from retained profits.

Q25. Because dividends are likely to fall if the firm borrows too much, retains too much profit or issues new shares. Unless shareholders are convinced that dividends and the share price will increase in the long run, they may sell their shares. The resulting fall in share prices will make the firm vulnerable to a takeover bid.

Q26. C. Vertical integration may be seen to reduce the flexibility of a firm, by making it more difficult to switch to new competitive suppliers, or to adjust its production to changing market conditions.

Q27. Diversification may spread risks for a firm where different products follow different cycles of production. A firm committed to a single product line may face the risk that it may be hit by a recession in the demand for that product. By diversifying into different product lines risk is reduced, as it may be unlikely that all products will be hit simultaneously by a fall in demand – especially if the new products are chosen carefully.

Q28. *(a)* conglomerate.
(b) vertical.
(c) horizontal.

Q29. Answers could include: to achieve economies of scale; to gain greater market power; to obtain an increased share price; to reduce uncertainty; to take advantage of an opportunity that arises; to reduce the likelihood of being taken over; to defend another firm from a hostile takeover bid; asset stripping (i.e. selling off the profitable bits of the newly acquired company); empire building; broadening the geographical base of the company.

Q30. *(a)* All could be argued to be! This is an example of the problem with the theory of long-run profit maximisation: virtually any action could be justified as potentially leading to increased profits.

(b) To achieve economies of scale; (to take advantage of an opportunity that arises); to reduce the likelihood of being taken over; empire building; broadening the geographical base of the company. These could be argued to lead directly to a faster growth in the size of the firm. Some of the others could be argued to be consistent under certain circumstances.

Q31. C. The growth-maximising firm will be prepared to sacrifice profit in order to achieve higher output and sales. Note: in the case of E, the growth-maximising firm will be operating at a lower point on its *AR* curve. This will correspond to a lower level of *MR* and hence a *lower* price elasticity of demand.

Q32. D.

Q33. Yes, (a), (b), (c), (d), (e) and (f). These may all be seen as advantages of a strategic alliance, although whether the benefits will actually be reaped may depend on the circumstances surrounding a particular alliance. One great advantage of a strategic alliance as opposed to a full-blown merger is that an alliance is much more easily dismantled than a merger – hence (f) there is less of a long-term commitment attached to a strategic alliance. As far as (g) cost-cutting is concerned, the picture is less clear. It is possible that costs will be reduced as a result of a strategic alliance, through some of the items already mentioned. However, by remaining as separate enterprises, it is likely that some scope for rationalisation is forgone. For example, both partners in an alliance will need to maintain separate finance or human resource divisions, and there is likely to be duplication of other management functions that could be avoided in a merger.

Q34. *No*: if there is any trade-off between the objectives. For example, in order to sell more, a firm may have to accept lower profits. In such cases only one of the objectives can be maximised. Alternatively one of the objectives could be maximised *subject* to achieving a target level of another objective. For example, the firm could maximise sales revenue subject to achieving a *satisfactory* level of profits.

Q35. A. In a multi-department firm there may be many different potentially conflicting interests of different managers. In such cases, unless one manager is dominant, it is likely that managers will have to be prepared to be 'satisficers' rather than 'maximisers'.

Q36. *search.*

Q37. *Where managers allow spare capacity to exist in their department, thereby enabling them to respond more easily to changed circumstances.*

Q38. *All of them.* Organisational slack is likely to increase when firms face uncertain times and when they are not forced by competition to cut their slack.

Q39. *No.* The changes in targets may result from the fact that senior managers have built slack into their departments and can afford the 'luxury' of changing targets: perhaps experimentally. At the same time, the junior managers, fearing changed targets, may well be trying to increase the amount of organisational slack in their domain (but hoping not to let their bosses know for fear of being given tougher targets).

Q40. *True.* The greater the number of goals, and hence the greater the chance of conflict, the more likely firms are to build in organisational slack, and therefore the less they will need to change their level of production as market conditions change.

Q41. *False.* The choice of the level of mark-up may reflect the firm's assessment of what price the 'market will bear': what price will maximise profits. By not using marginal cost and marginal revenue, the firm may well not arrive at the profit-maximising price and output immediately (and in this sense the statement is true), but if the firm is willing to adjust its mark-up in the light of the perceived strength of demand, then it may, by an 'iterative' approach (i.e. a step-by-step approach), arrive at the profit-maximising mark-up. Note that even if a firm does try to equate marginal cost and marginal revenue, a lack of information, especially about the shape of the demand curve for its product, and hence its marginal revenue, may prevent it from arriving directly at the profit-maximising price. It may still, therefore, have to use an iterative approach.

Q42. *True.* A firm that is a profit maximiser will need to adjust its price (i.e. its mark-up) as revenue and cost curves shift. A profit satisficer, given the probability of a degree of organisational slack, will not need to be so responsive to changes in demand and costs.

Q43. D. As its output increases, it will need a smaller (average) profit mark-up on top of average cost in order to achieve a given level of *total* profit.

Chapter 9

The Theory of Distribution of Income

 A | ***REVIEW***

In this chapter we consider what determines the incomes earned by different factors of production.

We start by having a look at the income earned by labour. This takes the form of wages. We will look at wage determination in both perfect and imperfect markets. In doing so we will attempt to establish why wage rates can differ substantially from one occupation to another: why there can be substantial inequality in wages.

We then look at the rewards to non-human factors of production. We first look at the determination of the return to capital: at the *price of capital* that is either hired or sold and at the incomes – *profit* and *interest* – earned from the use of capital by its owners (capitalists).

Finally we look at the rewards to owners of land (landlords). This consists of the *rent* earned from hiring out land or using it to produce goods.

9.1 Wage determination under perfect competition

(Pages 248–9) In a *perfect* market the rewards to factors are determined by the interaction of demand and supply.

Figure 9.1 shows a local market for plasterers. It is assumed that it is a perfect market. This assumption means that **Q1.** *the price of plaster/the wage rate of plasterers/the profitability of employers of plasterers* cannot be affected by individual **Q2.** *employers/workers/employers or workers.* This means that **Q3.** *the supply curve of labour to/the demand curve for labour by* an individual employer is perfectly elastic, and that **Q4.** *the supply curve of labour by/the demand curve for labour from* an individual worker is perfectly elastic too.

 Q5. In Figure 9.1(b), which of the two curves would shift and in which direction as a result of each of the following changes?

Figure 9.1 Local market for plasterers

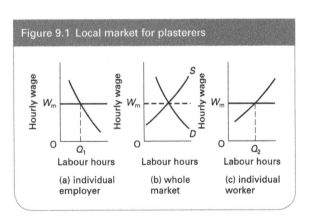

(a) individual employer
(b) whole market
(c) individual worker

(a) A deterioration in the working conditions for plasterers.

demand/supply; left/right

(b) A decrease in the price of plaster.

demand/supply; left/right

 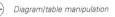

(c) A decrease in the demand for new houses.

demand/supply; left/right

(d) An increased demand for plasterers in other parts of the country. *demand/supply; left/right*

(e) Increased wages in other parts of the building trade (as a result of union activity).

demand/supply; left/right

(f) Increased costs associated with employing plasterers (e.g. employers having to pay higher insurance premiums for accidents to plasterers).

demand/supply; left/right

Q6. From Q5(c) it can be seen that the demand for a factor of production is:

A. a substitute demand.

B. a direct demand.

C. an elastic demand.

D. an inelastic demand.

E. a derived demand.

(Pages 249–51) The supply of labour

We can look at the supply of labour at three levels: the supply of hours by an individual worker, the supply of workers to an individual employer and the total market supply of a given category of labour.

When an individual worker works longer hours, each extra hour worked will involve additional sacrifice.

Q7. This additional sacrifice is known as

....

This sacrifice consists of two elements: the sacrifice of leisure and the extra effort/unpleasantness incurred from the extra work. As people work extra hours, these two sacrifices are likely to increase. As a result the supply curve will normally be **Q8.** *upward sloping/downward sloping.*

Under certain circumstances, however, the supply curve can bend backwards at higher wages. To understand why, we must distinguish between the *income* and *substitution* effects of a wage increase.

Q9. Which of the following is the income effect and which is the substitution effect?

(a) As wage rates rise, people will tend to work more hours, since taking leisure would now involve a greater sacrifice of income and hence consumption.

income effect/substitution effect

(b) At higher wage rates, people do not need to work such long hours. *income effect/substitution effect*

Thus the income effect is **Q10.** *positive/negative* and the substitution effect is **Q11.** *positive/negative.* The supply curve will thus become backward bending at high wage rates if the **Q12.** *income effect/substitution effect* becomes dominant.

Q13. The supply curve of labour to an *individual employer* in perfect competition will be perfectly elastic.

True/False

Q14. The *market* supply curve of labour will tend to be upward sloping. The position of this curve will depend on three main determinants. Of the following:

 (i) the number of qualified people,

 (ii) the wage rate,

(iii) the productivity of labour,

(iv) the pleasantness/unpleasantness of the job,

 (v) the wages and non-wage benefits of alternative jobs,

which three determine the position of the supply curve?

A. (i), (ii) and (iii).

B. (i), (iii) and (iv).

C. (iii), (iv) and (v).

D. (i), (iv) and (v).

E. (ii), (iii) and (iv).

(Pages 251–2 and Web case 9.1) Elasticity of supply

The elasticity of the market supply of labour will depend on how readily workers are willing and able to move into jobs as their wage rate increases relative to other jobs. What we are referring to here is the mobility of labour. The less the mobility (the greater the immobility), the less elastic the supply.

Q15. There are several causes of immobility. In each one of the following cases, identify whether it is a cause of geographical immobility, occupational immobility or both.

(a) Social and family ties. *geographical/occupational/both*

(b) Ignorance of available jobs.

geographical/occupational/both

(c) Difficulty in acquiring new qualifications.

geographical/occupational/both

(d) Inconvenience of moving house.

geographical/occupational/both

(e) Fear of the unknown. *geographical/occupational/both*

(f) Less desirable working conditions in alternative jobs.

geographical/occupational/both

(Web case 9.1) The elasticity of supply of labour will determine what proportion of wages consists of *transfer earnings* and what proportion consists of *economic rent*. The definition of a person's **Q16.** *transfer earnings/economic rent* is 'anything over and above what that person must be paid to prevent him or her moving to another job'.

Q17. A fashion model could earn £160 per week as a gardener, £320 per week working on a building site or £480 as a lorry driver. As a model, however, he earns £640. Assuming he likes all four jobs equally and that there are no costs associated with changing jobs, what is his economic rent from being a fashion model?

A. £160
B. £320
C. £480
D. £640
E. £960

Q18. In Figure 9.2, which area represents transfer earnings?
A. (i)
B. (ii)
C. (iii)
D. (i) + (ii)
E. (ii) + (iii)

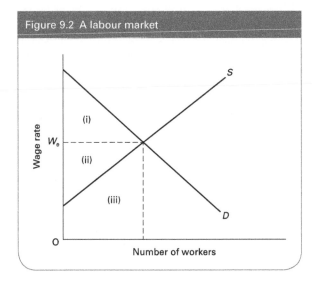

Figure 9.2 A labour market

Q19. In Figure 9.2, which area represents economic rent?
A. (i)
B. (ii)
C. (iii)
D. (i) + (ii)
E. (ii) + (iii)

(Pages 253–4) The demand for labour: the marginal productivity theory

We turn now to the *demand* for labour. How many workers will a profit-maximising firm want to employ? What will be its demand for labour?

There are a number of concepts you will need to be clear about here.

Q20. Match the concepts (i)–(vii) to the definitions (a)–(g).
 (i) Marginal cost (*MC*)
 (ii) Marginal cost of labour (MC_L)
 (iii) Average cost of labour (AC_L)
 (iv) Marginal revenue (*MR*)
 (v) Average revenue (*AR*)
 (vi) Marginal physical product of labour (MPP_L)
 (vii) Marginal revenue product of labour (MRP_L)

(a) The extra revenue a firm earns from the employment of one more worker.

....

(b) The wage rate.   ....

(c) The price of the good.   ....
(d) The extra cost of producing one more unit of output.

....

(e) The extra output gained from the employment of one more worker.

....

(f) The extra revenue from producing one more unit of output.

....

(g) The extra cost of employing one more worker.

....

The most important of these concepts in understanding the demand for labour is the marginal revenue product (MRP_L). This can be derived by multiplying **Q21.** MPP_L by *MR/AR* by MC_L/*MR* by AC_L.

The rule for profit maximising can thus be stated as 'whenever MC_L exceeds MRP_L the firm should employ **Q22.** *more/fewer* workers, and whenever MRP_L exceeds MC_L the firm should employ **Q23.** *more/fewer*'.

Q24. The firm's demand curve for labour under perfect competition is given by the MRP_L curve.   *True/False*

(Page 254) We can conclude that under perfect competition, there are three main determinants of the amount of labour that a firm will demand: the productivity of labour (MPP_L), the wage rate (*W*) and the price of the good (*P* = *MR*).

Q25. Will a change in each of the following determinants lead to a shift in or a movement along the demand curve for labour?
(a) A change in the productivity of labour (MPP_L).
                              shift/movement along
(b) A change in the wage rate (*W*). *shift/movement along*
(c) A change in the price of the good (*P* = *MR*).
                              shift/movement along

(Pages 254–5) The demand curve for labour by the *whole industry* will not simply be the horizontal sum of the demand curves by individual firms.

Q26. The (wage) elasticity of demand for labour will depend on a number of factors. Elasticity will be greater:
(a) the greater the price elasticity of demand for the good.
                              True/False
(b) the harder it is to substitute labour for other factors and vice versa.   *True/False*

(c) the greater the elasticity of supply of complementary factors. *True/False*

(d) the lower the elasticity of supply of substitute factors. *True/False*

(e) the smaller the wage cost as a proportion of total costs. *True/False*

(f) the longer the time period. *True/False*

(Pages 255–6) Even in a perfect market, inequality will exist between the earnings of different factors.

Q27. Which one of the following would be a cause of inequality of wages between different occupations in the long run even if all labour markets were perfect?

A. There is short-run geographical immobility of labour.

B. Different jobs require people with different skills.

C. There is perfect knowledge of wages throughout the economy.

D. Everyone has to accept wages as given by the market.

E. Labour is homogeneous within any one particular labour market.

(Page 256) In practice, of course, factor markets are not perfect and this will provide a further reason for inequality in factor earnings.

Q28. Name three types of market imperfection in factor markets.

1. ....

2. ....

3. ....

9.2 Wage determination in imperfect markets

(Page 257) In this section we shall consider the effect of economic power on wages.

Q29. There are a number of types of economic power. These include:

 (i) monopoly in goods markets
 (ii) monopoly in labour markets
 (iii) monopsony in goods markets
 (iv) monopsony in labour markets
 (v) bilateral monopoly

Match each of the following examples of economic power to the above five types.

(a) A group of local authorities get together as a purchasing consortium in order to be able to buy cheaper easy-empty wheelie bins from the manufacturers (bins that will be provided free to residents).

....

(b) A trade union operates a closed shop. ....

(c) A firm is the only domestic coal merchant supplying the area.

....

(d) The wages of postal workers are determined by a process of collective bargaining between the Post Office and the Communication Workers Union.

....

(e) A factory is the only employer of certain types of skilled labour in the area.

....

(Page 257) Let us examine the situation where firms have power in the labour market. This is the case of *monopsony*, where a firm is the sole employer in a particular labour market (or *oligopsony*, where the firm is one of only a few employers). A monopsonist, unlike a perfectly competitive employer, will face **Q30.** *a downward-sloping/an upward-sloping/a horizontal* **Q31.** *supply curve of/demand curve for* labour.

Q32. Assume that a monopsonist faces the supply-of-labour schedule given in Table 9.1.

(a) Fill in the figures for TC_L and MC_L.

(b) Plot the figures for AC_L and MC_L on Figure 9.3, which also shows the firm's MRP_L curve.

(c) How many workers will the firm choose to employ in order to maximise profits?

(d) What wage rate will it pay?

(e) If Figure 9.3 were to illustrate a perfectly competitive market for labour (i.e. the sum of all firms), how many workers would now be employed and at what wage rate?

(Pages 258–60) What happens when labour also has economic power? Let us assume that a union is formed and that it has sole negotiating rights with a monopsony employer. What we have here is a case of *bilateral monopoly*. Wages are set by a process of collective bargaining, and once the wage rate has been agreed, the firm has to accept that wage. It cannot therefore then drive the wage rate down by employing fewer workers. The firm thus now faces **Q33.** *an upward-sloping/a downward-sloping/a horizontal* supply-of-labour curve which is therefore **Q34.** *below/above/equal* to the new MC_L curve.

Table 9.1 A monopsonist's supply-of-labour schedule

Wage rate (AC_L)	£100	£120	£140	£160	£180	£200	£220	£240
Number of workers	1	2	3	4	5	6	7	8
Total wage bill (TC_L)	...	...	...	...	...	...	...	...
Marginal cost of labour (MC_L)		...	...	...	...	...	...	...

Q35. Referring still to Figure 9.3, assume that a union now represents labour and that wage rates are set by a process of collective bargaining.

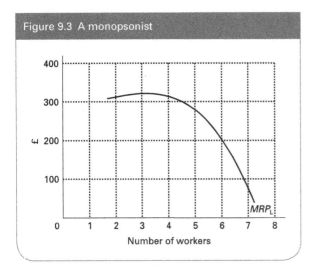

Figure 9.3 A monopsonist

(a) Draw the AC_L and MC_L if the agreed wage rate is £200 per week.

(b) How many workers will the firm now choose to employ?

....

(c) Explain briefly why the firm is willing to take on *more* workers than before despite now having to pay a higher wage rate.

....

....

(d) What is the highest negotiated wage rate at which the firm would still wish to employ the same number of workers as before the union was formed?

....

(e) What is the equilibrium wage rate under bilateral monopoly?

....

(Pages 261–6) Let us now look at the process of collective bargaining.

The outcome of the negotiations will depend on the attitudes of both sides, their skills in negotiating, the information they possess about the other side and the amount they are prepared to give ground. In particular, the outcome will depend on the relative power of both sides to pursue their objectives.

Q36. How will each of the following affect the *power of a union* to cause the employer to give ground at the negotiating table?

(a) New figures showing that the firm's profits for the last year were less than anticipated.
Increase/Decrease the union's power.

(b) A rise in unemployment.
Increase/Decrease the union's power.

(c) New figures showing that inflation has risen.
Increase/Decrease the union's power.

(d) A successful recruiting drive for union membership.
Increase/Decrease the union's power.

(e) Increased competition for the firm's product from imports.
Increase/Decrease the union's power.

(f) A rapidly growing demand for the firm's product.
Increase/Decrease the union's power.

(g) A closed shop agreement.
Increase/Decrease the union's power.

(h) The firm has substantial monopoly power in the goods market.
Increase/Decrease the union's power.

(Pages 266–9) Power is not the only factor that makes actual wage determination different from the perfectly competitive model. There are various other imperfections that cause labour markets to be distorted.

Q37. Give three different types of labour market imperfection.

1. ....

2. ....

3. ....

Q38. Which *one* of the following is not a feature of the efficiency wage hypothesis?

A. It is efficient for a firm to offer a market-clearing wage to its workers.

B. Asymmetric information makes it difficult for firms to judge the quality and qualities of its workers and potential workers.

C. Workers respond to the incentive of higher wages by shirking less.

D. Paying an efficiency wage helps to reduce labour turnover and encourages firms to offer more training to their workers.

E. There are circumstances in which a firm will find it desirable to offer wages above the market-clearing rate.

Q39. Which of the following could explain why the average wage of women tends to be lower than that of men?

(a) Some employers are prejudiced against women. *Yes/No*

(b) Women are less strong physically. *Yes/No*

(c) Women tend to be less geographically mobile than men. *Yes/No*

(d) A lower proportion of female workers are in unions than male workers. *Yes/No*

(e) Women tend to work in more labour-intensive industries. *Yes/No (f)* A lower proportion of the female population seeks employment than that of the male population.

Yes/No

(g) A lower proportion of women have higher education qualifications. *Yes/No*

Q40. A particular industry (which operates in a competitive labour market) discriminates against black workers. Which one of the following effects is likely? (Assume no discrimination in other industries.)

A. White workers will be paid a lower wage rate in that industry than they would have been otherwise.

B. Black workers in other industries will be paid a higher wage rate than they would otherwise.

C. White workers in other industries will be paid a lower wage rate than they would otherwise.

D. The discriminating industry will employ more black workers than it would if it did not discriminate, because it will pay black workers lower wage rates than white workers.

E. The profits of the industry that discriminates will fall.

Q41. The marginal productivity theory states that firms will employ workers up to the point where their MRP_L is equal to their MC_L. Some labour market imperfections are consistent with this theory; some contradict it. From the following list of imperfections, which ones are consistent with the marginal productivity theory?

(i) Firms discriminate against certain groups of workers.

(ii) Firms have monopsony power.

(iii) An industry has nationally negotiated wage rates.

(iv) When reducing its labour force, a firm adopts a 'last in, first out' policy.

(v) Firms are growth maximisers and profit satisficers.

(vi) Wage rates (but not employment) are set by a process of collective bargaining.

A. (iv) only.

B. (iii) and (vi).

C. (ii), (iii) and (vi).

D. (i), (iv) and (v).

E. all six.

9.3 Capital and profit

(Page 270) As with wages, the incomes accruing to the owners of capital and land are the outcome of the forces of demand and supply: forces affected to varying degrees by market distortions.

At the outset it is necessary to make an important distinction. This is between the money received from selling capital and land outright, and the income from the *services* of capital and land (i.e. income or interest from using or hiring out capital, and rent from land). The first is the price of the factor. The second is the price of the services of the factor.

Q42. Wage rates are the price of labour. *True/False*

Q43. As with labour, the profit-maximising employment of land and capital *services* will be where the factor's *MRP* is equal to its *MC* (= price under perfect competition).

True/False

(Page 270) Capital for hire

If Firm A owns capital equipment, what determines the rate at which the firm can rent it out? The answer is that it will be determined by demand and supply.

The demand for capital services by Firm B is given by the *MRP* of capital curve.

Q44. Draw the MRP_K, AC_K and MC_K curves for a firm that has monopsony power when hiring capital equipment. Mark the amount of capital equipment it will choose to hire and show what hire charge it will pay.

(Pages 272–3) The supply of capital services is determined in much the same way as the supply of goods. A firm will supply capital services up to the point where their marginal cost equals their marginal revenue. For a small firm supplying capital services (e.g. a tool hire company) the rental is given by the market and thus is the same as the **Q45.** *marginal revenue/marginal cost/average cost* from renting out equipment. The marginal cost will be the marginal *opportunity cost*.

Q46. Assume that a tool hire company already has a stock of tools. Which of the following are opportunity costs of hiring out the tools?

(a) The cost of replacing the equipment. *Yes/No*

(b) The depreciation of the equipment due to wear and tear. *Yes/No*

(c) The depreciation of the equipment due to ageing.

Yes/No

(d) Maintenance costs of the equipment. *Yes/No*

(e) Handling costs associated with hiring out the equipment. *Yes/No*

(Page 273) The price of capital services in a perfect market will be determined by market demand and supply.

Q47. The price of capital services will be higher:

A. the lower the marginal physical productivity of capital.

B. the lower the price of the goods produced with the capital equipment.

C. the lower the opportunity costs of supplying the capital services.

D. the lower the demand for the goods produced with the capital equipment.

E. the lower the price of complementary factors.

*(Pages 273–5) Capital for purchase: investment

The demand for capital for purchase (investment) will depend on the income it earns for the firm. To calculate the value of this income we need to use *discounted cash flow* (DCF) techniques.

These techniques allow us to reduce the future value of an investment back to a *present value* which we can then compare with the cost of the investment. If the present value exceeds the cost of the investment, the investment is worthwhile.

To find the present value we *discount* (i.e. reduce) the future values using an appropriate *rate of discount*.

✗ *Q48.* What is the present value of an investment in a project lasting one year that yields £110 at the end, assuming that the rate of discount is 10 per cent?

....

To work out the present value we use the following formula:

$$PV = \frac{R_1}{(1+r)} + \frac{R_2}{(1+r)^2} + \frac{R_3}{(1+r)^3} \cdots + \frac{R_n}{(1+r)^n}$$

where:

PV is the discounted present value of the investment;

R_1 is the revenue from the investment earned in year 1, R_2 in year 2 and so on;

r is the rate of discount expressed as a decimal (e.g. 10% = 0.1).

✗ *Q49.* Suppose an investment costs £12 000 and yields £5000 per year for three years. At the end of the three years, the equipment has no value. Work out whether the investment will be profitable if the rate of discount is:

(a) 5 per cent ....

....

....

(b) 10 per cent ....

....

....

(c) 20 per cent ....

....

....

(Page 276) The rate of interest
The rate of interest is the price of loanable funds. This depends on the supply of savings and the demand for finance (which includes investment demand).

◗ *Q50.* Would the following changes cause the rate of interest to rise or fall?

(a) People become more thrifty. *Rise/Fall*

(b) The productivity of investments generally increases.

Rise/Fall

(c) The demand for goods increases. *Rise/Fall*

(d) The cost of machinery rises. *Rise/Fall*

(Pages 276–9) Financing investment
A firm can raise finance for investment in various ways.

◗ *Q51.* Which of the following are categorised as internal sources and which as external sources of finance?

(a) Borrowing from the UK banking sector.

Internal/External

(b) Retained profits. *Internal/External*

(c) Borrowing from abroad. *Internal/External*

(d) Issuing new shares. *Internal/External*

The stock market operates as both a primary and a secondary market in capital. As a primary market, it is where public limited companies can raise finance by issuing new shares or debentures. As a secondary market, it enables the buying and selling of existing shares and debentures.

? *Q52.* Give two advantages and two disadvantages of using the stock market for raising new capital.

Advantages ....

....

Disadvantages ....

....

♟ *Q53.* Stock markets can lead to an efficient pricing of shares. This efficiency of pricing can be of three different levels.

(i) Weak form of efficiency.

(ii) Semi-strong form of efficiency.

(iii) Strong form of efficiency.

Match each of the above to the following definitions.

(a) Where share prices adjust quickly, fully and accurately to all available information, both public and that only available to insiders.

....

(b) Where share dealing prevents cyclical movements in shares.

....

(c) Where share prices adjust quickly, fully and accurately to publicly available information.

....

9.4 Land and rent

(Pages 280–3) Rent on land, like the price of other factor services, will be determined by the interaction of demand and supply.

Q54. What effect would the following have on the rent on arable farmland?

(a) A rise in the demand for wheat.   *rise/fall*

(b) A substantial rise in the demand for beef (but no fall in the demand for cereals).   *rise/fall*

(c) A major coastal land reclamation scheme is completed.   *rise/fall*

(d) The ending of the EU system of setting an artificially high price for grains.   *rise/fall*

(e) The introduction of a government scheme to 'set aside' 20 per cent of all farm land. Farmers would be prohibited from growing crops on such land. (What would happen to the rent on land remaining in use?)   *rise/fall*

Q55. In what sense has the supply of land an elasticity:

(a) equal to zero?   ....

(b) greater than zero?   ....

Q56. The following are possible explanations of why rents are higher in city centres than in rural areas:

  (i) Land in city centres is of more use to commerce.

 (ii) Transport costs are lower for people living in city centres.

(iii) The supply of agricultural land is elastic.

(iv) The marginal productivity of land is higher for shop and office use than for agricultural use.

 (v) City centres are more congested than out-of-town areas.

(vi) Costs of living (other than rents) are higher in towns than in the countryside.

Which are valid explanations?

A. (i), (ii) and (iv).

B. (i), (iv) and (v).

C. (iii), (iv) and (vi).

D. (i), (iii), (iv) and (vi).

E. (i), (ii), (iii), (iv), (v) and (vi).

Q57. If land is totally fixed in supply, then

A. all rent is economic rent.

B. all rent is transfer earnings.

C. the proportions of total rent that are economic rent and transfer earnings will depend entirely on demand.

D. the size of transfer earnings will depend on the *position* of the demand curve.

E. the amount of economic rent depends entirely on the position of the supply curve.

(Page 281) Not all land is rented. Much of it is bought and sold outright. Nevertheless the price of land will depend on its potential annual rental value (*R*) and on the market rate of interest (*i*). The formula for working out the equilibrium price of land is *R/i*.

Q58. How much would a piece of land be worth that produces £2000 in rent each year if the market rate of interest were:

(a) 10 per cent per annum? ....

(b) 20 per cent per annum? ....

B ## PROBLEMS, EXERCISES AND PROJECTS

Q59. Assume that you are offered some part-time evening work serving in a bar. You need this to supplement your meagre income/allowance. How many hours would you work if you were offered 50p per hour, £1, £2, £5, £20, £100, £1000? Is your behaviour rational? Do you have a backward-bending supply curve of labour and if so over what range? How would your behaviour differ if you were offered the job for 1 day, 1 week, 1 year, 40 years?

To what extent does your supply of labour per week depend on the number of weeks you *anticipate* being able to work at those rates? How would your behaviour differ if you were not allowed to save your wages or to invest them in shares, property, etc?

Try discussing this question with other students. Note down their answers and tabulate the information. Does a common pattern emerge?

Q60. Access the UK National Statistics website (www. statistics.gov.uk) and download the latest version of the

Annual Survey of Hours and Earnings (ASHE): Analyses by occupation. In Tables 2.1a, 2.5a and 2.9a (Average gross weekly earnings, hourly earnings and weekly hours) identify six occupations, each from a separate major group. Provide an explanation of the following:

(a) Differences in average gross hourly earnings between the six occupations for full-time males.

(b) Differences in average gross hourly earnings between the six occupations for full-time females.

(c) Differences in average weekly hours for males between the six occupations.

(d) Differences between female and male average gross hourly earnings between the six occupations.

(e) Compare your answers with other students to arrive at a set of conclusions about the differences in earnings between occupations and between women and men.

Q61. Table 9.2 shows how a firm's output of a good increases as it employs more workers. It is assumed that all

Table 9.2 Total physical product of labour (weekly)

Number of workers	Total physical product (units)	Marginal physical product (units)	Marginal revenue product (£)
1	500		
2	1100	600	...
3	1700	...	...
4	2200	...	...
5	2600	...	...
6	...	300	...
7	...	...	400
8	...	150	...

other factors of production are fixed. The firm operates under perfect competition in both the goods and labour markets. The market price of the good is £2.

(a) Fill in the missing figures in Table 9.2.
(b) How many workers will the firm employ (to maximise profits) if the wage rate is (i) £500 per week, (ii) £1100 per week, (iii) £1000 per week?

Q62. A profit-maximising firm has monopsony power in the labour market but its employees are not initially members of a trade union. Labour is the only variable factor and its supply schedule to the firm and the firm's total physical product of labour are shown in Table 9.3. The firm's product sells for £2.

(a) Fill in the columns for the total wage bill, MC_L, TRP_L and MRP_L. (Remember that the MC_L is the extra cost of employing *one* more worker not ten; similarly the MRP_L is the extra revenue earned from employing *one* more worker.)
(b) How many workers will the firm employ in order to maximise profits?

....

(c) What wage will the firm pay? ....

Table 9.3 A monopsonist's labour supply and output (hourly data)

Workers (number)	Wage rate (AC_L) (£)	Total wages (TC_L) (£)	MC_L (£)	TPP_L (units)	TRP_L (£)	MRP_L (£)
10	6	...		500	...	
20	7	...	...	600	...	...
30	8	...	...	680	...	...
40	9	...	...	750	...	...
50	10	...	...	810	...	...
60	11	...	...	860	...	...
70	12	...	...	900	...	...

(d) Assuming that the fixed costs of production are £600 per hour, what will be the firm's hourly profit?

....

(e) If the fixed costs increase to £1200 per hour, what will be the effect on the firm's output?

....

(f) Assume now that the price of the good rises to £4. How many workers will the firm now employ to maximise profits?

....

(g) Returning to the original price of £2, assume now that the workers form a trade union and that a situation of bilateral monopoly is the result. What is the maximum wage the trade union could negotiate without causing the firm to try to reduce the size of the labour force below that in (b) above?

....

(h) How much profit will the firm make, assuming that fixed costs were at the original £600 per hour level?

....

(i) What has happened to the level of profits and the wage bill compared with (c) and (d) above?

....

(j) If the union only succeeds in pushing the wage up to £11 per hour, what will happen to the level of employment?

....

(k) If, as a result of industrial action, the union succeeds in achieving a wage rate of £14 per hour with no reduction in the workforce below the level of that in (b) above, what will the firm's level of profit be now?

....

Q63. Collect data on office rental prices in different locations throughout your town/city (or nearest one). To collect your data, try visiting local estate agents which deal in business letting or look at advertisements in local papers.

(a) Explain the differences in rents.
(b) How would a profit-maximising firm decide whether to locate its offices in high-rent accommodation in a city centre or in low-rent accommodation in a less central location?

C — DISCUSSION TOPICS AND ESSAYS

Q64. What is the relationship between the mobility of labour and the proportion of wages that consists of economic rent? (See Web Case 9.1.)

Q65. To what extent will a perfect market economy lead to equality of wage rates (a) within any given labour market and (b) between labour markets?

Q66. If, unlike a perfectly competitive employer, a monopsonist has to pay a higher wage to attract more workers, why, other things being equal, will a monopsonist pay a lower wage than a perfectly competitive employer?

Q67. Why do the most pleasant jobs often pay the highest wages? Why does a Premiership football player get paid more than a National Health Service nurse?

Q68. Use the bilateral monopoly model to explain why a statutory minimum wage does not necessarily lead to a lower level of employment in a firm which would otherwise pay a lower wage rate.

Q69. Why is it impossible to identify an 'equilibrium wage' under bilateral monopoly?

Q70. Successive Acts of Parliament after 1979 reduced the power of the trade unions in the UK. Discuss the extent to which this has made workers in general worse or better off.

Q71. Why should employers decide to offer wages above the market-clearing rate?

Q72. Would a higher national average wage for men than women in a country be evidence of sexual discrimination in the labour market? Consider the impact on the labour market of equal pay legislation.

*Q73. Should a profit-maximising firm always go ahead with a project that has a present value greater than the cost of the investment?

*Q74. If a project's costs occur throughout the life of the project, how will this affect the appraisal of whether the project is profitable?

*Q75. A government wishes to encourage firms to invest more, and thus holds the rate of interest at an artificially low level. Discuss whether this will have the desired effect.

Q76. How can the concept of marginal revenue product be used to explain why rents are higher in city centres than in out-of-town areas?

Q77. Mary Giles, a farmer, earns £100 000 from her farm where she owns all the land. After paying the wage bills of the two workers employed on the farm, and the bills for seeds, fertiliser, equipment, maintenance, fuel, etc. she has £20 000 left over. How should this £20 000 be classified: as her wages, her profit, her rent, or a combination of all three?

Q78. To what extent can marginal productivity theory explain inequality of income?

Q79. Debate
A society where wages are based on productivity will be an unfair and unjust society.

D — ANSWERS

Q1. *the wage rate of plasterers*. We are referring to a perfect factor market: i.e. the market for plasterers, *not* the market for plaster or plastered walls. (These may or may not be perfect.)

Q2. *employers or workers*. Both demanders (employers) and suppliers (workers) are 'wage takers', under perfect competition.

Q3. *the supply curve of labour to*.

Q4. *the demand curve for labour from*.

Q5. (a) *supply; left*. Plasterers will be prepared to work fewer hours at any given wage rate.

    (b) *demand; right*. Plaster is a complementary good. Thus as its price comes down, more of it will be demanded *and* hence also more plasterers will be demanded to use it.

    (c) *demand; left*. As fewer houses are demanded, so fewer plasterers will be needed.

    (d) *supply; left*. This will push up plasterers' wages in other parts of the country and hence encourage plasterers to leave this part of the country to get jobs elsewhere.

    (e) *demand; left*. This will push up the price of new buildings and hence lead to a lower quantity of them being demanded and hence a lower demand for plasterers. Also: *supply; left*. Plasterers will be encouraged to move into other parts of the building trade.

    (f) *demand; left*. Employers will try to economise on the number of plasterers they employ. Many small builders may do the plastering themselves instead.

Q6. E. The demand for a factor of production is derived from the demand for the good it is used to produce: the more of the good that is demanded, the more of the factor that will be demanded to produce it.

Q7. *marginal disutility* (the opportunity cost of work).

Q8. *upward sloping*. A higher wage rate will be necessary to persuade a person to work extra hours.

Q9. (a) *substitution effect*. People substitute income for leisure (leisure has a higher opportunity cost).
(b) *income effect*. People can afford to take more leisure.

Q10. *negative*. Here higher wage rates will encourage people to work *less*.

Q11. *positive*. Here higher wage rates encourage people to work *more*.

Q12. *income effect*. If this becomes dominant above a certain wage, the number of hours offered by the worker will get *less* as the wage rate rises.

Q13. *True*. The firm is a 'wage taker': i.e. it has to pay the market wage, but at that wage can employ as many workers as it likes.

Q14. D. (ii) is not correct because a change in the wage rate is shown by a movement *along* the supply curve. (iii) is not correct because it determines the *demand* for labour not the supply.

Q15. (a) *geographical*.
(b) *both*.
(c) *occupational*.
(d) *geographical*.
(e) *both*.
(f) *occupational*.

Q16. *economic rent*.

Q17. A. He earns £160 more than he could in the next best paid job (as a lorry driver). Thus he earns £160 more than is necessary to prevent him giving up being a model and becoming a lorry driver instead.

Q18. C. The vertical distance below the supply curve shows the wage the marginal worker must receive to persuade him or her to move to this job: it shows the marginal worker's transfer earnings. When all these transfer earnings are added together we get the total area under the supply curve.

Q19. B. The area between the supply curve and the wage rate (W_e) shows the excess of actual wages over the minimum needed to persuade workers to stay in this job.

Q20. (a) (vii); (b) (iii); (c) (v); (d) (i); (e) (vi); (f) (iv); (g) (ii).

Q21. MPP_L by MR.

Q22. *fewer*.

Q23. *more*.

Q24. *True*. Under perfect competition the firm will always demand that quantity of workers where $MRP_L = W$. Thus, like the demand-for-labour curve, the MRP_L curve shows for each wage the number of workers the firm will employ.

Q25. (a) *shift*.
(b) *movement along* (given that the wage rate is measured on the vertical axis).
(c) *shift*.

Q26. (a) *True*. A fall in W will lead to higher employment and more output. This will drive P down. If the demand for the good is elastic, this fall in P will lead to a lot more being sold and hence a lot more people being employed.
(b) *False*. If labour can be *readily* substituted for other factors, then a reduction in W will lead to a large increase in labour used to replace these other factors.
(c) *True*. If wage rates fall, a lot more labour will be demanded if plenty of complementary factors can be obtained at little increase in their price.
(d) *False*. If wage rates fall and more labour is used, less substitute factors will be demanded and their price will fall. If their supply is *elastic*, a lot less will be supplied and therefore a lot more labour will be used instead.
(e) *False*. If wages are a *large* proportion of total costs and wage rates fall, total costs will fall significantly; therefore production will increase significantly, and so, therefore, will the demand for labour.
(f) *True*. Given sufficient time, firms can respond to a fall in wage rates by reorganising their production processes to make use of the now relatively cheap labour.

Q27. B. The perfect labour market will cause people with the *same* skills to be paid the same in the long run, but it will not cause people with a high level of skills to be paid the same as those with a low level of skills.

Q28. Market power; barriers to entry into various markets; imperfect knowledge.

Q29. (a) (iii); (b) (ii); (c) (i); (d) (v); (e) (iv).

Q30. *upward sloping*.

Q31. *supply curve of* labour. If the firm wants to employ extra workers, it will have to offer higher wages to attract the necessary labour into the market. Conversely, by cutting back on the number of workers it can force down the wage rate.

Q32. (a) See following table.

Wage rate (AC_L) (£)	50	60	70	80	90	100	110	120
Number of workers	1	2	3	4	5	6	7	8
Total wage bill (TC_L) (£)		100	240	220	640	900	1200	1540	1920
Marginal cost of labour (MC_L) (£)		140	180	220	260	300	340	380

(b) See Figure A9.1.
(c) *5 workers* (where $MRP_L = MC_L$).

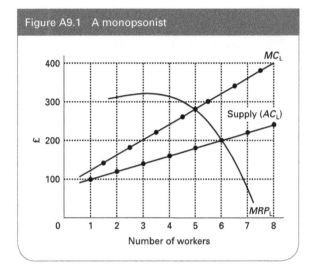

Figure A9.1   A monopsonist

(d) £180 (as given by the supply curve).

(e) 6 workers at £200 (where MRP_L = supply of labour).

Q33. *horizontal* (along to the point where it reaches the old supply curve: if it wants to employ beyond *that* point, it will have to pay *above* the negotiated rate in order to attract sufficient workers).

Q34. *equal to* (along to the point where it reaches the old supply curve: then it jumps up to the old MC_L curve).

Q35. (a) They are the same horizontal straight line at £200 up to 6 workers. Above that number of workers they are the same as the original curves.

(b) *6 workers* (where $MC_L = MRP_L$).

(c) Because it is no longer in the position to be able to drive down the wage rate by cutting down on the number of employees. The MC_L has now become the same as the AC_L (a horizontal straight line).

(d) £180. If this is the negotiated wage rate, it will now be the MC_L as well as the AC_L. Thus the firm will choose to employ 5 workers (the pre-union number) since this is where $MC_L = MRP_L$.

(e) There is none! The actual wage will depend on the outcome of the bargain, but that cannot be predicted with any accuracy. It depends on how successful each side is in the negotiations.

Q36. (a) *Decrease* the union's power. The union will have less scope to press its claim.

(b) *Decrease* the union's power. The firm can threaten to employ non-union labour; it can threaten redundancies (a greater threat when unemployment is high).

(c) *Increase* the union's power. The firm will be more able to pass on any wage increases in higher prices (given that it expects inflation to cause competitor firms to raise their prices).

(d) *Increase* the union's power. This will make it easier for the union to finance industrial action. It

will also create more solidarity among workers and make it more difficult for the firm to recruit non-union labour.

(e) *Decrease* the union's power. It will make the firm more resolved to resist high wage claims so that it can keep its prices competitive.

(f) *Increase* the union's power. The firm will be more anxious to avoid a dispute so as not to allow other firms to capture this market. The firm may be anxious to take on extra labour. Also if the firm's profits have increased, it may be in a better position to pay higher wages.

(g) *Increase* the union's power. The firm will not be able to use non-union labour or to divide the workforce by making separate (lower) offers to less militant groups of workers.

(h) *Increase* the union's power. The firm will find it easier to pass on wage increases to the consumer in higher prices.

Q37. *Discrimination* (by race, sex, age, class, etc., i.e. not based on differences in productivity), *imperfect knowledge of labour market conditions* (by workers and/or employers), *non-maximising behaviour*.

Q38. A.

Q39. Yes: all except (f).

Q40. E. If it is discriminating, it is preferring to employ white workers to black even when black workers are more able. It is thus sacrificing profit. (Note that D is wrong because the lower wages are the *result* of lower demand for black workers by the employers in the industry in question.)

Q41. C. These imperfections, although they affect wages, will not affect a firm's choosing to employ people up to the point where $MRP_L = MC_L$.

Q42. *False.* Wage rates are the price of labour *services.* When a firm pays a person a week's wages, the wages are for the person's labour. The firm has not purchased the actual person.

Q43. *True.* The principle is the same.

Q44. The diagram will be similar to Figure A9.1, but with the amount of capital measured on the horizontal axis. The amount of capital equipment the firm will hire is given by the intersection of the MC_K and MRP_K curves. The hire charge is given by the AC_K curve (i.e. the supply of capital curve).

Q45. *marginal revenue.*

Q46. Yes: (b), (d) and (e). These are all opportunity costs since they vary with the amount that the equipment is hired out.

Q47. E. The lower the price of complementary factors, the more of them will be demanded and hence the more capital equipment will be demanded. This will push up its market price.

*Q48. £100 (i.e. £100 invested at 10 per cent will be worth £110 after one year).

*Q49. Using the discounting formula gives:

(a) $PV = £5000/1.05 + £5000/1.05^2 + £5000/1.05^3$
    $= £4761.90 + £4535.15 + £4319.19$
    $= £13\ 616.24$

Therefore the investment is profitable at a 5 per cent discount rate.

(b) $PV = £5000/1.1 + £5000/1.1^2 + £5000/1.1^3$
    $= £4545.45 + £4132.23 + £3756.57$
    $= £12\ 434.25$

Therefore the investment is also profitable at a 10 per cent discount rate.

(c) $PV = £5000/1.2 + £5000/1.2^2 + £5000/1.2^3$
    $= £4166.67 + £3472.22 + £2893.52$
    $= £10\ 532.41$

Therefore the investment is not profitable at a 20 per cent discount rate.

Q50. (a) *Fall.* Caused by an increase in the supply of loanable funds.

(b) *Rise.* Caused by firms wanting to invest more and thus demanding more loans.

(c) *Rise.* Caused by a rise in investment demand as firms respond to the rise in consumer demand; also by a decrease in savings as a result of the increased spending.

(d) *Rise*: if the demand for machinery is inelastic. More will now be spent on machinery and thus more funds will be required. *Fall*: if the demand for machinery is elastic and thus less funds will be demanded.

Q51. (a) *External*; (b) *Internal*; (c) *External*; (d) *External*. 'Internal' means financed from within the firm.

Q52. *Advantages*: (a) It enables savings to be mobilised to generate output. (b) Firms listed on the stock exchange are subject to regulations. This is likely to stimulate investor confidence, making it easier for business to raise finance. (c) It makes mergers and takeovers easier, thereby increasing competition for corporate control.

Disadvantages: (a) The cost to a business of getting listed can be immense; (b) Directors' and senior managers' decisions will often be driven by how the market is likely to react, rather than by what they perceive to be in the business's best interests. (c) It can encourage short-termism.

Q53. (a) (iii); (b) (i); (c) (ii).

Q54. (a) *rise.* Being a derived demand, the *demand* for arable land would *rise* and hence the rent would *rise*.

(b) *rise.* The rise in the demand for beef would encourage farmers to move from cereals to beef production. This would cause a shortage of cereals and hence a rise in the price of cereals. This would cause the *demand* for arable land to *rise*. Also the switching of land to beef production would cause a *fall* in the *supply* of land for cereal production. Both effects will lead to a *rise* in rent on arable land.

(c) *fall.* The reclamation scheme would *increase* the *supply* of land.

(d) *fall.* The quantity of grain supplied would fall and hence the *demand* for arable land would *fall*.

(e) *rise.* The set-aside scheme would *reduce* the *supply* of arable land.

Q55. (a) *Land in total*: i.e. for all uses (assuming that land cannot be reclaimed from the sea or from deserts).

(b) *Land for specific uses*. The higher the rent or price of land for a specific use (e.g. building houses), the more land will be offered for sale for that purpose and thus transferred from other uses (e.g. agriculture).

Q56. A. All these cause a higher demand for land in city centres.

Q57. A. If the supply curve is totally inelastic, there are no transfer earnings: all rent is economic rent. The *size* of the economic rent will depend on the position of the demand curve relative to the supply curve.

Q58. (a) $£2000/0.1 = £20\ 000$.

(b) $£2000/0.2 = £10\ 000$.

Chapter 10

Inequality, Poverty and Policies to Redistribute Incomes

 A **REVIEW**

In this chapter we examine the distribution of income in practice and ask why incomes are unequally distributed. We start by looking at different ways of measuring inequality and poverty, and then examine their causes.

We then turn to look at what can be done. In particular, we look at the role of taxes and benefits as means of redistributing incomes.

10.1 Inequality and poverty

(Pages 288–9) There are a number of different ways of looking at the distribution of income and wealth. Each way highlights a different aspect of inequality.

Q1. Match the following measures of inequality (i)–(x) to the examples (a)–(j).

(i) Size distribution of income.
(ii) Functional distribution of income: broad factor categories.
(iii) Functional distribution of income: narrow factor categories.
(iv) Functional distribution of income: occupational.
(v) Distribution of income by recipient: class of person.
(vi) Distribution of income by recipient: geographical.
(vii) Size distribution of wealth.
(viii) Distribution of wealth by class of holder.
(ix) Absolute poverty.
(x) Relative poverty.

(a) The average income of manual workers compared with non-manual.

....

(b) The percentage of people with an income below what is considered to be a minimum acceptable level.

....

(c) The average level of income in the south-east compared with that in the north-west.

....

(d) Profits as a proportion of national income.

....

(e) The proportion of total savings held by people over retirement age.

....

(f) The ratio of the income of the richest 20 per cent to that of the poorest 40 per cent.

....

▤ Multiple choice   Written answer ◗ Delete wrong word ⊖ Diagram/table manipulation ⊗ Calculation   Matching/ordering

(g) The average income of doctors compared with that of nurses.

....

(h) The number of people without adequate food and shelter.

....

(i) The proportion of the nation's assets held by the richest 1 per cent of the population.

....

(j) The average income of one-parent families as a proportion of the national average income.

....

(Pages 289–92) The size distribution of income can be measured by the use of *Lorenz curves* and *Gini coefficients*.

⊖ **Q2.** Assume that the economy is grouped into five equal-sized groups of households according to income. The figures (imaginary) are shown in Table 10.1.

Draw two Lorenz curves corresponding to these two sets of figures on Figure 10.1.

Table 10.1 Percentage size distribution of income by quintile groups of households

| | Quintile groups | | | |
Lowest 20%	Next 20%	Middle 20%	Next 20%	Highest 20%
Income before taxes and benefits				
1.0	6.0	15.0	25.0	53.0
Income after taxes and benefits				
6.0	10.0	17.0	22.0	45.0

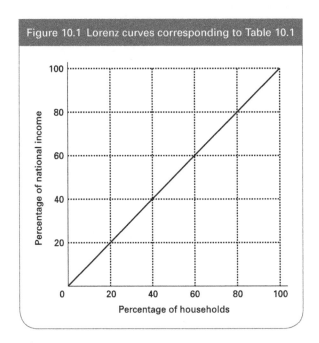

Figure 10.1 Lorenz curves corresponding to Table 10.1

(?) **Q3.** If the government pursues a policy of cutting taxes for the very rich but providing increased benefits for the very poor, and pays for this by increasing taxes on those with middle incomes, what will happen to the shape of the after-tax-and-benefits Lorenz curve?

....

....

The Gini coefficient is a way of measuring in a single figure the information contained in the Lorenz curve.

▤ **Q4.** In Figure 10.2 the Gini coefficient is the ratio of areas:

A. Y to Z

B. Z to $(X + Y + Z)$

C. Z to $(Y + Z)$

D. Y to $(Y + Z)$

E. Y to $(X + Y + Z)$

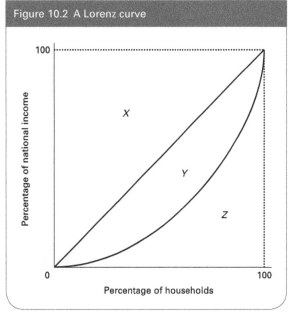

Figure 10.2 A Lorenz curve

◗ **Q5.** If the Gini coefficient rises, this means that income distribution has become more equal. *True/False*

(Pages 292–7) A common way of representing the degree of inequality in a country is to look at the functional distribution of income by source.

⊖ **Q6.** Table 10.2 shows the sources of UK household income by quintile groups. What do the figures suggest are the major causes of inequality in incomes?

....

....

Table 10.2 Sources of UK household income as a percentage of total household income: 2009

Gross household weekly incomes (quintiles)	Wages and salaries (1)	Income from self-employment (2)	Income from investments (3)	Pensions and annuities (4)	Social security benefits (5)	Other (6)	Total (7)
Lowest 20%	8	2	2	9	77	2	100
Next 20%	28	4	2	17	46	3	100
Middle 20%	55	6	2	11	21	2	100
Next 20%	74	7	2	8	8	1	100
Highest 20%	79	11	3	4	2	0	100
All households	67	9	3	7	13	1	100

Source: *Family Spending* (National Statistics, 2010). Crown copyright material is reproduced under the terms and conditions of the Open Government Licence (OGL).

There is marked inequality of income between females and males. The average gross hourly earnings of full-time adult female workers is only about 84 per cent of those of full-time adult male workers.

Q7. Although the average wage of women is less than that of men, the average wage of women is approximately the same as that for men *in the same occupation*.   *True/False*

Q8. The distribution of wealth in the UK is less equal than the distribution of income.   *True/False*

Q9. Give four different causes of the inequality of wealth.

1.   ....

2.   ....

3.   ....

4.   ....

Q10. The following are possible causes of inequality:
  (i) Differences in wealth.
 (ii) Differences in attitudes.
(iii) Differences in power.
(iv) Differences in household composition.
 (v) The proportion of the population over retirement age.
(vi) The proportion of the population below working age.

Which can help to explain inequality in wage rates?
A. (iii) only.
B. (ii) and (iii).
C. (i), (ii) and (iii).
D. (i), (ii), (iii) and (iv).
E. (i)–(vi).

Q11. Referring to the same list of possible causes of inequality as in Q10, which can help to explain inequality between households?

A. (iv) only.
B. (i) and (iv).
C. (iv), (v) and (vi).
D. (i), (iv), (v) and (vi).
E. (i)–(vi).

Q12. Figure 10.3 depicts a labour market for an industry.
(a) Identify the equilibrium wage and quantity of labour assuming that the labour market is perfectly competitive.

....

(b) What would be the effect on the wage rate paid and quantity of labour if a minimum wage of W_{min} was applied in this market?

....

Suppose now that the market is operated by a monopsony buyer of labour, such that S_L is now seen as the average cost of labour (AC_L).
(c) Add on the MC_L and identify the market wage and employment level.

....

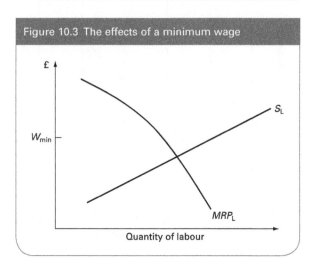

Figure 10.3 The effects of a minimum wage

(d) What would now be the effect on the wage and quantity of labour if a minimum wage of W_{min} was applied in the market?

....

(e) Comment on the effectiveness of using a minimum wage as a way of combating poverty.

....

10.2 Taxes, benefits and the redistribution of income

(Pages 299–303) We turn now to the role of the government in redistributing incomes more equally. The two means of redistributing income that we shall consider are taxes and benefits. We first examine taxation.

Principles of taxation

⬢ **Q13.** The following is a list of requirements that people have argued should be met by a good tax system:
  (i) Equitable between recipients of benefits (the benefits principle).
  (ii) Convenient to the government.
  (iii) Horizontally equitable.
  (iv) Minimal disincentive effects.
  (v) Non-distortionary.
  (vi) Vertically equitable.
  (vii) Difficult to avoid.
  (viii) Difficult to evade.
  (ix) Convenient to the taxpayer.
  (x) Cheap to collect.

Match the following descriptions to each of the above requirements.

(a) Taxes whose amount paid is the same for people in the same economic circumstances.

....

(b) Taxes whose rates can be quickly and simply adjusted.

....

(c) Taxes where the authorities can easily prevent illegal non-payment.

....

(d) Taxes with minimal administrative costs.

....

(e) Taxes where people pay in proportion to the amount of public services they use.

....

(f) Taxes that do not alter market signals in an undesirable direction.

....

(g) Taxes that people cannot escape paying by finding legal loopholes.

....

(h) Taxes that do not discourage initiative or effort.

....

(i) Taxes whose method of payment is easily understood and straightforward.

....

(j) Taxes whose rates depend on people's ability to pay.

....

(?) **Q14.** Why may there be a conflict between the principle of vertical equity and the benefits principle?

....

....

(?) **Q15.** How well do the following two taxes meet (i) the vertical equity principle and (ii) the benefits principle?
(a) Income tax:

  (i) ....
  ....

  (ii) ....
  ....

(b) A flat charge on all individuals, such as the community charge (poll tax), used in the UK in the early 1990s:

  (i) ....
  ....

  (ii) ....
  ....

(Pages 303–4) Taxes as a means of redistributing incomes
The degree of redistribution will depend on the degree of progressiveness of the tax.

Taxes can be categorised as *progressive, regressive, proportional* or *lump sum* (where lump-sum taxes are an extreme form of regressive tax).

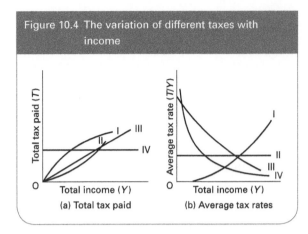

Figure 10.4 The variation of different taxes with income

(a) Total tax paid

(b) Average tax rates

Q16. Figure 10.4 shows how these four different categories of tax vary with income. Diagram (a) shows the total amount of tax paid. Diagram (b) shows the average tax rate. On each diagram which of the four curves correspond to which category of tax?

(a) Progressive   Curve........................

      Regressive   Curve........................

      Proportional   Curve........................

      Lump sum   Curve........................

(b) Progressive   Curve........................

      Regressive   Curve........................

      Proportional   Curve........................

      Lump sum   Curve........................

Q17. If Clyde's income tax goes up from £1000 to £1100 as a result of a rise in his income from £10 000 to £10 400:

(a) What was his original average rate of tax? ....

(b) What is his new average rate of tax?...........................

(c) What is his marginal rate of tax? ....

Q18. An income tax levied at a constant marginal rate with a tax-free allowance of £5000 will be a proportional tax. *True/False*

Q19. Indirect taxes levied at the same rate on all goods would be:
A. progressive.
B. regressive.
C. proportional.
D. lump sum.
E. progressive at low levels of national income and regressive at high levels.

(Pages 304–6) There are various problems in using taxes to redistribute incomes. For example, there are difficulties in helping the very poor.

Q20. Since taxes *take away* incomes, changing taxes alone cannot benefit the poor. To give additional help to the poor will require additional *benefits*. *True/False*

Q21. Which of the following will provide most help to the very poorest people in society? (In each case assume the total reduction in tax revenue for the government is the same.)
A. Cutting the rate of income tax.
B. Increasing tax thresholds on income tax.
C. Reducing excise duties.
D. Reducing the main rate for national insurance contributions.
E. Reducing VAT on basic goods.

Q22. Which of the following will provide most help to those on low incomes but who nevertheless are still liable to income tax? (As before, in each case assume the total reduction in tax revenue for the government is the same.)
A. Cutting the rate of income tax.
B. Increasing tax thresholds on income tax.
C. Reducing excise duties.
D. Reducing the main rate for national insurance contributions.
E. Reducing VAT on basic goods.

The effectiveness of a rise in income tax in redistributing incomes away from high-paid workers will depend on the elasticity of supply of labour.

Q23. The more elastic the supply of high-paid workers, the more effective will be an income tax in redistributing income away from this group. *True/False*

(Pages 306–8) Taxes and incentives
Perhaps the biggest drawback of using taxes to redistribute incomes is that they create *disincentives*.

Q24. The effects of imposing an income tax can be divided into an *income effect* and a *substitution effect*. Which of these two effects will be to:
(a) increase the amount people work?
           Income effect/Substitution effect
(b) decrease the amount people work?
           Income effect/Substitution effect
Whether people thus work more or less after a rise in income tax will depend on which of the two effects is the larger.

Q25. Which of the two effects of a rise in the rates of income tax is likely to be the larger in each of the following cases?

(a) For people with large long-term commitments (e.g. mortgages). *Income effect/Substitution effect*

(b) For second income earners in a family where the second income is not relied upon for 'essential' consumption. *Income effect/Substitution effect*

(c) For those on very high incomes.
Income effect/Substitution effect

(d) For people with large families.
Income effect/Substitution effect

(e) For those just above the tax threshold.
Income effect/Substitution effect

Q26. The Laffer curve shows that:

A. At very high levels of income tax, the government can expect to earn very high levels of revenue.

B. The government's tax revenue will be highest when the marginal rate of income tax is 50 per cent.

C. A rise in income tax beyond a certain level will reduce the government's tax revenue.

D. The government's tax revenue is at a maximum when the substitution effect begins to outweigh the income effect.

E. Tax revenues will be at a maximum when the marginal rate of tax is equal to the average rate.

Q27. Raising the higher rate(s) of income tax (but leaving the basic rate unchanged) will have a relatively small income effect and a relatively large substitution effect.
True/False

Q28. For all those above the old tax threshold, reducing tax allowances will have no disincentive effect at all.
True/False

The relationship between income taxes and incentives can be examined in the context of tax *cuts* as well as that of tax increases. If income tax rates are cut, people will choose to work *more* if the income effect **Q29.** *outweighs/ is outweighed by* the substitution effect. For people already above the tax threshold, this will only be likely if tax cuts come in the form of **Q30.** *cuts in the basic rate of income tax/increases in tax allowances.*

(Pages 308–10) State benefits
Some benefits are *means tested* and some are *universal.*

Q31. Which of the following are universal benefits and which are means-tested benefits?

(a) State pensions *universal/means tested*
(b) Child benefit *universal/means tested*
(c) Contribution-based jobseeker's allowance
universal/means tested
(d) Income-based jobseeker's allowance
universal/means tested
(e) Working tax credit *universal/means tested*
(f) Housing benefit *universal/means tested*
(g) Income support *universal/means tested*
(see: http://www.dwp.gov.uk)

Q32. Four of the following are possible problems with means-tested benefits. Which one is *not* a problem?

A. They tend to have a lower take-up rate than universal benefits.

B. They cost the taxpayer more to provide a given amount of help to the poor than do universal benefits.

C. The application procedure may deter some potential claimants.

D. If based solely on income, they may ignore the special needs of certain people.

E. They may act as a disincentive to getting a job.

(Pages 310–4) When means-tested benefits are combined with a progressive tax system there can be a serious problem with disincentives. A situation known as the 'poverty trap' can arise.

Q33. What is meant by the *poverty trap*?

....

....

....

Q34. If the marginal tax rate is 25 per cent and if for each extra £10 of take-home pay a person loses benefits of £6, what is the marginal tax-plus-lost-benefit rate?

....

One simple combined system of taxes and benefits which avoids the poverty trap is that of the *negative income tax*.

Q35. If everyone were entitled to a tax credit of £1000 per annum (a 'negative income tax') paid by the tax authorities, and if the tax rate were 20 per cent, what would your net tax liability be if your income were:

(a) zero? ....

(b) £1000? ....

(c) £5000? ....

(d) £10 000? ....

(e) What is the marginal rate of tax-plus-lost-benefit?

....

Q36. What is the major drawback of a tax credit (negative income tax) system?

....

....

PROBLEMS, EXERCISES AND PROJECTS

Q37. Refer to the latest edition of *Social Trends* (published annually by National Statistics). This can be downloaded from the National Statistics website: http://www.statistics.gov.uk. Find the chapter on income and wealth.

(a) Provide a summary of income distribution in the UK as described in this chapter.

(b) To what extent does the tax and benefit system redistribute incomes more equally?

(c) How has income distribution and redistribution changed between the years illustrated in the various tables? (You could also look at earlier editions of *Social Trends* for a more complete analysis, but be careful that the methods of calculating the statistics have not changed.)

(d) Identify any measures of inequality for which you think figures ought to be given if a more comprehensive analysis is to be provided.

Another, more complete, source is *Family Spending*, again published by National Statistics. Like *Social Trends*, it can be downloaded from the National Statistics website.

Q38. In groups of two or three, write a report on the changing pattern of poverty in the UK since 1980. This report should include the use of five different indicators of poverty, a clear description of the pattern and an explanation of why changes in the pattern may have occurred. Conduct your own search for sources of information. To help in this, try using a search engine, such as http://www.google.co.uk. You should also find the Joseph Rowntree Foundation site useful at http://www.jrf.org.uk.

Q39. To which of the four categories in Q16 do each of the following types of tax belong?

(a) Income £10 000, tax £1000; income £20 000, tax £2000

....

(b) Income £10 000, tax £5000; income £20 000, tax £9000

....

(c) Income £10 000, tax £2000; income £20 000, tax £5000

....

(d) Income £10 000, tax £0; income £20 000, tax £400

....

(e) Income £10 000, tax £400; income £20 000, tax £400

....

(f) Income £10 000, tax £400; income £20 000, tax £4000

....

(g) Income £10 000, tax £8000; income £20 000, tax £12 000

....

Q40. Figure 10.5 shows the effect of imposing an indirect tax on a good produced under conditions of perfect competition. It can be used to illustrate the resource costs of the tax. The tax has the effect of raising the equilibrium price from P_1 to P_2 and reducing the equilibrium quantity from Q_1 to Q_2.

(a) Which area(s) represent(s) the original level of consumer surplus?

....

(b) Which area(s) represent(s) the loss in consumer surplus after the imposition of the tax?

....

(c) Which area(s) represent(s) the original level of profits for the producers?

....

(d) Which area(s) represent(s) the loss in profits after the imposition of the tax?

....

(e) Which area(s) represent(s) the total loss to consumers and producers after the imposition of the tax?

....

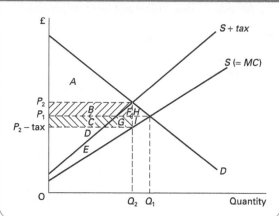

Figure 10.5 The effect of imposing an indirect tax on a good

(f) Which area(s) represent(s) the gain in tax revenue to the government after the imposition of the tax?

....

(g) Which area(s), therefore, represent(s) the net loss to society as a whole after the imposition of the tax?

....

(h) Name two weaknesses in using this type of analysis to criticise the imposition of taxes.

1. ....

2. ....

*Q41. Figure 10.6 uses indifference analysis to show the effect of a tax cut on a person's choice between income and leisure. Assume that the person has 14 hours per day to distribute between work and leisure.

(a) Which of the two budget lines show the person's available choices *after* the tax cut? B_1/B_2

(b) How many hours will the person work before the tax cut?

....

(c) How many hours will the person work after the tax cut?

....

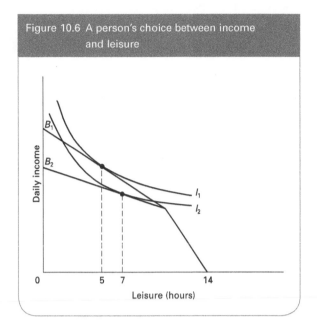

Figure 10.6 A person's choice between income and leisure

(d) What is the size of the income effect? ....

(e) What is the size of the substitution effect? ....

(f) Draw new indifference curves to illustrate the situation where the income effect outweighs the substitution effect.

(g) How would you illustrate an increase in tax allowances on this type of diagram?

....

 ## DISCUSSION TOPICS AND ESSAYS

Q42. What limitations are there in using Gini coefficients to compare the degree of inequality in different countries?

Q43. How well do the following taxes meet the requirements of a good tax system: (a) highly progressive income taxes; (b) VAT at a single rate on all goods and services; (c) excise duty on cigarettes?

Q44. What are the (UK) working tax credit and the child tax credit? (Details can be found on the Treasury website at www.hm-treasury.gov.uk.) Why might these be a better means of reducing poverty than a universal welfare benefit, such as child benefit before 2012?

Q45. 'The economic costs of an indirect tax will exceed the benefits.' Discuss with reference to its effect on producer and consumer surplus.

Q46. What effects will (a) cuts in basic rates of income tax and (b) increases in income tax allowances have on the labour supply of (i) high income earners, (ii) low income earners and (iii) those currently choosing not to work?

Q47. Discuss whether it is possible to reduce income inequality without creating disincentives to effort.

Q48. What is meant by the *poverty trap*? Will the targeting of benefits to those in greatest need necessarily increase the problem of the poverty trap?

Q49. Debate
Government intervention through tax-and-spend policies is the only solution to the problem of income inequality.

ANSWERS

Q1. (a) (iii), (b) (x), (c) (vi), (d) (ii), (e) (viii), (f) (i), (g) (iv), (h) (ix), (i) (vii), (j) (v).

Q2. See Figure A10.1.

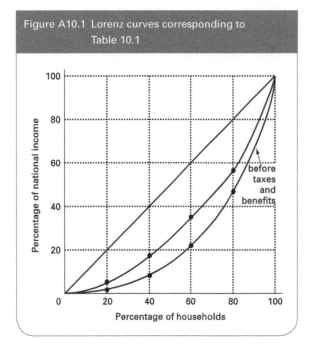

Figure A10.1 Lorenz curves corresponding to Table 10.1

before taxes and benefits

Q3. Moving up the curve, the new curve would initially be above the original one. It would then cross the original one and thereafter be below it up to the top right-hand corner.

Q4. D.

Q5. *False.* In Figure 10.2, as income distribution becomes more equal, the Lorenz curve will move closer to the 45° line and thus area Y will get smaller and hence the Gini coefficient will *fall* not rise.

Q6. (i) Differences in wages and salaries between different occupations, (ii) differences between incomes from self-employment and employment and (iii) differences between incomes from employment and self-employment on the one hand and social security benefits on the other.

Q7. *False.* Women are paid less even in the same occupation. The causes include: men promoted to more senior positions; the average age of full-time female workers is lower; women do less overtime; discrimination.

Q8. *True.* The wealthiest 10 per cent owned 53 per cent of UK wealth in 2003.

Q9. 1. *Inheritance*: this allows income inequality to be perpetuated and deepened from one generation to another.

2. *Income inequality*: people with higher incomes can save more.

3. *Different propensities to save*: people who save more will build up a bigger stock of wealth.

4. *Entrepreneurial and investment talent/luck*: some people are more successful than others in investing their wealth and making it grow.

Q10. B (possibly C). Wage rates will reflect workers' and employers' attitudes and their power in the labour market. The distribution of wealth will affect wages to the extent that it affects the distribution of economic power.

Q11. E. Household income is affected by wage rates (i.e. (ii) and (iii)), by income from assets (i.e. (i)) and by household composition (i.e. (iv), (v) and (vi)).

Q12. *(a)* W_{pc} and L_{pc} in Figure A10.2.

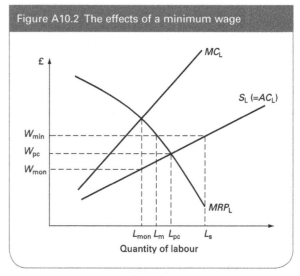

Figure A10.2 The effects of a minimum wage

(b) With a minimum wage of W_{min}, the wage paid rises to W_{min}, but the quantity of labour falls to L_m. However, there is now increased unemployment, partly because less labour is employed and partly because more workers offer themselves for work at the higher wage rate. Unemployment is the distance $L_s - L_m$.

(c) MC_L is marked in Figure A10.2; the firm sets the wage at W_{mon} and the quantity of labour is L_{mon}. Employment is thus lower than under perfect competition.

(d) A minimum wage of W_{min} again takes the market to L_m – with a wage of W_{min}, of course. However, in this instance the quantity of labour has increased from the level that pertained without the minimum wage, although there is still some unemployment. If the minimum wage had been set at W_{pc}, the market would have been forced to the perfectly competitive position.

(e) The effect of a minimum wage on overall poverty is ambiguous. Those workers who now receive the minimum wage having previously been paid less will be better off. However, those who are not in work are not clearly better off.

Q13. (a) (iii), (b) (ii), (c) (viii), (d) (x), (e) (i), (f) (v), (g) (vii), (h) (iv), (i) (ix), (j) (vi).

Q14. Because those who use a service the most (e.g. the sick using the health service) may be the least able to pay.

Q15. *(a)* (i) *relatively well*, if the rate of tax increases as people's incomes increase. Note, however, that income tax in the UK is not very progressive. Most people on the basic rate of income tax pay a marginal rate of 32 per cent (i.e. 22 per cent income tax and 10 per cent national insurance). People on very high incomes pay a marginal rate of 40 per cent (i.e. 40 per cent income tax and 0 per cent national insurance). Thus the difference in marginal rate between the moderately poor and the very rich is only 8 per cent.

   (ii) *badly*, given that poor people (who pay less income taxes) will be in receipt of larger amounts of state benefit.

  (b) (i) *very badly*, given that all except the very poor paid exactly the same amount per head within any given local authority area.

   (ii) *well*, for services which were consumed relatively equally (e.g. refuse services and street lighting), but *moderately badly* for services which were consumed unequally (e.g. education).

Q16. *(a)* Progressive – curve II; regressive – curve I; proportional – curve III; lump sum – curve IV.

  (b) Progressive – curve I; regressive – curve III; proportional – curve II; lump sum – curve IV.

Q17. *(a)* *10 per cent* (i.e. (£1000/£10 000) × 100)

  (b) *10.58 per cent* (i.e. (£1100/£10 400) × 100)

  (c) *25 per cent* (i.e. $\Delta T/\Delta Y$ = (£100/£400) × 100)

Q18. *False.* It will be progressive. Although the marginal rate is constant, the average rate will rise as income rises because the tax-free allowance will account for a smaller and smaller proportion of total income.

Q19. B. The rich tend to save proportionately more than the poor and hence spend proportionately less. This means that they would pay proportionately less of this type of tax.

Q20. *False.* Provided the poor pay some taxes, *cutting* taxes for the poor *will* provide additional help. The problem comes for the very poor, who do not pay income taxes in the first place.

Q21. E. This will target the tax cuts to the poorest people, who spend a large portion of their meagre incomes on basic goods. (Note, in the case of B, that increasing tax thresholds will not help the very poor, who are too poor to pay income tax in the first place.)

Q22. B. Everyone paying income tax will have the same *absolute* reduction in taxes. This will represent a larger *percentage* the lower a person's income (provided that they were paying at least as much in the first place as the size of the total tax cut).

Q23. *False.* In this case the main tax burden falls on employers: a significantly higher (pre-tax) wage will have to be offered in order to continue attacting enough workers. The employers' share of the tax is thus high.

Q24. *(a)* *Income effect.* Higher taxes reduce people's disposable income. They thus feel it necessary to work more or harder in order to try to recoup some of this lost income.

  (b) *Substitution effect.* As an hour's work now brings in less income (and hence enables less consumption), people are likely to substitute leisure for income.

Q25. *(a)* *Income effect.* People will feel a greater need to maintain their level of disposable income and will thus work harder.

  (b) *Substitution effect.* The second income earner will now be more inclined to stay at home or at least to work fewer hours.

  (c) *Income effect.* A rise in income tax will cause them to have a *substantial* fall in income and may thus cause them to work harder to compensate.

  (d) *Income effect.* These people will find it difficult to sustain a fall in income and will thus probably work harder.

  (e) *Substitution effect.* For these people the rise in income tax will have virtually *no* effect on disposable income. The income effect will be negligible. Each *additional* pound earned, however, will be at the higher tax rate and thus the disincentive effect will still exist. Thus the substitution effect is likely to outweigh the income effect even though the marginal utility of money is greater for poor people.

Q26. C. Note that B is wrong because that there is no reason why the curve should peak at a 50 per cent marginal (or average) tax rate. D is wrong because the point where the substitution effect begins to outweigh the income effect will be to the *left* of the peak of the curve; even when the substitution effect is bigger than the income effect and thus people work fewer hours, they could still pay more tax if the percentage reduction in hours is less than the percentage rise in tax.

Q27. *True.* The total income of higher tax payers will only be moderately affected if the basic rate is unchanged and thus the income effect is relatively small (except for extremely well-paid people). The substitution effect, however, could be quite large given that the rich tend to have a lower marginal utility of income than the poor.

Q28. *True.* The rate of tax has not changed and thus there is no substitution effect. There is an income effect, however. People will suddenly have been made poorer and are thus likely to work harder to compensate for the lost income. Thus reducing tax allowances will act as an incentive.

Q29. *is outweighed by.* The income effect (people can now afford to take more leisure) will cause people to work less. The substitution effect (the opportunity cost of leisure has now increased) will cause people to work more.

Q30. *cuts in the basic rate of income tax.* With increases in tax thresholds, there will be *no* substitution effect because the marginal rate of tax has not changed. There will only be an income effect. Thus with increases in tax allowances, people will be encouraged to work less.

Q31. (a), and (c) are *universal.* (d), (e), (f) and (g) are *means tested.* Child benefit (b) was universal until 2012, after which families with at least one higher-rate taxpayer were no longer eligible.

Q32. B. *Universal* benefits cost more to provide a given amount of help to the poor. The reason is that some will go to those who are not poor. For example, child benefit was an expensive way of relieving child poverty because rich parents as well as poor were entitled to child benefit until 2012.

Q33. Where poor people are discouraged from working or getting a better job because any extra income they earn will be largely or wholly taken away in taxes and lost benefits.

Q34. *70 per cent* (i.e. 25% + (60% × 75%)). In other words, if a person earned an extra £10, £2.50 would be taken off as taxes. Take-home pay would thus be £7.50, of which 6/10 (i.e. £4.50) would go in lost benefits, leaving a mere £3. Thus 70 per cent of the increase in pay has been lost.

Q35. *(a)* *–£1000.* The tax authorities would *pay you* a cash benefit (a negative tax) of £1000.

  (b) *–£800.* The tax authorities would *pay you* £1000 benefit minus £200 tax.

  (c) *zero.* You would be liable to a tax of £1000 which exactly offsets the benefit.

  (d) *+£1000.* You would be liable to a net tax of £2000 minus the £1000 benefit.

  (e) *20 per cent.* There is *no* lost benefit. Everyone is entitled to the benefit, which is offset against their tax liability. Thus the marginal tax-plus-lost-benefit rate is the same as the marginal tax rate.

Q36. If the marginal rate of tax is to be kept reasonably low (so as to avoid creating a disincentive to work), the benefit (i.e. the negative element) will have to be small, which reduces its effectiveness in providing help to the poor. If, on the contrary, the benefit were large but still only declined slowly (a low marginal rate of tax), the tax would only start to yield revenues from people with very high incomes and thus the tax would yield very little, if any, net revenue for the government!

Chapter 11

Markets, Efficiency and the Public Interest

A   REVIEW

In this chapter we examine the question of *social efficiency* in the allocation of resources. It is the failure of markets to achieve social efficiency that provides much of the argument for government intervention in the economy. But likewise it is the failure of governments to achieve social efficiency in the allocation of resources that provides much of the argument for *laissez-faire*.

We start by seeing how, under certain conditions, a perfect market economy will lead to social efficiency. We then see how in the real world the market will fail to do so and we examine the causes and types of market failure. We see how a government can intervene to correct these failures and then look at *cost–benefit analysis* – a means of establishing whether a particular public project is desirable or not. We turn finally to the other side of the argument and consider the case against government intervention.

11.1 Efficiency under perfect competition
(Pages 318–9) Simple analysis: MB = MC
A socially efficient economy is defined as one that is *Pareto optimal* (named after Vilfredo Pareto (1848–1923)).

Q1. A situation of Pareto optimality is one where:
A. resources are allocated in the fairest possible way.
B. people can be made better off with no one being made worse off.
C. losses to the rich will be more than offset by gains to the poor.
D. there is no X inefficiency.
E. it is not possible to make anyone better off without making at least one other person worse off.

Q2. In any economy there will be many different possible Pareto-optimal situations, some of which will involve greater equality than others. *True/False*

Q3. Bill and Ben both like apples and currently have 8 apples each in their respective fruit bowls. This is shown in Figure 11.1 as point *X*. Various other alternative quantities of apples are also shown (points *A–H*).

(a) Which points would represent a Pareto improvement compared with point *X*?

....

(b) Is point *X* a Pareto improvement on any other points? If so, which?

....

(c) With the information given, can we say anything about the relative efficiency of point *B* compared with point *X*?

....

 Multiple choice   Written answer   Delete wrong word   Diagram/table manipulation   Calculation   Matching/ordering

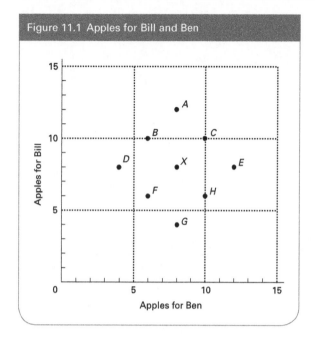

Figure 11.1 Apples for Bill and Ben

(Pages 318–9) Will a free-market economy lead to Pareto optimality, to social efficiency? The answer is that it will only do so under very strict conditions.

(?) Q4. What two conditions must be fulfilled for the free market to be socially efficient?

1. ....

2. ....

Under perfect competition we assume that individuals behave *rationally*. Rational behaviour involves doing more of any activity whose **Q5.** *total cost/marginal cost/average cost* is **Q6.** *greater than/less than* its **Q7.** *total benefit/marginal benefit/average benefit*. Such behaviour will lead to *private efficiency*.

(Pages 319–22) In the absence of externalities and with perfect competition in all markets, the achievement of private efficiency in each individual market will lead to a *general equilibrium* throughout the whole economy which is *socially efficient*: i.e. Pareto optimal.

Q8. In a perfect market, social efficiency in any activity will be maximised where the activity's:

A. marginal benefit equals marginal cost.
B. total benefit equals total cost.
C. marginal social benefit exceeds marginal social cost.
D. marginal social benefit equals marginal social cost.
E. total social benefit exceeds total social cost.

In a perfectly competitive goods market, the consumer will achieve private efficiency where **Q9.** *marginal utility/marginal cost/marginal revenue* equals the price of the good. The producer will achieve private efficiency where the price of the

good equals the firm's **Q10.** *marginal revenue/marginal revenue product/marginal cost*.

(?) Q11. Describe the process whereby social efficiency would be restored in all markets if the marginal social benefit of good X were to rise, causing initial disequilibrium. (Assume perfect competition and an absence of externalities.)

(a) Effects on the market for good X ....

....

(b) Effects on the market for factors used in producing good X ....

....

(c) Effects on other goods markets ....

....

(d) Effects on other factor markets...................................

....

(e) The final equilibrium state ....

....

*(Pages 322–5) Intermediate analysis: MB ratios equal MC ratios

(?) *Q12. If for two goods X and Y, MU_X/MU_Y (MRS) were greater than P_X/P_Y, what would a rational consumer do?

....

(?) *Q13. A firm produces two goods X and Y. If it finds that MC_X/MC_Y (MRT) is greater than P_X/P_Y what should it do to maximise profits?

....

(?) *Q14. If MU_X/MU_Y for person A exceeded MU_X/MU_Y for person B (i.e. $MRS_A > MRS_B$):
(a) How could a Pareto improvement be achieved?

....

(b) What would the Pareto optimum be?

....

*Q15. Assuming no externalities, social efficiency will be achieved where $MRS = MRT$ for all goods.   *True/False*

*Q16. Figure 11.2 shows social indifference curves (I_1 to I_4) and a social transformation curve (production

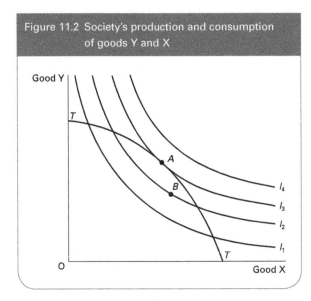

Figure 11.2 Society's production and consumption of goods Y and X

possibility curve) (*TT*) between two goods X and Y. It is assumed that there are no externalities.

(a) What does the slope of the social indifference curves give? ....

(b) What does the slope of the production possibility curve give? ....

(c) Draw a line showing the *equilibrium* price ratio P_X/P_Y

....

(d) Why are all points other than point *A* socially inefficient?

....

....

(e) If production were at point *B*, how could a Pareto improvement be achieved?

....

....

Q17. General equilibrium is where all the millions of markets throughout the economy are in a simultaneous state of equilibrium. *True/False*

11.2 The case for government intervention

(Page 326) Real-world markets will fail to achieve social efficiency. What is more, efficiency is not the only economic objective, and real-world markets may fail to achieve these other objectives too.

(?) Q18. Give two other economic objectives.

1. ....

2. ....

There are several reasons why real-world markets will fail to achieve a socially efficient allocation of resources.

Q19. The following are problems that cause market failings:
  (i)   Externalities.
  (ii)   Monopoly/oligopoly power.
  (iii) Monopsony/oligopsony power.
  (iv)   Ignorance and uncertainty.
  (v)   Public goods and services.
  (vi)   Persistent disequilibria.
  (vii) Dependants.
  (viii) Merit goods.

Match each of the above problems to the following examples of failures of the free market. In each case assume that everything has to be provided by private enterprise: that there is no government provision or intervention whatsoever. Note that there may be more than one example of each problem. Also each case may be an example of more than one market problem.

(a) There is an inadequate provision of street lighting because it is impossible for companies to charge all people benefiting from it.

....

(b) Advertising allows firms to sell people goods that they do not really want.

....

(c) A firm tips toxic waste into a river because it can do so at no cost to itself.

....

(d) Firms pay workers less than their marginal revenue product.

....

(e) Prices take a time to adjust to changes in consumer demand.

....

(f) People may not know what is in their best interests and thus may underconsume certain goods or services (such as education).

....

(g) Firms' marginal revenue is not equal to the price of the good and thus they do not equate *MC* and price.

....

(h) Firms provide an inadequate amount of training because they are afraid that other firms will simply come along and 'poach' the labour they have trained.

....

(i) In families one person may do the shopping for everyone and may buy things that other family members do not like.

....

(j) Farmers cannot predict the weather.

....

(Pages 326–7) As we saw in the previous section, externalities are spillover costs or benefits.

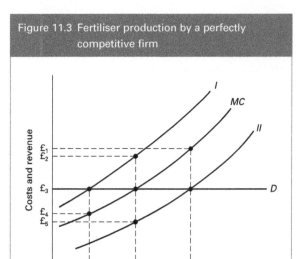

Figure 11.3 Fertiliser production by a perfectly competitive firm

Q20. Figure 11.3 shows the production of fertiliser by a perfectly competitive profit-maximising firm. Production of the good leads to pollution of the environment, however. This pollution is an external cost to the firm.

(a) Which of the two curves, *I* or *II*, represents the marginal social cost curve?   *I/II*

(b) What output will the firm produce if it takes no account of the pollution?

....

(c) What is the level of the marginal external cost at this output?

....

(d) What is the socially efficient level of output?

....

Q21. Give two examples of each of the following:

(a) External benefits of production...................................

(b) External benefits of consumption ....

(c) External costs of consumption....................................

Q22. In the absence of externalities, a monopoly will charge a price above the level where *MSC = MSB* and produce an output below the level where *MSC = MSB*.
True/False

(Pages 327–8) There is a category of goods that the free market, whether perfect or imperfect, will underproduce or fail to produce at all. These are *public goods*.

Q23. Which two of the following features distinguish public goods from other types of good?

(i) Large external benefits relative to private benefits.

(ii) Large external costs relative to private costs.

(iii) A price elasticity of demand only slightly greater than zero.

(iv) The impossibility of excluding free riders.

(v) Ignorance by consumers of the benefits of the good.

(vi) Goods where the government feels it knows better than consumers what people ought to consume.

A. (i) and (iv).

B. (ii) and (iii).

C. (v) and (vi).

D. (ii) and (v).

E. (iv) and (v).

Q24. Which of the following are examples of public goods (or services)? (Note that we are not merely referring to goods or services that just happen to be provided by the public sector.)

(a) Museums	Yes/No
(b) Roads in town	Yes/No
(c) Motorways	Yes/No
(d) National defence	Yes/No
(e) Health care	Yes/No
(f) Community policing	Yes/No
(g) Street drains	Yes/No
(h) Secondary education	Yes/No

Q25. The equilibrium price for a pure public good is zero.   *True/False*

(Pages 328–30) Some resources are not privately owned: they are available free of charge to anyone. Examples include fishing grounds and common land. These common resources are likely to be **Q26.** *overused/underused*. This is because, despite being publicly available, there is **Q27.** *rivalry/no rivalry* in their use. Also their use involves **Q28.** *positive externalities/negative externalities/no externalities*.

Q29. Figure 11.4 shows the number of privately owned cattle grazing an area of common land. There are many cattle owners. As more cattle graze the land, so grass intake per cow declines, and so milk yields fall. This is shown by a falling *MRP* and *ARP* (it is assumed that the price of milk is constant). These costs of purchasing a cow, milking it and storing, processing and selling the milk are assumed to be constant and are shown by the horizontal *AC* and *MC* curves. As long as the revenue from an additional cow exceeds the costs, it will be worth owners purchasing more cows and grazing them on the land.

Assuming owners are concerned to maximise profits:

(a) How many cows will be put to graze the land?...........

(b) What will be the *MRP* at this output?
Positive/Negative

(c) How many cows will maximise the collective profits of all owners?

....

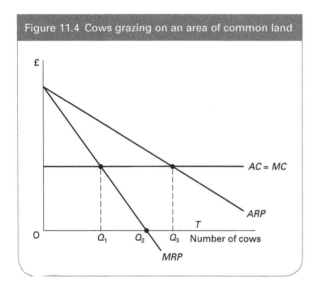

Figure 11.4 Cows grazing on an area of common land

(d) Explain whether there will be more or less total expenditure on fertilising and maintaining the land for grazing than if it had been privately owned.

....

(Pages 330–2) A monopoly will be socially inefficient because it will result in *deadweight welfare loss*.

Q30. Which one of the following is a definition of *deadweight welfare loss* under monopoly?
A. The loss in output compared with perfect competition.
B. The increase in price compared with perfect competition.
C. The loss of total consumer surplus compared with perfect competition.
D. The increase in total profit compared with perfect competition.
E. The loss of total consumer-plus-producer surplus compared with perfect competition.

(Pages 332–3)

Q31. If the provision of health care were left to the free market, there would be a number of reasons why the market would fail to provide an optimum allocation of health-care resources. Give an example from health care of each of the following categories of market failure:
(a) Externalities

....

(b) Market power

....

(c) Ignorance

....

(d) Uncertainty about the future

....

(e) Dependants

....

(f) Inequality

....

(g) Poor economic decision making by people on their own behalf

....

11.3 Forms of government intervention

(Pages 335–6) If there were a market distortion in just one part of the economy and elsewhere there were perfect competition and an absence of externalities, then the *first-best* solution to the distortion would be possible.

Q32. Define the first-best solution.

....

....

In the real world, where there are countless distortions, the first-best solution of correcting all these distortions simultaneously will be totally impossible. In this case the answer to a specific distortion is to adopt the *second-best* solution.

Q33. Which of the following represents the second-best solution to a market distortion?
A. Concentrating on making *MSB* equal *MSC* solely in the industry in question.
B. Correcting all the distortions in other parts of the economy that can be *identified*.
C. Concentrating on questions of equity and ignoring questions of efficiency.
D. Minimising the distortion relative to other distortions in the economy.
E. Tackling distortions one at a time.

(Pages 336–8) The use of taxes and subsidies
A policy instrument particularly favoured by many economists is that of taxes and subsidies.

Q34. In the first-best world, where there are no other market distortions, the problem of externalities can be corrected by imposing a tax equal to marginal social cost (at the optimum level of output) and a subsidy equal to marginal social benefit (at the optimum level of output).
True/False

Q35. Referring to Figure 11.3 (see Q20):

(a) Assume that the government imposes a 'pollution tax' on the firm at a constant rate per unit of output. What must the size of the tax per unit be in order to persuade the firm to produce the socially efficient level of output?

....

(b) Assuming that this firm is the only polluter in the industry, what effect will the tax have on the market price?

....

Q36. Give two advantages and two disadvantages of using taxes and subsidies to correct market imperfections.

Advantage 1 ....

Advantage 2 ....

Disadvantage 1...

Disadvantage 2...

Q37. Figure 11.5 shows the effects of an indirect tax. *D* represents market demand.

(a) Which of the supply curves S_1 and S_2 represents the supply curve *without* the tax?

....

(b) Identify the equilibrium price and quantity without the tax. Which areas represent consumer and producer surplus in this situation?

....

(c) Identify the price and quantity after the imposition of an indirect tax.

....

(d) Which area represents the revenue that the government receives from the tax?

....

(e) Comment on the extent to which the burden of the tax is borne by consumers and/or producers.

....

(f) Identify the areas that represent consumer and producer surplus after the imposition of the tax.

....

(g) What is the excess burden of the tax?

....

(Pages 338–9) Extending property rights
An alternative to taxes and subsidies is to extend individuals' private property rights. That way individuals may be able to prevent others from imposing costs on them. For example, people living by a river may be granted ownership rights which allow them to decide whether a firm can dump waste into it and if so whether to charge it for so doing. Such a solution will be impractical, however, when **Q38.** *many/few* people are **Q39.** *highly/slightly* inconvenienced and when there are **Q40.** *many/few* culprits imposing the costs.

(Pages 339–40) Legal controls
Another alternative is to use laws. Laws can be used to prohibit or regulate activities that impose external costs; to prevent or control monopolies and oligopolies; and to provide consumer protection.

Q41. From each of the following pairs of problems select the one where legal controls would be more appropriate. (Tick.)

(a) (i) preventing accidents from worn car tyres

....

(ii) encouraging people to use public transport

....

(b) (i) preventing monopolists from charging excessive prices

....

(ii) preventing manufacturers from setting the *retail* price

....

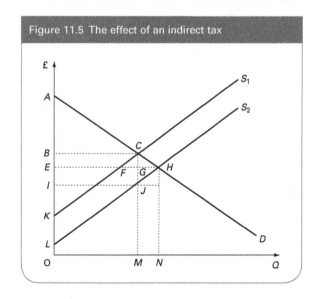

Figure 11.5 The effect of an indirect tax

(c) (i) preventing false claims by tobacco companies about the 'benefits' of smoking

....

(ii) preventing ignorance about the spread of infectious diseases

....

(Pages 340–1) Other policies

In addition to taxes and subsidies, extending property rights, and legal controls, there are other ways that a government can offset market failures. These include regulatory bodies, price controls, the provision of information, the direct provision of goods and services and public ownership.

♟ **Q42.** Match the methods of intervention (i)–(viii) to the examples (a)–(h).

(i) Taxes and subsidies.
(ii) Extending property rights.
(iii) Legal controls.
(iv) Regulatory bodies.
(v) Price controls.
(vi) The provision of information.
(vii) The direct provision of goods and services.
(viii) Public ownership.

(a) Government job centres. ....

(b) Nationalising an industry. ....

(c) Ofgem, Ofwat, Ofcom. ....

(d) Driving tests. ....

(e) State education. ....

(f) Grants for fitting loft insulation. ....

(g) Tightening the laws on trespass. ....

(h) Setting maximum rents that can be charged for private rented accommodation.

....

*11.4 Cost–benefit analysis

(Pages 343–6) If the government decides to replace or modify the market, it will need a means of assessing whether particular goods or services should be produced and, if so, in what quantities. *Cost–benefit analysis (CBA)* can help a government decide whether or not to go ahead with a public project.

♟ **Q43.** All costs and benefits associated with the project should be identified. These include:

(i) direct private monetary costs,
(ii) external monetary costs,
(iii) external non-monetary costs,
(iv) direct private monetary benefits,
(v) private non-monetary benefits,
(vi) external monetary benefits,
(vii) external non-monetary benefits.

Assume that a cost–benefit study is conducted to decide whether to build a road bridge across an estuary. At present the only way across is by ferry. Assume that building the bridge will drive the ferry operators out of business. Into which of the above seven categories should each of the following costs and benefits of the bridge be placed?

(a) Loss in profits to ferry operators. ....

(b) Tolls paid by the users of the bridge. ....

(c) Damage to local wildlife from constructing the bridge.

....

(d) The difference between what people would be prepared to pay in tolls and what they will actually be charged.

....

(e) Removal of the nuisance to local residents of people queuing for the ferry.

....

(f) Wages of the toll collectors ....

(g) Increased profits from fishing in the estuary now that the ferry boats no longer disturb the fish.

....

One way of estimating both private and external non-monetary costs and benefits is to make inferences from people's behaviour.

◗ **Q44.** Which of the following might be used to estimate the non-monetary benefits of a new by-pass round a village?
(a) The costs of its construction. *Yes/No*
(b) The difference in house prices in villages with a by-pass and villages with a main road running through them.
Yes/No
(c) The amount that people are prepared to pay for a quicker mode of transport. *Yes/No*
(d) The loss in profits to local traders. *Yes/No*
(e) The savings on future road maintenance in the village.
Yes/No

Another approach is to use questionnaires: to ask people how much they will suffer or gain from a project.

(?) **Q45.** Give two problems with using questionnaires to assess cost and benefits.

1. ....

2. ....

◗ **Q46.** Figures can be adjusted for *risk* by multiplying the value of the benefit or cost by the probability of its occurrence. *True/False*

⁇ **Q47.** What would be the expected value of a possible outcome if there was a 40% chance of receiving a benefit of £200?

....

But what if the costs and benefits are *uncertain*? One answer to this problem is to use *sensitivity analysis*.

◗ **Q48.** A project has a number of costs whose magnitudes are uncertain. Estimates for these costs range from a total of £4m to £10m. Is the project's desirability sensitive to this possible variation in costs, if the project's projected surplus of revenue over all *other* costs is:

(a) £20m?	*Yes/No*
(b) £6m?	*Yes/No*
(c) £1m?	*Yes/No*

Assume all costs and benefits are in present values.

(Pages 346–7) In a public project, the benefits and some of the costs can be expected to occur over many years. Thus to get an accurate assessment of benefits and costs, *discounting procedures* must be used.

◉ **Q49.** Put the following steps in the discounting procedure in the correct sequence. (Number them.)

(a) Discount each year's net benefit to give it a present value. ....

(b) Recommend accepting the project if the net present value is greater than zero. ....

(c) Estimate the costs and benefits for each year of the life of the project. ....

(d) Add up the present values of each year's net benefit to give a total net present value of the project.

....

(e) Subtract the costs from the benefits for each year, to give a net benefit for each year. ....

It is argued that the rate of discount chosen should be a *social* rate of discount: i.e. one that reflects society's preferences for the present over the future. Just what this rate should be, however, is controversial.

⁇ **Q50.** How may sensitivity analysis be used to ease the difficulty in choosing a social discount rate?

....

....

(Page 347) How may the *distribution* of costs and benefits be taken into account?

▤ **Q51.** One alternative is to use the Hicks–Kaldor version of the Pareto criterion. This states that a project will be desirable if:

A. the gainers fully compensate the losers and still have a net gain.

B. the government fully compensates the losers and there is still a net gain.

C. if it is impossible for people to make any further gains from the project without others losing.

D. if the gainers could in principle fully compensate the losers and still have a net gain, even though in practice no compensation is paid.

E. there are no losers.

⁇ **Q52.** What is the problem with the Hicks–Kaldor criterion?

....

11.5 Government failure and the case for the market

(Pages 350–3)

⁇ **Q53.** Give six possible drawbacks of government intervention: i.e. reasons why the government may fail to ensure an optimum allocation of resources.

1. ....

2. ....

3. ....

4. ....

5. ....

6. ....

◉ **Q54.** Match the following words to the blanks in the statement about the *neo-Austrian* support for free-market capitalism.

dynamic; longer-term; risk taking; monopoly; growth; oligopolies; efficiency; free-market; innovation.

The neo-Austrian school of economics argues that, rather than focusing on questions of (a).................... in the allocation of resources, we ought to judge (b).................... capitalism in its (c).................... context. The chances of (d).................... profits encourage (e)...................., (f).................... and (g).................... Thus governments ought to take a (h).................... view and not attempt excessive (or indeed *any*) regulation of monopolies and (i)....................

Q55. Even if a firm is currently a monopoly producer in the country, there are various reasons why in practice its market power may be limited. Four of these reasons are given below. One, however, is not a reason. Which one?
A. It faces a continuously falling *LRAC* curve.
B. The market may be contestable.
C. There may be competition from closely related industries.
D. The firm may face countervailing power from its customers.
E. It may face competition from imports.

B | PROBLEMS, EXERCISES AND PROJECTS

Q56. Conduct an audit of your activities during the course of a day.
(a) What external costs and benefits resulted from your activities? Make sure you try to identify *all* externalities you created. You may need to think very carefully.
(b) Were you aware of the externalities at the time? If so, did the existence of them make any difference to your actions?
(c) Were there any pressures on you to avoid generating external costs? If so, were these pressures social, moral or what?
(d) How could you best be encouraged/persuaded/forced to take the externalities fully into account? Are there any costs in such methods?
(e) Present your findings in groups and discuss each other's assessments of the externalities you create. Do your findings differ substantially one from another?

Q57. Assume that a firm produces organic waste that has the effect of increasing the fertility of neighbouring farmland and thus reducing the farmers' costs. It is impractical, however, to sell the waste to the farmers. Table 11.1 shows the firm's private marginal costs and these external benefits to farmers from the firm's production.
(a) How much will the firm produce to maximise profits?

....

Table 11.1 A firm's costs and revenue (daily figures)

Output (units)	Price (£)	Marginal (private) cost (£)	Marginal external benefit (£)
1	20	16	6
2	20	15	5
3	20	15	4
4	20	16	3
5	20	17	2
6	20	18	2
7	20	20	2
8	20	22	2
9	20	24	2
10	20	27	1

(b) What is the marginal social cost of producing 3 units of output per day?

....

(c) What is the socially optimum level of output?

....

(d) What subsidy per unit would the government have to pay the firm to encourage it to produce this level of output?

....

(e) What would it cost the government?

....

(f) If new farming technology doubled the benefit of the waste to the farmer, what would be the socially optimum level of the firm's output?

....

Q58. Figure 11.6 shows an industry which was previously perfectly competitive but is now organised as a monopoly. Cost and revenue curves are assumed to be the same in both situations. (Assume that there are no fixed costs of production.)
(a) What is the perfectly competitive price and output?

....

(b) What is the monopoly price and output?...................

(c) What areas represent consumer surplus in the perfectly competitive situation?

....

(d) What areas represent consumer surplus after the industry has become a monopoly?

....

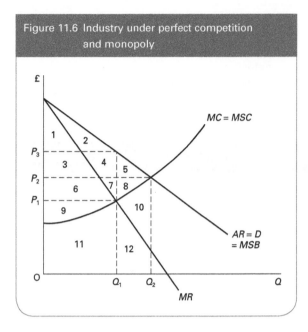

Figure 11.6 Industry under perfect competition and monopoly

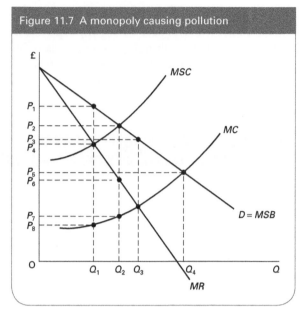

Figure 11.7 A monopoly causing pollution

(e) What areas represent the loss in consumer surplus after the industry has become a monopoly?

....

(f) What areas represent producer surplus in the perfectly competitive situation?

....

(g) What areas represent producer surplus after the industry has become a monopoly?

....

(h) What areas represent the gain in producer surplus after the industry has become a monopoly?

....

(i) What areas represent total deadweight welfare loss under monopoly?

....

Q59. Figure 11.7 illustrates the situation where a firm produces *two* market distortions. It creates a marginal external cost in the form of pollution, and it also has monopoly power. (Assume that it is possible for the firm to make a profit.)

(a) What is its profit-maximising price and output?

....

(b) What is the socially optimum price and output, assuming no distortions in other parts of the economy?

....

(c) If a tax were imposed equal to the marginal pollution cost, what would be the level of the tax rate?

....

(d) If there were no attempt to correct the monopoly power, what would be the new price and output resulting from the imposition of this pollution tax?

....

(e) Would this be socially efficient?   *Yes/No*

(f) If the monopoly problem were not to be corrected directly, what would be the size of the socially most efficient pollution tax?

....

(g) Would this be greater than or less than the marginal pollution cost and how much so?

greater than/less than

(h) If the marginal pollution cost were not as shown but were in fact smaller, so that *MSC* intersected with *MSB* at a higher output than Q_3, what would be the socially efficient solution if the problem of monopoly could not be tackled directly or by price controls?

....

(i) What would be the problem with this solution?

....

....

(j) How could this problem be dealt with without affecting the price and output (which with the subsidy would now be at the sociably optimal level)?

....

....

Q60. In groups of two or three, write a report on the consumption of fossil fuels in the UK (or another specific country) since 1980. You should conduct an Internet search to find information.

Your report should first include a description of the changing pattern of fossil fuel consumption over the period and then explain why this has occurred. Finally, you should describe and explain the likely consequences of an introduction of a carbon tax on fossil fuels (a tax on the use of fossil fuels).

C DISCUSSION TOPICS AND ESSAYS

Q61. Why is the Pareto test for social welfare said to be a 'weak' test?

Q62. Why will general equilibrium under perfect competition be socially efficient provided there are no externalities?

Q63. Would it be desirable for all pollution to be prevented?

Q64. Why will a free market fail to achieve an optimum allocation of resources in education? Is this an argument for the abolition of private education?

Q65. Examine the case for a 'carbon tax' (i.e. a tax on the use of fossil fuels). Why might different groups of people take opposing views on the desirability of such a tax?

Q66. Compare the relative advantages and disadvantages of taxation and regulation as means of dealing with the problem of external costs.

Q67. Examine whether the imposition of an indirect tax benefits society as a whole if the government spends all of the tax revenue responsibly.

Q68. When you visit your dentist for a check-up, she tells you that you have a filling that needs to be replaced to avoid future problems. In what sense is there a potential market failure present?

*Q69. How would you set about measuring the value of a human life?

Q70. Go through each of the types of failing of a free-market economy and assess whether a government is more or less likely to fail in these respects if it tries to take over from the market.

Q71. Consider the neo-Austrian argument that the possibility of large monopoly profits is of vital importance for encouraging risk taking and innovation. Does this imply that criticising a market economy for being imperfect and allocatively inefficient is to focus on the wrong issues?

Q72. Debate
Despite the weaknesses of a free market, replacing the market by the government generally makes the problem worse.

D ANSWERS

Q1. E. This is the case when all Pareto improvements have been made. A Pareto improvement is where it is possible to make people better off *without* making anyone worse off. Note that B is not correct because if improvements can still be made the optimum cannot yet have been reached. A and C are not correct: Pareto optimality has to do with efficiency, not fairness. D is not correct because Pareto optimality is concerned with *allocative* efficiency not X efficiency.

Q2. *True*. The Pareto criterion is concerned with *efficiency* not with equity. A totally equal and a highly unequal distribution of income can both be Pareto optimal (i.e. efficient).

Q3. *(a)* A, C and E. Compared with point X, C represents a gain to both Bill and Ben. A and E represent a gain to one but no loss to the other.

(b) D, F and G. Compared with point F, X represents a gain to both. Compared with points D and G, X represents a gain to one and no loss to the other.

(c) No. Bill's gain is Ben's loss. The choice then is one of distribution rather than efficiency.

Q4. 1. Perfect competition in all markets.
2. No externalities.

Q5. *marginal cost.*

Q6. *less than.*

Q7. *marginal benefit.*

Q8. D. It is merely an extension of the general proposition that the optimum level of any activity will be where $MB = MC$, only in this case it is marginal *social* costs and marginal *social* benefits that are relevant. (Note that A would be true in the absence of externalities.)

Q9. *marginal utility.*

Q10. *marginal cost.*

Q11. (a) People would consume more. MU (and MSB) would fall (diminishing marginal utility) and price would rise until once more $MSB = P$.

(b) The rise in the price of the good would raise the MRP of factors and thus the demand for factors would rise. The resulting shortage would increase the price of factors and encourage more supply of factors until $MRP_f = P_f = MC_f$ (where MRP_f is the marginal benefit from using a factor and MC_f is the marginal cost of supplying a factor (= MDU in the case of labour)). With no externalities this means that MSB of factor use equals MSC of factor supply.

(c) To the extent that good X is a complement or substitute for other goods, so the changes in the price of good X will affect the MU of other goods. To the extent that factors used for producing good X are used for producing other goods, so the change in factor prices will affect the MC of other goods. The resulting disequilibria will lead to adjustments in these other goods markets until in each case $MSB = MSC$ once more.

(d) To the extent that factors used for good X are complements or substitutes for other factors, so the demand for these other factors will change. The resulting disequilibria will lead to adjustments in these other factor markets until in each case $MSB_f = MSC_f$ once more.

(e) These ripple effects will continue until a general equilibrium is restored where $MSB = MSC$ in all goods and factor markets.

*Q12. Buy relatively more X and relatively less Y until $MU_X/MU_Y = P_X/P_Y$.

*Q13. Produce relatively more Y and relatively less X until $MC_X/MC_Y = P_X/P_Y$.

*Q14. (a) By B giving A some X in exchange for some Y. Both A and B would gain.

(b) Where MU_X/MU_Y for person A equals MU_X/MU_Y for person B.

*Q15. *True.* For any pair of goods, where $MRS = MRT$ there are no further Pareto improvements that can be made.

*Q16. (a) (social) $MRS = MU_X/MU_Y = MSB_X/MSB_Y$.

(b) (social) $MRT = MC_X/MC_Y = MSC_X/MSC_Y$.

(c) The line is the tangent to point A since this is the point where MRS equals MRT.

(d) Because production cannot take place beyond the production possibility curve and point A is the point where the production possibility curve reaches the highest social indifference curve.

(e) (i) By moving out towards the production possibility curve. There could be a gain in production by some producers with no loss in production by others. (ii) There could be a move to a higher social indifference curve. A reallocation of consumption could lead to some consumers gaining with no one losing.

Q17. *True.*

Q18. Examples include: greater equality and faster economic growth, but we might also consider other objectives such as full employment or stable prices.

Q19. (a) (v), (i); (b) (iv), (ii); (c) (i); (d) (iii), (iv); (e) (vi); (f) (viii), (iv); (g) (ii); (h) (i); (i) (vii), (ii) (but there are the benefits of economies of scale: for example, if another family member buys you the wrong flavour of yoghurt, the disappointment of this may be outweighed by the fact that you did not have to go out and buy it!); (j) (iv).

Q20. (a) I.

(b) Q_2 (where $P = MC$).

(c) £$_2$ – £$_3$.

(d) Q_1 (where $P = MSC$).

Q21. See *pages 326–7* of Sloman, *Economics* (this edition). Two additional examples of each are:

(a) An attractive new shopping centre built on previously ugly derelict land; the use of new cheaper, but less polluting, technology.

(b) A person decorating the outside of their house (thus making the street more attractive); travel by bus (thus relieving congestion).

(c) People visiting beauty spots and causing damage to wildlife; the consumption of alcohol and the effects of drunken behaviour on other people.

Q22. *True.* See Figure 11.7 on page 330 of Sloman, *Economics* (this edition).

Q23. A. Large external costs relative to private costs make the goods socially desirable but privately unprofitable to produce. Once provided it is not possible to exclude people from consuming the goods or services without paying (i.e. from getting a 'free ride').

Q24. *Yes:* (b), (d), (f) and (g). In each of these cases the free market would simply not provide these services.
No: (a), (c), (e) and (h). In each of these cases the free market would provide the good or service, but probably imperfectly. There would be only a relatively small free-rider problem.

Q25. *True.* Since people cannot be excluded from consuming the good without paying, the market price would be zero (and hence it would be privately unprofitable to produce the good).

Q26. *overused.*

Q27. *rivalry.* One person's use of the resource will reduce its yield for others.

Q28. *negative externalities.* People's use of the resource adversely affects other people.

Q29. (a) Q_3 (where *MC* equals the marginal revenue to the *individual* user, which will be the *ARP* of the land, given that the individual user is too small to affect the yield. The individual owner is a 'yield taker'.)

(b) *Negative.*

(c) Q_1 (where *MC = MRP*).

(d) *Less.* This is a classic example of positive externalities. Why should the individual spend money on improving the land if most of the gain is going to *other* owners, who will therefore gain a 'free ride'?

Q30. E. It is the loss in *total* surplus. The gain in producers' surplus (profit) will be more than offset by a loss in consumers' surplus, giving an overall net loss.

Q31. (a) People with infectious diseases passing them on to other people.

(b) Hospitals or doctors colluding to keep up the price of treatment.

(c) Patient ignorance about their condition. They may be persuaded to have more expensive treatment than is necessary.

(d) People taking out expensive private insurance for fear of their future health.

(e) Uncaring parents not buying adequate treatment for their children. Children not buying adequate treatment for their elderly parents.

(f) Poor people not being able to afford reasonable health. The belief that people have a moral right to health care according to need and not ability to pay.

(g) People may neglect their health. The government may regard health care as a merit good.

Q32. The solution of correcting a specific market distortion so as to restore the condition that *MSB = MSC* in all parts of the economy.

Q33. D. Thus if prices in the rest of the economy are on average 10 per cent above marginal cost, the minimum *relative* distortion would be for prices in this industry to be set at 10 per cent above marginal cost.

Q34. *False.* The tax should be equal to marginal *external* cost. (Marginal *social* cost equals marginal external cost *plus* marginal private cost.) Likewise the subsidy should be equal to marginal *external* benefit not marginal *social* benefit.

Q35. (a) $£_3 - £_4$.

(b) *None: it will remain at $£_3$.*

Q36. Advantages: they 'internalise externalities'; rates can be adjusted according to the magnitude of the problem, thus allowing *MSB* to equal *MSC*; firms are encouraged to find ways of reducing external costs and of increasing external benefits.

Disadvantages: impractical to use when a different tax or subsidy rate is required for each case; rates would have to be frequently adjusted as external costs and benefits changed; knowledge is imperfect (for example, there is a danger of underestimating external costs such as pollution) – it might be safer to ban certain activities.

Q37. (a) S_2.

(b) Price *E*, quantity *N*. Consumer surplus is the area *AEH*, and producer surplus is *EHL*.

(c) Price is now *B*, and quantity is *M*.

(d) *BCJI.*

(e) As the price rises by less than the amount of the tax (the vertical distance between S_1 and S_2), the burden of the tax is shared by consumers and producers. In this case, the consumers' share is *BCGE*; the producers' share is *EGJI*. The way that the burden is shared depends upon the elasticities of demand and supply.

(f) Consumer surplus is now *ABC* and producer surplus is *IJL*.

(g) *CHJ.* The excess burden is the difference between the original sum of consumer surplus and producer surplus (i.e. area *AHL*) and the after-tax sum of consumer, producer and government surplus (i.e. *ACJL*).

Q38. *many* (it will be difficult to co-ordinate their actions).

Q39. *slightly* (it may not be worth the effort of pursuing the culprits).

Q40. *many* (it makes pursuing the culprits more difficult and costly).

Q41. (a) (i) (it is illegal to have below a minimum tread).

(b) (ii) ('resale price maintenance' is against the law).

(c) (i) (cigarette advertising is banned on television and is being phased out on hoardings and in magazines).

Q42. (a) (vi), (b) (viii), (c) (iv), (d) (iii), (e) (vii), (f) (i), (g) (ii), (h) (v).

Q43. (a) (ii), (b) (iv), (c) (iii), (d) (v), (e) (vii), (f) (i), (g) (vi).

Q44. (b) and (c). These can give an indication of the non-monetary benefits to local residents from a quieter village – (b); and to road users from the time saved – (c).

Q45. *Ignorance*: people are unlikely to know beforehand just how much they will gain or lose. *Dishonesty*: people may exaggerate the costs or benefits to them in order to influence the outcome.

Q46. *True.*

Q47. *£80*. This is known as the expected value of the outcome.

Q48. *(a)* *No*. No matter whether the uncertain costs turned out to be £4 or £10, the project would still be *profitable*.

    (b) *Yes*. The project would be profitable only if the uncertain costs turned out to be less than £6m.

    (c) *No*. No matter whether the uncertain costs turned out to be £4 or £10, the project would still be *unprofitable*.

Q49. 1 (c), 2 (e), 3 (a), 4 (d), 5 (b).

Q50. Two or three alternative discount rates can be tried to see if the project's desirability is sensitive to the choice of discount rate. If it is, then the project will be seen as borderline.

Q51. D. The criterion is merely that there be a *potential* Pareto improvement. The question of *actual* compensation is seen to be a question of equity and should thus be considered separately from the social efficiency of the project.

Q52. In practice compensation may not be paid. An actual Pareto improvement, therefore, may not take place.

Q53. Reasons include: shortages and surpluses, poor information, bureaucracy and government inefficiency, lack of market incentives, inconsistent government policy, unrepresentative government, unaccountable government and voters' ignorance.

Q54. (a) efficiency, (b) free-market, (c) dynamic, (d) monopoly, (e)–(g) risk taking, innovation, growth, (h) longer-term, (i) oligopolies.

Q55. A. This will *strengthen* its power: it is a barrier to the entry of new firms. Any new entrants (at less than the output of the existing firm) would find that their costs were higher than this firm's and would thus find it hard to survive.

12

Environmental Policy

A REVIEW

Environmental issues have been highly contentious in recent years, raising important questions about how market failure should be tackled. In particular, there are many instances where there are externality effects that affect the environment. This chapter examines the possible strengths and weaknesses of both the market and government intervention in dealing with these issues. These relate first to the economics of the environment and second to traffic congestion and urban transport policies.

12.1 Economics of the environment

(Pages 356–7) People draw various benefits from the environment. The three main benefits are as: (1) an amenity; (2) a source of primary products; (3) a dump for waste. These three uses tend to conflict with each other.

 Q1. In what ways do the above uses come into conflict?...

....

Q2. As population increases, so environmental degradation is likely to:

A. reduce.
B. stay constant.
C. increase at a decelerating rate.
D. increase at a constant rate.
E. increase at an accelerating rate.

Q3. Which of the following are likely to reduce pressures on the environment?

(a) An increased price of non-renewable resources.
Yes/No

(b) Growth in national income. Yes/No

(c) Technological progress. Yes/No

(d) An increase in living standards in developing countries.
Yes/No

(e) An increased recognition of global interdependence.
Yes/No

Q4. Sir Nicholas Stern claimed that climate change is the 'greatest and widest-ranging market failure ever seen'.
True/False

Q5. Which of the following did the Stern Report *not* identify as being necessary in order to cut emissions of greenhouse gases to a sustainable level?

A. Reducing consumer demand for emissions-intensive goods and services.
B. Increasing efficiency, which can save both money and emissions.
C. Taking action on non-energy emissions, such as avoiding deforestation.
D. Encouraging less-developed countries to increase their use of coal-fired power generation.
E. Switching to lower-carbon technologies for power, heat and transport.

(Pages 357–61) What is the optimum use of the environment? The answer depends on people's attitudes towards sustainability.

🎳 **Q6.** The following are four different approaches to sustainability:
(i) The free-market approach.
(ii) The social efficiency approach.
(iii) The conservationist approach.
(iv) The Gaia approach.

Match each one of the following four descriptions to one of the above approaches:
(a) Downplaying the importance of material consumption and economic growth and putting greater emphasis on the maintenance of the ecosystems.

....

(b) Emphasising the importance of private property and the pressures this puts on using the environment as a productive resource – a resource which, like other resources, should not be wasted.

....

(c) Regarding the environment as having rights of its own, with humans having an obligation to live in harmony with it.

....

(d) Taking explicit account of environmental costs and benefits in decision making.

....

🌓 **Q7.** Figure 12.1 shows the net private benefit from producing a good (curve *MB – MC*) and the marginal pollution cost to society (*MC*_{pollution}). Which output would be seen as optimum under each of the following approaches?

(a) The social efficiency approach $Q_1/Q_2/Q_3/Q_4$
(b) The Gaia approach $Q_1/Q_2/Q_3/Q_4$
(c) The conservationist approach $Q_1/Q_2/Q_3/Q_4$
(d) The free-market approach $Q_1/Q_2/Q_3/Q_4$

12.2 Policies to tackle pollution and its effects

(Pages 361–2) There are various policy alternatives for dealing with environmental problems. One is to extend private property rights; another is to use green taxes. The next two questions again refer to Figure 12.1.

📃 **Q8.** According to the Coase theorem, the extension of private property rights to sufferers from pollution would allow them to levy a charge on the polluter which would (a) fully compensate the sufferers and (b) result in a profit-maximising output:
A. of Q_1.
B. between Q_1 and Q_3.
C. of Q_3.
D. between Q_3 and Q_4.
E. of Q_4.

📃 **Q9.** The socially efficient green tax would be an amount equal to:
A. zero.
B. OP_4.
C. $MB – MC$.
D. $MC_{pollution}$.
E. $OP_4 – OP_3$.

(Pages 362–4) An alternative means of protecting the environment is to use command-and-control systems. Minimum environmental standards could be set. These could be any of three types: technology-based standards, ambient-based standards, social-impact standards.

❓ **Q10.** Define these terms:

Technology-based standards..

....

Ambient-based standards..

....

Social-impact standards..

....

🌓 **Q11.** Command-and-control systems have the following advantages over green taxes:
(a) They are more appropriate when it is impossible to predict the precise environmental impact of pollution.
True/False

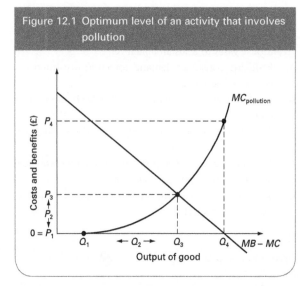

Figure 12.1 Optimum level of an activity that involves pollution

(b) They have the effect of making the polluter pay for the amount of pollution generated. *True/False*

(c) They are easier to administer than green taxes. *True/False*

(d) They act as a continuous incentive for polluters to reduce the amount of pollution they generate. *True/False*

(Pages 364–70) An alternative that has been much debated in recent years is the use of tradable permits.

⊗ **Q12.** Assume that two firms, A and B, are currently emitting 100 units of a pollutant each. Now assume that a standard is set permitting them to emit only 50 units of pollutant each. If either firm emits less than 50 units, it will be given a credit for the difference. This credit can then be sold to the other firm, allowing it to go over the 50-unit limit by the amount of the credit. Assume that the marginal cost of pollution reduction for firm A is £2000 per unit and for firm B it is £1000 per unit, irrespective of the current level of emission.

(a) How many units of pollution will each firm emit after trade in credits between the two firms has taken place?

Firm A .... Firm B ....

(b) What can we say about the price at which the credits will be traded?

....

Now assume that the marginal private cost to the firms of reducing pollution below 100 units is given in Table 12.1. (Assume for firm B that there is a straight-line *MC* curve: for example, the *MC* of reducing emissions by a 25th unit to 75 units is £4500.)

(c) How many units of pollution will each firm emit this time after trade has taken place in the permits?

Firm A .... Firm B ....

Table 12.1 Marginal cost of pollution reduction by firms A and B

Number of units of pollutant emitted	MC of reducing pollution by 1 unit (£000)	
	Firm A	Firm B
100	4	1
90	4	2
80	4	3
70	4	4
60	4	5
50	4	6
40	4	7
30	4	8
20	4	9
10	4	10

(d) What can we say about the price at which the credits will be traded?

....

⬤ **Q13.** Which of the following are features of a tradable permits scheme?

(a) The authorities need specific information about the polluting behaviour of individual firms. *Yes/No*

(b) Such a scheme penalises firms already using clean technology. *Yes/No*

(c) Firms have a financial incentive to reduce pollution. *Yes/No*

(d) Although the authorities decide the level of pollution permits, the market allocates the actual level of pollution that firms produce. *Yes/No*

(e) Trading of permits may lead to geographical concentration of polluting activities. *Yes/No*

(f) Such a scheme would be impractical in an international context. *Yes/No*

(Pages 370–1) It is difficult to reach international agreements on pollution reduction.

(?) **Q14.** Give three reasons why.

1. ....

2. ....

3. ....

⬤ **Q15.** Assume that a country is considering whether to honour a new international agreement to cut the emission of greenhouse gases. Assume also that it is considering purely its own domestic gains from the cutting of these gases and its own domestic costs of so doing.

(a) What would be the *maximax* strategy? *Stick to agreement/Break the agreement*

(b) What would be the *maximin* strategy? *Stick to agreement/Break the agreement*

(c) Why could this be described as a *prisoners' dilemma game*?

....

....

12.3 The economics of traffic congestion

(Pages 371–3) The demand for road space can be seen largely as a *derived* demand.

▤ **Q16.** Which one of the following demands for road space is *not* a derived demand?

A. Using a car to go to work.

B. Using a bus to go to work.

C. Using a car to go for a Sunday afternoon drive.

D. Using a car to go shopping.

E. Lorries using roads to deliver goods.

There are various determinants of the demand for road space by car users. One of the most important is the 'price' to the motorist of the journey. This is not paid directly for using a particular stretch of road, except in the case of **Q17.** *tolls/taxes/congestion/the price paid for the car*, but instead can be seen as the various **Q18.** *total/average/marginal* **Q19.** *costs/benefits* to the motorist.

◗ **Q20.** This 'price' will vary according to the level of congestion. *True/False*

◗ **Q21.** Which of the following motoring costs are marginal (private) costs to the motorist?

(a) Fuel consumption.   *Yes/No*

(b) Fuel tax.   *Yes/No*

(c) Road fund tax.   *Yes/No*

(d) Congestion.   *Yes/No*

(e) Car maintenance costs.   *Yes/No*

(f) Depreciation due to wear and tear.   *Yes/No*

(g) Depreciation due to ageing of the vehicle. *Yes/No*

(h) Time spent making a journey.   *Yes/No*

One of the reasons why it is difficult to tackle the problem of a growing level of traffic has to do with elasticity of demand.

▤ **Q22.** Which one of the following is likely to be elastic?

A. Price elasticity of demand for road space (with respect to the direct marginal motoring costs).

B. Income elasticity of demand for road space.

C. Cross-price elasticity of demand for road space with respect to rail fares.

D. Cross-price elasticity of demand for road space for private cars with respect to bus fares.

E. Cross-price elasticity of demand for road space with respect to the price of new cars.

◗ **Q23.** The high price elasticity of demand for motoring suggests that schemes to tackle traffic congestion that involve raising the cost of motoring will be highly successful.

True/False

(Pages 373–5) A problem is that when people use their cars they impose external costs on other people.

⁇ **Q24.** Give three examples of external costs of motoring.

1. ....

2. ....

3. ....

What, then, is the optimum level of road usage?

◗ **Q25.** The optimum level of road usage would be that at which the external costs of motoring were zero.

True/False

⁇ **Q26.** Figure 12.2 shows the effects of increasing traffic along a particular stretch of road. At first, additional cars have no effect on the speed of traffic: it flows freely. But after a point, additional cars slow down the traffic and thus impose a 'congestion cost' (an externality) on other car users. Beyond this point, therefore, the marginal social cost (*MSC*) of using the road is greater than the marginal private cost (*MC*).

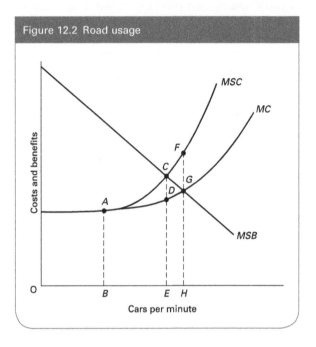

Figure 12.2 Road usage

(a) Assuming that there are no externalities on the demand side, so that marginal social benefit and marginal private benefit are the same, what will be the actual level of road use?

....

(b) What is the socially optimal level of road use?

....

(c) What is the marginal external cost at *OH*?

....

(d) What level of 'congestion tax' (e.g. tolls) would be necessary to achieve the optimal level of road use?

....

▤ **Q27.** In the long run, the supply of road space is not fixed. In identifying the socially efficient level of road construction, the authorities need to find the point at which:

A. Marginal private benefit of construction is equal to marginal private cost.

B. Marginal social benefit of construction is equal to marginal private cost.

C. Marginal social benefit of construction is equal to marginal social cost.

D. Marginal private benefit of construction is equal to marginal social cost.

E. Marginal social benefit of construction is greater than marginal social cost.

12.4 Urban transport policies

(Pages 376–80) Various policies have been adopted for tackling the problem of traffic congestion, which can be grouped into three broad types.

(?) **Q28.** Give three broad types of solution to traffic congestion.

1. ....

2. ....

3. ....

(?) **Q29.** Give three problems arising from building more roads as the means of reducing traffic congestion.

1. ....

2. ....

3. ....

Q30. Which one of the following is *not* a supply-side solution to traffic congestion?

A. Improved provision of public transport.

B. Electronic road pricing.

C. Park-and-ride schemes.

D. Expanding the capacity of existing roads.

E. Building new roads.

Q31. Which of the following are solutions to traffic congestion that rely on regulation and legislation?

(i) Improved provision of public transport.

(ii) Electronic road pricing.

(iii) Restricting access to the city centre depending on whether a taxi number plate is odd or even.

(iv) Introducing bus lanes.

(v) Parking restrictions.

A. (i) and (ii).

B. (i) and (v).

C. (ii) and (iii).

D. (iii), (iv) and (v).

E. (i), (iii), (iv) and (v).

Q32. In order to reduce congestion, the marginal tax rate must increase as the level of congestion increases.

True/False

Q33. Four of the following are advantages of electronic road pricing. Which one is not?

A. The charge can be varied according to the time of day.

B. The charge can be varied according to the level of congestion.

C. The socially efficient rate to charge can easily be ascertained.

D. The revenues can be used to subsidise public transport.

E. It can be used to 'internalise' motoring externalities.

(?) **Q34.** Under what circumstances will electronic road pricing be most effective in reducing the level of traffic congestion?

....

....

....

B   PROBLEMS, EXERCISES AND PROJECTS

Q35. The way in which the quality of life is affected by environmental change is monitored by DEFRA on behalf of the government. Visit the sustainable development website (at http://sd.defra.gov.uk/progress/national/) and evaluate the progress that has been made. By clicking on 'Key indicators and themes', you will see the range of measures that have been identified as ways of monitoring progress.

Q36. Table 12.2 shows the time taken to travel between two points along a given road.

Column (1) gives the traffic density: i.e. the number of cars per minute entering that stretch of road.

Column (2) gives the journey time per car: i.e. the number of minutes taken for a car to travel along that stretch of road.

Column (3) gives the sum of the journey times: i.e. the total number of minutes for *all* the cars per minute entering the road to travel along that stretch of road.

Column (4) gives the extra total journey time as traffic density increases by one more car.

Column (5) gives the additional time costs imposed on *other* road users by one more car entering that stretch of road: i.e. column (4) minus column (2).

Table 12.2 Time taken to travel between two points along a given road

Cars per minute (1)	Marginal private time cost: in minutes (2)	Total time cost: in minutes (3)	Marginal social time cost: in minutes (4)	Marginal external time cost: in minutes (5)
1	4	...	...	...
2	4	...	...	...
3	5	...	...	...
4	7	...	...	...
5	10	...	...	...
6	15	...	...	...
7	25	...	...	...

(a) Fill in the figures for columns (3), (4) and (5).

(b) Assume that tolls are now imposed on this road in order to reduce congestion to the socially optimal level. If time were valued at 10p per minute, what level of toll should be imposed per car when traffic density reaches:

(i)   6 cars per minute?...

(ii) 7 cars per minute?...

(c) Assume that the non-time costs of using the road are constant at 40p per car, that the marginal social benefit for the first car per minute using the road is £2.00, and that this decreases by 10p for each additional car per minute. What is the socially optimal level of road use (in cars per minute)?

....

(d) What level of toll should be imposed per car to achieve the socially optimal level of traffic on this road?

....

Q37. Undertake a web search to discover how effective has been the Congestion Charge in reducing congestion in central London.

DISCUSSION TOPICS AND ESSAYS

Q38. Compare the relative merits of green taxes and command-and-control systems as means of achieving an optimum use of the environment.

Q39. (a) For what reasons is it difficult to reach international agreements on global environmental protection? (b) Why is it difficult to stop overfishing in international waters?

Q40. To what extent are urban traffic problems the result of externalities?

Q41. Compare the relative merits of road pricing in cities with schemes to restrict the entry of traffic into city centres.

Q42. Imagine you were called upon by the government to offer advice on (i) whether to introduce tolls and, if so, at what rate on a particular motorway; (ii) whether to build an extra lane on a congested motorway. On what basis would you arrive at your recommendations?

Q43. To what extent can the provision of public transport solve the problem of urban traffic congestion?

Q44. Discuss whether the onset of a recession is likely to lead to slower or faster environmental degradation.

Q45. Debate
Taxation of motorists in the UK is excessive and unfair.

ANSWERS

Q1. Use of the environment for mining, farming, etc. reduces its amenity value. Use of the environment as a dump reduces its productivity for producing primary products. Use of the environment as a dump reduces its amenity value.

Q2. E.

Q3. *Yes*: (a), (c) and (e); *No*: (b) and (d). In the case of (c), technological progress has tended to be environmentally friendly (but not always so). The reasons include: greater miniaturisation, and hence a lower demand for raw materials; higher raw material prices leading to pressures to develop more resource-efficient products and processes; the pressure of public opinion; government policies (laws, taxes and subsidies promoting more environmentally friendly technology).

Q4. *True.*

Q5. D. Coal-fired power generation is certainly not to be encouraged, as it is a prime source of greenhouse gas emissions. The heavy dependence of China on coal has been a major concern during its period of rapid economic growth.

Q6. (a) (iii), (b) (i), (c) (iv), (d) (ii).

Q7. (a) Q_3, (b) Q_1, (c) Q_2, (d) Q_4.

Q8. C. By levying a charge that would fully compensate sufferers (i.e. a charge equal to the marginal pollution cost), the $MB - MC$ line would shift downwards by the amount of the charge (i.e. by the height of the $MC_{pollution}$ curve). Profits for the polluter would be maximised where the new $MB - MC$ curve crosses the horizontal axis: at Q_3.

Q9. D. The socially efficient tax rate is equal to the marginal external cost of pollution: i.e. $MC_{pollution}$. At the socially efficient level of output (Q_3), this will be equal to an amount OP_3.

Q10. *Technology-based standards.* Here the focus is on restricting the amount of pollution generated, irrespective of its impact.

Ambient-based standards. Here the focus is on restricting the environmental impact of the pollution.

Social-impact standards. Here the focus is on restricting the undesirable effects on people.

Q11. (a) and (c) *True.*

(b) and (d) *False.*

Q12. *(a)* Firm A 100 units; Firm B zero. (It is more expensive for firm A to reduce the emission of the pollutant than for firm B, and so it would be profitable for both firms if firm B reduced its emission by the full 100 units and then sold its 50 units of credits to firm A, permitting firm A to continue emitting 100 units.)

(b) The price would be somewhere between £1000 per unit (the lower limit for firm B to gain) and £2000 per unit (the upper limit for firm A to gain). This is a bilateral monopoly situation (i.e. only one seller and one buyer) and thus there is no unique equilibrium price. The actual price would depend on the outcome of negotiations between A and B.

(c) Firm A 30 units (a reduction of 70 units); Firm B 70 units (a reduction of 30 units). Firm B can reduce emissions of the pollutant by up to 30 units at an MC less than £4000, and hence more cheaply than A. Beyond this level, however, it would be cheaper for A to make the necessary reductions and sell the credits to B (allowing B to continue emitting 70 units).

(d) Again, given that the firms are operating under bilateral monopoly, the price would be negotiated. If a separate price is negotiated for each credit traded, then the upper price limit for each one would be the MC to B and the lower limit would be £4000, the MC to A.

Q13. *(a)* No: this is in fact one of the key attractions of a tradable permit scheme.

(b) No; such firms are able to sell their allocated permits, so do not suffer from the scheme.

(c) Yes.

(d) Yes.

(e) Yes, it could happen. This is one possible drawback of such schemes.

(f) Not entirely. The Kyoto Protocol has been somewhat hindered by not being universally accepted (most notably by the USA), but the EU carbon trading system has been in place since January 2005.

Q14. There may not be the political will, given that governments are concerned about *domestic* interests; it is difficult to measure the amount of pollution caused by each country; it is difficult to identify the global effects of individual countries reducing their pollution; it is difficult to agree on the amount that each country should reduce emissions.

Q15. *(a)* *Break the agreement.* (If it is assumed that other countries will stick to the agreement, this country would save costs by not sticking to the agreement, but would gain most of the benefits from the other countries sticking to it.)

(b) *Break the agreement.* (If it is assumed that other countries will *not* stick to the agreement, this country will save costs by not sticking to it, and would only sacrifice the small benefit it would get directly by sticking to it.)

(c) Because either strategy would lead to a breakdown of the agreement and hence all countries being worse off than without the agreement.

Q16. C. In all the other cases the demand for roads is to serve some *other* purpose than mere travelling: whether to go to work, to go shopping or to deliver goods. In the case of going for a Sunday afternoon drive, the pleasure is gained directly from the journey.

Q17. *tolls* (note that some taxes are nevertheless included in the 'price' of motoring, even though the motorist does not pay them for using a particular stretch of road).

Q18. *marginal.*

Q19. *costs.*

Q20. *True.* The higher the level of congestion, the longer will be the time taken to make a journey and the greater will be the level of frustration experienced. These are both costs to the motorists of that specific journey and are thus marginal costs.

Q21. (c) and (g) *No.* These are *fixed* costs of owning a car. There is no *additional* cost incurred under these two headings each time the motorist makes a journey. All the other costs, however, *are* variable costs with respect to car usage and therefore have a positive marginal cost. Note that (d) and (h) are not direct *monetary* costs, but nevertheless are a cost to the motorist of making the journey. In the case of (d) we are only referring to the cost the specific motorist experiences from the congestion; we are not referring to the congestion costs imposed on others by the motorist's journey.

Q22. B. As incomes grow, so the demand for road use grows rapidly: more people feel they can afford private transport rather than public transport; people use cars increasingly for leisure purposes; more families can afford more than one car. The price and cross-price elasticities of demand, on the other hand, are relatively inelastic: many people feel that there is no close substitute for private motoring.

Q23. *False.* In fact, the price elasticity of demand for motoring is seen to be low, so that schemes that involve raising the cost of motoring are not likely to be very successful.

Q24. Examples include: congestion; pollution (from exhaust fumes); accidents; noise.

Q25. *False.* The optimum level would be that where the marginal social benefit is equal to the marginal social cost. This may well be at a level of road use where there are some external costs. (If environmentalists object that this involves putting too little weight on protecting the environment, an economist would reply that the answer would be simply to attach a higher value to these external costs. This value, however, would have to be very high indeed, if not infinite, if the optimum level of road use were to generate *no* environmental externalities.)

Q26. *(a)* *OH*: where marginal private cost (*MC*) equals marginal private benefit, which, in the absence of externalities on the demand side, equals marginal social benefit (*MSB*).

(b) *OE*: where *MSC* = *MSB*.

(c) *FG*.

(d) A level equal to the marginal external cost: i.e. *CD* at the optimum level of road use, *OE*.

Q27. C.

Q28. The three broad types of solution to traffic congestion are: (1) direct provision; (2) regulation and legislation; and (3) changing market signals.

Q29. Environmental costs.
Equity: losers are unlikely to be compensated.
Congestion may not be solved. It may encourage a faster rate of growth of traffic.

Q30. B.

Q31. D.

Q32. *False.* Any positive marginal congestion tax rate will *reduce* congestion. To reduce congestion to the *optimum* level, however, the congestion tax would have to equal the size of the congestion externality at the optimum level of road use.

Q33. C. It is very difficult to measure the exact size of the congestion externalities and therefore difficult to determine the socially optimal level of charge.

Q34. When there are ready alternatives for the motorist: in terms of altering the timing of journeys, or the route, or the means of transport. For example, road pricing will be more effective if there is an attractive form of public transport available.

Chapter 13

Government Policy Towards Business

 REVIEW

This chapter continues the examination of government policy to tackle market imperfections, focusing on the potential problem that arises if firms have market power. The chapter explores the use of competition policy – measures introduced by the government to encourage competition in order to prevent monopolies and oligopolies from abusing their market power. The second part of the chapter investigates privatisation, and the extent to which regulation is needed to ensure that privatisation does not lead to the abuse of market power.

Although most markets in the real world are imperfect, it is not necessarily the case that this will always be against the public interest. The competition authorities need to be aware of this when implementing competition policy.

13.1 Competition policy

(Pages 384–5) There are a number of possible targets of government policy concerning competition and market power.

 Q1. Figure 13.1 shows a market that can operate either as a monopoly or under perfect competition. $AR = D$ is the market demand curve, and MR its associated marginal revenue curve. Under perfect competition, $MC (= \text{Supply})_{pc}$ is the (short-run) supply curve, but the monopoly is able to achieve economies of scale, and thus faces the marginal cost curve given by $MC_{monopoly}$.

(a) Identify the price and quantity that would result if the market were operating under perfect competition.

....

(b) Identify the output chosen by a profit-maximising monopolist, and the price that would be charged.

....

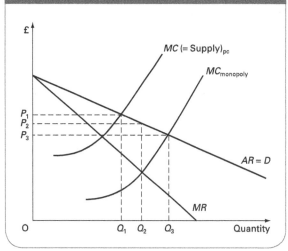

Figure 13.1 Monopoly and perfect competition with differing cost conditions

(c) At what price would the monopoly sell its output if it were subject to regulation that prohibited charging a price above marginal cost?

....

(?) **Q2.** Identify *three* possible targets of competition policy.

1. ....

2. ....

3. ....

Q3. The following are problems that have been the target of various government policies:
   (i) An increase in industrial concentration.
  (ii) The exercise of monopoly power.
 (iii) Restrictive practices.
  (iv) Resale price maintenance.
   (v) Excessive industrial concentration.
  (vi) Natural monopolies.
 (vii) Cross-subsidisation.

On which of the above problems would each of the following policies be primarily targeted?
(a) A government makes it illegal for manufacturers to set the price at which their products must be sold by shops.

....

(b) A government nationalises the national electricity grid.

....

(c) A government makes collusive agreements between oligopolists illegal.

....

(d) A government sets up a body which can investigate any firm with a share of the market above a certain level.

....

(e) Firms are prohibited from using 'unfair competitive practices' whereby they use profits in one market to charge prices below cost in another, and thereby to drive competitors out of business.

....

(f) A regulatory body has the power to limit a firm's price increases where this would result in 'excessive' super-normal profits.

....

(g) A government passes legislation that enables an investigation of any mergers that will lead to the merged firms having more than a certain percentage share of the market.

....

Q4. Which one of the above three problems is addressed by the following types of policy?
(a) Restrictive practices policy   *(i)/(ii)/(iii)*
(b) Monopoly policy   *(i)/(ii)/(iii)*
(c) Merger policy   *(i)/(ii)/(iii)*

Q5. Monopoly policy, under both EU and UK legislation, is directed purely towards monopolies.   *True/False*

(Pages 385–91) Because the relative costs and benefits of monopolies and oligopolies will differ from firm to firm and industry to industry, governments in the UK, like many other governments round the world, have tended to prefer to judge each case on its merits.

Q6. What is the main criterion used under both EU and UK legislation when deciding whether action should be taken against a firm with monopoly power?
A. The firm's market share.
B. Whether its behaviour is anti-competitive.
C. Whether it is achieving economies of scale.
D. Whether it engages in excessive advertising.
E. How high its profits are.

There are various types of anti-competitive practice in which firms can engage.

Q7. The following is a list of anti-competitive practices:
   (i) Tie-in sales.
  (ii) Collusive tendering.
 (iii) Selective distribution.
  (iv) Price rings.
   (v) Price discrimination.
  (vi) Rental-only contracts.
 (vii) Market-sharing agreements.
(viii) Vertical price squeezing.
  (ix) Predatory pricing.

Match the above practices to the following definitions.
(a) Where a firm is only prepared to supply certain selected retail outlets.

....

(b) Where a vertically integrated firm, which controls the supply of an input, charges competitors a high price for that input so that they cannot compete with it in selling the finished good.

....

(c) Where firms divide up the market between them, agreeing not to compete in each other's part of the market.

....

(d) Where firms bidding for a contract (e.g. to supply building materials for a new office development) agree beforehand all to bid high prices.

....

(e) Where a firm sells the same good at a different price (relative to costs) in different sectors of the market.

....

(f) Where a firm is only prepared to hire out equipment and not sell it outright.

....

(g) Where a firm controlling the supply of a first product insists that its customers also buy a second product from it rather than from its rivals.

....

(h) Selling a product below cost in order to drive competitors from the industry.

....

(i) Where firms get together to agree on a common price.

....

Q8. Which of the nine anti-competitive practices in Q7 are:

(a) forms of oligopolistic collusion (restrictive practices)?

....

(b) directly concerned with controlling prices?

....

(c) directly concerned with controlling supply or sales?

....

Q9. The EU and UK approaches to restrictive practices are very similar. Article 101 of the Treaty of the Functioning of the European Union and Chapter I of the UK's 1998 Competition Act do not seek to ban all agreements between oligopolies but rather to ban various types of anti-competitive *behaviour* by oligopolists. *True/False*

Q10. Which type of merger is likely to be most damaging to competition?

horizontal/vertical/conglomerate

(?) Q11. Give three ways in which a merger could be in the public interest.

1. ....

2. ....

3. ....

(?) Q12. Article 102 of the Treaty of the Functioning of the European Union is concerned with European monopolies and mergers. Under this Article, what is the main criterion in judging the desirability of a merger?

....

Q13. The EU merger control measures were adopted in 1990 and amended in 2004. Which of the following are characteristics of the measures?

(a) The process of control is very slow, laborious and administratively expensive. *Yes/No*

(b) The control is weak. *Yes/No*

(c) The regulations are highly inflexible. *Yes/No*

(d) Investigators have been too flexible and too easily persuaded by the firms under investigation. *Yes/No*

Q14. If, under the 1990 regulations (amended in 2004), the European Commission decides on a full investigation of a proposed merger, it can prevent the merger if it is found to be anti-competitive. *True/False*

Q15. The conduct of the Office of Fair Trading (OFT) is governed by the 1998 Competition Act and the 2002 Enterprise Act. Which of the following statements describe how the OFT operates?

(a) In investigating a cartel, the OFT can enter premises, seize documents and require people to answer questions or provide information as part of a criminal investigation. *True/False*

(b) In seeking to establish whether a firm has a dominant position in a market, the OFT checks whether the firm has at least a 40 per cent share of the relevant market. *True/False*

(c) The OFT's prime concern in investigating a firm with dominance in a market is whether the firm is abusing its dominance in such a way as to restrict competition. *True/False*

(d) The OFT investigates mergers in which the combined market share would exceed 25 per cent, and where annual turnover is £70 million or more. *True/False*

Q16. Under UK legislation governing mergers (covered by the 2002 Enterprise Act):

(a) Companies must give details of any proposed merger to the Office of Fair Trading. *True/False*

(b) The Director General of Fair Trading then makes recommendations to the Secretary of State for Trade and Industry. *True/False*

(c) The Secretary of State must then refer the merger proposal to the Competition Commission (CC). *True/False*

(d) When the CC investigates merger proposals, there is no initial assumption that the merger is against the public interest. Instead the arguments for and against are weighed up. *True/False*

(e) The CC reports its findings to the Secretary of State, who must then carry out the wishes of the CC and either prevent or permit the merger, or impose conditions on the future behaviour of the merged firm. *True/False*

(f) It is a criminal offence to engage in cartel agreements. *True/False*

13.2 Privatisation and regulation

(Pages 391–4) Privatisation can take various forms.

(?) **Q17.** Give three forms that privatisation can take other than the complete sale of state-owned corporations by a public sale of shares.

1. ....

2. ....

3. ....

One of the major arguments used to justify privatisation was the low level of profits of nationalised industries.

(?) **Q18.** Give three reasons why the level of profits may have been a poor indicator of the economic performance of nationalised industries.

1. ....

2. ....

3. ....

(◑) **Q19.** Imagine you are an economic consultant given the responsibility of preparing a report on the desirability of privatising the railways in a country where the railways are currently wholly stated owned. Classify the following arguments as being generally for privatisation, against privatisation or inconclusive.

(a) Many socially desirable lines are currently being run at a loss. *for/against/inconclusive*

(b) There are various ways in which competition could be injected into the industry. *for/against/inconclusive*

(c) The 'price' per mile to road users is well below the marginal social cost. *for/against/inconclusive*

(d) Studies show that the efficiency of the railways has been approximately the same as that in other countries.
for/against/inconclusive

(e) The proceeds from the privatisation sale can be used to reduce taxes. *for/against/inconclusive*

(f) There would no longer be any government interference in setting fares. *for/against/inconclusive*

(g) The railways have had a very poor profit record.
for/against/inconclusive

(h) A new genuinely independent body, Ofrail, would be given substantial regulatory powers.
for/against/inconclusive

(?) **Q20.** Assume that a government wants to raise the maximum revenue from a privatisation sale and also wants to inject the maximum amount of competition into the industry. Why may these two objectives come into conflict?

....

....

(Pages 394–5) If a nationalised industry is run 'in the public interest', or if the industry is privately owned but regulated so that it is required to operate in the public interest, how much should it produce and at what price? Take the case of industry X.

(▤) **Q21.** If all other industries were operating under perfect competition and there were no externalities, then the 'first-best' policy for industry X would be to produce where:

A. $P = AR$

B. $AR = AC$

C. $MR = MC$

D. $MC = P$

E. $MC = AC$

(▤) **Q22.** Consider now what price industry X should charge when the first-best situation does not apply. Assume that firms typically throughout the economy (including related industries to industry X) charge a price 15 per cent above marginal cost and that industry X's marginal cost is 5 per cent above its marginal social cost. Assume also that on average other firms' externalities are zero. The second-best price for industry X will be:

A. 10 per cent above its marginal cost.

B. 10 per cent above its average cost.

C. 20 per cent above its marginal cost.

D. 20 per cent above its average cost.

E. 15 per cent above its marginal cost.

(▤) **Q23.** If it is regarded as socially desirable for reasons of equity to provide loss-making rural bus services, what is the least distortionary solution to this problem?

A. Raise the fares on the urban bus services to cover the losses of the rural services so as to retain the same overall level of profit as before.

B. Keep urban fares the same and pay for the rural services from reduced bus company profits.

C. Subsidise the rural services from increased local taxes in rural areas.

D. Subsidise the rural services from increased income tax.

E. Subsidise the rural services from increased taxes on the motorist.

(Pages 395–7) In the UK, the major privatised industries have had substantial market power. It was felt at the time of their privatisation that the OFT and the MMC would not be sufficient to ensure that they operate in the public interest, and so the government set up independent bodies to regulate their behaviour.

(◑) **Q24.** Which of the following are features of UK regulation?

(a) Each regulatory body is responsible for just one industry. *Yes/No*

(b) *All* pricing decisions in the regulated industries are subject to regulation. *Yes/No*

(c) Price regulation is normally of the form: *RPI* plus *X*.

Yes/No

(d) The *X* in the formula is designed to take account of expected increases in efficiency. *Yes/No*

(e) Price regulation takes account of cost increases beyond the control of the industries. *Yes/No*

(f) Price regulation can involve industries having to reduce their prices even when there is inflation. *Yes/No*

(g) If there is no agreement between the regulator and the industry when reviewing price-setting formulae, an appeal can be made to the Competition Commission for settlement of the dispute. *Yes/No*

(h) Once the price-setting formula has been set for a specified number of years, it cannot be changed until the end of that period. *Yes/No*

(i) Regulators are only concerned with pricing decisions.

Yes/No

(j) The system of regulation is discretionary, with the regulator able to judge individual examples of the behaviour of the industry on their own merits.

Yes/No

Q25. In the USA, the main form of regulation has been 'rate-of-return' regulation, which involves restricting the amount of profit a firm can make. This has the major advantage that it encourages firms to find ways of reducing costs. *True/False*

Q26. One of the dangers with regulation is that of 'regulatory capture'. This can be defined as a situation where:

A. the regulator is only concerned about carrying out government policy.

B. the regulator totally dominates the industry, leaving the managers no discretion to make pricing and investment decisions which might be in the *long-term* interests of the industry and the country.

C. the regulator captures an ever *increasing* amount of the decisions of the industry.

D. the managers become obsessed with doing what the regulator wants rather than what is genuinely in the interests of the industry.

E. the regulator starts seeing things from the managers' point of view rather than the consumers'.

Q27. Give three advantages and three disadvantages of the UK system of regulation.

Advantages

1. ....

2. ....

3. ....

Disadvantages

1. ....

2. ....

3. ....

Q28. Assume that a country has a single interconnected system of natural gas pipelines owned by a recently privatised company. Give three ways in which the government could attempt to inject competition into the supply of gas to customers.

1. ....

2. ....

3. ....

B   PROBLEMS, EXERCISES AND PROJECTS

Q29. Figure 13.2 shows an industry that was originally perfectly competitive, but which has been taken over by a monopoly. It is assumed that this has resulted in lower costs of production. (This is illustrated by the two sets of *MC* curves.) It is also assumed that the monopoly produces no external costs or benefits. The government decides to regulate the firm's pricing behaviour.

(a) What price will the unregulated monopoly charge if it wishes to maximise profits?

....

(b) What price will the government set if it wishes the monopoly to charge the socially efficient price?

....

(c) What price will the government set if it wishes the monopoly to make only normal profits?

....

(d) What price will the government set if it wishes the price to be that which would have occurred had the industry remained under perfect competition?

....

Q30. Visit the OFT website at www.oft.gov.uk or the Competition Commission at www.competition-commission.org.uk and peruse some recent merger investigations. Identify and evaluate the economic arguments brought to bear on the cases.

Figure 13.2 Industry under perfect competition and monopoly

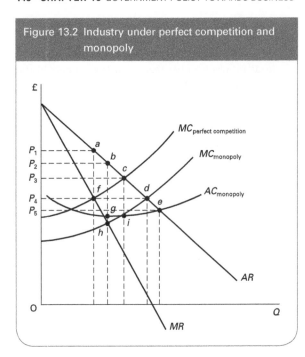

Q31. Select an industry that has been privatised and which has a government regulatory agency (such as Ofwat) concerned with its activities. Do a library and/or Web search to find articles on the industry's performance and pricing policies and on any competition it faces. See the hotlinks section of the Sloman website (www.pearsoned.co.uk/sloman) for useful websites.

You should use these articles to write two brief reports on the industry's performance in the private sector, and on the effectiveness of regulation and attempts to inject competition into the industry. One report should be critical of the industry's performance and one should be in support. You should then write a conclusion stating (a) where the balance of the arguments lies; (b) in what ways regulation could be made more effective; (c) in what ways additional competition could be introduced into the industry.

DISCUSSION TOPICS AND ESSAYS

Q32. Should certain monopolistic and restrictive practices be banned or should firms' practices be judged on a case-by-case basis? Use relevant examples to illustrate your answer.

Q33. Is it best to define the 'public interest' in terms of the level of deadweight welfare loss, when considering whether a firm should be referred to the Competition Commission?

Q34. Compare the differences of approach to (a) monopolies and restrictive practices and (b) mergers, in UK and EU legislation.

Q35. Discuss the relevance of contestability in investigating possible dominance within a market.

Q36. What *evidence* could you provide to a court of law in order to establish that a firm had engaged in predatory pricing? Explain your answer.

Q37. In the first 15 years of EU merger policy only 19 of the 2648 mergers notified were prohibited. Discuss whether this means that the policy was ineffective.

Q38. Give two examples of industries that are in part natural monopolies and which were once nationalised and then privatised. In each case consider whether any competition has been injected into the industry by or since privatisation. Consider ways of injecting further competition and any difficulties in so doing.

Q39. 'In the UK of today, there is no economic justification for nationalisation.' Discuss.

Q40. How successfully does the UK system of regulating privatised utilities protect the consumer's interest?

Q41. Debate
Regulation is always inferior to competition as a means of protecting the consumers' interests.

D **ANSWERS**

Q1. *(a)* Price P_1 and quantity Q_1. This is the point at which demand is equal to market supply.

(b) Under monopoly, the firm would choose to produce at the level of output at which $MC = MR$, which is Q_2, and would then set the price at P_2. Notice that what is happening here is that the monopoly firm enjoys such a cost advantage over a perfectly competitive industry that it sets a lower price, and sells more output.

(c) If forced to set price equal to marginal cost, the monopoly would produce Q_3 output, and sell it at a price P_3. Although this delivers much larger consumer surplus, the firm would make lower profits, and may have limited incentives to remain cost-efficient.

Q2. The three key targets of competition policy are: (1) abuse of the existing power of monopolies and oligopolies; (2) the growth of power of monopolies and oligopolies; and (3) the growth of power through mergers and acquisitions.

Q3. (a) (iv), (b) (vi), (c) (iii), (d) (v), (e) (vii), (f) (ii), (g) (i).

Q4. (a) (ii), (b) (i), (c) (iii).

Q5. *False*. Any firm in a dominant market position (whether a monopolist or an oligopolist) can be investigated if it is suspected of abusing its market power.

Q6. B. The mere possession of power is not seen to be important. What is important is how the firm exercises its power: whether it abuses its power by acting to restrict competition.

Q7. (a) (iii), (b) (viii), (c) (vii), (d) (ii), (e) (v), (f) (vi), (g) (i), (h) (ix), (i) (iv).

Q8. *(a)* (ii), (iv) and (vii).

(b) (ii), (iv), (v), (viii) and (ix).

(c) (i), (iii), (vi) and (vii).

Q9. *True*.

Q10. *horizontal*. This type of merger will reduce the number of firms in the relevant segment of the market.

Q11. Ways include: economies of scale from rationalisation, greater countervailing power to drive down prices charged by suppliers to the firm, increased power to compete more effectively against an already established large firm, increased ability to afford costly research and development.

Q12. Whether the merger is likely to impede effective competition.

Q13. *(a)* No, on the contrary: once it is decided to investigate a merger (which normally takes less than 25 days), the formal investigation must then be completed within 90 days, unless the case is especially complex.

(b) No: the regulations are potentially quite tough.

(c) No again: the regulations are flexible in recognising that mergers *may* be in the interests of consumers if they result in cost reductions.

(d) Before the 2004 amendments, this was a criticism levelled at the Commission, but the process is now overseen by a Chief Competition Economist and a panel to scrutinise the conclusions of the investigating team.

Q14. *True*. It can decide to block the merger, permit it, or permit it subject to various conditions to safeguard competition.

Q15. All are *true*.

Q16. *True*. (a), (b), (d) and (f). *False* (c) (the Secretary of State can choose whether or not to refer the proposed merger to the CC), (e) (the Secretary of State can choose whether or not to accept the recommendations of the CC).

Q17. Ways include: sale of a nationalised firm directly to a private-sector firm (e.g. Rover Group to British Aerospace); sale of government's shares in otherwise private company (e.g. BP); introduction of private contractors into parts of the public sector (e.g. contract cleaners in National Health Service hospitals); introduction of private firms selling directly to the public in otherwise nationalised industries (e.g. private canteens); sale of public sector assets (e.g. council houses).

Q18. Reasons include: poor profitability may be a reflection of low demand rather than ownership; prices may be kept deliberately low by the government for social/political/macroeconomic reasons; costs may be similarly high if it were under private ownership.

Q19. Although (b), (e), (f), (g) and (h) would seem at first sight to be arguments in favour of privatisation and (a) and (c) against, most of the arguments are inconclusive (which is part of the reason why politicians will continue to argue). The extent to which any industry, private or public, operates in the public interest depends on the way in which it is run, the degree of government intervention and the amount of competition faced, and these will not necessarily depend on whether the industry is publicly or privately owned. (How would you reply to argument (e)?)

Q20. To maximise revenue from the sale, the government will want the industry to be as attractive (profitable) as possible to potential shareholders. This will be the case if the industry is sold as a monopoly with the prospect of large supernormal profits. But this will conflict with the second objective of making the industry as competitive as possible.

Q21. D. The socially efficient output for a firm is where $MSB = MSC$. In the absence of externalities and in the first-best situation this will be where $P = MC$.

Q22. A. The second-best pricing formula is $P = MSC + X$ (where X is the average of other industries' price above their MSC). Given that, on average, other firms' externalities are zero, this formula gives $P = (MC - 5\%) + 15\% = MC + 10\%$.

Q23. D. If for reasons of equity it is desired to help a particular section of the community, it is best (*ceteris paribus*) to do this from *general* taxation, otherwise it would be unfair on those who have to pay the subsidy. For example, in A, why should urban bus users have any greater obligation than others to help the rural users?

Q24. *(a)* *Yes.* There are separate regulatory bodies for each regulated industry, such as Ofgem for the fuel (gas and electricity) industry, Ofcom for the telecommunications industry and Ofwat for the water industry.

(b) *No.* Only those parts where it is felt by the government that there is inadequate competition.

(c) *No.* It is of the form *RPI* minus *X*.

(d) *Yes.*

(e) *Yes.* This enters the formula as an extra term *Y*, so that the formula becomes *RPI* – *X* + *Y*.

(f) *Yes*, if *X* – *Y* is greater than the rate of inflation.

(g) *Yes.*

(h) *No.* The price-setting formula may be changed before the end of the period if circumstances change, such as a larger value for *X* than had been anticipated.

(i) *No.* They are also concerned to prevent practices which could be anti-competitive (e.g. attempts to compete unfairly against rivals in order to prevent them getting a larger share of the market).

(j) *Yes.*

Q25. *False.* It does just the opposite: it removes the incentive to reduce costs. What is the point of reducing costs if the regulators simply reduce prices to prevent profits rising?

Q26. E. The regulator is 'captured' by the industry.

Q27. Advantages: it gives the regulator discretion to take account of the specific circumstances of the industry; it is flexible, allowing the licence and price formula to be changed as circumstances change; the price formula gives the industry an incentive to be as efficient as possible, since that way it will be able to make more profit *and keep it* (provided that this does not then lead to a higher value being given to *X*).

Disadvantages: if the value of *X* is too low (which it might become if there are substantial technical advances in the industry), the firm might make excessive profits; if, on the other hand, *X* is changed to reflect reductions in costs, this then removes the incentive referred to above in the list of advantages; a large amount of power is vested in the regulator, who is not democratically accountable; regulation has become increasingly complex, which makes it more difficult for the industries to plan; regulation can involve a time-consuming 'game' between the regulator and the industry; regulatory capture.

Q28. Dividing up the industry into a separate company owning the pipelines and other companies using the pipelines and supplying the customers; forcing the pipeline company to charge the same rates to all companies using the pipelines (including itself, if it is still allowed to supply gas); forcing the pipeline company to allow any supplier meeting safety standards to use the pipelines; breaking up the part of the industry producing gas and supplying gas to customers into several companies; allowing customers to choose from a number of different suppliers (this is possible through metering, provided that central records are kept of the gas metered into the system by each company and the gas used by each consumer allocated to that company).

Chapter 14

The National Economy

 A **REVIEW**

Chapters 14 and 15 offer a basic overview of the principal macroeconomic issues and debates: *growth, unemployment, inflation* and *the balance of payments*. In this chapter we focus on national output and income and how they are measured. We also look at economic growth – the way in which national output and income grow over time.

14.1 The scope of macroeconomics

(Pages 404–6) Macroeconomics often triggers lively debate amongst economists. There can be different views about the importance of macroeconomic issues, their causes and how policy should be designed. Debates can arise about the difficulty of forecasting the path of the economy, about the way in which people form expectations about the future (a critical element in macroeconomic activity), and about the stance that governments may take to influence the economy.

Q1. Which of the following are macroeconomics issues?
(a) An increase in the number of job vacancies.   *Yes/No*
(b) The problems faced by a firm relocating in the south of England.   *Yes/No*
(c) Industrial action by the teaching unions.   *Yes/No*
(d) An increase in the level of taxation.   *Yes/No*
(e) A slowdown in the growth of the economy.   *Yes/No*
(f) The privatisation of the electricity industry.   *Yes/No*
(g) Unemployment in the coal industry.   *Yes/No*
(h) A rise in interest rates.   *Yes/No*

The four key macroeconomic topics to be considered are economic growth, unemployment, inflation and economic relationships with the rest of the world.

Q2. Economies suffer from inherent instability.
True/False

Q3. (Actual) economic growth is defined as

....

Q4. Unemployment in the UK has been lower than in the EU since the 1960s.   *True/False*

Q5. Inflation is defined as:
A. The difference in the price level this year compared with the same time last year.
B. The rise in costs over the previous 12 months.
C. The absolute increase in *average* prices over the previous 12 months.
D. The percentage increase in the average level of prices over the previous 12 months.
E. The percentage expansion of the economy over the previous 12 months.

Q6. Which of the following must happen if a country starts to spend more foreign currency than it earns?
 (i) The balance of payments will go into deficit.
 (ii) The balance of payments will go into surplus.
 (iii) The exchange rate will rise.
 (iv) The exchange rate will fall.

A. (i) or (iii).
B. (ii) or (iv).

 Multiple choice   Written answer   Delete wrong word   Diagram/table manipulation   Calculation   Matching/ordering

C. (i) or (iv).

D. (ii) or (iii).

E. None of the above.

14.2 The circular flow of income

(Pages 406–9) An important diagram for understanding how the macroeconomy works is the *circular flow of income diagram*. It can be used to show the relationship between changes in aggregate demand and the four macroeconomic objectives.

⊖ **Q7.** Figure 14.1 shows a circular flow of income. Attach the correct label (*Cd, G, I, M, S, T, X, Y*) to each of the eight flows.

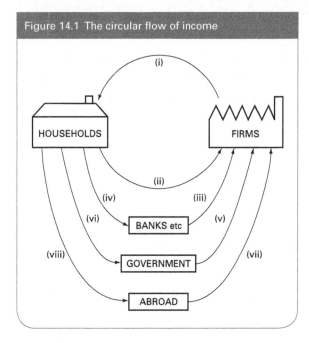

Figure 14.1 The circular flow of income

⬤ **Q8.** Which of the following are changes in injections and which are changes in withdrawals in the UK circular flow of income? In each case specify whether the change is an increase or a decrease. In each case assume *ceteris paribus*.

(a) The government raises tax allowances.

Withdrawal/Injection Increase/Decrease

(b) The government cuts spending on roads.

Withdrawal/Injection Increase/Decrease

(c) Firms borrow more money in order to build up their stocks in preparation for an anticipated rise in consumer demand.

Withdrawal/Injection Increase/Decrease

(d) A depreciation in the exchange rate affects the popularity of holidays abroad.

Withdrawal/Injection Increase/Decrease

(e) Saving is affected by a redistribution of income from the rich to the poor.

Withdrawal/Injection Increase/Decrease

(f) Consumers demand more goods that are domestically produced (but total consumption does not change).

Withdrawal/Injection Increase/Decrease

(g) People invest more money in building societies.

Withdrawal/Injection Increase/Decrease

⊗ **Q9.** The following represent flows in the economy of a small country:

	(£m)
Saving	200
Consumption of domestic goods	1550
Income tax revenue	750
Indirect tax revenue	475
Import expenditure	600
Export expenditure	850
Government expenditure	900
Investment	575

(where government expenditure and investment include only the amount spent in the domestic economy: i.e. exclude any imported component).

Calculate the level of withdrawals from the circular flow.

....

▤ **Q10.** Referring to the data in Q7, what is the level of aggregate demand?

A. £4075m

B. £3875m

C. £3275m

D. £2325m

E. £1550m

(Pages 409–10) Assume initially that injections equal withdrawals. Now assume that injections rise (or withdrawals fall), so that injections exceed withdrawals. This will cause a **Q11.** *rise/fall* in national income. This in turn will cause a **Q12.** *rise/fall* in **Q13.** *injections/withdrawals/both injections and withdrawals* until a new equilibrium level of income is reached where withdrawals once more equal injections. This change in income will tend to be **Q14.** *larger/smaller* than the initial change in injections.

◖ **Q15.** What will happen to the level of national income in an economy if the following changes occur? (In each case assume other things remain unchanged.)

(a) The Chancellor of the Exchequer raises income tax.

Rise/Fall/Impossible to tell without more information

(b) Firms are encouraged by lower interest rates to build new factories.

Rise/Fall/Impossible to tell without more information

(c) French buyers are deterred from buying British-made goods.

Rise/Fall/Impossible to tell without more information

(d) Both taxation and government expenditure are reduced.

Rise/Fall/Impossible to tell without more information

(e) People decide to save a larger proportion of their income.
Rise/Fall/Impossible to tell without more information

(f) Other countries begin to recover from recession.
Rise/Fall/Impossible to tell without more information

14.3 Measuring national income and output

(Pages 410–14) Gross domestic product (GDP) can be calculated in three different ways – the product, income and expenditure methods **Q16.** *true/false* – and the three methods will always produce the same result **Q17.** *true/false*.

Q18. Gross domestic product (GDP) may be defined as

....

In considering data for GDP and many other macroeconomic variables, it is crucial to distinguish between *real* and *nominal* values. This is Threshold Concept 12. The reason is that we need to adjust figures measured in current prices for the rate of inflation, and come to a measurement of real GDP relative to a base year. This may be done using the *GDP deflator*.

Q19. The GDP deflator is the same as the consumer price index (CPI). *True/False*

Q20. Nominal GDP figures show the *variability* of economic growth more clearly than real GDP figures. *True/False*

Q21. Assume that GDP in current prices grows from £120bn in year 1 to £160bn in year 2 and that the GDP deflator rises from 100 in year 1 to 130 in year 2. By how much has real GDP grown (as a percentage)?

....

Q22. In a particular country in 2011, it was announced that nominal GDP had increased by 5 per cent, and prices (as measured by the GDP deflator) had increased by 2 per cent. Which one of the following can be inferred from these facts?

A. Real GDP decreased by 3 per cent.

B. Real GDP increased by 5 per cent.

C. Real GDP increased by 3 per cent.

D. All inhabitants of the country became better off.

E. All inhabitants of the country became worse off.

When comparing national income statistics of different countries, they have to be converted into a common currency (e.g. dollars or euros). But the current market exchange rate may be a poor indicator of the purchasing power of a country's currency. To correct for this, *purchasing-power parity* (PPP) exchange rates can be used. PPP rates are those at which a given amount of money would buy the same in any country after exchanging it into the local currency. GDP measured at PPP exchange rates is known as *purchasing-power standard* GDP (PPS GDP).

Q23. If country A has a national income of $10bn and country B has a national income of $12bn at current exchange rates, and if, in PPP terms, current exchange rates overvalue the currency of B relative to A by 1.5 times, what is the ratio of the PPS GDP of country A to country B?

....

Q24. Identify five reasons why real GDP may not provide a good indication of a country's standard of living.

1. ....

2. ....

3. ....

4. ....

5. ....

14.4 Short-term economic growth and the business cycle

(Pages 415–17) When discussing economic growth we need to distinguish between *actual* and *potential* economic growth.

Q25. What would be the result of each of the following events: actual growth, potential growth, both or neither? (In each case assume that other things remain constant.)

(a) The discovery of new raw materials.
Actual growth/potential growth/both/neither

(b) Firms take on more labour in response to an increase in consumer demand.
Actual growth/potential growth/both/neither

(c) A reduction in the number of vacancies in the economy.
Actual growth/potential growth/both/neither

(d) An increase in the level of investment.
Actual growth/potential growth/both/neither

(e) A reduction in the working week.
Actual growth/potential growth/both/neither

(f) The discovery of new more efficient techniques which could benefit industry generally.
Actual growth/potential growth/both/neither

(g) Increased expenditure on training.
Actual growth/potential growth/both/neither

The output gap is calculated as **Q26.** *actual output – potential output/potential output – actual output*. Generally, the gap will be **Q27.** *negative/positive* in a boom and **Q28.** *negative/positive* in a recession. The **Q29.** *de-trending/production function* approach provides a way of measuring the output gap based on economic theory.

Q30. Actual growth can never be greater than potential growth. *True/False*

The awareness that such fluctuations are normal is part of thinking like an economist. It is our thirteenth Threshold Concept.

(Pages 415–17) Actual growth will tend to fluctuate over the course of the business cycle. The cycle can be broken down into four phases: the upturn, the boom, the peaking out and the slowdown or recession. In the **Q31.** *upturn/expansion/ peaking out/slowdown or recession* phase the rate of growth will be at its highest, whereas in the **Q32.** *upturn/expansion/ peaking out/slowdown or recession* phase growth may actually cease or even become negative. Actual and potential outputs are closest during the **Q33.** *upturn/expansion/peaking out/ slowdown or recession* phase of the business cycle.

Q34. With reference to Figure 14.2, match the following with the three lines on the graph (I, II, and III).
(a) Trend output.   I/II/III
(b) Potential output.   I/II/III
(c) Actual output.   I/II/III

Q35. Again with reference to Figure 14.2 match the points 1, 2, 3, 4, 5 with the following.
(a) The peaking out.   1/2/3/4/5
(b) The expansion.   1/2/3/4/5
(c) The slowdown.   1/2/3/4/5
(d) The upturn.   1/2/3/4/5

(?) Q36. Why is it unlikely that actual and potential outputs would ever be equal?

....

....

Q37. Which of the following can be a cause of business cycles?
(a) Government policy   *Yes/No*
(b) Consumer spending   *Yes/No*
(c) Export sales   *Yes/No*
(d) Firms' investment expenditure   *Yes/No*

14.5 Long-term economic growth

(Pages 420–6) When we look at economic growth over the *longer* term, it is growth in *potential* output that we need to examine.

(?) Q38. The potential output of an economy depends upon which two factors?

1. ....

2. ....

This idea that long-term growth depends on the growth in the quantity and/or productivity of its resources is the fourteenth Threshold Concept.

Q39. Which of the following affects the *quantity* of factors of production in an economy, and which affects their *productivity*?
(a) An inflow of immigrant workers.   *Quantity/Productivity*
(b) Technological progress.   *Quantity/Productivity*
(c) Education and training.   *Quantity/Productivity*
(d) A fall in unemployment.   *Quantity/Productivity*
(e) An increase in the capital stock.   *Quantity/Productivity*
(f) A more flexible labour market.   *Quantity/Productivity*

Q40. The relationship between investment as a proportion of national income (*i*) and the potential rate of economic growth (g_p) is given by the formula:
A. $g_p = i / MEC$
B. $g_p = MEC / i$
C. $g_p = MEC - i$
D. $g_p = i - MEC$
E. $g_p = i \times MEC$

where *MEC* stands for the marginal efficiency of capital: the annual extra income (ΔY) as a proportion of the investment (*i*) that yielded it.

(X) Q41. Given that investment of £100m yields an extra £50m annual national income, and given that 25 per cent of national income is put into new investment, what will be the growth in potential output?

....

Q42. If there is an increase in the size of the population, this will cause the level of output per head to increase.
True/False

Appendix: Calculating GDP

There are three methods of calculating GDP: the product method, the income method and the expenditure method.

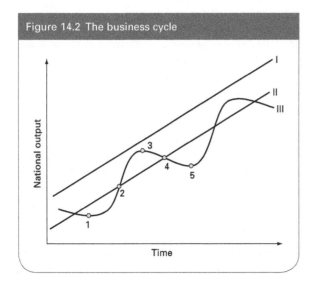

Figure 14.2 The business cycle

(Pages 426–7) The product method

In order to avoid double counting we measure the value added to a product or service as it passes through each phase of its production.

⊗ **Q43.** If a raw material supplier, firm A, sells some raw materials to firm B for £120, which then processes them and sells them to firm C for £160; and if firm C fashions them and sells them to firm D for £240, which uses them to produce a finished good which it sells to a wholesaler for £300, which then sells it to a retailer for £350, which then adds a £25 mark-up – what has been the total value of production? Use a value-added approach to work out the answer.

....

◗ **Q44.** Which of the following would be included in the measurement of the UK's GDP?

(a) The appreciation of stock due to price increases.

Yes/No

(b) A service provided by government. *Yes/No*

(c) A raw material that is imported. *Yes/No*

(d) Stocks carried over from previous years. *Yes/No*

(e) The profits from the output produced in the UK by foreign-owned firms. *Yes/No*

(f) The benefits derived by owner occupiers from living in a property. *Yes/No*

(g) Additions to stocks made during the year. *Yes/No*

(h) The incomes earned by UK residents from the production of overseas companies. *Yes/No*

(Pages 427–30) The income approach

◗ **Q45.** The factor incomes generated from the production of goods and services will be exactly equal to the sum of all values added. *True/False*

⊗ **Q46.** Table 14.1 represents a simplified national income account.

(a) What is the level of gross value added?

....

(b) What is the level of gross domestic product (at market prices)?

....

Table 14.1 Items from a national income account

	(£m)
Compensation of employees	3000
Gross profit	500
Gross rent and interest	100
Mixed incomes	90
Taxes on products	150
Subsidies on products	60

(Page 430) The expenditure approach

◗ **Q47.** Which of the following items would be included in measuring the UK's GDP by the expenditure method?

(a) Spending on domestically produced consumer durables. *Yes/No*

(b) The purchase of British clothes in Europe. *Yes/No*

(c) Government spending on social security. *Yes/No*

(d) Government spending on educational services.

Yes/No

(e) The purchase of new machinery by private industry.

Yes/No

(f) Expenditure on new private housing.

Yes/No

(g) Local government expenditure on new council housing. *Yes/No*

(h) Private expenditure on old (unimproved) housing.

Yes/No

⊗ **Q48.** Table 14.2 shows GDP by category of expenditure. Calculate

(a) GDP (at market prices) ....

(b) GVA ....

(Pages 430–1) Other measures

Three other measures that are frequently used are gross national income (GNY), net national income (NNY) and households' disposable income.

⊗ **Q49.** Using the figures in Table 14.2, calculate the following:

(a) GNY..

(b) NNY..

▤ **Q50.** Households' disposable income is:

A. GDP (at market prices) + taxes paid by firms – subsidies received by firms + personal taxes – benefits.

Table 14.2 GDP by category of expenditure

	(£m)
Consumer expenditure	1050
Government final consumption	600
Gross domestic fixed capital formation	500
Exports of goods and services	850
Imports of goods and services	950
Taxes on products	500
Subsidies on products	50
Net income from abroad	60
Capital consumption (depreciation)	120

B. GDP (at market prices) – taxes paid by firms + subsidies received by firms – depreciation – undistributed profits + personal taxes – benefits.

C. GDP (at market prices) – taxes paid by firms + subsidies received by firms – depreciation – undistributed profits – personal taxes + benefits.

D. GNY (at market prices) – taxes paid by firms + subsidies received by firms – undistributed profits + personal taxes – benefits.

E. GDY (at market prices) – taxes paid by firms + subsidies received by firms – depreciation – undistributed profits – personal taxes + benefits.

B PROBLEMS, EXERCISES AND PROJECTS

Q51. In small groups, find four items from this week's newspapers that are macroeconomic items. What makes them macroeconomic? To what extent is each of the items related to any of the four macroeconomic objectives that we have identified? Are any of the items related to macroeconomic policy and, if so, how is the policy supposed to improve the macroeconomic situation?

Q52. Given the following data:

	£m
Consumers' expenditure	290 000
Government final consumption	91 000
Gross domestic fixed capital formation	80 000
Exports of goods and services	110 000
Imports of goods and services	125 000

Calculate the level of aggregate demand (*AD*)........................

Q53. Using available statistical sources, find time-series data for the past ten years for the following macroeconomic variables:

- Consumer expenditure.
- Government expenditure.
- Gross fixed capital formation.
- Imports and exports.

Calculate the level of aggregate demand for each of the years found (a bar chart may be effective here) and describe the implications of your findings. Does there appear to be a regular business cycle? What is the length of time between peaks? Data may be obtained from the *Annual Abstract of Statistics* or *Blue Book*, available on the National Statistics website at www.statistics.gov.uk. See, in particular, the 'Time series data' section.

Q54. In small groups, find data for economic growth, unemployment, inflation and current account deficits as a proportion of GDP for the UK and two other developed countries from 1980 to the current time. Data can be found from *OECD Economic Outlook* (http://www.oecd.org).

(a) When has economic growth been the highest in the UK and when has it been negative? Has the pattern been cyclical? Have the 'ups and downs' in economic growth since 1980 been similar in all three countries?

(b) Which of the countries has had the highest long-term growth?

(c) What explanations can you offer for (i) differences in the amount by which economic growth fluctuates in the three countries; (ii) differences in long-term economic growth in the three countries?

(d) How do the four indicators vary with each other over the course of the business cycle in the three countries?

Q55. Table 14.3 shows UK National Income Accounts for 2009 by category of expenditure. Calculate the following:
(a) GDP.
(b) GVA.
(c) GNY.
(d) NNY.

Table 14.3 UK national income by category of expenditure

	(£m at constant 2006 prices)
Consumption of households and NPISH	846 947
General government final consumption	296 306
Gross fixed capital formation	196 997
Changes in inventories	−14 790
Exports of goods and services	334 601
Imports of goods and services	362 026
Statistical discrepancy	−1 346
Taxes on products *less* subsidies	137 540
Net income from abroad	28 247
Capital consumption	150 413

DISCUSSION TOPICS AND ESSAYS

Q56. Assume that country A has higher economic growth, lower unemployment and lower inflation than country B. Discuss whether this makes country A (a) more successful economically; (b) a better place to live in than country B.

Q57. Sketch a circular flow of income diagram and describe its components. Explain the effect of (a) a decrease in saving and (b) an increase in direct taxation.

Q58. Suppose that the proportion of the 18–30 age group participating in higher education rises from 40 to 50 per cent. Explain what is likely to happen to the level and rate of growth of GDP in (a) the short run and (b) the long run. Specify your assumptions.

Q59. (a) What is the relationship between actual and potential output? (b) What is the relationship between actual and potential growth?

Q60. At what stage of the business cycle is the economy at the present time? Are all the macroeconomic variables behaving in the way you would expect?

Q61. How might the government set about increasing the overall level of investment in the economy? What problems is it likely to encounter in attempting to do so?

Q62. Why can GDP be measured in three different ways? What adjustments have to be made to ensure that all these methods yield the same figure?

Q63. There are difficulties in making useful national income comparisons not only of different countries, but also of the same country over time. Why?

Q64. A number of measures have been proposed to augment GDP as a measure of economic well-being. Evaluate the extent to which these circumvent the weaknesses of GDP.

Q65. Debate
Comparing the welfare of different countries' citizens by the use of GNY statistics is so misleading that it is better not to use these statistics at all for comparative purposes.

Q66. Debate
The pursuit of economic growth is not in society's best long-term interests.

ANSWERS

Q1. (a), (d), (e) and (h) are macroeconomic issues as they concern the whole economy rather than a segment of it.

Q2. *True.*

Q3. Economic growth can be defined as the percentage increase in national output over a 12-month period.

Q4. *False.* Unemployment in the UK in the early 1990s and the early years of the 21st century was lower than in the EU (12), especially countries like France and Germany. However, before that, the UK experienced unemployment that was above the average for the EU (12). (See Table 14.1 on page 405 of Sloman, *Economics*, this edition.)

Q5. D.

Q6. (i) *Y*, (ii) *Cd*, (iii) *I*, (iv) *S*, (v) *G*, (vi) *T*, (vii) *X*, (viii) *M*.

Q7. C.

Q8. (a) *withdrawal, decrease*; (b) *injection, decrease*; (c) *injection, increase* (building up stocks counts as investment); (d) *withdrawal, decrease*; (e) *withdrawal, decrease* (the poor save proportionally less and spend proportionally more than the rich); (f) *withdrawal (imports), decrease*; (g) *withdrawal (saving), increase* (note that whereas it is normal in everyday

language to refer to depositors 'investing' in building societies, economists refer to this as 'saving'; they reserve the term 'investment' to refer to the spending by firms on capital (plant, equipment, stocks, etc.) which is an *injection*).

Q9. £2025m ($S + T$ (both) $+ M$).

Q10. B. $C_d + I + G + X$. Notice that C_d excludes imports: if the consumption figure was for *total* consumption, we would have to subtract imports: i.e. $C - M + I + G + X$.

Q11. *rise.*

Q12. *rise.*

Q13. *withdrawals.* (In the simple model, injections are not affected by the level of income.)

Q14. *larger.* The reason is that additional injections will subsequently flow round and round the circular flow of income, generating additional expenditure and additional income. There is a 'multiplied' rise in income (see Chapter 17). But the process will not go on for ever, because eventually all the additional injections will leak away as additional withdrawals.

Q15. (a) *fall* (increase in withdrawals); (b) *rise* (increase in injections); (c) *fall* (fall in injections); (d) *impossible* *to tell without further information* (both withdrawals and injections fall); (e) *fall* (increase in withdrawals); (f) *rise* (increase in injections: i.e. exports to these countries rise as a result of their increased incomes).

Q16. *True.*

Q17. *False*: although in principle the three methods should produce the same result, measurement inaccuracies means that the three methods will produce slightly different results in practice.

Q18. The value of output produced within the economy over a 12-month period.

Q19. *False.* The GDP deflator, unlike the CPI, includes not just the prices of consumer goods, but also the prices of investment goods, the prices of goods and services consumed by the government and the prices of exports: in other words, it includes the weighted prices of all the components of GDP. However, it is the rate of change of the CPI that is used as the target rate for inflation.

Q20. *False*: the variability of economic growth is shown more clearly in the real GDP values. This is masked in the nominal values by the effect of changing prices.

Q21. 2.56 per cent.

This is calculated as follows:

Real GDP = Nominal GDP/GDP deflator $\times$ 100

Thus in year 1, real GDP = £120bn/100 $\times$ 100 = £120bn

and in year 2, real GDP = £160bn/130 $\times$ 100 = £123.07bn.

∴ real GDP has grown by (123.07 − 120)/120 $\times$ 100 = 2.56%.

Q22. C. The formula is: nominal GDP growth minus the rate of inflation. Note that answer *D* is wrong because, although it is possible that all inhabitants became better off (*D*), the data cannot tell us this, partly because GDP is not informative about the distribution of income, and partly because whether people are better or worse off does not only depend on things that are measured in GDP.

Q23. The ratio of country A's GDP to country B's is 10/12 at current exchange rates. Given, however, that country B's currency is overvalued by 1.5 times in PPP terms, the ratio of country A's PPS GDP to country B's PPS GDP is 10/12 $\times$ 1.5 = 1.25.

Q24. Reasons include: real GDP needs to be adjusted for population size; it is not informative about the distribution of income; in international comparison we need to take account of exchange rate issues; real GDP does not take account of items that are not marketed; it ignores externalities.

Q25. (a) *potential growth.* (Only if they are *used* will there be actual growth.)

(b) *actual growth.*

(c) *neither.* (A reduction in vacancies usually signals a reduction in output. It *could*, however, be a sign

of increased labour productivity, in which case there would be *potential growth*, or more vacancies being filled, in which case there would be *actual growth.*)

(d) *both.* (Increased investment, by increasing the stock of capital, increases potential output. The purchase of new machinery and equipment stimulates growth in the industries producing the equipment.)

(e) *neither.* (Other things being equal, it will lead to a *reduction* in output.)

(f) *potential.* (It would only lead to actual growth if these techniques were used.)

(g) *both.* (It will increase labour productivity and hence lead to potential growth. The employment of instructors and other money spent on the training will stimulate demand and hence encourage an increased output in the economy.)

Q26. *actual output − potential output.*

Q27. *positive.*

Q28. *negative.*

Q29. *production function.* Using de-trending techniques is a purely mechanistic way of measuring the output gap.

Q30. *False.* Provided there is some slack in the economy (i.e. production is inside the production possibility curve), actual growth can take place by using some of the idle capacity. Only when the economy is operating at full capacity will potential growth be a necessary condition for actual growth.

Q31. The *expansion* phase.

Q32. The *peaking out* and the *slowdown or recession* phases.

Q33. The *peaking out* phase. During this phase the economy will be running closest to full capacity.

Q34. (a) II; (b) I; (c) III.

Q35. (a) 3; (b) 2; (c) 4; (d) 1 and 5.

Q36. In a perfect market situation it might be possible for all resources to be fully utilised. In real-world markets, however, either as a result of imperfect information, or as a consequence of other market failures, some resources will remain idle.

Q37. All of these items can cause fluctuations in economic activity. These are explored in more detail in section 17.4 of Sloman, *Economics*, this edition (see pages 517–21).

Q38. Potential output depends on the growth in the quantity and/or the productivity of its resources.

Q39. *Quantity*: (a), (d) and (e).

Productivity: (b), (c) and (f).

Q40. E.

Q41. The MEC = 50/100 = 0.5. In order to find the potential growth rate we use the formula $g = i \times MEC$, where i is the level of investment as a percentage of national income (i = 25%). Thus g = 25% $\times$ 0.5 = 12.5%.

Q42. *False.* Whether output per head rises or not depends upon the proportion of the population as a whole that is working, and whether the marginal product of labour of new workers is above the average product of labour.

Q43. £120 + £40 + £80 + £60 + £50 + £25 = £375 (which is the retail price).

Q44. *Yes*: (b), (e), (f) and (g). (Note that if we had been referring to gross *national income*, then (e) would not have been included but (h) would have been.)

Q45. *True.* The value added in production is simply the difference between a firm's revenue from sales and the costs of its purchases from other firms. This difference is made up of the wages, rent, interest and profit generated in the production process.

Q46. *(a)* £3690m: i.e. income from employment + gross profits + gross rent and interest + mixed incomes.
 (b) £3780m, i.e. *GVA* + taxes on products − subsidies on products.

Q47. All except (c) and (h) would be included in the expenditure method of calculating GDP (since all except (c) and (h) involve the production of goods and/or services).

Q48. *(a)* £2050m (i.e. $C + G + I + X - M$).
 (b) £1600m (i.e. GDP − taxes on products + subsidies on products).

Q49. *(a)* £2110m (i.e. GDP at market prices + net income from abroad).
 (b) £1990m (i.e. GNY − depreciation).

Q50. E. It is the income available for people to spend after all deductions and additions.

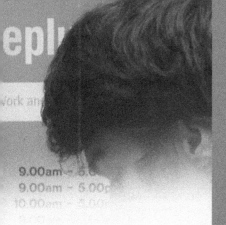

Chapter 15

Macroeconomic Issues and Analysis: an Overview

 A   REVIEW

In the previous chapter we examined economic growth. In this chapter, we explore the other three key macroeconomic issues – namely, unemployment, inflation and the balance of payments. The chapter introduces the important tool of aggregate demand and supply analysis.

15.1 Unemployment

(Pages 434–43) We start by examining the meaning and measurement of unemployment.

Q1. If there are 3 million people unemployed and 24 million people employed, the rate of unemployment will be:
A. 3 per cent
B. 8 per cent
C. 9 per cent
D. 11.1 per cent
E. 12.5 per cent

Q2. There are two major measures of unemployment: the claimant count and the standardised measure used by the ILO and OECD. Why is claimant unemployment likely to be lower than standardised unemployment?

....

....

Q3. The stock of unemployment at the end of year *t* equals the stock of unemployment at the beginning of year *t* minus the outflows of people from unemployment to work or to outside the labour force, plus the inflows of people to unemployment from jobs and from outside the labour force.   *True/False*

Q4. Which one of the following will increase the level of unemployment?
A. More people retire.
B. More unemployed people become disheartened and give up looking for work.
C. The school leaving age is raised.
D. The retirement age is lowered.
E. More people resign from low-paid jobs.

We now turn to the different types of unemployment.

Q5. Which of the following defines *real-wage* unemployment?
A. Real wages being set above the equilibrium level by trade unions, or minimum wage legislation.
B. Inflation causing an erosion of real wages and hence a rise in unemployment.
C. Increased aggregate demand in the economy driving up equilibrium real wages.
D. Increased aggregate demand in the economy causing money wages to rise faster than real wages.
E. Real wages falling below the equilibrium level as a result of deficiency of demand.

Q6. Why is demand-deficient unemployment sometimes referred to as *cyclical unemployment*?

....

....

Q7. Frictional unemployment is the result of:
A. a shift in the pattern of consumer demand.
B. workers and employers being ill-informed about the labour market.
C. the introduction of new technology.
D. the economy entering the recessionary phase of the business cycle.
E. employers responding to the time of year and cutting back on their level of production.

Q8. Which of the following will affect the level of *structural* unemployment?
(*a*) The concentration of a particular industry within a particular region.   *Yes/No*
(*b*) The speed at which structural change within the economy is taking place.   *Yes/No*
(*c*) The immobility of labour.   *Yes/No*

Q9. Given the following possible types of unemployment – *demand-deficient/real-wage/frictional/ structural/technological/seasonal* – which one is likely to worsen in which of the following cases?
(*a*) The introduction of robots in manufacturing.

....

(*b*) The economy moves into recession.

....

(*c*) Legislation is passed guaranteeing everyone a minimum wage rate that is 60 per cent of the national average.

....

(*d*) The development of the single market in Europe leads to a movement of capital to the 'centre of gravity' in Europe.

....

(*e*) The government decides to close job centres in an attempt to save money.

....

(*f*) The government raises interest rates.

....

(*g*) More people are forced to take their annual holidays when the schools are on holiday.

....

Q10. Figure 15.1 shows the aggregate labour market, where AD_L shows the aggregate demand for labour, AS_L shows the aggregate supply of labour, and N shows the total number in the labour force.

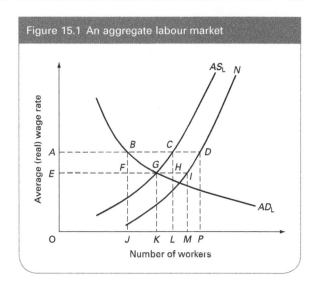

Figure 15.1 An aggregate labour market

(*a*) Identify the equilibrium wage and the number of workers employed.

....

(*b*) What is unemployment in this situation?

....

(*c*) Why does unemployment arise if the labour market is in equilibrium?

....

(*d*) Suppose that the wage rate is set at *OA*. Identify employment and unemployment, distinguishing between equilibrium and disequilibrium unemployment.

....

(*e*) Why might such a situation arise?

....

5.2 Aggregate demand and supply and the level of prices

(Pages 444–6) Before we examine the causes of inflation (the rate of increase in prices), we need to look at how the *level* of prices in the economy is determined.

It is determined by the interaction of aggregate demand and aggregate supply.

Q11. As the price level in the economy rises, which of the following occurs?
(i) The quantity of 'real money' decreases.
(ii) Real aggregate demand decreases.
(iii) Total spending in *money* terms decreases.

A. (i) only.
B. (ii) only.
C. (i) and (ii).
D. (i) and (iii).
E. (i), (ii) and (iii).

The aggregate demand curve slopes downwards. This is largely because of a *substitution effect* of a rise in the price level.

Q12. Of the following, which account for the substitution effect of a rise in the price level?

(a) Higher domestic prices lead to people purchasing fewer domestic goods and more imports.

Yes/No

(b) Exports become less competitive and thus fewer are sold. *Yes/No*

(c) People cannot afford to buy so much at higher prices. *Yes/No*

(d) As the price level rises, so the value of people's money balances will fall. They will therefore *spend* less in order to increase their money balances and go some way to protecting their real value.

Yes/No

(e) The government is likely to raise taxes as prices rise. Higher taxes will mean that people will be able to purchase less. *Yes/No*

(f) Higher wages and prices cause a higher demand for money. With a given supply of money in the economy, this will drive up interest rates and encourage people to spend less and save more. This will have the effect of reducing real aggregate demand.

Yes/No

(g) Higher prices will encourage the government to reduce the money supply in an attempt to reduce inflation. The reduction in money supply will reduce spending. *Yes/No*

Q13. There are various factors that can cause the aggregate demand curve to shift. What effect will the following have on the aggregate demand curve?

(a) The government increases the money supply.

Leftward shift/rightward shift/
no shift (movement along)

(b) The government increases taxes.

Leftward shift/rightward shift/
no shift (movement along)

(c) The government increases its spending.

Leftward shift/rightward shift/
no shift (movement along)

(d) People anticipate a rise in the rate of inflation.

Leftward shift/rightward shift/
no shift (movement along)

(e) Higher prices lead to higher interest rates.

Leftward shift/rightward shift/
no shift (movement along)

(f) The government reduces interest rates.

Leftward shift/rightward shift/
no shift (movement along)

(g) Higher UK prices lead to a fall in the exchange rate.

Leftward shift/rightward shift/
no shift (movement along)

(h) A reduction in prices abroad leads to a fall in the demand for UK exports.

Leftward shift/rightward shift/
no shift (movement along)

(?) Q14. Why is the aggregate supply curve upward sloping?

....

....

Figure 15.2 shows aggregate demand and aggregate supply curves for an economy. The equilibrium price level is **Q15.** $P_1/P_2/P_3$. If the price level were to be at P_2, there would be an overall **Q16.** *equilibrium/shortage/surplus*. In response, prices would be driven **Q17.** *down/up*, which would encourage firms to produce **Q18.** *more/less* and there would be a movement **Q19.** *of/up* along the *AS* curve. At the same time, there would be a movement **Q20.** *of/up* along the *AD* curve until the equilibrium was reached.

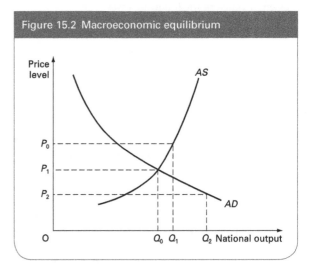

Figure 15.2 Macroeconomic equilibrium

15.3 Inflation

(Pages 446–9) The rate of inflation in the UK is normally calculated by taking the percentage increase in the consumer price index (CPI).

Q21. If the CPI increased by 14 points over a 12-month period, the standard of living must have fallen.

True/False

Q22. Suppose that the CPI in a country increases from 150 to 153 over a period of a year. What is the rate of inflation?

A.   3 per cent

B.   2 per cent

C.   1.02 per cent

D.   0.03 per cent

E.   0.02 per cent

Q23. The consumer price index is sometimes known as the *GDP deflator*.   *True/False*

Q24. In a period of rapid inflation, which of the following would be the least desirable store of wealth?
A. Vintage wine.
B. Money.
C. Property.
D. Land.
E. Stocks and shares.

Q25. Debtors are likely to benefit from inflation.
                                                 True/False

Q26. Why is a high rate of domestic inflation likely to make the country's foreign trade balance (exports minus imports) worse?

....

....

Q27. Why might a higher rate of inflation cause economic growth to slow down?

....

....

(*Pages 449–57*) Inflation is caused by persistent **Q28.** *rightward/leftward* shifts in the aggregate demand curve and/or persistent **Q29.** *rightward/leftward* shifts in the aggregate supply curve.

Q30. Assume that the following factors lead to inflation. Which ones will result in demand-pull inflation and which will result in cost-push inflation? (In each case assume *ceteris paribus*.)
(*a*) A cut in the rate of income tax.
                                  demand-pull/cost-push
(*b*) The expansion of public-sector works.
                                  demand-pull/cost-push
(*c*) An attempt by unions to increase real wages
                                  demand-pull/cost-push
(*d*) An increase in the price of oil.   *demand-pull/cost-push*
(*e*) VAT is imposed on domestic fuel.
                                  demand-pull/cost-push
(*f*) A company decides to increase its profits by increasing its prices.   *demand-pull/cost-push*

Q31. Explain the phenomenon of the wage–price spiral.

....

....

Anti-inflationary policy can focus on reducing the rate of growth in aggregate demand ('demand-side policy') or on reducing the rate of increase in costs ('supply-side policy').

Q32. Which of the following are examples of demand-side policies and which of supply-side policies?
(*a*) A cut in government expenditure.
                                  demand-side/supply-side
(*b*) A rise in taxation.   *demand-side/supply-side*
(*c*) Tougher anti-monopoly policy.
                                  demand-side/supply-side
(*d*) Reducing the bargaining power of trade unions.
                                  demand-side/supply-side
(*e*) Increasing the rate of interest. *demand-side/supply-side*
(*f*) Offering tax incentives to encourage increased productivity.   *demand-side/supply-side*

Q33. How will expectations influence the rate of inflation?

....

....

....

(*Pages 454–5*) The Phillips curve was claimed to reveal a trade-off relationship between inflation and unemployment.

Q34. What use could a Phillips curve serve for economic policy makers (assuming that it painted an accurate picture)?
A. Predicting the phase of the business cycle.
B. Showing the relationship between the level of aggregate demand and aggregate supply.
C. Showing the relationship between rates of unemployment and rates of inflation.
D. Showing the relationship between overseas trade and economic growth.
E. Showing the effects of expectations on the level of investment.

During the late 1950s and 1960s, policy makers interpreted the Phillips curve as follows: demand management policy would lead to a **Q35.** *shift in/movement along* the Phillips curve. Thus it would only be possible to reduce both inflation and unemployment together by **Q36.** *expansionary demand management policies/contractionary demand management policies/keeping the level of aggregate demand the same/using policies to influence non-demand factors causing inflation and unemployment*.

After 1966 the Phillips curve appeared to break down, and economies began to experience both higher unemployment *and* higher inflation.

Q37. Today the evidence suggests that there is no longer any relationship between inflation and unemployment.
                                                 True/False

15.4 The balance of payments and exchange rates

(Page 457)

Q38. The balance of payments for country A is defined as the balance of all money transactions between the residents of country A and the residents of all other countries over a specified period of time. *True/False*

Q39. Receipts of money from abroad are counted as *credits* on the balance of payments, whereas outflows of money are regarded as *debits*. *True/False*

Q40. Which of the following are debit items and which are credit items on the UK balance of payments account?

(a) The purchase of imports. *debit/credit*

(b) Loans made to non-UK residents by UK banks. *debit/credit*

(c) Investment by UK companies abroad. *debit/credit*

(d) Dividends earned by UK shareholders on overseas investment by UK companies. *debit/credit*

(e) Investment in the UK by non-UK companies. *debit/credit*

(f) Money placed on short-term deposit in the UK by non-residents. *debit/credit*

(g) Drawing on reserves. *debit/credit*

(Pages 457–60) The balance of payments account is composed of a number of parts.

Q41. A country has the following items in its balance of payments:

Exports of goods	£120m
Imports of services	£60m
Income flows and current transfers from abroad	£80m
Imports of goods	£150m
Exports of services	£50m
Income flows and current transfers going abroad	£30m

Its balance on trade in goods and services is a:

A. deficit of £40m.

B. deficit of £30m.

C. deficit of £20m.

D. deficit of £10m.

E. surplus of £10m.

Q42. Referring to the data of Q41, the country's balance of payments on current account is a:

A. deficit of £40m.

B. deficit of £30m.

C. deficit of £20m.

D. deficit of £10m.

E. surplus of £10m.

Q43. If there is a current account deficit of £1bn, then:

A. there must be a surplus of £1bn on trade in services.

B. there must be an equivalent deficit on the capital plus financial accounts.

C. there must be a net errors and omissions item of +£1bn.

D. the overall capital plus financial accounts (including net errors and omissions) must be in surplus by £1bn.

E. the financial account must be +£1bn.

Q44. The following are the various elements in the UK balance of payments account:

(i) Imports of goods (–)

(ii) Exports of goods (+)

(iii) Imports of services (–)

(iv) Exports of services (+)

(v) Incomes and current transfers to the UK from abroad (+)

(vi) Incomes and current transfers abroad from the UK (–)

(vii) Transfers of capital to the UK from abroad (+)

(viii) Transfers of capital abroad from the UK (–)

(ix) Long-term UK investment abroad (–)

(x) Long-term investment in the UK from abroad (+)

(xi) Short-term financial outflows (–)

(xii) Short-term financial inflows (+)

(xiii) Adding to reserves (–)

(xiv) Drawing on reserves (+)

Into which of the above categories would you put the following items (there can be more than one item in each category)?

(a) A car imported from Germany.

....

(b) Insurance cover purchased by an overseas company at Lloyd's in London.

....

(c) The UK pays a contribution to EU Budget.

....

(d) A Japanese car company builds a factory in the UK.

....

(e) A UK resident takes a holiday in Florida.

....

(f) Interest earned by non-UK residents on assets held in the UK.

....

(g) A UK insurance company sets up a branch in Canada.

....

(h) Running down the stock of foreign exchange in the Bank of England.

....

(i) Deposits in UK banks by foreigners.

....

(j) Scotch whisky sold in France.

....

(k) Aid given by the UK to developing countries for the construction of infrastructure.

....

⊗ **Q45.** The following are items in country X's balance of payments accounts for 2011:

Exports of services	£80bn
Exports of goods	£74bn
Income flows and current transfers from abroad to country X	£43bn
Net investment abroad by country X	£70bn
Imports of services	£78bn
Imports of goods	£82bn
Net investment in country X from abroad	£56bn
Financial derivatives (net)	£12bn
Drawing on reserves	£1bn
Income flows and current transfers abroad from country X	£40bn
Transfers of capital to country X from abroad	£7bn
Transfers of capital abroad from country X	£5bn

Work out the following balances in country X's balance of payments:

(a) the balance on trade in goods

....

(b) the balance on trade in goods and services

....

(c) the balance of payments on current account

....

(d) the capital account balance

....

(e) the financial account balance

....

(f) the current plus capital plus financial account balances

....

(g) net errors and omissions

....

(?) **Q46.** Explain why the overall balance of payments always balances.

....

....

◗ **Q47.** The current account of the balance of payments tends to fluctuate with the business cycle. The current account tends to improve during a recession and deteriorate during a boom.   *True/False*

(Pages 461–5) The balance of payments is closely related to the rate of exchange. The rate of exchange is the rate at which one currency exchanges for another. If the rate of exchange of a pound sterling alters from 200 to 210 Japanese yen, this means that the pound has **Q48.** *appreciated/depreciated* relative to the yen, and that the yen has **Q49.** *appreciated/depreciated* relative to the pound. This means that Japanese imports will now be **Q50.** *cheaper/more expensive* in the UK and that, therefore, they will **Q51.** *rise/fall* in volume.

⊖ **Q52.** Sketch a demand curve for sterling and a supply curve of sterling against the euro on Figure 15.3 and mark the equilibrium exchange rate. Make sure you label the axes correctly.

(a) Who is demanding sterling in the diagram and for what purpose?

....

Figure 15.3 Demand for and supply of sterling

(b) Who is supplying sterling in the diagram and for what purpose?

....

(c) Now illustrate what happens to the exchange rate when there is an increased demand for sterling and a decreased supply.

Q53. The demand for sterling results from the credit items in the UK balance of payments and the supply of sterling results from the debit items.   *True/False*

Q54. Only one of the following flows represents a *demand* for sterling. Which one?
A. Imports of goods and services into the UK.
B. UK investment abroad.
C. Short-term financial outflows from the UK.
D. Profit earned from UK investment abroad.
E. Overseas aid by the UK government.

Q55. Assume that there is a free-floating exchange rate. Will the following cause the exchange rate to appreciate or depreciate? In each case you should consider whether there is a shift in the demand or supply curves of sterling (or both) and which way the curve(s) shift(s).
(a) More video recorders are imported from Japan.
Demand curve shifts *left/right/no shift*
Supply curve shifts *left/right/no shift*
Exchange rate *appreciates/depreciates*

(b) Non-UK residents increase their purchases of UK government securities.
Demand curve shifts *left/right/no shift*
Supply curve shifts *left/right/no shift*
Exchange rate *appreciates/depreciates*

(c) UK interest rates fall relative to those abroad.
Demand curve shifts *left/right/no shift*
Supply curve shifts *left/right/no shift*
Exchange rate *appreciates/depreciates*

(d) The UK experiences a higher rate of inflation than other countries.
Demand curve shifts *left/right/no shift*
Supply curve shifts *left/right/no shift*
Exchange rate *appreciates/depreciates*

(e) The result of the development of the single market in the EU is for investment in the UK by the rest of the EU to increase by a greater amount than UK investment in other EU countries.
Demand curve shifts *left/right/no shift*
Supply curve shifts *left/right/no shift*
Exchange *rate appreciates/depreciates*

(f) Speculators believe that the rate of exchange will fall.
Demand curve shifts *left/right/no shift*
Supply curve shifts *left/right/no shift*
Exchange *rate appreciates/depreciates*

(Pages 465–6) The government may be unwilling to let the pound float freely. Instead it may attempt to fix the exchange rate, or at least attempt to reduce exchange rate fluctuations.

Q56. Which one of the following is likely to lead to persistent balance of payments deficits for country X under fixed exchange rates?
A. A lower income elasticity of demand for the country's exports than for its imports.
B. A lower rate of growth at home than abroad.
C. A higher rate of inflation abroad than in the domestic economy.
D. The long-term development of import substitutes at home.
E. A growth in the country's monopoly power in the export market.

Q57. Which one of the following would help to prevent an appreciation of sterling resulting from an excess demand for sterling?
A. An increase in interest rates.
B. Building up reserves.
C. The Bank of England purchasing sterling on the foreign exchange market.
D. A reduction in government expenditure and an increase in taxation, but with no change in interest rates.
E. A decrease in the supply of money.

(?) Q58. Assume that, as a result of inflation, there was downward pressure on the exchange rate. List three short-term measures the government could adopt in order to prevent the exchange rate depreciating.

1. ....

2. ....

3. ....

15.5 The relationship between the four macroeconomic objectives

(Pages 466–8) In the short term, the four macroeconomic objectives – faster economic growth, lower unemployment, lower inflation and the avoidance of excessive current account balance of payments deficits – are all related.

Q59. Fill in the blanks in Table 15.1, which relates the state of the economy to each phase of the business cycle. You should insert one of the following words in each of the blanks: *high/low/rising/falling/surplus/deficit*.

Table 15.1

	The upturn	The expansion	The peaking out	The slow-down
Inflation	.....	.....	.....	.....
Unemployment	.....	.....	.....	.....
Balance of trade	.....	.....	.....	.....
Growth	.....	.....	.....	.....
Investment	.....	.....	.....	.....
Business confidence	.....	.....	.....	.....

There are, however, various time lags involved in the response of the four objectives to changes in aggregate demand. This means that at some points in the business cycle, the objectives are collectively looking more favourable than at other points.

Q60. At which of the following points in the business cycle would a government be more likely to call an election (assuming that it can choose)?

A. The bottom of a recession.

B. The peak of the boom.

C. Mid-recovery, where growth is fastest.

D. Shortly after the peak, where the economy is slowing down.

E. Where the economy is just beginning to recover from a recession.

B PROBLEMS, EXERCISES AND PROJECTS

Q61. Referring to Table 15.2, how did the duration of unemployment change between 1997 and 2010? How did this relate to the rate of unemployment?

Table 15.2 UK claimant unemployment by duration

	Up to 26 weeks	Over 26 weeks and up to 52 weeks	Over 52 weeks	Total
Oct 1997 (thousands)	773.4	236.1	444.8	1454.3
(per cent)	53.2	16.2	30.6	100.0
Oct 1999 (thousands)	695.5	204.9	287.5	1187.9
(per cent)	58.5	17.2	24.2	100.0
Oct 2001 (thousands)	604.2	159.1	179.4	942.7
(per cent)	64.1	16.9	19.0	100.0
Oct 2003 (thousands)	604.4	168.0	141.0	913.4
(per cent)	66.2	18.4	15.4	100.0
Oct 2005 (thousands)	595.0	161.7	124.8	881.5
(per cent)	67.5	18.3	14.2	100.0
Oct 2006 (thousands)	609.3	184.5	160.1	953.9
(per cent)	63.9	19.3	16.8	100.0
Oct 2007 (thousands)	567.3	135.0	130.9	833.2
(per cent)	68.1	16.2	15.7	100.0
Oct 2008 (thousands)	756.2	151.3	101.7	1009.2
(per cent)	74.9	15.0	10.1	100.0
Oct 2009 (thousands)	1073.0	364.6	182.7	1620.3
(per cent)	66.2	22.5	11.3	100.0
Oct 2010 (thousands)	952.7	251.9	253.4	1458.0
(per cent)	65.3	17.3	17.4	100.0

Source: *Labour Market Statistics – integrated FR* (National Statistics), available online at www.statistics.gov.uk/StatBase/TSDtables1.asp, accessed August 2011. Crown copyright material is reproduced under the terms and conditions of the Open Government Licence (OGL).

Q62. Table 15.3 shows the aggregate demand and supply of labour at various average wage rates.

(a) Plot the labour demand and labour supply curves.

(b) How might we explain the inelastic nature of the labour supply curve?

....

(c) If the wage rate were set at £7.00, what would be the level of employment and unemployment?

employment = ... *unemployment* = ...

(d) What type of *unemployment* is this?

....

(e) If the wage level were to increase to £7.50, how many workers would be classified as *disequilibrium* and how many as *equilibrium* unemployed?

disequilibrium = ... *equilibrium* = ...

Table 15.3

Average real wage (£ per hour)	Labour demand (000s)	Labour supply (000s)	Labour force (000s)
6.00	200	100	118
6.50	170	120	136
7.00	140	140	154
7.50	110	160	172
8.00	80	180	190

Table 15.4

Commodity	Average price in base year	Average price in year x	Weight
A	£0.70	£0.75	4
B	£1.20	£1.35	1
C	£45.00	£55.00	1
D	£0.35	£0.37	2
E	£3.20	£3.55	2

Q63. From the information in Table 15.4 calculate the price index in year X for the basket of commodities.

....

Q64. In small groups, write a report on changes in unemployment since 1980. Your report should include the following: (a) a description of changes in the unemployment rate over the period; (b) a description of changes in (i) the duration of unemployment and (ii) the gender balance of unemployment since 1990; (c) an assessment of the extent to which unemployment is cyclical; (d) an explanation of changes in unemployment from 1980 to the present day. The best sources of information are *Labour Market Statistics* and *The Annual Abstract of Statistics*. Both are available on the National Statistics website (www.statistics.gov.uk) and also as separate time-series tables in the 'Time series data' section.

Q65. Find data on the composition of the UK balance of payments current account for the period since 1990 and answer the questions that follow. The best place to find these data is *The Pink Book*, which is available on the National Statistics website.

(a) Explain the terms 'Services', 'Income' and 'Current transfers'.

(b) Which parts of the current account are subject to the greatest short-term fluctuations? What explanations can you offer for this?

(c) Which parts of the current account fluctuate with the course of the business cycle and in which direction? What explanations can you offer for this? Why do other parts appear not to fluctuate with the course of the business cycle?

Q66. Table 15.5 shows a simplified balance of payments account for the UK in 2009.

(a) What was the UK's balance on trade in goods and services?

....

(b) Calculate the deficit/surplus on the current account.

....

Table 15.5 UK balance of payments (2009)

Item	£bn
Net direct investment	−15.4
Balance of services	+49.9
Capital account	+3.2
Net current transfers	−14.8
Net errors and omissions	+6.7
Portfolio investment (balance)	+34.8
Balance of financial derivatives	+29.1
Income balance	+31.3
Exports of goods	386.6
Imports of goods	418.7
Other investment (balance)	−37.2
Changes in reserves	...

(c) Calculate the deficit/surplus on the capital plus financial accounts (excluding reserves and net errors and omissions).

....

(d) Establish whether there was a loss or addition to the country's reserves and of how much. (You will first have to take net errors and omissions into account.)

....

Q67. Let us assume that there is a free-floating exchange rate: i.e. that the exchange rate is determined by free-market forces. The demand and supply schedules in Table 15.6 relate the price of sterling to the euro for a given day.

(a) What is the equilibrium rate of exchange?.................

(b) A sharp fall in UK interest rates causes the demand for sterling to fall by £8m per day at all exchange rates. Assuming other things remain equal, what will happen to the exchange rate for sterling in euros?

....

(c) If we relax the assumption that other things remain equal in (b) above, what might happen to the supply of sterling?

....

Table 15.6 Demand for and supply of sterling

Price of sterling in euros	1.10	1.20	1.30	1.40	1.50	1.60	1.70	1.80
£m demanded per day	40	36	32	28	24	20	16	12
£m supplied per day	16	20	24	28	32	36	40	44

(d) Assume that, in addition to the fall in demand for sterling of £8m per day, the supply of sterling to purchase euros rises by £8m. What will the equilibrium exchange rate be now?

....

(e) Suppose now that the authorities decide to fix the exchange rate value between the pound and the euro. They decide on a rate of £1 = €1.60. How can the reserves be used to maintain this rate of exchange?

....

(f) What will be the effect on trade between the UK and the eurozone countries of this policy of fixing the exchange rate at £1 = €1.60?

....

(g) In order to address the problem of the over-valued pound, the authorities may be forced in the long run to reassess the fixed exchange-rate value. They might be forced to *devalue/revalue* the currency.

Q68. In pairs, find data for (i) economic growth and (ii) current account deficits as a percentage of GDP for four separate countries. Data can be found from the *OECD Economic Outlook*, which is available to download from http://www.oecd.org.

(a) To what extent do the two indicators move together over time in each of the countries?

(b) Can you observe any time lags? If so, explain them.

(c) If an economy grows rapidly, what is likely to happen to (i) interest rates; (ii) the exchange rate? How will these impact on the current account?

 DISCUSSION TOPICS AND ESSAYS

Q69. How do (a) the flows into and out of unemployment and (b) the average duration of unemployment vary with the course of the business cycle?

Q70. To what extent is it appropriate to classify either some or all of unemployment as 'voluntary'?

Q71. What are the arguments for and against raising the benefits paid to (a) the unemployed; (b) their families?

Q72. What factors have been most important in explaining the changing level of unemployment in the UK over the past 10 years?

Q73. If we were to devise a series of policies to tackle the plight of the unemployed, what factors other than the actual *number* unemployed ought we to take into account?

Q74. Solutions to the unemployment problem can be classified as interventionist or market orientated, although there is some common ground. List as many solutions to unemployment as you can, suggesting which would be supported by 'free marketeers' and which by 'interventionists'.

Q75. What are the economic consequences of inflation?

Q76. Would it be desirable to achieve a permanent zero rate of inflation? Explain.

Q77. If the government insisted that everyone had wage increases to match the rate of inflation, would it matter how high the rate of inflation was?

Q78. Distinguish between demand-pull and cost-push inflation. Why in practice might it be difficult to establish the extent to which a given rate of inflation were demand-pull or cost-push?

Q79. For what reasons were both inflation and unemployment generally higher in the 1980s than in the 1960s? For what reasons were both generally lower in the 2000s than in the 1980s?

Q80. Under what circumstances are policies to reduce unemployment likely to lead to higher inflation? Are there any policies that a government could pursue that would reduce both inflation and unemployment?

Q81. In what sense is it true to say that a current account deficit will always be matched by an equal surplus elsewhere in the balance of payments?

Q82. What effect will a rise in interest rates be likely to have on the various parts of the balance of payments account?

Q83. For what reasons may the rate of exchange depreciate? What measures could the government adopt to prevent this depreciation?

Q84. Why should a government ever be concerned about the balance of payments, if a deficit on the current account is always offset exactly by a surplus on the capital plus financial account?

Q85. What are the advantages and disadvantages of a depreciation in the exchange rate? To what extent do these advantages and disadvantages depend on the causes, magnitude and timing of the depreciation?

Q86. If it is assumed that a Japanese firm opened a car plant in the UK, what would be the likely impacts on the various parts of the balance of payments in (a) the short term; (b) the long term?

Q87. Assume that the exchange rate has been depreciating over time. What are the likely causes of this? What are the likely economic consequences? What policies can the government introduce to stop the depreciation in the currency?

Q88. If a government or central bank decides to reduce unemployment through changing the interest rate, what should it do to the interest rate? Explain the likely consequences for the other macroeconomic objectives.

Q89. What problems face a government in attempting to achieve all its principal macroeconomic objectives simultaneously?

Q90. At what point of the business cycle is the country at present? Do you think that the government has managed to get the economy to the right point of the cycle in order to improve its chances of success at the next general election?

Q91. Debate
Keeping inflation low should be the overriding macroeconomic objective of the government.

Q92. Debate
A persistent and substantial current account deficit is a symptom of a fundamental weakness in the structure of the economy.

D ANSWERS

Q1. D. The formula is $U/(U + E) \times 100\%$ (where U is the number unemployed and E is the number employed): i.e. $3/(3 + 24) \times 100\% = 11.1\%$.

Q2. The claimant figures exclude those who are unemployed but are ineligible for benefit. In the UK the following categories of unemployed people are ineligible for benefit: people returning to the workforce, people over 55, people temporarily unemployed, people seeking part-time work rather than full-time work.

Q3. *True.* The level of unemployment at the end of a period is equal to that at the beginning plus the inflows and minus the outflows.

Q4. E. (Note that A will have no effect, B will have the effect of reducing unemployment, and C and D will either reduce unemployment or leave it the same depending on whether those now staying on at school and retiring were previously recorded in the statistics.)

Q5. A. The result is that the supply of labour exceeds the demand, causing disequilibrium unemployment.

Q6. Because such unemployment is closely related to the business cycle and grows in periods of recession.

Q7. B. Frictional unemployment would be reduced if workers had better knowledge of jobs available and employers had better knowledge of what workers were available. This improved knowledge would reduce the search time of workers looking for a job and firms in recruiting labour.

Q8. (a), (b) and (c). The more industrially diverse a region, the slower the rate of change and the more flexible the workforce, the less of a problem structural unemployment will be. Those made unemployed over a period of time can more easily move to alternative employment either within the existing area or elsewhere.

Q9. (a) *technological*; (b) *demand-deficient*; (c) *real-wage*; (d) *structural*; (e) *frictional*; (f) *demand-deficient*; (g) *seasonal* (holiday areas have higher unemployment during school terms).

Q10. (a) Wage E; number of workers K.
(b) GI (or KM).
(c) Because there are some workers in the labour force who are not prepared to accept jobs at the going wage rate.
(d) Employment J; total unemployment is BD (JP), of which BC (JL) is disequilibrium unemployment and CD (LP) is equilibrium unemployment.
(e) There may be a number of reasons. It may be that there has been a negative demand shock, but that the wage is sluggish to adjust downwards in response. Or it may be that trade unions have used their power to negotiate for wages above the equilibrium level.

Q11. C. The higher prices will mean that the current stock of money will purchase fewer goods and services:

i.e. the 'real' money supply has decreased (i). The movement up along the aggregate demand curve shows that fewer goods and services will be demanded: i.e. that real aggregate demand has decreased (ii). With the rise in prices and a constant nominal money supply, however, it is highly unlikely that *money* expenditure will decrease (iii).

Q12. *(a) Yes.* This is part of the *foreign trade substitution effect.* People substitute imports for home-produced goods and services.

(b) Yes. This is the other part of the foreign trade substitution effect. People abroad substitute non-UK goods for UK exports.

(c) No. This is the income effect. (For this to occur, prices would have to rise faster than wages.)

(d) Yes. This is the *real balance effect.* People substitute increased money balances for expenditure on goods and services.

(e) No. This will shift the curve. It is not a direct consequence of the rise in the price level: it is something the government chooses to do.

(f) Yes. The higher interest rates are a direct consequence of the higher price level.

(g) No. The reason is the same as in the case of (e).

Q13. *Leftward shift* (b), (h). (These are causes of a fall in aggregate demand other than a rise in the price level.)

Rightward shift (a), (c), (d), (f). (These are causes of a rise in aggregate demand other than a fall in the price level.) Note in the case of (d), if people believe that inflation is going to rise, they will buy more now in order to beat the price rises.

No shift (movement along) (e), (g). (These are changes in the price level that will affect aggregate demand and will thus be shown by the curve itself.)

Q14. Firms' marginal cost curves are likely to slope upwards. They would thus need to receive higher prices to encourage them to produce more. (This assumes that they believe that their cost curves will not *shift*: only that costs will rise as they move upward *along* their marginal cost curves.)

Q15. P_1.

Q16. *shortage.*

Q17. *up.*

Q18. *more.*

Q19. *up along.*

Q20. *up along.*

Q21. *False.* The CPI does not measure the standard of living as it takes no account of incomes.

Q22. B. (= 100 × (153 − 150)/150).

Q23. *False.* The GDP deflator is also a price index, but it is defined as the ratio of real GDP to nominal GDP, whereas the CPI is based on collecting data about prices. The RPI is yet another different index.

Q24. B. In a period of rapid inflation the real value of money falls.

Q25. *True.* Debtors will see the value of their debt fall as prices rise. High inflation is often accompanied by low *real* rates of interest (i.e. interest rates relative to the rate of inflation). This benefits debtors.

Q26. A high rate of domestic inflation relative to those with whom we trade will cause the competitiveness of exports to fall as they become more expensive. Equally the demand for imported goods will increase since they will appear relatively cheaper than domestically produced products.

Q27. Inflation creates uncertainty for businesspeople: costs and hence profits are difficult to predict. As a consequence businesses may be reluctant to invest, thereby reducing the actual and potential levels of growth.

Q28. *rightward.*

Q29. *leftward.*

Q30. (a) and (b) are demand-pull while the rest are cost-push.

Q31. Higher wages increase firms' costs of production and thus cause them to put up their prices. These higher prices then cause unions to demand higher wages to compensate for the higher cost of living. Thus wages and prices chase each other in a spiral.

Q32. (a), (b) and (e) are demand-side policies. They have the effect of reducing the growth in aggregate demand. The others are supply-side policies. If successful, they will reduce the rate of increase in costs.

Q33. The higher the rate of inflation that employers and employees expect, the bigger will be the rate of increase in wages and prices that are set. The higher the current rate of inflation, the higher people will expect it to be in the future. (This question is examined in Chapter 21.)

Q34. C. The Phillips curve showed the apparent trade-off between rates of unemployment and rates of inflation.

Q35. *movement along.* In other words, the government could trade off inflation against unemployment.

Q36. *using policies to influence non-demand factors causing inflation and unemployment.* It was believed that demand management policies could only be used to trade off inflation against unemployment: i.e. to cause a movement along the curve. Thus if the government wanted to reduce *both* inflation *and* unemployment, it would have to attempt to shift the curve inwards. This would involve policies other than demand management policies: policies to tackle cost-push inflation and equilibrium unemployment.

Q37. *False.* There is still an apparent inverse relationship between them, albeit a worse trade-off than in the 1950s and 1960s but better than in the 1980s. Indeed, there is some evidence that the Phillips curve has been moving to different positions at different times, partly connected with people's expectations about inflation.

Q38. *True.*

Q39. *True.*

Q40. *debits* (a), (b), (c). These all represent a monetary flow from the UK to the rest of the world.

credits (d), (e), (f), (g). These all represent a monetary flow to the UK. Note that drawing on reserves is a credit item because it credits the balance of payments (even though it represents a debit to the reserves).

Q41. A. The balance on trade in goods and services equals exports of goods and services minus imports of goods and services: i.e. (£120m + £50m) − (£150m + £60m) = −£40m.

Q42. E. It equals the balance on trade in goods and services plus net income flows and current transfers: i.e. −£40 + £80m − £30m = +£10m.

Q43. D. The three accounts, the current account, capital account and financial account (plus any net errors and omissions), must add up to zero: they must balance. Thus a deficit on the current account must be balanced by a surplus of the same amount on the sum of the other two accounts plus net errors and omissions.

Q44. (a) (i), (b) (iv), (c) (vi), (d) (x), (e) (iii), (f) (vi), (g) (ix), (h) (xiv), (i) (xii), (j) (ii), (k) (viii).

Q45. *(a)* £74bn − £82bn = −£8bn.
(b) £74bn − £82bn + £80bn − £78bn = −£6bn.
(c) −£74bn − £82bn + £80bn − £78bn + £43bn − £40bn = −£3bn.
(d) £7bn − £5bn = £2bn.
(e) £56bn − £70bn + £12bn + £1bn = −£1bn.
(f) £3bn + £2bn − £1bn = −£2bn.
(g) +£2bn.

Q46. After taking account of any errors and omissions, any deficit on the current account must be matched by an equal and opposite surplus on the total of the other two accounts, and vice versa.

Q47. *True.* In a boom, higher incomes lead to more imports, and higher inflation leads to both less exports and more imports. Therefore the balance of payments on current account tends to deteriorate. The reverse is true in a recession.

Q48. *appreciated.*

Q49. *depreciated.*

Q50. *cheaper.*

Q51. *rise.*

Q52. *(a)* Non-UK residents are buying sterling with euros in order to obtain UK exports of goods and services and to invest in the UK.
(b) UK residents are supplying sterling in order to purchase euros in order to obtain imports of goods and services from the eurozone countries and to invest in the eurozone.
(c) The demand and supply curves in Figure A15.1 shift to D_2 and S_2 respectively. The exchange rate will appreciate to r/e_2.

Q53. *True.*

Q54. D. It is a credit item on the balance of payments. The others are debit items. The profit earned abroad on

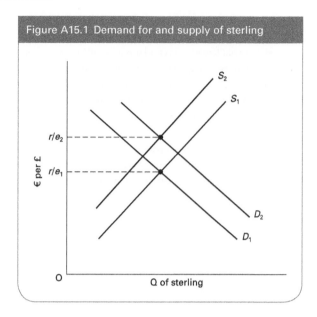

Figure A15.1 Demand for and supply of sterling

UK investment will be in foreign currency. When this is exchanged for sterling in order to pay the dividends to UK shareholders, this will create a demand for sterling.

Q55. *(a)* Demand curve *no shift*; supply curve shifts to the *right*; exchange rate *depreciates*.
(b) Demand curve shifts to the *right*; supply curve *no shift*; exchange rate *appreciates*.
(c) Demand curve shifts to the *left*; supply curve shifts to the *right*; exchange rate *depreciates*.
(d) Demand curve shifts to the *left*; supply curve shifts to the *right*; exchange rate *depreciates*.
(e) Demand curve shifts to the *right*; supply curve shifts to the *right* (but less so than the demand curve); exchange rate *appreciates*.
(f) Demand curve shifts to the *left*; supply curve shifts to the *right*; exchange rate *depreciates*.

Q56. A. This will mean that as world incomes grow, exports will grow less rapidly than imports. Note in the case of B that a lower rate of growth in country X will lead to a lower rate of growth in demand for imports than in other countries, and hence a lower rate of growth in demand for country X's imports than its exports.

Q57. B. Building up reserves results from the Bank of England selling sterling on the foreign exchange market. This increased supply of sterling helps to prevent an appreciation. All the other options will tend to *cause* an appreciation. In the case of option A, higher interest rates increase the demand for sterling and decrease the supply, as short-term finance flows into the country. With option C, the Bank of England is adding to the demand for sterling. With option D, there will be a reduction in aggregate demand and hence a reduction in the demand for imports (and hence the supply of sterling) and, via lower prices, an increase in exports (and hence the demand for sterling).

Q58. 1. The use of reserves to buy sterling.

2. Borrowing from abroad to buy sterling.

3. Increased interest rates to attract short-term money inflows.

Q59. See the table below.

	The upturn	The expansion	The peaking out	The slow-down
Inflation	*low*	*rising*	*high*	*falling*
Unemployment	*high*	*falling*	*low*	*rising*
Balance of trade	*surplus*	*deficit*	*deficit*	*surplus*
Growth	*rising*	*high*	*falling*	*low*
Investment	*rising*	*high*	*falling*	*low*
Business confidence	*rising*	*high*	*low*	*low*

Q60. C. In mid-recovery, growth is fastest and unemployment is falling (both popular with the electorate), but inflation has probably not started rising yet, given the fact that most firms are still able to respond to the higher demand by raising their output. Also, there is unlikely to be a severe current account deficit and downward pressure on the exchange rate. Thus there is good news and no bad news – yet!

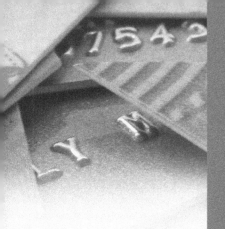

16

The Roots of Modern Macroeconomics

A **REVIEW**

'The ideas of economists and political philosophers, both when they are right and when they are wrong, are more powerful than is commonly understood. Indeed the world is ruled by little else. Practical men, who believe themselves to be quite exempt from any intellectual influences, are usually the slaves of some defunct economist.'

J.M. Keynes, *The General Theory of Employment, Interest and Money* (1936)

In this chapter we examine the development of macroeconomic ideas and their influence on economic policy.

16.1 The macroeconomic environment and debates

(Pages 474–5) Debates within macroeconomics have tended to reflect current macroeconomic issues of the time.

Macroeconomics as a separate branch of economics had its birth in the mass unemployment experienced in the **Q1.** *1900s and 1920s/1920s and 1930s/1940s and 1950s*. The 'old classical theories of the time essentially said that free markets would provide a **Q2.** *healthy/stagnant/declining* economy. The new analysis of the economy put forward by Keynes advocated active intervention by governments, especially through **Q3.** *fiscal/monetary* policy. In the 1970s, the macroeconomic consensus broke down, as both inflation and unemployment **Q4.** *fell/rose* and economic growth **Q5.** *accelerated/slowed down*. The 1990s saw general improvements in the macroeconomic environment but the financial crisis of the late 2000s and the subsequent global economic downturn again highlighted differences amongst macroeconomists.

 Q6. Macroeconomic problems are the result of too much government intervention. *True/False/Cannot tell*

16.2 Setting the scene: three key issues

(Pages 475–7) The different schools of economic thought make different assumptions about how the economy operates. The classical and new classical schools argue that prices and wages are **Q7.** *flexible/inflexible*; that aggregate supply is **Q8.** *responsive/unresponsive* to a change in aggregate demand; and that individual producers and consumers have **Q9.** *quickly adjusting/slowly adjusting* expectations concerning economic events. As a result of these assumptions, supporters of the classical position argue that the main role of government economic policy is **Q10.** *to manage the level of aggregate demand so as to maintain full employment/remove impediments to the free play of market forces/ensure that no slack is allowed to develop in the economy*. This they argue is the only way to guarantee long-term growth.

(?) **Q11.** Go through questions 7–10 and summarise the key assumptions of the *Keynesian* school.

....

....

Much of the disagreement between the different schools of thought centres on the responsiveness of aggregate supply to changes in aggregate demand.

(?) **Q12.** Aggregate supply may be defined as ....

....

(—) **Q13.** Consider the aggregate supply curves shown in Figure 16.1.

Which of the three curves would be most likely to represent the views of:

(a) Extreme free-market economists?

....

(b) Those who argue that an expansion of demand will have no effect upon inflation?

....

(c) Those who argue that the degree of slack in the economy will determine the impact of a change in aggregate demand on aggregate supply?

....

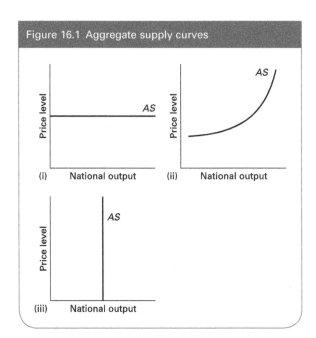

Figure 16.1 Aggregate supply curves

(?) **Q14.** One of the arguments used by those advocating government intervention in the economy is that people's expectations are slow to adjust to changes in the economic environment. *True/False*

(≡) **Q15.** Supply-side economics is an approach that focuses on:

A. how to influence the shape of the *AS* curve.
B. aggregate supply and how to shift the *AS* curve inwards.
C. attempts to manipulate aggregate demand.
D. aggregate supply and how to shift the *AS* curve outwards.
E. aggregate supply and how to induce a movement along the *AS* curve.

16.3 Classical macroeconomics

(Pages 477–8) The classical school of the 19th and early 20th centuries advocated minimal state intervention in the running of economic affairs, and the development of a system of free trade. Providing the government balanced its budget, in other words that it made *T* equal to **Q16.** *I/G/X/S/M/C*, achievement of full-employment macroeconomic equilibrium could be left to the free market. The free market would ensure that *S* was equal to **Q17.** *I/T/G/X/M/C*, and that *M* was equal to **Q18.** *I/T/G/X/S/C*.

(?) **Q19.** What, according to the classical economists, would be the effect of a rise in saving on the level of investment?

....

....

The operation of the gold standard was supposed to ensure that the balance of payments was kept in equilibrium (*X = M*). The gold standard was a system of **Q20.** *fixed/freely flexible/ partly flexible* exchange rates.

(●) **Q21.** Assume that there is a balance of payments deficit (*M > X*). Trace through the steps by which the gold standard could correct this deficit.

(a) The deficit leads to an *inflow/outflow* of gold.
(b) This leads to an *increase/decrease* in interest rates.
(c) This leads to an *increase/decrease* in the price level.
(d) This leads to an *increase/decrease* in imports and an *increase/decrease* in exports.

(Page 479) The classical economists argued that because the markets for loanable funds and for imports and exports would clear, then Say's law would apply.

(≡) **Q22.** Say's law states that, at a macroeconomic level:

A. supply will always adjust to equal demand.
B. markets are always in a state of disequilibrium.
C. demand creates its own supply.
D. supply creates its own demand.
E. price and quantity are directly related.

Q23. Say's law implied that there could be no deficiency of demand in the economy. *True/False*

Q24. In terms of the circular flow of income diagram, Say's law would imply that *flexible prices* (as opposed to changes in national income) would ensure that withdrawals equalled injections. *True/False*

(Pages 479–81) The classical economists also supported the *quantity theory of money*.

Q25. This states that $MV = PY$. *True/False*

Q26. If real national income (i.e. measured in base-year prices) were £30bn, if prices had doubled since the base year, and if the velocity of circulation were 5, then the level of money supply would be:
A. £300bn
B. £75bn
C. £60bn
D. £12bn
E. £3bn

The classical economists had predicted that, provided markets were allowed to clear, there would never be a problem of **Q27.** *high inflation/mass unemployment.*

Q28. Which of the following policy decisions would have been characteristic of the classical economists' approach to the Great Depression?
(a) Encourage workers to take wage cuts. *Yes/No*
(b) Increase the rate of interest. *Yes/No*
(c) Expand the public sector's provision of goods and services. *Yes/No*
(d) Reduce unemployment benefits. *Yes/No*
(e) Increase the supply of money in circulation. *Yes/No*
(f) The government should aim to balance its budget. *Yes/No*
(g) Encourage people to save. *Yes/No*

16.4 The Keynesian revolution

(Pages 482–3) J.M. Keynes rejected many of the assumptions made by the classical school, key among which was the notion that markets would clear. According to Keynes, disequilibrium was the natural state of the market and such disequilibrium would persist unless the government intervened. For example, in the labour market, if there were a fall in aggregate demand, as occurred during the Great Depression, workers would resist wage cuts and the result would be demand-deficient unemployment.

Q29. Show, using Figure 16.2, the effect of a fall in the aggregate demand for labour and the subsequent level of disequilibrium unemployment that would result. (Assume that the labour market is initially in equilibrium.)

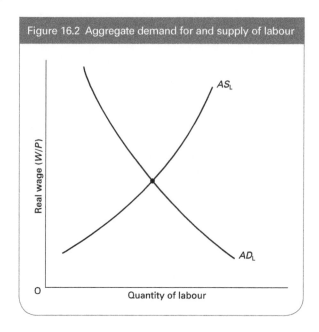

Figure 16.2 Aggregate demand for and supply of labour

But even if workers *were* willing to accept cuts in real wages, there would still be a problem of unemployment.

Q30. Why, according to Keynes, might a successful cut in workers' wages, as advocated by the classical school, deepen the recession and not improve it?

....

....

Q31. Disequilibrium could also persist in the market for loanable funds. Assume, for example, that there was an increase in saving. Why might the resulting fall in interest rates fail to stimulate a rise in investment and restore equilibrium?

....

....

(Pages 483–4) Keynes also rejected the simple quantity theory of money. Under certain circumstances, a rise in money supply may have little or no effect on prices.

Q32. If there was an expansion of the money supply, what, according to Keynes, would happen to each of the following?
(a) V *rise/fall/stay the same*
(b) Y – if there was substantial unemployment *rise/fall/stay the same*
(c) Y – if there was full employment *rise/fall/stay the same*

(Page 484) Keynesian theory stresses that equilibrium in the economy is brought about, not so much by changes in prices, but by changes in the level of national income.

Q33. Describe the process whereby a new equilibrium national income will be achieved, following a rise in aggregate demand.

....

....

....

....

(Pages 484–6) Keynesian theory emphasised an active role for government in maintaining the full-employment level of national income. There are two major methods a government can use to control the level of aggregate demand. These are *fiscal policy* and *monetary policy*.

Q34. Fiscal policy involves

....

Q35. Monetary policy involves

....

Following the Second World War, Keynesian views became the accepted orthodoxy. If the economy was experiencing rising inflation then **Q36.** *expansionary/deflationary* fiscal and monetary policy was to be used. Alternatively, an economy suffering low rates of growth and unemployment would require **Q37.** *expansionary/deflationary* policy measures.

Because of the cyclical nature of the economy, the policies alternated between deflationary and reflationary (i.e. expansionary) measures.

Q38. As a result the policies became known as

....

Q39. List four criticisms of Keynesian demand management policy that were to grow over the 1960s.

1.   ....

2.   ....

3.   ....

4.   ....

16.5 The Monetarist–Keynesian debate

(Pages 486–7) The problems encountered with the Keynesian model of the economy led certain economists to return to the old classical theory of income determination. The monetarists, led by Milton Friedman, returned to the quantity theory of money. They reasserted that both V (the velocity of circulation) and Y (the level of real national income) were **Q40.** *endogenous/exogenous* variables, meaning that V and Y are determined **Q41.** *by the supply of money/independently of the supply of money.* The implication was that any change in the money supply would have a direct effect upon the level of **Q42.** *prices/ national income.*

An important element of the monetarist analysis was that there was no trade-off in the long run between unemployment and inflation: that the long-run Phillips curve is **Q43.** *horizontal/vertical/upward sloping/a downward-sloping line at 45° to the axes.*

Q44. What arguments do monetarists use to justify a long-run Phillips curve of this shape?

....

....

....

Q45. What effect would the following have on the natural rate of unemployment?
(a) A reduction in the level of information concerning available work.   *Rise/Fall*
(b) The decline in traditional heavy industry.   *Rise/Fall*
(c) An increase in the power trade unions have within the wage-negotiating process.   *Rise/Fall*
(d) An expansion of job retraining schemes.   *Rise/Fall*
(e) A more rapid and widespread introduction of new technology into the workplace.   *Rise/Fall*
(f) An increase in unemployment benefits.   *Rise/Fall*

(Pages 487–9) Not surprisingly, modern-day Keynesians reject much of the monetarist analysis.

Q46. The modern *Keynesian* analysis of a rightward shift in the Phillips curve after 1970 focuses on a *variety* of factors, some that are argued to have influenced the rate of inflation and some the level of unemployment. List three causes of inflation and three of unemployment given by Keynesians to explain higher levels of both occurring simultaneously.
(a) Inflation

1.   ....

2.   ....

3.   ....

(b) Unemployment

1. ....

2. ....

3. ....

One reason given by Keynesians for unemployment being higher in the 1980s and early 1990s than in the 1970s was the problem of *hysteresis*.

Q47. In the context of unemployment, hysteresis can be defined as the persistence of unemployment that occurred in a recession even when the economy has recovered from the recession. *True/False*

Q48. Keynesians criticised monetarism for various reasons. These include:

(a) Monetarists place too much reliance on markets.
True/False

(b) Market imperfections prevent an optimum allocation of resources. *True/False*

(c) Firms may be discouraged from undertaking investment if markets (for example, stock markets, money markets or foreign exchange markets) are volatile in the face of short-term pressures. *True/False*

(d) Problems of inflation, unemployment and industrial decline cannot be controlled via money supply and unregulated market forces. *True/False*

(e) Monetarists encourage governments to take too interventionist a stance in trying to maintain aggregate demand. *True/False*

16.6 An emerging consensus?

(Pages 489–92) In the 1990s, the focus of macroeconomic policy shifted towards one of fostering a stable economic environment conducive to long-term economic growth and prosperity.

Fiscal policy became more **Q49.** *active/passive,* and became subject to rules, leading to the birth of what some economists called *constrained discretion.*

(?) Q50. Constrained discretion may be defined as............

....

Monetary policy also became more rule-based, with the Bank of England being given independence to determine interest rates in order to meet a target for **Q51.** *growth/ inflation/unemployment.*

Policy in this period before the economic and financial upheaval of the late 2000s was, in essence, drawing on ideas that had emerged from the debates of the past. Although this seemed to be creating a 'mainstream consensus', this did not mean that all macroeconomists agreed, and a whole range of ideas can be identified.

Q52. The following are four schools of thought:
(i) New classical
(ii) Moderate monetarist
(iii) Moderate Keynesian/new Keynesian
(iv) Extreme Keynesians

Members of which school of thought hold each of the following views?

(a) A rise in aggregate demand (caused by an increase in money supply) can lead only to a temporary reduction in unemployment. As price expectations adjust upwards, so within a few months the extra demand will be translated into higher prices and unemployment will return to the natural level. *(i)/(ii)/(iii)/(iv)*

(b) Equilibrium in the economy can persist at a very high level of unemployment and there is no automatic mechanism for bringing the economy out of recession. Indeed, recessions are likely to persist as expectations remain pessimistic. It is important, therefore, for the government to take an active role in maintaining sufficient aggregate demand. This will help to stimulate investment and lead to faster long-term growth.
(i)/(ii)/(iii)/(iv)

(c) Markets clear virtually instantaneously. Any increase in aggregate demand by the government will be entirely reflected in higher prices. *(i)/(ii)/(iii)/(iv)*

(d) Wage rates are sticky downwards. Unemployment can take a long time, therefore, to be eliminated by a fall in real wages. The government should take responsibility for maintaining an adequate (but not excessive) level of aggregate demand. *(i)/(ii)/(iii)/(iv)*

Q53. New classical 'real business cycle theory' explains cyclical fluctuations in the economy in terms of *shifts in aggregate demand/shifts in aggregate supply/changes in the output of goods rather than services.*

Despite disagreements between economists, some general points of agreement have emerged in recent years.

Q54. Associate each of the following definitions with the appropriate school of thought.

(a) A group of economists that seeks to explain the downward stickiness of real wages and the resulting persistence of unemployment.
New classical/moderate monetarist/new Keynesian/post-Keynesian

(b) Economists who stress the importance of institutional and behavioural factors, and the role of business confidence in explaining the state of the economy. They argue that firms are more likely to respond to changes in demand by changing output rather than prices.
New classical/moderate monetarist/new Keynesian/post-Keynesian

(c) A body of economists who believe that markets are highly competitive and clear very rapidly; any expansion of demand will feed through virtually instantaneously

into higher prices, giving a vertical short-run as well as a vertical long-run Phillips curve.

New classical/moderate monetarist/new Keynesian/post-Keynesian

(d) Economists who reject the new classical notion of a vertical short-run aggregate supply curve and vertical short-run Phillips curve, but still maintain that markets adjust fairly quickly.

New classical/moderate monetarist/new Keynesian/post-Keynesian

(Pages 492–3) The financial crisis of the later 2000s stimulated much debate amongst economists and policy-makers, given the impact on the wider economy and public finances.

(?) **Q55.** List the two immediate priorities of policy-makers at this time.

1. ....

2. ....

Economists on the right tended to argue that the banking crisis was the result of **Q56.** *too little/too much* intervention, whereas economists on the left argued that it was because of **Q57.** *too little/too much* intervention. One impact of the global economic and financial crisis was that governments experienced **Q58.** *a deterioration/an improvement* in their public finances. Those on the political right argued for **Q59.** *gradual/no/rapid* deficit reduction, whereas those on the political left took a more Keynesian line, arguing that cutting the deficit too **Q60.** *quickly/slowly* would endanger the economic recovery.

(◗) **Q61.** Which of the following propositions were general points of agreement that have emerged in recent years?

(a) Excessive growth in the money supply will lead to inflation.   *Yes/No*

(b) Governments' ability to control their country's economy is being increasingly eroded by the process of globalisation.   *Yes/No*

(c) In the short run, changes in aggregate demand will have only a minor effect on output and employment.
                                                    Yes/No

(d) There is a clear long-run trade-off between inflation and unemployment.   *Yes/No*

(e) Long-term growth depends primarily on changes in aggregate supply.   *Yes/No*

(f) Expectations have an important effect on the economy.
                                                    Yes/No

B PROBLEMS, EXERCISES AND PROJECTS

Q62. In the version of the quantity theory of money $MV = PY$:

(a) What are meant by the following terms?
   (i) M

   ....

   (ii) V

   ....

   (iii) P

   ....

   (iv) Y

   ....

(b) If the money supply were £20bn and money on average were spent 5 times per year on buying goods and services that make up national income, what would be the level of national income (in nominal terms)?

   ....

(c) Continuing with the same assumptions as in (b), what would be the price index if real national income, measured in base-year prices, were £50bn?

   ....

(d) If money supply increases by 50 per cent and neither the price level nor the velocity of circulation changes, how much will real national income increase?

more than 50 per cent/50 per cent/ less than 50 per cent

(e) If money supply increases by 50 per cent and neither real income nor the velocity of circulation changes, how much will the price level rise?

more than 50 per cent/50 per cent/ less than 50 per cent

(f) What did the classical economists assume about:
   (i) V?

   ....

   (ii) Y?

   ....

(g) What do Keynesian economists assume about:

(i) *V*?

....

(ii) *Y*?

....

Q63. The kingdom of Never Had It So Good is having it bad! Inflation has risen steadily following a series of expansionary budgets and the current account of the balance of payments has slipped into deficit. High interest rates, used to tackle the high inflation by curbing domestic demand, have led to a steady fall in household consumption. Firms have responded by cutting back on production and reducing their demand for labour, as well as postponing future investment.

Write two reports advising the chancellor of Never Had It So Good on a course of action to solve the country's economic problems. One report should emphasise the policies and beliefs of the classical school of economics, whereas the second should focus on Keynesian strategies.

 C **DISCUSSION TOPICS AND ESSAYS**

Q64. Explain the contrasting views of Keynesians and new classical economists concerning the nature of the aggregate supply curve. What implications do their respective analyses have for the effect of a rise in aggregate demand on prices and output?

Q65. What are the implications of the quantity theory of money for (a) the control of inflation, and (b) the use of monetary policy to stimulate an economy in recession?

Q66. What assumptions must be made about the terms in the equation of exchange if the strict quantity theory of money is to hold? How would changes in the money supply affect the economy if you changed these assumptions?

Q67. Describe the working of the economy using classical economic theory. Clearly state your assumptions. Why did classical economists maintain that the economy would tend towards a situation of full employment?

Q68. Explain the reasoning behind Keynes' rejection of Say's law.

Q69. Keynesian demand management policies, although initially appearing to be successful, began to run into problems in the mid-1960s. What were these problems?

Q70. 'The monetarist counter-revolution is simply the restating of classical theory.' Discuss.

Q71. Describe how monetarist and Keynesian views differ regarding the Phillips curve.

Q72. What are the distinguishing features of the following schools of thought: new classical economists, moderate monetarists, moderate Keynesians, extreme Keynesians?

Q73. What is meant by 'hysteresis' (in the context of unemployment)? How do Keynesians explain this phenomenon?

Q74. To what extent is there common ground between economists over the following: (a) the effect of changes in aggregate demand on real national income; (b) the relationship between inflation and unemployment; (c) appropriate policies for increasing the rate of economic growth over the longer term?

Q75. Debate
Leaving the economy to private enterprise and the market system is more likely to lead to recessions and instability than to sustained economic growth.

Q76. Debate
The financial crisis of the late 2000s was due to over-active intervention by governments.

 D **ANSWERS**

Q1. *1920s and 1930s.*
Q2. *healthy.*
Q3. *fiscal.*
Q4. *rose.*
Q5. *slowed down.*
Q6. *Cannot tell*: sometimes problems arise from too much intervention, and sometimes from too little.

Q7. *flexible.*
Q8. *unresponsive.*
Q9. *quickly adjusting.*
Q10. *remove impediments to the free play of market forces.*
Q11. The Keynesian school argues that prices and wages are relatively inflexible; that aggregate supply is relatively responsive to changes in aggregate demand; and that

expectations are relatively slow to adjust. Keynesians advocate government intervention to manage aggregate demand so as to avoid recessions.

Q12. Aggregate supply may be defined as the quantity of goods and services that the nation's producers would be willing to supply at any given price.

Q13. *(a)* (iii). They argue that changes in aggregate demand will have no effect on output and therefore the aggregate supply 'curve' is vertical.

(b) (i). They argue that aggregate supply is totally elastic and that therefore output depends entirely on aggregate demand.

(c) (ii). The lower the level of output and the higher the level of unemployment, and hence the greater the degree of 'slack' in the economy, the more will output be able to increase in response to an increase in aggregate demand, and hence the shallower the curve will be. As full employment is approached, however, the curve will get steeper, as firms find it increasingly difficult to increase output and instead respond to an increase in aggregate demand by putting up their prices.

Q14. *True.* Because expectations take time to adjust, interventionist policies can have a significant impact on the economy. For example, a rise in aggregate demand can lead to firms producing more if they do not expect that the rise in aggregate demand is also likely to raise inflation and hence raise their costs of production.

Q15. D.

Q16. G.

Q17. I.

Q18. X.

Q19. The rise in saving would cause a surplus of loanable funds. This would drive the rate of interest down. This in turn would cause an increase in the level of investment and a reduction in the level of saving (a movement along the investment curve and the new saving curve), until equilibrium was restored where saving equalled investment.

Q20. *Fixed.* The value of each country's currency was fixed in terms of a certain amount of gold. Each country's exchange rate was therefore fixed.

Q21. (a) *outflow*; (b) *increase*; (c) *decrease*; (d) *decrease* in imports, *increase* in exports.

Q22. D. The production of goods and services will generate incomes, which in turn will generate spending, thereby creating a demand for the goods and services which have been produced. Any proportion of income that is saved will generate extra investment, and any proportion going on imports, via the gold standard, will generate extra exports. Thus, when production generates extra income, *all* of it will come back as extra spending.

Q23. *True.* Any change in aggregate supply would automatically bring about a corresponding change in

aggregate demand, via the effects on aggregate demand of a change in prices and interest rates.

Q24. *True.*

Q25. *False.* The quantity theory of money states that the level of prices (*P*) depends on the quantity of money: if money supply increases faster than output, then prices will rise. The equation $MV = PY$ is called the 'quantity equation', not the 'quantity theory of money'.

Q26. D. The level of national income (at current prices) is equal to the real level of national income at base-year prices ($Y = £30bn$) multiplied by the price level as a proportion of the base year price ($P = 2$): $PY = £60bn$. Thus MV is also equal to £60bn. Given that the velocity of circulation (V) = 5, money supply must be £60bn/5 = £12bn.

Q27. *mass unemployment.*

Q28. Yes (a), (b), (d), (f) and (g). These were all advocated by classical economists during the 1920s and early 1930s.

Q29. The AD_L curve shifts to the left, but, with no resulting fall in the real wage rate, the level of aggregate labour supply now exceeds the level of aggregate labour demand, the gap between them giving the level of disequilibrium unemployment.

Q30. As workers took a wage cut, their ability to consume goods and services would fall. This would deepen the recession as firms would consequently have less demand for their output.

Q31. As saving increased, consumers would consequently have less money to spend on consumption of domestic goods and services. Businesses would respond to this fall in demand by cutting back on their level of investment.

Q32. *(a)* *fall.* The average speed at which money circulates may slow down. (The reasons for this are examined in Chapter 19.)

(b) *rise.* The increased spending will stimulate extra production and extra employment.

(c) *stay the same.* Output and employment cannot be stimulated by a rise in spending as there is no slack in the economy.

Q33. The rise in injections will mean that injections exceed withdrawals. This will cause a rise in national income. This will cause withdrawals (and consumption) to rise until withdrawals equal injections. At that point income will stop rising: income will be in equilibrium.

Q34. Changing government expenditure (an injection) and/or taxes (a withdrawal).

Q35. Changing money supply or interest rates, and thereby affecting the level of spending.

Q36. *deflationary.*

Q37. *expansionary.*

Q38. *Stop/go policies*, or less provocatively, *demand management policies*.

Q39. Criticisms included: policies failed to stabilise the economy; policies were short term rather than long term; the Phillips curve relationship appeared to be breaking down; balance of payments problems meant that deflationary policies had to be pursued even when unemployment was high; it was difficult to predict the magnitude of the effects of the policy (difficult to predict size of the multiplier); there were time lags involved with the policy (see Chapter 20, section 20.1).

Q40. exogenous.

Q41. *independently of the supply of money.*

Q42. *prices.*

Q43. *vertical.*

Q44. If the government expands aggregate demand in order to reduce unemployment, eventually people's expectations of inflation will increase until all the extra demand is absorbed in higher prices with no increase in output or employment. Thus in the long run the Phillips curve is vertical.

Q45. All will cause the natural rate of unemployment to rise except (d), which will cause it to fall.

Q46. *(a)* Examples include: rising costs, changes in the pattern of demand in the economy and expectations.

(b) Examples include: deficient demand, poor business expectations, structural changes in the economy, hysteresis.

Q47. *True.*

Q48. *True.* All except (e).

Q49. *passive.*

Q50. *Constrained discretion is a set of principles or rules within which economic policy operates – these can be informal or enshrined in law.*

Q51. *inflation.*

Q52. (a) (ii), (b) (iv), (c) (i), (d) (iii).

Q53. *shifts in aggregate supply.*

Q54. *(a)* New Keynesian.

(b) Post-Keynesian.

(c) New classical.

(d) Moderate monetarist.

Q55. to ensure the stability of the financial system and to try and mitigate the effects on aggregate demand of the limited levels of credit available for households and firms.

Q56. *too much.*

Q57. *too little.*

Q58. *deterioration.*

Q59. *rapid.*

Q60. *quickly.*

Q61. *Yes:* (a), (b), (e) and (f).

No: (c) and (d).

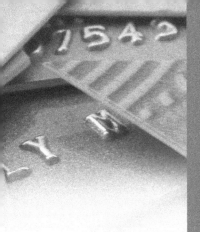

Chapter 17

Short-run Macroeconomic Equilibrium

 REVIEW

In order to analyse the workings of the macroeconomy in the short run, we use a model based on a Keynesian view of the world. This builds in the idea that aggregate demand determines the level of economic activity in the short run. For the moment, we also assume that the rate of interest is fixed.

17.1 Background to the theory

(Pages 496–7) In order to understand the Keynesian model, it is necessary that you are fully familiar with the circular flow of income diagram that we looked at in Chapter 14.

Q1. By way of revision, sketch the circular flow diagram and label the inner flow and all the injections and withdrawals.

The relationship between national income and the various components of the circular flow are shown in the *Keynesian 45° line diagram*.

Q2. In the model, it is assumed that consumption and withdrawals are determined by the level of national income, whereas injections are not. Which would we classify as endogenous and which as exogenous variables?

(*a*) Withdrawals are   *endogenous/exogenous*
(*b*) Injections are   *endogenous/exogenous*
(*c*) Consumption is   *endogenous/exogenous*

Q3. In the 45° line diagram, which of the following is given by the 45° line?

A. National expenditure.
B. Consumption of domestic goods and services.
C. Consumption of domestic goods and services plus withdrawals.

D. Consumption of domestic goods and services plus injections.
E. Withdrawals plus injections.

(Pages 497–500) The consumption function
The consumption function shows the relationship between consumption and national income.

Q4. This question is based on Table 17.1.
(*a*) Plot the consumption function shown in Table 17.1 on Figure 17.1 and add the 45° line.

Table 17.1

National income (£bn)	Consumption (£bn)	
50	70	...
75	90	...
100	110	...
125	130	...
150	150	...
175	170	...
200	190	...
225	210	...
250	230	...

 Multiple choice   Written answer   Delete wrong word   Diagram/table manipulation   Calculation   ⬡ Matching/ordering

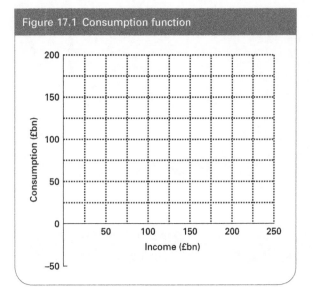

Figure 17.1 Consumption function

(b) Explain why the consumption function lies above the 45° line at low levels of national income and below it at high levels.

....

....

(c) What is meant by the term *marginal propensity to consume*? Give its formula.

....

....

(d) Calculate the marginal propensity to consume between the following levels of national income:

(i) £50bn and £75bn...

(ii) £125bn and £150bn...

(e) The marginal propensity to consume is given by the slope of the consumption function/the height of the consumption function above the horizontal axis.

(f) If the marginal propensity to consume diminished as national income rose, what shape would the consumption function be?

....

....

In the long run the marginal propensity to consume will be *Q5. higher/lower* than in the short run. This is the result of individuals responding relatively *Q6. quickly/slowly* to changes in their level of income.

? *Q7.* What is the difference between the marginal propensity to consume (*mpc*) and the marginal propensity to consume domestically produced goods and services (*mpc*$_d$)?

....

◑ *Q8.* For each of the following possible influences on consumption, indicate the most likely result:
(a) An increase in the rate of income tax.
decrease/increase/cannot tell
(b) A decrease in expected future income.
decrease/increase/cannot tell
(c) An increase in the availability of credit
decrease/increase/cannot tell
(d) An increase in the mortgage rate
decrease/increase/cannot tell
(e) An increase in uncertainty about the future
decrease/increase/cannot tell
(f) An expectation that future prices of consumer durables will be higher. *decrease/increase/cannot tell*
(g) A redistribution of income from the rich to the poor.
decrease/increase/cannot tell

? *Q9.* Define what is meant by consumption smoothing:

....

The household balance sheet summarises the sector's holdings of financial assets and liabilities. The balance of financial assets over liabilities is the household sector's *Q10. gross financial worth/net financial worth/net worth*. A worsening balance sheet may *Q11. weaken/strengthen* spending.

(Pages 500–6) Withdrawals and injections
? *Q12.* The major determinant of saving in the Keynesian model is

....

⊖ *Q13.* Label the last column in Table 17.1 'Saving (£bn)'.
(a) Assuming that saving is the only withdrawal, fill in the figures for saving in Table 17.1.
(b) Plot the saving function on Figure 17.1.
(c) Over which range of national income is there dissaving?

....

(d) What is the marginal propensity to save between a national income of £175bn and £200bn?

....

◑ *Q14.* What effect will the following have on saving? In each case state whether there will be a rise or fall in saving and whether there will be a shift in or a movement along the saving function.

(a) An increase in personal taxation.

rise/fall; shift/movement along

(b) Christmas. *rise/fall; shift/movement along*

(c) An increase in the rate of interest.

rise/fall; shift/movement along

(d) Expectations of a fall in prices.

rise/fall; shift/movement along

(e) Moving into the recessionary phase of the business cycle. *rise/fall; shift/movement along*

Q15. The marginal propensity to pay taxes (*mpt*) is the same as the marginal tax rate. *True/False*

Q16. The marginal propensity to import is the proportion of a rise in national income that goes on imports. If a country were predominantly an importer of luxury goods, what effect would this have on (a) the shape of the import function and (b) the marginal propensity to import?

(a) ....

(b) ....

Q17. Injections are assumed in the Keynesian model to be exogenously determined. This means:

(a) That injections are constant with respect to changes in national income. *True/False*

(b) That injections are constant with respect to time. *True/False*

(c) That injections in the 45° line diagram are given by a horizontal straight line. *True/False*

Q18. For each of the following possible influences on investment, indicate the most likely result. In each case assume *ceteris paribus*.

(a) Increased consumer demand.

decrease/increase/cannot tell

(b) Firms have improved expectations about future market conditions. *decrease/increase/cannot tell*

(c) An increase in the cost of capital.

decrease/increase/cannot tell

(d) Improved efficiency of capital.

decrease/increase/cannot tell

(e) An increase in the interest rate.

decrease/increase/cannot tell

(f) Improved availability of finance.

decrease/increase/cannot tell

17.2 The determination of national income

(Pages 508–11) The injections and withdrawals approach

Q19. Figure 17.2 shows a withdrawals and an injections function.

(a) Equilibrium national income is

....

Figure 17.2 National income determination: withdrawals and injections approach

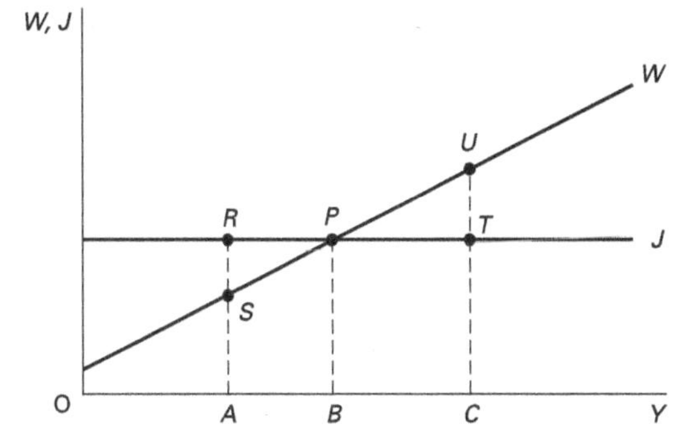

(b) Assume that the current level of national income is *OA*. Describe the process whereby equilibrium will be achieved.

....

(c) Illustrate on Figure 17.2 the effect of an increase in government spending by an amount *UT* on the level of national income.

Q20. The multiplier can be defined as

....

Q21. In symbols the (injections) multiplier can be defined as:

A. $\Delta Y/\Delta J$

B. $\Delta J/\Delta Y$

C. $\Delta J/\Delta W$

D. $\Delta W/\Delta J$

E. $\Delta W \times \Delta J$

Q22. Referring back to Figure 17.2, the multiplier is given by:

A. *UT/PT*

B. *PT/UT*

C. *PU/PT*

D. *PU/UT*

E. *PT/PU*

Q23. The multiplier is the inverse of the *mpw*.

True/False

Q24. What are the answers to the following?

(a) $mpw + mpc_d =$

....

(b) $(1 - mpc_d) - (mps + mpm + mpt) =$

....

(where mps, mpm and mpt are from gross income).

⊗ **Q25.** What is the value of the multiplier in the following cases?

(a) $mpw = 1/3$

....

(b) $mpc_d = 0.75$

....

The full multiplier effect does not occur instantaneously. It takes time for the additional incomes to build up as they go round and round the circular flow of income. The multiplier is an example of *cumulative causation* – the idea that economic effects can snowball. This is the fifteenth, and final, Threshold Concept.

◑ **Q26.** Which of the following are examples of cumulative causation?

(a) A falling stock market leads to a loss of confidence on the part of investors, and to further falls in share prices. *Yes/No*

(b) An expanding region attracts migrant workers and grows even more rapidly. *Yes/No*

(c) Microsoft gains network economies, and is able to tap even more economies of scale. *Yes/No*

(d) A buoyant house market leads to further rises in house prices. *Yes/No*

(e) Some firms withdraw investment from a country whose economy seems to be in trouble, and other firms follow. *Yes/No*

(f) The multiplier. *Yes/No*

The following question demonstrates the cumulative causation that underlies the multiplier process.

⊖ **Q27.** Assume that the $mpw = 1/2$ and that there is an initial injection of £200m into the economy. Fill in the missing values in Table 17.2 and calculate by how much income has increased after five periods.

Table 17.2 The multiplier

Period	ΔJ(£m)	ΔY(£m)	ΔC_d(£m)	ΔW(£m)
1	200	200	...	...
2	–	...	...	...
3	–	...	...	...
4	–	...	...	...
5	–	...	...	...
Totals				

▤ **Q28.** Which of the following would cause the value of the multiplier to fall?

A. A cut in the level of government spending.

B. An increase in the marginal propensity to consume.

C. A fall in the level of investment.

D. The population becomes more thrifty, and saves a larger proportion of any rise in income.

E. A balance of payments surplus.

(Pages 511–3) The income and expenditure approach
The multiplier can also be demonstrated using the income/expenditure approach.

⑦ **Q29.** Consumption of domestically produced goods and services plus injections ($C_d + J$) is otherwise known as:

....

⑦ **Q30.** Figure 17.3 shows a Keynesian national income and expenditure diagram.

(a) Assuming that the expenditure function is given by E_1 by how much do injections exceed withdrawals at an income of OC?

....

(b) If the expenditure line now shifts upwards from E_1 to E_2 as the result of an increase in planned consumer spending, what will be the new equilibrium level of national income?

....

(c) What is the size of the multiplier given a rise in expenditure from E_1 to E_2?

....

Figure 17.3 National income determination: income and expenditure approach

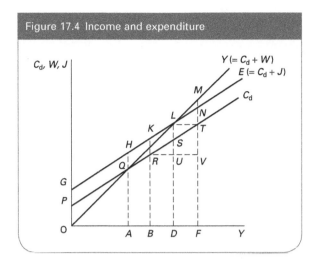

Figure 17.4 Income and expenditure

Q31. A rise in the marginal propensity to save is shown by a swing downwards of the expenditure function (i.e. the curve becomes less steep). *True/False*

Q32. Examine Figure 17.4.
Identify the correct letters for each of the following:
(a) Equilibrium national income. *OA/OB/OD/OF*
(b) Injections at income *OA*. *AQ/AH/QH/(AQ – QH)*
(c) Withdrawals at income *OF*. *FT/TN/TM/NM/VT*
(d) mpc_d. $RU \div SU/SU \div RU/TM \div LT/RT \div VT$
(e) The amount that withdrawals rise when national income rises from *OD* to *OF*. *TN/NM/TM/LN/LM*
(f) *mpw*. $TN \div DF/NM \div DF/DF \div TN/DF \div NM$
(g) The multiplier. $TN \div DF/NM \div DF/DF \div TN/DF \div NM$

(Pages 512–13) The formula for the multiplier is $1/(1 – mpc_d)$. Remember that mpc_d refers to consumption of *domestic* goods, from *gross* income and after the deduction of indirect taxes. When people decide how much of a rise in income to spend (their *mpc*), however, their decision is based on *disposable* income, they do not distinguish between domestic and imported goods and their spending includes the indirect taxes on the goods they purchase. How, then, do we derive the mpc_d from the *mpc* (from disposable income)? We use the formula:

$$mpc_d = mpc(1 – t_E)(1 – t_Y) – mpm$$

where t_Y is the marginal rate of income tax, and t_E is the marginal rate of expenditure tax.

*Q33. If the *mpc* is 0.75, the *mpm* is 0.1, the rate of expenditure tax is 10 per cent and the rate of income tax is 25 per cent:
(a) What is the mpc_d?

....

(b) What is the size of the multiplier?

....

17.3 The simple Keynesian analysis of unemployment and inflation
(Pages 514–17)

Q34. When the economy is at the 'full-employment' level of national income, this means that:
A. everybody is employed.
B. there is no deficiency of demand.
C. the amount of money in the economy is at its maximum level.
D. the economy is in the expansionary phase of the business cycle.
E. the multiplier effect will generate a large number of jobs.

If the equilibrium level of national income (Y_e) is below the full-employment level (Y_f), there will be a **Q35.** *deflationary gap/inflationary gap*. Alternatively, if the level of national expenditure exceeds the full-employment level of national income, there will be a **Q36.** *deflationary gap/inflationary gap*.

Q37. Which of the following define a *deflationary* gap?
(i) The amount by which equilibrium national income exceeds the full-employment level.
(ii) The amount by which the full-employment level of national income exceeds the equilibrium level.
(iii) The amount by which injections exceed withdrawals at the full-employment level of national income.
(iv) The amount by which withdrawals exceed injections at the full-employment level of national income.
(v) The amount by which national income exceeds national expenditure at the full-employment level of national income.
(vi) The amount by which national expenditure exceeds national income at the full-employment level of national income.

A. (ii)
B. (ii) + (v)
C. (iv)
D. (iv) + (v)
E. (iii) + (vi)

Q38. Referring to the same list as in Q37, which define an *inflationary* gap?
A. (i)
B. (i) + (vi)
C. (iii)
D. (iv) + (v)
E. (iii) + (vi)

Q39. Using Figure 17.5:
(a) Mark a full-employment level of national income above Y_e. Identify the deflationary gap. Use two methods to do this.
(b) Now assume that injections rise such as to increase equilibrium national income beyond Y_f. Illustrate this

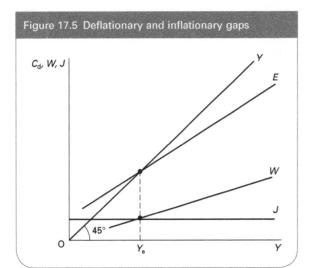

Figure 17.5 Deflationary and inflationary gaps

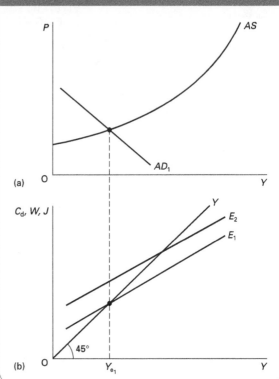

Figure 17.6 National income determination: upward-sloping *AS* curve

and identify the resulting inflationary gap. Again use two methods to do this.

⊗ **Q40.** Table 17.3 gives country A's withdrawals schedule. Assume that the full-employment level of national income is £250bn, and that there is an inflationary gap of £10bn.

Table 17.3

National income (£bn)	50	100	150	200	250	300	350	400
Withdrawals (£bn)	0	10	20	30	40	50	60	70

(a) What is the size of the multiplier?

....

(b) What is the current equilibrium level of national income?

....

(c) If technological progress and increased labour productivity led to a rise of £150bn in the full-employment level of national income, and if there were no change in the equilibrium level of national income, what sort of gap would there be now and what would be its size?

....

▤ **Q41.** An economy currently has a deflationary gap of £20bn and an equilibrium level of national income £60bn below the full-employment level of national income. This means that it must have an mpc_d of:

A. 3
B. 3/2
C. 2/3
D. 1/3
E. 1/6

In practice, inflation is likely to occur before the full-employment level of national income is reached. This means that the aggregate supply curve, rather than being horizontal up to the full-employment level of national income and then vertical at that point, is in fact upward sloping. How do we analyse this using a 45° line diagram?

⊖ **Q42.** Figure 17.6 shows an aggregate demand and supply diagram and a 45° line diagram. Assume that national income is initially in equilibrium at Y_{e_1} where $Y = E_1$ and $AS = AD_1$. Now assume that there is an increase in injections such that expenditure increases to E_2.

(a) Illustrate the effect on national income in diagram (b), assuming *no* rise in prices.

(b) Draw in the new *AD* curve on diagram (a) and again assuming no rise in the price level (i.e. a horizontal *AS* curve) mark the equilibrium level of national income.

(c) Now allowing for the fact that the *AS* curve is upward sloping, show the actual effect on income of the shift in the *AD* curve that you drew in question (b).

(d) Given that diagram (b) shows *real* national income and expenditure, mark the eventual (reduced) rise in the expenditure curve after allowing for the price rise.

17.4 The Keynesian analysis of the business cycle

(Pages 517–22) Keynesians seek to manage the level of aggregate demand and thereby stabilise the fluctuations in the

business cycle. They argue that one of the major causes of cyclical fluctuations is the instability of investment.

Q43. The *accelerator* theory of investment states that the level of investment depends upon:
A. the rate of interest.
B. the level of saving.
C. the level of national income.
D. the size of changes in national income.
E. the degree of slack in the economy.

Q44. The marginal capital/output ratio refers to:
A. the change in investment.
B. the change in investment over a year.
C. the amount output must change in order to lead to more investment.
D. the amount of additional capital required to produce an additional unit of output.
E. the level of investment needed to achieve full employment.

The relationship between induced investment (I_i) and changes in national income (ΔY) can be expressed in the formula:

$$I_i = \alpha \Delta Y$$

where *a* is known as the 'accelerator coefficient'.

Q45. The accelerator coefficient is the marginal capital/output ratio. *True/False*

Q46. The accelerator gets its title because of the amount by which investment changes following a change in national income. *True/False*

Q47. Table 17.4 illustrates the accelerator effect by looking at the case of an individual firm. Assume that each of its machines produces 100 units of output and that one machine each year will need replacing.
Assume that the firm decides to increase the number of machines as necessary in order to supply consumer demand.

Table 17.4 The accelerator effect

	0	1	2	3	4	5	6
Quantity demanded by consumers	500	500	1000	2000	2500	2500	2300
Number of machines required	...	...	...	...	...	...	...
Induced investment (I_i)	...	...	...	...	...	...	...
Replacement investment (I_r)	...	...	...	...	...	...	...
Total investment ($I_i + I_r$)							

(a) Fill in the missing values.
(b) Between years 3 and 4 demand has continued to grow but total investment has fallen. Why is this?

....

....

Q48. List four difficulties we might encounter when trying to calculate the size of the real-world accelerator effect.

1. ....

2. ....

3. ....

4. ....

(Pages 519–22) The multiplier/accelerator interaction is important when analysing changes in national income. A single injection will cause a cycle of economic activity.

Q49. Describe the interaction between the multiplier and accelerator following an increase in government spending.

....

....

....

Q50. The magnitude of cyclical fluctuations resulting from any initial shock to the economy will be greater:
A. the greater the value of both the multiplier and the accelerator.
B. the smaller the value of both the multiplier and the accelerator.
C. the greater the value of the multiplier and the smaller the value of the accelerator.
D. the smaller the value of the multiplier and the greater the value of the accelerator.
E. the greater the difference in the values of the multiplier and accelerator.

Q51. If firms hold stocks, this will increase the speed with which the economy will recover from recession. *True/False*

Q52. Decide in which phase of the business cycle (*upturn/expansion/peaking out/recession*) each of the following effects is most likely to appear.

(a) The accelerator leads to an increase in investment.

....

(b) Low interest rates result from only limited borrowing.

....

(c) Firms reach their full productive capacity.

....

(d) Rising stocks force firms to cut back on production.

....

(e) Firms attempt to rebuild their level of stocks.

....

(f) Replacement investment re-emerges.

....

 B **PROBLEMS, EXERCISES AND PROJECTS**

Q53. Table 17.5 shows how national income and the consumption of domestically produced goods and services (C_d) are related. Government expenditure is £5 million, investment is £2 million and exports are £3 million.

(a) Fill in the missing figures in Table 17.5.

(b) Equilibrium national income is at a level of £40 million.
True/False

(c) Using Figure 17.7, plot the line showing $C_d + W$ against income (the 45° line).

(d) Plot the *J*, *W* and *E* functions.

(e) Identify the equilibrium level of national income from the diagram, verifying that the same result is obtained using both the injections and withdrawals approach and the income and expenditure approach.

....

Table 17.5

Income (*Y*) (£m)	20	40	60	80	100	120
Consumption (C_d) (£m)	25	40	55	70	85	100
Withdrawals (*W*) (£m)	...	...	...	...	...	...
Injections (*J*) (£m)	...	...	...	...	...	...
Expenditure (*E*) (£m)	...	...	...	...	...	...

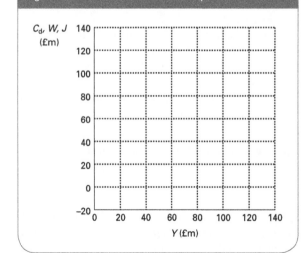

Figure 17.7 National income and expenditure

(f) Assume that withdrawals now fall by £5 million at all levels of national income. Plot the new *W* and *E* functions on Figure 17.7.

(g) What is the new equilibrium level of national income?

....

(h) What is the value of the mpc_d?....................................

(i) What is the value of the *mpw*?.....................................

(j) What is the value of the multiplier?............................

(k) Verify that the rise in equilibrium in question (g) accords with the value of the multiplier you have just given.

....

....

Q54. At present a country has the following: exports £15bn, investment £1.5bn, government expenditure £6.5bn, *total* consumer expenditure £42bn, imports £10bn, indirect taxes £6bn. The economy is currently in equilibrium. It is estimated that the full-employment level of national income is £60bn. The *mpw* is 0.5.

(a) What is the equilibrium level of national income?

....

(b) Is there an inflationary or deflationary gap?
inflationary/deflationary

(c) What is the size of the gap?

....

(d) If the government wished to close this gap by fiscal policy but did not want to alter taxes, by how much would it have to adjust its level of spending?

....

Q55. Assume that there is an initial increase in injections to the economy of £100m. Assume that the mpc_d is 0.5 and the accelerator coefficient (α) is 1.5. Each period, therefore, C_d rises by 0.5 times the rise in income last period (i.e. ΔC_{dt} = $0.5\Delta Y_{t-1}$). The level of I is 1.5 times the rise in income last period (i.e. $I_t = 1.5\Delta Y_{t-1}$); this means that the *rise in I* is 1.5 times the rise in ΔY.

The effects of the initial rise in J are shown in Table 17.6 for three periods.

(a) Fill in the figures up to period 7.

(b) Does a cyclical effect occur?

Table 17.6 Effects of a rise in injections (£m)

Period	Initial rise in J	ΔC_d ($C_{dt} - C_{dt-1}$)	ΔI ($I_t - I_{t-1}$)	ΔY ($Y_t - Y_{t-1}$)	Cumulative rise in income ($Y_t - Y_0$)
1	100	–	–	100	100
2	–	50	150	200	300
3	–	100	150	250	550
4	–	...	...	...	...
5	–	...	...	...	...
6	–	...	...	...	...
7	–	...	...	...	...

Q56. Table 17.7 gives data comparing the investment performance of six industrialised countries.

(a) Plot the UK's investment performance, plus that of two other countries. How does the UK compare?

(b) Using Table 17.8, assess how investment changes with output. Can you identify any time lags between changes in output and the level of investment?

(c) What are the implications for an economy of a lower level of investment than that of its main rivals?

Table 17.7 Growth of total fixed capital formation (real percentage change over 12 months)

	1997	1998	1999	2000	2001	2002	2003	2004	2005	2006	2007	2008	2009	2010*	2011*	2012*
USA	8.1	9.7	9.0	6.8	−1.0	−2.7	3.1	6.2	5.3	2.5	−1.2	−4.5	−14.8	3.3	4.2	8.0
Japan	−0.3	−7.2	−0.8	1.2	−0.9	−4.9	−0.5	1.4	3.1	0.5	−1.2	−3.6	−11.7	−0.2	0.0	6.5
Germany	0.8	3.6	4.4	3.7	−3.4	−6.1	−0.3	−1.3	1.1	8.7	4.9	1.8	−10.0	5.7	6.3	4.0
France	0.4	7.2	8.1	7.5	2.3	−1.6	2.2	3.3	4.5	4.5	5.9	0.3	−6.9	−1.1	4.0	4.6
Italy	1.9	3.6	3.7	7.1	2.4	3.7	−0.9	1.5	1.4	3.2	1.4	−3.8	−12.0	2.3	1.2	2.5
UK	6.8	13.7	3.0	2.7	2.6	3.6	1.1	5.1	2.4	6.4	7.8	−5.0	−15.4	3.0	1.7	4.2

Source: Based on data from table "Demand and output", OECD Economic Outlook No. 89 Annex Tables, www.oecd.org/oecdEconomicOutlook.

Table 17.8 Growth of real GDP (percentage change over 12 months)

	1997	1998	1999	2000	2001	2002	2003	2004	2005	2006	2007	2008	2009	2010*	2011*	2012*
USA	4.5	4.4	4.8	4.1	1.1	1.8	2.5	3.6	3.1	2.7	1.9	0.0	−2.6	2.9	2.6	3.1
Japan	1.6	−2.0	−0.1	2.9	0.2	0.3	1.4	2.7	1.9	2.0	2.4	−1.2	−6.3	4.0	−0.9	2.2
Germany	1.8	1.8	1.9	3.5	1.4	0.0	−0.2	0.7	0.9	2.6	2.8	0.7	−4.7	3.5	3.4	2.5
France	2.2	3.5	3.2	4.1	1.8	1.1	1.1	2.3	2.0	2.4	2.3	0.1	−2.7	1.4	2.2	2.1
Italy	1.9	1.3	1.4	3.9	1.7	0.5	0.1	1.4	0.8	2.1	1.4	−1.3	−5.2	1.2	1.1	1.6
UK	3.3	3.6	3.5	3.9	2.5	2.1	2.8	3.0	2.2	2.8	2.7	−0.1	−4.9	1.3	1.4	1.8

Source: Based on data from table "Demand and output", OECD Economic Outlook No. 89 Annex Tables, www.oecd.org/oecdEconomicOutlook.

DISCUSSION TOPICS AND ESSAYS

Q57. Describe the main determinants of consumption and consider whether changes in these determinants are likely to cause simply a parallel shift in the consumption function or whether they will also affect the *mpc*.

Q58. In what ways and for what reasons is a country's long-run consumption function likely to differ from its short-run consumption function?

Q59. The simple Keynesian model assumes that injections are exogenously determined. What does this mean? Are there any elements of injections that might in fact be *endogenously* determined?

Q60. Using (a) a withdrawals and injections diagram and (b) an income and expenditure diagram, illustrate and explain what you understand by the 'multiplier' effect and what determines its magnitude.

Q61. Why is it difficult to predict the size of the multiplier?

Q62. Why does the size of the multiplier vary from country to country? Which country is likely to have the bigger multiplier: the USA or Singapore? Explain.

Q63. Distinguish between an inflationary gap and a deflationary gap and explain the importance of this information for policy makers. What are the weaknesses of the analysis?

Q64. Explain the accelerator theory of investment and suggest some of the reasons why it is difficult to forecast the accelerator effect with any degree of accuracy.

Q65. Fluctuations in the level of stocks are an important feature of the business cycle. Explain how stocks are likely to change over the course of a business cycle and what effect these changes have on the cycle.

Q66. Why do booms and recessions come to an end?

Q67. Identify three key 'leading' indicators which are likely to signal the end of a recession and the recovery of the economy. Explain why they act as indicators and consider how reliable they are.

Q68. Debate

The Keynesian model presents such a simplified view of reality that it is misleading.

 ANSWERS

Q1. See Chapter 14, Q7.

Q2. Withdrawals and consumption are *endogenous* in the model of national income determination: that is, they are determined (in part) by the level of national income. Injections, however, are *exogenous*: that is, they are determined by factors other than the level of national income.

Q3. C. Assuming that the scale of the two axes is the same, then a 45° line shows that whatever is measured on one axis *must* under all circumstances equal what is measured on the other axis. With national income measured on the horizontal axis, a 45° line shows whatever must equal national income. This is consumption of domestic goods and services plus withdrawals ($C_d + W$): income must be either spent on domestically produced goods and services or withdrawn – there is nothing else that can happen to income.

Q4. (a) See Figure A17.1.
   (b) At low levels of income, people may be forced to spend more than they earn, by either borrowing or drawing on savings. By contrast, at high levels of income individuals will be able to save part of their income.
   (c) The marginal propensity to consume represents the proportion of a rise in national income that goes on consumption. The formula is $\Delta C/\Delta Y$.
   (d) (i) $(90 – 70) \div (75 – 50) = 0.8$
        (ii) $(150 – 130) \div (150 – 125) = 0.8$
   (e) *the slope of the consumption function.*
   (f) It would be curved, with the slope diminishing as national income rose.

Q5. *higher*. In the long run, individuals will have time to adjust their consumption patterns.

Q6. *slowly*.

Q7. The mpc_d includes only that part of a rise in national income that accrues to domestic firms. It thus excludes

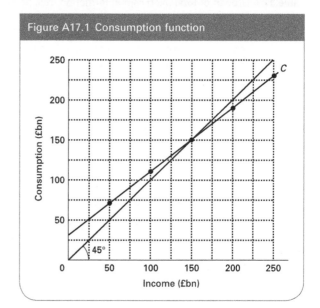

Figure A17.1 Consumption function

that part of a rise in consumption that goes in expenditure taxes (VAT, excise duties, etc.) and also excludes the consumption of imports. It includes, however, sales subsidies to firms.

Q8. (a) *decrease:* an increase in the income tax rate reduces disposable income, which in turn affects consumption.
   (b) *decrease:* with lower expected income in the future, consumers may be less prepared to borrow to finance consumption now because of the need to repay debt in the future.
   (c) *increase.*
   (d) *decrease.*
   (e) *decrease:* this effect is sometimes known as a response to consumer sentiment: if people are uncertain about the future, they are likely to be more cautious about spending in the present.

(f) *increase:* if people expect the price of consumer durables to increase in the future, they may choose to buy now to save money.

(g) *increase:* poor households tend to have a higher marginal propensity to consume.

Q9. Consumption smoothing is where households make use of the financial system to smooth consumption in the face of volatile levels of income.

Q10. *net financial worth.*

Q11. *weaken.*

Q12. *Income.*

Q13. *(a)* See the following table.

National income (£bn)	Saving (£bn)
50	−20
75	−15
100	−10
125	−5
150	0
175	5
200	10
225	15
250	20

(b) See Figure A17.2.

(c) At levels of national income below £150bn.

(d) $mps = \Delta S/\Delta Y = (10 - 5) \div (200 - 175) = 0.2$.

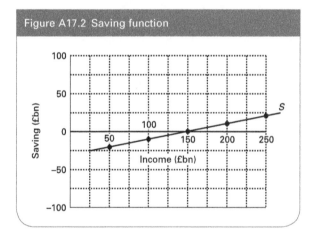

Figure A17.2 Saving function

Q14. *(a)* *fall; shift.*
(b) *fall; shift.*
(c) *rise; shift.*
(d) *rise; shift.*
(e) *fall; movement along.* (The fall in saving is due to the fall in income.)

Q15. *True.* It is the weighted average of all the marginal tax rates for each person in the country.

Q16. The import function would become progressively steeper as imports would account for a larger proportion of any rise in national income. The *mpm* would thus rise as income rose.

Q17. (a) *True* (b) *False* (c) *True.*

Q18. *(a)* *increase.*   *(d)* *increase.*
(b) *increase.*   *(e)* *decrease.*
(c) *decrease.*   *(f)* *increase.*

Q19. *(a)* *OB* (where $W = J$).

(b) At income *OA* injections exceed withdrawals. There will be a movement towards point *P* as the additional net expenditures $(J - W)$ encourage producers to increase output, which in turn lead to higher levels of national income. As income rises, so will the level of withdrawals (a movement along the *W* curve). The movement along the withdrawals curve will continue until $W = J$.

(c) The injections curve will shift upwards by an amount *UT*. Equilibrium will now be achieved at point *U* (where the new injections curve intersects the withdrawals curve). National income will thus have risen by an amount *BC*.

Q20. The ratio of a rise in national income to the rise in injections that caused it.

Q21. A.

Q22. B.

Q23. *True.* The multiplier = $1/mpw$. The larger the *mpw*, the less of any rise in income will be spent on domestic goods and services, and thus the less will recirculate round the circular flow of income each time.

Q24. *(a)* 1.
(b) 0.

Q25. *(a)* 3.
(b) 4 (i.e. $1/(1 - 0.75)$).

Q26. All items are examples of cumulative causation, including the multiplier (f). In the case of (e), one of the causes of the Asian financial crisis of 1997/8 (see Web cases 26.3 and 26.4) is said to be that when some foreign investors began withdrawing their investments from Thailand and Korea, others began to follow suit.

Q27. See Table A17.1.

Table A17.1 The multiplier

Period	ΔJ(£m)	ΔY(£m)	ΔC_d(£m)	ΔW(£m)
1	200	200	100	100
2	–	100	50	50
3	–	50	25	25
4	–	25	12.5	12.5
5	–	12.5	6.25	6.25
Totals		387.5	193.75	193.75

Q28. D. An increase in the marginal propensity to save will cause the *mpw* to increase: hence the value of the multiplier will fall.

Q29. *National expenditure* (which is the same as aggregate demand).

Q30. (a) *VZ* (b) *OB* (c) *AB/UG*.

Q31. *True.* The mpc_d will fall, and thus the slope of the C_d function and hence the *E* function will fall.

Q32. (a) OD (where $Y = E$).

    (b) QH (i.e. $E - C_d$).

    (c) TM (i.e. $Y - C_d$).

    (d) $SU \div RU$ (i.e. $\Delta C_d \div \Delta Y$).

    (e) NM (i.e. $TM - SL$).

    (f) $NM \div DF$ (i.e. $\Delta W \div \Delta Y$).

    (g) $DF \div NM$ (i.e. $1 \div mpw$).

*Q33. (a) $(0.75 \times 0.9 \times 0.75) - 0.1 = 0.40625$.

    (b) $1/(1 - 0.40625) = 1.68$.

Q34. B. National output is at a maximum and the level of national income is such as to ensure that all such output produced is bought, i.e. there is no deficiency in demand.

Q35. deflationary gap.

Q36. inflationary gap.

Q37. D. Note that (ii) is *not* a definition. The deflationary gap will be less than the shortfall of national income below the full-employment level. If the government adopts policies to close the deflationary gap, the multiplier will then ensure that the full shortfall is made up.

Q38. E.

Q39. (a) See Figure A17.3.

    (b) The J and E lines will shift upward so that they now intersect with the W and Y lines respectively to the right of Y_f. The inflationary gap is now the amount by which E exceeds Y and J exceeds W at Y_f.

Q40. (a) 5. (i.e. $1/mpw$. The mpw is $1/5$, since for every rise in national income of £50bn, withdrawals rise by £10bn.)

    (b) *£300bn.* (With an inflationary gap of £10bn and a multiplier of 5, the equilibrium national income must be £50bn above the full-employment level.)

    (c) *Deflationary gap of £20bn.* (The full-employment level of national income has risen by £150bn to £400bn. This means that the full-employment

level of national income is now £100bn above the equilibrium level of national income (of £300bn). With a multiplier of 5, the deflationary gap must be £100bn/5 = £20bn.)

Q41. C. If an increase in injections to fill a gap of £20bn leads to a rise in national income of £60bn, the multiplier must have a value of 3. Given that the multiplier $= 1/(1 - mpc_d)$, the mpc_d must equal $^2/_3$.

Q42. (a) In Figure A17.4, part (b), national income rises to Y_{e_2}.

    (b) The AD curve shifts to AD_2, and if the price level remained at P_1 (i.e. if the AS curve were horizontal), income would rise to Y_{e_2}.

    (c) With the upward-sloping aggregate supply curve illustrated, equilibrium will be at point X. National income will be Y_{e_3}.

    (d) The expenditure curve will be E_3.

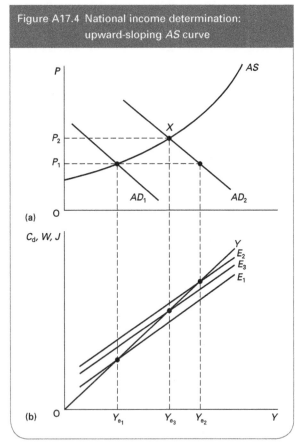

Figure A17.4 National income determination: upward-sloping *AS* curve

Q43. D.

Q44. D.

Q45. *True.*

Q46. *True.* Relatively small changes in national income can lead to relatively large changes in the level of investment, which in turn lead to further rises in national income.

Q47. (a) See Table A17.2.

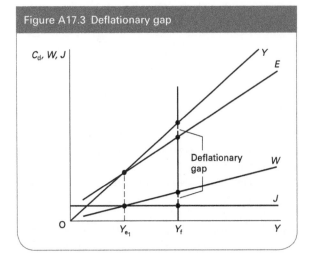

Figure A17.3 Deflationary gap

Table A17.2 The accelerator effect

	0	1	2	3	4	5	6
Quantity demanded by consumers	500	500	1000	2000	2500	2500	2300
Number of machines required	5	5	10	20	25	25	23
Induced investment (I_i)	–	0	5	10	5	0	0
Replacement investment (I_r)	–	1	1	1	1	1	0
Total investment ($I_i + I_r$)		1	6	11	6	1	0

(b) Even though demand has continued to grow, it has done so at a slower rate. Induced investment is determined by the rate of growth of demand.

Q48. Firms often have spare capacity or carry stocks and thus do not need to invest more when demand rises; expectations of future demand will vary; producer goods industries may not be able to supply additional machines; replacement investment is unpredictable; firms make investment plans into the future and it may take time to change them.

Q49. Following an increase in government spending, national income will rise (multiplier effect). This rise in national income will stimulate investment (the accelerator effect). This represents a further injection into the circular flow (causing a multiplier effect). Whether the subsequent effect on national income is greater than the previous change in national income will determine whether investment continues to increase. If the change in national income is bigger, investment will rise and there will be a resulting multiplied rise in income. If it is smaller, investment will fall and there will be a resulting multiplied fall in income. The interactions continue indefinitely.

Q50. A.

Q51. *False.* It will slow down the recovery. The firm, rather than employing more labour to increase output, may simply draw on its stocks to meet the additional rise in demand.

Q52. (a) *expansion*; (b) *recession or early part of upturn*; (c) *peaking out*; (d) *recession*; (e) *expansion*; (f) *upturn*. For discussion of this, see Web case 17.8.

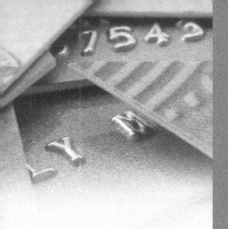

Chapter 18

Banking, Money and Interest Rates

 A **REVIEW**

The financial sector has changed a great deal in recent years, primarily as a result of the introduction of new technology and of the policy of deregulation.

This chapter and the next will review the monetary sector of the economy, examining how it operates and how it is controlled. We will also consider the banking sector and the relationship between money and interest rates, and examine the importance of money and interest rates in determining the level of activity in the economy.

18.1 The meaning and functions of money

(Pages 525–6) The starting point is to define precisely what is meant by 'money'. The main component of a country's money is not cash, but deposits in banks and other financial institutions **Q1.** *true/false.* Fortunately, the chances of banks running out of cash are very low indeed **Q2.** *true/false.*

(?) **Q3.** Identify two steps that the central bank or government could take if faced with a serious 'run on the bank'.

1. ....

2. ....

(|) **Q4.** The supply of money in the economy is a flow concept since money circulates by being passed from hand to hand. *True/False*

(?) **Q5.** Money has four main functions. These are:

1. ....

2. ....

3. ....

4. ....

(?) **Q6.** Which of the following items would be included in:
(i) both narrow and broad definitions of money?
(ii) broad definitions alone?
(iii) neither narrow nor broad definitions?

(a) Current accounts in banks. ....

(b) Share certificates. ....

(c) Cash in banks' tills. ....

(d) Cash in a person's pocket. ....

(e) Deposits in savings accounts in banks and building societies.
....

(f) A debit card. ....

(g) Wholesale deposits in financial institutions.
....

The amount of money in the economy influences the level of economic activity. It does this by affecting aggregate demand.

Before we can examine just how money supply affects the economy, we must see what determines money supply itself. We begin by looking at the various financial institutions involved.

18.2 The financial system

(Pages 526–8) Financial intermediaries provide a number of important services, two of which are in providing expert advice to their customers, and channelling funds to those areas that will yield the greatest return. They also lend long and borrow short. This is known as **Q7.** *risk transformation/maturity transformation/credit creation.* Also by lending to a large number of individuals they reduce the impact of loan defaults by any one borrower. This is known as **Q8.** *risk transformation/maturity transformation/ credit creation.*

Banking can be divided into two main types; retail banking and wholesale banking. However, most banks today conduct both types of business, and are thus known as 'universal banks'.

Q9. Which of the following characteristics do you mainly associate with retail banking, and which with wholesale banking?
(a) The business conducted by the familiar high street banks. *retail/wholesale*
(b) Bank operations dealing in large-scale deposits and loans, mainly with companies and other banks and financial institutions. *retail/wholesale*
(c) Branch, telephone, postal and Internet banking for individuals and businesses at published rates of interest and charges. *retail/wholesale*
(d) Banking services in which interest rates and charges may be negotiable. *retail/wholesale*
(e) The operation of extensive branch networks. *retail/wholesale*

Q10. There is a clear distinction between banks and building societies, with the latter focusing on loans for house purchase. *True/False*

Q11. Which of the following are classified as monetary financial institutions (MFIs)?
(i) Retail banks.
(ii) The Bank of England.
(iii) Building societies.
(iv) Universal banks.

A. (i) and (iv).
B. (ii) and (iv).
C. (i), (iii) and (iv).
D. (iii) and (iv).
E. (i), (ii), (iii) and (iv).

During the financial crisis of 2008/09, many forms of inter-bank lending **Q12.** *expanded rapidly/virtually dried up.* In response to the crisis, the Bank of England **Q13.** *supplied extra money to/withdrew funds from* MFIs to ensure the security of these institutions and the stability of the financial system.

(Pages 528–35) The deposits made in banks and building societies are **Q14.** *liabilities/losses/costs/assets/profits* of these institutions. The loans they make to their customers are **Q15.** *liabilities/losses/costs/assets/profits* of these institutions.

An important distinction is between wholesale and retail loans and deposits.

Q16. Match the following types of deposit with their definitions.
(i) Sight deposits.
(ii) Time deposits.
(iii) Certificates of deposit.
(iv) Sale and repurchase agreements (repos).

(a) Agreements between financial institutions whereby one in effect borrows from another by selling its assets, agreeing to buy them back at a fixed price and at a fixed date.
....
(b) Deposits that can be withdrawn on demand without penalty.
....
(c) Resalable certificates issued by banks for fixed-term interest-bearing deposits.
....
(d) Deposits that require notice of withdrawal or where a penalty is charged for withdrawal on demand.
....

Q17. Which of the following are wholesale and which are retail?
(a) Large-scale deposits made by firms at negotiated rates of interest. *retail/wholesale*
(b) Loans made by high street banks at published rates of interest. *retail/wholesale*
(c) Deposits in savings accounts in high street banks. *retail/wholesale*
(d) Deposits in savings accounts in building societies. *retail/wholesale*
(e) Large-scale loans to industry syndicated through several banks. *retail/wholesale*

Banks must have sufficient capital (i.e. funds) to allow them to meet all demands from depositors and to cover losses if borrowers default on payment.

Q18. Identify each of the following as part of either Tier 1 or Tier 2 capital under Basel II:

(a) Bank reserves from retained profits   *Tier 1/Tier 2*
(b) Preference shares   *Tier 1/Tier 2*
(c) Ordinary share capital   *Tier 1/Tier 2*

Q19. Which of the following defines the capital adequacy ratio?
A. The ratio of bank reserves from retained profits to the bank's assets.
B. The ratio of a bank's capital (reserves and shares) to its total assets.
C. The ratio of the value of a bank's shares to its assets.
D. The ratio of a bank's capital (reserves and shares) to its risk weighted assets.
E. The ratio of bank reserves from retained profits to the bank's risk weighted assets.

Q20. Under the internationally agreed Basel II accord, banks are required to have a capital adequacy ratio of at least:
A. 2 per cent.
B. 4 per cent.
C. 5 per cent.
D. 8 per cent.
E. 10 per cent.

Financial institutions keep a range of liabilities and assets. The balance of items is dictated by considerations of *profitability* and *liquidity*.

Basel III tightened the requirements, holding the minimum overall CAR at 8 per cent, but increasing the minimum Tier 1 capital ratio to **Q21.** *2 per cent/4 per cent/ 6 per cent* by 2015 and the minimum ordinary share capital ratio to **Q22.** *1.5 per cent/2 per cent/4.5 per cent* by the same date.

(?) Q23. Define macro-prudential regulation.

....

Q24. Rank the following assets of a commercial bank in order of decreasing liquidity.
(a) Money at call with money market institutions.
(b) Government bonds.
(c) Bills of exchange.
(d) Operational balances with the Bank of England.
(e) Cash.
(f) Personal loans.

High liquidity

(i) ....

(ii) ....

(iii) ....

(iv) ....

(v) ....

(vi) ....

Low liquidity

(?) Q25. Profitability is the major aim of most financial institutions. Why does the motive of profitability tend to conflict with the need for liquidity?

....

....

....

Q26. The liquidity ratio of a bank refers to:
A. the ratio of Treasury bills to government bonds that it holds.
B. the ratio of liquid to illiquid assets.
C. the ratio of cash to advances.
D. the ratio of liquid assets to total liabilities.
E. the ratio of total assets to total liabilities.

(?) Q27. What adverse consequence for a bank might follow if it maintained a liquidity ratio that was:

(a) too low? ....

....

(b) higher than necessary? ....

....

Another way of reconciling the conflicting aims of liquidity and profitability is through secondary marketing, either through instruments (such as certificates of deposit) or through securitisation.

Q28. Figure 18.1 shows the securitisation chain. Match the following terms with their place in the chain.
(a) Originator/lender.   *(i)/(ii)/(iii)*
(b) Bond holders (noteholders).   *(i)/(ii)/(iii)*
(c) Special purpose vehicle (SPV).   *(i)/(ii)/(iii)*

Figure 18.1 The securitisation chain

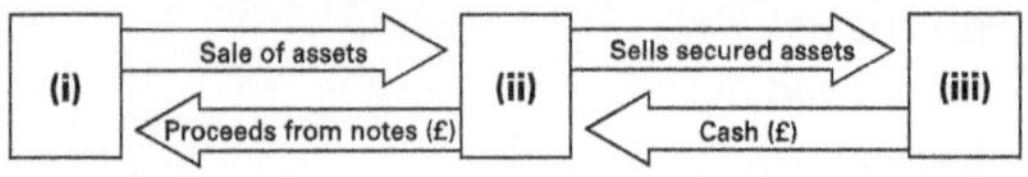

The effect of secondary marketing is to **Q29.** *reduce/widen* the liquidity ratio that banks feel they need to keep; it has the effect of **Q30.** *decreasing/increasing* their maturity gap.

Q31. Which of the following is *not* a danger of secondary marketing?
A. A lower national liquidity ratio.
B. A banking collapse.
C. A weakened securitisation chain if individual financial institutions move into riskier market segments such as the sub-prime residential mortgage markets.
D. A higher national liquidity ratio.
E. The risk of loan defaults.

Q32. Moral hazard is the temptation to take more risks when you know that someone else will cover the risks if you get into difficulties. *True/False*

Financial intermediation is underpinned by the process of maturity transformation, where financial institutions borrow **Q33.** *long/short* and lend **Q34.** *long/short*. Financial deregulation and innovation resulted in an expansion of the aggregate balance sheets of financial institutions and **Q35.** *a decrease/an increase* in leverage. This can be seen as a form of co-ordination failure.

Q36. Co-ordination failure is a form of market failure and arises when

....

(Pages 535–7)) The Bank of England is the UK's central bank. All countries with their own currency have a central bank to fulfil two vital roles in the economy.

Q37. Identify the two key roles of the central bank.

1. ....

2. ....

Q38. Which of the following statements about the Bank of England are true?
(*a*) The Bank of England is the sole issuer of banknotes in the UK. *True/False*
(*b*) The Bank of England acts as banker to the banks. *True/False*
(*c*) No matter whether the government runs a budget surplus or a budget deficit, the Bank of England still has to manage the national debt. *True/False*
(*d*) The Bank of England is lender of last resort to the banking system. *True/False*
(*e*) The Bank of England not only operates domestic monetary policy but also manages the country's exchange rate policy. *True/False*

Q39. The amount of banknotes issued by the Bank of England depends largely on the demand for notes from the general public. *True/False*

Q40. The following items relate to the balance sheet of the Banking Department of the Bank of England in August 2011 in £billion. Please note that short-term open market operations (which appear on both sides of the balance sheet) registered zero in this period.

Long-term reverse repos	1.7
Reserve balances of banks	128.0
Foreign currency public securities issued	3.7
Bonds and other securities acquired	8.7
APF loan investment in corporate bonds and commercial papers	1.1
Cash ratio deposits of banks	2.4
Other liabilities	90.1
Other non-APF assets	14.6

Using this information, calculate the amount of APF loan investment in gilts.

....

Q41. The Asset Purchase Facility (APF) was introduced in 2009 in order to reduce nominal spending growth. *True/False*

(Pages 535–41) The Monetary Policy Committee (MPC) of the Bank of England sets Bank Rate at its monthly meetings. The Bank of England keeps interest rates in line with level set by the MPC using open-market operations to manage liquidity. If shortages of liquidity are driving up short-term interest rates, the Bank of England **Q42.** *purchases/sells* securities on the open market, thus **Q43.** *reducing/releasing* liquidity and putting **Q44.** *downward/upward* pressure on interest rates.

Arbitrage is the practice of taking advantage of price differentials in markets by **Q45.** *buying/selling* in the low-priced markets and **Q46.** *buying/selling* in the high-priced ones. This practice will tend to **Q47.** *eliminate/widen* the price differentials.

The money market plays a central role in the financial system.

Q48. There are two parts of the London money market:

(*a*) the ...., and

(*b*) the ....

Q49. Bills of exchange are one major type of monetary instrument. Bills pay no interest. Why, then, is it profitable for banks to buy bills (thereby providing liquidity to the issuers of the bills – the government in the case of Treasury bills and firms in the case of commercial bills)?

....

Q50. The process of purchasing bills from the banks and discount houses by the Bank of England is known as 'rediscounting'. *True/False*

Q51. Another major type of monetary instrument is a sale and repurchase agreement (repo). Which of the following describes a repo?

A. Where a bank agrees to buy certain assets from an institution for cash in return for being able to borrow from that institution in the future.

B. Where a bank sells some assets (e.g. bonds) and agrees to buy them back at a particular price after a set period of time.

C. Where bank A lends to bank B provided that bank B is prepared to lend to bank A in the future.

D. Where a bank sells assets to person or institution A in return for buying assets from person or institution B.

E. All of the above.

Q52. Give three reasons why the parallel money market has grown in importance in recent years.

1. ....

2. ....

3. ....

Q53. Significant changes to monetary policy began in March 2009 when the Bank of England began creating reserves to fund a programme of gilt purchases. This process became known as:

....

18.3 The supply of money

(Page 542) If the money supply is to be monitored and controlled then it must be measured. The most usual measure that countries use for money supply is broad money, which in the UK is known as **Q54.** *M1/M2/M3/M4.*

(Pages 544–50) The process by which banks increase the money supply is known as **Q55.** *maturity transformation/ credit creation/profit generation/liquidity preference.* The amount by which the money supply can increase depends on their liquidity ratio.

Q56. If banks operate with a liquidity ratio of 20 per cent, by how much would they eventually increase their advances if they received an additional £175m from a government investment project?

....

Q57. If the banks decide to hold a lower liquidity ratio, what effect will this have on the bank multiplier?

Increase it/Reduce it

Explain ....

....

Q58. Which of the following will cause the UK money supply to rise; which will cause it to fall; and which will cause no direct change?

(a) A fixed exchange rate where the demand for sterling is greater than the supply. *Rise/Fall/No change*

(b) The government finances its PSNCR by selling securities to the Bank of England. *Rise/Fall/No change*

(c) The government decides to increase the proportion of the national debt financed by bonds rather than by bills. *Rise/Fall/No change*

(d) The government finances its PSNCR by selling bonds and bills to the general public and non-bank private sector. *Rise/Fall/No change*

(e) The government imposes a statutory liquidity ratio on banks higher than their current ratio.

Rise/Fall/No change

(Page 550) The various effects on money supply can be shown in a *flow-of-funds equation.*

Q59. Decide whether each of the following elements should be added (+) or subtracted (–) to arrive at the total change in money supply.

(a) The PSNCR. +/–

(b) Sales of public-sector debt to the non-bank private sector. +/–

(c) Bank lending to the private sector. +/–

(d) A total currency flow deficit (on the balance of payments). +/–

(Pages 550–1) The relationship between the money supply and the rate of interest is one of debate.

Q60. What does it mean in simple monetary theory when it is assumed that the money supply is *exogenously* determined?

....

....

Q61. Give two reasons why Keynesian models assume that the money supply is *endogenous.*

1. ....

2. ....

18.4 The demand for money

(Pages 552–5)

Q62. What do we mean by the term the 'demand for money'? Is it:

A. the demand by individuals for greater wealth?

B. the demand to hold financial assets in money form?

C. a means of controlling the money supply?

D. a sign of individuals wishing to change from sight to time deposits?

E. a term used by the Bank of England to refer to the demands placed upon it by the banking sector?

It is common to distinguish three motives for holding money: the transactions motive, the precautionary motive and the speculative motive. The principal determinant of the size of transactions balances is **Q63.** *national income/interest rates/the exchange rate/tastes*, and the principal determinant of the size of speculative balances is **Q64.** *national income/interest rates/the exchange rate/tastes*.

Q65. Peter and Jane receive the same annual income, but Peter, who gets paid monthly, will have a much higher demand for active balances than Jane, who gets paid weekly. *True/False*

Q66. Indicate whether the following reasons for holding money are based on the transactions, precautionary or speculative motive.

(a) To purchase household items.
Transactions/Precautionary/Speculative

(b) To purchase shares at some future date.
Transactions/Precautionary/Speculative

(c) To pay rent. *Transactions/Precautionary/Speculative*

(d) To be able to purchase goods and services if your wages are not paid on time.
Transactions/Precautionary/Speculative

Q67. What will be the effect on the demand for money curve (*L*) of the following?

(a) An increase in nominal GDP.
Shift right/Shift left/Movement up along/
Movement down along

(b) A rise in interest rates.
Shift right/Shift left/Movement up along/
Movement down along

(c) Growing expectations that share prices will fall.
Shift right/Shift left/Movement up along/
Movement down along

(d) A rise in bond prices.
Shift right/Shift left/Movement up along/
Movement down along

(e) People believe that foreign interest rates will fall, while domestic interest rates will be unchanged.
Shift right/Shift left/Movement up along/
Movement down along

18.5 Equilibrium

(Pages 556–7) Equilibrium in the money market is achieved where the demand for money is equal to the supply of money.

This is illustrated in Figure 18.2.

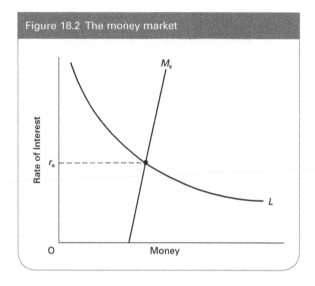

Figure 18.2 The money market

Q68. In each of the following cases, state which curve shifts and what the effect will be on the equilibrium rate of interest.

(a) The government funds the PSNCR by borrowing from the Bank of England.

....

(b) A rise in national income.

....

(c) Speculation that the domestic currency will appreciate on the foreign exchange market.

....

(d) The Bank of England sells more securities through open market operations.

....

Q69. An excess supply of money will cause people to buy securities, hence increasing their price and causing interest rates to fall. The lower interest rates eliminate the excess supply of money so that equilibrium in the money market is restored. *True/False*

Q70. Short-term rates of interest will rise relative to long-term rates of interest if the demand for long-term bonds increases relative to bills. *True/False*

(?) **Q71.** Trace through the effects of a reduction in money supply on the exchange rate.

....

....

B PROBLEMS, EXERCISES AND PROJECTS

Q72. Consider the items in Table 18.1 selected from Bank A's balance sheet.
(a) Using these items, compile a balance sheet for the bank. When doing so make sure you order the sterling assets in descending order of liquidity.
(b) What are the bank's total sterling assets (and liabilities)?
(c) What is the liquidity ratio?

Table 18.1 A range of sterling assets and liabilities of Bank A

	£bn
Notes and coin	3.5
Sight deposits by UK private sector	100.0
Time deposits by UK private sector	120.0
Investments in the public sector	16.0
Certificates of deposit in Bank A	50.0
Advances to UK private sector	200.0
Bills of exchange	14.0
Debit items in suspense and transmission	9.0
Time deposits by overseas customers	57.0
Operational balances with Bank of England	0.5
Market loans	102.0

Q73. Assume that banks choose to maintain a liquidity ratio of 25 per cent, that new cash deposits of £100m are made in the banking system and that all loans made are redeposited in the banking system.
(a) Complete Table 18.2.
(b) To what level will total deposits eventually increase (after an infinite number of rounds!)?

....

Table 18.2 The creation of money

	£m		£m
Banks receive	100	Hold	25
		Lend	75
Second round deposits rise by	...	Hold	...
	...	Lend	...
Third round deposits rise by	...	Hold	...
	...	Lend	...
Fourth round deposits rise by	...	Hold	...
	...	Lend	...
Fifth round deposits rise by	...	Hold	...
	...	Lend	...
Total deposits after five rounds	...		

(c) How much credit will have been created?

....

(d) What is the size of the bank multiplier?

....

Q74. Look up the liabilities and assets of the banking sector for the most recent month available and for 10 and 20 years ago. You will find the information in the Bankstats section of the Bank of England website at http://www.bankofengland.co.uk/Bankstats/. How has the balance of items changed over the years? How have the cash and liquidity ratios changed? What explanations can you offer for these changes?

C DISCUSSION TOPICS AND ESSAYS

Q75. Describe the main functions of money. What attributes should money have if it is to fulfil these functions?

Q76. 'The aims of profitability and liquidity tend to conflict.' Explain this statement in respect of the banking sector.

Q77. Define the term 'liquidity ratio'. How will changes in the liquidity ratio affect the process of credit creation? Why might a bank's liquidity ratio vary over time?

Q78. What have been the government's objectives in encouraging greater competition in the banking sector?

How are these objectives likely to conflict with the government's/central bank's objectives of maintaining stability and security in the banking sector and of carrying out effective control of the money supply?

Q79. Discuss the changes in the operation of monetary policy that followed the financial crisis of 2008/09.

Q80. What factors might cause the money supply to rise and why? To what extent are these factors within the government's (or central bank's) control?

Q81. Describe the main motives for holding money and the main determinants of each of these money balances.

Q82. Discuss how (a) the increased availability of cash machines, (b) the convenience of debit cards, (c) the ability to earn interest on current accounts and (d) the rise of Internet banking are each likely to affect the demand for money.

Q83. Trace through the effects of an increase in money supply on interest rates and exchange rates. How does the elasticity of demand for money affect the outcome? What determines this elasticity?

Q84. To what extent do you consider Britain's rescue plan for the banking system to have been effective following the financial crisis of 2008/09?

Q85. **Debate**
Total deregulation of banks is in the interests of their customers as it is the best way of ensuring maximum competition between banks.

 ANSWERS

Q1. *True.*

Q2. *True.* The chances of banks running out of cash in a country like the UK are low, but there are occasional instances where people have lost confidence in a bank. One example was that of Northern Rock in 2008.

Q3. There are two basic steps that the central bank or government could take if faced with a serious run on the bank. One would be to make more cash available to the bank. The second would be to nationalise the bank.

Q4. *False.* The amount of money in supply is a stock concept. At any one point in time there is a given amount of money in circulation.

Q5. The four main functions of money are: as a medium of exchange, a store of wealth, a means of valuing different types of goods and services, and a means of establishing future claims and payments, e.g. the setting of wages or an estimate from a builder tendering for a future contract.

Q6. *(a)* (i).

(b) (iii).

(c) (iii). Cash in banks is not included as a separate item because it has *already* been included under the heading of accounts. To count it again would be a case of 'double counting'.

(d) (i).

(e) (i). Under old definitions deposits in savings accounts were only included in broad definitions of money. Now, however, since savings accounts can normally be accessed rapidly (albeit with some loss of interest) they are also included in the narrow definition of money, M2. (M2 includes all *retail* deposits: i.e. deposits in branches of banks and building societies at published interest rates.)

(f) (iii).

(g) (ii).

Q7. *maturity transformation.* This process is possible because not all depositors wish to withdraw their deposits at the same time. If they did, the financial intermediary would be unable to return their money!

Q8. *risk transformation.* This is where the risks of lending are spread over a large number of borrowers.

Q9. *(a)* *retail.*

(b) *wholesale.*

(c) *retail.*

(d) *wholesale.*

(e) *retail.*

Q10. *false:* banks and building societies have become much more alike, with building societies offering current account facilities and cash machines.

Q11. E.

Q12. *virtually dried up.*

Q13. *supplied extra money to.*

Q14. *liabilities.* Institutions that take depositors' money are liable to the claims that the individuals may make on their money.

Q15. *assets.* These are claims that the financial institution has on others, e.g. personal loans to customers.

Q16. (a) (iv), (b) (i), (c) (iii), (d) (ii).

Q17. (a) *wholesale*, (b) *retail*, (c) *retail*, (d) *retail*, (e) *wholesale*.

Q18. *(a)* *Tier 1.*

(b) *Tier 2.*

(c) *Tier 1.*

Q19. D.

Q20. D. 8 per cent.

Q21. *6 per cent.*

Q22. *4.5 per cent.*

Q23. Regulation which focuses not on a single financial institution but on the financial system as a whole and which monitors its impact on the wider economy.

Q24. (i) (e) Cash, (ii) (d) Operational balances with the Bank of England, (iii) (a) Money at call, (iv) (c) Bills of exchange, (v) (b) Bonds, (vi) (f) Personal loans.

Q25. The more liquid an asset, the less profitable it is (the less interest it will earn). However, banks and other financial institutions must keep part of their assets liquid, e.g. to act as till money and cover day-to-day transactions.

Q26. D. The liquidity ratio refers to the bank's total assets held in liquid form as a percentage of the bank's total assets or liabilities (total assets equal total liabilities).

Q27. *(a)* The consequence of a liquidity ratio that is too low might be that customers' demands for cash cannot all be met. The bank may be forced to borrow, or in an extreme case it may be driven out of business.

(b) If the liquidity ratio is excessively high, the bank will not be making as much profit as it might.

Q28. *(a)* (i).

(b) (iii).

(c) (ii).

Q29. *reduce.*

Q30. *increasing.*

Q31. D.

Q32. *True.*

Q33. *short.*

Q34. *long.*

Q35. *an increase.*

Q36. a group of firms (e.g. banks) acting independently could have achieved a more desirable outcome if they had co-ordinated their decision making.

Q37. 1. to oversee the whole monetary system.

2. to act as the government's agent.

Q38. *(a) False.* The Bank of England is the sole issuer of banknotes in England and Wales. In Scotland and Northern Ireland the clearing banks can also issue notes.

(b) True. The banks keep operational balances with the Bank of England for clearing purposes.

(c) True. When the government runs a budget deficit, the Bank of England arranges the necessary borrowing. But even when the government runs a budget surplus, the Bank of England will still need to manage the national debt and the issuing of new bonds if the budget surplus is insufficient to repay all maturing bonds.

(d) True. The Bank of England thereby ensures there is always sufficient liquidity within the banking system.

(e) True. The Bank of England manages the nation's stock of foreign currency and its gold reserves.

Q39. *True.*

Q40. Total liabilities are $128.0 + 3.7 + 2.4 + 90.1 = £224.2b$. Assets listed amount to $1.7 + 8.7 + 13.6 + 1.1 = £25.1b$

So the APF loan investment in gilts is $224.2 - 25.1 = £199.1b$.

Q41. *False:* the APF was introduced when the Bank of England began to purchase assets in exchange for money in order to *boost* nominal spending growth.

Q42. *purchases.*

Q43. *releasing.*

Q44. *downward.*

Q45. *buying.*

Q46. *selling.*

Q47. *eliminate.*

Q48. (a) the *discount and repo markets*, (b) the *parallel money markets*.

Q49. The banks buy them at a discount (i.e. below their face value) but sell them back to the issuer on maturity at face value. The difference is the equivalent to interest. The rate of discount (i.e. the annualised return relative to the face value) will be determined by demand and supply and will reflect market rates of interest.

Q50. *True.* Rediscounting refers to the buying of bills by the Bank of England before they reach maturity. Banks and discount houses will only sell to the Bank of England in this way if they are short of liquidity as the rediscount rate will be a penal one (i.e. the Bank of England will pay a low price for these bills).

Q51. B. As with bills, the difference between the sale and repurchase price is the equivalent of interest. Repo rates may be determined by demand and supply. Alternatively, the central bank can set the repo rates at which it deals with the banks, and thereby seek to influence interest rates generally. Here we are talking about government bond (or 'gilt') repos between banks and the central bank (the Bank of England in the case of the UK). This is a means whereby the central bank, by temporarily buying back government bonds from the banks, provides them with a short-term source of liquidity.

Q52. The parallel money market has grown due to: the abolition of exchange controls and the expansion of international dealing, the deregulation of the money market, and the volatility of interest rates and exchange rates making it more desirable to have a stock of funds that can be quickly converted from one asset to another and from one currency to another.

Q53. *quantitative easing.*

Q54. *M4.*

Q55. *Credit creation* is the process whereby bank deposits expand by more than the cash base.

Q56. £700m. The *total* increase in bank deposits will equal $1/L \times \Delta R$ (where ΔR = the change in the reserve base).

$1/0.2 \times £175m = £875m$. The additional advances are found by deducting the initial increase in the reserve base (£175m).

Q57. If the bank decides to hold a lower liquidity ratio, the bank multiplier will increase. More will be lent to customers, thereby creating more money when it is redeposited back in the banking system.

Q58. *(a)* *Rise.* If the exchange rate is to be maintained at this value, additional pounds will need to be supplied to the market. These additional pounds will then find their way back to banks as deposits by those that trade overseas.

(b) *Rise.* If the government finances its PSNCR in this way, this will lead to the creation of new money. When the government spends the money, banks' accounts in the Bank of England will be credited, thereby increasing their liquid assets and allowing credit to be created.

(c) *Fall.* Changing the way the national debt is funded by substituting bonds for bills will cause the asset base of banks to become more illiquid. As a result, advances to customers will be reduced.

(d) *No change.* Funding the PSNCR in this manner will simply lead to a reshuffling of money between individuals and government. No new money is created.

(e) *Fall.* Statutory reserve requirements effectively mean that banks cannot lend as much as they would like to. Thus the initial imposition of such a ratio will cause the money supply to fall.

Q59. (a) *added*, (b) *subtracted* (given that this is the part of the PSNCR that does *not* lead to an increase in the money supply), (c) *added* (this is credit creation), (d) *subtracted* (a balance of payments deficit will mean that the Bank of England has to *purchase* the excess pounds on the foreign exchange market, thereby 'retiring' them from circulation).

Q60. That the level of the money supply is determined by government rather than by the demand for money.

Q61. Reasons include: higher demand for credit will force up interest rates, encouraging banks to supply more credit and causing the money supply to expand as a consequence; higher interest rates may encourage depositors to switch deposits from sight to time accounts, but since such money is less likely to be withdrawn quickly from time accounts, banks may be encouraged to lower their liquidity ratio and create more credit as a result; higher interest rates will attract deposits from overseas.

Q62. B. The term 'demand for money' reflects the desire by individuals to hold their assets in money form as opposed to any other (such as stocks and shares or property).

Q63. *national income.*

Q64. *interest rates.*

Q65. *True.* Peter will receive just over four times as much on each pay day as Jane, but this will have to last him a whole month. On average, therefore, he will hold a larger transactions balance of money than Jane.

Q66. (a) *Transactions*; (b) *Speculative*; (c) *Transactions*; (d) *Precautionary*.

Q67. (a) *Shift right*; (b) *Movement up along*; (c) *Shift right* (instead of buying shares now, people will prefer to hold money while they wait for share prices to fall); (d) *Movement down along* (bond prices and interest rates move inversely to each other; thus interest rates will fall, causing a movement down along the L curve); (e) *Shift right* (the demand for the domestic currency will rise as people anticipate that the fall in interest rates abroad will cause the domestic currency to appreciate).

Q68. *(a)* Supply curve shifts to the right; rate of interest falls.

(b) Demand curve shifts to the right; rate of interest rises.

(c) Demand curve shifts to the right; rate of interest rises.

(d) Supply curve shifts to the left; rate of interest rises.

Q69. *True.* As security prices rise, so the return on them (i.e. the interest relative to the price paid for them) falls. The lower interest rate will increase the demand for money, and possibly decrease the supply, until the demand for money equals the supply.

Q70. *True.* The increased demand for long-term bonds will drive up their price, and hence reduce their return (i.e. the long-term interest rate) relative to bills. In other words, short-term interest rates will rise relative to long-term ones.

Q71. A reduction in money supply will lead to fewer assets, including foreign ones, being purchased: the supply of the domestic currency on the foreign exchange market will fall. The reduction in money supply will also drive up the rate of interest: this will increase the demand for the domestic currency on the foreign exchange market. The net effect will be a rise in the rate of exchange. This will be compounded by the actions of speculators.

Chapter 19

The Relationship between the Money and Goods Markets

 A **REVIEW**

In Chapter 17 we saw how equilibrium national output was determined. In other words, we looked at macroeconomic equilibrium in goods markets. In Chapter 18 we saw how equilibrium was determined in the money market. In this chapter we combine the analysis of the two chapters. We see how monetary changes affect goods markets and how changes in the goods market affect interest rates.

19.1 The effects of monetary changes on national income

(Page 560) The quantity theory of money
The possible effects of monetary changes on aggregate demand can be shown by considering the *quantity theory of money*. This states that **Q1.** *money supply/the average level of prices* is a function of **Q2.** *money supply/the average level of prices/the velocity of circulation.*

Q3. The relationship between money supply and prices can be expressed in the *quantity equation*. One version is as follows:
A. $M/V = PY$
B. $M/V = Y/P$
C. $MY = VP$
D. $MV = PY$
E. $MP = VY$

Q4. If the money supply as measured by M4 = £150bn and GDP at current prices (nominal GDP) = £300bn:
(a) What will be the (GDP) velocity of circulation (of M4)?

....

(b) If the money supply were cut by 50 per cent, what must happen to the velocity of circulation if there were no change in the current value of final goods and services sold?

....

Q5. Monetarists and Keynesians disagree over the nature of V and Y. Who argues the following cases?
(a) Changes in V are small and predictable, hence any increase in the money supply M will have a significant effect upon total spending.
Keynesian view/monetarist view
(b) M and V vary inversely.
Keynesian view/monetarist view
(c) V is determined by people's desire to hold speculative balances, which in turn is determined by expectations.
Keynesian view/monetarist view
(d) V is exogenously determined.
Keynesian view/monetarist view
(e) If MV falls as a result of a tight monetary policy, then Y will fall as well as P.
Keynesian view/monetarist view

 Multiple choice   Written answer   Delete wrong word   Diagram/table manipulation   Calculation   Matching/ordering

(f) In the long run, *Y* is determined independently of the level of aggregate demand, such that any rise in *MV* will ultimately simply lead to a rise in prices.

Keynesian view/monetarist view

(Pages 560–3) The interest-rate transmission mechanism (the traditional Keynesian mechanism)

According to the interest-rate transmission mechanism, a rise in money supply will lead to a **Q6.** *rise/fall* in interest rates, which, in turn, will lead to a **Q7.** *rise/fall* in investment and hence a **Q8.** a *rise/fall* in aggregate demand. These effects of monetary policy on aggregate demand depend upon the elasticity of the money demand curve and the responsiveness of investment to a change in interest rates.

⊖ **Q9.** Figure 19.1 shows the relationship between changes in the money supply and the level of national income.

(a) On diagram (ii) draw a curve relating investment to the rate of interest. On diagram (iii) draw an injections 'curve' and a withdrawals curve.

(b) On diagram (i) illustrate the effect of a decrease in the money supply. Trace through the effects on to diagrams (ii) and (iii).

(c) The effect on national income will be greater:

   (i) The *steeper/flatter* the liquidity preference (demand for money) curve.

   (ii) The *steeper/flatter* the investment demand curve.

Keynesians and monetarists disagree over the shape and stability of the liquidity preference curve (the demand-for-money curve).

🔵 **Q10.** Distinguish which of the four propositions below reflect Keynesian views and which monetarist views.

(a) 'Money and financial assets are relatively close substitutes for each other. Thus, as interest rates rise, so will the demand for financial assets. Consequently the demand for money will fall significantly. The liquidity preference curve is therefore relatively elastic.'

Keynesian/monetarist

(b) 'Expectations concerning changes in the exchange rate, in interest rates and in inflation have important effects upon the holding of speculative balances.'

Keynesian/monetarist

(c) 'Money is not a close substitute for financial assets. Hence changes in the rate of interest will have little effect upon money demand. The liquidity preference curve is thus relatively inelastic.' *Keynesian/monetarist*

(d) 'The liquidity preference curve is stable and relatively inelastic, as speculative balances are relatively insignificant.' *Keynesian/monetarist*

⑦ **Q11.** Figure 19.2 illustrates the interest-rate transmission mechanism.

(a) Of the four curves, L_A, L_B, I_A and I_B in Figure 19.2, which two are based on monetarist assumptions?

....

(The other two are based on Keynesian assumptions.)

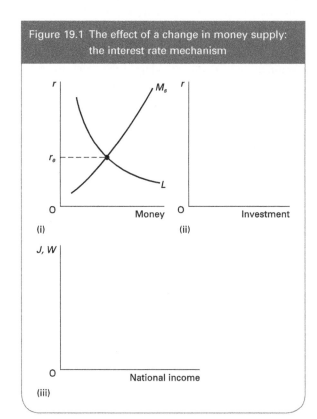

Figure 19.1 The effect of a change in money supply: the interest rate mechanism

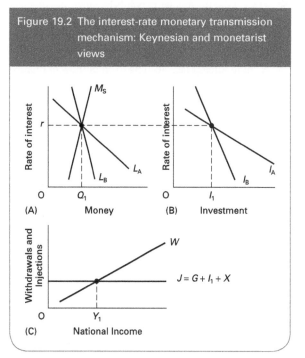

Figure 19.2 The interest-rate monetary transmission mechanism: Keynesian and monetarist views

(b) Using Figure 19.2, show the effect of an increase in the money supply on the level of national income using both monetarist and Keynesian curves.

(c) Under which assumption does a change in money supply have the greater impact?

monetarist/Keynesian

(d) The money supply curve in diagram (a) has been drawn as upward sloping (albeit steeply) rather than vertical. The assumption here is that money supply in the model is: *endogenous/exogenous*

(e) If the money supply curve had been drawn under strict monetarist assumptions, would there have been a bigger or smaller effect on national income from an increase in money supply? *bigger/smaller*

Keynes argued that an economy could find itself in a liquidity trap. This would happen when people believe that the interest rate cannot go **Q12.** *any higher/any lower.* In the financial crisis of the late 2000s, policy-makers responded by **Q13.** *decreasing/increasing* money supply through quantitative easing.

(?) **Q14.** Keynesians argue not only that changes in money supply will have a relatively small effect on investment, but also that the relationship between money supply and investment is an *unstable* one. Why?

....

....

(Pages 563–4) The Keynesian analysis of the exchange-rate transmission mechanism

♟ **Q15.** Order the following points in a logical sequence, assuming that there is a free-floating exchange rate.

(a) A rise in demand for exports and a fall in demand for imports.

(b) A fall in interest rates leading to an outflow of finance overseas.

(c) A rise in the money supply.

(d) A multiplied rise in national income.

(e) A depreciation of the exchange rate.

Order: (c)..

⊝ **Q16.** What effect would a fixed exchange rate have on the exchange-rate transmission mechanism?

....

....

(Pages 565–9) The portfolio balance effect
Money can also affect the economy through a process of portfolio adjustment, a mechanism that is stressed by monetarists.

≣ **Q17.** The monetarist analysis is based on the theory of portfolio balance. This states that:

A. in times of recession individuals will use up their savings rather than cutting down on excess spending.

B. people hold their wealth in a number of different forms, the balance depending on their relative profitability and liquidity.

C. individuals will keep an equal balance between financial assets and money in their portfolios, irrespective of the rate of interest.

D. individuals with stocks and shares spread their risks by having a broadly balanced portfolio of equities.

E. high inflation will cause people to sell their low-earning financial assets and substitute them for cash, which, by definition, is totally liquid.

(?) **Q18.** How does the theory of portfolio balances help to explain the direct transmission mechanism between money supply and aggregate demand?

....

....

....

Many Keynesian economists argue that the portfolio balance effect may be weak and unreliable.

◑ **Q19.** Suppose there is an increase in government expenditure financed by purchases of Treasury bills by the banking system. The impact on output and prices will come from: *extra liquidity of households and firms/the higher government expenditure/we cannot tell.*

◐ **Q20.** The effect of extra liquidity created through quantitative easing will depend upon the extent to which banks use it to extend new credit – which in turn depends upon the demand for credit. *True/False*

≣ **Q21.** Many economists claim that the velocity of circulation (*V*) is relatively stable over the longer run. Of the following, which can be used to support this claim?

(i) Sufficient time has elapsed for the direct mechanism to have worked fully through.

(ii) The demand for money is relatively elastic in the long run.

(iii) Increased money supply would lead to inflation and hence a higher nominal rate of interest, thus offsetting any fall in the real rate of interest (and any initial fall in *V*).

(iv) Increased money supply would lead to inflation and hence people holding smaller money balances, thus offsetting any initial tendency for *V* to rise.

A. (i) and (ii).

B. (i) and (iii).

C. (ii) and (iii).

D. (ii) and (iv).

E. (iii) and (iv).

19.2 The monetary effects of changes in the goods market

(Pages 570–3)

(?) Q22. Assume that the government runs a budget deficit. Describe what will happen to:

(a) The supply of money...

....

(b) The demand for money...

....

(c) Interest rates   *rise/fall/either/neither*

   Explain ....

....

Assume that, despite an increase in government expenditure and a resulting budget deficit, the government does not allow the money supply to increase. Interest rates will **Q23.** *rise/fall.* This in turn will cause the level of investment to **Q24.** *rise/fall.* As a consequence **Q25.** *crowding in/crowding out/additional investment/pump priming* will occur. The level of injections into the circular flow will **Q26.** *increase further/fall back again*, causing the level of national income to **Q27.** *increase further/fall back again*.

If the government operates an expansionary fiscal policy but does not allow money supply to increase at all, this is known as *pure* fiscal policy.

(◐) Q28. Which of the following analyses of the crowding-out effects of pure fiscal policy are Keynesian and which are monetarist?

(a) The increased demand for money will cause a relatively large rise in interest rates.   *Keynesian/monetarist*

(b) The increased demand for money will cause a relatively small rise in interest rates.   *Keynesian/monetarist*

(c) The increased interest rates will cause a relatively large fall in investment.   *Keynesian/monetarist*

(d) The increased interest rates will cause a relatively small fall in investment.   *Keynesian/monetarist*

(e) Crowding out is thus substantial and possibly total.
                                       Keynesian/monetarist

(f) Crowding out is thus relatively minor and may even be non-existent.   *Keynesian/monetarist*

The extreme monetarist position is that money supply is wholly **Q29.** *endogenous/exogenous*, whereas the extreme Keynesian position is that it is **Q30.** *endogenous/exogenous*.

*19.3 ISLM analysis: the integration of the goods and money market models

(Pages 573–4) The *ISLM* model is an attempt to combine in one diagram the analysis of the goods market (i.e. the injec-tions/withdrawals model) with the analysis of the money market (i.e. the demand and supply of money model). The *ISLM* model involves two curves: an *IS* curve and an *LM* curve. Let us look at each in turn.

(Pages 574–5) The IS curve

The *IS* curve represents equilibrium in the **Q31.** *goods market/money market*.

(?) Q32. The *IS* curve slopes downwards from left to right because, as interest rates fall,

....

....

The elasticity of the *IS* curve is determined by the responsiveness of investment (and saving) to changes in the rate of interest and by the size of the multiplier. The more responsive are investment and saving to changes in interest rates, the more **Q33.** *elastic/inelastic* will the *IS* curve be. The smaller the value of the multiplier, the more **Q34.** *elastic/inelastic* will the *IS* curve be.

Keynesians argue that the *IS* curve is relatively **Q35.** *elastic/inelastic*. Monetarists by contrast argue that the *IS* curve is relatively **Q36.** *elastic/inelastic*.

(?) Q37. Why do Keynesians and monetarists disagree over the slope of the *IS* curve?

....

....

....

(◐) Q38. What effect will the following have on the *IS* curve?

(a) Business expectations of the future improve.
                                       Shift left/Shift right

(b) Minimum deposits are required before mortgages are given.   *Shift left/Shift right*

(c) Consumer durables fall in price as VAT is cut.
                                       Shift left/Shift right

(d) The economy experiences a consumer boom.
                                       Shift left/Shift right

(e) Firms anticipate an oncoming recession.
                                       Shift left/Shift right

(Pages 575–6) The LM curve

(◐) Q39. The *LM* curve represents those points where the demand for money is equal to the equilibrium rate of interest.   *True/False*

? Q40. The *LM* curve slopes upwards from left to right because, as national income rises,

....

....

The elasticity of the *LM* curve is determined by (i) the responsiveness of the demand for money to changes in national income and (ii) the responsiveness of the demand for money to changes in the rate of interest.

In the case of (i), the greater the marginal propensity to consume, the more the money demand curve (*L*) will shift to the **Q41.** *left/right* with a given increase in national income. Hence the more will the equilibrium rate of interest rise and the **Q42.** *steeper/shallower* will the *LM* curve become.

In the case of (ii), the more elastic the money demand curve, the **Q43.** *more/less* will the equilibrium interest rate change from a given shift in the money demand curve caused by an increase in national income. Hence the **Q44.** *steeper/shallower* will the *LM* curve be.

The Keynesians argue that the *LM* curve is relatively **Q45.** *steep/shallow*, whereas the monetarists argue that it is relatively **Q46.** *steep/shallow*.

? Q47. Why do Keynesians and monetarists disagree over the slope of the *LM* curve?

....

....

....

◗ Q48. What effect will the following have on the *LM* curve?
(a) Banks decide to hold a higher liquidity ratio.
Shift upwards/Shift downwards
(b) Speculation that the price of securities is about to fall. *Shift upwards/Shift downwards*
(c) The government funds the PSNCR by selling bonds to overseas purchasers. *Shift upwards/Shift downwards*
(d) People are paid on a less frequent basis.
Shift upwards/Shift downwards
(e) It is expected that the foreign exchange value of the domestic currency will fall.
Shift upwards/Shift downwards

▤ Q49. What would be the slope of the *LM* curve for an economy in the liquidity trap?
A. Vertical.
B. Steeply upward sloping.
C. Gently upward sloping.
D. Horizontal.
E. Downward sloping.

(Pages 576–9) Equilibrium in the ISLM model

? Q50. Figure 19.3 shows an *IS* and an *LM* curve, with equilibrium in the goods and money markets respectively.
(a) Equilibrium in both markets simultaneously is identified by which point?

....

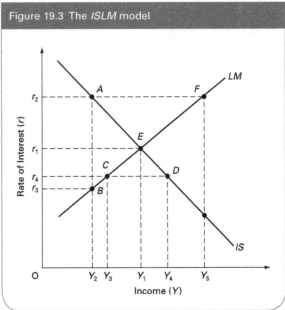

Figure 19.3 The *ISLM* model

(b) Describe the position of the economy at point *A*, referring to both the goods and the money markets.

....

....

(c) By what process would the economy return to an equilibrium position?

....

(d) Describe the position of the economy at point *C*, again referring to both the goods and the money markets.

....

....

(e) By what process would the economy return to an equilibrium position this time?

....

....

(f) Using Figure 19.3, demonstrate the effects of the following:
(i) An inflow of funds coming from abroad as the result of a balance of payments surplus.
(ii) An increase in business confidence.

19.4 Taking inflation into account

(Pages 580–4) Many countries today have inflation targets and change interest rates as necessary to keep inflation at its target rate. What will be the implications of a change in aggregate demand under these circumstances?

Q51. When inflation is above target, action by the central bank will lead to a fall in aggregate demand and hence a fall in real national income.   *True/False*

Figure 19.4 shows the impact of changes in aggregate demand when inflation is targeted at the rate of π_{target}.

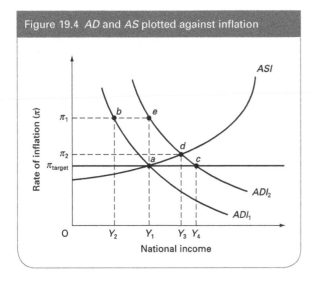

Figure 19.4 *AD* and *AS* plotted against inflation

Q52. The *ADI* curve is downward sloping because:

A. A higher national income will cause inflation to fall.

B. The central bank will raise interest rates if national income falls.

C. The government will set a lower inflation target if national income rises above its sustainable level.

D. The central bank will lower interest rates if inflation falls below its target level.

E. A lower level of aggregate demand will cause national income to fall and inflation to rise.

Q53. The *ADI* curve will be steeper:

(*a*) the more quickly the central bank wants to get inflation back on target if it should diverge from the target.
                                             True/False

(*b*) the more the central bank is concerned to avoid a recession if inflation is above target.   *True/False*

(*c*) the more responsive the components of aggregate demand are to a change in interest rates.   *True/False*

Q54. Assume in Figure 19.4 that equilibrium is initially at point *a*, but that inflation is currently at π_1 with national income at Y_2. Explain what will cause a movement from point *b* to point *a*.

....

....

Q55. All of the following except one would cause the *ADI* curve to shift to the right (e.g. from ADI_1 to ADI_2 in Figure 19.4). Which one would not?

A. A reduction in interest rates because inflation is currently below target.

B. The government sets a higher target rate of inflation.

C. An increase in government expenditure because real income is below the level the government desires.

D. An increase in business confidence.

E. An increase in consumer confidence.

Q56. Assume that equilibrium in Figure 19.4 is initially at point *a*. Now assume that aggregate demand rises to ADI_2.

(*a*) Assuming *no* initial change in inflation, what will be the new initial level of real national income?
                                             $Y_1/Y_2/Y_3/Y_4$

(*b*) What will be the new equilibrium level of national income after prices have responded to this new higher level of aggregate demand? $Y_1/Y_2/Y_3/Y_4$

(*c*) Assuming that the central bank adjusts its target rate of interest in order to keep inflation at the target level, what will be the equilibrium level after the economy has adjusted to the central bank's actions?
                                             $Y_1/Y_2/Y_3/Y_4$

Q57. On Figure 19.4, draw the effect of a permanent increase in aggregate supply in (a) the short run; (b) the long run.

Q58. A temporary supply shock will cause a movement along the *ADI* curve, whereas a permanent supply-side change will lead to a shift in the *ADI* curve. *True/False*

PROBLEMS, EXERCISES AND PROJECTS

Q59. Using diagrams (such as those in Figure 19.7 on page 564 of Sloman, *Economics*, this edition), illustrates the effect on aggregate demand, via the exchange-rate transmission mechanism, of a contraction in the money supply, making (a) Keynesian assumptions; (b) monetarist/new classical assumptions.

Q60. Using data for the money supply (M4) and GDP (where $GDP = PY$), calculate values for the velocity of circulation for each of the past 15 years. How has the value of V changed over the period? What explanations can you offer for these changes?

Figures for GDP and the various money supply measures can be found in the *Annual Abstract of Statistics*, available on the National Statistics website (www.statistics.gov.uk) with separate time-series tables in the 'Time series data' section.

*Q61. In Figure 19.5, simultaneous goods and money market equilibria are achieved at point E (r_1, Y_1). Two alternative *LM* curves are shown, one representing the monetarist position, the other the Keynesian position.

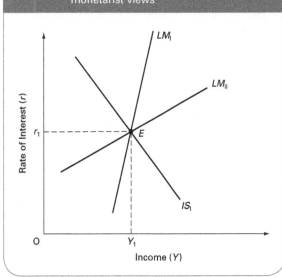

Figure 19.5 The effect of fiscal policy: Keynesian and monetarist views

(a) Which *LM* curve represents the monetarist position?

LM_I/LM_{II}

(b) Which *LM* curve represents the Keynesian position?

LM_I/LM_{II}

(c) Draw on Figure 19.5 the new *IS* curve following an expansionary fiscal policy. Clearly identify the new rates of interest and levels of national income for each *LM* curve.

(d) Extend the line from r_1 to the new *IS* curve. What would be the full multiplied rise in national income from the shift in *IS*, assuming that money supply expanded sufficiently to keep the rate of interest at r_1?

....

(e) Dropping the assumption of a constant rate of interest, identify the crowding out that occurs from the shift in the *IS* curve if the *LM* curve is:

(i) LM_I ....

(ii) LM_{II} ....

(f) What would the *LM* curve look like if there were no crowding out?

....

(g) What would the *LM* curve look like if crowding out were total?

....

 DISCUSSION TOPICS AND ESSAYS

Q62. 'The dismantling of controls on international financial flows and the integration of international financial markets have made the transmission mechanism from exchange rates to the money supply to prices far more important.' Discuss and consider the implications for the conduct of monetary policy.

Q63. 'The quantity equation $MV = PY$ is true by definition.' Explain why this is so. Does it imply that a rise in money supply will necessarily lead to a rise in the price level? Discuss how monetarists and Keynesians have disagreed over the nature of V and Y. What are the implications of this disagreement for the effectiveness of monetary policy in controlling inflation?

Q64. 'The effectiveness of discretionary fiscal policy is reduced by the phenomenon of crowding out.' Explain what is meant by 'crowding out'. What determines its magnitude?

Q65. How does a change in money supply affect the output of goods and services? How does the size of this effect depend on (a) the responsiveness of the demand for money to changes in interest rates; (b) the responsiveness of aggregate demand to changes in interest rates; (c) the size of the multiplier; (d) the responsiveness of international financial flows into and out of the country to changes in interest rates; (e) the responsiveness of the demand for imports and exports to changes in the exchange rate?

Q66. To what extent did the UK economy suffer from a 'liquidity trap' in the aftermath of the financial crisis? In this context, why may monetary policy be totally ineffective in bringing an economy out of recession?

Q67. Explain the 'portfolio balance' transmission mechanism. What determines the strength of this mechanism?

Q68. Under what circumstances would an increase in private investment lead to a reduction in private investment elsewhere in the economy? How does the size of this effect depend on the government's/central bank's attitude towards the size of the money supply and the rate of interest?

Q69. Why and how much does crowding out depend on the central bank's attitudes towards the money supply and interest rates? If the money supply were totally endogenous, would there be any crowding out?

Q70. How does inflation targeting affect the impact of (a) a temporary supply-side shock; (b) a permanent increase in aggregate supply?

Q71. If inflation is targeted and if the aggregate supply curve (with respect to inflation) does not shift, explain why a reduction in aggregate demand will lead to only a temporary decrease in real national income. What determines the speed with which the economy rises back to the sustainable level of real national income?

Q72. Debate

An increase in aggregate demand can never lead to more than a temporary increase in real national income.

 ANSWERS

Q1. *the average level of prices.*

Q2. *the money supply.*

Q3. D. The quantity theory of money is $MV = PY$. PY, the money value of national output, is equal to MV, the total spending on national output.

Q4. *(a)* If we rearrange the quantity theory of money equation, then $V = PY/M$. Thus if $PY = GDP$ at current prices = £300bn and M = M4 = £150, V = 300/150 = 2. Hence money (M4) is spent, on average, twice a year on final goods and services.

(b) If the money supply were to be cut by 50 per cent, then the velocity of circulation would have to *double* in order for total spending to remain the same and hence for there to be no change in the value of final goods and services sold.

Q5. (a), (d) and (f) are all monetarist arguments, (b), (c) and (e) are Keynesian. (For a full explanation of these views, see Sloman, *Economics*, this edn, pp. 560–70.)

Q6. *fall.*

Q7. *rise.*

Q8. *rise.*

Q9. *(a)* and *(b)* See Figure A19.1.

(c) (i) *steeper.* The steeper the demand-for-money curve, the bigger the change in interest rates for any given change in money supply.

(ii) *flatter.* The flatter the demand for investment curve, the bigger the effect on investment for any given change in interest rates.

Q10. (a) and (b) are the Keynesian views. The demand-for-money curve is elastic and unstable. By contrast the monetarists see the demand-for-money curve as inelastic and stable. (The reasons for this can be found in Sloman, *Economics* (this edn), pp. 560–3.)

Q11. *(a)* The monetarist curves are L_B and I_A. The Keynesian curves are L_A and I_B.

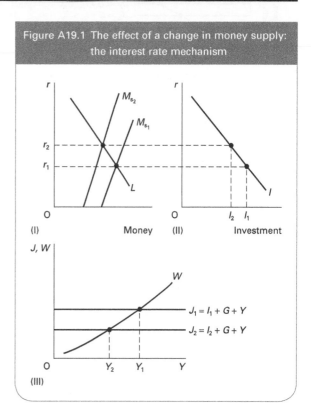

Figure A19.1 The effect of a change in money supply: the interest rate mechanism

(b) See Figure A19.2. A rise in money supply to M_{S_2} leads to a fall in the rate of interest to r_{2_K} (Keynesian assumptions about L) or r_{2_M} (monetarist assumptions about L). This fall in the rate of interest leads to a rise in investment to I_{2_K} (Keynesian assumptions about I) or I_{2_M} (monetarist assumptions about I). This rise in investment leads to a rise in injections to J_{2_K} (Keynesian assumptions about I) or J_{2_K} (monetarist assumptions about I) and a resulting rise in national income to Y_{2_K} (Keynesian assumptions) or Y_{2_M} (monetarist assumptions).

(c) *monetarist.* (National income rises to Y_{2_M} in Figure A19.2 (c).)

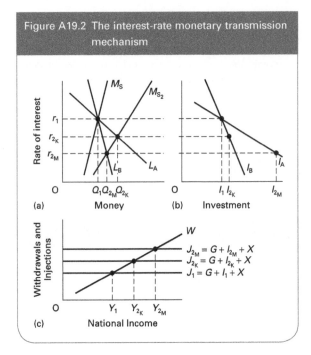

Figure A19.2 The interest-rate monetary transmission mechanism

(a) Money

(b) Investment

(c) National Income

(d) *endogenous*. With an upward-sloping M_S curve, the level of money supply depends on the rate of interest, which in turn depends on the demand for money.

(e) *bigger*. If the money supply were exogenous (the strict monetarist assumption), the M_S curve would be vertical. A given rightward shift would lead to a bigger reduction in the rate of interest and hence a bigger increase in aggregate demand.

Q12. *any lower.*

Q13. *increasing.* The policy was intended to increase bond prices, thus reducing interest rates and generate higher rates of spending growth. However, in the event the liquidity trap prevented this from happening – at least initially.

Q14. Because the other determinants of investment, and especially business confidence, are themselves subject to considerable fluctuations.

Q15. The points should be ordered in the following sequence: (c), (b), (e), (a) and (d). They show the effect of an increase in money supply on national income via the exchange-rate transmission mechanism.

Q16. The more rigidly fixed the exchange rate, the less its value will appreciate or depreciate. Hence the less effect changes in money supply will have via this mechanism. In fact, any attempt to alter the money supply will be largely frustrated. For example, a rise in the money supply would cause the balance of payments to go into deficit. This would then cause the money supply to fall again as reserves were used to buy in excess sterling and as interest rates had to rise again to protect the overvalued exchange rate (see Sloman, *Economics*, this edn, Chapter 25, Section 25.2, page 754).

Q17. B. The theory of portfolio balances argues that individuals hold their assets in various forms – money, financial assets and physical assets such as housing.

Q18. Assume that the money supply expands. As it does so, people find that their portfolios change as well: they become more liquid. The additional money may be used to purchase more securities (driving up their price and forcing down the rate of interest), or more goods and services. This readjusting of individuals' portfolios will continue until balance has been restored. In the process, spending will have increased.

Q19. *we cannot tell.*

Q20. *True.*

Q21. B. In the case of (ii), monetarists argue that the demand for money is relatively *inelastic*. In the case of (iv), the initial tendency would be for V to *fall* as increased money supply drove down the rate of interest and encouraged people to hold *larger* money balances.

Q22. *(a)* The increased PSNCR will lead to an increase in the money supply if it is financed by borrowing from the Bank of England or by selling bills to the banking sector.

(b) The increased aggregate demand will lead to an increased transactions demand for money.

(c) *either.* The effect of (b) will be to increase interest rates. The effect of (a) will be to offset this. Whether interest rates do rise, and whether as a result some crowding out will occur, will depend on just how much the money supply increases.

Q23. *rise.*

Q24. *fall.*

Q25. *crowding out.*

Q26. *fall back again.*

Q27. *fall back again.*

Q28. (a), (c) and (e) are monetarist. (b), (d) and (f) are Keynesian.

Q29. *exogenous.*

Q30. *endogenous.*

Q31. *goods market.*

Q32. As interest rates fall, investment will expand and the level of saving will decrease. Both will cause a multiplied rise in national income.

Q33. *elastic.*

Q34. *inelastic.*

Q35. *inelastic.*

Q36. *elastic.*

Q37. They disagree over the responsiveness of investment and saving to changes in the rate of interest. Keynesians argue that investment and saving are relatively unresponsive, whereas the monetarists argue that they are relatively responsive.

Q38. (a), (c) and (d) will all lead to shifts to the right. They will all lead to a higher level of national income for any given rate of interest.

Q39. *False.* The *LM* curve shows all the various combinations of interest rates and national income at which the demand for money equals the supply ($L = M$).

Q40. As national income rises, transactions and precautionary demands for money increase, shifting the liquidity preference curve to the right. Assuming the money supply is fixed, this will lead to a rise in the rate of interest.

Q41. *right.*

Q42. *steeper.*

Q43. *less.*

Q44. *shallower.*

Q45. *shallow.*

Q46. *steep.*

Q47. The disagreement between the two groups centres on the speculative demand for money and its responsiveness to changes in the rate of interest. Keynesians argue that the speculative demand is significant and responsive to interest rate changes, and that the *LM* curve is therefore correspondingly shallow. Monetarists argue that the demand for money is relatively inelastic, and that therefore the *LM* curve is relatively steep.

Q48. *(a)* *Shift upwards.* A higher liquidity ratio will cause the supply of money to fall. This, in turn, will cause the rate of interest to rise. Thus for any given level of national income the rate of interest will be higher.

(b) *Shift upwards.* As speculation mounts, there will be an increase in the demand for money. This will cause the money demand curve to shift to the right. The rate of interest will rise at the current level of national income.

(c) *Shift downwards.* If the PSNCR is funded in this manner, the money supply will increase. The rate of interest will fall at the current level of national income.

(d) *Shift upwards.* The transactions demand for money will rise. Thus the same reasoning as in (b) applies.

(e) *Shift downwards.* If domestic currency is expected to fall in value, the demand for it will fall. The liquidity preference curve will shift left, causing the rate of interest to fall at the current level of national income.

Q49. *D.*

Q50. *(a)* *E.*

(b) At point *A*, given national income of Y_2 and a rate of interest of r_2, the economy is in goods market equilibrium and money market disequilibrium. The rate of interest r_2 would lead to a national income of Y_2. But at this level of income the demand for money is less than the supply (point *A* is above the *LM* curve). At this level of income, the money market would be in equilibrium at point *B*, at a rate of interest of r_3.

(c) The excess supply of money will cause the rate of interest to fall. This will lead to a movement along the *IS* curve as saving declines and investment picks up. National income will rise (maintaining the balance between saving and investment). The higher national income will lead to an increased transactions demand for money and hence a movement up along the *LM* curve. The process will continue until point *E* is reached.

(d) At point *C*, given national income of Y_3 and a rate of interest of r_4, the economy is in money market equilibrium and goods market disequilibrium. At this low rate of interest, the desired level of investment and saving are equal at point *D*.

(e) The excess of investment over saving at point *C* will cause the level of national income to rise. This will lead to a movement up along the *LM* curve and a rise in the rate of interest. As the rate of interest rises, the desired level of investment will fall and saving increase. This will cause a movement back along the *IS* curve until equilibrium is reached at point *E*.

(f) (i) This will cause the *LM* curve to shift downwards (towards a point such as *D*) as the money supply expands. The equilibrium rate of interest will fall and the level of national income will rise. The new equilibrium in both markets will be where the new *LM* curve intersects with the *IS* curve. (Thus in the case of point *D*, the equilibrium rate of interest would be r_4 and the equilibrium level of national income would be Y_4.)

(ii) This will cause the *IS* curve to shift right, towards a point such as *F*. This pushes interest rates and national income upwards. The new equilibrium is where the new *IS* curve intersects with the *LM* curve. In the case of point *F*, this would give a national income of Y_5 and a rate of interest of r_2.

Q51. *True.* This is shown by a movement up along the *ADI* curve (e.g. from point *a* to point *b* in Figure 19.4).

Q52. *D.* The lower interest rates will cause a higher level of aggregate demand (a movement down along the curve) and hence a higher level of real national income. Similarly, the central bank will raise interest rates if inflation rises above its target level, thereby reducing real national income.

Q53. *(a)* *False.* The more rapidly the central bank wants to get inflation back to target, the more it will change interest rates and hence the more real income will change and hence the *shallower* will be the curve.

(b) *True.* It will only change the rate of interest by a small amount, so as not to have a big effect on aggregate demand and hence on real national income.

(c) *False.* The more responsive the components of aggregate demand are to a change in interest rates, the bigger will be the effect on real national income and hence the *shallower* the curve.

Q54. Real national income is at Y_2 because the central bank has raised interest rates in response to the higher inflation. As inflation falls in response to the higher interest rate, so the rate of interest can be reduced somewhat. There will be a move back down the curve towards point *a*.

Q55. A. This is a movement along the curve. A rate of inflation below target will cause the central bank to reduce interest rates. This will raise real national income. Note that in B, a higher target rate of inflation will lead to a lower interest rate being set for each rate of inflation, thereby shifting the *ADI* curve to the right.

Q56. (a) Y_4 (where ADI_2 crosses the target rate of inflation line).

(b) Y_3. The upward-sloping *ASI* curve illustrates the effects of both quantity *and* inflation adjustment to changes in the level of aggregate demand. Equilibrium is at point *b*.

(c) Y_2. Since point *b* is above the target rate of inflation, the central bank will have to raise its target rate of interest, so as to shift the *ADI* curve back to ADI_1, giving equilibrium back at point *a*.

Q57. (a) The rightward shift in the *ASI* curve will cause it to cross the *ADI* curve (ADI_1) at a rate of inflation below target.

(b) Assume that the permanent increase in aggregate supply is represented by a new *ASI* curve passing through point *c*. Once the central bank realises that this is a permanent increase in aggregate supply, it will lower the target rate of interest. This will shift the *ADI* curve to the right. Long-run equilibrium will be at point *c*.

Q58. *True.* In the case of a temporary supply shock, the central bank will adjust the actual rate of interest to bring the economy back to target at the sustainable level of real national income. There will be a movement along the *ADI* curve. In the case of a permanent supply-side change, the target rate of interest will have to be changed in order to cause a shift in the *ADI* curve to match the shift in the *ASI* curve.

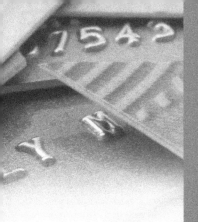

Chapter 20

Fiscal and Monetary Policy

 A **REVIEW**

In this chapter we look at the two types of policy for controlling aggregate demand: fiscal and monetary policy. Fiscal policy seeks to control aggregate demand by altering the balance between government expenditure (an injection into the circular flow of income) and taxation (a withdrawal). Monetary policy seeks to control aggregate demand by directly controlling the money supply, or by altering the rate of interest and then backing this up by any necessary change in money supply.

20.1 Fiscal policy

(Pages 587–93) Fiscal policy involves altering the size of the *budget deficit* or *budget surplus*.

(?) **Q1.** Identify the two possible roles of fiscal policy in the management of aggregate demand.

1. ....

2. ....

Q2. The national debt is defined as:
A. the amount that the government borrows during a fiscal year.
B. a country's overseas borrowing.
C. the accumulation of past government borrowing.
D. a country's accumulated overseas debt.
E. the government's accumulated budget deficit over the past business cycle.

Q3. The whole public sector includes which of the following?
(i) Central government.
(ii) Local government.
(iii) Public corporations.

A. (i) only.
B. (ii) only.
C. (iii) only.
D. (i) and (iii).
E. (i), (ii) and (iii).

Q4. Privatisation and nationalisation can distort the public finance statistics. *True/False*

Q5. Match the following terms with their definitions.
(a) Recurrent spending on goods and factor payments.
*capital expenditure/current expenditure/
final expenditure/transfers*
(b) Expenditure on goods and services.
*capital expenditure/current expenditure/
final expenditure/transfers*
(c) Transfers of money from taxpayers to recipients of benefits and subsidies.
*capital expenditure/current expenditure/
final expenditure/transfers*
(d) Investment expenditure; expenditure on assets.
*capital expenditure/current expenditure/
final expenditure/transfers*

◑ **Q6.** Between 1990 and 2010, the UK's public expenditure was typically split 93 to 7 per cent between current and capital expenditure, whereas the split had been 80 to 20 per cent in the 1960s and 1970s.   *True/False*

If the sum of the public sector's current expenditure is less than it earns, then it runs a **Q7.** *deficit/surplus* in the current budget, and **Q8.** *cannot contribute to/can meet* some of the cost of its net investment.

The size of the budget deficit or surplus is linked to the size of the *public-sector net cash requirement* (PSNCR).

▤ **Q9.** The public-sector net cash requirement is defined as:

A. the amount central government has to borrow in a given year.

B. the national debt.

C. the increase in government securities in a given year.

D. the excess of public-sector spending over public-sector receipts in a given year.

E. the budget deficit in a given year.

⑦ **Q10.** Explain why the size of the public-sector deficit or surplus will be influenced by the level of national income.

....

....

▤ **Q11.** Fiscal stance refers to:

A. the total level of government spending.

B. whether the government supports the use of fiscal policies to manage the economy.

C. the effect of the budget deficit or surplus on the level of aggregate demand.

D. the existence of inflationary or deflationary gaps in the economy.

E. the size of the government's budget surplus or deficit.

The public sector structural deficit (or surplus) is that which would occur if the economy were operating **Q12.** *above/at/below* the potential level of national output, that is, where there is a **Q13.** *negative/positive/zero* output gap.

⑦ **Q14.** Those taxes and government expenditures that increase and decrease respectively as national income rises are called:

....

▤ **Q15.** Which one of the following is not a drawback of automatic stabilisers?

A. High marginal tax rates may discourage effort and initiative.

B. Fiscal drag.

C. They come into effect without the need for conscious government intervention.

D. High unemployment benefits may increase equilibrium unemployment.

E. High income-related benefits may create a poverty trap.

The more that taxes increase and government expenditure decreases as national income rises, the **Q16.** *larger/smaller* will be the multiplier. What is more, if taxes are progressive, then *ceteris paribus*, a rise in national income will cause the multiplier to **Q17.** *rise/fall*.

(Pages 593–6) Discretionary fiscal policy refers to the specific adjustment of government expenditure and/or taxation with the aim of influencing the level of aggregate demand.

In the financial crisis of the late 2000s, the initial response from many governments was to use **Q18.** *contractionary/expansionary* fiscal policy, but as national economies began to emerge from the global slowdown, there was a move (especially in Europe) towards reducing fiscal **Q19.** *deficits/surpluses* and to rebalance aggregate demand towards the **Q20.** *private/public* sector.

◑ **Q21.** Which of the following fiscal policy measures would have an expansionary and which a contractionary impact upon the level of economic activity?

(a) A cut in direct taxation.   *expansionary/contractionary*

(b) A rise in personal allowances.

                                          expansionary/contractionary

(c) An increase in the PSNCR.

                                          expansionary/contractionary

(d) A reduction in social security benefits.

                                          expansionary/contractionary

(e) A move from a budget deficit to a budget surplus.

                                          expansionary/contractionary

The multiplier effect of increasing government expenditure by £xm is different from that of reducing taxes by £xm. The tax multiplier is given by $\Delta Y/\Delta T$.

◑ **Q22.** The tax multiplier is smaller than the government expenditure multiplier.   *True/False*

▤ **Q23.** If the mpc_d is 0.75, the tax multiplier is:

A. 4

B. −4

C. 3

D. −3

E. −1$^1/_3$

▤ **Q24.** If investment exceeds saving by £10m and there is a balance of payments surplus of £30m, then for the economy to be in equilibrium there must be a:

A. budget deficit of £40m.

B. budget surplus of £40m.

C. budget deficit of £20m.

D. budget surplus of £20m.

E. budget balance.

(Pages 596–602) One problem with fiscal policy is that it can lead to 'crowding out'.

Q25. Crowding out is defined as:

A. increased public expenditure replacing private-sector expenditure.

B. increased taxes pushing up interest rates.

C. when there are insufficient tax revenues to finance increased government expenditure.

D. the difficulty some people find in paying their taxes.

E. that part of public expenditure financed from borrowing.

Q26. The government tries to raise national output using pure fiscal policy (i.e. without increasing money supply). State how each of the following influences the extent of crowding out.

(a) If the *L* curve is flat.

....

(b) If money supply is endogenous.

....

(c) If consumers' expenditure is not responsive to changes in the rate of interest.

....

(d) If firms' investment expenditure is highly sensitive to changes in the rate of interest.

....

Q27. Give three reasons why it is difficult to forecast the magnitude of the impact of fiscal policy on the economy.

1. ....

2. ....

3. ....

Q28. Fiscal policy suffers from a number of timing problems. Match the following problems to the various time lags between a problem occurring and the full final effect of fiscal policy measures taken to correct the problem.

(i) The time taken for the multiplier process to work.

(ii) The long-run consumption function is different from the short-run one.

(iii) The business cycle is irregular.

(iv) Administrative delays.

(v) The Budget occurs only once a year.

(a) Time lag to recognition. ....

(b) Time lag between recognition and changes being announced.

....

(c) Time lag between changes being announced and changes coming into force.

....

(d) Time lag between changes in taxes and government expenditure and the resulting changes in national income.

....

(e) Time lag before people's spending patterns adjust fully to changes in incomes.

....

Q29. The golden rule of fiscal policy adopted by the Labour government in 1998 was that public-sector receipts should cover all current and capital spending. *True/False*

Q30. The UK government held to the golden rule even through the financial crisis of the late 2000s and its aftermath. *True/False*

20.2 Monetary policy

(Page 603)

Q31. Which of the following would be classified as monetary policy? The attempt to:

(a) reduce the level of taxation. *Yes/No*

(b) control the supply of money by various means.

Yes/No

(c) regulate wages by the use of formal agreements with unions. *Yes/No*

(d) ration credit. *Yes/No*

(e) manipulate aggregate demand via the use of interest rates. *Yes/No*

(f) regulate aggregate demand through changes in government spending. *Yes/No*

Q32. Since 1997, the main instrument of monetary policy has been the interest rate, which is set monthly by the government. *True/False*

(Pages 603–5) Controlling the growth of the money supply over the medium and long term

Q33. Which one of the following would not be a cause of growth in the money supply?

A. The banks decide to hold a lower liquidity ratio.

B. There is a total currency flow surplus on the balance of payments.

C. Public sector borrowing is financed by selling Treasury bills to the banking sector.

D. The government imposes a statutory reserve ratio on banks that is higher than their current reserve ratio.

E. National income rises and money supply is endogenous.

If over the longer term the government wishes to control the growth of the money supply, it will have to tackle the underlying causes.

(?) **Q34.** Give the two major sources of a long-term growth in the money supply.

1. ....

2. ....

One way in which the central bank could influence the growth of money supply would be to impose a statutory minimum reserve ratio on the banks that was **Q35.** *above/below/equal to* the level that banks would otherwise choose to hold. This would also have the effect of **Q36.** *increasing/reducing* the bank multiplier. The **Q37.** *excessive/inadequate* lending of the mid-2000s showed that banks were **Q38.** *keen/reluctant* to lend, resulting in calls for **Q39.** *greater/less* regulation.

If there is a substantial PSNCR, it is nevertheless possible to avoid an increase in the money supply by financing the PSNCR by government borrowing from **Q40.** *the banking sector/the non-bank private sector.* If the government does this, however, there is likely to be a problem of financial crowding out. This will involve **Q41.** *higher/lower* interest rates and **Q42.** *more/less* private-sector borrowing.

(≣) **Q43.** In the long run, increasing the money supply will affect:
A. Real output.
B. Real income.
C. The productive capacity of the economy.
D. Prices.
E. Employment.

(Pages 605–6) The operation of monetary policy in the short term
There are three approaches to short-term monetary control: controlling the *supply* of money; controlling the *demand* for money by controlling interest rates; and rationing credit.

(?) **Q44.** Figure 20.1 shows the demand for and supply of money in an economy. In the initial period, money supply is given by M_{s0}, and L represents the demand for money.
(a) Identify the equilibrium rate of interest and quantity of money.

....

(b) If the monetary authorities were to operate a tighter monetary policy by reducing money supply to M_{s1}, what would be the equilibrium rate of interest?

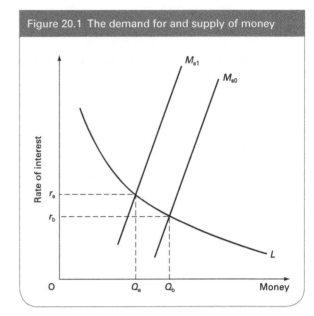

Figure 20.1 The demand for and supply of money

(c) If instead the authorities raise the interest rate to r_a, how could equilibrium in the market be restored?

....

(d) If the authorities were to reduce money supply to M_{s1} and also hold the rate of interest at r_b, what would be the market situation?

....

Controlling the supply of money will involve manipulating the liquid assets of the banking sector.

(♦) **Q45.** The following are methods of controlling banks' liquidity base:
 (i) open-market operations
 (ii) the central bank changing the amount it lends to banks
 (iii) funding
 (iv) changing minimum reserve ratios

Match each of the following actions of a central bank to the above methods of control, and in each case state whether money supply will *increase* or *decrease*. (In each case, assume that the actions are not in response to changes in the PSNCR.)
(a) It sells more government bonds but reduces the value of Treasury bills sold by the same amount, thereby keeping total government borrowing the same.
(i)/(ii)/(iii)/(iv); increase/decrease
(b) It sells more government bonds (but the same amount of Treasury bills).   *(i)/(ii)/(iii)/(iv); increase/decrease*
(c) It buys back bonds from banks under a repo agreement.   *(i)/(ii)/(iii)/(iv); increase/decrease*
(d) It requires banks to hold a larger proportion of liquid assets.   *(i)/(ii)/(iii)/(iv); increase/decrease*

(e) It sells fewer bonds and bills.

(i)/(ii)/(iii)/(iv); increase/decrease

(f) It replaces £1m of gilts that are maturing with £1m extra Treasury bills. *(i)/(ii)/(iii)/(iv); increase/decrease*

(g) It keeps its interest rate to the banks below market rates, but then reduces the amount it allows banks to borrow at that rate. *(i)/(ii)/(iii)/(iv); increase/decrease*

⊗ **Q46.** If banks operate a rigid 10 per cent liquidity ratio and the Bank of England repurchases £10m of government bonds on the open market, what will be the eventual size of the change in the level of bank advances?

(Pages 604–5) It is difficult to control the growth of the money supply over the medium and longer term without controlling the size of the PSNCR. This can also be difficult, however.

🌓 **Q47.** Which of the following make the control of PSNCR difficult?

(a) The political desirability of cutting taxes. *Yes/No*

(b) The political desirability of increasing government expenditure. *Yes/No*

(c) Automatic fiscal stabilisers in times of a boom. *Yes/No*

(d) Automatic fiscal stabilisers in times of stagflation (recession plus inflation). *Yes/No*

(e) Pressure on the government to increase expenditure on education, R&D and transport infrastructure as a means of improving productivity and long-term growth. *Yes/No*

(f) An ageing population. *Yes/No*

(Pages 606–10) Controlling the money supply is difficult whether the authorities use monetary base control or attempt to control broad liquidity.

❓ **Q48.** What is meant by 'monetary base control'?

....

....

🏛 **Q49.** Four of the following are problems associated with monetary base control. One is not. Which one?

A. Banks could currently have a cash ratio above their prudent (or statutory) level.

B. Goodhart's law.

C. Disintermediation.

D. There may be a high demand for liquidity in the financial system.

E. The Bank of England will always lend money to banks if demanded.

❓ **Q50.** Give two problems for the authorities in attempting to control broad liquidity.

1. ....

2. ....

🌓 **Q51.** If the government is successful in keeping the money supply stable, it will have succeeded in keeping interest rates stable too. *True/False*

(Pages 611–16) The prime form of monetary policy in the UK has been to control *interest rates*.

🌓 **Q52.** Interest rates are controlled by the Bank of England through its operations in the discount and repo markets. *True/False*

🌓 **Q53.** Assume that the Bank of England decides that it wants a rise in the rate of interest and conducts open-market operations in the discount market to achieve this. What should it do if:

(a) banks have excess liquidity? *Buy/Sell more/fewer* bills.

(b) banks are currently having to borrow from the Bank of England? *Buy/Sell more/fewer* bills.

🏛 **Q54.** If there is a shortage of liquidity in the banking system, which one of the following operations in the gilt repo market would the Bank of England conduct to maintain interest rates at the level chosen by the Monetary Policy Committee?

A. It buys bonds from the banks at its chosen interest rate on condition that the banks must sell the bonds to other banks later.

B. It sells bonds to the banks at its chosen interest rate on condition that the banks must sell the bonds to other banks later.

C. It buys bonds from the banks at its chosen interest rate on condition that the banks must buy them back again later from the Bank of England.

D. It sells bonds to the banks at its chosen interest rate on condition that the banks sell them back to the Bank of England later.

E. It buys bonds from the non-bank sector at its chosen interest rate on condition that the banks must buy them later from the Bank of England.

🏛 **Q55.** Which of the following may cause problems for the Bank of England in seeking to control interest rates?

(i) The demand for loans is unresponsive to interest rate changes.

(ii) Different interest rates respond differently to changes in the Bank Rate.

(iii) The demand for loans is very stable.

(iv) The demand for loans is unstable.

(v) The demand for loans is highly responsive to interest rate changes.

A. (i) and (iii).

B. (i), (ii) and (iv).

C. (ii), (iii) and (iv).

D. (i) and (v).

E. (ii) and (v).

Q56. Goodhart's law states that 'to control an indicator is to distort its accuracy as an indicator'. An example of this law when applied to monetary policy is that:

A. all forms of intervention in financial markets will have little impact on the money supply.

B. regulation in one part of the financial system will divert business to other areas of the financial system.

C. government borrowing will lead to financial crowding out.

D. control of the money supply will not be possible without control of the PSNCR.

E. private-sector borrowing is a more important determinant of monetary growth than is public-sector borrowing.

(?) Q57. In the short run the supply of money is to a large extent demand determined. Why?

....

....

(Pages 614–5) Because the supply of money is demand determined in the short run, monetary policy has tended to concentrate on controlling the demand for loans via the control of interest rates. This, however, may require the authorities setting very high interest rates. This is because the demand for loans is relatively interest **Q58.** *elastic/inelastic.*

Q59. A tight monetary policy involving high interest rates can lead to a number of related problems. Identify which of the following might be a consequence of such a policy.

(a) Reduced investment. *Yes/No*

(b) A deteriorating competitive position overseas. *Yes/No*

(c) Increased costs of production. *Yes/No*

(d) Slow growth in potential output. *Yes/No*

(e) Expensive for the government to maintain. *Yes/No*

(f) Increased cost-push pressures. *Yes/No*

20.3 ISLM analysis of fiscal and monetary policy

(Pages 618–21) Fiscal and monetary policy

Q60. Using the two diagrams in Figure 20.2, illustrate the following situations.

(a) Government expenditure grows and is financed by an expansion in the money supply. Avoid any crowding out in your model.

(b) Business expectations deteriorate and in response the government expands the money supply in order to maintain the level of aggregate demand.

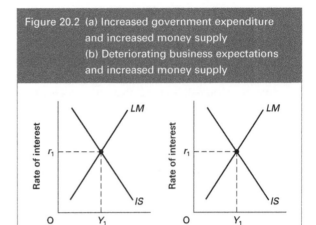

Figure 20.2 (a) Increased government expenditure and increased money supply
(b) Deteriorating business expectations and increased money supply

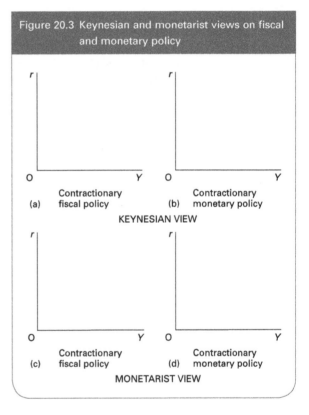

Figure 20.3 Keynesian and monetarist views on fiscal and monetary policy

Q61. Using Figure 20.3, sketch the following effects of government policy. On diagrams (a) and (b) sketch *ISLM* curves to represent a contractionary fiscal and contractionary monetary policy from a Keynesian perspective. On (c) and (d) sketch *ISLM* curves to represent contractionary fiscal and contractionary monetary policy from a monetarist perspective.

20.4 Fiscal and monetary policy in the UK

(Pages 621–31)

Q62. Which of the following arguments would a Keynesian use concerning government macroeconomic intervention in the economy?

(a) The management of aggregate demand by the government can reduce the degree of instability in the economy. *Yes/No*

(b) Control over the money supply is the best way to regulate aggregate demand in the short run. *Yes/No*

(c) Control over the money supply is the best way to regulate aggregate demand in long run. *Yes/No*

(d) The 'natural' state of the market system is one of disequilibrium. *Yes/No*

(e) 'Intervention' should focus on removing government barriers to the free operation of the market. *Yes/No*

(f) The business cycle is damaging to economic performance. *Yes/No*

(g) Fine tuning can reduce cyclical fluctuations. *Yes/No*

Q63. What was the dominant constraint on demand-led growth policies in the 1950s and 1960s?

A. The level of unemployment.
B. Time lags.
C. Money supply targets.
D. The balance of payments.
E. The size of the budget deficit.

Q64. List five possible causes of the stagflation experienced by the UK economy in the 1970s.

1. ....

2. ....

3. ....

4. ....

5. ....

Q65. Which of the following policies were pursued by the Thatcher government in the early 1980s?

(a) The setting of targets for the growth in the money supply. *Yes/No*

(b) Attempts to cut the PSNCR. *Yes/No*

(c) The implementation of statutory requirements. *Yes/No*

(d) Reductions in the rate of income tax. *Yes/No*

(e) The use of incomes policy to regulate the growth of wages. *Yes/No*

(f) The tendering of public-sector services to the private sector. *Yes/No*

Q66. List three problems that were encountered.

1. ....

2. ....

3. ....

Q67. Were any economic indicators targeted in the late 1980s, and if so, what?

....

Q68. UK entry into the ERM (the exchange rate mechanism of the European Monetary System) meant that government had less discretion in monetary policy than before. *True/False*

Q69. Which one of the following was a direct consequence of UK membership of the ERM?

A. The rate of inflation was driven up to the European average.
B. Fiscal policy was dominated by European budgetary issues.
C. The money supply grew more rapidly.
D. Aggregate demand was caused to expand faster than the government had wished.
E. Interest rates had to be set at whatever level was necessary to maintain the exchange rate.

Q70. Since 1992, the main focus of UK demand-side policy has been the control of inflation. *True/False/Partly true*

Q71. If the UK rate of inflation is forecast to be below 2 per cent, the Monetary Policy Committee of the Bank of England is obliged to reduce the rate of interest. *True/False*

Q72. Under the golden rule of fiscal policy adopted by the Labour government between 1997 and 2007, fiscal policy had no influence on aggregate demand. *True/False*

Q73. Under the inflation targeting regime followed since 1997, if inflation is more than 1 percentage point higher or lower than the target, the Governor of the Bank of England is required to write an open letter to the Chancellor to explain why the divergence has happened. *True/False*

In 2007/08 the UK faced a policy dilemma. To meet the inflation target there was pressure to **Q74.** *lower/raise* the Bank Rate, but to avert a recession there was pressure to **Q75.** *lower/raise* it. By March 2009, Bank Rate had fallen to just **Q76.** *0.5/1.0/1.5 per cent* and the Bank of England was embarking on a process of **Q77.** *expanding/reducing* money supply.

Q78. Which of the following describes the early fiscal priority of the coalition government in 2010?

A. To increase borrowing in order to tackle the recession.
B. To reduce borrowing and start to bring down the stock of public debt.
C. To raise interest rates to reduce aggregate demand.
D. To lower interest rates to stimulate aggregate demand.
E. To raise government expenditure and lower taxes.

20.5 Rules versus discretion

(Pages 632–5)

(?) **Q79.** State two important arguments against discretionary policy.

....

....

(?) **Q80.** Outline the Keynesian case in favour of discretion.

....

....

....

 Q81. To take account of the fact that achieving the target rate of inflation may nevertheless still be consistent with fluctuations in national income, some economists have advocated following a 'Taylor rule'. This means that:

A. National output is targeted rather than inflation.
B. The central bank will *reduce* interest rates if inflation is above target, for fear of an impending recession.
C. Real national income and inflation will, as a result, vary inversely.
D. The amount that interest rates rise when inflation rises depends on the relative weights attached to divergences of inflation and real national income from their respective targets.
E. Inflation is less likely to diverge from its target.

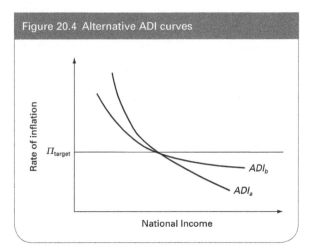

Figure 20.4 Alternative ADI curves

(—) **Q82.** Figure 20.4 shows alternative *ADI* curves, one of which is drawn under the assumption that the central bank's prime concern is with controlling inflation, whilst the other assumes that the central bank is more concerned about stabilising national income.

(a) Which *ADI* curve is drawn under the assumption that the central bank is most concerned about controlling inflation?   *ADI_a/ADI_b*
(b) Which *ADI* curve is drawn under the assumption that the central bank is most concerned about stabilising national income?   *ADI_a/ADI_b*
(c) If inflation rises, under which rule will the central bank raise interest rates by more? *controlling inflation/ stabilising national income*
(d) Explain your answer.

B PROBLEMS, EXERCISES AND PROJECTS

Q83. Table 20.1 shows the consumption schedule for a closed economy (i.e. one that does not trade with other countries). Investment is currently £40bn.

(a) Assuming that the government is currently spending £20bn, what is the equilibrium level of national income?

....

(b) Assuming that at this equilibrium level of national income the government is running a budget deficit of £5bn, what must be the level of saving in the economy?

....

(c) What is the government expenditure multiplier?

....

(d) What is the tax multiplier?

....

Q84. Referring to Q83, assume that full employment is achieved at a national income of £240bn.

(a) What is the size of the deflationary gap?

....

(b) How much would government expenditure have to be raised (assuming no change in tax rates) in order to close this gap?

....

Table 20.1 National income and consumption for country A (£bn)

National income	30	60	90	120	150	180	210	240	270	300
Consumption		20	40	60	80	100	120	140	160	180	200

(c) Alternatively, how much would taxes have to be changed (assuming no change in government expenditure) in order to close the gap?

....

(d) Alternatively, assume now that the government decides that it wants to close the gap and *also* to balance its budget (i.e. to raise taxes £5bn more than it raises government expenditure). How much must it raise government expenditure and how much must it raise taxes?

....

....

Q85. The Budget is when the Chancellor of the Exchequer announces changes in taxation and government expenditure for the coming financial year commencing 5 April. Using references that you have available, find out the main fiscal measures in the most recent Budget. Assess how these measures related to the state of the economy at the time of the Budget, and how the economy was forecast to change in the future. This may require your referring to government statistics. These can be found in *Financial Statistics* (NS) and the *Annual Abstract of Statistics* (NS). Forecasts of economic performance can be found in the Treasury's *Financial Statement and Budget Report* (published at the time of the Budget). Independent forecasts and assessments can be found in the quality press. There is usually a wealth of information in the press concerning the Budget and the state of the economy at the end of March (when the Budget is usually held). Information on the Budget can also be found at the following two web addresses:
http://www.hm-treasury.gov.uk
http://www.ft.com

Q86. Using relevant statistical sources, such as *Financial Statistics* (NS) or the *Annual Abstract of Statistics* (NS), investigate recent movements in the various monetary aggregates. See also the National Statistics website at http://www.statistics.gov.uk and the Statistics part of the Bank of England's website at http://www.bankofengland.co.uk/statistics/index.htm. How do such movements compare with those in earlier years? Does this tell you anything about the current tightness of monetary policy and the economic position of the UK economy?

Q87. Assume that the banking sector's assets and liabilities consist of the following items: cash £10m; advances £60m; time deposits £50m; bonds £15m; market loans £10m; bills £5m; sight deposits £40m; certificates of deposit in the banking system £10m. Assume that there are no other items.

(a) Compile a balance sheet for the banking sector.
(b) What is its current cash ratio?
(c) What is its current liquidity ratio?

Assume in each of the following that banks want to maintain the *cash* ratio in (b) above. What will be the effect of each of the following?
(d) An open-market purchase by the central bank of £1m of bonds.
(e) An open-market sale by the central bank of £5m of bonds.
(f) An open-market sale by the central bank of £2m of bills, where these bills are purchased by the banking sector.
(g) An open-market sale by the central bank of £2m of bills, where these bills are purchased by the non-banking sector.

Assume in each of the following that banks want to maintain the *liquidity* ratio in (c) above. What will be the effect of each of the following?
(h) An open-market purchase by the central bank of £1m of bonds.
(i) An open-market sale by the central bank of £5m of bonds.
(j) An open-market sale by the central bank of £2m of bills, where these bills are purchased by the banking sector.
(k) An open-market sale by the central bank of £2m of bills, where these bills are purchased by the non-banking sector.

Q88. Using the Bank of England and Treasury websites, http://www.bankofengland.co.uk and http://www.hm-treasury.gov.uk, and the Bank of England's *Inflation Report*, trace the decisions of the Bank of England's Monetary Policy Committee on interest rates over the past two years. Were changes made? In retrospect, do you think this was the appropriate course of action?

Alternatively you could answer this question in terms of the interest rate decisions of another central bank, such as the European Central Bank (see http://www.ecb.int) or the US Federal Reserve Bank (see http://www.federalreserve.gov).

Q89. In small groups, write a commentary on the use of demand management policy in the UK over the past three years.

The report should include (a) evidence on the performance of economic growth, unemployment and inflation and (b) a description of the fiscal and monetary policy measures that were taken.

By examining the evidence and reading commentaries, you should attempt to assess how successful the fiscal and monetary policies have been. Remember that fiscal and monetary policies take a time to work and therefore you will need to look at the lagged effects of policies taken some time before.

Consider whether there have been any 'economic shocks' (such as wars, trade disputes, stock market turbulence, etc.) and whether fiscal and monetary policies have been able to offset the effects of these shocks.

Good sources of evidence are the Treasury, Bank of England and Financial Times websites (see Hotlinks section on the Sloman *Economics* website at http://www.pearsoned.co.uk/sloman).

 # DISCUSSION TOPICS AND ESSAYS

Q90. 'The existence of a budget deficit or a budget surplus tells us very little about the stance of fiscal policy.' Explain and discuss.

Q91. What factors might prevent the government from effectively fine-tuning the economy?

Q92. Adam Smith remarked in *The Wealth of Nations* concerning the balancing of budgets, 'What is prudence in the conduct of every private family can scarce be folly in that of a great kingdom.' Should the government follow a balanced budget approach to its spending?

Q93. Aaron Wildavsky refers to the Treasury's forecasting as 'a compound of knowledge, hunch and intuition'. What difficulties are there in forecasting the effects of changes in fiscal policy? What are the future policy implications if past and present policies are based on inaccurate forecasts? Give some hypothetical examples.

Q94. The UK Labour government has established a 'golden rule' for fiscal policy which states that over the economic cycle, government borrowing would only be for investment, and not to fund current spending. Examine the rationale for such a rule, and discuss the advantages and disadvantages of such a rule-based approach to fiscal policy.

Q95. 'The problems of magnitude and the problems of timing conspire to make fiscal policy unpredictable. As such, intervention of this sort should be avoided and the government should aim to balance its budget.' Discuss.

Q96. What is the relationship between the money supply and the public-sector net cash requirement?

Q97. When the Bank of England's Monetary Policy Committee announces that it is putting up interest rates,

how will it achieve this, given that interest rates are determined by supply and demand?

Q98. How might the targeting of a foreign exchange rate value be a means of controlling inflation?

Q99. 'It is impossible to target both the money supply and the rate of interest. If you control one, you have to let the other be as it will.' Discuss.

Q100. Are targeting the rate of inflation and targeting the rate of growth in the money supply compatible policies?

Q101. Use *ISLM* analysis to explain the difference in monetarist and Keynesian views on the efficacy of fiscal and monetary policies.

Q102. What was stagflation? What reasons have been advanced to explain the stagflation experienced by the British economy during the 1970s? What problems did stagflation create for the management of economic affairs during this period?

Q103. Outline and assess the success or otherwise of the monetarist experiment in the 1980s.

Q104. To what extent has the policy of targeting a 2 per cent rate of inflation in the UK, with the Bank of England independently setting interest rates to achieve this, been a successful macroeconomic strategy?

Q105. Discuss the way that fiscal and monetary policy were used to cope with the financial crisis and the subsequent global slowdown.

Q106. Debate
The only way of achieving a stable macroeconomic environment is to set clear macroeconomic targets and then stick to them.

 # ANSWERS

Q1. Fiscal policy can be used to prevent the occurrence of fundamental disequilibrium in the economy and to smooth out fluctuations in the economy associated with the business cycle.

Q2. C.

Q3. E.

Q4. *True:* privatisation takes corporations out of the public sector into the private sector, whereas nationalisation has the reverse effect – such as happened when banking groups were taken into the public sector during the financial crisis of the late 2000s.

Q5. *(a)* *current expenditure*

(b) *final expenditure*

(c) *transfers*

(d) *capital expenditure*

Q6. *True.*

Q7. *surplus.*

Q8. *can meet.*

Q9. D. The answer is not A, C or E, because the PSNCR refers to the borrowing of the *whole* public sector: central government, local government and public corporations. The answer is not B, because the national debt refers to the accumulated debt over the years, not just to this year's borrowing.

Q10. As national income rises, so tax revenue will rise. Conversely, if national income rises fast enough for unemployment to fall, government expenditure on transfer payments such as unemployment benefit will fall. The net effect is that the budget deficit will fall (or the surplus rise). The opposite will happen if national income falls.

Q11. C. Fiscal stance refers to the effect of the government's fiscal policy on total aggregate demand: will the effect be reflationary or deflationary, and how much so? The answer is not E because the mere size of the deficit or surplus alone is not enough to determine whether aggregate demand will increase or decrease and by how much. It is also necessary to know what is happening to the other two injections and the other two withdrawals.

Q12. *at.*

Q13. *zero.*

Q14. *automatic fiscal stabilisers.*

Q15. C.

Q16. *smaller.* The more that taxes increase, the higher the *mpt* and hence the higher the *mpw* and the smaller the multiplier. The smaller the multiplier, the more stable will the economy be.

Q17. *fall.* The *mpt* will rise.

Q18. *expansionary.*

Q19. *deficits.*

Q20. *private.*

Q21. (a), (b) and (c) are expansionary. (d) and (e) are contractionary.

Q22. *True.*

Q23. D. The full multiplier is 4, but only $3/4$ of the cut in taxes is spent on domestic goods and services. Thus the rise in income is only $3/4$ as much as with the full multiplier. In fact, you can easily demonstrate that the tax multiplier is always 1 less than the full multiplier. (Note that the tax multiplier is negative: this is because a *fall* in taxes leads to a *rise* in income and vice versa.)

Q24. B. In equilibrium $I + X + G = S + M + T$. Thus if I exceeds S by £10m, and X exceeds M by £30m, $I + X$

must exceed $S + M$ by £10m + £30m = £40m. Thus for the economy to be in equilibrium T must exceed G by £40m: i.e. there must be a budget surplus of £40m.

Q25. A. Increased public expenditure can lead to a shortage of resources available for the private sector (resource crowding out) or a shortage of finance for private sector borrowing (financial crowding out).

Q26. *(a)* The flatter the L curve, the less will interest rates rise, so the less will be the crowding-out effect.

(b) If the money supply is endogenous – for example, if the increase in the demand for money results in the banks creating additional credit, then the increase in money supply will limit the rise in the interest rate – again, this will mean less of a crowding-out effect.

(c) If consumers' expenditure is unresponsive to an increase in the interest rate, then there will be less crowding out than if consumers greatly reduce their expenditure as interest rates rise in response to greater government borrowing.

(d) If investment is highly sensitive to interest rates, then as the government increases its borrowing to finance its higher expenditure, firms will find it more difficult to raise funds for investment, and there will be strong crowding out.

Q27. Reasons include: the amount of crowding out is difficult to predict; the impact of tax cuts (or benefit increases) will depend on how consumers decide to allocate additional incomes (which in turn depends on expectations of future price and income changes); the size of the accelerator is difficult to predict and subsequent multiplier/accelerator interactions are virtually impossible to predict; random shocks.

Q28. (a) (iii), (b) (v), (c) (iv), (d) (i), (e) (ii).

Q29. *False.* The golden rule does not cover capital spending, which is seen as investment for the benefit of future generations.

Q30. *False:* during the crisis fiscal rules were temporarily abandoned in the UK and elsewhere as governments resorted to discretionary fiscal policy. However, rules were generally reinstated as the global economy pulled out of recession.

Q31. (b), (d) and (e) are all examples of monetary policy. (a) and (f) are examples of fiscal policy, and (c) incomes policy.

Q32. *False.* The interest rate is not set by the government, but by the Monetary Policy Committee of the Bank of England.

Q33. D. This will reduce the credit multiplier. For the current reserve base, banks will now have to reduce the amount of non-reserve assets (i.e. loans, etc.).

Q34. The two major sources are: increased government borrowing (a PSNCR) and increased private-sector borrowing (from banks being prepared to operate with a lower liquidity ratio).

Q35. *above.*

Q36. *reducing.*

Q37. *excessive.*

Q38. *keen.*

Q39. *greater.*

Q40. *the non-bank private sector.* If the borrowing is not from the banks, there will be no expansion of the money base and no resulting credit creation.

Q41. *higher.* The excess government spending will increase the demand for money, and so, with no increase in the supply of money, there will be a rise in interest rates.

Q42. *less.* Higher interest rates will reduce private-sector borrowing, including private-sector investment. This 'crowding-out' of investment is seen by monetarists to be a serious problem of attempting to restrain the growth of the money supply *without* also reducing the PSNCR.

Q43. D. In the long run, increasing the money supply will not affect the real economy, so the only lasting effect is on prices. This is often referred to as the long-run neutrality of money.

Q44. (a) r_b

(b) r_a

(c) By manipulating money supply to M_{s_1}.

(d) The market would remain in disequilibrium, and some form of credit rationing would have to be introduced.

Q45. (a) (iii): *decrease,* (b) (i): *decrease,* (c) (i): *increase,* (d) (iv): *decrease,* (e) (i): *increase,* (f) (iii): *increase,* (g) (ii): *decrease.*

Open-market operations will involve altering the total amount of government borrowing on the open market (as opposed to from the central bank). If the central bank deliberately keeps banks short of liquidity and then manipulates the amount that it lends to them, this will directly affect banks' liquid base. Funding involves altering the *type* of government borrowing (e.g. switching from bills to bonds). In some countries (but not the UK), the central bank requires banks to maintain a minimum ratio of reserve assets to total assets – a ratio which is above the ratio banks would choose. By raising this ratio it can force banks to contract credit.

Those actions that increase the liquidity base of the banking sector will increase the credit creation. Those that decrease the liquidity base will decrease credit creation.

Q46. £90m. The liquidity base will expand by £10m, on which banks can create £90m credit, making a total increase in the money supply of £100m (a bank multiplier of 10).

Q47. (a) *Yes.* If the government cuts taxes, then other things being equal this will increase the PSNCR.

(b) *Yes.* Similarly, if the government wants to increase government expenditure, this will increase the PSNCR.

(c) *No.* A booming economy will automatically lead to higher tax revenues and reduced government expenditure (e.g. on unemployment benefits).

(d) *Yes.* In a recession, however, the PSNCR will increase as tax revenues fall and government expenditure automatically rises.

(e) *Yes* (short term). The extra government expenditure will raise the PSNCR.
No (long term). A faster growth in output will lead to a faster growth in tax revenues.

(f) *Yes.* This will reduce the tax base and increase government expenditure on health care, pensions and other benefits.

Q48. This is where the authorities seek to control cash and banks' balances with the central bank.

Q49. D. In this case, any reduction in the cash base is likely to 'bite' more effectively. In the case of A, banks could suffer a loss of liquidity without reducing loans; in the case of B and C, there is a diversion of business between institutions, which will limit the size of the total reduction in loans; in the case of E, the Bank of England is supplying liquidity on demand (albeit at a price).

Q50. Banks may reduce their liquidity ratios; they may initially have surplus liquidity; disintermediation may occur (possibly abroad).

Q51. *False.* If the supply of money is stable, but the *demand* for money is unstable, then the rate of interest will fluctuate as the level of demand fluctuates.

Q52. *True.* When banks run short of liquidity they will borrow from the Bank of England through gilt repos or offer bills of exchange for rediscounting. The Bank of England can dictate the repo and discount rates. This then has a knock-on effect on interest rates generally throughout the financial system.

Q53. (a) *Sell more.* If banks have surplus liquidity, they will be buying bills. If the Bank of England sells them more, this will force down the price of bills and hence force up the rate of discount and hence the rate of interest.

(b) *Buy fewer.* If banks are short of liquidity, they will be 'in the Bank' (selling bills to the Bank of England). If the Bank of England is prepared to buy fewer at any given price, this will force down the bill price and hence force up the rate of rediscount and hence the rate of interest.

Q54. C. Given that the Bank of England generally keeps banks short of liquidity, the banks have to borrow from the Bank of England. They do this through gilt repos. The Bank of England is prepared to buy bonds from the banks (thereby providing them with liquidity) on condition that the banks buy them back later (generally two weeks later). The price difference is set to be equivalent to the interest rate chosen by the Monetary Policy Committee.

Q55. B.

Q56. B. Goodhart's law states that regulation of one part of the financial system would cause unregulated parts to expand. Thus the amount of lending by the regulated institutions would be a poor indicator of total lending: 'to control is to distort'.

Q57. If people wish to borrow (demand), then the financial institutions will attempt to lend (supply), even if controls are in place restricting institutions from doing so.

Q58. *inelastic.*

Q59. All are possible consequences of a policy of high interest rates. Note that in case of (b), higher interest rates will lead to an appreciation of the exchange rate, which will make exports and home-produced import substitutes less competitive. In the case of (d), higher interest rates will discourage investment, which will reduce the rate of growth of capital and of technical progress.

Q60. **(a)** In Figure A20.1(a), the increase in government expenditure causes an increase in aggregate demand and a rightward shift in the *IS* curve to IS_2. If it is financed by an increase in the money supply, the *LM* curve will shift to LM_2. The rate of interest remains at r_1. Hence there is no crowding out and there is a full multiplier rise in income to Y_2.

   (b) In Figure A20.1(b), the deterioration in business expectations causes a leftward shift in the *IS* curve to IS_2. If the government increases the money supply, this will shift the *LM* curve downwards. If income is to be maintained at Y_1, the *LM* curve must shift downwards to LM_2 and the rate of interest fall to r_3.

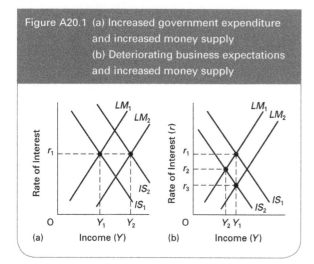

Figure A20.1 (a) Increased government expenditure and increased money supply
(b) Deteriorating business expectations and increased money supply

Q61. See Figure A20.2. Given their assumptions about the shapes of the curves, Keynesians conclude that fiscal policy has a relatively large effect on aggregate demand, whereas monetary policy has a relatively small effect. Monetarists conclude the opposite.

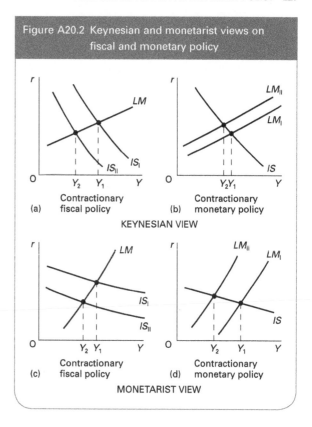

Figure A20.2 Keynesian and monetarist views on fiscal and monetary policy

Q62. (a), (d), (f) and (g) are all justifications used by the Keynesians for government intervention in the economy.

Q63. D. As the balance of payments moved into deficit, a deflationary policy was adopted in order to stop people buying imports and to improve the competitive position of UK exports by reducing the rate of inflation. As the economy slowed down and inflation fell, the balance payments would move into surplus. This was the cue for government to reflate the economy, and the start of a new cycle.

Q64. There are many arguments put forward to explain the stagflation of the 1970s. These include: a relaxation of monetary controls; a massive increase in the money supply in 1972/73; the move to floating exchange rates; the rise in oil prices; rising costs in the domestic economy; the decline in the UK's competitive position overseas; the effects of technology on jobs; poor expectations of future economic performance. (For a more comprehensive consideration of these points, see Sloman, *Economics* (this edition), pp. 623–5.)

Q65. (a), (b), (d) and (f) are all policies that characterised the approach to economic management in the early 1980s.

Q66. A range of problems were encountered: the PSNCR was very difficult to reduce; money supply measures moved in different directions and proved difficult to control; the decision to allow the pound to float freely, and the subsequent large-scale appreciation, created a great deal of uncertainty for those businesses trading overseas; the removing of credit controls contributed to the credit boom of the mid-1980s that proved to be too large to be sustainable; the reliance on high interest rates to curb spending created great difficulties for businesses and consumers. (For a more comprehensive assessment of these policy problems, see Sloman, *Economics* (this edition), pp. 625–6.)

Q67. The D-Mark exchange rate was effectively targeted in the late 1980s (before entry to the ERM).

Q68. *True.* The ERM imposed an exchange rate band. If the exchange rate moved to the limits of its band, then the government had to adopt appropriate policies to maintain the exchange rate value. For example, it could have been forced to raise interest rates if the value of the pound moved towards the bottom of its band.

Q69. E. With a fixed exchange rate, monetary policy has to be geared to maintaining that exchange rate. This substantially reduces flexibility in the use of monetary policy. In the case of A, the UK inflation rate was *higher* than the European average. In the case of B, fiscal policy was largely dominated by the domestic issue of reducing the growing PSNCR. In the case of C and D, maintaining the exchange rate meant maintaining high rates of interest, and this tended to reduce the growth of the money supply and the growth of aggregate demand.

Q70. *Partly true*: the control of inflation has been the focus for most of the period since 1992, but this changed a bit when the global recession began to bite, and inflation was allowed to drift up a bit.

Q71. *True.* The Monetary Policy Committee (MPC) is charged with targeting a rate of inflation of 2 per cent. It has to reduce interest rates if it believes that otherwise inflation would be below 2 per cent, and raise interest rates if it believes that otherwise inflation would be above 2 per cent.

Q72. *False*: fiscal policy still affected aggregate demand through the operation of automatic stabilisers.

Q73. *True.*

Q74. *raise.*

Q75. *lower.*

Q76. *0.5 per cent.*

Q77. *expanding*: the process was known as quantitative easing.

Q78. B.

Q79. 1. Political behaviour.
2. Time lags.

Q80. Keynesians favour discretion because the economic environment is always changing; hence government must change its policy in response. Better forecasting and speedier action will help to increase the effectiveness of discretionary policy.

Q81. D. The Taylor rule seeks to obtain the optimum degree of stability of both inflation and real national income by assigning weights to each. The higher the weight attached to achieving the inflation target, the more the central bank will be prepared to allow real national income to fluctuate. The higher the weight attached to achieving stability in real national income, the more the central bank will be prepared to allow inflation to diverge from its target.

Q82. *(a)* ADI_b.
(b) ADI_a.
(c) *controlling inflation.*
(d) If the main concern is to control inflation, then the central bank will be ready to adjust interest rates in order to bring inflation back under control, even if this means allowing national income to be lower. On the other hand, if the central bank is most keen to stabilise national income, it would allow inflation to increase a bit without rushing to raise interest rates.

Chapter 21

Aggregate Supply, Unemployment and Inflation

A REVIEW

To what extent will aggregate supply respond to changes in aggregate demand? Will the effects be solely on prices? Or will they be solely on output and employment? Or will the effects be partly on prices and partly on output and employment, and if so, in what combination? As you will discover, the different schools of economics give different answers to these questions.

The nature of aggregate supply and its responsiveness to changes in aggregate demand will also determine the shape of the *Phillips curve*. It is the shape of the Phillips curve that has been at the centre of the *expectations revolution* in economics. Later in the chapter we will look at the theories of expectations and their implications for policies to tackle inflation and unemployment.

21.1 Aggregate supply

(Page 643) The effect that a change in aggregate demand has on the economy is determined by the nature and shape of the aggregate supply curve.

 Figure 21.1 illustrates two extreme aggregate supply curves. Aggregate supply curve I represents the extreme **Q1.** *Keynesian/new classical* position, whereas aggregate supply curve II represents the extreme **Q2.** *Keynesian/new classical* position.

Q3. Consider Figure 21.1. To which of the aggregate supply curves will the following statements apply?

(a) Up to the full-employment level of national income, an expansion in aggregate demand will progressively close a deflationary gap. AS_I/AS_{II}

(b) A rise in aggregate demand will have no effect on output and employment. AS_I/AS_{II}

(c) The only way to achieve higher levels of national income in the long run is through the use of supply-side policies. AS_I/AS_{II}

Figure 21.1 Different-shaped aggregate supply curves

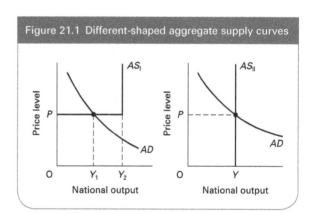

(d) Fiscal and monetary policy used to regulate aggregate demand will have a significant effect upon economic activity. AS_I/AS_{II}

When looking at aggregate supply we must distinguish between short-run and long-run *AS* curves.

(Pages 643–4) Short-run aggregate supply

To understand the short-run aggregate supply curve we need to look at its *microeconomic* foundations.

In the short run we assume that individual firms respond to a rise in demand for their product **Q4.** *by considering/ without considering* the effects of a general rise in demand on their suppliers and on the economy as a whole.

⊖ **Q5.** Figure 21.2 shows the profit-maximising price and output of a firm facing a downward-sloping demand curve. Look back to Chapters 5 and 6 (sections 5.6 and 6.3) in Sloman, *Economics* (this edition), if you are uncertain of this material.

(*a*) Using Figure 21.2, show the effect of a rise in demand on price and output.

(*b*) Add a further *MC* curve that is flatter than the one already shown in the diagram (but still passes through point *x*). How does this influence the effect upon price and output of a rise in demand?

....

....

(*c*) Near full capacity, is the *MC* curve likely to become steeper or flatter?   *steeper/flatter*

(*d*) Explain your answer to (c).

....

....

....

If there is now a *general* rise in demand in the economy, but firms assume that their cost curves are given (i.e. that the rise in demand for their products is not accompanied by a shift in their cost curves), then the aggregate supply curve will be **Q6.** *horizontal/similar in shape to the MC curve illustrated in Figure 21.2/horizontal then vertical/vertical.*

(Pages 644–5) Long-run aggregate supply

In the long run (which might not be very long at all), we cannot assume that firms' cost curves are unaffected by a change in aggregate demand. Three factors will have an important influence on the aggregate supply curve in the long run: the *interdependence* of firms, *investment* and *expectations*.

⊖ **Q7.** Figure 21.3 illustrates two situations (diagrams (a) and (b)) in which the slope of the long-run aggregate supply curve is different from that of the short-run *AS* curve. In each diagram there is an initial increase in aggregate demand. In each situation we assume that in the long run firms' cost curves are affected by the change in aggregate demand. One situation is the result of firms being interdependent; the other, the result of investment by firms in response to the change in aggregate demand.

(*a*) In which diagram is the interdependence of firms the dominant effect on the long-run *AS* curve?

                      Diagram(a)/Diagram(b)

(*b*) Explain the reason for your answer.

....

....

(*c*) Explain why the diagram you did not select in (a) represents the impact of new investment on aggregate supply.

....

....

....

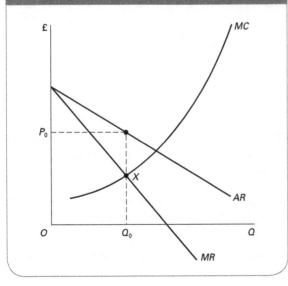

Figure 21.2 Profit-maximising price and output for a firm in an imperfect market

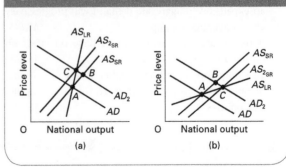

Figure 21.3 Long-run aggregate supply curves

Q8. Expectations can make the long-run *AS* curve either steeper or shallower than the short-run *AS* curve. Which of the following effects of a rise in aggregate demand will make the long-run *AS* curve steeper, and which will make it shallower?

(a) People expect that the rise in aggregate demand will lead to a general rise in prices. *steeper/shallower*

(b) People expect that the rise in aggregate demand will lead to firms increasing the level of investment.
steeper/shallower

(c) People expect that the rise in aggregate demand will cause unemployment to fall. *steeper/shallower*

(d) People expect that the rise in aggregate demand will cause a general rise in wages throughout the economy.
steeper/shallower

(e) People expect that the rise in aggregate demand will lead to increased economic growth. *steeper/shallower*

(f) People expect that the rise in aggregate demand will strengthen the bargaining position of trade unions.
steeper/shallower

(Pages 645–7) Aggregate supply, the labour market and unemployment
What is the relationship between aggregate supply and unemployment?

Q9. Figure 21.4 shows short-run aggregate demand and supply of labour curves. The total labour force is shown by curve *N*; the effective supply of labour (those working plus others willing and able to work) is shown by curve AS_L. Aggregate demand for labour is initially given by AD_{L1} and the wage rate by W_1.
(a) How much is equilibrium unemployment?

....

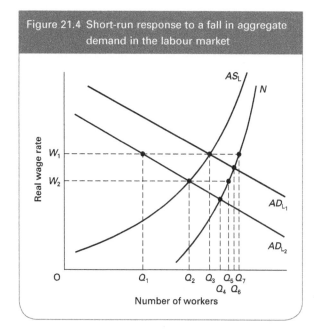

Figure 21.4 Short-run response to a fall in aggregate demand in the labour market

(b) How much is disequilibrium unemployment?

....

Now assume that aggregate demand falls to AD_{L2} and that wages are *flexible* downwards.
(c) How much is total unemployment now? ....
(d) How much is disequilibrium unemployment?

....

(e) How much is equilibrium unemployment?

....

Now assume that aggregate demand has again fallen from AD_{L1} to AD_{L2}, but that this time wages are fixed at W_1.
(f) How much is total unemployment this time?

....

(g) How much is disequilibrium unemployment?

....

(h) How much is equilibrium unemployment?

....

Q10. The natural level of output is just another name for the potential level of output. *True/False*

Q11. In monetarist analysis, with long-run employment being at the natural rate, the long-run aggregate supply curve will be horizontal at the natural level of output.
True/False

Q12. Keynesian models of long-run aggregate supply make one or more of four assumptions. Which of the following is *not* one of these four?
A. The existence of money illusion.
B. Firms will take on more labour only if there is a fall in the real wage rate.
C. Downward stickiness of wages.
D. Expectations by firms that changes in aggregate demand will affect sales.
E. Hysteresis.

(Pages 647–51) Aggregate demand and supply, and inflation
So far we have used aggregate supply and demand analysis to illustrate the effect of a single increase in aggregate demand and a single increase in the price level. Aggregate demand and aggregate supply analysis can also be used to illustrate the causes of *inflation* (the rate of *increase* in prices). It can be used to distinguish between demand-pull and cost-push pressures on inflation.

Q13. This question is based on Figure 21.5 and illustrates an inflationary sequence that starts with *demand-pull* pressures. The economy is initially at point *X* on curves AD_1 and AS_1. Each of the following events will shift either the *AD* or the *AS* curve. Assuming they occur in a sequence,

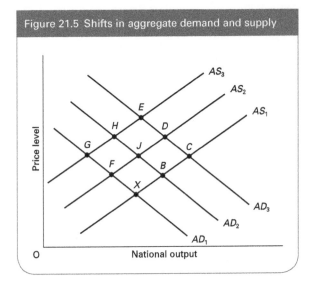

Figure 21.5 Shifts in aggregate demand and supply

to which point on the diagram will the economy move after each event?

(a) The government undertakes an extensive new programme of public works.

point ....

(b) Subsequently the government decides to fund the programme by selling bonds to the banking sector in an attempt to prevent crowding out.

point ....

(c) Higher production costs have a knock-on effect throughout industry.

point ....

(d) Workers demand higher wages to cover rising costs of living.

point ....

⊖ **Q14.** This question is also based on Figure 21.5 but this time illustrates an inflationary sequence that starts with *cost-push* pressures. To which point on the diagram will the economy move after each of the following events, which, as before, shift either the *AD* or the *AS* curve? Again assume that point X is the starting point and that each event follows the previous one.

(a) Firms expect their suppliers' prices to rise following the collapse of an agreement between government and unions over pay restraint.

point ....

(b) Trade unions demand and get higher wages.

point ....

(c) Falling national output and rising unemployment persuade the government to increase public expenditure.

point ....

(d) The government, believing that its fiscal policy is inadequate, decides to cut interest rates.

point ....

The use of interest rate changes in order to achieve an inflation target implies that inflation is generally of the

cost-push/demand-pull variety, so forecasts of inflation tend to concentrate on factors that affect **Q16.** *aggregate demand/aggregate supply*. An increase in oil prices would affect **Q17.** *aggregate demand/aggregate supply*, and under inflation targeting the response would need to be to slow the rate of growth of **Q18.** *aggregate demand/aggregate supply*.

(?) **Q19.** The economy shown in Figure 21.6 is operating under inflation targeting, with the inflation target set at π_{target}. In the initial position, aggregate demand is given by ADI_1 and aggregate supply by ASI_1.

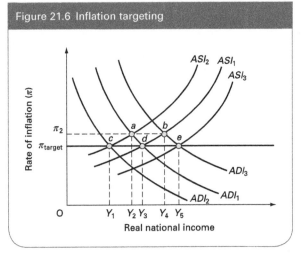

Figure 21.6 Inflation targeting

(a) Identify the equilibrium level of real national income.

....

Suppose now that there is an increase in oil prices.

(b) Which new curve represents the effect of this?
ASI_2 ASI_3 ADI_2 ADI_3

(c) How does this affect equilibrium in the short run?

....

(d) Identify the sustainable level of real national income.

....

(e) What action would the central bank need to take in order to maintain the original inflation target?

....

(f) Suppose that the central bank is given a new higher inflation target at π_2. Comment on whether this will enable a new sustainable equilibrium of Y_2 to be achieved.

....

Q20. This question is also based on Figure 21.6, with the economy starting in the same initial equilibrium. From this initial position, suppose there is an increase in government expenditure.

(a) Which new curve represents the effect of this?

ASI_2 ASI_3 ADI_2 ADI_3

(b) How does this affect equilibrium in the short run?

....

(c) Identify the sustainable level of real national income.

....

(d) What action would the central bank need to take in order to maintain the original inflation target?

....

(e) Suppose that the central bank is given a new higher inflation target of π_2. Comment on whether this will enable a new sustainable equilibrium of Y_4 to be achieved.

....

21.2 The expectations-augmented Phillips curve

(Pages 651–8) The Phillips curve had an important influence upon economic thinking and analysis during the 1960s and 1970s.

Q21. The original Phillips curve showed:

A. the influence of fiscal policy on the level of inflation and unemployment.

B. the direct relationship between price inflation and unemployment.

C. the relationship between aggregate labour demand and aggregate labour supply in the long run.

D. the inverse relationship between wage inflation and unemployment.

E. the effect of expectations about changes in economic activity on the level of unemployment.

The main contribution of the monetarists to the study of the Phillips curve was to introduce the effects of expectations. They based their theory upon adaptive expectations.

Q22. Adaptive expectations state that:

A. people never make the same mistake twice.

B. people adapt their expectations according to the policies the government is currently pursuing.

C. expectations are formed on the basis of information from the past.

D. expectations are based upon forecasts made about the future performance of the economy.

E. government economic policy will always be predicted and hence people will adapt to it before it takes effect.

Q23. Which of the following equations are consistent with the adaptive expectations theory?

(i) $\pi_t^e = a\pi_t$

(ii) $\pi_t^e = a\pi_{t-1}$

(iii) $\pi_t = b + c(1/U) + d\pi_t^e$

(iv) $\pi_t = b + c(1/U) + d\pi_{t-1}^e$

where π is the percentage annual rate of inflation, π^e is the expected rate of inflation, t is the time period and U is the percentage rate of unemployment.

A. (i) and (iii).

B. (ii) and (iii).

C. (i) and (iv).

D. (ii) and (iv).

E. (iv) only.

Q24. Why is the adaptive expectations theory of the Phillips curve sometimes referred to as the *accelerationist theory*?

....

....

According to the adaptive expectations model, in the long run the Phillips curve is **Q25.** *horizontal/vertical*. At this rate of unemployment, real *AD* is equal to real *AS*. Monetarists call this rate of unemployment the **Q26.** *natural rate/accelerating rate* of unemployment. The implications this has for government policy are that expansionary monetary (and fiscal) policy will only have the effect of reducing unemployment in **Q27.** *the long run/the short run*. In the **Q28.** *long run/short run*, the effect of expansionary policy will be purely inflationary.

Q29. Figure 21.7 shows an economy moving clockwise over time from points *A* to *J* and back to *A* again.

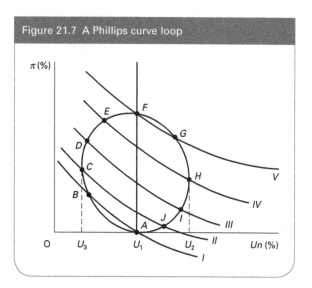

Figure 21.7 A Phillips curve loop

(a) What is the natural rate of unemployment?

$U_1/U_2/U_3$

(b) What is the non-accelerating inflation rate of unemployment (NAIRU)?

$U_1/U_2/U_3$

(c) Between what points will the economy experience positive demand-pull pressures on inflation?

....

(d) Between what points will the economy experience stagflation?

....

(e) How could the economy move from point *F* back to point *A* more rapidly?

....

Q30. A fall in the rate of frictional unemployment will cause the Phillips curve to shift to the right.

True/False

Q31. In late 2008, the Bank of England announced substantial reductions in bank rate, even though inflation at the time was above its target. Which of the following most closely describes what was happening?

A. The Bank had abandoned inflation targeting.

B. The Bank was more concerned about the impending recession than about inflation, and had adopted a Taylor rule approach.

C. The Bank had come under pressure from the government to lower interest rates in spite of the high inflation.

D. The Bank believed that the relationship between interest rates and inflation had broken down.

E. Given the expected recession, the Bank's prediction two years ahead was that there was danger of inflation falling well below the 2% target.

The Bank of England faced a policy dilemma in 2010/11 as inflation picked up with economic growth remaining **Q32.** *fragile/robust* and unemployment **Q33.** *falling/rising*. Despite inflation consistently **Q34.** *exceeding/falling below* the upper bound of the target, the MPC kept Bank Rate at 0.5 per cent throughout 2010 and into 2011.

21.3 Inflation and unemployment: the new classical position

(Pages 658–62) The *new* classical economists take an extreme view of the Phillips curve and the aggregate supply curve. They argue that both curves are vertical in **Q35.** *the short run alone/the long run alone/both the short run and the long run/neither the short run nor the long run*. Therefore the effect of any expansionary monetary policy will be simply to **Q36.** *raise prices/increase output and employment*.

The new classical school assumes that markets clear **Q37.** *very slowly/virtually instantaneously*. Therefore all unemployment is **Q38.** *voluntary/involuntary*.

The new classical economists reject adaptive expectations theory. Instead they base their analysis on *rational expectations*.

Q39. Rational expectations theory states that:

(a) Expectations are formed using currently available information. *True/False*

(b) Errors in prediction are made at random and therefore do not result in systematic divergences between the actual and expected rate of inflation. *True/False*

(c) The current economic situation will have only limited impact on expectations. *True/False*

(d) Expectations are based on imperfect information.

True/False

Q40. Figure 21.8 shows the effects upon price and output of a rise in the level of aggregate demand under rational expectations. Aggregate demand rises from AD_1 to AD_2.

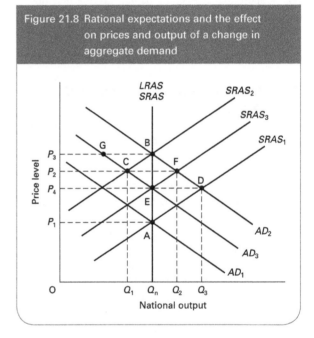

Figure 21.8 Rational expectations and the effect on prices and output of a change in aggregate demand

(a) Assuming the long-run *AS* curve is vertical, then given rational expectations theory, to which point on Figure 21.8 will the economy move in the *short run*, assuming that people correctly predict that the *AD* curve will shift to AD_2?

....

(b) If expectations prove to be incorrect, and people anticipate that aggregate demand will rise only to AD_3 and that the price level will rise only to P_4, to what point will the economy move in the short run?

....

(c) Returning to point *A*, assume now that aggregate demand in reality only increases to AD_3, but that people *over*predict the rate of inflation and believe in

effect that aggregate demand will rise to AD_2 and that prices will rise to P_3. To what point will the economy move in the short run?

....

(?) Q41. What happens to the Phillips curve if inflation is (a) underpredicted and (b) overpredicted?

(a) ....

....

(b) ....

....

One of the major criticisms made of the new classical approach concerns the assumption of perfect wage and price flexibility.

Q42. If the new classical analysis is correct, anticipated changes in aggregate demand will have no effect on output or employment. *True/False*

Q43. To which of the following statements would a new classical economist *not* subscribe?
A. Keynesian demand management should be rejected except in the short run.
B. Fiscal policy should not be used to increase output and employment.
C. Monetary policy should not be used to increase output and employment.
D. Monetary policy should be used to control inflation.
E. Output and unemployment will remain at the natural level.

(Pages 662–3) If new classical economists argue that unemployment deviates from its natural rate only very temporarily and by chance, how do they explain cyclical fluctuations in unemployment and output? They have developed 'real business cycle theory' to explain this.

Q44. Real business cycle theory explains cyclical fluctuations in terms of:
A. fluctuations in real aggregate demand (i.e. after correcting for inflation).
B. fluctuations in the money supply, caused by banks expanding credit in anticipation of real increases in output and hence demand.
C. the effects of changes in rational expectations on real output.
D. fluctuations in aggregate supply, caused by technological or structural changes in the economy that take place over a number of months.
E. fluctuations in real output causing changes in expectations.

21.4 Inflation and unemployment: the modern Keynesian position

(Pages 664–7)

Q45. Which of the following are given as reasons by Keynesians for the problem of both higher inflation and higher unemployment in the 1980s and 1990s (or at least a worse trade-off) than in the 1950s and 1960s?
(a) An increase in equilibrium unemployment (at least up to the early 1990s). *Yes/No*
(b) Expectations of higher inflation and/or higher unemployment. *Yes/No*
(c) High unemployment persisting after the end of a recession (hysteresis). *Yes/No*
(d) The absence of a trade-off, even in the short run, between inflation and unemployment. *Yes/No*

Long-term unemployment rose markedly with the recession that followed the financial crisis of 2007/08. The labour market was **Q46.** *less/more* flexible than before, which **Q47.** *dampened/magnified* the increase in the NAIRU.

Q48. Firms may pay a wage rate that is above the market-clearing real wage in order to maintain a well-motivated labour force, thus cutting down on labour turnover and making it easier to attract well-qualified workers.

True/False

(?) Q49. Why are 'insider workers' in firms able to secure higher wage rates, if there are 'outsiders' willing to work at lower wage rates?

....

....

Q50. According to Keynesians, which of the following are suitable policies to tackle the problem of hysteresis?
(a) An increase in aggregate demand. *Yes/No*
(b) Retraining programmes. *Yes/No*
(c) Grants to firms to take on the long-term unemployed. *Yes/No*
(d) A tight monetary policy. *Yes/No*

Q51. Modern Keynesians argue that structural changes experienced by the economy over recent years have resulted in higher levels of technological, structural and frictional unemployment. They argue that freer markets would solve this problem. *True/False*

(?) Q52. Give two reasons why modern Keynesians reject the notion of a natural rate of unemployment.

1. ....

2. ....

Q53. Modern Keynesians are critical of free-market thinking, arguing that government policy should involve the maintenance of a steady expansion of demand.

True/False

21.5 Postscript: common ground among economists?

(Pages 607–8)

Whilst there is some disagreement among economists over some aspects of the aggregate supply and Phillips curves, there is quite a lot of common ground over some issues.

Q54. With the exception of extreme new classical economists, other economists would accept that the short-run aggregate supply curve is upward-sloping, albeit getting steeper as full-capacity output is approached. Which of the following are implied by this?

(i) Reductions in aggregate demand can cause reductions in output and increases in unemployment.

(ii) Reductions in aggregate demand will have no effect whatsoever on output or unemployment.

(iii) An increase in aggregate demand by the government will have no effect in times of recession.

(iv) An increase in aggregate demand by the government will help to pull an economy out of recession.

A. (i) and (iii).

B. (i) and (iv).

C. (ii) and (iii).

D. (ii) and (iv).

E. (iii) only.

Q55. New classical and most Keynesian economists would agree that both the long-run aggregate supply curve and the long-run Phillips curve are vertical. *True/False*

Q56. New classical and most Keynesian economists would agree that expectations have important effects on the economy. *True/False*

PROBLEMS, EXERCISES AND PROJECTS

Q57. Assume that inflation depends on two things: the level of aggregate demand, indicated by the inverse of the rate of unemployment $(1/U)$, and the expected rate of inflation (π_t^e). Assume that the rate of inflation (π_t) is given by the equation:

$$\pi_t = 40/U - 4 + \pi_t^e$$

Assume initially (year 0) that the actual and expected rate of inflation is zero.

(a) What is the current (natural) rate of unemployment?

....

(b) Now assume in year 1 that the government wishes to reduce unemployment to 5 per cent and continues to expand aggregate demand by as much as is necessary to achieve this. Fill in the rows for years 0 to 4 of Table 21.1. It is assumed for simplicity that the

expected rate of inflation in a given year (π_t^e) is equal to the actual rate of inflation in the previous year (π_{t-1}).

(c) Now assume in year 5 that the government, worried about rising inflation, reduces aggregate demand sufficiently to reduce inflation by 2 per cent in that year. What must the rate of unemployment be raised to in that year?

....

(d) Assuming that unemployment stays at this high level, continue Table 21.1 for years 5 to 7.

Q58. In Tables 21.2 and 21.3, you are provided with unemployment and consumer price inflation data for three countries from 1974 to 2004.

(a) Using the data, plot inflation against unemployment for each country, clearly marking the year of each point.

(b) Can you identify any Phillips curve loops?

(c) Does the evidence suggest that the Phillips curves shifted to the right during this period?

(d) Do you think that the Phillips curve relationship is of any value to economic policy makers?

Q59. Figure 21.9 gives a monetarist/adaptive expectations perspective of the relationship between real GDP, unemployment and inflation over the course of the business cycle.

(a) Explain the relationship between actual and real GDP, unemployment and inflation at each of the points 1–7 in the top part of the diagram. Why does the top of

Table 21.1 An expectations-augmented inflation function: $\pi_t = (40/U - 4) + \pi_t^e$

Year	U	$40/U - 4$	.	π^e	=	π
0	...	...	.	+	=	...
1	...	...	.	+	=	...
2	...	...	.	+	=	...
3	...	...	.	+	=	...
4	...	...	.	+	=	...
5	...	...	.	+	=	...
6	...	...	.	+	=	...
7	...	...	.	+	=	...

Table 21.2 Unemployment rates (percentage)

	1973	1974	1975	1976	1977	1978	1979	1980	1981	1982	1983	1984	1985	1986	1987	1988
USA	4.9	5.6	8.3	7.7	7.0	6.1	5.8	7.2	7.6	9.7	9.6	7.1	7.1	7.0	6.2	5.5
Japan	1.3	1.4	1.9	2.0	2.0	2.2	2.1	2.0	2.2	2.3	2.7	2.6	2.6	2.8	2.8	2.5
France	2.7	3.0	4.3	4.5	5.0	5.4	6.0	6.4	7.6	8.2	7.9	9.4	9.8	9.9	9.9	9.4

	1989	1990	1991	1992	1993	1994	1995	1996	1997	1998	1999	2000	2001	2002	2003	2004
	5.3	5.6	6.8	7.5	6.9	6.0	5.6	5.4	4.9	4.5	4.2	4.0	4.7	5.8	6.0	5.5
	2.3	2.1	2.1	2.2	2.5	2.9	3.1	3.4	3.4	4.1	4.7	4.7	5.0	5.4	5.3	4.7
	8.9	8.5	9.0	9.9	11.1	11.7	11.1	11.6	11.5	11.1	10.5	9.1	8.4	8.9	9.5	9.7

Source: Based on data from *Consumer Prices* (MEI) under Prices and Price Indices under Prices and Purchasing Power Parities from OECD. Stat Extracts, http://stats.oecd.org/index.aspx, accessed on 5/10/11.

Table 21.3 Consumer prices (annual percentage increase)

	1973	1974	1975	1976	1977	1978	1979	1980	1981	1982	1983	1984	1985	1986	1987	1988
USA	6.2	11.1	9.1	5.7	6.5	7.6	11.2	13.5	10.3	6.1	3.2	4.3	3.5	1.9	3.6	4.1
Japan	11.7	24.5	11.8	9.3	8.1	3.8	3.6	8.0	4.9	2.7	1.9	2.2	2.1	0.4	−0.2	0.5
France	7.3	13.7	11.8	9.6	9.4	9.1	10.8	13.6	13.4	11.8	9.6	7.4	5.8	2.5	3.3	2.7

	1989	1990	1991	1992	1993	1994	1995	1996	1997	1998	1999	2000	2001	2002	2003	2004
	4.8	5.4	4.2	3.0	3.0	2.6	2.8	2.9	2.3	1.5	2.2	3.4	2.8	1.8	2.3	2.7
	2.3	3.1	3.3	1.6	1.3	0.7	−0.1	0.0	1.7	0.7	−0.3	−0.7	−0.7	−0.9	−0.3	0.0
	3.5	3.6	3.4	2.4	2.2	1.7	1.8	2.1	1.3	0.7	0.6	1.8	1.8	1.9	2.2	2.3

Source: Based on data from *Consumer Prices* (MEI) under Prices and Price Indices under Prices and Purchasing Power Parities from OECD. Stat Extracts, http://stats.oecd.org/index.aspx, accessed on 5/10/11.

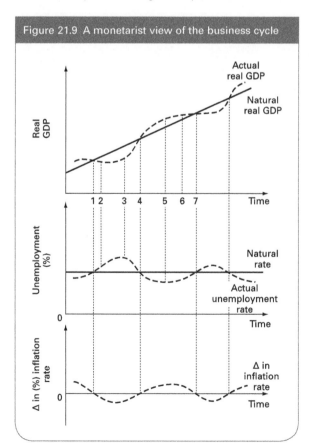

Figure 21.9 A monetarist view of the business cycle

the curve in the top diagram (point 6) not correspond to the bottom and top respectively of the curves in the other two parts of the diagram (point 5)?

(*b*) If the magnitude of the cycle in the top part of the diagram became greater, would there be a similar change in magnitude in the fluctuations in unemployment and inflation?

(*c*) To what extent would (i) a Keynesian and (ii) a new classicist agree with the relationships portrayed in the diagram?

DISCUSSION TOPICS AND ESSAYS

Q60. How does the shape of the aggregate supply curve affect the relationship between inflation and unemployment?

Q61. Why will the long-run aggregate supply curve have a different slope from the short-run aggregate supply curve? What determines the relationship between the two?

Q62. What is meant by the 'natural' rate of unemployment? Is it possible to reduce unemployment below the natural rate in (a) the short run and (b) the long run?

Q63. Distinguish between adaptive and rational expectations and describe how they are formed. What effect will each type of expectation have on the relationship between inflation and unemployment?

Q64. Outline the main assumptions made by the new classical school and describe the implications these assumptions have for macroeconomic policy.

Q65. If real wages are 'sticky' downwards, what implications does this have for the shape of the Phillips curve and for government macroeconomic policy?

Q66. How do new Keynesians explain the persistence of unemployment in the recoveries of the mid-1980s and mid-1990s?

Q67. Discuss the respective roles of monetary and fiscal policy under a regime of inflation targeting.

Q68. Discuss the proposition that the only effective way of reducing *both* inflation *and* unemployment is to use supply-side policies.

Q69. Debate
Governments invariably resort to demand-side policies for short-term political gain. But such policies are useless in the long run as a means of increasing aggregate supply.

ANSWERS

Q1. *Keynesian.*

Q2. *new classical.*

Q3. (a) and (d) relate to the Keynesian aggregate supply curve, AS_I. Changes in aggregate demand will have no effect on prices until the full-employment level of income (Y_2) is reached. (b) and (c) relate to the monetarist aggregate supply curve, AS_{II}. Changes in aggregate demand will have no effect on output, but instead will be reflected solely in changes in the price level.

Q4. *without considering.* We assume that firms assume that a rise in demand is confined to their product.

Q5. (a) See Figure A21.1. The average and marginal curves shift to AR_2 and MR_2 respectively, giving a new profit-maximising price and output of P_2 and Q_2.

(b) See Figure A21.2. The flatter the MC curve, the more will a rise in demand affect output rather than price.

(c) *steeper.*

(d) The nearer a firm gets to full capacity, the more costs per unit will rise for each extra unit produced. This is in accordance with the principle of diminishing marginal returns.

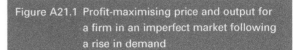

Figure A21.1 Profit-maximising price and output for a firm in an imperfect market following a rise in demand

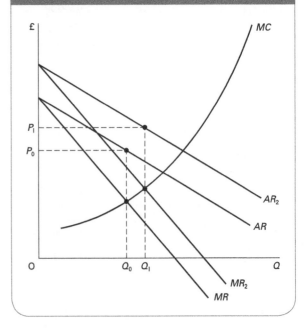

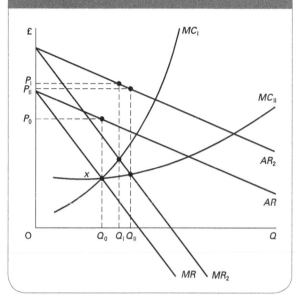

Figure A21.2 Profit-maximising price and output for a firm with alternative cost curves

Q6. similar in shape to the MC curve illustrated in Figure 21.2.

Q7. (a) Diagram (a).

(b) As AD rises, prices throughout the economy also rise. Because firms are interdependent, the price rise by one firm will be passed on as additional costs of production to another firm. This will cause the short-run AS curve to shift upwards.

(c) As demand rises, firms will be encouraged to invest. As a result they will be able to increase output without significantly increasing prices.

Q8. (a), (d) and (f) will tend to make the AS curve *steeper*. All of these will tend to stimulate inflation and lead firms to believe that they can raise their prices without losing market share. The effect will therefore be to shift the short-run AS curve upwards and hence make the long-run AS curve steeper.

(b), (c) and (e) will tend to make the AS curve shallower. They will all encourage firms to invest, in the belief that their market is expanding. The effect will therefore be to shift the short-run AS curve to the right and hence make the long-run AS curve shallower.

Q9. (a) $Q_7 - Q_3$ (the gap between AS_L and N at W_1).

(b) There is no disequilibrium unemployment. The wage rate is at the equilibrium.

(c) $Q_5 - Q_2$.

(d) It is still zero, because the wage rate has fallen to the new equilibrium.

(e) $Q_5 - Q_2$. Note that this is higher than before when the wage rate was W_1. Given that wages are lower, unemployed workers are inclined to search for longer before being prepared to accept job offers.

(f) $Q_7 - Q_1$ ($N - AD_{L2}$ at W_1).

(g) $Q_3 - Q_1$.

(h) $Q_7 - Q_3$.

Q10. True.

Q11. False: it would be vertical.

Q12. B. Keynesians assume that firms will take on more labour in response to an increase in the demand for the goods that they produce. A fall in the real wage rate is not a precondition.

Q13. The economy will move from point X through points B, C, D and E. Both (a) and (b) will cause aggregate demand to shift to the right, whereas (c) and (d) will cause aggregate supply to shift upwards.

Q14. The economy will move from point X through points F, G, H and E. Both (a) and (b) will cause aggregate supply to shift upwards. If, in response to falling output and rising unemployment, the government then stimulates economic activity, as in (c) and (d), aggregate demand will shift to the right.

Q15. demand-pull.

Q16. aggregate demand.

Q17. aggregate supply.

Q18. aggregate demand.

Q19. (a) Y_3.

(b) ASI_2.

(c) Real national income falls to Y_2 and inflation rises above the target level to π_2.

(d) The sustainable output level is now at Y_1.

(e) In order to maintain the original inflation target, the central bank needs to introduce contractionary policies to reduce aggregate demand to ADI_2 (point c) in order to restore equilibrium at the new sustainable level of real national income.

(f) Adopting a new higher inflation target will not be effective in the long run, as eventually the economy must find its way to the sustainable equilibrium level of Y_1; this will happen through further movements of the aggregate supply curve. The point is that the ASI curves shown in the diagram are short-run curves. In the long run, they are much steeper, if not vertical.

Q20. (a) ADI_3.

(b) Output in the short run moves to Y_4 (point b): a movement along curve ASI_1.

(c) Sustainable real national income is unchanged at Y_3.

(d) The central bank needs to tighten fiscal and monetary policy to shift the aggregate demand curve back to its original position.

(e) Adopting a new target will not be effective in the long run, as eventually the economy must find its way to the sustainable level of real national income through upward shifts in the short-run ASI curve as people come to expect higher inflation.

Q21. D. The Phillips curve showed the inverse relationship between wage inflation and unemployment. Wage inflation was replaced in later modifications by price inflation.

Q22. C. Adaptive expectations are based upon past events. It is assumed that people learn from experience. Hence, if the rate of inflation is underpredicted one year, the following year expectations will be adapted and revised upwards.

Q23. B. (ii) states that the expected rate of inflation (π^e) depends on the actual rate of inflation in the last time period (π_{t-1}): i.e. expectations adapt to what was actually the case previously.

(iii) states that actual inflation (π_t) depends on some constant amount (b), on the inverse of unemployment ($1/U$) and on the expected rate of inflation in the current time period (π_t^e).

Q24. It is sometimes called the accelerationist theory because, in order to keep unemployment below the equilibrium rate, price increases must accelerate: i.e. inflation must rise. As long as unemployment is kept below the equilibrium rate, each year expectations will underpredict the rate of inflation and hence adapt and rise the following year. Thus the trade-off is not between unemployment and inflation but between unemployment and the rate of *increase* in inflation.

Q25. vertical.

Q26. natural rate.

Q27. short run.

Q28. long run.

Q29. *(a)* U_1. This is where real aggregate demand equals real aggregate supply.

(b) U_1. In this model, the NAIRU is the same as the natural rate. It is the rate of unemployment consistent with a stable rate of inflation.

(c) Between points *A* and *F*. Unemployment is reduced (temporarily) below the natural rate, but inflation rises.

(d) Between points *C* and *F*. Between these points both inflation and unemployment rise.

(e) By a more drastic contraction of aggregate demand. Unemployment would rise above U_2, but inflation would fall more rapidly.

Q30. *False*. A fall in the rate of frictional unemployment will shift the Phillips curve to the left.

Q31. E.

Q32. fragile.

Q33. rising.

Q34. exceeding.

Q35. both the short run and the long run.

Q36. raise prices.

Q37. virtually instantaneously.

Q38. voluntary.

Q39. *(a)* *True*. Expectations are formed using currently available information. People look not merely at what has happened to inflation in the past, but also at *current* economic indicators and government policies and project forward.

(b) *True*. If errors in prediction are made at random, it can be assumed that on *average* forecasts will be correct. (The mean forecasted value will be correct over time, but there will be random divergences around the mean.)

(c) *False*. Rational expectations theory argues that the current state of the economy, or the current policies being pursued by the government, will have a crucial impact upon expectations.

(d) *True*. Expectations are based on the information available. Such information might well be incomplete or even wrong.

Q40. *(a)* The economy will move to point B. Here the effect of rising demand is correctly anticipated and simply causes aggregate supply to shift upwards to $SRAS_2$ as aggregate demand expands to AD_2. The price level rises to P_3.

(b) F. As firms believe that aggregate demand will only rise to AD_3 and the price level to P_4 the aggregate supply curve will only shift up to $SRAS_3$. The excess demand at P_4 of $D - E$ will push up the level of prices. Believing that this represents a *real* rise in prices, firms increase output (they move up along $SRAS_3$.) Short-run equilibrium is achieved at point F with a higher price and output of P_2 and Q_2. Eventually, when people realise their mistake, long-run equilibrium will be achieved at point B.

(c) C. The converse of (b) occurs. The *AS* curve shifts up to $SRAS_2$. Firms believe that there is a fall in real demand (they perceive a demand deficiency of $B - G$). They thus reduce prices and output. Short-run equilibrium is achieved at point C with a price and output of P_2 and Q_1. Eventually, when people realise their mistake, long-run equilibrium will be achieved at point E.

Q41. The Phillips curve will always be vertical in the long run as errors in prediction are made at random. However, underprediction will shift the short-run Phillips curve to the left: unemployment temporarily falls below the natural rate. Overprediction will shift the short-run Phillips curve to the right: unemployment will be temporarily above its natural rate.

Q42. *True*.

Q43. A. The new classical school would argue that Keynesian demand management should not be used in any circumstances – even in the short run.

Q44. D. The new classical school explains the business cycle in terms of fluctuations in aggregate supply, rather than fluctuations in aggregate demand. These changes in aggregate supply may be the result of changes in technology or other supply-side factors.

The effects do not take place instantaneously, but over a period of time. These 'build-up' effects cause periods of expansion (or contraction) in the economy.

Q45. *Yes.* All except (d).

Q46. *more.*

Q47. *dampened.*

Q48. *True.* This is known as the efficiency wage argument.

Q49. Because there would be additional costs to employers from employing outsiders, including training costs and the costs of demotivating the insiders. Also insiders may be members of unions who might be able to push their wage rates above market rates. Alternatively, insiders may simply have power and influence within the firm, as a result of having become established members of staff. For these reasons, firms may be willing to pay insiders more, rather than attempting to bring in outsiders.

Q50. (a) *No*; (b) *Yes*; (c) *Yes*; (d) *No*. Supply-side policies are needed to tackle the supply-side problems that have been caused by previous recessions.

Q51. *False.* Keynesians tend to argue that free markets will not offer sufficient incentives to cure this problem.

They will fail to encourage sufficient people to retrain or move to where employment might be found.

Q52. Two reasons are: rising demand makes firms more confident about their future sales and encourages them to invest and consider expanding their labour force; if existing rates of unemployment include a high level of long-term unemployed or those unemployed due to structural change, the inflationary impact of their employment and retraining may be offset in the long run by higher levels of productivity.

Q53. *True.* Leaving things to the market is seen by modern Keynesians as a slow and highly ineffective way to deal with economic problems such as unemployment.

Q54. B.

Q55. *False.* This would be the view of the new classical economists, but many Keynesian economists would hold that changes in aggregate demand, if steady, will have effects on output and employment in the long term through changes in investment and thus in potential output.

Q56. *True.* Although they may not agree on what those effects would be!

Chapter 22

Long-term Economic Growth

 A ▶ **REVIEW**

If an economy is to achieve sustained economic growth over the longer term, there must be a sustained increase in potential output. This means that there has to be a continuous rightward shift in the aggregate supply curve. This chapter examines the determinants of long-term economic growth.

22.1 Long-run economic growth in industrialised countries

(Pages 671–3)

Although industrialised countries experienced recessions in the early 1980s, the early 1990s and the early and late 2000s, most developed countries have averaged rates of economic growth of **Q1.** *between 0 and 2 per cent/2 and 4 per cent/over 4 per cent* per annum over the past 50 years. The fluctuations in output in this period appear **Q2.** *minor/ substantial* compared with the long-term growth in output. Such growth **Q3.** *can/cannot* be explained by a closing of the gap between actual and potential output.

Q4. Which of the following stylised facts about economic growth are valid?

(a) In general, the richer developed countries have grown at a slower rate than the less rich ones in recent years.
Yes/No

(b) As a result, the gap in living standards amongst the industrialised countries has narrowed.   *Yes/No*

(c) This convergence in average incomes is also evident globally, with countries in sub-Saharan Africa beginning to close the gap on more developed countries.
Yes/No

(d) Economic growth has been a continuous process spanning the past 2000 years.   *Yes/No*

(e) Economic growth has only been significant once countries have undergone an industrial revolution.
Yes/No

Q5. As richer countries have grown at a slower rate than less rich ones, there has been a process of convergence taking place around the world.   *True/False*

Q6. If an economy were to grow steadily at an annual rate of 5 per cent, how long would it take for it to double in size?

....

Q7. Which of the following are major explanations of this sustained economic growth?

(a) A closing of the gap between actual and potential output.   *Yes/No*

(b) Increases in labour productivity.   *Yes/No*

(c) Technological progress.   *Yes/No*

(d) Sustained increases in the capital stock.   *Yes/No*

(e) Reductions in unemployment.   *Yes/No*

(f) Increases in human capital.   *Yes/No*

22.2 Economic growth without technological progress

(Pages 673–8) We begin an analysis of economic growth by considering the effects of an increase in the rate of capital investment when there is no change in technology.

An increase in capital per worker will generally **Q8.** *increase/decrease* output, but to increase capital requires **Q9.** *consumption/investment* expenditure, which in turn requires resources that could have been used for producing **Q10.** *consumer/investment* goods.

(?) **Q11.** What is the opportunity cost of investment?

....

⊖ **Q12.** Figure 22.1 shows a simple model of economic growth. Assume that the economy currently has a capital stock of K_0.

(a) What is the level of total investment?

....

(b) What is the level of net investment?

....

(c) What is the current level of national income?

....

(d) Explain the process whereby national income increases.

....

....

(e) Will national income go on rising for ever? Explain.

....

(f) Now assume that there is an increase in the rate of saving and hence investment. Illustrate the effect on Figure 22.1.

....

(g) Why will national income not go on rising for ever as a result of this higher rate of investment?

....

Capital intensity (the amount of capital per person employed) is an important component of many economic growth models. We would expect that the higher the capital intensity, the

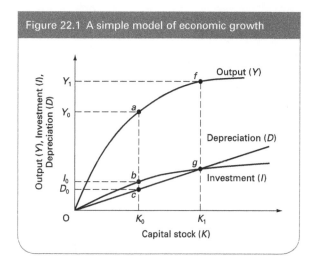

Figure 22.1 A simple model of economic growth

Q13. *greater/lower* would be the level of output per worker. Capital intensity in the UK increased between 1960 and 2012 by a factor of **Q14.** *1.5/2.3/6.5.*

(▤) **Q15.** Given that an increase in saving means a reduction in current consumption, and has a declining effect in terms of extra long-term output, economists have developed the concept of a 'golden-rule saving rate'. This can be defined as the rate of saving that leads to:

A. the maximum level of output.
B. the maximum rate of growth.
C. the maximum level of consumption.
D. the minimum rate of depreciation.
E. the maximum level of investment.

(◗) **Q16.** In the simple Solow model:

(a) As capital stock increases, so output increases, but at a diminishing rate because of the law of diminishing returns. *Yes/No*
(b) There is no depreciation. *Yes/No*
(c) A permanent increase in the saving rate will lead to a higher equilibrium level of real national income, but not to a rise in the long-term growth rate. *Yes/No*
(d) An increase in human capital increases the steady-state level of real national income. *Yes/No*

22.3 Economic growth with technological progress

(Pages 678–83) Technological progress has the effect of increasing the output from a given amount of investment. Technological progress thus needs to be incorporated into the growth model.

(◗) **Q17.** An increase in technological progress is the main condition for achieving a faster rate of economic growth. *True/False*

⊖ **Q18.** Use Figure 22.1 to show the effect of a one-off technological advance.

Q19. An economy is experiencing continuing technological progress through time. Figure 22.2 shows the steady-state growth path.

(a) On Figure 22.2, show the effect of an increase in the saving rate at time t_1 on the steady-state growth path and the actual path followed by the economy.

(b) If the increase in the saving rate is sustained, does this result in an increase in the long-term growth rate?

....

....

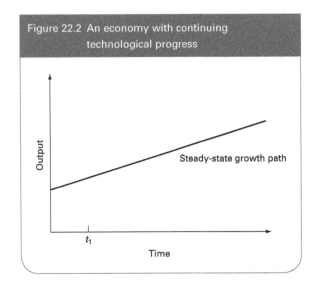

Figure 22.2 An economy with continuing technological progress

Q20. Which of the following can affect the long-run rate of economic growth?

(a) An increase in the rate of saving. *Yes/No*

(b) Devoting more resources to research and development. *Yes/No*

(c) Investment in human capital by providing more education and training. *Yes/No*

(d) Improving the rate at which new technology is disseminated. *Yes/No*

Q21. According to endogenous growth theory:

A. increases in aggregate supply depend on increases in aggregate demand.

B. the rate of technological progress depends purely on developments in science and engineering which, in turn, depend on random inventions and discoveries.

C. economic growth can only be a temporary phenomenon caused by 'one-off' discoveries.

D. the rate of technological progress and diffusion can be increased by appropriate incentives and government policies.

E. a faster rate of economic growth is likely to lead to a lower rate of technological progress.

Q22. In a model of endogenous growth, it is argued that investment is composed of two elements, I_c (investment in capital that uses current technology) and I_n (investment in research and development of new technology). Identify the effect on the growth path of the following:

(a) An increase in I_n relative to I_c.

....

(b) An increase in the responsiveness of output to an increase in I_n.

....

(c) The provision of tax incentives to encourage I_n.

....

(d) An increase in competition between firms over the development of new products.

....

(e) An increase in the popularity of engineering as a subject to study at university.

....

(f) Improved dissemination of information about new technology.

....

Q23. The following are common ways of measuring productivity:

(i) output per person working.

(ii) output per hour worked.

(iii) output per person in the workforce.

(iv) total factor productivity.

Match each of the following with one of the above measures.

(a) The average number of hours worked can vary significantly between countries: for example, UK full-time employees typically work longer hours than those in France or Germany.

(b) It is important to recognise that productivity depends upon the efficiency in use of both labour and capital.

(c) It is useful to have a measure that is straightforward to calculate.

(d) There are differences between countries in unemployment and participation rates.

Q24. Which of the following help to influence the rate of growth of productivity?

(a) Private investment in new physical capital and in R&D. *Yes/No*

(b) Public investment in education, R&D and infrastructure. *Yes/No*

(c) Training and the development of labour skills. *Yes/No*

(d) Innovation and the application of new technology. *Yes/No*

(e) The organisation and management of factors of production. *Yes/No*

(f) The rate of entry of new firms into market. *Yes/No*

(g) The competitive business environment in which firms operate. *Yes/No*

 Q25. Which of the following statements apply to the neoclassical growth model, and which to endogenous growth models?

(a) Without technological progress, the economy will reach a steady-state where economic growth slows to the rate at which labour input is growing.

endogenous/neoclassical

(b) No policy prescriptions are offered.

endogenous/neoclassical

(c) Technological advancement is explicitly modelled.

endogenous/neoclassical

(d) Policy prescriptions are offered.

endogenous/neoclassical

B PROBLEMS, EXERCISES AND PROJECTS

Q26. In small groups, find some data on economic growth in a number of industrialised countries over the past 50 years and investigate whether average income levels have tended to converge. You will need to think about how to measure convergence. A useful source is OECD (www.oecd.org).

Q27. With reference to recent Budget statements, investigate whether the government has introduced or updated measures designed to influence long-run economic growth: for example, tax incentives to encourage research and development.

C DISCUSSION TOPICS AND ESSAYS

Q28. Discuss whether industrialised countries will eventually all converge on the same steady state. What factors might prevent this from happening?

Q29. Under what circumstances will an increase in the rate of saving lead to a faster rate of *long-term* economic growth?

Q30. What do you understand by 'endogenous growth theory'? What implications does the theory have for a

government wishing to achieve a more rapid rate of long-term economic growth?

Q31. Discuss how differences in education and training levels between countries may affect their relative growth rates.

Q32. **Debate**
Increased university tuition fees will lead to more rapid long-term growth by enabling improved education of engineers, scientists and economists.

D ANSWERS

Q1. *Between 2 and 4 per cent* per annum. For example, the average annual percentage growth rate in the UK between 1961 and 2012 was 2.3 per cent. For the USA it was 3.1 per cent, whilst Japan registered 4.1 per cent.

Q2. *minor.*

Q3. *cannot*: Over this period, the economic capacity of countries increased.

Q4. *(a)* *Yes.* This has been a feature of recent years, although the growth performance of the industrialised countries has been very mixed.

(b) *Yes.* It is valid to argue that the gap in living standards has narrowed, if we take a long view of the process.

(c) *No.* Regrettably countries in sub-Saharan Africa have not shared in the process of development and growth, and have experienced virtually static (or even falling) output per head.

(d) *No.* Economic growth is a relatively recent phenomenon.

(e) *Yes.* It does seem that an industrial revolution has been an important ingredient of economic growth.

Q5. *False.* Although some countries such as China, India and various other Asian countries have grown very rapidly, there are many others (especially in sub-Saharan Africa) that have not.

Q6. 14.2 years.

Q7. *Yes*: (b), (c), (d) and (f). These all help to explain the rightward shifts in the aggregate supply curve. In the case of (a), closing the gap between actual and potential output has not taken place, and even if it had, would be insignificant over the long run compared with increases in potential output. In the case of (e), reductions in unemployment have not occurred, except in the last few years, and do not help to explain long-term growth.

Q8. *increase.*

Q9. *investment.*

Q10. *consumer.*

Q11. The opportunity cost of investment is the consumer goods that could have been produced, but which must be forgone in order for investment to take place.

Q12. *(a)* I_0 (point *b*).

(b) $I_0 - D_0$ (points *b* – *c*). D_0 has to be subtracted for capital depreciation.

(c) Y_0.

(d) The net investment of $I_0 - D_0$ leads to an expansion of the capital stock and hence a rise in national income. As national income rises, however, diminishing returns to capital take place (the *Y* and *I* curves get less and less steep). Eventually all the new investment is taken up with replacing worn-out capital (it all goes on depreciation) and national income stops rising. A steady state has been reached at Y_1 and K_1.

(e) No (see answer to (d)).

(f) The *I* line will shift upwards and a new equilibrium will be reached where it crosses the *D* line.

(g) Because all the extra investment will be eventually absorbed by depreciation (see answer to (d)).

Q13. *greater.*

Q14. 2.3.

Q15. C (see Figure 22.4 on page 675 in Sloman, *Economics*, (this edition)).

Q16. *(a)* *Yes.*

(b) *No*: depreciation is included in the model.

(c) *Yes.*

(d) *Yes.*

Q17. *True.*

Q18. The *Y* line will shift upwards and there will be a corresponding upward shift in the *I* line. If it is a 'one-off' technological advance, rather than progress that goes on building over several years, there will be a single upward shift in the *Y* and *I* curves and a 'one-off' increase in national income. The new equilibrium national income will correspond to the level of capital stock where the new *I* line crosses the *D* line.

Q19. *(a)* See Figure A22.1. The dotted line represents the new steady-state growth path, and the continuous line shows the adjustment towards the new steady state.

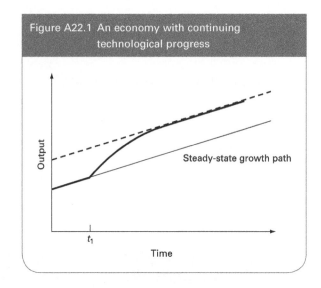

Figure A22.1 An economy with continuing technological progress

(b) *No*: the economy converges to a new steady-state path – but although the *level* of output has increased, the growth rate is as it was – reflecting the rate of technological progress.

Q20. *(a)* *No*: an increase in saving leads to a new *level* of aggregate output, but not to a higher growth rate unless the saving is used in such a way as to lead to a higher rate of technological progress.

(b) *Yes*: more research and development can lead to a higher rate of technological progress.

(c) *No*: an increase in human capital leads to a higher level of national income, not to an increase in the long-run rate of economic growth – but again, if the higher human capital allows a more rapid rate of technological progress, then it could affect the growth rate.

(d) *Yes*: if new technology spreads more rapidly through the economy, then this could affect the rate of growth.

Q21. D. It is important for the government to create the right climate (through appropriate supply-side policies) to encourage more research and development and a correspondingly faster rate of technological progress and hence economic growth.

Q22. *(a)* An increase in I_n (investment in research and development) relative to I_c (investment in current technology) will shift the growth path upwards, and make the steady-state growth path steeper.

(b) The more responsive output is to an increase in I_n, the steeper will be the steady-state growth path.

(c) The provision of tax incentives to encourage I_n should thus lead to a steeper steady-state growth path.

(d) If firms compete in the development of new products, this should also steepen the steady-state growth path by accelerating the pace of technological change.

(e) If engineering becomes more popular as a subject of study at university, this should enable more rapid technological change, provided that these new engineers continue in the profession, and firms hire them.

(f) The more rapidly information about new technology can be disseminated, the more rapidly will firms be able to adopt best practice techniques, again enabling a steeper steady-state growth path to be reached more quickly.

Q23. *(a)* (ii)
   (b) (iv)
   (c) (i)
   (d) (iii)

Q24. *(a)–(g)*: *Yes*: all of these factors help to influence the rate of growth of productivity.

Q25. (a) and (b) relate to the neoclassical model, whereas (c) and (d) apply to endogenous growth models.

Chapter 23

Supply-side Policies

 REVIEW

We saw in the previous chapter that long-term economic growth entails an increase in aggregate supply, which in turn requires an increase in productivity. In this chapter we look at various policies to increase aggregate supply and examine how developments on the supply side can affect the other macroeconomic objectives of achieving low unemployment and low inflation.

23.1 Supply-side policies and the macroeconomy

(Pages 685) Given the importance of achieving sustainable economic growth, governments in many countries across the world have increasingly focused on supply-side policies designed to increase the productive capacity of their economies by influencing aggregate supply.

(?) **Q1.** Define supply-side policies

....

(≣) **Q2.** In endogenous growth models, which one of the following factors cannot influence technological progress?
A. The size and composition of the capital stock.
B. Investment in research and development.
C. Externality effects, as there are knowledge spillovers between firms.
D. The use of patents and copyrights.
E. Hours worked per worker.

(≣) **Q3.** In the context of endogenous growth models, which of the following is not a suggested focus for a supply-side policy to encourage faster economic growth?

A. Education and training.
B. Research and development.
C. Industrial organisation.
D. Labour force growth.
E. Hours worked per worker.

(◑) **Q4.** Supply-side policies are exclusively concerned with promoting technological progress. *True/False*

It is important to distinguish clearly between policies that affect the supply side of the economy and those that operate on the demand side.

(◑) **Q5.** Which of the following measures to cure unemployment would we call supply-side and which demand-side solutions, and which have elements of both?
(a) The encouragement of pay restraint to keep costs down by preventing excessive wage increases.
Supply-side/Demand-side/Both
(b) The launch of a new government training programme for school leavers. *Supply-side/Demand-side/Both*
(c) A new computer network is set up to provide more detailed national information at job centres on vacancies. *Supply-side/Demand-side/Both*
(d) A government investment programme targeted on key growth industries. *Supply-side/Demand-side/Both*

 Multiple choice   Written answer   Delete wrong word   ⊖ Diagram/table manipulation   ⊗ Calculation   Matching/ordering

(e) Income tax is cut by 2p in the pound.

Supply-side/Demand-side/Both

(f) Lower interest rates to prevent the exchange rate appreciating. *Supply-side/Demand-side/Both*

Q6. Figure 23.1 shows an economy before and after a successful supply-side policy. The aggregate demand curve begins at AD_0.

(a) Identify the equilibrium position before the policy.

A/B/C/D

(b) Identify the equilibrium position after the policy.

A/B/C/D

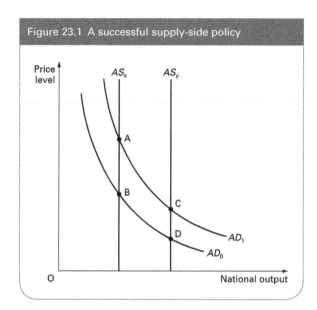

Figure 23.1 A successful supply-side policy

Q7. What effect will successful supply-side measures have on the following curves?

(a) The production possibility curve.

Outward shift/Inward shift/Movement along

(b) The aggregate supply curve.

Rightward shift/Leftward shift/Movement up along/Movement down along

(c) The aggregate demand curve.

Rightward shift/Leftward shift/Movement up along/Movement down along

(d) The Phillips curve.

Rightward shift/Leftward shift/Movement up along/Movement down along

(e) The withdrawals curve in the Keynesian 45° line diagram.

Upward shift/Downward shift/No shift in

(f) The injections 'curve' in the Keynesian 45° line diagram.

Upward shift/Downward shift/No shift in

(g) The full-employment level of income in the Keynesian 45° line diagram.

Rightward shift/Leftward shift/No shift in

Q8. List three supply-side policies which might be used to achieve the effect on the production possibility curve in Q7 (a) above.

1. ....

2. ....

3. ....

23.2 Approaches to supply-side policies

(Pages 686–7) The Keynesian and new classical schools of thought adopt differing positions in regard to supply-side policies, debating whether they should be interventionist or market-oriented.

Q9. Monetarists and new classical economists argue that there is a clear distinction between demand-side and supply-side policy. Which of the following would be maintained by such economists?

(a) In the long run, demand-side policy is suitable only for tackling inflation. *True/False*

(b) In the long run, only supply-side policy will reduce unemployment and increase output. *True/False*

(c) Supply-side policies will help to shift the Phillips curve to the right by reducing the natural rate of unemployment. *True/False*

(d) Supply-side policies should aim to make markets freer.

True/False

Keynesian arguments concerning the nature and role of demand-side and supply-side policies differ considerably from those of the new classical economists. Keynesians argue that demand-side policies **Q10.** *can/cannot* cause increase in output and employment. They also argue that, on their own, supply-side policies **Q11.** *can/cannot* lead to increases in output and employment *and* a reduction in inflation.

Q12. Keynesians maintain that supply-side policies can reduce the need for deflationary demand-side policies.

True/False

Q13. 'Third way' supply-side policies aim to help people to help themselves. Such policies involve a mixture of government support and market incentives. *True/False*

Q14. Some policies can have both demand-side and supply-side effects. *True/False*

23.3 Market-orientated supply-side policies

(Pages 687–8) The main emphasis of the supply-side policies of the UK, the USA and many other countries in the 1980s was on the liberation of market forces.

Q15. Which one of the following supply-side policies was not used in the UK in the 1980s?

A. Controls on both public- and private-sector prices and incomes to prevent inflation.

B. Deregulation and privatisation of British industry.

C. Attempts to reduce the PSNCR.

D. Regional grants to encourage industrial relocation.

E. Limiting the automatic entitlement to certain welfare benefits.

(Page 688) Reducing government expenditure.

(?) **Q16.** List four supply-side measures adopted by the UK government during the 1980s designed to reduce public expenditure.

1. ....

2. ....

3. ....

4. ....

(≣) **Q17.** Reducing the level of government expenditure, while at the same time adopting a tight monetary policy to reduce inflation, proved to be difficult. Which one of the following help to explain why this was so?

A. The government also wanted to cut taxes.

B. Reducing the PSNCR was itself inflationary.

C. Reducing the PSNCR increased the money supply.

D. Statutory reserve ratios for banks had been abolished.

E. The deflationary monetary policy triggered automatic fiscal stabilisers.

After the financial crisis and global slowdown of the late 2000s, many governments found themselves with high levels of public debt, and faced difficult choices in reducing expenditure, particularly concerning the level of services and the provision of infrastructure.

(Pages 688–90) Tax cuts

(◗) **Q18.** Cuts in the marginal rate of income tax are claimed to have various beneficial supply-side effects. These are:

(a) People work longer hours because the substitution effect from cutting the marginal rate of income tax is less than the income effect. *True/False*

(b) More people wish to work. *True/False*

(c) People work more enthusiastically. *True/False*

(d) Both equilibrium and disequilibrium unemployment fall even when wage rates are inflexible downwards. *True/False*

(e) Employment rises. *True/False*

(?) **Q19.** Comment on the incentive effects for (a) employers and (b) workers of a cut in the rate of income tax.

....

....

(≣) **Q20.** Which of the following are market-oriented supply policies designed to encourage investment?

 (i) Cuts in corporation tax.

 (ii) Grants awarded to firms in a certain industry.

 (iii) Increases in investment allowances.

 (iv) Increased ability to offset R&D expenditure against corporation tax.

A. (i) only.

B. (i) and (ii)

C. (i), (ii) and (iv)

D. (i), (iii) and (iv).

E. (i), (ii), (iii) and (iv).

(Pages 690–1) Reducing the power of labour

(◗) **Q21.** If the government succeeds in reducing the power of labour, equilibrium unemployment may well rise.

True/False

(⊖) **Q22.** Figure 23.2 shows an aggregate labour market. N is the total labour force; AS_L is the effective demand for labour; AD_L is the aggregate demand for labour. Assume that wages are fixed above the equilibrium at a rate of W_1.

(a) Mark on the diagram the levels of equilibrium and disequilibrium unemployment.

(b) Now assume that the government reduces union power, so that wages are freely set by forces of demand and supply. Mark the new wage rate and the resulting levels of equilibrium and disequilibrium unemployment.

(c) Now assume that the effect of reducing wages is to reduce the level of consumer expenditure. Illustrate the effect of this on aggregate demand.

(d) Illustrate the effect of this on employment (both equilibrium and disequilibrium), assuming that the wage rate is no longer flexible downwards below that in (b) above.

(e) Returning to (c) above, illustrate the effect of this on unemployment (both equilibrium and disequilibrium), assuming that the wage rate continues to be flexible downwards.

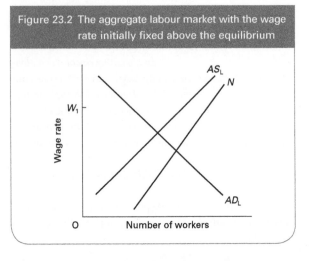

Figure 23.2 The aggregate labour market with the wage rate initially fixed above the equilibrium

Q23. The disequilibrium unemployment in Q22(d) above is of which type?

....

(Pages 691–3) Reducing welfare
Monetarists argue that a **Q24.** *small/large* difference between wages and welfare benefits will cause a high level of **Q25.** *frictional/structural* unemployment. The extra income that an individual would receive from taking employment would be small. We would say these individuals are caught in a **Q26.** *poverty/unemployment* trap. If the level of benefits were cut, the effective labour supply curve (*AS*_L) would shift to the **Q27.** *left/right*.

(Pages 693–5) Encouraging competition
(?) Q28. List three policies favoured by the Thatcher and Major governments as means of encouraging competition.

1. ....

2. ....

3. ....

Q29. The Conservatives and Liberal Democrats criticised the Private Finance Initiative when in opposition, and abandoned it immediately after coming to power.
True/False

Q30. Following the financial crisis of the late 2000s, many workers saw real wage rates fall, which helped to limit the rise in equilibrium unemployment. This was driven by greater labour market flexibility brought about through supply-side reforms. *True/False/Unproven*

23.4 Interventionist supply-side policy
(Pages 695–703) The market has some limitations in stimulating supply-side improvements, but there may be ways in which the government can intervene to encourage investment and economic growth.

Q31. Industrial policy is a set of measures designed to encourage industrial investment and greater industrial efficiency. *True/False*

Q32. Gross fixed capital formation as a percentage of GDP increased substantially in the UK between 1971–91 and 1992–2012. *True/False*

Q33. During the 2000s, the pattern of investment finance seemed to be changing, and one feature of the financial crisis was a dramatic decline in funds for investment.
True/False

(?) Q34. Give four arguments why the free market might lead to a sub-optimal level of investment.

1. ....

2. ....

3. ....

4. ....

Q35. Which of the following could be classified as *interventionist* supply-side policy?
(a) Government provision of infrastructure. *Yes/No*
(b) Privatisation. *Yes/No*
(c) Investment grants for private firms. *Yes/No*
(d) A reduction in corporation tax. *Yes/No*
(e) Government-funded workplace training schemes.
Yes/No

The most extreme form of interventionist supply-side policy is national economic planning.

Q36. Which of the following describes *indicative* planning?
A. A type of planning undertaken by a group of countries acting together.
B. Commands issued to different sectors of the economy to produce targeted amounts of output.
C. Consultation between government, business and unions in order to co-ordinate their policies and plans.
D. Government intervention in the operation of markets for short periods of time.
E. The nationalisation of large sections of the economy.

Q37. Although governments in most industrialised countries do not engage in national economic planning, virtually all intervene selectively in order to bring supply-side improvements. *True/False*

Private-sector research and development (R&D) is generally **Q38.** *higher/lower* in the UK than in other major industrialised countries, which has led to a productivity gap between the UK and other G7 countries which is beginning to **Q39.** *narrow/widen*.

(?) Q40. Give three arguments against interventionist industrial policy.

1. ....

2. ....

3. ....

Q41. Many advanced countries have adopted a new approach to industrial policy, focusing on improving those factors that shape a nation's competitiveness. Which one of the following would *not* figure as part of this approach?

A. The promotion of investment in physical and human capital.

B. Increases in employers' social security and pension contributions.

C. The promotion of innovation and encouragement of greater levels of research and development.

D. Support for small and medium-sized enterprises.

E. Improvement of infrastructure, including physical transport and information highways.

(Pages 701–3) There are significant regional and local disparities in the UK economy, many of which grew over the 1980s but then narrowed in the recession of the early 1990s.

 Q42. If market prices were perfectly flexible, and there were perfect factor mobility:

(a) There would be no specifically regional or local unemployment problem. *True/False*

(b) There would be no problem of regional or local inequality of wage rates for given occupations.
True/False

 Q43. If market prices were perfectly flexible, but there was significant factor immobility:

(a) There would be no specifically regional or local unemployment problem. *True/False*

(b) There would be no problem of regional or local inequality. *True/False*

 Q44. Regional multiplier effects:

(a) add to migration effects into more prosperous regions through the creation of additional jobs in response to higher demand. *True/False*

(b) add to migration effects out of depressed regions as loss of jobs in (say) manufacturing leads to lower demand for local service sectors. *True/False*

 Q45. Which of the following regional or urban policies would be classified as being market-oriented and which as interventionist?

(a) The offering of local facilities and improvement of local infrastructure for potential new business.
Market-oriented/Interventionist

(b) The migration of labour should be encouraged by the reduction of benefit levels.
Market-oriented/Interventionist

(c) Government should move some of its own activities into depressed areas. *Market-oriented/Interventionist*

(d) Nationally negotiated wage agreements should be replaced by locally negotiated ones.
Market-oriented/Interventionist

(e) The provision of a range of local subsidies and grants to firms. *Market-oriented/Interventionist*

B PROBLEMS, EXERCISES AND PROJECTS

Q46. Figure 23.3 illustrates the effect of a tax cut on the level of employment. N is the total labour force; AS_L is the effective aggregate supply of labour; AD_L is the aggregate demand for labour.

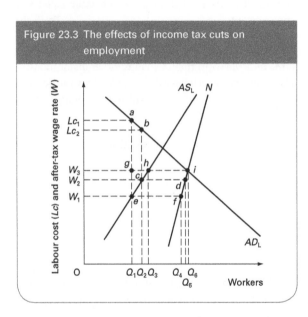

Figure 23.3 The effects of income tax cuts on employment

(a) Assume that Q_1 represents an equilibrium in the labour market, and that labour supply depends on the after-tax wage rate (W), whereas the demand for labour depends on unit labour costs: the pre-tax wage rate (Lc). What is the average level of income tax per worker?

....

(b) With employment at Q_1, what is the level of *equilibrium unemployment*?

....

(c) Assume now that income tax falls to $b - c$. What is the new unit labour cost to firms (pre-tax wage), assuming that wage rates are flexible?

....

(d) How many workers will now be employed?

....

(e) Has equilibrium unemployment risen or fallen?
Risen/Fallen

Q47. Referring still to Figure 23.3, assume now that (pre-tax) wage rates are inflexible downwards.

(a) Still assuming a cut in income tax to $b - c$: if the pre-tax wage rate did not fall, but instead the after-tax wage rate rose to W_1 (i.e. $a - g = b - c$), how many workers would be willing to work at this wage now?

....

(b) What would be the level of disequilibrium unemployment?

....

(c) What would be the level of equilibrium unemployment?

....

(d) Has total unemployment risen or fallen as a result of the tax cut, given that the pre-tax wage rate is not flexible downwards? *Risen/Fallen*

Q48. Either individually or in small groups, write a report on the changing geographical and social pattern of inequality in the UK (or some other country of your choice) since 1980.

Identify a range of economic and social inequalities and comment upon their growing (or declining) significance. Your report should include some assessment of whether these inequalities are likely to widen or narrow in the future. It should also review the main policies that might be adopted in order to remove or narrow such imbalances.

Sources of UK data for this question include *Social Trends* (NS) and *Regional Trends* (NS), which can be downloaded from the National Statistics website at http://www.statistics.gov.uk.

DISCUSSION TOPICS AND ESSAYS

Q49. Describe how Keynesian and new classical approaches to supply-side policy differ. Illustrate this difference with reference to policies concerned with reducing unemployment and inflation.

Q50. Has there been a supply-side 'miracle' in the UK?

Q51. Outline the main supply-side policies introduced by the Thatcher and Major governments. Does the evidence suggest that they achieved what they set out to do?

Q52. In what ways did the supply-side policies of the Blair government differ from those of the previous Conservative governments? Provide a comparative critique of the two sets of policies.

Q53. What normative objections and justifications can be put forward to criticise and support market-orientated supply-side policies?

Q54. What do you understand by the term 'deindustrialisation'? What arguments have been advanced to explain

the UK's experience of this phenomenon? What are the economic arguments for and against attempting to reverse the process? Consider the relative merits of alternative policies for reversing the process.

Q55. Given large regional and local variations in economic prosperity and economic performance, what problems might occur in using a free-market policy to rectify such imbalances?

Q56. To what extent is it possible for a government to make a significant impact on urban deprivation without spending considerable sums of money?

Q57. Discuss the importance of maintaining supply-side policies at a time when the budget deficit needs to be reduced.

Q58. Debate
If supply-side policy is to be successful in achieving more rapid economic growth, it must inevitably lead to greater inequality.

ANSWERS

Q1. Supply-side policies are government policies that attempt to influence aggregate supply directly, rather than through aggregate demand.

Q2. E.

Q3. D.

Q4. *False.* Supply-side policies can also be directed at other macroeconomic objectives, such as reducing some types of unemployment, improving the flexibility

of labour markets, encouraging competition, dealing with cost-push inflation, and so on.

Q5. (a), (b) and (c) are supply-side solutions. (f) is a demand-side solution. (d) and (e) can have an effect upon both the demand side and the supply side. In the case of (d), investment will stimulate aggregate demand, but it will also increase potential output and/or reduce costs by increasing the capital stock, especially if investment is targeted on key growth industries or to bottleneck sectors. In the case of (e), tax cuts, as well as stimulating aggregate demand, will also offer an incentive for workers to work (assuming the substitution effect outweighs the income effect). In the case of (f), lower interest rates will increase demand generally, and a lower exchange rate will increase the demand for exports at existing *sterling* prices. A lower exchange rate, however, will *not* reduce costs.

Q6. (a) B.

(b) D.

Q7. (a) *Outward shift*.

(b) *Rightward shift*.

(c) *Movement down along* (caused by the rightward shift in the aggregate supply curve).

(d) *Leftward shift* and/or *Movement down along*. The leftward shift would result from a lower equilibrium level of unemployment. The movement down along would result from increased output from a given quantity of labour, and thus less employment for any given level of real aggregate demand.

(e) *No shift in* (except as a side-effect: e.g. tax cuts to provide greater incentives would, *ceteris paribus*, shift the withdrawals curve downwards).

(f) *No shift in* (except as a side-effect: e.g. incentives for firms to conduct research and development or training may lead to an increase in net investment and hence a vertical shift upwards in the injections line).

(g) *Rightward shift*.

Q8. Three supply-side policies that could be used to push the production possibility curve outward are: incentives to encourage investment; the expansion of labour training programmes; the use of taxation policy to encourage more people to work or the same people to work harder.

Q9. (a) *True*. Demand-side policy for the monetarist is monetary policy which should be directed to the control of inflation. Given a long-run vertical Phillips curve, demand-side policy cannot be used to control long-run output and unemployment.

(b) *True*. In the long run only by shifting the natural rate of unemployment to the left will unemployment fall, or by shifting the production possibility curve outward will output rise.

(c) *False*. If supply-side policy causes the natural rate of unemployment to fall, the Phillips curve will shift to the *left*.

(d) *True*. Free-market philosophy dominates the monetarist view of supply-side policy.

Q10. *can*.

Q11. *can*. With an upward-sloping aggregate supply curve, a rightward shift in the curve will both reduce prices and increase output. With a downward-sloping Phillips

curve, a leftward shift in the curve can lead to lower unemployment and lower inflation too.

Q12. *True*. If supply-side policies can reduce inflation, there is less need for deflationary policies and the attendant problems of higher unemployment.

Q13. *True*. An example is the use of a mixture of tax incentives and the provision of training to encourage unemployed people to take up unemployment.

Q14. *True*. For example, a supply-side policy to cut taxes in order to improve incentives will also have an effect on aggregate demand. Similarly, a demand-side policy that leads to an increase in investment expenditure will boost the economy's productive potential and thus have an effect on aggregate supply.

Q15. A. Prices and incomes policy was not used during the 1980s. In the case of D, regional grants were used but were substantially reduced compared with previous periods.

Q16. Examples included: cash limits on government departments; reductions in grants and subsidies to private industry; reductions in central government grants to local authorities as a proportion of local authority revenue; reductions in public-sector capital projects; cuts in the size of the civil service; tough stance on public-sector pay; reductions in the amount of government support given to nationalised industries; rate capping of local authorities; privatisation.

Q17. E. As the deflationary monetary policy led to increased unemployment, so the expenditure on unemployment and other social security benefits increased. (In the case of A, the desire to cut taxes would further stimulate the need to cut government expenditure; in the case of B and C, reducing the PSNCR tends to lead to *reductions* in the money supply; in the case of D, this had no direct effect on government expenditure.)

Q18. (a) *False*. The supposed beneficial effect is that the tax cut will act as an incentive for workers to work more. This will occur only if the substitution effect (substituting work for leisure) is *larger* than the income effect (being able to afford to work less).

(b) *True*. Lower tax rates are seen as a work incentive to those who are not the main income earners: for example, parents looking after children.

(c) *Unsure*. This is very difficult to prove or disprove. The argument is that people will be prepared to put more effort into their work if they can keep more of their pay.

(d) *False*. If tax rates are cut, take-home pay will increase, and thus it becomes more worthwhile for unemployed people to accept job offers. The level of *equilibrium* unemployment will fall. However, if (pre-tax) wage rates are sticky downwards, firms will not be willing to take on the extra supply of labour. Thus *disequilibrium* unemployment will *rise*.

(e) *True.* Provided the increased supply of labour has some downward effect on *pre-tax* wages, firms will take on extra labour.

Q19. Employers face a lower total labour cost per worker, and are thus prepared to demand more labour. More people join the labour force at the higher after-tax wage, and more accept jobs. There is likely to be a reduction in unemployment because more additional workers accept jobs than join the labour force – i.e. N is steeper than AS_L (see Figure 23.2).

Q20. D. Grants awarded to firms in a specific industry would be categorised as an interventionist policy, not market-oriented.

Q21. *True.* As union power is reduced, wages will fall, leading to a fall in the incentive to find employment. (Note, however, that disequilibrium unemployment will fall.)

Q22. The following answers refer to Figure A23.1:

(a) Equilibrium unemployment equals $c - b$.
Disequilibrium unemployment equals $b - a$.

(b) Wage equals W_2.
Equilibrium unemployment equals $e - d$.
There is no disequilibrium unemployment.

(c) The aggregate demand for labour shifts to the left (e.g. to AD_{L_2}).

(d) Equilibrium unemployment equals $e - d$.
Disequilibrium unemployment equals $d - f$.

(e) Assuming no further fall in AD_L, the wage rate will fall to W_3.

There will be no disequilibrium unemployment, but equilibrium unemployment will now be $h - g$. (In practice, there may be a further fall in consumer demand – given a further redistribution away from wages to profits – and thus there will be a further leftward movement in AD_L. If there is any sluggishness downwards in wages, further disequilibrium unemployment will occur.)

Q23. Demand deficient.

Q24. *small.*

Q25. *frictional.*

Q26. *poverty.*

Q27. *right.* (More people would feel forced to look for a job.)

Q28. Examples include: privatisation; deregulation (e.g. financial markets and the bus industry); introducing market relationships into parts of the public sector, such as health and education; removing barriers to trade and international capital movements.

Q29. *False.* Although they criticised it when in opposition, when it came to power the Coalition government saw an important role for the PFI given its commitment to reducing the budget deficit and the consequent reluctance to fund public-sector investment directly.

Q30. *unproven.* The supply-side reforms may have contributed, but the rise in equilibrium unemployment may also have been limited by the fall in aggregate demand and by economic uncertainty.

Q31. *True.*

Q32. *False.* Gross fixed capital formation fell over this period – general government investment fell from 3.0 per cent to 1.7 per cent, and in the private sector it fell from 16.6 per cent to 15.4 per cent. See Table 23.1 on page 696 in Sloman, *Economics* (this edition).

Q33. *True.*

Q34. Reasons include: many markets are monopolistic (this removes some of the incentive for investment); firms may only be interested in short-term profits; investment might appear too risky, especially if the free market is subject to cyclical fluctuations; investment decisions by private firms may not take into account the social rate of return (e.g. the full benefits from the training of labour); financial institutions may be unwilling to finance long-term investment.

Q35. (a), (c) and (e).

Q36. C. The key feature of indicative planning is one of consultation. Targets and goals are agreed upon between government, firms and possibly unions, and become the basis of a national plan.

Q37. *True.* Examples include: government-financed training schemes, financing research and development, providing assistance to small firms, increasing expenditure on infrastructure projects as a means of increasing national productivity.

Q38. *lower.*

Q39. *narrow.* Only Swiss companies increased R&D at a faster rate than UK companies in the four-year period to 2008.

Q40. Arguments include: firms have no incentive to be efficient if they know they can rely on government subsidies; the provision of grants and subsidies distorts economic signals; the government may finance extravagant projects that would otherwise not be economically viable.

Q41. B.

Q42. *(a)* *True(?).* Prices and wages would simply adjust to equate demand and supply. There would be no

---

Figure A23.1 The effects of reducing the monopoly power of labour

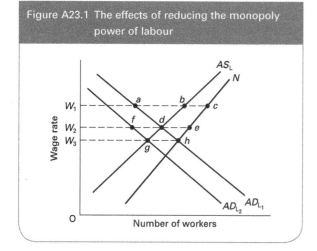

disequilibrium unemployment. There would merely be a residual frictional unemployment, which nevertheless could vary from one locality to another.

(b) *True(?)*. Workers would migrate to where wages were highest and businesses would locate where labour was cheapest. Any disparity in wages would be largely eliminated in this manner (unless there were significant non-monetary benefits from staying in the areas of reduced demand).

Q43. (a) *True(?)*. Prices and wages would simply adjust to equate demand and supply. There would be no disequilibrium unemployment. To the extent, however, that wages differed from one region to another, the lower-wage regions might have a slightly higher frictional unemployment (but expectations of a normal wage would also be lower in these regions, which might make people more willing to accept lower-paid jobs).

(b) *False*. Considerable regional disparities in wages might continue to exist if some regions were more productive/more rapidly growing than others.

Q44. Both (a) and (b) are *true*.

Q45. (a), (c) and (e) are all interventionist strategies. They have in common the fact that they all interfere with the free working of the market. The remainder are market-oriented proposals as they attempt to limit state or local authority intervention and/or to free up the market.

Chapter 24

International Trade

A REVIEW

In this chapter we will look at the advantages and disadvantages of international trade. We start by examining the arguments in favour of trade and then ask, if trade is potentially beneficial to all participating countries, why do countries frequently seek to restrict trade? We then turn to examine the case for establishing trading blocs between countries where the members give each other preferential treatment. The final topic is the European Union, probably the most famous of all preferential trading arrangements.

24.1 The advantages of trade

(Pages 708–15) The theory of comparative advantage
Countries can gain from trade if they specialise in producing those goods in which they have a comparative advantage.

Q1. Since 1950 world trade has stagnated, consistently growing more slowly than world GDP. *True/False*

Q2. The developed countries dominate world trade, but the most rapid growth in exports can be found in the developing world. *True/False*

Q3. A country has a comparative advantage in good X compared with good Y if:
A. it can produce more X than Y in total.
B. it can produce more X than Y for a given amount of resources.
C. it can produce more X than other countries.
D. it can produce more X relative to Y than other countries.
E. it can produce X with less resources than other countries.

Q4. Consider the following five situations for a world with just two countries. Each one shows alternative amounts of goods X and Y that the two countries F and G can produce for a given amount of resources. Assume constant costs. In each case give the (pre-trade) opportunity cost of X in terms of Y.

(i) Country F: 10 units of X or 20 units of Y.
$$1X = ...Y$$
Country G: 10 units of X or 10 units of Y.
$$1X = ...Y$$

(ii) Country F: 12 units of X or 12 units of Y.
$$1X = ...Y$$
Country G: 6 units of X or 8 units of Y.
$$1X = ...Y$$

(iii) Country F: 8 units of X or 8 units of Y.
$$1X = ...Y$$
Country G: 10 units of X or 10 units of Y.
$$1X = ...Y$$

(iv) Country F: 20 units of X or 5 units of Y.
$$1X = ...Y$$
Country G: 18 units of X or 2 units of Y.
$$1X = ...Y$$

(v) Country F: 10 units of X or 8 units of Y.
$$1X = ...Y$$
Country G: 6 units of X or 6 units of Y.
$$1X = ...Y$$

♟ **Q5.** Referring to the six different situations given in Q4, and assuming no transport costs:

(a) In which situations will country F export good X and import good Y?

....

(b) In which situations will country F export good Y and import good X?

....

(c) In which situations will country F either import or export both goods?

....

(d) In which situations will no trade take place?

....

⊗ **Q6.** In situation (i) in Q4, assume that before trade the price ratios of the two goods were equal to their opportunity cost ratios.

(a) What would the pre-trade price ratio (P_X/P_Y) be in country F?

....

(b) What would the pre-trade price ratio (P_X/P_Y) be in country G?

....

(c) Now assume that trade is opened up and that 1 unit of X exchanges for 1.5 of Y. Demonstrate how both countries have gained.

....

....

In what type of goods will countries have a comparative advantage? Which goods will they be able to produce at a low opportunity cost?

♟ **Q7.** The following are four items that are traded internationally:

(i) Wheat
(ii) Computers
(iii) Textiles
(iv) Insurance

In which one of the four is each of the following most likely to have a comparative advantage?

(a) India ....

(b) UK ....

(c) Canada ....

(d) Japan ....

These four countries have a comparative advantage in these four products because they are intensive in the respective country's **Q8.** *scarce/abundant/intermediate* factor.

Specialising in these goods and exporting them will have the effect of **Q9.** *reducing/increasing/maintaining existing* factor price inequalities.

In practice there will be a limit to specialisation and trade. This will result in part from **Q10.** *increasing/decreasing/constant* opportunity costs. In other words the country will face a **Q11.** *bowed in/bowed out/straight line* production possibility curve. As a country specialises and has to use resources that are less and less suited to producing its exports, so its comparative advantage will **Q12.** *increase/remain constant/disappear*.

⟨?⟩ **Q13.** There are other factors also which will have the effect of limiting specialisation and trade. Name two.

1. ....

2. ....

(Pages 715–9) The terms of trade
What will be the relative price of exports and imports? This is given by the *terms of trade*.

◗ **Q14.** In a simple world of just one export (X) and one import (M) the terms of trade are defined as P_M/P_X.

True/False

⊗ **Q15.** If 2 units of exports exchange for 3 units of imports, what are the terms of trade?

....

In the real world where countries have many imports and exports, the terms of trade are given by a weighted average price of exports divided by a weighted average price of imports, expressed as indices.

⊗ **Q16.** If in year 1 (the base year) the terms of trade index is 100, what will it be in year 5 if, over the period, the weighted average price of exports doubled while the weighted average price of imports went up by 50 per cent?

....

How will the trade price of each individual import and export be determined? Let us again assume for simplicity that there are just two countries.

⊖ **Q17.** Figure 24.1 shows the demand and supply of good Z in the two countries F and G.

(a) Which country will export the good?

....

(b) What will be the equilibrium trade price?

....

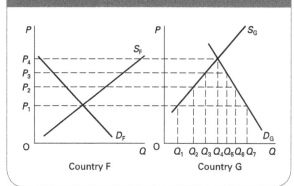

Figure 24.1 The demand and supply of good Z in countries F and G

(c) How much of good Z will be consumed in country G?

....

(d) How much will be traded?

....

The relative price of imports and exports, and hence the terms of trade, will also depend on the rate of exchange. For example, if the rate of exchange changes from £1 = €1.50 to £1 = €1.30, then, other things being equal, the UK terms of trade will have **Q18.** *improved/deteriorated.*

⊗ **Q19.** Suppose that country A imports 250 000 units of a manufactured good per year. The price in year 1 is £1 per unit. In order to pay for the product, country A exports 250 000 units of an agricultural good, also priced in year 1 at £1 per unit. In year 2, the price of the manufactured good rises to £1.20 per unit, but the price of the agricultural good falls to 96p.

(a) What are the terms of trade in year 2 relative to year 1?

....

(b) If country A still wants to import 250 000 units of the manufactured good, what volume of exports of the agricultural good will be needed?

....

(Pages 719–20) Other reasons for trade
Current comparative cost differences are not the only basis for trade.

🎯 **Q20.** The following is a list of other factors that can make trade beneficial:
 (i) Decreasing costs.
 (ii) Differences in demand.
 (iii) Increased competition.
 (iv) Trade is an engine of growth.
 (v) Non-economic factors.

Into which one of these five categories do the following examples fit?

(a) When the rest-of-the-world economy expands, this will increase the demand for a country's exports and also improve its terms of trade.

....

(b) By specialising in certain exports, the country may become increasingly skilled in their production.

....

(c) Free trade between countries may encourage closer political co-operation.

....

(d) Allowing imports freely into a country may stimulate domestic producers to be more efficient.

....

(e) The marginal utility ratios for products differ between different countries.

....

◗ **Q21.** The theory of comparative advantage shows how countries can gain from trade, but does not explain why countries come to have a comparative advantage in some goods rather than in others. *True/False*

🎯 **Q22.** Porter argued that there were four key determinants of a country's competitive advantage:
 (i) Available resources.
 (ii) Demand conditions in the home market.
 (iii) Strategy, structure and rivalry of firms.
 (iv) Existence of related and supported industries.

Match each of the following explanations with the above determinants.
(a) The more discerning customers are within the country, the more this will drive the development of each firm's products and the more competitive the firm will then become in international markets. ....*(i)/(ii)/(iii)/(iv)*
(b) Firms are more likely to be successful internationally if there are well-developed supporting industries within the home economy. ....*(i)/(ii)/(iii)/(iv)*
(c) The country has an endowment of resources, such as raw materials, population, climate, skills and capital. ....*(i)/(ii)/(iii)/(iv)*
(d) The very particular competitive conditions within each industry can have a profound effect on the development of firms within that industry. ....
....*(i)/(ii)/(iii)/(iv)*

24.2 Arguments for restricting trade

(Pages 721–2) Trade involves costs as well as benefits, and governments have a range of measures available to them if they wish to restrict trade.

📃 **Q23.** Which of the following is not a supply-side policy that could be used to influence a country's competitive advantage?

A. A supportive tax regime.

B. Investment in transport and communications infrastructure.

C. Expansionary fiscal and monetary policy.

D. Competition policy.

E. Investment in education and training.

Q24. Which of the following are methods that can be used by governments to restrict trade?

(i) Tariffs.

(ii) Quotas.

(iii) Exchange controls.

(iv) Administrative barriers.

(v) Procurement policies.

(vi) Dumping.

A. (i) and (ii).

B. (i), (ii), (iii) and (vi).

C. (i), (v) and (vi).

D. (v) and (vi).

E. All of the above.

Q25. Dumping is a strategy whereby exports are sold at prices below average cost – often as a result of government strategy. *True/False*

(Pages 722–6) Many arguments are used by governments to justify restricting imports or giving specific help to domestic industries. These arguments can be put into four categories: (i) those arguments with some general validity in a world context, (ii) those arguments with validity for specific countries, but where there is nevertheless a net world loss, (iii) non-economic arguments, (iv) fallacious arguments.

Q26. Into which of the above four categories do the following arguments belong?

(a) Putting tariffs on certain imports is desirable if it can thereby drive down the price-less-tariff.

....

(b) Industries that are subject to external economies of scale should be protected or promoted if that will result in their gaining a comparative advantage.

....

(c) Trade sanctions are desirable against countries that abuse human rights.

....

(d) The international community should permit countries to retaliate with equivalent-sized tariffs against countries that subsidise their exports.

....

(e) If imported goods undercut the price of home-produced goods, it is desirable to put tariffs on them to bring them up to the price of home-produced goods.

....

(f) A domestic computer firm should be protected from a giant competitor abroad if there is the danger that the domestic one will not survive the competition.

....

The growing penetration of US markets by imports from China and other countries has led to calls for strategic protection for US industries. Strategic trade theory also argues that protecting certain industries allows a net **Q27.** *gain/loss* in the **Q28.** *long run/short run* from **Q29.** *decreased/increased* competition.

Q30. Figure 24.2 shows a large country that as a whole has monopsony power in the purchase of a given import. Assume, however, that *individual* consumers in the country are price takers. What would be the size of the optimum tariff (assuming no externalities) to allow the country best to exploit its power?

A. HJ

B. OJ – FH

C. GH

D. FH

E. GJ – FH

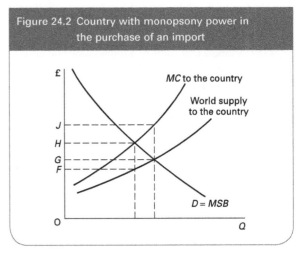

Figure 24.2 Country with monopsony power in the purchase of an import

(Pages 726–30) Even if there are valid arguments for government intervention, protection through trade restrictions will rarely be the optimum solution. The point is that trade restrictions impose costs. Take the case of a tariff.

Q31. Figure 24.3 shows a country's domestic demand and supply curves (D_{dom} and S_{dom}) for a product. Part of demand is satisfied by imports. The country is a price taker and the world price for the product is given by P_w with the world supply curve given by S_w. A tariff is then imposed on the product whose amount is shown by the vertical difference between S_w and $S_w + t$.

(a) How much is imported before the tariff is imposed?

....

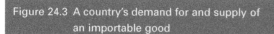

Figure 24.3 A country's demand for and supply of an importable good

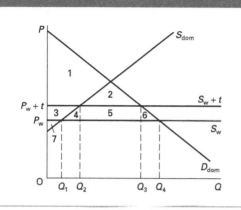

(b) How much is imported after the tariff is imposed?

....

(c) What area(s) represent(s) total consumer surplus before the tariff is imposed?

....

(d) What area(s) represent(s) total consumer surplus after the tariff is imposed?

....

(e) What area(s) represent(s) the loss in consumer surplus from the imposition of the tariff?

....

(f) What area(s) represent(s) the producer surplus before the tariff is imposed?

....

(g) What area(s) represent(s) the producer surplus after the tariff is imposed?

....

(h) What area(s) represent(s) the gain in producer surplus from the imposition of the tariff?

....

(i) How much revenue does the government gain from the imposition of the tariff?

....

(j) What area(s) represent(s) the total net loss from the tariff?

....

Part of these 'costs' may be warranted. For example, if there were negative externalities in consumption (e.g. from cars), then it might be desirable to reduce consumption to Q_3 in Figure 24.3. But it is not *also* desirable to increase domestic production from Q_1 to Q_2. This, after all, involves diverting production from **Q32.** *high-cost producers to low-cost producers/low-cost producers to high-cost producers*. Thus protection in this case would be **Q33.** *first best/definitely second best/at most second best.*

Q34. Referring to Figure 24.3, if there were external benefits of domestic production equal to $P_w + t - P_w$, but no externalities in domestic consumption such that $D_{dom} = MSB$, what would be the optimum form of government intervention?

A. A consumption tax so as to reduce consumption to Q_3 but leave production unchanged.

B. A tariff on imports, equal to $P_w + t - P_w$.

C. A production subsidy, equal to $P_w + t - P_w$.

D. A tax on the product, equal to $P_w + t - P_w$.

E. A complete ban on all imports of this product.

Q35. What would be the 'first-best' solution to negative externalities in consumption (as in Q32 and Q33)?

....

Q36. Name three other possible drawbacks from protectionism.

1. ....

2. ....

3. ....

Q37. Between them, the members of the World Trade Organisation account for some 96 per cent of world trade.

True/False

....

Q38. The World Trade Organisation (WTO) requires its members to operate under various rules, including:

(a) Any trade concession that a country makes to one member must be granted to *all* signatories. *Yes/No*

(b) Any nation benefiting from a tariff reduction by another country must reciprocate by making similar tariff reductions itself. *Yes/No*

(c) Tariffs must be reduced, but quota agreements are permitted. *Yes/No*

(d) WTO-sanctioned retaliatory action is permitted in response to unfair barriers to trade. *Yes/No*

24.3 Preferential trading

(Page 731) Countries may make a partial move towards free trade by removing trade restriction with selected other countries. These *preferential trading arrangements* may take different forms, but there are four broad types.

Q39. The four types of arrangement are as follows.

(i) Free trade areas.

(ii) Customs unions.

(iii) Common markets without full economic and monetary union.

(iv) Common markets with full economic and monetary union.

Match each of the above to the following definitions:

(a) Where countries have no tariffs or quotas between themselves and have common external tariffs and quotas with non-members.

....

(b) Where countries have no trade barriers whatsoever between themselves, whether in terms of tariffs, quotas, differences in regulations governing the activities of firms, restrictions on factor movements or differences in indirect taxation.

....

(c) Where countries have no tariffs or quotas between themselves and are free to impose whatever restrictions they each individually choose on non-members.

....

(d) Where countries have no trade or other economic restrictions between themselves, have a fixed exchange rate or even a common currency, and pursue common economic policies: fiscal, monetary, labour and industrial.

....

(Pages 731–4) When a country joins a preferential trading system its trading patterns will change. The result can be either *trade creation* or *trade diversion*.

◗ **Q40.** Trade creation is defined as a situation where production shifts from a higher-cost to a lower-cost source.

True/False

▤ **Q41.** Which of the following defines a situation of trade diversion resulting from the formation of a customs union?

A. Production is diverted from a higher-cost producer outside the union to a lower-cost producer within the union.

B. Production is diverted from a lower-cost producer outside the union to a higher-cost producer within the union.

C. Production is diverted away from trade within the union to trade with non-union members.

D. Production is diverted away from tradable goods to those which are not traded.

E. Trade between non-union members is diverted to trade with union members.

⊖ **Q42.** Figure 24.4 illustrates the process of trade diversion. It shows a product that country A partly produces itself and partly imports. Before joining the union, country A imposed a common tariff on imports of the product from all countries. This had the effect of shifting the supply curve of imports from S_w to $S_w +$ tariff. After joining the union, the country faced a (tariff-free) supply curve of the product from within the union of S_{union} (this curve includes the country's own domestic supply).

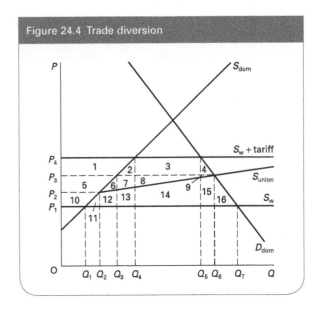

Figure 24.4 Trade diversion

(a) Before it joined the customs union, how much did country A import?

....

(b) Did it import the product from union countries or the rest of the world?

union countries/rest of the world

(c) Which are the higher-cost producers: union countries or the rest of the world?

union countries/rest of the world

(d) After joining the union, at what price could it now import the product?

....

(e) After it joined the customs union, how much did it import?

....

(f) Did production move to a higher- or a lower-cost producer?

higher-cost producer/lower-cost producer

(g) What area(s) represent the gain/loss in consumers' surplus from joining the union?

gain/loss of area(s)..............................

(h) What area(s) represent the gain/loss in domestic producers' surplus from joining the union?

gain/loss of area(s)..............................

(i) What area(s) represent the loss in tariff revenue for the government?

area(s)..................................

(j) What area(s) represent the net gain or loss from the trade diversion?

area(s)..................................

◗ **Q43.** A customs union is more likely to lead to trade diversion rather than trade creation when

(a) the union's external tariff is very high.   *True/False*

(b) there is a substantial cost difference between goods produced within and outside the union.   *True/False*

24.4 The European Union
(Pages 735–41)

📃 **Q44.** Which of the following best describes the European Community as it was in the 1980s?

A. A customs union.
B. A common market.
C. A free trade area.
D. An economic and monetary union.
E. A monetary system.

In 1993 the European Community (EC) was renamed the European Union (EU).

📃 **Q45.** Referring to the list in Q44, which one best describes the European Union today as envisaged in the Single European Act of 1987?

A. B. C. D. E.

Despite the elimination of tariffs between member states, there were significant *non-tariff* barriers before the completion of the single European market after 1992.

♟ **Q46.** The following are various types of non-tariff barrier:
  (i) Market-distorting barriers.
  (ii) Quotas imposed by individual members on imports from outside the EU.
  (iii) Tax barriers.
  (iv) Labour market barriers.
  (v) Regulations and norms.
  (vi) State procurement bias.
  (vii) Licensing.
  (viii) Financial barriers.
  (ix) Customs formalities.

Match each of the following examples from the pre-single market EU to the above types of barrier. There is one example of each type.

(a) A requirement by an EU country that all new buildings must be constructed using a certain type of girder made only in that country.

....

(b) The delays experienced by checking paperwork when goods cross from one EU country to another.

....

(c) Higher rates of excise duty on alcoholic drinks not produced in the country in question but produced elsewhere in the EU.

....

(d) A restriction on the quantity of shoes that one EU country allows to be imported from Poland, thereby encouraging Polish shoes to be diverted to other EU countries, making it harder for their domestic shoe industries to compete.

....

(e) Subsidies granted to domestic sheep farmers to enable them to compete unfairly in the EU lamb and wool markets.

....

(f) Professions that only recognise their own national qualifications.

....

(g) Governments or local authorities permitting only national firms to operate domestic coach and bus services.

....

(h) Governments preferring to buy military equipment from domestic armaments manufacturers.

....

(i) Credit controls that favour domestic firms.

....

❓ **Q47.** Give three advantages of the completion of the single market in the EU.

1. ....

2. ....

3. ....

A complete common market also entails problems.

❓ **Q48.** Give three disadvantages of the single market in the EU.

1. ....

2. ....

3. ....

◑ **Q49.** In which of the following cases are there most likely to be adverse regional multiplier effects from the development of the single market?

(a) Capital and labour move towards the geographical centre of the Union. *Yes/No*
(b) Firms gain substantial plant economies by centralising production. *Yes/No*
(c) Rents and land prices are flexible. *Yes/No*
(d) A larger proportion of the EU budget is spent on regional policy. *Yes/No*
(e) The impossibility of eurozone countries altering exchange rates between themselves. *Yes/No*
(f) The development of information technology reduces communication costs. *Yes/No*
(g) Infrastructure expenditure is financed locally. *Yes/No*

Although the development of the single market encourages trade creation, it can also encourage trade diversion.

Q50. Which of the following cases would make trade diversion more likely?

(a) Substantial initial internal barriers to trade are now completely abolished.

Yes/No

(b) External barriers remain high. *Yes/No*

(c) European industries have a wide range of available technologies and skills.

Yes/No

(d) Many European industries experience decreasing costs at the level of individual national markets. *Yes/No*

The nations that joined the EU in May 2004 have economic structures that are **Q51.** *similar/dissimilar* to those of existing members, so this allows **Q52.** *more/less* potential gains from the exploitation of comparative advantage. The existing members are likely to benefit by **Q53.** *more/less* than the new entrants.

B PROBLEMS, EXERCISES AND PROJECTS

Q54. Table 24.1 shows the pre-trade production possibilities of countries F and G per period of time.

Table 24.1 Pre-trade production possibilities for goods X and Y in countries F and G (per period of time)

Country F		Country G	
Good X (units)	Good Y (units)	Good X (units)	Good Y (units)
180	0	200	0
135	90	150	50
90	180	100	100
45	270	50	150
0	360	0	200

(a) Which country has a comparative advantage in good Y? *Country F/Country G*

(b) Assuming that $P = MC$, what would be the pre-trade price ratio (P_X/P_Y) in country F?

....

(c) Draw the production possibility curves for the two countries on Figure 24.5.

(d) Assuming that the exchange ratio after trade which balances the supply and demand for both imports and exports is $2X = 3Y$, draw a new line on each diagram showing the post-trade consumption possibilities if each country specialises completely in the good in which it has a comparative advantage.

(e) What will be the level of production and consumption in each country after trade has commenced, assuming that country F consumes 240 units of good Y?

Country F produces .... units of X and................ units of Y.

Country F consumes .... units of X and 240 units of Y.

Country G produces .... units of X and .... units of Y.

Country G consumes .... units of X and .... units of Y.

...................units of X are exported by country..................

...................units of Y are exported by country ....

(f) Mark the level of imports and exports of each country on diagrams (a) and (b) of Figure 24.5.

Q55. A country's domestic supply and demand schedules for good X are as follows:

$$Qs_{dom} = -10 + 10P$$
$$Qd_{dom} = 130 - 10P$$

(a) Using these two equations, fill in the figures in Table 24.2.

(b) What is the equilibrium price and quantity?

P = ... Q = ...

Table 24.2 Demand and supply of good X

Price (£)	0	1	2	3	4	5	6	7	8
Qs_{dom}	...	...	...	...	30	...	...	...	...
Qd_{dom}	...	...	110	...	...	...	...	...	...

(c) Plot the curves on Figure 24.6.

Now assume that the country starts to trade and faces an infinitely elastic world supply curve at a price of £3 per unit.

(d) How much will the country now consume?

............units

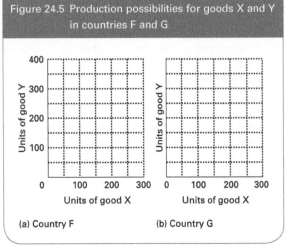

Figure 24.5 Production possibilities for goods X and Y in countries F and G

(a) Country F

(b) Country G

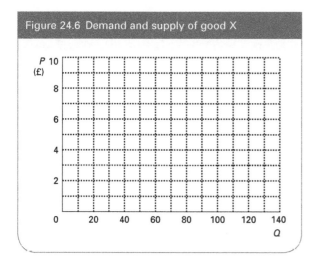

Figure 24.6 Demand and supply of good X

(e) How much will the country now produce?

.............units

(f) How much will the country now import?

.............units

(g) How much extra consumer surplus will consumers now gain?

....

(Clue: look at Figure 24.6 and work out the extra area gained.)

(h) How much producer surplus do domestic producers lose?

....

(i) What is the net welfare gain?

....

Q56. Given the information in Q55, now assume that a tariff of £2 per unit is imposed on the good.

(a) What will be the new market price?

....

(b) What will be the new level of imports?

.............units

(c) What is the reduction in consumer surplus?

....

(d) What is the increase in producer surplus?

....

(e) What is the tariff revenue for the government?

....

(f) What is the net welfare loss from the imposition of the tariff?

....

Now assume that the country joins a customs union, which has an infinitely elastic supply of good X at a price of £4.

(g) What is the new market price?

....

(h) What will be the new level of imports?

.............units

(i) Has there been trade creation or trade diversion?

trade creation/trade diversion

(j) What is the increase in consumer surplus?

....

(k) What is the reduction in producer surplus?

....

(l) What is the reduction in tariff revenue?

....

(m) What is the net gain or loss in terms of good X from joining the customs union?

....

Q57. Either individually or in small groups, find out how the composition of UK imports and exports has changed over the past 25 years. The best sources are *United Kingdom Balance of Payments (the 'Pink Book')* (NS) and *Annual Abstract of Statistics* (NS). Both of these can be downloaded from National Statistics website (www.statistics.gov.uk).

(a) How has the *area* composition changed? (What proportions of imports and exports come from which areas of the world?) Attempt an explanation for these changes.

(b) How has the *commodity* composition changed in primary products, semi-manufactures, manufactures and services? Have such changes reflected changes in comparative costs?

Q58. Find out what has happened to the UK's terms of trade over the past 15 years. Details are given in the *Annual Abstract of Statistics* (NS).

(a) Have these changes reflected changes in the exchange rate index (given in Financial Statistics – Freestanding (NS))?

(b) What else determines the terms of trade? Are the figures consistent with your answer here?

Q59. Write a report evaluating the economic issues surrounding three recent trade disputes submitted to the World Trade Organisation (WTO). Comment on which countries are involved in the dispute, and provide reasons as to why the complaints should be upheld or otherwise. You can find information on recent cases on the WTO website at http://www.wto.org.

Q60. Consult the trade statistics provided on the WTO website (see Q59) and examine the patterns in the direction of world trade. In particular, compare the shares of exports and imports that involve the USA, Western Europe and sub-Saharan Africa, and comment on the differences that you find. The information can be found by going to the WTO website and following links to resources then statistics.

C DISCUSSION TOPICS AND ESSAYS

Q61. Discuss the changing pattern of world trade since the 1960s.

Q62. Can different endowments of factors of production fully explain countries' differences in comparative costs?

Q63. Make out a case for restricting trade between the USA and the UK. Are there any arguments here that could not equally apply to a case for restricting trade between Scotland and England or between Liverpool and Manchester?

Q64. 'Far from leading to specialisation by country, free trade simply leads to a proliferation of products within any one country. The result is the relatively minor gain of an increased number of brands to choose from.' Discuss.

Q65. Are any of the arguments for restricting trade based on the criticism that free trade *prevents* countries from fully exploiting their comparative advantage?

Q66. Are import restrictions ever a first-best policy for aiding declining industries?

Q67. Discuss the economic consequences of the imposition of a tariff on a particular product. You should consider the effects on various types of consumers, firms and workers. Are tariffs ever superior to subsidies as a means of correcting market distortions?

Q68. Examine the benefits and costs of the strategic trade policy adopted towards Boeing and Airbus by the US and EU authorities.

Q69. 'Administrative barriers are a much more damaging form of protection than tariffs.' Discuss.

Q70. Discuss the economic implications for all relevant economic agents of a country joining a free trade area.

Q71. Discuss the extent to which the European single market is operating effectively. If the benefits from trade within the EU are so great, why should governments continue to try to introduce new restrictions on trade?

Q72. To what extent do non-EU countries gain or lose from the existence of the EU?

Q73. To what extent is the enlargement of the EU to include countries of eastern Europe and the Baltic likely to result in trade creation or trade diversion?

Q74. Discuss the issues faced by the eurozone countries during the financial crisis of the late 2000s and its aftermath.

Q75. Debate
All arguments for restricting trade boil down to special pleading for particular interest groups. Ultimately there will be a net social cost from any trade restrictions.

Q76. Debate
Free trade reinforces the pattern of the rich countries becoming richer and the poor countries becoming relatively poorer.

D ANSWERS

Q1. *False.* World trade has grown rapidly over the last sixty years, consistently outgrowing world GDP.

Q2. *True.* Developed countries account for 60 per cent of world exports and 65 per cent of imports. However, the so-called BRICS (Brazil, Russia, India, China and South Africa) increased their share of world exports from 6.5 per cent in 1994 to 16.3 per cent in 2010.

Q3. D. A country will have a comparative advantage over another in the production of a good if it can produce it at a lower opportunity cost. This will apply to case D: the opportunity cost of X in terms of Y is lower. Note that B does not apply because other countries could possibly produce even more X relative to Y. Also E does not apply because the country could produce Y with even less resources than other countries.

Q4.
  (i) Country F: $1X = 2Y$.
      Country G: $1X = 1Y$.
  (ii) Country F: $1X = 1Y$.
      Country G: $1X = 1.33Y$.
  (iii) Country F: $1X = 1Y$.
      Country G: $1X = 1Y$.
  (iv) Country F: $1X = 0.25Y$.
      Country G: $1X = 0.11Y$.
  (v) Country F: $1X = 0.8Y$.
      Country G: $1X = 1Y$.

Q5. *(a)* (ii) and (v). In these cases the opportunity cost of X in terms of Y is lower in country F than country G. Thus F specialises in good X and G in good Y.
  (b) (i) and (iv). In these cases the opportunity cost of X in terms of Y is lower in country G than country F. Thus G specialises in good X and F in good Y.

(c) None. If there are only two goods and two countries, trade must involve one good being exported in return for the other being imported.

(d) (iii). In this case the opportunity cost of X in terms of Y is the same in both countries. Thus although country G has an *absolute* advantage in both cases, no trade will take place.

Q6. *(a)* $P_X/P_Y = 2$. Since 1 unit of X exchanges for 2 of Y, X must be twice the price of Y.

(b) $P_X/P_Y = 1$.

(c) Country F has gained because, before trade, to obtain 1 unit of X it had to sacrifice 2 units of Y (the opportunity cost of *X* was 2*Y*); whereas with trade, it can import 1 unit of X by exporting only 1.5 units of Y (the opportunity cost of *X* is now only 1.5*Y*).

Country G has gained because, before trade, to obtain 1 unit of Y, it had to sacrifice 1 unit of X (the opportunity cost of *Y* was 1*X*); whereas with trade, it can import 1 unit of Y by exporting only 2/3 of a unit of X (the opportunity cost of *Y* is now only 0.67*X*).

Q7. (a) (iii), (b) (iv), (c) (i), (d) (ii).

Q8. *abundant.* Abundant factors will tend to have a relatively low price as will goods that are intensive in them.

Q9. *reducing.* The effect of countries specialising in goods that are abundant in their relatively cheap factor will be to increase the demand for this factor and push up its price, thereby reducing factor price differentials.

Q10. *increasing.*

Q11. *bowed out.*

Q12. *disappear.*

Q13. Factors include: transport costs; factors of production moving rather than goods (e.g. labour migration); government restrictions.

Q14. *False.* The terms of trade are defined as P_X/P_M.

Q15. If 2*X* exchange for 3*M*, then P_X/P_M must be 3/2.

Q16. Terms of trade equal $P_{\text{index of exports}} \div P_{\text{index of imports}} = 200/150 \times 100 = 133.3$.

Q17. *(a)* Country F.

(b) P_2 (where the exports from country F ($S_F - D_F$) equal the imports to country G ($D_G - S_G$)).

(c) Q_6.

(d) $Q_6 - Q_2$.

Q18. *deteriorated.* If the exchange rate depreciates, then less imports can be purchased for a given quantity of exports: P_X/P_M has fallen. This is known as deterioration in the terms of trade.

Q19. *(a)* 0.8.

(b) 312 500 units of exports are now needed. In other words, when there is a deterioration in the terms of trade, a greater volume of exports is needed in order to maintain a given volume of imports. Many less developed countries have found themselves facing this dilemma as their terms of trade have deteriorated over a long period.

Q20. (a) (iv), (b) (i), (c) (v), (d) (iii), (e) (ii).

Q21. *True.*

Q22. *(a)* (ii).

(b) (iv).

(c) (i).

(d) (iii).

Q23. C.

Q24. E. These are all methods that governments have used to restrict trade.

Q25. *False.* Dumping is where exports are sold below *marginal* cost.

Q26. *(a)* (ii) This is where the country is able to exercise its monopsony power.

(b) (i) This is the infant industry argument. It is justifying short-term protection (or better promotion) in order to be able to experience long-term comparative advantage.

(c) (iii) This is a political/moral argument.

(d) (i) This will prevent the move *away* from comparative advantage that dumping tends to create. Note, however, that the losers from dumping are *not* the consumers in the importing countries: they get the goods at a lower price! The losers are the firms in the importing country and the taxpayers in the dumping country.

(e) (iv) If followed, this policy would lead to a huge decline in trade, with no imports (however much more efficiently produced) being able to gain a price advantage.

(f) (i) This will help to prevent the establishment of a monopoly situation.

Q27. *gain.*

Q28. *long run.*

Q29. *increased.*

Q30. D. This is the amount of the tariff necessary to bring consumption to the point where *MC* to the country = *MSB*.

Q31. *(a)* $Q_4 - Q_1$.

(b) $Q_3 - Q_2$.

(c) $1 + 2 + 3 + 4 + 5 + 6$.

(d) $1 + 2$.

(e) $3 + 4 + 5 + 6$.

(f) 7.

(g) $3 + 7$.

(h) 3.

(i) 5.

(j) $4 + 6$ (i.e. the gain in producer surplus (3), plus revenue to the government from the tariff (5), minus the loss in consumer surplus ($3 + 4 + 5 + 6$)).

Q32. *low-cost* (foreign) *producers to high-cost* (domestic) *producers.*

Q33. *at most second best.* Some other policy (if such existed) which only increased production part of the way to Q_2 would be second best.

Q34. C. The production externalities but no consumption externalities imply that consumption should remain at Q_4 (where $P = MSB$), but that domestic production should be increased to Q_2. Both a production subsidy and a tariff (alternative B) will achieve the required increase in production, but a tariff, by raising the price to $P_w + t$, will also reduce consumption – side-effect distortion. A production subsidy, however, will not raise the price of imports. The product will continue to be sold at the world price of P_w.

Q35. A tax on consumption. This will have the desired effect on consumption, but by leaving the *producer* price unchanged, domestic production will remain unchanged and the reduced consumption will simply mean reduced imports. In terms of Figure 24.3, D_{dom} will shift downward by the amount of the tax, but domestic production will remain at Q_1.

Q36. Examples include: deflationary effects on the world economy may reduce demand for the country's exports; other countries may retaliate; protection may reduce competition and encourage firms to remain inefficient; protection may involve high administrative costs; it may encourage corruption as firms bribe officials to waive restrictions.

Q37. *True.*

Q38. *(a)* No: exceptions are allowed for free-trade areas and customs unions such as the EU.

(b) Yes: this is known as reciprocity.

(c) No: quotas are prohibited, although in some cases the process of removal of quota agreements has been slow.

(d) Yes: but explicit WTO permission is required.

Q39. (a) (ii), (b) (iii), (c) (i), (d) (iv).

Q40. *True.* Trade creation is where the removal of trade barriers allows greater specialisation according to comparative advantage.

Q41. B. The reduction in tariffs within the union may mean that members now buy imports from each other rather than from outside the union, even if the non-union members were more efficient producers of the product.

Q42. *(a)* $Q_5 - Q_4$ at a price of P_4.

(b) *rest of the world.* (S_{union} is at a higher price for each output than S_w. If there were equal tariffs, therefore, on both union and non-union imports, the country would import from non-union countries.)

(c) *union countries.*

(d) P_3.

(e) $Q_6 - Q_3$.

(f) *higher-cost producer.* Trade is diverted from non-union suppliers who without tariffs would have supplied at the lower price of P_1.

(g) *gain* of areas $1 + 2 + 3 + 4$.

(h) *loss* of area 1.

(i) $3 + 8 + 14$. (Since nothing is now imported from outside the union, the government loses the whole of the tariff revenue it had previously earned.)

(j) $(1 + 2 + 3 + 4) - 1 - (3 + 8 + 14) = 2 + 4 - 8 - 14$.

Q43. *(a)* *True.* The abolition of such a tariff between union members will lead to a large reduction in the price of goods imported from other union members.

(b) *False.* If there is a substantial cost difference, the abolition of tariffs between union members is less likely to divert trade away from the (very) low-cost non-union producers.

Q44. A. There was an absence of tariffs and quotas within the EC and common tariffs with the outside world.

Q45. B. The Act envisaged the complete abandonment of all barriers to inter-EC trade and factor movements.

Q46. (a) (v), (b) (ix), (c) (iii), (d) (ii), (e) (i), (f) (iv), (g) (vii), (h) (vi), (i) (viii).

Q47. Advantages include: trade creation; reduction in the direct costs associated with barriers (such as administrative costs and delays); economies of scale, with firms better able to operate on an EU-wide scale; greater competition.

Q48. Disadvantages include the costs of radical economic change, adverse regional multiplier effects, the possible development of monopoly or oligopoly power and trade diversion. A key issue is whether these potential costs will outweigh the benefits.

Q49. *(a)* *Yes.* If firms now see their market as the EU as a whole rather than mainly just their own country, they are likely to want to locate nearer the geographical centre of the EU.

(b) *Yes.* This encourages firms to merge and again to locate towards the geographical centre of the EU.

(c) *No.* A fall in rents and land prices tends to attract capital to the regions.

(d) *No.* This helps to offset regional problems.

(e) *Yes.* Individual eurozone countries with severe regional problems are unable to devalue in order to gain competitiveness.

(f) *No.* This reduces the need for centralising office functions.

(g) *Yes.* Depressed regions may be unable to afford the improvements to their infrastructure necessary to attract enough capital to halt their decline.

Q50. *(a)* *Yes.* This is likely to lead to a bigger switch in consumption from non-EU goods to EU goods, irrespective of whether many of them may be produced at higher cost. (On the other hand, the substantial increase in inter-EU competition may, over time, significantly reduce EU costs.)

(b) *Yes.* This would prevent low-cost non-EU products competing with higher-cost EU products.

(c) *No.* This tends to lead to trade creation as consumers are now able to purchase from lower-cost producers.

(d) *No.* The economies of scale from serving an EU-wide market tend to reduce costs of production and hence encourage trade creation.

Q51. *dissimilar.*

Q52. *more.*

Q53. *less.*

Chapter **25**

The Balance of Payments and Exchange Rates

A   REVIEW

In this chapter we will look at ways of dealing with problems of the balance of payments and exchange rates. We begin with an overview of the range of alternative types of exchange rate 'regime' and how the balance of payments is corrected under each. We then look in detail first at fixed exchange rates and then at free-floating exchange rates.

Next we look at the various intermediate exchange rate regimes that have been tried since 1945. We start with the adjustable peg – a semi-fixed exchange rate system that was used round the world from 1945 to 1971. Then we consider the system of 'dirty' floating that has been used since 1971.

Finally, there are some optional questions on the extension of the *ISLM* model (see Chapter 20) to take account of balance of payments issues.

25.1 Alternative exchange rate regimes

(Pages 744–5) A country is likely to have various internal and external policy objectives.

 Q1. Internal balance can be expressed in various ways depending on the model of the economy and the policy objectives being pursued. The following list different approaches that could be taken:
  (i) A Keynesian view.
  (ii) A new classical/monetarist view.
  (iii) An economy operating with an inflation target.

Match the above to the following states of internal balance.
(a) The economy is on the vertical Phillips curve with stable inflation.
....

(b) The economy is at the output level where *ADI = ASI* at the targeted inflation rate.
....

(c) The economy is in a situation in which equilibrium national income is equal to full-employment national income.
....

External balance in the narrow sense is where there is a current account balance in the context of **Q2.** *fixed/floating* exchange rates. More loosely, external balance is where there is a total currency flow balance under **Q3.** *fixed/floating* exchange rates.

 Q4. Suppose that an economy is initially in internal and external balance. Match each of the following shocks

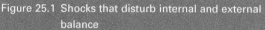

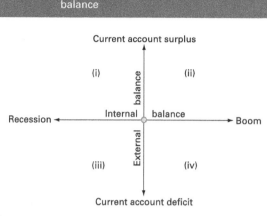

Figure 25.1 Shocks that disturb internal and external balance

with the appropriate quadrant of Figure 25.1 to show how internal and external balance are likely to be disturbed.

(a) Expansionary fiscal policy, higher consumption.

....

(b) Exchange rate depreciation, foreign boom.

....

(c) Contractionary fiscal policy, lower consumption.

....

(d) Exchange rate appreciation, foreign recession.

....

(Pages 745–7) It is important to distinguish between nominal and real exchange rates.

◗ **Q5.** Decide whether the following are true or false.
(a) The nominal exchange rate is simply the rate at which one currency exchanges for another. *True/False*
(b) The real exchange rate index is the nominal exchange rate index adjusted for the terms of trade. *True/False*
(c) The real exchange rate index can be defined as:
RERI = NERI $\times P_M/P_X$. *True/False*
(d) The nominal exchange rate provides a better idea of the quantity of imports that can be obtained from selling a given volume of exports. *True/False*
(e) If the real exchange rate rises, the economy can obtain more imports for a given volume of exports.
True/False

(Pages 748–50) Correction under fixed exchange rates
In order to maintain the exchange rate at a fixed level, the central bank will have to intervene in the foreign exchange market whenever there is a **Q6.** *current account/capital account/ currency flow* deficit or surplus. If the UK has a currency flow deficit, the Bank of England will have to **Q7.** *buy/sell* sterling.

Central bank intervention to maintain a fixed exchange rate will tend to affect the money supply.

If the Bank of England buys pounds to support the exchange rate when there is a total currency flow deficit, this will **Q8.** *reduce/increase* the money supply. In turn this will **Q9.** *lower/raise* the equilibrium rate of interest, causing financial **Q10.** *inflows/outflows* and also **Q11.** *stimulating/dampening* aggregate demand. The net effect is to **Q12.** *reduce/widen* the overall currency flow deficit, and may well lead to a **Q13.** *boom/recession.*

◗ **Q14.** Other things being equal, central bank intervention in the foreign exchange market to prevent a deficit leading to a depreciation in the exchange rate will increase the money supply. *True/False*

The effects on money supply can be offset by a process of *sterilisation.*

▤ **Q15.** Assume that there is a currency flow surplus and that the Bank of England intervenes in the foreign exchange market to prevent the pound appreciating. Which of the following additional actions by the Bank of England would sterilise (i.e. offset) the consequent effects on money supply?
A. A reduction in interest rates.
B. Buying government securities on the open market.
C. Selling government securities on the open market.
D. Buying pounds on the foreign exchange market.
E. Selling pounds on the foreign exchange market.

If a currency flow deficit persists and if the government is to maintain the fixed exchange rate, it will have to tackle the underlying deficit. One approach is to try to improve the current account balance. It can use **Q16.** *deflationary/ reflationary* fiscal or monetary policy for this purpose. This will lead to both 'expenditure changing' and 'expenditure switching' (an income effect and a substitution effect respectively).

◗ **Q17.** Which of the following are examples of expenditure changing and which are examples of expenditure switching?
(a) Relatively lower export prices lead to an increase in exports. *expenditure changing/expenditure switching*
(b) Lower aggregate demand leads to less imports.
expenditure changing/expenditure switching
(c) The resulting slowdown in economic activity leads to less demand for imports of raw materials and capital equipment from abroad.
expenditure changing/expenditure switching
(d) A fall in the rate of inflation makes home-produced goods more competitive relative to imports.
expenditure changing/expenditure switching

◗ **Q18.** Unlike expenditure changing, expenditure switching from deflationary policy will not have an adverse effect on unemployment. *True/False*

(Pages 750–2) Correction under free-floating exchange rates
Free-floating exchange rates automatically correct any balance of payments deficit or surplus by depreciation or appreciation respectively. As with a regime of fixed exchange rates, expenditure changing and expenditure switching will occur.

◗ Q19. Unlike with a fixed exchange rate, only expenditure changing will help to correct the disequilibrium: expenditure switching will make the problem worse. *True/False*

◗ Q20. The greater the price elasticities of demand for imports and exports, the greater will be the level of expenditure switching from a depreciation and the smaller will be the amount of depreciation necessary to restore equilibrium. *True/False*

(Pages 752–3) Intermediate exchange rate regimes
There are a number of alternative exchange rate regimes between the extremes of a completely fixed and a completely free-floating exchange rate.

▩ Q21. The following is a list of exchange rate regimes:
  (i) Crawling peg.
  (ii) Free floating.
  (iii) Adjustable peg.
  (iv) Totally fixed.
  (v) Dirty floating.
  (vi) Exchange rate band.
  (vii) Joint float.

Match the above to each of the following descriptions.
(a) Where a currency is allowed to float between an upper and lower exchange rate but is not allowed to move outside these limits.
....

(b) Where countries peg their exchange rate permanently to gold or to another currency.
....

(c) Where exchange rates are fixed for a period of time, but may be devalued (or revalued) if a deficit (or surplus) becomes substantial.
....

(d) Where a group of currencies are pegged to each other but collectively are free to fluctuate against other currencies.
....

(e) Where governments do not intervene at all in foreign exchange markets.
....

(f) Where the government allows a gradual adjustment of the exchange rate by small amounts.
....

(g) Where the government intervenes in the foreign exchange market to prevent excessive exchange rate fluctuations.
....

25.2 Fixed exchange rates

*(Pages 754–5) The effects of internal and external shocks under fixed exchange rates are analysed differently by new classical and Keynesian economists.

◗ *Q22. Assume that there is an *internal* shock affecting an economy operating under fixed exchange rates, stemming from a fall in aggregate demand caused by a fall in consumption. What will be the *short-run* effect on the following under the assumption that prices (especially wages) are inflexible, and that neither the government nor the central bank intervenes? Assume initial internal and external balance (in the narrow sense).
(a) Imports *fall/rise*
(b) The current account of the balance of payments
surplus/deficit
(c) The demand for money *falls/increases*
(d) Interest rates *fall/rise*
(e) The financial account of the balance of payments
surplus/deficit
(f) What more would we need to know in order to judge the overall effect on the balance of payments?

....

◗ *Q23. Under fixed exchange rates, interest rates are determined by the balance of payments. *True/False*

◗ *Q24. In the long run under fixed exchange rates, wage and price flexibility leads to flexibility in the real exchange rate, and helps to restore internal and external balance.
True/False

* Now consider the effect of an *external* shock under fixed exchange rates. Assume there is a rise in the demand for UK exports. In the short run, the current account will go into **Q25.** *surplus/deficit*. It also affects aggregate demand, causing a multiplied **Q26.** *fall/rise* in national income. This **Q27.** *reduces/increases* the demand for imports; the larger the *mpm*, the **Q28.** *larger/smaller* will be the impact on imports. The change in aggregate demand **Q29.** *reduces/increases* the transactions demand for money, putting **Q30.** *upward/downward* pressure on interest rates. If interest rates were allowed to adjust, this would lead to financial **Q31.** *inflows/outflows* and thus a **Q32.** *surplus/deficit* on the financial account. The central bank will then need to intervene by **Q33.** *increasing/reducing* money supply. In the long run, the **Q34.** *upward/downward* pressure on domestic inflation will **Q35.** *increase/reduce* the real exchange rate, thus restoring internal balance.

(Pages 755–6) Balance of payments problems do not simply arise from 'one-off' shocks. There are other factors that can lead to *persistent* balance of payments problems under fixed exchange rates.

▤ Q36. Which one of the following is likely to lead to persistent current account deficits under fixed exchange rates?

A. A lower income elasticity of demand for the country's exports than for its imports.

B. A lower rate of growth at home than abroad.

C. A higher rate of inflation abroad than in the domestic economy.

D. The long-term development of import substitutes at home.

E. A growth in the country's monopoly power in the export market.

(Pages 756–8) Under fixed exchange rates the government will probably have to use fiscal and/or monetary policy to control the level of demand for imports and the level of inflation.

Q37. Assume that there is a balance of payments deficit caused by a high rate of domestic inflation.

(a) What effect will a deflationary *monetary* policy (a reduction in money supply) have on interest rates?
Raise/Lower them.

(b) What effect will this have on the financial account?
Cause an *inflow/outflow* of finance.

(c) What effect will this have on the money supply?
Increase it again/Reduce it further.

(d) What effect will this have on inflation?
Help to reduce it/Increase it.

(e) What effect will a deflationary *fiscal* policy have on interest rates? *Raise/Lower* them.

(f) What effect will this have on the financial account?
Cause an *inflow/outflow* of finance.

(g) What effect will this have on money supply?
Increase/Reduce it.

(h) What effect will this have on inflation?
Help to reduce it/increase it.

(i) Which will be more effective under fixed exchange rates: fiscal or monetary policy? *fiscal/monetary*

Q38. Give three advantages of fixed exchange rates.

1. ....

2. ....

3. ....

Q39. Give three disadvantages of fixed exchange rates from a new classical perspective.

1. ....

2. ....

3. ....

Q40. Give three disadvantages of fixed exchange rates from a Keynesian perspective.

1. ....

2. ....

3. ....

25.3 Free-floating exchange rates

(Pages 758–66) Under a free-floating exchange rate, the balance of payments will automatically be kept in balance by movements in the exchange rate.

If there are any internal shocks, then, provided that monetary policy maintains interest rates at international levels, the purchasing-power parity theory will hold.

Q41. The purchasing-power parity theory states that:

A. inflation will adjust to the level of that abroad.

B. exchange rates will adjust so that the same quantity of internationally traded goods can be bought in all countries with a given amount of one currency.

C. interest rates will adjust so that the inflation rate is equalised in all countries so as to maintain the relative value of real incomes.

D. the exchange rate between currencies A and B and between B and C and between C and A will be such that all three rates are consistent.

E. the exchange rate between any two currencies at any one time will be the same in all foreign exchange dealing centres in any part of the world.

Q42. Assume initially that the exchange rate is £1 = $1.50. Assume also that UK inflation is 50 per cent, but that US inflation (and also that in other countries) is zero. According to the purchasing-power parity theory, what will be the exchange rate after one year?

....

If we drop the assumption that interest rates are maintained at the same level at home as abroad, the purchasing-power parity theory will break down.

Q43. Assume that UK inflation is 10 per cent more than the (trade-weighted) average of that in other countries and that there is an expansion of domestic money supply that forces interest rates below the level of those abroad.

(a) What will happen to the current account balance (assuming it was initially in balance)?
Move into *deficit/surplus.*

(b) What will happen to the financial account balance (assuming it was initially in balance)?
Move into *deficit/surplus.*

(c) By how much will sterling depreciate?
more than 10 per cent/10 per cent/ less than 10 per cent.

(Page 766) Let us consider how effective monetary and fiscal policies will be under free-floating exchange rates.

Q44. Exchange rate movements will reinforce monetary policy but will dampen fiscal policy.   *True/False*

Q45. Assume that the government wishes to pursue a deflationary policy.
(a) What will happen to the exchange rate if it uses deflationary *monetary* policy?   *Appreciate/Depreciate*
(b) What effect will this exchange rate movement have on aggregate demand?   *Increase it/Decrease it*
(c) What will happen to the exchange rate if it uses deflationary *fiscal* policy?   *Appreciate/Depreciate*
(d) What effect will this exchange rate movement have on aggregate demand?   *Increase it/Decrease it*

Q46. Give three advantages of free-floating exchange rates.

1. ....

2. ....

3. ....

Q47. Under which of the following conditions are fluctuations in exchange rates likely to be severe?
(a) The demand for imports and exports is highly price inelastic.   *Yes/No*
(b) Speculators believe that fluctuations in exchange rates are likely to be considerable.   *Yes/No*
(c) Governments pursue a policy of setting interest rates in accordance with international interest rates.   *Yes/No*
(d) Large amounts of the country's currency are held abroad.   *Yes/No*
(e) There are many substitutes abroad for the country's exports.   *Yes/No*

The uncertainty for importers and exporters associated with fluctuating exchange rates can be lessened in the **Q48.** *short term/long term* by firms dealing in the **Q49.** *spot/forward* exchange market. This allows traders to plan future purchases of imports and sales of exports at a known **Q50.** *price/exchange rate/interest rate/inflation rate.*

25.4 Exchange rate systems in practice
(Pages 767–9) After the Second World War, the world adopted an adjustable peg system where currencies were pegged to the US dollar. This was the Bretton Woods System (named after the town in the USA where the system was devised).

Q51. The following are various measures that can be taken under an adjustable peg system:
(i) Drawing on reserves.
(ii) Building up reserves.
(iii) Deflation.
(iv) Reflation.
(v) Devaluation.
(vi) Revaluation.

Which of the above measures is suitable for each of the following balance of payments problems?
(a) A severe and fundamental deficit.
          ....
(b) A temporary balance of payments surplus.
          ....
(c) A moderate surplus arising from the economy operating with a low level of aggregate demand.
          ....
(d) A mild deficit that is expected to disappear as the world economy recovers from recession.
          ....
(e) A large and persistent surplus because of the country's much lower underlying rate of inflation.
          ....
(f) A moderate deficit associated with a too rapid recovery from recession.
          ....

There were serious problems with the system.

Q52. Governments were sometimes reluctant to devalue, even when a deficit was fundamental. Why?

....

....

Q53. One problem of devaluation was the so-called 'J-curve effect'. This effect arose because:
A. governments tended to back up devaluation with deflationary fiscal and monetary policies.
B. after several months speculators came to believe that the balance of payments would begin to move into deficit again.
C. devaluation tended to make inflation worse in the long run.
D. the IMF only provided support for the exchange rate on a temporary basis.
E. the Marshall–Lerner condition was only satisfied in the long run.

Q54. Why was there a problem of excess liquidity in the late 1960s and early 1970s?

....

(Pages 769–76) Since 1972 the world has been largely on a dirty floating exchange rate system (although groups of countries, such as those in the former European Monetary System, may peg their rates to each other).

Q55. What are the two major ways in which countries seek to prevent short-term fluctuations in their exchange rate?

1. ....

2. ....

Q56. Floating exchange rates after 1972, by reducing the need for international liquid assets, reduced the inflationary pressures that were building up in the international economy. *True/False*

Q57. One of the problems experienced in the 1970s and 1980s was the growth in 'hot money'. Hot money may be defined as:

A. illegal exchange rate transactions designed to circumvent exchange controls.

B. currency deposits earning very high interest rates.

C. dollars that are used for international trade rather than transactions in the USA.

D. currency used for buying property and other assets abroad.

E. money put on short-term deposit in the country paying the most favourable interest rates relative to expected movements in the exchange rate.

The use of interest rates as the main weapon for stabilising the exchange rate has often led to conflicts with internal policy objectives.

Q58. In which of the following cases is there a clear conflict between internal and external policy objectives if interest rate changes are the only weapon available to the government?

(a) The government wants to prevent an appreciation of the exchange rate and to reduce demand-deficient unemployment. *Yes/No*

(b) The government wants to help UK exporters and to reduce the rate of inflation. *Yes/No*

(c) The government wants to reduce the price of imports and to curb the rate of growth in the money supply. *Yes/No*

(d) The government wants to prevent a depreciation of the exchange rate and to stimulate investment. *Yes/No*

(e) The government wants to halt a rise in the exchange rate and to reduce the rate of growth of the money supply. *Yes/No*

(f) The government wants to reverse a recent fall in the exchange rate and to reduce its unpopularity with home owners. *Yes/No*

Q59. Which of the following are likely to contribute to the volatility of exchange rates between the major currencies?

(a) A growth in the size of short-term financial flows relative to current account flows. *Yes/No*

(b) The abolition of exchange controls. *Yes/No*

(c) A harmonisation of international macroeconomic policies. *Yes/No*

(d) The adoption of money supply targets by individual countries. *Yes/No*

(e) The adoption of exchange rate targets by individual countries. *Yes/No*

(f) The adoption of inflation targets by individual countries. *Yes/No*

(g) A growing belief that speculation against exchange rate movements is likely to be stabilising. *Yes/No*

(h) A growing belief that speculation against exchange rates movements is likely to be destabilising. *Yes/No*

(i) A growing ease of international transfers of funds. *Yes/No*

(j) Countries' business cycles become more synchronised with each other. *Yes/No*

Appendix: The open economy and ISLM analysis

(Pages 777–80) ISLM analysis (see Chapter 20) can be extended to incorporate the balance of payments. This is done by introducing an additional curve to the *IS* and *LM* curves: this third curve is the *BP* curve.

Q60. Figure 25.2 illustrates a *BP* curve (we will look at the other two curves in the next question).

(a) What does the *BP* curve show?

....

(b) What will happen to the balance of payments if the rate of interest increases?

Current account/Financial account moves into deficit/surplus.

(c) What will happen to the balance of payments if the level of national income increases?

Current account/Financial account moves into deficit/surplus.

(d) Why does the *BP* curve slope upwards?

....

....

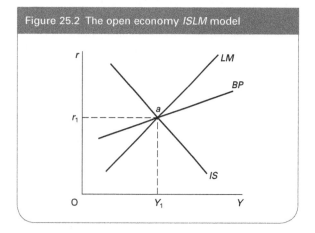

Figure 25.2 The open economy *ISLM* model

(e) What combinations of interest rate and national income would cause a surplus on the balance of payments?

Combinations in area of diagram *above/below* BP curve

(f) What will happen to the slope of the BP curve if the marginal propensity to import increases?

It will get *steeper/shallower.*

(g) What will happen to the slope of the curve if the elasticity of supply of international finance decreases?

It will get *steeper/shallower.*

(h) What will happen to the curve if there is an autonomous increase in exports?

It will shift *upwards/downwards.*

(i) What will happen to the curve if there is an appreciation of the exchange rate?

It will shift *upwards/downwards.*

 Q61. Figure 25.2 shows an economy which initially has an interest rate of r_1 and a level of income of Y_1 (point *a*). This is an equilibrium position because it is where $IS = LM$. Let us assume that the balance of payments is also in equilibrium (the BP curve passes through point *a* too). Assume a system of fixed exchange rates.

(a) What curve would initially shift and in which direction if the government pursued a deflationary fiscal policy? (It may help you answer the following questions if you draw the effects on Figure 25.2.)

The IS/LM curve would shift to the *left/right.*

(b) What effect would this have on the rate of interest?

rise/fall

(c) What effect would it have on national income?

rise/fall

(d) What effect would this have on the current account of the balance of payments? *improve/deteriorate*

(e) What effect would this have on the financial account of the balance of payments?

improve/deteriorate

(f) The way the diagram is drawn, what would be the overall effect on the balance of payments?

Move into *deficit/surplus.*

(g) If there were to be the opposite effect on the balance of payments, how would the diagram have to have been drawn?

(h) What effect will the balance of payments position in (f) above have on the money supply?

increase/decrease

(i) What effect will this have on the LM curve?

Shift it to the *left/right.*

(j) Where will equilibrium finally be achieved?

....

(k) Will the secondary monetary effects of a fixed exchange rate (i.e. the shift in the LM curve) have strengthened or weakened the deflationary effects of the fiscal policy?

strengthened/weakened

Q62. Monetary policy under fixed exchange rates will be ineffective because:

A. any initial shift in the LM curve will simply be reversed because of the monetary effects of the change in the balance of payments.

B. the BP curve will shift so as to eliminate the effect of any shift in the LM curve.

C. the IS curve will shift so as to eliminate the effect of any shift in the LM curve.

D. the BP curve is steeper than the LM curve.

E. the BP curve is shallower than the LM curve.

Q63. Illustrate on a diagram like Figure 25.2 the effects of a deflationary fiscal policy under a system of free-floating exchange rates. Assume initially that the economy is in equilibrium at a national income of Y_1 with a rate of interest of r_1.

B ## PROBLEMS, EXERCISES AND PROJECTS

Q64. Expenditure switching and expenditure changing are shown diagrammatically in Figure 25.3.

Assume initially that the total expenditure function is given by E_1. The balance of payments is given by the line $(X - M)_1$. This shows that the higher the level of national income, the higher the level of imports relative to exports.

(a) What is the initial equilibrium level of national income?

....

(b) What is the balance of payments surplus or deficit at this initial equilibrium level of income?

surplus/deficit of....................

(c) Beyond what level of national income will there be a balance of payments deficit?

....

Now assume that there is depreciation of the exchange rate. This will alter the relative price of imports and exports and cause expenditure switching.

(d) How is this expenditure switching illustrated in the diagram?

....

(e) Why will the E line shift upwards as a result of the expenditure switching?

....

(f) Why does the E line shift upwards to E_2, but no further?

....

Figure 25.3 Expenditure switching and expenditure changing

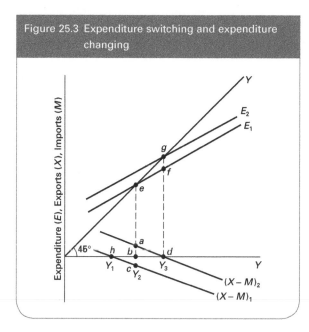

Figure 25.4 Alternative effects of exchange rate speculation

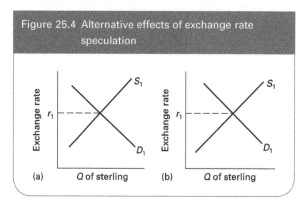

(g) What is the size of the multiplier? ....

(h) What is the size of the substitution effect (expenditure switching) on the balance of payments from the depreciation? *positive/negative effect of* ....

(i) What is the size of the income effect (expenditure changing) on the balance of payments from the depreciation? *positive/negative effect of* ....

(j) What is the total effect on the balance of payments of the depreciation?

positive/negative effect of ....

Q65. Free-floating exchange rates are likely to give rise to speculation. The two diagrams of Figure 25.4 both show an original demand and supply curve for sterling and an exchange rate of r_1. Assume that the UK experiences a lower rate of inflation than other countries.

(a) Show on each diagram the effect on the demand and supply curves and the exchange rate.

(b) Now assume that, as a result of the change in the exchange rate, people expect the government to cut interest rates and reflate the economy. On Figure 25.4(a) illustrate the effect on the demand and supply curves of these expectations.

(c) Alternatively assume that people expect inflation to continue falling and that as a result the exchange rate will continue to move in the same direction as in question (a). Use Figure 25.4(b) to illustrate the effect of these expectations.

(d) Which of the two diagrams represents destabilising speculation? *Figure 25.4(a)/Figure 25.4(b)*

(e) In which of the two diagrams is speculation self-fulfilling? *Figure 25.4(a)/Figure 25.4(b)/both/neither*

Q66. Construct a table showing the following figures for the UK economy since 1975: the exchange rate index, interest rates, the current account on the balance of payments, the rate of economic growth, the rate of growth in money supply (M4), the rate of inflation. Plot the figures on a graph (or two or three graphs if it is easier). The graph(s) should show time on the horizontal axis and the other variables on the vertical axis (you can use different scales up the *same* axis for the different variables).

(a) Comment on the movement of these variables over time and whether there are any apparent relationships between them.

(b) Are these relationships as you would expect? Explain.

(c) What other factors would influence the movement of these variables? Explain any apparent unexpected movements of one variable relative to others.

Sources: *The Pink Book* (NS); *Financial Statistics* (NS); *Annual Abstract of Statistics* (NS); *National Institute Economic Review (Quarterly)* (NIESR).

Q67. Compare movements in the volume of exports, the volume of imports, consumer prices, average earnings and the effective exchange rate over the past ten years for Germany, Japan, the UK and the USA. Plot these relationships on a separate graph for each country. (See Q66.) Explain the relative performance of the three countries.

Sources: *OECD Economic Outlook* (OECD); *National Institute Economic Review (Quarterly)* (NIESR). The first of these can be downloaded from the website: www.oecd.org.

DISCUSSION TOPICS AND ESSAYS

Q68. Discuss the effect on the balance of payments in both the short and long run of an increase in the domestic interest rate.

Q69. Why may an expansion of aggregate demand lead to a balance of payments surplus under a fixed exchange rate system?

Q70. What are the arguments for and against pursuing a policy of maintaining a high fixed exchange rate?

Q71. Explain whether it is a problem for a country to have a persistent current account balance of payments deficit over the long term (i.e. a structural deficit rather than a mere cyclical deficit). What policies could a government pursue to remove a structural current account deficit?

Q72. Explain the process by which, in the long run, the exchange rate restores purchasing-power parity following an external shock for an economy under free-floating exchange rates.

Q73. To what extent can dealing in forward exchange markets remove the problems of a free-floating exchange rate?

Q74. 'If a country moves from a system of floating exchange rates to fixed or pegged exchange rates, it should switch its emphasis from monetary policy to fiscal policy when attempting to manage the level of aggregate demand.' Discuss.

Q75. How do elasticities of demand and supply for imports and exports influence the effectiveness of (a) depreciation and (b) deflation as means of correcting a balance of payments disequilibrium?

Q76. Was a system of managed flexibility (dirty floating) the best compromise between fixed and free-floating exchange rates in the 1970s? Is it the best compromise today?

Q77. Discuss the events that led to the depreciation of sterling in 2008.

Q78. What are the causes of exchange rate volatility? What are the adverse effects of exchange rate volatility? Has the problem of exchange rate volatility become worse in the past ten years?

*Q79. Using *ISLMBP* analysis, compare the relative effectiveness of fiscal and monetary policy as means of controlling aggregate demand (a) under a system of fixed exchange rates and (b) under a system of free-floating exchange rates.

Q80. Debate
A movement towards fixed exchange rates is to be wholly regretted. It is a denial of political and economic sovereignty and can force countries to adopt quite inappropriate domestic macroeconomic policies.

ANSWERS

Q1. (a) (ii), (b) (iii), (c) (i).

Q2. *floating.*

Q3. *fixed.*

Q4. (a) (iv), (b) (ii), (c) (i), (d) (iii).

Q5. **(a)** *True.*
  (b) *True.*
  (c) *False:* it should be RERI = NERI × P_X/P_M.
  (d) *False:* the real exchange rate provides a better idea of the quantity of imports that can be obtained from a given quantity of exports.
  (e) *True.*

Q6. *currency flow.* Note that if a deficit on current account is offset by a surplus on the capital plus financial accounts (excluding reserves) or vice versa, there will be no need for intervention.

Q7. *buy* sterling (with currencies in the reserves).

Q8. *reduce.*

Q9. *raise.*

Q10. *inflows.*

Q11. *dampening.*

Q12. *reduce.*

Q13. *recession.*

Q14. *False.* Purchases of domestic currency by the central bank to support the exchange rate will reduce the money supply.

Q15. C. To prevent the pound rising on the foreign exchange market the Bank of England will sell pounds. This will increase the money supply; so to offset this – sterilise it – the Bank of England must reduce the money supply by selling government securities.

Q16. *deflationary.*

Q17. (a) and (d) are examples of *expenditure switching.*
  (b) and (c) are examples of *expenditure changing.*

Q18. *True.* Lower domestic prices will lead to an *increase* in demand for domestically produced goods.

Q19. *False.* It is the other way round. Expenditure changing from increased export demand and reduced import demand will, via the multiplier, cause an increase in national income and an *increase* in the demand for imports.

Q20. *True.*

Q21. (a) (vi), (b) (iv), (c) (iii), (d) (vii), (e) (ii), (f) (i), (g) (v).

Q22. (a) *fall.*

(b) *surplus.*

(c) *falls.*

(d) *fall.*

(e) *deficit.*

(f) The question is which will be the greater: the surplus on current account or the deficit on the financial account. This will depend on the marginal propensity to import, which will determine the size of the current account surplus, and on the mobility of capital, which will determine the size of the financial account deficit.

Q23. *True:* so monetary policy cannot be used for domestic stabilisation purposes.

Q24. *True:* but according to Keynesians, the long run may be a long time coming.

Q25. *surplus.*

Q26. *rise.*

Q27. *increases.*

Q28. *larger.*

Q29. *increases.*

Q30. *upward.*

Q31. *inflows.*

Q32. *surplus.*

Q33. *increasing.*

Q34. *upward.*

Q35. *increase.* Notice that prices tend to be more flexible upwards than downwards, so the long-run adjustment may be quicker for a positive shock than for a negative one.

Q36. A. As the world economy grows, so the growth in the country's exports will be less than the growth in its imports if the income elasticity of demand for exports is lower than that for imports.

Q37. (a) *Raise* them.

(b) Cause an *inflow* of finance.

(c) *Increase it again.*

(d) *Increase it.*

(e) *Lower* them.

(f) Cause an *outflow* of finance.

(g) *Reduce* it.

(h) *Help to reduce* it.

(i) *fiscal.*

Q38. Advantages include: certainty for the business community; little or no speculation (provided people believe that the rate will remain fixed); automatic correction of monetary errors; prevention of the government pursuing 'irresponsible' macroeconomic policies.

Q39. Disadvantages from the new classical perspective include: they make monetary policy totally ineffective; an imbalance between current and financial accounts may persist; they contradict the objective of having free markets.

Q40. Disadvantages from the Keynesian perspective include: deficits can lead to a recession, or if severe, to a depression; there may be problems of international liquidity to finance deficits; inability to adjust to shocks given sticky wages and prices; speculation if people believe that the fixed rate cannot be maintained. Furthermore, if a country has persistent current account deficits, it may need to have persistently higher interest rates than its competitors, and may suffer lower growth rates as a result.

Q41. B. The theory implies that the exchange rate will adjust so as to offset the effects of different inflation rates in different countries.

Q42. $1.00. To keep the purchasing power of the pound the same abroad as at home, the 50 per cent reduction in the purchasing power of the pound at home as a result of the 50 per cent inflation must be matched by a 50 per cent depreciation in the exchange rate (i.e. whereas originally £1 exchanged for $1.50, now £1.50 must exchange for $1.00).

Q43. (a) Move into *deficit.*

(b) Move into *deficit.*

(c) *more than 10 per cent.* The deficit on the financial account will cause the exchange rate to depreciate by more than that necessary to restore purchasing-power parity.

Q44. *True.*

Q45. (a) *Appreciate.* A deflationary monetary policy will lead to higher interest rates, which will cause an inflow of finance and thus extra demand for (and reduced supply of) the domestic currency on the foreign exchange market.

(b) *Decrease it.* The higher exchange rate will discourage exports (an injection) and encourage imports (a withdrawal).

(c) *Depreciate.* A deflationary fiscal policy will lead to a lower transactions demand for money and hence a lower interest rate. This will encourage an outflow of finance and thus an increased supply of (and reduced demand for) the domestic currency on the foreign exchange market.

(d) *Increase it.* The lower exchange rate will lead to increased exports and reduced imports.

Q46. Advantages include: automatic correction of external disequilibria; elimination of the need for reserves; governments have a greater independence to pursue their chosen domestic policy.

Q47. (a) *Yes:* the inelasticities of currency demand and supply will cause severe fluctuations unless changes in interest rates or other factors affecting the financial account caused the curves to shift in such a way as to offset exchange rate movements.

(b) *Yes:* speculation tends to be self-fulfilling.

(c) *No*: this will tend to prevent large-scale financial movements and thus avoid large-scale exchange rate fluctuations.

(d) *Yes*: this can cause large-scale financial movements.

(e) *No*: this will make the demand for the currency more elastic and thus the exchange rate more stable.

Q48. *short term*: long-term movements in exchange rates over a number of years *cannot* be offset by forward currency dealing. Forward exchange deals are only for a few weeks or months hence.

Q49. *forward*.

Q50. *exchange rate*.

Q51. (a) (v), (b) (ii), (c) (iv), (d) (i), (e) (vi), (f) (iii).

Q52. It could be very disruptive to firms and might be seen as a sign of weakness of the economy and of the government's political failure. If so, it could possibly lead to speculation about a further devaluation. Also it would be inflationary.

Q53. E. In the short run, the demand for both imports and exports may be relatively inelastic, given that consumers and producers take time to adjust to price changes (arising from the devaluation). Thus the current account may deteriorate directly after the devaluation and only improve after a number of months (the J-curve).

Q54. Because the USA ran persistent balance of payments deficits.

Q55. Using reserves to intervene on the foreign exchange market; changes in interest rates.

Q56. *False*. By reducing the need to deflate if a country was experiencing a deficit, the system encouraged the expansion of countries' money supply.

Q57. E. It is 'hot' because it can easily be switched from one country to another as interest rates or expected exchange rates change.

Q58. (a) No: external and internal $r \downarrow$.
(b) Yes: external $r \downarrow$; internal $r \uparrow$.
(c) No: external and internal $r \uparrow$.
(d) Yes: external $r \uparrow$; internal $r \downarrow$.
(e) Yes: external $r \downarrow$; internal $r \uparrow$.
(f) Yes: external $r \uparrow$; internal $r \downarrow$.

Q59. Yes: (a), (b), (d), (h) and (i).
No: (c), (e), (f), (g) and (j).
Note in the case of (d) that the adoption of money supply targets is likely to involve the government having to adjust interest rates to keep money supply within the target range and that this could lead to large inflows or outflows of short-term finance with a resulting effect on the exchange rate. In the case of (f) the adoption of inflation targets by countries (assuming that the targets are similar) will lead to greater harmonisation. In the short run, it could lead to greater exchange rate volatily if countries had different underlying inflation rates, but in the long run, it should lead to greater exchange rate

stability as harmonisation increases. In the case of (j), if business cycles become more synchronised, countries' consumption, interest rates and inflation rates are likely to be more synchronised.

Q60. (a) All those combinations of national income (Y) and the rate of interest (r) where the balance of payments is in equilibrium.

(b) *Financial account* moves into *surplus* (as finance is attracted into the country).

(c) *Current account* moves into *deficit* (as higher incomes cause an increase in imports).

(d) Because an increase in national income causes the current account to move into deficit and therefore if the balance of payments is to stay in balance there must be a rise in the rate of interest to cause a counterbalancing surplus on the financial account.

(e) Combinations in area of diagram *above* the *BP* curve. This area shows higher interest rates or lower levels of national income than are necessary to achieve a balance. Higher interest rates will improve the financial account. Lower national income will improve the current account.

(f) It will get *steeper*. A rise in national income will cause a bigger rise in imports and thus there will have to be a bigger rise in interest rates to cause the necessary counterbalancing inflow of finance.

(g) It will get *steeper*. A bigger rise in interest rates will be needed to attract the necessary inflow of finance to offset any deterioration on the current account from an increase in income.

(h) It will shift *downwards*. The current account will improve at any level of national income and thus a lower interest rate will be necessary to achieve the counterbalancing level on the financial account.

(i) It will shift *upwards*. If there is currently a balance of payments surplus (the economy is in the part of the diagram above the *BP* curve), the exchange rate will appreciate. The resulting increased imports and reduced exports will cause the balance of payments surplus to disappear. The *BP* curve will shift upwards.

Q61. (a) The *IS* curve would shift to the *left*.

(b) It would *fall*.

(c) It would *fall*.

(d) It would *improve*. A lower income would mean that less imports were purchased.

(e) It would *deteriorate*. A lower rate of interest will encourage an outflow of finance.

(f) It would move into *deficit*. The intersection of the new *IS* curve with *LM* is below the *BP* curve. The financial account effect is stronger than the current account effect (this is likely in the short run, given the massive financial flows that take place on the foreign exchanges).

(g) The *BP* curve would have to be steeper than the *LM* curve.

(h) *Decrease* as finance flows out of the country.

(i) Shift it to the *left*.

(j) Where the *LM* curve has shifted far enough to the left so that it intersects with the new *IS* curve *along* the *BP* curve. Only then will the balance of payments deficit be eliminated and thus money supply stop falling.

(k) *Strengthened*. The leftward shift of the *LM* curve will cause a further fall in equilibrium national income.

Q62. A. A rise in money supply (a rightward shift in the *LM* curve) will reduce interest rates. This will encourage an outflow of finance, which will reduce money supply again (a leftward shift in the *LM* curve).

Q63. See Figure A25.1. The deflationary fiscal policy shifts the *IS* curve to the left (say to IS_2). The resulting lower interest rate causes a balance of payments deficit (point *b* is below the *BP* curve). This causes the exchange rate to depreciate and thus the *BP* curve to shift downwards. But the depreciation

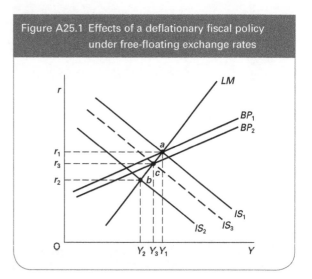

Figure A25.1 Effects of a deflationary fiscal policy under free-floating exchange rates

will encourage more exports (an injection) and discourage imports (a withdrawal) and thus cause a rise in aggregate demand. The *IS* curve will shift back towards the right, reducing the original deflationary effect. Eventual equilibrium is reached at a point such as *c*, where all three curves intersect.

Chapter 26

Global and Regional Interdependence

A **REVIEW**

A rapid growth in international trade and financial flows has made countries much more inter-dependent. The result has been that countries' domestic economies are increasingly being governed by the world economy and by world international financial movements. We start by seeing just how countries are inter-related. We then look at what can be done to create a greater co-ordination of international economic policies. The extreme solution to currency instability is for countries to adopt a common currency. We then turn to look at the euro and how economic and monetary union (EMU) operates. Finally we look at some alternative suggestions for reducing currency fluctuations.

26.1 Globalisation and the problem of instability

(Pages 783–5) There are two main ways in which countries are economically interdependent: through trade and through international financial markets.

When the US economy expands, assuming no change in US interest rates, this will lead to **Q1.** *an expansion of output in other countries/a contraction in other countries approximately equal to the expansion in the USA.* This is the international trade multiplier effect.

 Q2. Which one of the following defines the inter-national trade multiplier?

A. The amount by which international trade expands for each $1 expansion in exports of country A.

B. The amount that country A's income expands for each $1 increase in its exports.

C. The amount that country A's income declines for each $1 increase in its imports.

D. The amount that country B's imports grow for each $1 increase in country A's national income.

E. The amount that country B's national income rises (via an increase in exports to A) for each $1 rise in country A's national income.

As international trade grows as a proportion of world GDP, countries become more interdependent and vulnerable to world trade fluctuations. In 2009, world output fell by **Q3.** *0.5/1.5/2.5* per cent and worldwide exports fell by **Q4.** *8/12/16 per cent.*

Q5. Which of the following are consequences of increasing international financial interdependence?

(a) Each day, some $4 trillion of assets are traded across the foreign exchanges. *Yes/No*

(b) Pension funds, insurance companies and investment trusts have become important players on foreign exchange markets. *Yes/No*

(c) Financial institutions operating in one country have liabilities to foreign residents. *Yes/No*

(d) There are growing foreign holdings of government securities. *Yes/No*

(e) Securitisation enables financial institutions to raise capital from financial investors across the globe.

Yes/No

(f) Changes in interest rates in one country can affect the economies of other countries.   *Yes/No*

The effects of the international trade multiplier may be amplified by, or more than offset by, international financial flows.

Q6. Assume that the US economy expands. Assume also that the US Federal Reserve Bank (the central bank of the USA), worried by rising inflation, raises interest rates. What will be the consequences?

(a) There will be an outflow of finance from the USA.

True/False/Uncertain

(b) The US dollar will appreciate.   *True/False/Uncertain*

(c) This will lead to a fall in US exports.

True/False/Uncertain

(d) As a result of the action of the Federal Reserve Bank, US national income will fall below what it would otherwise have been.   *True/False/Uncertain*

(e) There will also be a fall in US imports.

True/False/Uncertain

(f) The current account of the USA's trading partners will improve.   *True/False/Uncertain*

(g) Interest rates in other countries will fall.

True/False/Uncertain

(h) Investment in other countries will rise.

True/False/Uncertain

(i) Other countries' national incomes will rise.

True/False/Uncertain

From the example given in Q6, it can be seen that a change in US monetary policy will probably have a **Q7.** *similar/opposite* effect on *other* countries' national incomes to that on US national income. This is the result of **Q8.** *the international trade multiplier effect/international financial flows*. The larger the level of international financial flows, the **Q9.** *more/less* will interest rate changes in one country affect the economies of other countries.

Q10. Consider the following policy changes in the USA:
(i) an expansionary fiscal policy, combined with lower interest rates.
(ii) an expansionary fiscal policy, combined with higher interest rates.
(iii) a contractionary fiscal policy, combined with lower interest rates.
(iv) a contractionary fiscal policy, combined with higher interest rates.

In which case(s) will international financial flows amplify the foreign trade multiplier effect on other countries?

A. (i) and (ii).

B. (iii) and (iv).

C. (i) and (iv).

D. (ii) and (iii).

E. (i) and (iii).

(Pages 785–7) As a consequence of both trade and financial interdependence, the world economy tends to experience an international business cycle. In this context, it is important for countries to adopt complementary economic policies and not to engage in 'beggar-my-neighbour' tactics.

Q11. Assume that the world is suffering from a recession. Which of the following policies adopted by country A would benefit other countries and which would hinder them in attempting to pull out of recession?

(a) An expansionary fiscal and monetary policy.

benefit/hinder other countries

(b) A devaluation of the currency.

benefit/hinder other countries

(c) Raising interest rates in an attempt to reduce inflation and make exports more competitive.

benefit/hinder other countries

(d) Using protectionism to help domestic industry.

benefit/hinder other countries

(e) Giving investment grants to industry.

benefit/hinder other countries

(Pages 788–90) Currency fluctuations could be lessened if countries' economies were harmonised: in other words, if they were at a similar stage in the business cycle and if they did not experience excessive exchange rate fluctuations. In order to achieve these objectives, the Group of 7 major industrialised countries (Canada, France, Germany, Italy, Japan, the UK and the USA) meet periodically to discuss joint economic policies.

Q12. During the 2000s, the USA operated with a massive current account deficit, financed by the acquisition of huge amounts of dollars by the rest of the world, especially in Asia. Which of the following are the likely consequences of such an imbalance?:
(i) A depreciation of the US dollar.
(ii) Overheating in China.
(iii) An appreciation of the US dollar.
(iv) Currency volatility.

A. (i), (ii) and (iv).

B. (ii), (iii) and (iv).

C. (i).

D. (ii).

E. (iv).

Q13. For which of the following reasons is it likely to be difficult for the G7 countries to achieve harmonisation of their economies?

(a) The G7 countries are usually more concerned about their own national interests than international ones.

Yes/No

(b) Countries today have little power, given the huge scale of international financial flows. *Yes/No*

(c) Monetary policy is generally determined by central banks. *Yes/No*

(d) Achieving similar rates of economic growth may involve considerable differences between the countries with respect to other macroeconomic indicators. *Yes/No*

(e) General harmonisation of policies is possible only if there is convergence of the G7 countries, and that has not been achieved. *Yes/No*

(?) **Q14.** For each of the following pairs of objectives, explain why it may be difficult to achieve harmonisation of *both* simultaneously.

(a) Interest rates and inflation rates

....

(b) Budget deficits and economic growth

....

(c) Inflation rates and exchange rate stability

....

Q15. If countries attempt to achieve similar rates of economic growth through demand management policy, for which of the following reasons may the equilibrium rate of exchange change over the longer term?

(i) The marginal propensity to import differs from one country to another.

(ii) The relative income elasticities of demand for imports and exports differ from one country to another.

(iii) The rate of growth of productivity differs from one country to another.

A. (i) and (ii).

B. (i) and (iii).

C. (ii) and (iii).

D. (ii) alone.

E. (i), (ii) and (iii).

Q16. In the global financial crisis of the late 2000s, countries that faced severe problems struggled to cope without assistance from international institutions. *True/False*

26.2 European Economic and Monetary Union (EMU)

(Pages 791–2) The ultimate way for a group of countries to achieve greater currency stability between themselves is to form an economic and monetary union (EMU), adopting a common currency and having a common central bank and common monetary policy. An example of this is the EU.

The forerunner to EMU was the exchange rate mechanism (ERM), which attempted to achieve greater exchange rate stability. It operated until the launch of the euro.

Q17. Which one of the following describes the ERM?

A. A fixed exchange rate system between member countries and a joint float with the rest of the world.

B. A dirty floating system between member countries and a clean float with the rest of the world.

C. A pegged exchange rate system at a single point between member countries and a joint float with the rest of the world.

D. A pegged exchange rate system within bands between member countries and a joint float with the rest of the world.

E. A fixed exchange rate system within bands between member countries and a crawling peg with a basket of rest-of-the-world currencies.

Q18. Under an exchange rate mechanism, which of the following could be used to reduce inflation if there is upward pressure on the exchange rate and if it is already near the top of its band?

(i) Raising interest rates.

(ii) Reducing aggregate demand through fiscal policy.

(iii) A prices and incomes policy.

A. (i) only.

B. (i) and (ii).

C. (i) and (iii).

D. (ii) and (iii).

E. (i), (ii) and (iii).

(Pages 792–6) The Maastricht Treaty, signed in February 1992, set out a three-stage process to lead to the establishment of a single currency by 1999 at the latest.

Q19. Which of the following convergence criteria did the Maastricht Treaty specify as conditions for joining the single currency?

(i) Inflation should be no more than 1.5 per cent above the average inflation rate of the three countries in the EU with the lowest inflation.

(ii) The interest rate on long-term government bonds should be no more than 2 per cent above the average of the three countries with the lowest inflation rates.

(iii) The budget deficit should be no more than 3 per cent of GDP at market prices.

(iv) The national debt should be no more than 60 per cent of GDP at market prices.

(v) The currency should have been within the normal ERM bands for at least two years with no realignments or excessive intervention.

A. (i), (ii) and (iv).

B. (ii), (iii) and (iv).

C. (i) and (v).

D. (ii), (iv) and (v).

E. All of the above.

Q20. As 1999 approached, so convergence between the economies of the ERM countries grew and exchange rate fluctuations diminished. *True/False*

Q21. At the time of the launch of the euro in 1999, only Britain, Denmark and Belgium did not join. *True/False*

In May 2004, **Q22.** *five/ten* new members joined the EU. **Q23.** *All/Most* of them stated their intention of joining the euro, but to qualify, they need to be members of ERM2 for at least **Q24.** *two/five* years. The first three countries to join ERM2 (in June 2004) were **Q25.**:

....

....

....

Q26. By 2011, there were 17 countries that had adopted the euro. *True/False*

Q27. According to the Maastricht Treaty, which of the following would apply to those countries adopting full EMU in Stage 3?

(a) A fixed exchange rate between their currencies.
Yes/No

(b) A pegged exchange rate between their currencies.
Yes/No

(c) A single central bank for all the countries. *Yes/No*

(d) A single currency for all the countries. *Yes/No*

(e) Identical tax rates. *Yes/No*

(f) Free trade between the countries. *Yes/No*

(g) Free financial movements between the countries.
Yes/No

(h) Common external tariffs. *Yes/No*

(i) The abolition of all special EU help for different regions of the various countries. *Yes/No*

(j) A common monetary policy. *Yes/No*

(?) Q28. Give two advantages of a single currency area.

1. ....

2. ....

(?) Q29. Give two disadvantages of a single currency area.

1. ....

2. ....

Q30. In 2010/11, many EU politicians were concerned that a two-track Europe would emerge, with some countries in recession pressing to have interest rates remain low whilst others were calling for interest rates to rise to prevent an acceleration of inflation. *True/False*

The success or otherwise of having a single currency in Europe will depend on how close the eurozone is to an 'optimal currency area'.

Q31. An optimal currency area can be defined as one which:

A. maximises the growth rates of the member countries.

B. minimises the degree of economic fluctuations between member countries.

C. maximises the amount of trade between the member countries.

D. minimises the average inflation rate between member countries.

E. would involve a decrease in net benefits from having a single currency if the size of the area were either to grow or to diminish.

Q32. The formation of the Coalition government in the UK in 2010 increased the possibility that the UK would join the euro. *True/False*

26.3 Achieving greater currency stability

(Pages 796–7) If there is a consensus in markets that a currency will depreciate, there is very little in the short term that governments can do to stop it.

Q33. If there were a 50 per cent chance that by this time next week a currency will have depreciated by 20 per cent, then selling the currency now will give an expected return of approximately 10 per cent for the week. *True/False*

Q34. The weekly interest in Q33 is equivalent to approximately 520 per cent per annum. *True/False*

Q35. If neither changes in interest rates nor central bank intervention from the reserves can halt a depreciation/appreciation of a currency that is perceived to be not at its equilibrium exchange rate, then which of the following exchange rate regimes are viable over the longer term?

(a) Free-floating exchange rate. *Yes/No*

(b) Adjustable peg system (with just occasional adjustments). *Yes/No*

(c) Fixed with an independent monetary policy. *Yes/No*

(d) Adopting the dollar or the euro or some other international currency as the domestic currency. *Yes/No*

(Pages 797–800) What then can be done to reduce the scale of speculative flows and create greater currency stability? One approach is to reduce the *mobility* of international finance by introducing controls over financial flows. Such controls pose problems of their own.

(?) **Q36.** Identify two problems of using controls over financial flows (sometimes known as 'capital controls').

1.   ....

2.   ....

(≣) **Q37.** Which one of the following is not a possible advantage of a Tobin tax on financial transactions?

A. It would dampen speculative currency movements.

B. It would generate significant revenue that could be used to tackle international problems.

C. It would restore to the nation state an element of control over monetary policy.

D. It would discourage tax avoidance.

E. It would reduce volatility in exchange rate movements.

(?) **Q38.** Controls are likely to dampen speculation, not eliminate it. Why might this be seen to be a desirable outcome?

....

....

(◗) **Q39.** An alternative to controlling financial flows would be to use a system of exchange rate target zones. This system would have the following features:

(a) Currencies would be allowed to fluctuate within bands.   *True/False*

(b) These bands would be very narrow, say ±1 per cent.   *True/False*

(c) Central parity would be set so as to maintain it at the 'fundamental equilibrium exchange rate'.   *True/False*

(d) The central parity would be adjusted very infrequently.   *True/False*

(e) There would be 'soft buffers', with exchange rates occasionally allowed to move outside their bands.   *True/False*

(?) **Q40.** Give two problems of the system of exchange rate target zones.

1.   ....

2.   ....

B   PROBLEMS, EXERCISES AND PROJECTS

Q41. Construct a table and four graphs showing the movements of the following rates of exchange over the last three years: \$/€, ¥/\$, €/£, \$/£. Plot the exchange rates at monthly intervals. Now plot interest rates for the four countries/areas over the same period. How closely have the exchange rate movements reflected interest rate movements? Identify any rapid changes in exchange rates and search through newspapers to find articles explaining such changes.

Sources: *International Financial Statistics* (IMF); *Datastream*; *The Economist*; newspapers; various websites, including the *Financial Times* (http://www.ft.com), Bank of England (http://www.bankofengland.co.uk), European Central Bank (http://www.ecb.int), Bank of Japan (http://www.boj.or.jp/en/index.htm), US Federal Reserve Bank (http://www.federalreserve.gov), International Monetary Fund (http://www.imf.org), Treasury Pocket Databank (http://www.

hm-treasury.gov.uk). Hotlinks to all these sites can be found in the hotlinks section of this book's website at http://www.pearsoned.co.uk/sloman.

Q42. Find data that will allow you to evaluate the extent to which the countries in the euro area have been closely aligned in terms of the business cycle in recent years. A helpful source of data is OECD (http://www.oecd.org), especially the statistical annex to the OECD Economic Outlook.

Q43. Undertake a web search to find articles considering whether or not the UK should adopt the euro. Prepare two reports, one putting the case for the UK adopting the euro and one putting the case against.

Sources: various newspapers (see the hotlinks section of this book's website at http://www.pearsoned.co.uk/sloman).

C   DISCUSSION TOPICS AND ESSAYS

Q44. Under what circumstances will the effect of international financial flows reinforce the international trade multiplier effect? Under what circumstances will the effect of such flows offset the international trade multiplier effect?

Q45. Why is it important for countries' economic policies to be harmonised?

Q46. What are the economic (as opposed to political) difficulties in achieving an international harmonisation of economic policies?

Q47. Using appropriate examples, explain how an economic crisis in one part of the world might lead to a global economic crisis. What would be the appropriate response by the G7 economies to a 'regional' economic crisis?

Q48. Discuss why it should be a problem for the global economy if the USA persists in running a substantial current account deficit.

Q49. To what extent were the benefits and costs of membership of the exchange rate mechanism of the European Monetary System similar to those experienced under the old Bretton Woods system?

Q50. Would economic and monetary union between a group of countries reduce any individual country's economic problems to those of a region *within* a country?

Q51. What are the arguments for and against a common currency for (a) the whole of the existing EU; (b) a considerably enlarged EU; (c) the whole world?

Q52. What difficulties are there for the eurozone countries in achieving continued convergence of their economies?

Q53. Discuss the extent to which countries in the eurozone were hampered in responding to the global financial crisis by the need to follow a common monetary policy.

Q54. Consider the arguments for and against the worldwide adoption of a Tobin tax.

Q55. Debate
A world of just three currencies (the dollar, euro and yen) would be one which was much more stable economically, where international economic policies could be much more easily harmonised and where international economic growth could be higher.

 ANSWERS

Q1. *an expansion of output in other countries.* This will occur via the following process. A rise in US national income will lead to a rise in US expenditure on imports. These increased US imports represent an increase in exports for other countries, and hence an injection into their economies. These increased injections lead to an expansion in output of these other countries.

Q2. E.

Q3. *0.5 per cent*: this may not sound much, but 0.5 per cent of world output is a lot of output!

Q4. *12 per cent.*

Q5. *(a)–(f): yes.* All of these are consequences of increasing international financial interdependence.

Q6. (a) *False.* The higher interest rate will attract an *inflow* of finance.

(b) *True.* The inflow of finance will drive up the exchange rate.

(c) *True.* The higher exchange rate will cause exports to be less competitive.

(d) *True.* The higher interest rate will cause lower investment. This, combined with lower exports, will cause national income to be lower than it would otherwise have been.

(e) *Uncertain.* A higher exchange rate will make imports relatively cheaper and hence increase them, but a lower national income will tend to reduce expenditure on imports.

(f) *True.* Lower US exports (and possibly higher imports) will mean lower imports (and possibly higher exports) for the USA's trading partners.

(g) *False.* A rise in US interest rates will tend to drive up interest rates in the rest of the world (albeit by probably not so much as in the USA).

(h) *Uncertain* (although probably *False*). Higher interest rates in other countries will cause their investment to fall and lead to a fall in confidence. It is possible, however, that higher exports to the USA (injections) combined with lower imports from the USA (withdrawals) could lead to *higher* national income, and, via the accelerator, to *higher* investment. It is likely, however, that the first effect would be the dominant one.

(i) *Uncertain* (although probably *False*). There are two effects here: (i) the fall in their imports (and possible rise in their exports) will cause their national income to rise; (ii) the rise in their interest rates and probable fall in investment will cause their national income to fall. Probably the interest rate effect will be the dominant one, leading to a net fall in national income.

Q7. *similar.*

Q8. *international financial flows.*

Q9. *more.*

Q10. C. In the case of (i), an expansionary fiscal policy in the USA will lead, via the international trade multiplier, to higher national incomes in other countries. This effect will be amplified by lower interest rates, transmitted to them from the USA via international financial flows. In the case of (iv), the contractionary international trade multiplier effects of a contractionary fiscal policy will be amplified by higher interest rates, again transmitted via international financial flows.

Q11. (a) and (e) will help to stimulate other countries too, via the international trade multiplier. They thus *benefit* other countries.

(b), (c) and (d) reduce other countries' exports and/or increase their imports and thus *hinder* their recovery.

Q12. A.

Q13. *Yes* for all of them. In the case of (c), with monetary policy determined by central banks, it makes it impossible for G7 politicians to use changes in interest rates as a means of achieving harmonisation. In the case of (d), with different rates of productivity growth, different underlying inflation rates, different propensities to import, and different sizes of budget deficits and national debts as a proportion of GDP, achieving similar growth rates may involve considerable interest rate differences and currency instability.

Q14. *(a)* With different underlying rates of inflation (e.g. different cost-push pressures), to achieve similar rates of inflation between countries may require quite different rates of interest.

(b) Budget deficits differ substantially from one country to another as does the balance between saving and investment. To achieve similar budget deficits will entail considerable fiscal policy changes between countries and different rates of economic growth.

(c) To achieve similar rates of inflation between countries will involve changing interest rates for this purpose. These changes in interest rates can cause considerable exchange rate volatility.

Q15. E. Each one would cause a different rate of growth of imports and exports (the last one because it would affect the rate of inflation) and thus a change in the equilibrium rate of exchange over time.

Q16. *False.* The IMF was a major player in providing rescue packages for countries such as Iceland, Ireland and Greece.

Q17. D. From August 1993 to the start of the euro in 1999, the band was fixed at a ±15 per cent divergence from any other ERM currency (the exception being the German mark and the Dutch guilder, where the band was ±2^1/$_4$ per cent). Previous to that the band was ±2^1/$_4$ per cent for all currencies other than those of Spain and Portugal (and the UK before it left the system in 1992), where the band was ±6 per cent.

Q18. D. Interest rates could not be raised because this would put further upward pressure on the exchange rate.

Q19. E. All of these convergence criteria were to be met.

Q20. *True.*

Q21. *False*: it was Britain, Denmark, Sweden and Greece. Greece subsequently joined in 2001.

Q22. *ten.*

Q23. *All.*

Q24. *two.*

Q25. Estonia, Lithuania and Slovenia.

Q26. *True*: Slovenia adopted the euro in 2007, Malta and Cyprus in 2008, Slovakia in 2009 and Estonia in 2011.

Q27. *Yes*: (c), (d), (f), (g), (h) and (j).

No: (a), (b), (e) and (i).

Note that since the euro has fully replaced the previous currencies there have been no 'exchange rates' between member countries – any more than there is between

England and Wales. Note also that, although types of tax must be harmonised and rates of indirect taxes should be similar, direct taxes could differ: they would be like different local taxes within a country.

Q28. Advantages include: elimination of the costs of converting currencies; elimination of uncertainties associated with possible exchange rate realignments and fluctuations within the permitted band; a lower average rate of inflation (provided that the European Central Bank is truly independent from short-term political considerations); greater macroeconomic stability which will promote higher levels of investment.

Q29. Disadvantages include: problems of domestic adjustment if the economy is not in harmony with other members (e.g. if it has higher cost-push inflationary pressures), with the country maybe becoming a depressed 'region' of the union; adjustment to asymmetric shocks (shocks that have different effects on the various member countries); loss of political sovereignty (some see this as an advantage).

Q30. *True.* This conflict would be less of a problem if convergence between the member economies were to increase.

Q31. E. The benefits (or costs) of a single currency are not confined to one indicator (such as inflation or trade or economic growth). An optimal currency area is one which maximises the *overall* benefit to the members. If the current area is the optimal size, then altering the size (either increasing it or decreasing it) will lead to a decrease in the overall benefit from having the currency area.

Q32. *False*: the Coalition has made it clear that there is now no possibility of the UK joining the euro.

Q33. *True* (50 per cent of 20 per cent).

Q34. *False.* 10 per cent per week compounded over a year is equivalent to over 14 000 per cent per annum.

Q35. *Yes*: (a) and (d). With a free-floating exchange rate, there is no need for exchange rate intervention at all. With a common currency, you give up monetary policy, but there can be no speculation as there is no possibility of a currency depreciating against itself! With anything other than these extremes, as soon as the pegged or fixed rate ceases to be the perceived equilibrium rate, speculation is likely to force an exchange rate adjustment.

Q36. They may discourage international investment; they may discourage international trade; they are disliked as 'anti-market'.

Q37. D. Preventing tax avoidance is one of the major challenges of operating a Tobin tax.

Q38. Because speculation, if dampened, is likely to be stabilising and may help force countries to move towards an equilibrium exchange rate, rather than maintaining one which does not reflect underlying economic fundamentals, such as purchasing power parities.

Q39. (a) *True*; (b) *False* (bands would be wide: e.g. ±10%); (c) *True*; (d) *False* (the central parity may have to be adjusted very frequently, if the country's rate of inflation diverges from the weighted average of its trading partners); (e) *True* (the closer the rate approached to these buffers, the greater would be the scale of exchange market intervention).

Q40. It removes pressure on high-inflation countries to bring their inflation under control; monetary policy may have to be geared to keeping the exchange rate within the bands, rather than being used for domestic purposes (though this problem is not as great as it would be with a more rigid exchange rate system).

Chapter **27**

Economics of Developing Countries

 A **REVIEW**

In this last chapter we look at some of the economic problems of the poorer countries of the world, problems beside which those of the affluent North pale into insignificance. We start by examining the nature and extent of poverty in developing countries. This poverty cannot be examined in isolation from these countries' relationships with the rest of the world and thus we turn to this topic next. We continue by looking at some specific internal problems such the neglect of agriculture and the huge scale of unemployment. Finally we examine the massive international debts that many poor countries have incurred and the difficulties in overcoming them.

27.1 The problem of underdevelopment

(Pages 803–5) One way of defining the level of development is the extent to which a country provides the basic needs of life.

Q1. Some 70 per cent of the world's population lives in developing countries (low- and middle-income countries) but earns only 30 per cent of the world's income.

True/False

Q2. Which of the following would you include as basic needs?
(a) Adequate food. *Yes/No*
(b) Free education for all children up to 12. *Yes/No*
(c) Sufficient time free from work to be able to rest and enjoy social interaction. *Yes/No*
(d) Adequate clothing, warmth and shelter. *Yes/No*
(e) Freedom to choose where to work and live. *Yes/No*
(f) Adequate health care. *Yes/No*
(g) Adequate care for the elderly and those without work. *Yes/No*
(h) Fulfilment at work. *Yes/No*

(i) Proper sanitation. *Yes/No*
(j) Self-esteem. *Yes/No*

Q3. Give three problems in defining development in terms of basic needs.

1. ....

2. ....

3. ....

(Pages 805–7) The single most commonly used measure of economic development is GNY per head, measured in some international currency such as the US dollar.

Q4. Which of the following are advantages of using GNY as an indicator of the level of a country's economic development?
(a) GNY statistics are available for all countries. *Yes/No*
(b) A sustained rise in GNY is generally considered to be a necessary condition for a sustained increase in economic welfare. *Yes/No*

 Multiple choice   Written answer   Delete wrong word   Diagram/table manipulation   Calculation   Matching/ordering

(c) A sustained rise in GNY is generally considered as a sufficient condition for a sustained increase in economic welfare. *Yes/No*

(d) Exchange rates accurately reflect domestic purchasing power. *Yes/No*

(e) Virtually all goods and services that are produced are included in GNY. *Yes/No*

(f) Prices, although not exactly equal to marginal costs, do roughly reflect the opportunity costs of production. *Yes/No*

(g) The rules for measurement of GNY are generally agreed. *Yes/No*

(h) GNY takes externalities into account. *Yes/No*

(i) There is a fairly close correlation between the ranking of countries by GNY per head and by other indicators of development (taken as a whole). *Yes/No*

As a country's economy grows, it is likely that there will be movement from subsistence agriculture to cash crops and industrial production. This structure of production means that GNY statistics for developing countries will tend to **Q5.** *overstate/understate* the level of production and **Q6.** *overstate/understate* the rate of growth of production.

Q7. GNY is based on market prices, but market prices are often distorted. Which of the following are typical market distortions in developing countries?

(a) Rates of interest in the towns are below the opportunity cost of capital. *Yes/No*

(b) Producers of manufactured goods often have considerable market power. *Yes/No*

(c) Wage rates in the modern sector are typically below the market-clearing level. *Yes/No*

(d) Exchange rates are typically overvalued. *Yes/No*

(e) Protection (in the form of tariffs or quotas) is given unevenly to different industries. *Yes/No*

(f) Rates of interest in the countryside are often much higher than those in the towns. *Yes/No*

(g) Prices of foodstuffs are kept artificially high. *Yes/No*

(h) Mine and plantation owners often have considerable monopsony power to drive down wages. *Yes/No*

Q8. Which of the following help to explain why country rankings based on GDP per head and on the HDI are likely to diverge?

(a) The HDI gives weighting to indicators of education and health. *Yes/No*

(b) Countries make use of their resources in different ways – for example, in giving greater weight to education and health care. *Yes/No*

(c) GDP per capita is one of the component indicators used to calculate the HDI. *Yes/No*

(d) Some countries may have better educational provision than the average for countries of their income level. *Yes/No*

(e) Some countries may have lower health care facilities than are typical of countries of their income level. *Yes/No*

27.2 International trade and development

(Pages 807–12) Trade is of vital importance for most developing countries, and yet most suffer from chronic balance of trade deficits. It is therefore of vital importance for countries to adopt the most appropriate trade policies.

Q9. The UN's trade and development index identifies three broad groups of influences or dimensions which interact and affect a country's trade and development performance. For each of the following indicators, state the dimension to which it relates:

(a) Human capital.

Structural and institutional/ Trade policies and process/Levels of development

(b) Openness to trade.

Structural and institutional/ Trade policies and process/Levels of development

(c) Physical infrastructure.

Structural and institutional/ Trade policies and process/Levels of development

(d) Gender development.

Structural and institutional/ Trade policies and process/Levels of development

(e) Financial environment

Structural and institutional/ Trade policies and process/Levels of development

(f) Social development.

Structural and institutional/ Trade policies and process/Levels of development

(g) Effective access to foreign markets.

Structural and institutional/ Trade policies and process/Levels of development

(h) Institutional quality.

Structural and institutional/ Trade policies and process/Levels of development

(i) Environmental sustainability.

Structural and institutional/ Trade policies and process/Levels of development

(j) Economic development.

Structural and institutional/ Trade policies and process/Levels of development

Traditionally, developing countries have been **Q10.** *primary/secondary* exporters and **Q11.** *primary/secondary* importers.

Q12. There are various arguments why developing countries should export food and raw materials. These include:

(i) the vent for surplus theory;

(ii) the Heckscher–Ohlin theory;

(iii) the engine for growth argument;

(iv) differences in technology and labour skills.

Match each of the following arguments to the above.

(a) As industrial expansion takes place in advanced countries, so their demand for developing countries' primary products will increase.

....

(b) Advanced countries can produce industrial goods with comparatively fewer resources than primary products when compared with developing countries.

....

(c) Developing countries have a relative abundance of labour and a relative scarcity of capital when compared with advanced countries.

....

(d) Trade allows developing countries to exploit resources that would not otherwise be used.

....

Q13. According to the Heckscher–Ohlin theory, international trade will lead to an increase in income inequalities.
True/False

Q14. In the late 2000s, almost 50 per cent of exports from the countries known as the heavily indebted poor countries comprised primary goods, compared with 22 per cent for advanced countries. *True/False*

Q15. Which of the following are problems that might arise from a policy of specialising in the production of primaries for export?

(a) Technological progress is less rapid in the production of primaries than in manufactures. *Yes/No*

(b) The benefits from the trade may only accrue in small part to the nationals of the country. *Yes/No*

(c) Primary products have a high income elasticity of demand. *Yes/No*

(d) The price elasticity of demand for primary products from an *individual* country is very low. *Yes/No*

(e) Relying on primary exports may lead to long-term balance of payments deficits. *Yes/No*

(f) Relying on primary exports may lead to long-term increases in the terms of trade. *Yes/No*

(g) The income elasticity of demand for manufactured imports is high. *Yes/No*

(h) The price elasticity of demand for manufactured imports is high. *Yes/No*

(i) The world price of primaries is subject to sharper price fluctuations than the world price of manufactures. *Yes/No*

(j) Exporting primary products may involve substantial external costs. *Yes/No*

(*Pages 812–15*) A second approach to trade is that of *import-substituting industrialisation* (ISI).

Q16. Define *import-substituting industrialisation*.

....

....

ISI has typically involved a process of *tariff escalation*.

Q17. Tariff escalation is where the government imposes larger and larger tariffs on products:
A. the closer they are to the finished stage.
B. over time.
C. the greater the monopolistic power of the foreign importers.
D. the more established the domestic producer becomes.
E. the higher the rate of domestic inflation.

Q18. Import substitution through protectionism is likely to encourage multinational investment in a country.
True/False

Despite its popularity with developing country governments, ISI has involved some serious disadvantages.

Q19. Which of the following have tended to result from ISI?

(a) It has encouraged the establishment of monopolies and oligopolies. *Yes/No*

(b) It has involved artificially high real interest rates. *Yes/No*

(c) It has led to an overvaluation of the exchange rate. *Yes/No*

(d) It has led to urban wages being kept down relative to rural wages. *Yes/No*

(e) It has led to a bias against the agricultural sector. *Yes/No*

(f) Effective protective rates have differed widely from one product to another. *Yes/No*

(g) Effective protective rates have generally been below nominal protective rates. *Yes/No*

Q20. Give three other problems with import-substituting industrialisation.

1. ....

2. ....

3. ....

(*Pages 815–19*) A third approach, and one that many countries have turned to after their experiences with the limitations of ISI, is export-orientated manufacturing.

Q21. The developing countries which have experienced the most rapid rates of economic growth have tended to be export-orientated manufacturing countries. *True/False*

(?) **Q22.** What does the Heckscher–Ohlin theory suggest about the type of manufactured goods in which developing countries should specialise?

....

(≣) **Q23.** Which of the following will help promote the development of export-orientated industries?
(i) Devaluation.
(ii) Removal of tariff barriers.
(iii) Reduction in taxes on employing labour.

A. (i).
B. (ii).
C. (i) and (ii).
D. (i) and (iii).
E. (i), (ii) and (iii).

The gains from an export-orientated manufacturing policy will tend to be greatest for **Q24.** *small/large* countries and when there are **Q25.** *minimal/substantial* internal economies of scale in the potential export industries.

(?) **Q26.** Give three possible drawbacks of pursuing a policy of export-orientated manufacturing.

1. ....

2. ....

3. ....

(≣) **Q27.** China's economic performance has been extraordinary in recent decades. Which of the following were key factors in this success?
(i) Specialisation to take advantage of China's comparative advantage, based in its increasingly well-trained and well-educated workforce.
(ii) Having an economy that is favourable to both domestic and inward investment.
(iii) Having an exchange rate that is overvalued in PPP terms.
(iv) Having an exchange rate that is undervalued in PPP terms.

A. (i) and (ii).
B. (i) and (iii).
C. (ii) and (iv).
D. (i), (ii) and (iii).
E. (i), (ii) and (iv).

27.3 Structural problems within developing countries

(Pages 820–1) The neglect of agriculture
Policies of import-substituting industrialisation have tended to involve an urban bias.

(◗) **Q28.** Examples of urban bias include:
(a) *High/Low* food prices.
(b) *High/Low* rural rates of interest.
(c) *Overvalued/Undervalued* exchange rates.
(d) *High/Low* manufactured prices.
(e) *High/Low* tariffs on imported manufactures.
(f) *High/Low* tariffs on imported foodstuffs.

(?) **Q29.** Give three examples of policies that can help to develop the agricultural sector.

1. ....

2. ....

3. ....

(Pages 821–3) Inappropriate technology
In the urban sector of developing countries, the wage/interest rate ratio has typically been **Q30.** *above/below* the market-clearing level. The effect has been to create a **Q31.** *capital/labour* intensity bias in the choice of techniques. This **Q32.** *is in accordance with/contradicts* the implications of the Heckscher–Ohlin theory.

Nevertheless, capital-intensive techniques may bring some advantages.

(≣) **Q33.** Which of the following are possible advantages for developing countries of capital-intensive techniques?
(i) They are in accordance with the law of comparative advantage.
(ii) They typically yield a higher rate of profit, which can be used for reinvestment.
(iii) They may have a lower capital/output ratio despite having a higher capital/labour ratio.

A. (i).
B. (ii).
C. (iii).
D. (i) and (ii).
E. (ii) and (iii).

(?) **Q34.** Give three possible disadvantages of capital-intensive technologies.

1. ....

2. ....

3. ....

(Pages 823–5) Unemployment
In addition to high rates of open unemployment, developing countries may suffer from considerable disguised unemployment and underemployment.

Q35. Which of the following two definitions is of disguised unemployment and which of underemployment?

(a) Where people are unable to find sufficient work to occupy them full time.

disguised unemployment/underemployment

(b) Where the same work could be done by fewer people.

disguised unemployment/underemployment

Q36. A cause of disguised unemployment in the countryside is the level of overcrowding on the land and the resulting low marginal productivity of labour. *True/False*

Q37. How may the creation of jobs in towns also create more open unemployment in the towns?

....

....

Q38. Rural–urban migration will be greater:
(a) The greater the income differential between the towns and the countryside. *True/False*
(b) The higher the level of unemployment in the towns. *True/False*
(c) The greater the level of disguised unemployment in the countryside. *True/False*
(d) The higher the cost of living in the towns. *True/False*
(e) The lower the costs of migration. *True/False*
(f) The more risk averse a potential migrant is. *True/False*
(g) The more attractive the potential migrant believes city life to be. *True/False*

Q39. Of the following, which will help to reduce urban unemployment?
 (i) Concentrating investment in the towns.
 (ii) The adoption of more capital-intensive techniques.
 (iii) Increasing food prices.
 (iv) Labour-intensive rural infrastructure projects.

A. (i) and (iv).
B. (ii) and (iii).
C. (iii) and (iv).
D. (i), (iii) and (iv).
E. (i), (ii), (iii) and (iv).

27.4 The problem of debt
(Pages 826–7) After the 1973 oil crisis, many developing countries borrowed heavily in order to finance their balance of trade deficits and maintain a programme of investment. After the 1979 oil price rises, however, the problem became much more serious.

Q40. In the world economy after 1979, when compared with the period after 1973:
(a) real interest rates were *higher/lower*.
(b) nominal interest rates were *higher/lower*.

(c) monetary policy was generally *tighter/more relaxed*.
(d) the resulting recession was *deeper/shallower*.
(e) the resulting recession was *shorter/longer lasting*.
(f) a greater proportion of debt was at *variable/fixed* interest rates.
(g) a greater proportion of debt was in the form of *official government/commercial bank* loans.
(h) the effect on developing countries was *more/less* severe.

(Pages 827–9) To cope with the debt crisis and the difficulties of servicing these debts, many countries' debts have been *rescheduled*.

Q41. Give three ways in which debts could be rescheduled.

1. ....

2. ....

3. ....

Official loans are renegotiated through the **Q42.** *London/ Paris/Houston/Toronto* Club, whereas commercial bank loans are often rescheduled by collective action of banks which form a Bank Advisory Committee. Such arrangements are referred to as the **Q43.** *London/Paris/Houston/Toronto* Club.

Q44. Which of the following policies for highly indebted developing countries are recommended by the IMF?
(a) Tight monetary policies. *Yes/No*
(b) Tight fiscal policies. *Yes/No*
(c) Greater economic planning to direct resources into investment. *Yes/No*
(d) Import controls in order to reduce balance of payments deficits. *Yes/No*
(e) Policies to promote greater national economic self-sufficiency. *Yes/No*
(f) Privatisation. *Yes/No*
(g) Devaluation. *Yes/No*
(h) Market-orientated supply-side policies. *Yes/No*
(i) A more open trade policy. *Yes/No*
(j) The abolition of price controls. *Yes/No*

Q45. Give three disadvantages of the policies recommended by the IMF.

1. ....

2. ....

3. ....

Q46. Biofuels offer a clear solution to the problems of environmental degradation, as burning the fuel is offset by the carbon absorbed by growing oil palm trees. *True/False*

(Pages 829–32) A long-term solution to the debt problem will involve a restructuring of the economies of developing countries and their relationships with the advanced countries.

Another requirement for a long-term solution to the debt problem is the cancellation of some of the debts of the most heavily indebted poor countries. Under the HIPC initiative of 1996, and revised in 1999, some of these countries would have a proportion of their debts cancelled.

Q47. The Heavily Indebted Poor Countries (HIPC) initiative was launched in 1996 with the aim of providing debt relief for poor countries in order to reduce their debt to sustainable levels. Which of the following is *not* a criticism that has been levelled at the scheme?

A. The qualifying period is too long.

B. The thresholds have been set too high so that the resulting reduction in debt servicing has been quite modest, or zero.

C. No attempt has been made to ensure that funds released by HIPC were appropriately used for poverty alleviation.

D. The IMF reform programmes have been too harsh.

E. There are countries not included within HIPC that are also suffering debts which divert a high percentage of their income from poverty relief.

In 2006, debt relief was extended under the Multilateral Debt Relief Initiative (MDRI). By 2011, a total of about **Q48.** *26/58/84 per cent* of HIPC countries' debt had been cancelled under HIPC and MDRI; the effect on various debt indicators had been **Q49.** *dramatic/negligible*.

Q50. The following are various types of swap arrangement for reducing countries' debt burden:

(i) Debt-for-cash swaps.

(ii) Debt-for-equity swaps.

(iii) Debt-for-development swaps.

(iv) Debt-for-bonds swaps.

(v) Debt-for-nature swaps.

(vi) Debt-for-export swaps.

(vii) Debt-to-local-debt swaps.

Match each of the above to the following definitions:

(a) Where banks help developing countries sell their products in rich countries on the condition that the revenues gained are used to pay off the debt.

(b) Where banks allow developing countries to buy back their own debt (i.e. repay it) at a discount.

(c) Where banks agree to convert debt into low-interest-rate securities.

(d) Where debt is sold to companies exporting to or investing in the debtor country. These companies then sell the debt to the central bank for local currency at a discount. This provides these companies with a cheap source of local currency.

(e) Where banks sell debt. The purchasers can then exchange this debt with the central bank of the debtor country for local currency to use for purchasing shares in companies in the debtor country.

(f) Where debts are sold to an international environmental agency. This agency then swaps this debt with the central bank of the debtor country for a local bond which pays interest. The interest is then used to finance environmental projects.

(g) As (f) except that the interest is used to finance a range of projects in such fields as education, health, transport infrastructure and agriculture.

B PROBLEMS, EXERCISES AND PROJECTS

We do not usually provide answers to questions in the discussion section, but we have made an exception this time.

Q51. Table 27.1 presents indicators for two less developed countries. Based on these data, which country would you judge to enjoy the higher standard of living? Which would you expect to have the higher level of GNY per capita?

Q52. Either individually or in small groups, you should select two of the most highly indebted developing countries and write a report that analyses their economic situation.

The report should: (a) identify the level and nature of their international debt using appropriate debt indicators; (b) paint an economic profile of each of the two countries; (c) explain why they reached a position of severe indebtedness; (d) identify similarities and differences in the causes of their situation; (e) consider the extent to which debt

Table 27.1

	Country A	Country B
Life expectancy at birth (years)	52.0	73.7
Mean years of schooling	8.2	9.6
Infant mortality (per 1000 live births)	48	22
Human Development Index	0.597	0.723
Employed people living on less than $1.25 per day (% of total employment)	44.4	9.0
Number of internet users per 100 population	8.6	24.7
Population without electricity (%)	24.2	22.5
Gini coefficient	0.578	0.505
HIV prevalence (% of adults aged 15–49)	18.1	0.5

Source: United Nations Development Programme, Human Development Report 2010, published 2010, reproduced with permission of Palgrave Macmillan.

relief has enabled your chosen countries to benefit in terms of economic growth and the alleviation of poverty.

References include the World Bank website (http://www.worldbank.org) and the One World portal site (http://www.oneworld.net). Other sources of information on your chosen countries can be found by using a search engine, such as Google (http://www.google.com).

Q53. At the Millennium summit meeting of the United Nations in September 2000, the 189 member states agreed the following declaration: '. . . we will spare no effort to free our fellow men, women and children from the abject and dehumanising conditions of extreme poverty to which more than a billion of them are currently subjected'. As part of the agreement reached, specific targets were set to allow the monitoring of progress towards what have become known as the *Millennium Development Goals (MDGs)*. These goals were to be met by the year 2015. Visit the MDG website at (http://www.developmentgoals.org), choose two or three less developed countries from different regions of the world, and assess the extent to which progress is being made towards the targets.

 ## DISCUSSION TOPICS AND ESSAYS

Q54. Is GNY a suitable measure of the level of a country's development?

Q55. Why do developing countries tend to suffer from chronic balance of payments problems?

Q56. Developing countries generally have a comparative advantage in primary products. Why should this be so? Does this imply that investment should be focused in the primary sector?

Q57. What are the problems of using protectionism as a means of encouraging industrialisation?

Q58. Does import-substituting industrialisation inevitably involve a bias against agriculture?

Q59. Is increased inward investment by multinational companies the best means of improving economic growth rates in developing economies?

Q60. Should labour-abundant countries always adopt labour-intensive techniques?

Q61. Do all farmers gain equally from the Green Revolution? In what ways could the government help to ensure that the poorest farmers benefit from new agricultural technologies?

Q62. To what extent has unemployment in developing countries been caused by an 'urban bias' in development policy?

Q63. Discuss the problems that may arise in a society that is characterised by dualism.

Q64. To what extent is developing countries' debt problem the direct result of mistaken development policies of the 1960s and 1970s?

Q65. Would it be desirable to cancel *all* the debts of developing countries? Why might there be a problem of 'moral hazard' if this occurred?

Q66. Debate
The problems of the developing countries have generally been exacerbated by trade and other economic relationships with the developed world.

Q67. Debate
Making debt relief for developing countries conditional on their making 'structural adjustments' to their economies is the best way of ensuring their long-term development.

 ## ANSWERS

Q1. *False.* In fact, some 84 per cent of the world's population lives in developing countries – and they earn only 24 per cent of the world's income.

Q2. Deciding on what constitutes a *basic need* is to some extent a normative judgement. Clearly, adequate food, shelter, clothing, warmth, health care, sanitation, care for the elderly and those without work, etc. can be regarded as basic needs, but there is still the problem of deciding what constitutes 'adequate'. The other items in the list could *all* be regarded as basic needs: it depends on people's value judgements. This is clearly a problem for defining development.

Q3. Problems are: what items to include, how to measure them, how to weight them (given that they are

Q4. *Yes*: (a), (b), (f), (g) and (i).

No: (c), (d), (e) and (h).

Q5. *understate*. Many subsistence items will not be included.

Q6. *overstate*. As people now begin to purchase items (which thus get included in GNY statistics) that they would previously have produced themselves (and which would not have been included in GNY statistics), so it appears that production is growing faster than it really is.

Q7. *(a)* *Yes*. Real rates of interest are often kept deliberately low by governments in order to encourage investment. This has the effect, however, of worsening the shortage of saving.

(b) *Yes*. The market is often too small to allow effective competition.

(c) *No*. Although wage rates are very low, they are typically *above* the market-clearing level (perhaps because of minimum wage legislation). There is often high unemployment as a result.

(d) *Yes*. This is often the result of import restrictions, which thus improve the balance of trade. Foodstuffs and raw materials thus come cheaply into the country, while exporters find it difficult to export profitably.

(e) *Yes*. There is often huge variation in protection rates.

(f) *Yes*. The only source of loans is often the local moneylender, who may charge exorbitant interest rates.

(g) *No*. Typically they are kept artificially low by price controls. This makes farming less profitable.

(h) *Yes*.

Q8. *(a)* *Yes*.

(b) *Yes*.

(c) *No*.

(d) *Yes*.

(e) *Yes*.

Q9. *(a)* *Structural and institutional*.

(b) *Trade policies and process*.

(c) *Structural and institutional*.

(d) *Levels of development*.

(e) *Structural and institutional*.

(f) *Levels of development*.

(g) *Trade policies and process*.

(h) *Structural and institutional*.

(i) *Structural and institutional*.

(j) *Levels of development*.

Q10. *primary* (food and minerals).

Q11. *secondary* (manufactures).

Q12. (a) (iii), (b) (iv), (c) (ii), (d) (i).

Q13. *False*. By countries specialising in goods which are intensive in the abundant (and hence relatively low-priced) factors of production, this will result in an increase in the demand for these factors, an increase in their relative price, and hence an erosion of inequalities.

Q14. *False*. The figure was closer to 80 per cent.

Q15. *(a)* *Yes*: the rate of growth in GNY may thus be correspondingly less for primary producers.

(b) *Yes*: especially if mines and plantations are foreign *owned* and if they have monopsony power in employing local labour.

(c) *No*: they have a low income elasticity of demand. The demand for primaries therefore grows only slowly as the world economy grows.

(d) *No*: developing countries tend to be price takers (facing a virtually infinitely elastic demand curve).

(e) *Yes*: the demand for developing countries' primary exports is likely to grow less rapidly than the demand by developing countries for manufactured imports.

(f) *No*: the terms of trade are likely to decline: the price of manufactured imports is likely to grow more rapidly than the price of primary exports.

(g) *Yes*: and hence their demand grows rapidly over time.

(h) *No*: there are few if any domestic substitutes.

(i) *Yes*: their world demand and supply is less price elastic and the supply curve is subject to shifts.

(j) *Yes*: mining can lead to the despoiling of the countryside, damage to the health of miners and the breaking up of communities. Plantations can also lead to undesirable ecological, social and cultural effects.

Q16. A strategy of building up domestic manufacturing industries by protecting them from competing imports.

Q17. A. Thus a finished product would have higher tariff protection than component parts. This therefore allows a firm setting up in assembly to import the components at a lower tariff than that protecting it from imports of the finished good.

Q18. *True*. By setting up plants in the developing country, the multinationals will receive the protection themselves. If, however, they were to attempt to export to the country from plants abroad, they would be faced by the trade barriers.

Q19. *(a)* *Yes*: firms are protected from foreign competition.

(b) *No*: often governments have kept interest rates low in order to encourage investment. Also with less pressure on the current account of the balance of payments, there is less need for a surplus on the short-term financial account.

(c) *Yes*: the improvement in the balance of payments from the protectionism pushes up the exchange rate.

(d) *No*: it has led to relatively higher urban wages compared with rural wages.

(e) *Yes*: the overvalued exchange rate has made it less profitable to export primaries. The higher prices of manufactured goods, combined with low food prices, have worsened the rural–urban terms of trade (a unit of agricultural produce buys fewer manufactured products than before).

(f) *Yes*: enormous differences in effective rates occur from one product to another, thus causing huge market distortions.

(g) *No*: given tariff escalation, effective protective rates have generally been above nominal rates.

Q20. Other problems include: social/cultural problems of urban living, often in appalling conditions; environmental costs of industrialisation; increased inequality (between the urban and rural sectors, between the employed and unemployed, between relatively high-paid jobs in some industries and pittance wages in others); increased dependence on specific imports (raw materials, capital equipment and component parts) often from monopoly suppliers; inefficiency due to lack of competition.

Q21. *True.* Export-orientated countries such as South Korea and Singapore have had exceptionally high growth rates (except during the Asian crisis of 1997–8).

Q22. They should be labour-intensive goods (or at least be produced using relatively labour-intensive techniques).

Q23. E. Devaluation increases the profits from exports; removal of tariff barriers helps to reduce the exchange rate and also reverse the bias towards the home market; reductions in employment taxes reduce the costs of producing (labour-intensive) exports.

Q24. *small*: such countries are likely to have a much more limited home market.

Q25. *substantial*: the domestic market under such circumstances is likely to be too small for production at minimum costs.

Q26. Drawbacks include: possible continuing neglect of agricultural sector; trade barriers to developing countries' manufactured exports erected by advanced countries; difficulties in competing against other developing country exporters already established in various markets; risks of shifts in world trading conditions and a rise in protectionism.

Q27. E.

Q28. (a) *Low*, (b) *High*, (c) *Overvalued*, (d) *High*, (e) *High*, (f) *Low*.

Q29. Examples include: increasing food prices; provision of rural infrastructure (roads, irrigation schemes, distribution agencies, etc.); provision of low-interest finance to the rural sector; education and training in new techniques; land reform; the encouragement of rural co-operatives.

Q30. *above.*

Q31. *capital.*

Q32. *contradicts.* The Heckscher–Ohlin theory suggests that a labour-abundant country ought to choose labour-intensive techniques.

Q33. E. (i) is incorrect (see answer to Q32). In the case of (iii), if the techniques are more sophisticated they may economise not only on labour, but also (to a lesser extent) on capital costs and thus have a lower capital/output ratio as well as a lower labour/capital and labour/output ratio.

Q34. Possible disadvantages include: capital-intensive techniques may require more maintenance; they may require more imported raw materials, equipment and components; they may involve more pollution; they may provide only very limited employment.

Q35. *(a)* *underemployment.*
(b) *disguised unemployment.*

Q36. *True.* This 'surplus' labour is supported because they are either the owners of the land themselves or are part of a family which owns the land and is therefore prepared to support its relatives.

Q37. Because the extra jobs encourage people to migrate from the countryside to the towns, but more than one person migrates for each extra job created.

Q38. *True*: (a), (c), (e) and (g).
False: (b), (d) and (f).

Q39. C. Higher food prices will discourage migration, as will rural infrastructure projects. Investment in the towns may create more urban jobs, but it is likely to encourage more migration and thereby increase urban unemployment.

Q40. (a) *higher*, (b) *lower* (inflation was generally lower), (c) *tighter*, (d) *deeper*, (e) *longer lasting*, (f) *variable*, (g) *commercial bank*, (h) *more*.

Q41. The length of loan could be extended; a temporary delay could be granted in repaying loans due to mature; countries could be allowed to pay interest only (rather than capital as well) for a period of time; countries could acquire new loans on more favourable terms and use them to pay off the old debts.

Q42. *Paris.* (Note that the Toronto and Houston terms were new Paris Club agreements negotiated at these two places. These new terms allowed greater concessions to be made to low-income debtor countries and lower-middle-income debtor countries respectively.)

Q43. *London.*

Q44. The IMF generally favours market-based solutions combined with tight demand-side policies. These include (a), (b), (f), (g), (h), (i) and (j).

Q45. Disadvantages include: economic recession while inflation is being squeezed out of the economy – this may take a long time; higher initial inflation as price controls are removed; greater inequality; increased structural unemployment; more vulnerability of the economy to world economic fluctuations.

Q46. *False*. This has turned out to be only part of the story. The production of the additional palm oil has involved either cutting down rain forest, which, apart from being a much more efficient carbon absorber than oil palm trees, is habitat for many endangered species, or the draining and burning of peat lands, which sends huge amounts of carbon dioxide into the atmosphere.

Q47. C. There were attempts made to ensure that funds released by HIPC would be used for poverty alleviation – one of the conditions for receiving debt forgiveness under HIPC was that countries should develop a Poverty Reduction Strategy paper to show how debt relief would help to relieve poverty.

Q48. *84 per cent.*

Q49. *dramatic.*

Q50. (a) (vi), (b) (i), (c) (iv), (d) (vii), (e) (ii), (f) (v), (g) (iii).

Q51. It is clear that country B shows more favourable performance on all of these indicators. However, country A (South Africa) has GNY per capita of US$5678, whereas country B (Peru) has GNY per capita of only US$4477. This reminds us that GNY per capita is not wholly informative about living standards in different countries. Notice that for these countries, the discrepancy in GNY per capita when measured in PPP$ is also striking, with South Africa having GNY per capita of PPP$9812 compared with Peru's PPP$8424.